# Oracle DBA on Unix and Linux

Michael Wessler

201 West 103rd St., Indianapolis, Indiana, 46290 USA

P9-CCG-392

# Oracle DBA on Unix and Linux

Copyright © 2002 by Sams

All rights reserved. No part of this book shall be reproduced, stored in a retrieval system, or transmitted by any means, electronic, mechanical, photocopying, recording, or otherwise, without written permission from the publisher. No patent liability is assumed with respect to the use of the information contained herein. Although every precaution has been taken in the preparation of this book, the publisher and author assume no responsibility for errors or omissions. Nor is any liability assumed for damages resulting from the use of the information contained herein.

International Standard Book Number: 0-672-32158-0

Library of Congress Catalog Card Number: 2001089580

Printed in the United States of America

First Printing: November 2001

04   03   02   01      4   3   2   1

## Trademarks

All terms mentioned in this book that are known to be trademarks or service marks have been appropriately capitalized. Sams cannot attest to the accuracy of this information. Use of a term in this book should not be regarded as affecting the validity of any trademark or service mark.

## Warning and Disclaimer

Every effort has been made to make this book as complete and as accurate as possible, but no warranty or fitness is implied. The information provided is on an "as is" basis. The author and the publisher shall have neither liability nor responsibility to any person or entity with respect to any loss or damages arising from the information contained in this book.

**ASSOCIATE PUBLISHER**
*Jeff Koch*

**ACQUISITIONS EDITOR**
*Kathryn Purdum*

**DEVELOPMENT EDITOR**
*Kevin Howard*

**MANAGING EDITOR**
*Matt Purcell*

**PROJECT EDITOR**
*Natalie F. Harris*

**COPY EDITOR**
*Kezia Endsley*

**INDEXER**
*Erika Millen*

**PROOFREADER**
*Jody Larsen*

**TECHNICAL EDITORS**
*Jim Kotan*
*Paul Love*

**TEAM COORDINATOR**
*Vicki Harding*
*Denni Bannister*

**INTERIOR DESIGNER**
*Dan Armstrong*

**COVER DESIGNER**
*Aren Howell*

**PAGE LAYOUT**
*Lizbeth Patterson*
*Heather Stephenson*

# Contents at a Glance

# Contents

# About the Author

**Michael Wessler** received his B.S. in Computer Technology from Purdue University in West Lafayette, IN. He is an Oracle Certified Database Administrator for Oracle 8 and 8i. He has administered Oracle databases on NT, and various flavors of Unix, and Linux at several different companies ranging from a handful of employees to IT staffs in the thousands. Included in this experience is working at a true .com startup and managing a mission-critical OPS database on a Sun Cluster. Michael has also programmed professionally in COBOL, SQL, and PL/SQL. Currently, he is an Oracle consultant for Perpetual Technologies working at the Department of Defense in Indianapolis, Indiana. Michael is coauthor of *Oracle Unleashed, Second Edition*; *Unix Primer Plus, Third Edition*; and *COBOL Unleashed*. Michael can be reached at mwessler@yahoo.com.

# About the Technical Editor

Residing in Omaha, Nebraska, **Jim Kotan** has been in the Information Technology field since 1987 as a Unix System Administrator, Oracle DBA, Programmer, Consultant, and Manager. Jim has also written numerous articles for Inside SCO Unix Systems Magazine. He is currently a Production Oracle Database Administration Engineer for Qwest Communications, International where he specializes in Shell Programming, Backup & Recovery, Migrations of High Availability databases and Database Creations. Jim's favorite activities are Bible Study, bicycle riding, writing code and target shooting.

# Dedication

*I would like to dedicate this work to the memory of my grandfather Robert Johnson. We miss you, Daddy Bob!!!*

# Acknowledgments

No one writes a book like this in total isolation. This book is certainly no exception and I'd like to thank the following people.

All the hard working people at Sams. Katie Purdum, my Acquisitions Editor, for making this work possible. Kevin Howard for developing this book. Natalie Harris for all her hard work. Kezia Endsley for helping out with the grammar. Thanks to Jim Kotan for his skilled technical review. It certainly was a pleasure to work with all of you on this project.

I'd like to thank fellow author Rich Blum for his overall support and advice during this project. Rich's experience with writing and wisdom made this project much easier. I'd also like to thank the following people for the miscellaneous support they provided, particularly in terms of networking and hardware: Tige Chastain, Ben Styring, John Pahos, Brian Conant, and Ed Lewis. Thanks guys!

The following people have helped me professionally and technically to get to the point where I could write this book. First, a very special thanks to Dan Wilson for always being there to help, guide, and answer questions. Bill Pierce for giving me that first opportunity and showing me how an MIS shop ought to be run. The following System Administrators showed incredible patience with me in the early days: Mark Hinkle, Karl Buchman, and Greg Hartman. Thanks to the Purdue University Computer Technology Department, particularly Professors Goldman, Weaver, and Boggess. Finally, thanks to Ryan, Ron, and Chris for providing me such a great opportunity at Perpetual.

Finally, I'd like to thank my family and friends for being so understanding when I said, "Sorry, I can't do X, I have to write." Anyone who has ever authored a book understands just how much time it takes to do it right. Mom, Dad, Grandma, Nanny, Joe, Angie, Tim, Emily, Rob, Marsha, Zach, Travis; I'll actually be around more often! For my friends Erik, Kalynn, JJ, Brian, John, Mark, Sam, Zach, Josh, Bob, Becky, Ben, and Wendy; I'll actually be able to go out again!

# Tell Us What You Think!

As the reader of this book, *you* are our most important critic and commentator. We value your opinion and want to know what we're doing right, what we could do better, what areas you'd like to see us publish in, and any other words of wisdom you're willing to pass our way.

As an Associate Publisher for Sams, I welcome your comments. You can fax, email, or write me directly to let me know what you did or didn't like about this book—as well as what we can do to make our books stronger.

*Please note that I cannot help you with technical problems related to the topic of this book, and that due to the high volume of mail I receive, I might not be able to reply to every message.*

When you write, please be sure to include this book's title and author as well as your name and phone or fax number. I will carefully review your comments and share them with the author and editors who worked on the book.

| | |
|---|---|
| Fax: | 317-581-4770 |
| Email: | feedback@samspublishing.com |
| Mail: | Jeff Koch |
| | Sams |
| | 201 West 103rd Street |
| | Indianapolis, IN 46290 USA |

# Introduction

Oracle is a complex Object Relational Database Management System and is probably the best database that money can buy. People know this and that is why they trust their businesses to Oracle. Furthermore, when they do buy Oracle they usually run it on a Unix or Linux system. Experience shows that Unix operating systems are robust, dependable, and scalable. That is why most companies use Unix when they have to develop large or critical systems to support their businesses.

At the other end of the spectrum, Linux systems were initially introduced as testing and development systems. Basically, people loaded Linux on old machines to learn and test with. Recently, however, Linux has become a respected operating system that many companies, particularly Internet startups, use to run their businesses. As a result of these factors, there are a large number of Oracle systems running on both Unix and Linux.

Unfortunately, however, there are relatively few people who know Oracle and Unix/Linux. To be an effective DBA, however, you must understand how the database interacts with the operation system. Oracle and the Unix/Linux operating systems are tied closely together. Anything that impacts the operating system will likely impact the database. Likewise, the behavior of the database will impact the performance of the server. Despite efforts by Oracle and various operating system vendors to simplify administration, this is still an inescapable fact. The key here is to view Oracle and Unix/Linux as a total system, not as separate, isolated pieces.

I have worked with many people who were trained as Oracle DBAs, but couldn't perform basic tasks, such as install software or apply patches, if their lives depended on it. Usually they went to some school or class that taught them about Oracle in a vacuum, but never provided any information in the context of the operation system. This "one size fits all" approach to training isn't sufficient. The reality is that when they come into the industry as DBAs, they are almost helpless because they understand only half of the Oracle and Unix/Linux equation.

I have also worked with some Unix System Administrators who thought of Oracle as just another application. In reality, this is far from the truth. In fact, Oracle is more of an operating system than an application. These people had a very difficult time understanding why and how they needed to configure their servers to run Oracle optimally. Once again, their "one size fits all" mentality resulted in failure.

To manage this system, whereby Oracle is tied closely to Unix and Linux, you need to understand both sides of the equation. However, the reality often is that DBAs only understand Oracle and SAs only understand Unix/Linux. This is indeed a problem.

My solution in this book is to show DBAs what they need to know to run Oracle on Unix and Linux. That way, they are not dependent on finding the rare System Administrator who understands Oracle. In this way, you also understand how and why Unix and Linux work the way they do.

My goal with this book is two-fold:

- Write a book that shows database administration in a way that combines the skills of the DBA with the knowledge of a Unix/Linux System Administrator. This allows you to manage the database and Unix/Linux server as a total system.

- Write a book that is for the *working* DBA. I have written this book as if I'm writing notes and procedures for a co-worker. I combine solid theoretical database and system administration knowledge with practical examples of what I do on the job. I think it is important to know how and *why* the database and operating system works the way they do, so I cover some theory. On the other hand, I give detailed examples of how to perform regular DBA tasks. If I've had to struggle to get something working, you'll find that information in this book.

First I cover what a DBA's job really is and how you can survive as one. Next, I cover Oracle architecture so you understand how and why Oracle works the way it does. I also cover the initial steps, from planning your database, to setting up your Unix/Linux server, and then installing Oracle. I then cover how to intelligently create databases and manage them on a daily basis. I spend a lot of time showing you how to solve problems as they occur, both from an Oracle and a Unix/Linux perspective. Chapters are dedicated to tuning both the database and Unix/Linux servers. Additionally, I show you how to Web-enable your system using Java and iAS. Finally, I explain some of the new features of Oracle's new database, 9i.

## Who Should Read This Book?

This book is geared for the person who knows what a database is and has basic SQL skills, but wants to learn how to build and manage Oracle databases on either Unix or Linux. This book isn't geared towards certification, but rather towards becoming a proficient and seasoned DBA in the Unix/Linux environments.

The following people will get the most benefit out of this book:

- Computer professionals who are starting their first jobs as Oracle DBAs.

- Experienced Oracle DBAs from NT or other platforms making the move to the Unix and Linux platforms.

- DBAs with experience on other databases, such as SQL Server or DB2. This experience can be on Unix and Linux or any other platform.

- System Administrators who have to support database servers and want to know more about the database they indirectly support.

- Developers who need to understand how Oracle works on the platform they support.

- People new to databases who want to install Oracle on a Linux box so they can learn the technology.

- Computer science and technology students.

I have written this book assuming the reader has basic skills regarding computers, understands what a database is, and knows basic SQL. If you have these skills and have access to either a Unix or Linux machine, you should be able to create a database and do all the examples in this book. This should prepare you for most of what you will run into on the job as a DBA.

## What Makes This Book Different?

There are many books written about Oracle database administration, but very few, if any, focus on DBA work in the Unix and Linux environments. Most books on the Oracle subject try to separate the DBA from the operation system. Although that might make a book easier to write, it doesn't work in the real world.

What this book offers is a solid DBA guide, but tailored to the Unix and Linux platforms. This book is more than just a generic DBA book where all the examples happen to be on a Unix or Linux machine. Rather, I show you the "tricks of the trade" that'll help you support Unix and Linux systems. I show you what working DBAs do on a daily basis and why.

Part of this book deliberately touches on subjects that are traditionally reserved for System Administrators. I try to blur the distinction between a DBA and an SA task so you will know how to manage Oracle on Unix/Linux as a total system.

Key differences between this book and others include:

- This book is written specifically for the Unix and Linux platforms. Most of the focus is on Sun Solaris, HP-UX, and RedHat Linux, which are three of the most common operating systems supporting Oracle. However, if you are running another flavor of Unix or Linux, the concepts will easily transfer.

- I provide detailed information about how and why the database works as it does. I don't think it is sufficient just to give the DBA the basics. There are too many "point-and-click" DBAs with minimal skills already. Rather, I cover topics in detail so you understand *why* things work the way they do.

- I wrote this book as though I was making notes to myself or explaining topics to another DBA. I focus on what's important and what actually works.

- As I explain topics, I provide detailed examples and walk you through them. If you have a system at home, you can follow along and practice. If you can do what is covered in this book and understand the reasoning behind it, you should do well in a work environment.

- You will not find marketing material or find me pushing products I wouldn't run on my own system. I'm not going to tell you to do something I wouldn't do myself.

- The book includes coverage of Oracle 9i, Java, and iAS. As of this writing, 9i is being released. Although I have a chapter dedicated to 9i new features, I also cover differences between 8i and 9i throughout the book. Also, few DBA books attempt to address Java and iAS. I cover these topics in a manner so you will know the fundamentals when you encounter these technologies.

I feel this book is different from most DBA books. I know that they don't give the Unix- and Linux-specific details you find here. That alone separates this book from other books. However, I take this one step further by covering the topic from a working DBA's standpoint, and I refuse to water down the technical content. There's plenty of explanation and theory for you Oracle purists. Finally, this might well be the first book to cover Oracle 9i and it is one of the first to address Java and iAS. For those reasons, this book is a more complete and practical guide than others on the market. I hope you enjoy the book!

# Role of the DBA

## ESSENTIALS

- The official roles and responsibilities of the DBA depend largely on the particular company or organization.

- A DBA is the person tasked with making sure the data is safe and available to the organization.

- The DBA has both technical responsibilities dealing with the database and non-technical responsibilities outside the database.

- Skills required by the successful DBA range from the obvious technical database skills to having "people" skills and understanding the business of the organization.

# What Is a DBA?

In its simplest terms, a DBA is the person held responsible and accountable for the safety and practical availability of the organization's data. Today, this is typically implemented with a Relational Database Management System (RDBMS) or an Object Relational Database Management System (ORDBMS). Most people tend to agree on that definition regardless of whether dealing with Oracle or another database. Before we look at the duties of the Oracle DBA on Unix and Linux, we should look at some of the factors affecting the generic DBA's job description.

## Depends on the Shop

The roles and responsibilities of the DBA can vary greatly from company to company. In fact, the job of the DBA is continually evolving as new technologies appear, such as the Internet. As organizations change and receive new management, the role of the DBA can also change to meet new requirements. Also, as old DBAs leave and new DBAs join an organization, the scope of the DBA's responsibilities can change as well, depending on each person's personality and experience.

The size of the organization (the *shop*) has a major influence on the role of the DBA. In a large environment there are often many DBAs, so there may be well-defined responsibilities given to each person. Within the shop there may be, for example, a dedicated performance tuning team while other administrators are assigned individual systems to manage. Also, there may be many different departments or organizations, each with its own (and sometimes competing) group of DBAs. If geographically distributed environments are included, the situation becomes even more complex. These can become tricky environments for a person to navigate because exact responsibilities and expectations may not be clearly defined or they may be changing. This is when "turf battles" and organizational politics become problematic.

On the other hand, a small shop might have only one or two DBAs to manage everything. This is common in Web/Internet startups, for example. In even smaller shops, the DBA might also be the System Administrator (SA) and may have programming responsibilities as well. I have found that the smaller shops usually allow greater personal initiative with a wider range of responsibilities. This can be an exciting place to be, with many great opportunities for a motivated DBA.

## Where DBAs Come From

The background the DBA comes from will naturally influence how this person views the position. How do people become DBAs and where do they come from? Usually they grow into the position from another IT-related position, but there are exceptions. The following sections describe some of the more common paths to becoming a DBA, which are illustrated in Figure 1.1. Keep in mind how each would likely influence how the new DBA views the position.

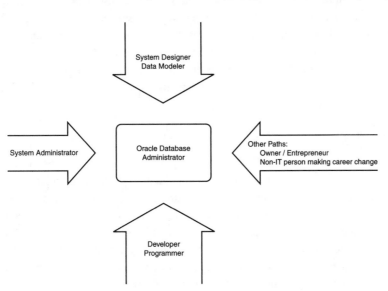

**FIGURE 1.1**
*Some of the more common paths to becoming a DBA.*

# Paths to Becoming a DBA

## System Administrator (SA)

The SA is the person responsible for making sure the organization's servers and overall computer system are secure and available. In many ways this is very similar to the job of being the DBA. Usually the SA manages systems supporting the database, so she is already familiar with its needs. The SA and DBA usually (or at least *should*) work very closely together to support their systems. It is for these very good reasons that a SA can pick up the job of being a DBA. As a DBA, expect these people to look at the database as part of a larger system. For example, they will view Oracle more as a system supporting users than PL/SQL code needing support.

## Developer/Programmer

The developer or programmer is the person who writes code. Whether it is COBOL, C, Java, or PL/SQL, these are the people who should know how their code is implemented within the system. These people usually have a very good understanding of what their organization does and how it works because they wrote the program to do it. They typically work with the DBA in terms of requesting tables or tuning SQL for an individual subsystem. As a DBA, expect these people to look at Oracle initially in terms of packages and procedures rather than backup and recovery.

## Systems Designer/Data Modeler

These people design the system from a conceptual view. They use data flow diagrams and Entity Relationship Diagrams (ERDs) to decide how a system should be organized, but not necessarily how it is implemented. At some sites they may have the role of data administrator, whose responsibility is to manage the data from a theoretical standpoint. They will work with the DBA on how their logical models are actually implemented as tables. They will likely look at the job of being DBA in terms of managing data and processes rather than the fine details or advanced features of Oracle.

## Other Paths

Some people simply grow into the DBA position by doing DBA tasks until someday someone says "You're a DBA." This is more common in small environments than in larger shops, but it does happen. It may be an entrepreneur implementing his own idea. In that case he is more likely to view the database as a means to an end rather than to get caught up in the technology. Others may be computer operators or even non-technical people making a move to being a DBA as a way to break into IT. This may be something they wanted and have lobbied for or it may be forced on them because of a vacancy. It is difficult to tell how they will view the DBA position, but they will likely be more influenced by their mentors and training material than by a history of practical experience.

# Types of DBAs

Just as there are several roads to becoming a DBA, there are several types of DBA. These classifications apply more toward large shops because of the need for defining responsibilities. Also, within each classification, sometimes new DBAs are referred to as Junior DBAs while more experienced people get senior status. I've never been a fan of classifying people that way because it can be divisive. However, the following descriptions are applicable in some situations. Just remember that these titles and responsibilities also vary greatly, depending on the organization.

## Application DBA

This person is responsible for a specific application(s) and all the corresponding database objects at the schema/user level. This DBA works closely with the developers and data modelers to assist with table definitions and schema creation. He also focuses on tuning a particular application by adding indexes or tuning SQL and PL/SQL. Ultimately this person becomes an expert on the application and database objects involved. It is common to assign new DBAs to this position initially.

## Systems DBA

This type of DBA manages the database at the database level. Specifically, she makes sure the actual database is running, backups are implemented, and everything is interfacing well with the other systems (such as the OS). This DBA works very closely with the System Administrator(s) to ensure that the total system is available and secure. While not every shop has someone assigned as an Application DBA, every shop does have someone fulfilling the tasks of the Systems DBA. When most people imagine the DBA position, they are usually thinking of the Systems DBA.

## Maintenance DBA

This is a person tasked with supporting preexisting systems. There usually isn't much new development on these systems, just making sure they are available as needed. This type of work can involve converting old systems (such as SQL Server to Oracle), doing upgrades, and applying patches. This type of DBA will often work with the creators of the original system to maintain and occasionally improve it. This designation is not as common as Application or Systems DBA, but it does exist in some larger organizations.

The three classifications of DBAs just discussed are generic. I have seen each classification implemented, but usually a working DBA is a combination of all three. Especially in smaller to mid-size shops, a DBA will be expected to do everything. This means to support the application and the developers (Applications DBA), maintain and upgrade existing systems (Maintenance DBA), and manage all the databases as a total system (Systems DBA). For the purposes of this book, I will assume the DBA is tasked with all classifications because that is most common. Now let's look more in depth at what exactly a DBA is expected to do.

# Database Administration Principles

To be truly successful and be a person that adds real value to an organization, the DBA must take the position seriously. Being a DBA is far more than just creating tables and taking backups; it means being responsible for *everything* affecting the organization's data. This responsibility encompasses both the data and RDBMS directly. It also involves every other entity that affects the data directly or indirectly, its safety, and its availability. Does this sound like a big job? It should, because this is probably the most important job in IT. If the SA has a bad day and people lose some e-mail, life goes on. If the DBA has a bad day and loses some data, the company can get sued, lose customers, and go out of business. Now let's look at the two key principles of database administration: data protection and data availability.

## Data Protection

If the DBA does only one thing, it should be to make sure the organization's data is safe and recoverable. If the DBA cannot do that, he is not much of a DBA. It doesn't matter how well tuned or technologically advanced a system is; without data it is worthless. Make no mistake about it; protecting the data is absolutely the most important part of being a DBA.

Systems fail all the time for a variety of reasons. Even the most advanced 24/7 shop isn't really 24/7; it's just a matter of time before something breaks. While that is not what most people want to hear, that's the reality of it. Computer systems are designed by humans and are therefore fallible. This fact of life is acceptable. However, it is not acceptable for data to be lost because of something the DBA should have planned for.

There are numerous effective ways to make data secure and recoverable. Each method has its benefits and costs. The methods usually provide varying degrees of effectiveness, but come at the expense of performance, complexity, or recoverability. It is up to the DBA to find the right mix of multiple methods to ensure the integrity of the organization's data, based on business requirements. This will likely involve consultations with the System Administrator, the customers, and management, but it is the DBA's responsibility to ensure a secure system is implemented.

The DBA should have planned for most of the likely problems and outages the organization will face. These will depend on the business nature of the organization, but I have seen precautions for everything from an accidentally dropped table to limited nuclear war. It is up to the DBA to assess the risks rationally and plan accordingly. The level of protection and recoverability must also involve a buy-in from management as well, so that they know what to expect in terms of recoverablity.

Once the risks are planned for as much as humanly possible, recovery plans should be tested and refined. This is where most problems occur. DBAs often plan on how to respond to an outage, but never really test their plans under realistic conditions until something actually happens. It is here where things go wrong and data and databases are lost. There is no excuse for this, and no one will have any sympathy for the DBA if this occurs. It is excusable to not have a plan for a totally unforeseen event, but failing to prepare for something you should have expected is not excusable. Also, this is not a one-time event; the process of risk assessment, planning, and recovery training is continual. Recovery plans need to be documented and provided to everyone in the organization who could conceivably perform a recovery. When the DBA leaves the organization, he should pass this information on to the replacement if at all possible.

Once something actually fails (eventually it will) and the organization's data is put on the line, the DBA truly earns her money. This is a stressful situation, and these failures never occur at a convenient time. Management usually wants everything up immediately because they think they are losing money. People are looking over your shoulder and someone always has a suggestion or comment on how they would do things *if* it were their show. This may well be the first time anyone has ever really noticed you, because administrators are typically ignored until there is a problem. Expect to be working until the problem is solved, even if that's 3:00 in the morning. That is why you are paid the big dollars, get the DBA title, and have the responsibility of protecting the organization's data. Hopefully you will be well versed in recovery procedures and will have tested the procedure you are using for that particular case. If things go well, you are a hero (no bonus though, since this was unscheduled downtime). If things go bad, you probably should have an updated resume.

## Data Availability

Data availability is keeping the data—and therefore the database—open and available for normal use. This is the second most important responsibility of a DBA. It does the organization no good to have an elaborate information system if it is not operational. Indeed, some sites measure this downtime in hundreds of thousands of dollars lost per hour. If the system is down for too long, the business can go under.

This is a DBA responsibility, but it is not something the DBA always has control over. For example, the Unix server could crash and require recovery. This is out of the DBA's hands, but it affects the database. In that case the DBA could have planned to have a standby database ready to go until the normal system is restored. Contingency planning such as this is a DBA's responsibility that must be taken seriously. It is the DBA's job to have ways to keep the data available even when unavoidable problems occur. Other events affecting data availability, such as rebuilding tables or applying patches, are controlled directly by the DBA and should be scheduled at a time when their impact is minimized. If this means the DBA comes in on a Sunday to apply a patch, then the DBA does this. Ideally, management will recognize this kind of effort, but working odd or extra hours really is part of the DBA's job.

Data availability is often tied to data protection. One idea is that if the data is damaged or lost, it certainly is not available. While that is true, it is important to realize that protection and availability are often at odds with each other. The simplest example of this is with backups. Depending on the backup methods used, the database may be shut down or performance reduced, thus affecting availability, but this is a necessary evil.

The balance between availability and protection must be struck by the DBA, but again other parties such as the users, customers, and management will certainly want to have input. This is often a very difficult situation because most people push for availability over data protection because they never really expect to have to recover their data. The DBA must be careful not to be bullied into unreasonably exposing the data to risks. A very common example is when a DBA has to fight to get a cold backup scheduled even though it will take the system offline temporarily. Once something bad does happen (and it will eventually), the conversations about backups versus availability will likely be forgotten in favor of dealing with the DBA who didn't protect the data. To protect against this, it is highly recommended that the DBA provide to management a document confirming the shop's policies regarding data availability, protection, and procedures. This should allow management to know what to expect from the DBA and will hopefully provide some protection for the DBA in the aftermath of a crisis.

One other facet of data availability is performance. If the system is so slow that work cannot be completed successfully, it may as well not be running. This can be a tricky problem to solve because it may not even have anything to do with the database *per se*. For example, a network problem or bad piece of application code could be the real culprit. Regardless of the real cause, it is usually the DBA who gets called initially to figure out "why is the database so slow today?". If it affects the database, it is the DBA's responsibility to find out what is wrong and make sure it is fixed regardless of where the problem originates.

Those are the two main principles of being a DBA: data protection and data availability. Every other activity a DBA undertakes supports one or both of those principles. Either he is taking action to protect the data or he is taking action to make it available. As long as those two principles are faithfully served, the DBA is doing fine.

# Database Administration Responsibilities

Once the two guiding principles of database administration have been established, everything else tends to fall into either technical responsibilities or non-technical responsibilities. While the principles remain the same no matter where you go, the responsibilities assigned to a particular DBA may vary.

## Database Technical Responsibilities

Core technical responsibilities of the DBA can be broken roughly into the following areas: systems activities, application support, tuning, backup and recovery, and troubleshooting. These have a great deal of overlap, but they do provide a basis to begin with.

### System Activities

The DBA is, or at least should be, responsible for planning and designing how the database system is implemented. Once the system is designed the DBA builds it and then tests it. From there on, it is a continual cycle of maintenance and upgrades for the life of the system. Of course, that makes the often unrealistic assumptions of an ideal situation and a DBA staying with one system for its entire life. In reality, a DBA may come into a project at any given stage, and that system may or may not be doing very well.

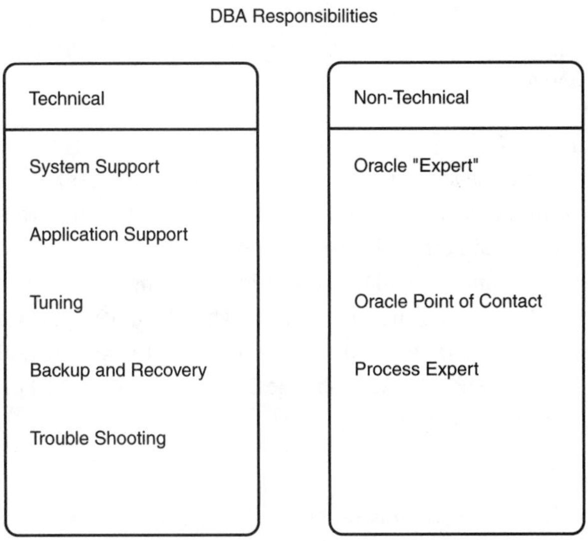

DBA Responsibilities

| Technical | Non-Technical |
|---|---|
| System Support | Oracle "Expert" |
| Application Support | |
| Tuning | Oracle Point of Contact |
| Backup and Recovery | Process Expert |
| Trouble Shooting | |

**FIGURE 1.2**

*DBA Responsibilities*

The planning and design phase of any system or project is the most critical of any project. Unfortunately, it is often unappreciated or not properly completed. The DBA usually comes out of this phase with an ERD of tables to build and some general ideas about system response requirements and activity. Hopefully the DBA has had an opportunity to work with the data modeler to come up with a practical design for the tables. It is good if the DBA has met with the developers and has a feel for the type of application the database will be supporting. Finally, hopefully the DBA has had a good dialogue with the System Administrator regarding server sizing and configuration. Entire books have been written on each of these subjects, but ultimately the DBA will have a set list of requirements for the system.

Once the DBA has the system requirements, it is up to that DBA to build it. Usually this means a Unix or Linux server has been selected, purchased, and loaded with the basic operating system by the System Administrator. At this stage the DBA installs and patches Oracle Server and any other related database software. Next the DBA creates the actual database, using the plans generated before. This results in a blank database running on a server with no data. The DBA will then create the tables, populate them with data, and establish connectivity with the application. A basic backup and recovery schedule should also be established at this stage. After a period of initial testing, the application will go live.

Maintaining the system is the next phase. The idea behind maintaining the system is to take proactive steps so the data and application is available for use to the end users. Typically this involves mundane daily tasks such as creating users, monitoring database growth, making sure backups and production jobs run successfully, and reacting to change requests. Applying patches and performing database upgrades and migrations are also part of normal system maintenance for the DBA.

## Application Support

The application(s) the database supports is written by the developer(s). Typically, developers work in conjunction with the data modeler and the DBAs to determine what tables and indexes are needed. They will then send the table specifications to the DBA to review and implement. The DBA will usually fine-tune the table specifications in terms of storage and indexing to improve performance, but the basic structure will be what the developer wants. Once the application is built, the developers will usually have changes to existing tables or request new indexes, which will keep the DBA busy. In the meantime, it is up to the DBA to monitor the application and look for ways to improve it.

## Tuning

Tuning is a key part of database administration and can be split into three areas: application tuning, database tuning, and system tuning. Each area is important and tied with the other areas. It is important to note that tuning is never really done and that something running fine today may be unacceptable tomorrow. The DBA should know that user perception is important. If the users and management believe one part of the system is running well, the DBA should focus on other areas perceived as having problems.

Application tuning is typically the most visible tuning activity for a DBA. In its simplest terms, it means making things run faster for the users. If this is done well, it is noticed and makes a positive effect on the organization. Ideally this process begins early in the planning process when tables and data flows are being designed. Once the application is built, the DBA usually can only add or remove indexes and tune SQL and PL/SQL code. Often this involves working closely with the developers. I have seen cases where adding a missing index has made dramatic improvements for the end users. This can be rewarding work for the DBA because it can have an immediate positive impact on the user community.

Database tuning is the process of tuning the actual database server and processes and is a core DBA function. Tuning the database can involve topics such as optimizing memory allocation, datafile placement and size, locks and latches, and instance parameters. This is where the DBA becomes an expert on the specifics of the database. It is also where the DBA needs to be especially careful because a minor mistake can have wide-reaching effects on the system.

System tuning involves tuning the environment the database and application run in. It involves those areas outside the database that affect the database either directly or indirectly. This could mean, for example, working with the operations staff to determine when batch jobs are run. It could also mean working with the SA on networking issues. This is a difficult topic to define because it involves working with areas outside the database and application that affect the data and database. This is an area in which DBAs with a wide range of IT experience can really excel.

## Backup and Recovery

This is the most important part of the job for a DBA, but it is often not given the attention it deserves. The DBA is responsible for selecting a mix of backup and recovery methods based on the specific needs of the system. What may be great for one system might be totally unacceptable for another. It is up to the DBA to meet with key management and customer groups to determine what is an acceptable balance between data protection and data availability. Once those requirements have been established in writing, typically as a Service Level Agreement (SLA), the DBA selects the appropriate backup methods.

The next step is actually to implement, test, and document the various backup and recovery scenarios. Regular testing of the backups and practicing recoveries are key. At this stage the DBA should be working in conjunction with the System Administrator. Problems seldom occur in isolation, and a failure of one system will likely affect other systems. For example, a failure of the server or operating system will affect the database as well. Also, recovering a database will likely involve the SA restoring files from tape or implementing special backups. The DBA and SA must have an understanding of what is needed to recover the entire system. Full-scale practice recoveries should take place whenever possible. The DBA should also consult developers and business analysts to see what to do from a business and process standpoint when problems occur. Finally, the DBA should document these tested procedures.

## Troubleshooting

This is a catchall area for the DBA. Problems, both real and perceived, are common to all computer systems. The DBA may receive a call saying the system is down and then find that the person calling had a locked login account. The DBA may be told that an important month-end batch job failed and that he needs to fix the problem by adding a larger rollback segment to the database. Sometimes the problem and solution will clearly be DBA responsibilities; other times they won't even involve the database. It is at this stage that the DBA really becomes an administrator who must evaluate problems and develop solutions (both technical and non-technical) in a practical manner. This is where a DBA's knowledge, experience, and personality are tested. Problem-solving skills are a must at this level. Troubleshooting is where the DBA really has a chance to shine in crisis situations.

### One Problem Often Leads to Another

Any time you start to fix a problem ask yourself if you are really fixing the problem or just a symptom of a larger issue. Many small problems you see and fix are related to bigger technical problems. Even more disturbing, the technical problem you are fixing is caused by a problem in the business process or human logic.

I was called to fix a "crisis" whereby the USERS tablespace had ran out of space. When developers were running scripts to create test tables, they were receiving errors saying the USERS tablespace was full and Oracle couldn't allocate space. This was deemed an emergency that was stopping development for scores of PL/SQL programmers working on a project. It was of the utmost importance that I add more space to the USERS tablespace immediately.

I asked why not put the table in a different tablespace. There were plenty of other tablespaces with gigabytes of free space, so why not use those? The answer was that the scripts didn't come with those tablespaces specified, so they couldn't have the developers edit their own scripts to use them. I considered this silly from a purely technical standpoint, but since it was their database and their rules, I added more space to USERS.

## Non-Technical Responsibilities

Fulfilling non-technical responsibilities is a key part of being a successful DBA. These are the skills not normally taught in class or detailed in database manuals, but they are what determine who really adds value to an organization.

### Oracle "Expert"

As an Oracle DBA, you are expected to know everything about Oracle, all of its products, the future direction of the technology, and the business practices of the database vendors. This is an impossible task, so it is acceptable just to be highly knowledgeable but willing to research the questions you cannot answer. Most of the people a DBA deals with will not know the difference between Oracle database server products and, for example, development tools. While some questions technically might not fall under the role of a DBA, it is your responsibility to find answers because you are "the Oracle expert." Don't shirk this responsibility, because a large part of your job is inspiring confidence that you are knowledgeable about Oracle and database administration. In pursuit of this goal, don't be surprised if you even have to teach classes for your own organization.

Don't expect all the questions you receive to be about Oracle or even technical. Often the DBA is asked questions that really fall under the realm of the System Administrator. If you can provide accurate answers to these questions, doing so adds value to your position. If you honestly cannot answer a question, either find the answer or refer the person to someone who can. That is part of being a computer *administrator*. It is also beneficial to keep Oracle Corporation press releases, announcements, and stock prices. Again, this might not technically be a DBA task, but you will look pretty silly if you don't even know who is the CEO of Oracle Corporation.

Stay current with computer technology in general. This means reading non-database books and experimenting on your own. This makes you more knowledgeable, more effective, and ultimately more marketable. Most of the new technologies will eventually integrate with Oracle in one form or another so it is definitely worth the time to learn them early on. Java is a prime example. Just a few years ago, Java was simply a new programming language. Now it is integral to the database and future of Oracle. Lightweight Directory Access Protocol (LDAP) is another new technology that a DBA should have at least a basic understanding of. This will help you because as new ideas are passed around the office, it will be you (and not someone else) determining the technical direction of your organization.

## Oracle Point of Contact

Just as you are expected to know everything about Oracle, you will likely be the person assigned to deal with Oracle Corporation. Again, this may not be a DBA technical task, but it is a responsibility of the DBA.

As the DBA you will recommend the level of Oracle support and make sure it is used by your organization. These days online support via MetaLink and phone support are part of most Oracle contracts. It is your job to make sure all the technical people in your organization (such as the developers and System Administrators) have access to online support services. When your people call Oracle Support, it is your job to make sure they get the answers they need. If they don't, it is your job to step in and get a satisfactory resolution. Oracle Support is a great resource, and it is something the DBA should make sure is fully utilized.

Oracle training is often another responsibility of the DBA. Whether it is signing up the people for Oracle University (formerly Oracle Education) courses or sending people to another training organization such as Perpetual Technologies (`http://www.perptech.com`), often it is the DBA's job. You should keep current on what classes are available so that the right people get the necessary training in a timely manner. This might mean knowing what classes are needed to get a Master's Certificate or are needed for Oracle Certified Professional (OCP) tests.

The DBA is supposed to know all of the Oracle products and what they do, so it is logical that the DBA have input when creating the contracts. For example, does the organization really need the Parallel Server option added to the contract? That is something the DBA should know. Oracle contracts can cost a great deal of money, and the DBA is responsible for making sure unneeded features are not purchased. The DBA should also expect to have to justify these costs to management. It is entirely understandable when managers ask for justification as to why they are spending several hundred thousand dollars a year on support. The DBA should be prepared to answer these questions. Depending on the organization, the DBA will have differing roles on determining how much money to spend and when to spend it. The DBA might have a great deal of power and authority in this area or it might be completely out of the DBA's hands. Regardless, the DBA should be kept up to date on the status of the contract and make sure it is paid.

## Process Expert

The DBA is expected to have a solid working knowledge of the core business processes of the organization. The DBA should have a greater understanding of what the organization actually does than simply the tables involved. This is a key area where the DBA can really add value. Because the DBA has access to the data and application processes of the organization, the DBA is in a unique position to optimize those processes as a system. This goes far beyond adding a needed index or parameter; it means being able to identify both needed processes and inefficient processes. If the DBA is able to understand both the "how" and "why" of the business, this person can become the most valuable person in that organization.

## Skills Needed

Not everyone can or should be a DBA. Doing the job well requires a mix of skills more than just being technically competent. Just as you can teach someone the syntax of Java, there is more to programming than typing code. The same applies to being a DBA. It is not enough just to know how the Oracle database server operates; you must be able to think logically and solve problems. Plus you need to be able to deal with people and understand your organization's business processes. If it seems that you must be "a jack of all trades," then you are correct. In its simplest form, an effective DBA needs to possess talents in the areas of technical skills, business skills, and human interaction (Figure 1.3).

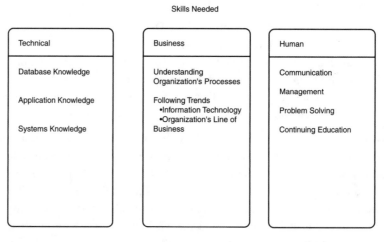

**FIGURE 1.3**

*Skill areas required for DBA.*

## Skills Needed by the DBA Technical

The most obvious area in which the DBA needs skills is the technical arena. This is where most DBAs are at their strongest. Technical skills for the DBA break down into three main categories: database, application, and system.

### Database Knowledge

This is the core technical area of the DBA. It is the RDBMS the DBA is responsible for. The DBA will monitor this on a daily basis and will provide all the maintenance for it. He will know everything about the database and will have it fully documented. It is the database that the DBA is well paid to protect and manage, so the DBA needs to treat it as such. The skills necessary to perform this task are what this book will explain.

### Application Knowledge

The DBA is responsible for understanding and supporting the program code affecting the database. The DBA does not necessarily write code, but he needs to know what it does. If it is stored inside the database, such as PL/SQL packages or Java procedures, the DBA needs to support this. If it runs outside the database, such as Pro*C, the DBA needs to know where it is and how it connects to the database. Installation and maintenance of development tools such as Oracle Developer typically are the responsibility of the DBA. Tuning the code, especially SQL and PL/SQL, is a joint responsibility between the DBA and the application developers.

### Systems Knowledge

These are the technical skills not directly related to managing the database that the DBA is responsible for. In this book we will focus on Unix and Linux skills. There is a strong link between how Oracle and Unix/Linux tie together, and the DBA needs to understand this. Ideally, the DBA should be able to serve as a backup System Administrator if needed.

The more systems administration and networking skills the DBA has, the better. For example, even if the DBA is not responsible for creating a swap file, he should know what it is and how its use affects performance. This book will not teach you how to be a full-time SA, but it will show you the aspects of systems administration that affect your database.

## Business Knowledge

Most production database systems are not isolated, nor are they merely for research. Database systems are typically built to support a larger system that supports a business process. It is this process that the DBA needs to understand.

### Understanding Organization's Processes

The DBA needs to have a clear understanding of what the database is supporting. It is not enough merely to create tables to implement an ERD without understanding the process as a whole. The "how" and "why" need to be understood. Then the DBA can apply relevant experience and knowledge of all the tools and features provided by Oracle, not just the database server, and provide a better technical solution.

More importantly, the DBA will be able to address the business process as a whole. This is where the DBA will add value to the process and to the organization. Eliminating inefficiencies at this level provides a far greater benefit than any amount of tuning at the database level.

### Following Industry Trends

There is another level of business knowledge the DBA must understand. The DBA should follow the industry the organization is in. By watching industry trends and the competition, the DBA can have an idea of what to expect. In large organizations, this usually equates only to a heads up; a single DBA will not be able to influence a major industry change. On the other hand, one person in a small shop (such as an Internet startup) could see a trend and find a way to capitalize on it. This does not fall under the traditional DBA job description. However, considering the detailed knowledge of business, core processes, and data that a DBA should already have, the DBA is in a good position to come up with new ideas.

It is also important for the DBA to keep up with the IT industry. This is different from just staying current with new technologies (both database and non-database related). The DBA should be familiar with major IT industry news. For example, the DBA may use a third-party backup utility. If that software company is bought by a larger company, the DBA should learn what impact this will have on the product's future. This sort of activity occurs all the time, and the DBA should be aware of the potential impact.

## Human Interaction

Human interaction is sometimes the most difficult skill for a technical person to master. This is sometimes referred to as "people skills," the ability to communicate effectively with others, both inside and outside the organization.

I will take this one step further: The DBA should be able to communicate effectively *and* professionally. I have seen some brilliant technical people fail miserably as administrators and managers because they could not interact professionally with others. This is not to say that a DBA or even an SA needs to be everyone's friend, but it is necessary for an administrator to be perceived as a professional and to be able to work effectively with others.

### Communication

A good administrator (DBA or SA) needs to be able to communicate with others. This includes both technical people within the organization and non-technical people outside the organization or even outside the company.

On the technical side, communication is necessary not only to foster productivity, but also to avoid accidental mishaps. I have seen quite a few cases in which administrators have destroyed each other's work or imposed system downtime because of a lack of communication. For example, suppose an administrator wants to apply a patch to a machine that she thinks is not critical. After the patch is applied, it is shut down and restarted (*bounced*), at which point the administrator learns the hard way that someone was using that machine or database. That sort of accident happens quite often, especially in larger shops, because administrators either have not documented their procedures or the communication process is not working.

Accidents are even more common when there is a new administrator in the shop who does not know the environment. Senior team members should take it upon themselves to explain the technical environment and site procedures to new people. It is also the responsibility of new team members to make sure they understand the environment and site standards. By taking the time to communicate effectively with the entire technical staff, many misunderstandings and accidents can be avoided.

## Management

DBAs are often assigned management responsibilities. This often relates to the fact that DBAs are the people who know the system from a technical standpoint, understand the business processes, and already have a relationship with people from different groups. Knowledge of the entire system (not just the database) and how it supports the business makes the DBA a very knowledgeable person and often qualifies him to take on project management responsibilities. The people he manages may not be just DBAs; it might include SAs and programmers in support of a project. More traditional managerial responsibilities such as project planning and budgeting may also be required.

## Problem Solving

DBAs ideally should be natural problem solvers. The people who really add value to their positions are those who can solve both technical and non-technical problems. Much of what a DBA or SA does involves gathering information and making judgments. It is imperative that they be logical, analytical, and detailed in this process.

Many mundane tasks can be automated or simplified with wizards, but complex systems require an experienced human to make judgements. This is especially true when systems experience problems. Many times the real source of an error is hidden and will be found only by someone who understands how the database, operating system, and application interact with each other. Other problems will be of a human nature and will require skills in negotiation and compromise.

## Continuing Education

A good DBA is curious and is willing to take the initiative to learn new technologies. Many DBAs suggest that at least one hour a day be spent reviewing technical manuals or studying new technologies. I agree with that number. It would be easy to say the DBA should get *x* number of hours of classroom training per year, but education does not work that way.

The DBA should get some training outside of work, but each DBA should also have a test database on a test server to play with, and the shop should have an environment that encourages this type of learning. A shop that encourages its technical staff to stay sharp will reap benefits in higher morale and less system downtime. If management frowns on DBAs using company time to learn, the DBA should take the initiative anyway or leave for a more progressive organization. DBAs who do not actively continue their professional education will be left behind by the industry until they are ineffective anywhere but on a legacy system.

# Roles Within the IT Organization

Most IT shops are essentially comprised of developers and programmers, DBAs, System Administrators, and management. The titles might change, and in larger organizations these groups might be split into dedicated groups such as networking/telecommunications, LAN and PC support, data modeling, operations, and help desk.

In every IT shop there is a power structure and an organizational hierarchy. This is more apparent in larger shops, but it exists everywhere. It is very important for the DBA—or any IT professional, for that matter—to understand the hierarchy of that particular shop. This will dictate who reports to whom and how the DBA will interact with other elements within the organization. The hierarchy will probably have been established well before the DBA joins the organization. Additionally, that power structure may have been based on political consideration as much as technical considerations. Regardless, the DBA needs to recognize this and do the job at hand anyway. The following sections discuss consistencies that I have seen from shop to shop and how they affect the typical DBA.

## System Administrators

The role of the SA is very much like that of the DBA, except the SA has a wider range of responsibilities. The main concern of the SA is keeping all the boxes running efficiently and in a secure manner. If this sounds a lot like the DBA's job it should, because both have similar responsibilities.

The DBA will interact with the SA frequently, especially when building a new database or server. The DBA needs to know the server's backup strategy, the disk layout, RAID level, machine memory, and if there are any major non-database applications planned. All these factors will affect the database, and the SA is obligated to provide this information to the DBA.

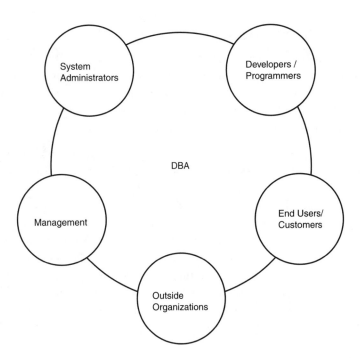

**FIGURE 1.4**

*Interaction with Other Groups.*

Not only is the SA obligated to provide relevant information to the DBA, the SA also needs to provide resources to support Oracle. The DBA will typically have one constant request from the SA: more disk space. Oracle installations and databases can be large, and this requires substantial disk space. The DBA should not expect the SA to hand over gig after gig of space blindly; he should expect to be questioned about why it is needed. Also, if the SA is new to Oracle, don't be surprised if she shows concern about the huge amount of memory being consumed. Oracle can easily use over 250M of memory for just one medium-size database.

With the interaction between the SA and DBA, you might assume it to be a very close and cordial relationship. That is not always the case. In fact, there can be contention between the two. The DBA, rightfully so, is concerned with the welfare of the database. The SA, also quite correctly, is concerned about her box. There is often contention between the administrators on such issues as when to reboot the machine, use of system resources (disk space and memory), backup and recovery procedures, and user policy. This contention is normal, but the DBA needs to make sure above all that data safety and availability are not compromised.

## Programmers/Developers

Programmers are usually the group the DBA will spend the most time supporting and troubleshooting. As programs are written, there are always database or environment changes that need to be implemented by the DBA. The DBA will be involved in code walk-throughs and tuning sessions as well. When working with large or complex applications, it is not uncommon to have Application DBAs dedicated to supporting the developers.

DBAs are also kept busy by developers in another respect: troubleshooting. Most problems in production and most database errors are the result of bad program code. This is not in any way to knock the developer community; it is simply a fact of the IT industry. Whenever the database starts generating trace files or messages in the error logs, the DBA should seriously examine the code being executed, particularly new code. The same applies to problems in production. If there are problems, the DBA should look first at what has been changed in the application. The DBA should ask the developers if they have changed anything. If they say they haven't, the DBA should take it with a grain of salt. Unfortunately, that "no" sometimes means the change actually made was really small and should not have caused problems. In those cases, the DBA should continue to investigate the problem because developers don't always volunteer information if it is their code causing problems.

## Management

As an administrator, the DBA must report to management. A manager may be technical or may be from a non-technical background. Managers typically will look to the DBA for accountability in terms of data availability first and data safety second. The administrator needs to understand that the typical manager doesn't care about how technically advanced a system is, he just wants it to be available to serve its business function. The manager will see seemingly large amounts of money going into the IT shop, and he will be quite upset if problems still occur. The problem might not even be related to the database, but the DBA may have to provide an explanation anyway.

Just as there can be friction with management, there can be a good working relationship. Many managers realize that they don't understand IT and are fearful of trusting their IT staffs completely. An administrator who can address this issue and gain the trust of management can later enjoy a great deal of management support. A good DBA should be able to educate even a non-technical manager. This means explaining to the manager the different parts of a system (at a high level) and explaining how they are dependent on each other. The DBA can explain what it takes to provide high system uptime, both in terms of hardware and in terms of trained IT professionals. If communication is good, the manager can become a champion for the system and will have a good relationship with the staff.

# Customers and End Users

Technical people, especially administrators, must communicate with non-technical people. The population may be inside the organization, outside the organization, or even outside the company. Each will have a different background and needs, but all will expect a level of support from the IT staff.

The administrator regularly must deal with users who are often frustrated with IT. The DBA or SA needs to have the patience to listen to what is being said and provide answers that are understandable. IT sometimes has a bad reputation with users; the administrator needs to recognize this and respond in a professional manner. It may not always be popular to give the answers the customer or user wants to hear, but the administrator needs to be able to do this anyway.

---

### Don't Kill the Messenger

Often times you have to tell management things they don't want to hear. I once had to inform the senior management of a company that if they wanted to upgrade their database and application it was going to take an entire weekend. These people normally got upset at one or two hours of downtime, an entire weekend was nearly out of the question.

Next the SA told them the expensive cluster they had was so outdated it would be more cost efficient to scrap the whole thing and rebuild the system on a smaller, faster server. That really angered them. However, we knew what had to be done. We approached them with the facts and explained to them why this was the case.

They didn't like it at all, especially when we told them that if normal upgrades had been allowed previously this step might not have been necessary. Basically, a large amount of the blame rested on them because they never allowed maintenance downtime. However, they listened and ultimately approved the purchase of the new system and the upgrade. This happened because we explained the situation in a manner they could understand and backed it up with proof.

---

By the same token, the administrator needs to really listen to what is being said. Often it is the end user who is the first to notice a problem with the system, even before the IT staff does. Also, simply asking users if there is anything they think could be improved with the system will promote goodwill and an occasional good idea. Above all, the administrator needs to remember that the system and therefore the administrator exist to support the business and the customers.

## Outside Organizations

The DBA will often have to represent the organization to outside parties. This could mean meeting with vendors and salespeople on a sporadic basis. It could mean negotiating with companies such as Oracle who have preexisting contracts.

At a minimum the DBA will have to interact with Oracle Corporation. This will mean choosing products and negotiating support contracts. This usually involves varying degrees of management approval and consultations with other branches of IT, but it should never negate the technical input of the DBA. Other interactions with Oracle Corporation include signing up for training classes (highly recommended), pursuing technical support issues, and occasionally working with members of Oracle Consulting. The DBA should address these issues on a case-by-case basis, but should not forget that the organization is paying a large amount of money and should therefore receive satisfactory service.

Just as the DBA will deal with Oracle Corporation, there is a host of other outside companies that may demand interaction. There is a seemingly endless supply of vendors continually trying to sell products to IT shops. The DBA should stay abreast with these products, but that could become a full-time job. Instead, the DBA should focus on what the organization actually needs, rather than what the salesperson is pushing.

It is important to keep in mind that the IT shop exists to support the business, not to be a showcase of extraneous technology. The DBA is also responsible for making sure that any new software implemented, related to both database and non-database uses, does not adversely affect data protection or availability. Just because a product is purchased and installed doesn't necessarily mean it will work well with other products. It is up to the DBA to do the actual research and testing needed to guarantee that no unexpected problems or bugs occur because of a new software addition.

## DBA Mindset

Now that we have discussed what a DBA actually does, it is important to discuss the mindset the DBA should have at all times. The DBA needs to be very territorial and protective of the system. No one but the DBA touches the database. Anything that could conceivably affect it is the DBA's business. If application developers want to run new program code, that's fine, but the DBA has the final say in what is run in the RDBMS.

The same goes with anything the System Administrator wants to do. It might be the SA's box, but it is the DBA's database. No server patches or downtime should be allowed without the notification and approval of the DBA. It is the database that the DBA is well paid to protect and manage, so the DBA needs to treat it as such. Don't rely on SAs or developers to consider the effect on the database; that is clearly the DBA's job. Support of the database may sometimes conflict with

**1**

plans of the developers, SAs, or even management. Protecting the safety and integrity of the data may also be an issue when a manager is demanding a down system be made available ASAP, regardless of whether a precautionary backup needs to be made. It is in stressful situations like this that the DBA needs to take a stand and protect the data and database.

## Summary

The database administrator is the person responsible for making sure the organization's data is safe and available. Depending on the shop, the DBA can have different titles or varying responsibilities, but the two principles of data safety and availability remain the same.

DBAs come from many different backgrounds, each shaping how the DBA perceives this new position. Regardless of where DBAs come from, they will require a mix of both technical and non-technical skills to successfully perform the role as the DBA.

# Architecture of the Oracle Server

## ESSENTIALS

- A solid understanding of the architecture of an Oracle database is essential to the success of the DBA.

- A running Oracle database consists of database files, memory structures, and background processes.

- There are three types of Oracle files: software installation files, configuration/parameter files, and actual database files.

- An Oracle instance consists of memory structures and background processes.

- Most of the components of an Oracle database are tunable by the DBA; therefore, the DBA must understand them.

The knowledge of how and why an Oracle database works is essential for the successful DBA. Oracle databases function more as a Unix operating system than as a standalone application. Just as the Unix System Administrator knows the details of how the operating system runs, the DBA must know the equivalent information for the database. Administration of an Oracle database requires fundamental knowledge of its files, memory structures, and processes. There is no GUI that can (or even should) replace this kind of knowledge. Oracle on the Unix/Linux platform gives the DBA such a high degree of control that understanding how the database actually functions is key to building, tuning, and troubleshooting a system.

This chapter details the anatomy and processes of an Oracle database, hereafter referred to as an Oracle server. The chapter assumes that you are familiar with basic relational database theory, as it focuses on the Oracle implementation for the Unix and Linux platforms.

## Oracle Products Relating to Database Servers

Before we dive into the core components of the database server, we should look at the larger picture. Specifically, where does the database reside in relation to the user? Figure 2.1 shows an example of a typical system.

The database resides on a Unix server. Users log into their workstations. They then start up an Oracle application such as SQL*Plus. This tool connects across a TCP/IP network using the Oracle Net8 protocol to establish connectivity with the Unix server running the database. The user is then authenticated and receives a connection with the database. From here the user issues SQL statements that are sent across the network to the database for processing, and results are sent back to the user.

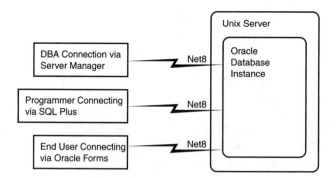

**FIGURE 2.1**
*Oracle Server Overview*

This represents the most rudimentary example of a user accessing a database. In fact, this is about as simple as it gets. We will discuss more advanced architectures in later chapters. In this example we introduced several fundamental components: a user, a user's application, a network, and a database residing on a Unix/Linux server. We will now look at some of the key components in more detail.

# SQL*Plus

SQL*Plus is the most common user interface to the database. It is essentially a command-line utility that enables the user to enter SQL commands for the database. In many respects, it is very similar to a DOS or Unix prompt. The main idea is to provide the user a direct way to interface with the database without a cumbersome GUI.

SQL*Plus can be installed on PCs, workstations, or servers. It can be used to connect to any database accessible via the network. In Oracle 8.1.7, iSQL*Plus will be released to provide the same access from a Web browser. SQL*Plus provides an easy way to access virtually any database as long as the user has the correct security permissions and the network is configured properly. It is this availability that makes this a practical tool. SQL*Plus is available with any installation of an Oracle database and most Oracle desktop products.

Not only is SQL*Plus a widely available tool, it is extremely powerful. Starting with Oracle 8i, any database command can be entered using SQL*Plus. Originally, SQL*Plus was used primarily by users and developers to issue normal SQL statements, write PL/SQL, run scripts, and generate text-based reports. DBAs used a similar but separate tool, Server Manager, to issue DBA-type commands. Now, since Oracle 8i, DBAs can use SQL*Plus to do such activities as start-up and shut down databases, alter database settings, or add users.

As a DBA, most of what you do will be executed via SQL*Plus. In fact, it is preferable for the DBA to be more knowledgeable about SQL*Plus than the GUI management tools. SQL*Plus provides everything you need without a cumbersome GUI. As long as the DBA can reach any PC and use Telnet to connect to the Unix/Linux server hosting the database, the DBA is fully functional because access to SQL*Plus will always be available.

Just as SQL*Plus is a powerful tool and is widely available, it is a potential security risk. While you cannot actually drop a database with SQL*Plus, a user with DBA privileges can practically destroy a database. It is amazing the number of regular users with SQL*Plus on their desktops who don't know how much power they have. The DBA should be conscious of this and be selective with which PCs are loaded with SQL*Plus. While users can connect to a database without SQL*Plus loaded on their PCs, not having it loaded reduces the possibility. Better yet, the DBA should enforce a high degree of security at the user level to prevent users from logging in with excessive permissions.

## Server Manager

Server Manager is very similar to SQL*Plus, but it is geared specifically toward DBAs. It replaced a product called SQL*DBA which was a previous DBA utility. Server Manager has a line mode and a graphical mode, but we will focus on the more common line mode. It is capable of issuing the same SQL statements as SQL*Plus, but it lacks the extensive formatting and report-generating features. All DBA commands can be issued from Server Manager, assuming the user has the correct level of permissions.

In versions of Oracle before 8i, Server Manager was the only command-line tool available to issue DBA commands directly. If the DBAs wanted to start or stop a database, they had to log in using Server Manager. This functionality was not available in SQL*Plus. Starting with Oracle 8i, the DBA functionality of Server Manager was included in SQL*Plus. Oracle has decided to phase out Server Manager as a product, and it will likely no longer be available after 8i. DBAs should now be using SQL*Plus instead of Server Manager. All of the security concerns with SQL*Plus apply equally to Server Manager.

## Net8

Net8 is the network software used to connect to Oracle databases. Originally called SQL*Net, starting in Oracle 8 it was renamed Net8. Anytime you install Oracle products to connect to an Oracle database, you are using Net8. Net8 can be used over such networking protocols as IPX/SPX, DECnet, and IBM LU6.2, but in the Unix/Linux world it is TCP/IP that is used. Net8 can be used for more than just establishing database connectivity. Net8 and its extra features can provide additional security measures, encryption, load balancing, and other management features.

In the example in Figure 2.1, a very simple architecture was introduced. The user had SQL*Plus loaded on a PC connected to a Unix server hosting an Oracle database. A TCP/IP network was established so the PC could connect to the Unix server. A specific Net8 configuration file called tnsnames.ora was configured on the PC. This file contained the IP address of the Unix server and the names of the database(s) on that server. The Unix server had a server-side Net8 file called listener.ora containing the names of the server's databases and basic connect information.

In our example, the user starts SQL*Plus and enters a username, password, and database name. This information, referred to as a *connect string*, is resolved to the desired database server via the client-side tnsnames.ora. The information is sent from the PC across the TCP/IP network on the Net8 layer to the Unix server. On the Unix server, the listener.ora file configures a listener process used to connect the user request to the appropriate database where the username and password are authenticated. Once this is successful, a connection is established between the user running SQL*Plus and the Oracle database. The user can then enter SQL commands on the PC running SQL*Plus. Those commands are sent across the network to the database to be executed, and the results are sent back across the network to the user.

These are the bare fundamentals of how a database is accessed by a user. This example is certainly not intended to provide a high degree of networking knowledge, but only to provide an overview of basic Oracle DBA products and how they interface with the database. Now that we have the context of the Oracle database server, we will examine its anatomy in detail.

## Database Versus Instance

A running Oracle database is composed of three components: files, memory, and processes. Each component is configured and managed by the DBA. Much like the Unix operating system, Oracle runs more as an operating system than a standalone application. Figure 2.2 shows these components.

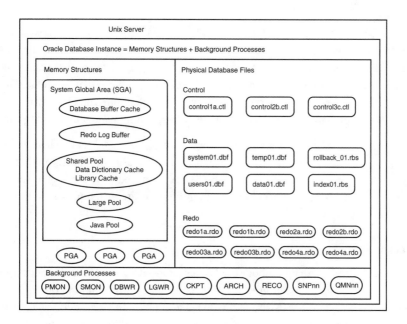

**FIGURE 2.2**

*An Oracle Database Instance*

An Oracle database is different from an Oracle instance. Specifically, a database is just the physical files on disk, but an instance is the memory structures and background processes. The physical database files are simply storage containers for data. It is a database instance that the DBA starts up and shuts down and that users access. Data in the data files cannot be accessed without the supporting memory and background processes.

It is the Oracle background and server processes (similar to Unix daemons) that actually access and manipulate data. These processes move data from disk into shared memory areas for short-term storage, access, and modification. They also move data between memory areas and eventually write data back to disk.

Everything that happens with an Oracle database occurs in memory first before it is moved to disk. Also, these memory structures and, to a lessor degree, background processes are highly configurable by the DBA. Managing these components is where knowledge of Oracle and Unix architecture is essential for the successful DBA.

# Oracle File Types

A running Oracle database is composed of three main components: physical files on disk, several different memory buffers, and background processes. Since physical files are easiest to visualize, we will begin with file types.

If you were to examine all the files related to Oracle on a Unix/Linux server, you would find quite a few. As you can see in Figure 2.3, these files can be broken roughly into three categories: shared software installation files that are loaded via the installation CD, database parameter and logging files, and the actual files composing the database. Most of these files are related to the software installation, and few of those require extensive DBA attention. The DBA typically is more focused on the files of the actual database and the corresponding parameter and log files.

An Oracle database consists of three types of files: control, data, and redo. These three file types are what actually compose a physical database. A database will usually include a mix of at least 10 different files, and if any of them are lost or damaged a severe loss of service could result. The care, maintenance, and function of each file type are different, so the DBA needs to understand these files.

## Control Files

The control file stores information about the file structure of the database. It keeps track of every file in the database, its location, and a time stamp. The time stamp in our case is referred to as a System Change Number (SCN) and is the last time the file's header was modified. Control files also contain the database name, character set, and file type limits.

An Oracle database requires only one control file, but typically three or more identical control files are used. The reason for the redundancy is that control files are absolutely essential for the database to run. If any control file is damaged or lost (such as in a disk crash), the database will need to be shut down and repaired. At this stage the redundancy of the files comes in to play. If there is still an existing good copy, the DBA simply copies the good copy over the damaged file and restarts the database with a minimal loss of service. If all the files are lost or damaged, the DBA will have to perform what can be a tricky and time-consuming database recovery, and lost data may result.

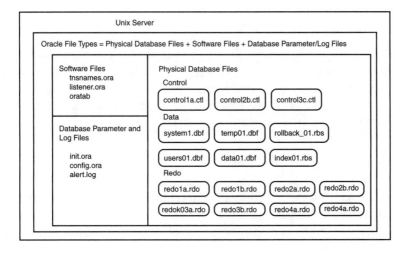

**FIGURE 2.3**
*Oracle Database File Types*

Control files are relatively small in size, and there is no real performance overhead in having multiple copies. The DBA should create the database with no fewer than three control files, located on separate disks with separate controllers. Oracle will automatically take care of writing to each of these files. Therefore, there is very little DBA interaction involved after the control files are created. Control files typically are named with the suffix CTL.

> **TIP**
>
> Never try to open a data, control, or redo files with an editor. You cannot see anything useful (most files are binary) and will only risk corrupting the file. If you want to see a control file's content, issue the statement ALTER DATABASE BACKUP CONTROLFILE TO TRACE. This will create a text file in the background dump area that can safely be viewed using an editor such as `vi`.

## Data Files

The most common type of file is the data file, which stores the information accessed by the database. There are five categories of data files, each distinguished by the type of information it stores. They have different functions and differing degrees of importance.

> **NOTE**
>
> The term *data file* refers to a single physical file. Data files are physical objects, but they are organized logically within the database as tablespaces. One or more of the same type of data file compose a logical tablespace. We will discuss this relationship in greater detail in Chapter 6, "Daily Activities," but for the purposes of this discussion we will use the terms interchangeably.

## System

The most critical data file is the system data file. It contains all the information about the database. This is stored in the data dictionary, which is a read-only collection of tables and views owned by the user SYS. The data dictionary can be considered the "brains" of the database. While control files contain information about the database's physical structure, the system data file contains relational tables containing internal database information of both a physical and logical nature. All of the information about the database, its layout, objects, and their status is stored in the data dictionary.

Normal user tables and sort areas should never be stored in the system tablespace, even though it is technically possible. There are only two users who should own any objects in this file. User SYS owns V$VIEWS, V_$TABLES, and X$TABLES, and the SYSTEM user owns other critical tables. Most of the SYS and SYSTEM tables are too cryptic for the average user to use, so views such as V$ and DBA_XXX are created during database creation. The DBA will become very familiar with many of the V$ and DBA_XXX views because they provide a window into the database.

This is the most critical data file for running the database. If the system data file becomes damaged or lost, the database will crash immediately and require recovery. If the system data file is lost, the database is rendered useless. Unlike control files, the system data file is much larger, often exceeding 250M. There is no way to keep identical copies as with control files. The system data file typically ends with a DBF suffix.

## Data

These are the files most people consider when they think of a database. Generic data files contain all the normal users' data tables such as CUSTOMER and EMPLOYEE tables.

Any user can write to a data file if he has a space quota for that tablespace. Each user is assigned one default tablespace containing one or more data files in which the user can create tables. However, users almost always create and write to tables in an assortment of tablespaces containing multiple data files. Also, tablespaces and data files are not owned by any specific user, so they may be written to by anyone with a quota of space in that tablespace.

For example, a table called CUSTOMER may be created in the CUSTOMERS tablespace, containing one data file called customers.dbf. All the users in the database can add rows to the CUSTOMER table, each signifying a new customer. Additionally, tables logically containing customer type data, such as address information, could be created in the CUSTOMERS tablespace as well as written to the same data file.

There usually are many data files in a database. Tablespaces are often composed of several data files. The file sizes typically range anywhere from 50M to over the 2G limit. Note that some Unix platforms with some operating systems now support files over 2G. Baseline examples include Solaris 2.6 and HP-UX 10.20, but you should verify this for your own platform. There are performance concerns regarding the size of data files, but basically you do not want to use only a few large files if you can spread smaller files over multiple disks.

Data files are not actually required for a database, but this would seemingly defeat the whole idea of having a database. If you lose a data file while the database is running, it should not crash. However, you will lose access to any data contained in that file. Depending on the importance of the data in the lost file, this may or may not stop the business. The DBA should restore an old file from a backup and then recover it to the time of its loss. A data file typically has the DBF suffix.

> **NOTE**
>
> Files for the tablespace USERS and TOOLS are simply subsets of the data file type. These tablespaces are optional, but they are recommended. If a user creates an object without specifying the tablespace, it will typically be created in the USERS tablespace. Oracle add-on productions, such as Oracle Enterprise Manager, sometimes need tables in a database. When this is the case, they are created in the TOOLS tablespace.

## Index

Index files are the sisters to the data files. Tables are created in data files and hold actual data. Optionally, that data can be indexed to provide faster access. Just as you could read through this entire book to find a specific topic, it is much faster to use the index at the end to find the specific page where the topic is located. Indexes created on tables provide the same functionality as indexes in a book, but in a database they are stored in index files.

The same general rules that apply to data files apply to indexes. They are optional, but it doesn't make any sense not to use them. If you lose an index file, the database will still continue to operate, but the associated loss of performance and some index-dependent operations may render the database useless from a business perspective. On the plus side, index files are the easiest for the DBA to recover.

Index files are stored in tablespaces just as data files are stored. Each index file may contain indexes from multiple tables. They typically range from 50M to over 2G as well. Just as with data files, there are performance issues associated with their size and placement. Index files typically end with the IDX suffix.

## Temp

Temp (temporary) data files are simply locations on disk for sorting operations. Some SQL queries require data to be selected and then sorted before it is returned to the user. For example, if a user wanted all employees' names, identification numbers, and salary, starting with the most highly paid employee and ending with the lowest-paid employee, a sorting operation would be necessary. Oracle would find all the employees and their corresponding data, but it would be necessary to sort them based on salary because the rows would most likely not be stored in that order. For performance reasons, Oracle will do a sort in memory until it exceeds a DBA-specified size. Then the sort will occur on disk, which is the temp file.

In Oracle 7 and 8, the temporary sorting area was typically called temp. In Oracle 8i it is usually called sort, but the functionality is the same. Also, in previous versions of Oracle, permanent tables and indexes could be created in temp files, although that was usually not a good idea. That option has been removed in Oracle 8i, so only temporary objects can be written to these areas.

Temp data files require special handling from the DBA. They should be monitored by the DBA because if they are used often, it could be a sign of excessive sorting, which affects performance. Also, the DBA should make sure the temp data file does not run out of space when large sort operations are needed. Each user is assigned a default tablespace and corresponding data file(s) for sorting operations. Temp files usually end with the DBF suffix.

## Rollback

When a user changes a row of data, its old value is stored in a rollback segment. The reason for this relates to the three "R's" of rollback:

- **Transaction Rollback**   When a user updates a row in a table, the old value is stored in the rollback segment in the event the user decides to roll back (or undo) the statement. Actually, the old value really isn't stored. A statement to reverse the row to its previous value is stored. For example, if a user inserts a row into a table, a corresponding delete statement is stored in the rollback segment.

- **Transaction Recovery**   If the database instance crashes before the statement can be committed, the statement will be rolled back (undone) during instance recovery. This is made possible by storing the value in both the rollback segment and the redo log files.

- **Read Consistency**  Oracle promises that users will see data in a read-consistent state within their own transactions. Once the users start modifying data, they will be the only person seeing those changes until they are made permanent with a commit. Other users on the system will not see the uncommitted changes. If a user updates a row, that modification will exist within the rollback segment and will be visible only to that user. Also, the user will not see changes committed by other users that did not exist at the beginning of a statement. Once the update is committed, everyone will see the new value. Oracle automatically applies row-level locks to updated data to prevent two users from modifying the same data.

Rollback segments are stored in rollback tablespaces, which are made up of one or more files. A rollback tablespace typically contains multiple rollback segments. Each rollback segment is a circular chain of extents. Rollback segments are created with a specified number of extents allocated. For example, rollback segment rbs2 (see Figure 2.4) has 10 extents at 500K each. As a transaction grows and more rollback space is needed, the next extent is acquired. If all 10 extents are used, an eleventh is allocated, assuming there is still space in the data file. This also will happen if the transaction needs to write to the next extent, but that extent is already occupied by another transaction. Oracle cannot "jump" over an extent, so it will allocate a new extent.

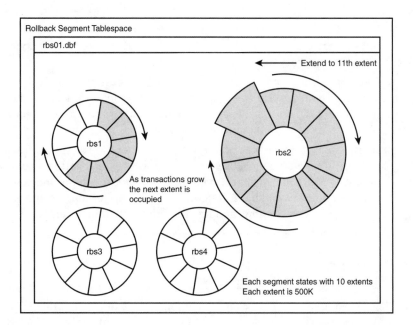

**FIGURE 2.4**
*Rollback Segments*

When a rollback segment extends like this, called an extend, the circular segment has been increased. If the new extent fills, another will be allocated as an extend. This will continue until either the transaction commits or rolls back, the DBA-defined maximum number of extents is exceeded, or the rollback segment runs out of disk space. While this extend is necessary, it does represent a performance hit.

The SYSTEM tablespace automatically has one small rollback segment for use with objects, but the segments we are discussing are for normal users. The DBA should also note that only inserts, updates, and deletes generate rollback. Index changes resulting from these changes are also stored in the rollback segment. Data Definition Language (DDL) changes such as DROP TABLE and TRUNCATE do not generate rollback and cannot be undone.

Files containing rollback segments demand a great deal of DBA attention. They are planned carefully, created, and constantly monitored because they have a large impact on performance. There are also serious implications to the database if any of these files are damaged or destroyed. These issues will be covered in Chapter 9, "Backup and Recovery," and Chapter 11, "Oracle Server Tuning." These files typically end with the RBS suffix.

### Know and Understand the Technical Details

Understanding how and why Oracle does things will often prevent you from doing silly or dangerous things to the database. There are many people who know enough about Oracle to be extremely dangerous. It takes a skilled DBA to be able to identify and stop bad advice before it takes place.

I once had a PL/SQL programmer ask me to drastically increase the size of the rollback segments inside the database. He was going to do large scale processing and wanted to make sure he didn't blowout a rollback segment. By itself that is a fair request and I almost did it without really thinking to ask for details.

It turns out that his script would was going to commit every 10 rows, thus freeing the rollback. It's doubtful he would have used more than one extent before a commit, much less run out of space. I explained to him how rollback segments and commits work and why his request would have done nothing to help his job. Instead we increased the time between commits and left the rollback segments alone.

## Online Redo Logs

The third type of file in an actual database is the online redo log file (also called a redo log file). Every change within the database such as modifying a row of data is written from a memory area (the redo log buffer, described later in this chapter in the section "Memory Structures") to one of the online redo log files. In effect, these files are a transaction log for every change in the database.

There is a large amount of data continually being written to the active online redo log file. When one of the two log files fills up with data, Oracle begins writing to the next online redo log file. This is referred to as a *log switch*. Once the second redo log is filled, Oracle will either write to the next empty redo log (if one exists) or it will begin overwriting the first online redo log file. This is a continuous circular process in which each redo log file is written to in a serial fashion.

Oracle requires that at least two online redo log files exist for the database to run. Actually, Oracle requires two redo log groups. A *redo log group* consists of one or more files called *members*. When Oracle performs a log switch, it stops writing to one group and begins writing to the next group. For performance reasons, the DBA often creates more than the default two groups. Three or four different groups is common for most databases. Also, because the database will crash and lose data if one group is lost or damaged, DBAs often multiplex their redo log files. *Multiplexing* involves creating multiple members (usually two) for each group. Each member is the same size but is located on a different disk and controller to minimize the chance of losing both members.

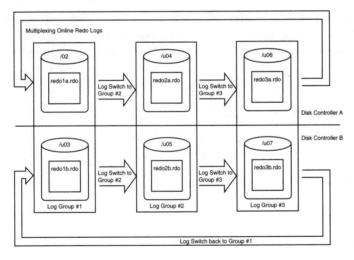

## FIGURE 2.5
*Multiplexing Online Redo Log Files*

Many common performance problems can be attributed to inappropriate size or layout of the redo log files, as well as the frequency of log switches. As a result, they demand a high degree of planning and monitoring by the DBA. These high-activity files should be located on separate disks, preferably away from any other I/O (input/output)–intensive files. Details of how to avoid I/O contention are in Chapter 3, "Planning a Database." Redo log files usually have the RDO suffix.

# Memory Structures

As was stated earlier, a running Oracle database is composed of files, memory structures, and processes. In the previous section we focused on the three types of database files on the server: control files, data files (and their subtypes), and redo log files. We will now focus on database memory structures. There are three memory structures the DBA focuses on: SGA, PGA, and UGA. The SGA is what the DBA is most concerned about because it services the entire database and requires a high degree of configuration and monitoring. PGA and UGA processes exist for individual processes and are not as maintenance intensive as the SGA.

## Shared Global Area (SGA)

The Shared Global Area (also referred to as System Global Area) is the largest and most important memory area for the DBA to understand. The SGA is a collection of several smaller memory pools that are allocated when the database is started. This shared memory area is where all the action within the database occurs. If the system data file is the brains of the database, the SGA is its heartbeat. Without the SGA, the data in the data files is inaccessible.

The SGA includes the database buffer cache, the redo log buffer, the shared pool, the large pool, and the Java pool (new in 8i). Each of these memory areas is configurable by the DBA and has a large impact on performance. The values for the SGA are displayed on SQL*Plus at instance startup. They can also be displayed by either SELECT * FROM V$SGA or SHOW SGA, as can be seen here:

```
SQL> select * from v$sga;

NAME                      VALUE
-------------------- ----------
Fixed Size                69616
Variable Size         111783936
Database Buffers       98304000
Redo Buffers             548864

SQL> show sga

Total System Global Area  210706416 bytes
Fixed Size                    69616 bytes
Variable Size             111783936 bytes
Database Buffers           98304000 bytes
Redo Buffers                 548864 bytes
```

As you can see, the SGA is quite large, over 200M. This is normal for many databases. The composition of the SGA is derived as follows:

SGA =  Database Buffers (database buffer cache)

+      Redo Buffers (redo log buffer)

+      Variable Size (shared pool + large pool + Java pool)

+      Fixed Size

> **NOTE**
>
> Examine the SGA
>
> V$SGASTAT gives a complete breakdown of the SGA. Use this to see how your pools are allocated.

The value Fixed Size is small and not configurable. It contains information about the database used by the background processes. Variable Size is really a sum of the shared, large, and Java pools. To see a listing of their values, enter the following from a SQL*Plus prompt:

```
SHOW PARAMETER pool
```

Each parameter with `pool` will be displayed. To see all published parameters and their settings, just enter SHOW PARAMETER.

This is typically the largest memory area in the SGA. The database buffer cache is a shared memory area used to cache copies of data blocks read from the data files on disk. These blocks can be actual data blocks or they can be from index, rollback, temp, or data dictionary segments. A user will issue a SQL statement requiring a specific piece of data stored in a block. Oracle will quickly read through the buffer cache to see if a current unmodified "clean" copy is present. If so, that copy will be used. If it is not found, Oracle will go to disk to get that block and write it to the buffer cache. Once the data block is in the buffer cache, it can be manipulated to meet the user's request.

A block in the buffer cache can be in one of three states: current, dirty, or pinned. A block is *current* if it is the same in the buffer as it is on disk. These blocks can be accessed immediately as needed. *Dirty* blocks are those blocks that have been modified by a process and must be written to disk before they can be reused. A *pinned* block buffer is one that is currently being used. Note that several copies of the same block, each in a different state, can be found in the cache simultaneously. In this case, one is considered current (consistent with the disk copy), and the others are kept to provide read consistency for other users.

Keeping the data blocks needed by Oracle in the buffer cache is key to performance. Every time a user needs a row of data, that data block will need to be in the buffer cache before it can be accessed. If the block is already in the cache, the user process can proceed. If the block is not in the cache, Oracle must make an expensive disk ready to retrieve that data block and place it in the buffer. It is between 10,000 and 100,000 times faster to access data in memory then on disk. Therefore, it is in the DBA's best interest to make sure buffer cache is properly sized so the data blocks most commonly accessed are found there. The DBA does this by making sure there are enough buffers to keep the most frequently accessed data in the cache.

The size of the buffer cache and therefore the number of blocks it can hold are configured by the DBA. Each buffer in the buffer cache corresponds to one database block. Therefore, the total size of the buffer cache is equal to the size of a database block multiplied by the number of buffers:

$$\text{Database Buffer Cache} = \text{DB\_BLOCK\_SIZE} \times \text{DB\_BLOCK\_BUFFERS}$$

Sizing, measuring performance, and tuning multiple database buffer caches are covered in detail in Chapter 11.

The buffer cache has a finite size, so some blocks are kept in the cache and others are written back to disk to free up space. Oracle manages this process by using two lists: a Least Recently Used (LRU) list and a "dirty blocks" list.

The LRU list is a linked list where blocks are stored. The list has a Most Recently Used (MRU) end and a Least Recently Used (LRU) end. As blocks are read into the cache, they are placed on the MRU end. As time passes and newer blocks are placed at the MRU end, the older blocks are moved down the chain toward the LRU end. Eventually the cache will fill and Oracle will need to make room in the cache for a new block. Modified blocks (on the dirty list) are written to disk to make room. Consistent (unmodified) blocks at the end of the LRU list do not need to be written to disk, so that space is simply reclaimed. When that block is needed again, it is read from disk and again placed on the MRU end. If the block is already in the cache and is needed, it will be moved back to the MRU end, thus giving it more time in the cache. See Figure 2.6.

Note that there is an exception to the rule of putting new blocks at the MRU end. If a Full Table Scan (FTS) is taking place, where an entire table is being read, those blocks will be placed at the LRU end of the list. This is done because these blocks are typically not needed for very long.

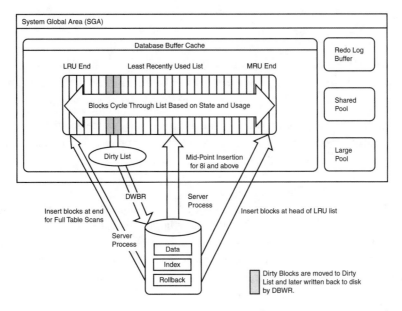

**FIGURE 2.6**

*LRU and Dirty Block Lists in the Buffer Cache.*

The dirty blocks list is technically called the LRUW (LRU Write) list, but most DBAs use the more descriptive name. The dirty block list identifies those blocks that have been modified but not yet written to disk. As Oracle scans the LRU list, any dirty blocks found are moved to this list. These blocks represent data that has not been committed but cannot simply be overwritten. Therefore, they must be written to disk before the space in the cache can be reclaimed. The details of when they are written to disk is covered later in this chapter in the DBWn section.

The previous information is specific to Oracle 7 and Oracle 8, but the buffer cache in Oracle 8i is managed slightly differently. The exact algorithm for how blocks are handled in 8i and above is internal to Oracle Corporation and has not been released to the public. However, based on what information is available, the process seems similar, but with two new concepts: midpoint insertion and touch count. Midpoint insertion is the process of placing new blocks in the middle of the LRU list, rather than at the head of the MRU side. Apparently the idea is that since some blocks are used only once, there is no need to place them at the MRU side if they are only going to be aged out. These blocks are promoted forward to the MRU end by using a touch count algorithm. Each time a block is used, that counts as a "touch." Based on the number of touches a block receives, Oracle moves the block to the "hot" MRU end or toward the "cold" LRU end of the list. This may become tunable by the DBA in future releases.

# Shared Pool

The shared pool provides caching in memory to improve performance for the same reasons as does the database buffer cache. The shared pool, however, caches data dictionary information and parsed SQL statements rather than data blocks. Like the database buffer cache, proper sizing and management of the shared pool is critical for good database performance.

The shared pool is composed of two caches: the data dictionary cache and the library cache. Database control data regarding the status of the instance, its processes, locks, and other attributes is also contained within the shared pool.

## Data Dictionary Cache

The data dictionary cache holds information about database objects such as table definitions and privileges in memory. This is the data dictionary information stored in the system table-space. Upon instance startup this cache is empty, but it will fill up as more SYS objects are queried. This cache is smaller than the library cache, and it is not heavily tuned by the DBA. An LRU algorithm manages the contents of the data dictionary cache.

## Library Cache

The library cache stores the text of SQL and PL/SQL blocks, the corresponding parsed SQL and PL/SQL statements, and their execution plans. These are retained for reuse by future user requests in an area called the *shared SQL area.*

Storing parsed SQL and PL/SQL is a key point in database tuning. Before they can be executed, new SQL and PL/SQL statements must be parsed and plans for their execution must be created. This is a relatively time-consuming process, especially since a SQL query can be executed thousands of times within the database. If each statement could go through this parsing process only once and then be saved in the cache, it would represent a major time savings.

This is exactly what the shared SQL area is for. Each new SQL and PL/SQL statement is parsed, analyzed, and stored in this area. A quick hash algorithm is applied to the statement, and the resulting value is saved. As more statements are issued by users, their SQL is quickly hashed and a value is determined. Oracle then searches the shared SQL area for any parsed statement with the same hash value. If a matching value is found, the two statements match and the normal parsing steps are skipped. Oracle simply executes the old SQL statement again and returns the value to the new user process.

Writing SQL code that is reusable is one of the most effective ways to tune a database. It is the DBA's responsibility to make sure the developers write code that is reusable in this manner. Details on this will be discussed in Chapter 11.

Within the shared SQL area, a LRU algorithm is used to age out old SQL statements. Existing statements in the shared SQL area are also flushed/invalidated under certain conditions. If an object is analyzed with the ANALYZE command, all statements referencing that object are flushed because new execution plans will be created reflecting the new statistics. Also, when a database object is altered, any dependent SQL statements are invalidated. They will be reparsed and new execution plans will be generated next time the statement is reissued.

Neither the data dictionary cache nor the library cache can be sized directly. Both are sized together with the database parameter SHARED_POOL_SIZE. This value is in bytes, not buffers or blocks. Typically, DBAs size the shared pool to optimize the library cache rather than the data dictionary cache. The general consensus is that if the library cache is sized properly, the data dictionary cache will be as well.

## Redo Log Buffer

The redo log buffer contains a record of any change to the database. These include any type of insert, update, or delete activity in Data Manipulation Language (DML), as well as any changes to the database such as creating or dropping objects in Data Definition Language (DDL). These changes are recorded in the log buffer in case the database crashes. As the database is recovered, these changes are replayed (or redone) to bring the database to the exact same condition it was before it crashed; hence it is called a *redo* log buffer.

When a user process makes a change to a row or data object, Oracle writes that to this buffer. While that change may later be rolled back (assuming it is a change to data), it is still recorded. The only exception to the rule of redo activity being written to the log buffer is when an operation is specified as NOLOGGING. Normally this is used only when a large amount of data needs to be loaded but the overhead of generating redo would be too intensive. If the database crashes during the load, that data will be lost, but the DBA should know this and have a workaround solution. NOLOGGING is available with the Oracle data-loading utility SQL*Loader (see Chapter 8, "DBA Utilities") and some SQL statements (see the SQL Reference manual).

Obviously there is a great deal of activity within this memory area. However, it is a relatively small area when compared to other parts of the SGA. The reason is that the redo log buffer is written to disk very frequently. Also, unlike the database buffer cache, the entire redo log buffer is flushed to disk rather than just some blocks. The Log Writer process (see the section "Log Writer Process (LGWR)," later in this chapter) is responsible for writing this buffer to the active online redo log group.

The redo log buffer is sized by the database start-up parameter LOG_BUFFER. This is not the actual number of buffers, but is the total size in bytes. To be the actual number of buffers, divide LOG_BUFFER by DB_BLOCK_SIZE, which is the size in bytes of each Oracle data block. Remember that the value for these parameters may be viewed by issuing the SHOW PARAMETER statement in SQL*Plus. There is an enforced minimum size of $4 \times$ DB_BLOCK_SIZE for this buffer. Tuning-specific details are covered in Chapter 11.

**2**

**ARCHITECTURE OF THE ORACLE SERVER**

## Large Pool

The large pool is an optional memory structure in the SGA first introduced in Oracle 8. It is used to provide memory for specific activities that normally would come at the expense of the shared pool.

The large pool is used to aid the following:

- User Global Area (UGA) session memory when using a Multi Threaded Server (MTS) configuration.
- Extended Architecture (XA)
- I/O slaves
- Recovery Manager (RMAN) backup and restore activities

In many systems there is no real need to configure the large pool. I/O slaves are used only occasionally. Unless the system has a very high number of users or is supporting Enterprise Java Beans (EJBs) or CORBA servers, there is no reason to use MTS. RMAN is being used increasingly on NT systems, but it still is not entirely embraced by most Unix DBAs.

This has to be CORBA. The parameter LARGE_POOL_SIZE configures the size of this memory area in bytes.

## Java Pool

The Java pool is a relatively new memory structure first introduced in Oracle 8i. It is used to store shared Java objects. The more stored Java procedures and EJBs you use, the larger this parameter should be. This pool is used especially during loading of classes, but compiling objects will also use it.

The parameter JAVA_POOL_SIZE sizes the Java pool in bytes. The default size is 20M, with 50M common for systems using more Java. However, a JAVA_POOL_SIZE of 100M or more is needed if `initjvm.sql` is being used to install Java Virtual Machine (JVM) manually, but after the JVM is loaded this parameter can be downsized. If Java is not going to be actively used in the database, the Java pool can be set to 1M without problems.

The SGA is shared memory for the entire database instance and demands most of the DBA's attention. However, there are two other memory areas that the DBA should be familiar with: PGA and UGA.

The Program Global Area (PGA) is also referred to as the Process Global Area. One PGA is allocated for each dedicated server process spawned. The PGA contains user session data, stack space, and cursor state information for its process. This memory area is not shared between processes because each is specific to one server process.

The User Global Area (UGA) is a subset of the PGA. It contains the user session data and cursor information. Sorts for each user occur first in this area. If the sort exceeds the value set in SORT_AREA_SIZE, it will be moved to disk in the temporary tablespace.

When using the dedicated server configuration, the PGA contains user session data, stack space, and cursor state information and is located outside the SGA. Therefore the corresponding UGA (session and cursor information) is also stored outside the SGA. This is a factor because sorts will occur outside the SGA, which is good from a performance standpoint. See Figure 2.7.

If the Multi Threaded Server option is used (see the following section, "Oracle Processes"), the session information and cursor state (UGA) are stored in the SGA, with only stack space stored outside the SGA. This is because the shared server process may need to access any user's session information. If the large pool memory area is allocated, it will store each process's UGA. Otherwise the UGA is stored in the shared SQL area. This can have a negative effect because it takes away space that could be used for caching. Also, any sorts that take place in memory will occur in the shared SQL area, thus consuming even more valuable cache space.

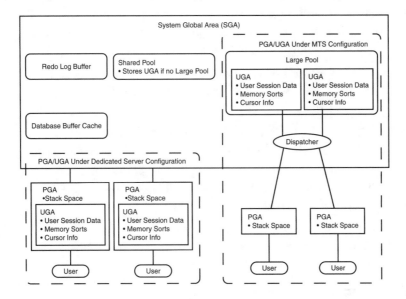

**FIGURE 2.7**
*SGA/PGA and Multi Threaded Server*

# Oracle Processes

The second component of an Oracle instance is the Oracle process. There are two main types of process: user processes and Oracle processes. User processes are on the client side and are requesting data from the server. Oracle processes are those that run on the database server. These fall into two categories: server processes and background processes.

# Server Processes

A server process acts as a go-between for the user process and the Oracle memory structures. When a user process has a request for work, that work is done by a server process. Reading data from disk and placing it in memory also is done by the server process. For example, when a user process requests data, it is the server process that scans the database buffer cache to find it and, if the data is not in the cache, the server process reads the data block from memory into the buffer cache.

The method by which server processes support user processes depends on the database's configuration.

## Dedicated Server

Every time a user process is created, a corresponding server process is created. That server process is dedicated to fulfilling the work requests of that specific user process. The user process will pass its work requests to its server process. The server process will perform the work and return the results directly to the user process.

Information about the user's session is stored in PGA by the server process. The one-to-one relationship between the user's session and server process exists for the life of the user process. When the user process terminates, so does the server process. If the user process does not make any requests, the server process will remain idle.

Oracle requires a dedicated server process for any DBA session attempting media recoveries or a database startup/shutdown. Ideally, user processes running large batch jobs should have dedicated server processes as well. This is because any user process requiring a high degree of service should have a dedicated server process.

The dedicated server configuration is the default for Oracle. It is fairly efficient, robust, easy to monitor, and simple to implement. Generally speaking, unless you need MTS for a specific reason, use the dedicated configuration.

## Multi Threaded Server (MTS)

In some cases, it is preferable to have a few server processes servicing many user processes. Under these circumstances, Oracle's Multi Threaded Server option should be considered.

For example, people working at a call center will need to query a customer record and sometimes enter an order. This is called On Line Transaction Processing (OLTP). In an OLTP situation, users are issuing brief requests to the database on a relatively infrequent basis (in terms of CPU time). Most of the time, the user process is waiting idle for a command from the user.

During this time, the corresponding server process is also sitting idle. This represents a chunk of memory that is not being used. While this may seem trivial, the issue becomes serious if the system is attempting to support hundreds or thousands of users simultaneously.

MTS seeks to reduce the amount of unused memory by allocating a few shared server processes to service multiple user processes. This results in a one-to-many ratio for server-to-user processes (see Figure 2.8).

Under this configuration, when a user logs in the listener identifies this as a new user process. The listener hands off the client process to a dispatcher process. The dispatcher will listen to multiple clients and place their requests in a shared request queue. Shared server processes will take the user's requests from the request queue and process them. When the work is done, the shared server process will place the results in the response queue for the particular dispatcher handling the request. The dispatcher will then pass the return response to the client process.

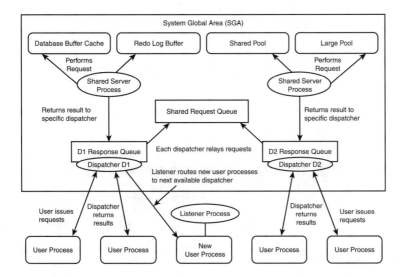

**FIGURE 2.8**
*Multi Threaded Server (MTS)*

MTS requires the use of Net8 and a running listener process even if the clients are on the same machine as the server. Once the user process is assigned to a dispatcher, only that dispatcher process will be used. Requests are placed in a shared request queue for all dispatchers and are processed in a first in, first out basis. Each dispatcher has a private response queue where the finished results are placed by the shared server processes.

Although MTS can be used to support large numbers of OLTP users, it sometimes must be used in support of Java. Specifically, when using Enterprise Java Beans (EJBs) or CORBA

(Common Object Request Broker Architecture) servers, MTS is a requirement. This is detailed in Chapter 16, "Java Inside the Database Server."

MTS is used in conjunction with dedicated server processes. Even if MTS is configured, a DBA will need a dedicated server connection to start up or shut down the database. In addition, Oracle can be configured to enable some normal users to log in as MTS users and others, such as batch jobs, to log in and receive a dedicated server connection.

Configuration of Oracle for MTS requires modification of the init.ora parameter file and the listener.ora file. See Appendix C for an example of an MTS configuration.

## Background Processes

Background processes perform much of the legwork between the memory structures and disks. Anytime data is written from memory to disk, it is done by a background process. The DBA needs to know what each process does and how to configure it. This is critical to understanding how Oracle actually functions.

Like memory structures, background structures exist only when the database instance is running. To see the background processes for a particular database instance, enter the following Unix command:

```
ps -ef | grep -i database_sid
```

Figure 2.9 shows the processes for an Oracle instance.

**FIGURE 2.9**

*Oracle Background Processes*

As you can see, there are multiple processes here. System Identifier (SID) identifies the instance and will be discussed in Chapter 5, "Creating a Database."

Some are server processes and can be identified with:

```
oracleSID (DESCRIPTION=(LOCAL=no)(ADDRESS=(PROTOCOL=BEQ)))
```

or

```
oracleSID (DESCRIPTION=(LOCAL=YES)(ADDRESS=(PROTOCOL=beq)))
```

The background processes are the remaining processes. We will cover each in detail, but for now it is important to note that some are mandatory and others are optional. Specifically, PMON, SMON, LGWR, DBWR, and CKPT (starting in Oracle 8) are required. If any of these processes die or are accidentally killed, the database will crash. The database instance cannot survive without all of these processes. Other processes, such as QMN*n* or ARCH, are required to provide additional database functionality.

## System Monitor Process (SMON)

The System Monitor process is a required Oracle process that is normally sleeping. It wakes up periodically and performs its tasks automatically without any interaction from the DBA.

SMON automatically performs the following activities:

- Instance recovery after a crash. This is the "roll forward" and "roll back" stage in which transactions are resolved to the last completed checkpoint.

- Coalesces (merges) free space on disk within dictionary managed tablespaces if the PCTFREE parameter is greater than 0. This applies to tables and indexes.

- Recovery of space used by temporary segments.

## Process Monitor Process (PMON)

Process Monitor (PMON) cleans up abnormally terminated user processes. This includes rolling back a process's transaction and releasing its resources such as transaction locks and memory. PMON also detects and resolves deadlocks by rolling back the deadlocking transaction. If the database is set to use MTS, PMON will restart dispatcher and server processes that have died unnaturally.

PMON can take a while to wake-up because killed user processes can exist for quite some time. I have seen user logins that have been killed at the Oracle level survive on the database for several days.

Although there are five required Oracle background processes for a running database instance (SMON, PMON, DBWR, LGWR, and CKPT), most DBAs verify if a database is up or down by checking for PMON. It is common to use the Unix command string ps -ef | grep -i pmon to verify if a database is running. This method is often used in Unix shell scripts to check if the database is up before attempting to access a database.

## Database Writer Process (DBWn)

The database writer (DBWn, also called DBWR) writes modified (dirty) blocks from the database buffer to disk. DBWR does this to clear out old dirty blocks to make room for new blocks in the cache. The DBA should note that this includes both committed and uncommitted data.

Oracle will be able to keep track of which data is not yet committed, so it will move out those blocks when necessary. DBWR does not write unmodified (clean) blocks to disk because there is no reason to do so. Multiple DBWRs and slaves can be configured as needed.

DBWR writes blocks at the following times:

- Every three seconds.
- When Oracle cannot find a free block in the LRU list as dictated by the Least Recently Used (LRU) algorithm.
- When the number of dirty blocks in the buffer exceeds the DB_BLOCK_MAX_DIRTY_TARGET setting. This is a value defined by the DBA in the start-up parameter file (init.ora).
- At any system checkpoint (CKPT).
- When an object is dropped from the database.
- When a tablespace is offlined.
- At the beginning of a hot tablespace backup (ALTER TABLESPACE BEGIN BACKUP).

There is normally one database writer process per database instance, but up to 10 DBWRs may be configured. Also, DBWR slave processes may also be used in some cases. These options are further described in Chapter 11.

## Log Writer Process (LGWR)

Log Writer (LGWR) writes all the entries from the redo log buffer to the active online redo log group. If there are two or more files in the online redo log group (as there ideally should be), LGWR will write to all the members in that group simultaneously. If LGWR can write to only one member of the active redo log group, it will do so, but it will issue an error in the alert log. In the event that LGWR cannot write to any of the online redo log members, the database will require a more in-depth recovery, as detailed in Chapter 9. In that case, the DBA must exercise caution because it is easy to lose data accidentally in this scenario.

LGWR writes to the active log group under the following conditions:

- Every three seconds.
- After a commit is issued.
- When the redo log buffer reaches one third full.
- When DBWR writes.
- During a checkpoint.

LGWR also periodically updates file headers during the checkpoint process.

# Checkpoint Process (CKPT)

A checkpoint process (CKPT) is when Oracle takes a moment to flush its buffers and synchronize all its files. During a checkpoint, all the database file headers and control files are updated with the checkpoint sequence number. This number is used to synchronize all the files in the database to a specific point in time and state.

The exception to the rule of all file headers being updated during checkpoints is those data files that are part of read-only tablespaces. Their file headers are frozen at the time they are made read-only.

Memory buffers are also cleared during a checkpoint. All the modified (dirty) blocks in the database buffer cache are written to disk by the DBWR process. Also, the entire redo log buffer is written to disk by LGWR. This guarantees that transactions can be correctly applied (committed) or revoked (rolled back) if the database instance suddenly crashes, because the buffer information would be located on disk rather than in memory.

A checkpoint occurs at the following times:

- Every time a redo low switch occurs.
- When manually initiated by the DBA with ALTER SYSTEM CHECKPOINT.
- Just before any database shutdown except for a shutdown abort.
- When a tablespace is taken offline.
- At the beginning of a hot tablespace backup.
- After the specified time (in seconds) since the last checkpoint as defined by the parameter LOG_CHECKPOINT_TIMEOUT.
- After the specified number of OS blocks have been written to the online redo log files since the last checkpoint. This parameter is set with LOG_CHECKPOINT_INTERVAL.

2

**ARCHITECTURE OF THE ORACLE SERVER**

> **NOTE**
>
> Use of the parameters LOG_CHECKPOINT_TIMEOUT and LOG_CHECKPOINT_INTERVAL is mutually exclusive. You can use one or the other but not both.

Checkpoints do have performance implications. Performance is affected during a checkpoint, so the DBA does not want continual checkpointing. However, if the database instance crashes, the time to recover is also affected. The closer the last checkpoint is to the database instance crash, the faster the instance will be able to recover. There is a tradeoff, and it will be discussed further in Chapter 11. The database parameter LOG_CHECKPOINTS_TO_ALERT should be set to TRUE so that each checkpoint occurrence is recorded in the database alert log.

## Archiver Process (ARCn)

The archiver process (ARCn, also called ARCH) automatically copies online redo log files (which will eventually be overwritten) to permanent archive log files. This is to preserve all the changes to the database in the event a database recovery is needed. This process is active only if the database is in ARCHIVELOG mode and automatic archiving is enabled. There may be up to 10 archiver processes if needed. Details about using the archiver process are found in Chapter 9 and Chapter 10, "When Things Go Wrong."

## Recover Process (RECO)

The recover process (RECO) exists only in distributed database environments. It automatically cleans up failed transactions and tries to resolve in-doubt transactions. This means that if a transaction is occurring between two separate databases and fails, RECO will take the appropriate rollback steps.

## Job Queue Processes (SNPnn)

Job queue processes perform several tasks. They execute jobs submitted by the DBMS_JOB package. They also refresh snapshots of tables in distributed database environments. There may be up to 36 job queue processes.

## Queue Monitor Processes (QMNnn)

Queue monitor processes support the Oracle Advanced Queuing (AQ) option. Up to 10 of these processes can be configured to support message queuing.

## Dispatcher Processes (Dnnn)

Dispatchers are present only when MTS is implemented. The listener process directs incoming user processes to a dispatcher process. The dispatcher process places user requests in a request queue to be picked up by the next available server process. Once the shared server process has preformed the request, the dispatcher retrieves the results from its response queue and relays them to the user.

## Shared Server Processes (Snnn)

Shared server processes are allocated only when MTS is used. These are the shared processes that service the user processes as directed by the dispatcher process. Once the shared server has retrieved the information for the user process, the results are placed in the dispatcher's response queue.

# Transaction Control

Now that we have looked at the Oracle architecture, we will look at a sample transaction in detail to see how everything works together. This sample transaction is shown in Figure 2.10.

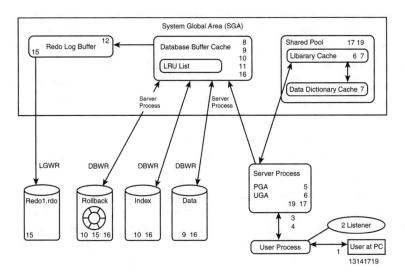

**FIGURE 2.10**

*A sample Oracle transaction.*

The following covers a basic transaction inside Oracle:

1. A user logs starts SQL*Plus and enters a username, password, and database name (referred to as a *connect string*). On the client side, Oracle finds the database name in tnsnames.ora. Using the specified IP address, port number, and connect string, the user process establishes a connection with the database server.

2. The Oracle listener process on the database server receives the user process connection. It looks for the databases in listener.ora and routes the user process to the specified database. At this point we are assuming a dedicated (not MTS) connection.

3. A new server process inside the database is spawned and establishes contact with the user process. At this stage the listener process is no longer involved. After password authentication, the user process is connected.

4. The user process issues a SQL statement to update a row of data in a table. This statement goes across the network to the dedicated server process.

5. Information inside the PGA for the server process is updated to reflect the new SQL statement.

6. The server process runs a quick hash algorithm on the statement and receives a value. It then scans the shared SQL area for any statements with the same hash value. For this example, it does not find a matching hash value.

7. The server process scans and finds a free area within the shared SQL area to work. It parses the user's SQL statement and checks the syntax. Oracle verifies that the table exists in the data dictionary and verifies the user's object-level permissions on the table being modified. Then it looks at the statement and the stored statistics it has about the table and any indexes to develop an execution plan. Oracle then issues an exclusive lock on the row of data and attempts to execute the statement. Oracle reads the current System Change Number (SCN) for the system and uses this value to maintain consistency throughout the transaction.

8. The server process scans the database buffer cache to see if the data block is already cached. In our example the server process does not find a copy of the block in the buffer cache, so it must read in a copy.

9. A scan of the database buffer cache finds a consistent data block buffer that can be reused. The server process follows the prescribed execution plan and retrieves the block containing the row to be modified. It overwrites the buffer cache buffer with the new block. The block is marked as being at the MRU end of the Least Recently Used list. In Oracle 8i it is believed that a block will be placed in the middle of the LRU list using Mid Point Insertion, but there isn't enough public information to confirm this.

10. A slot in the rollback segment header is briefly acquired, and space in a rollback segment extent is found. The block of this rollback segment extent is moved to the database buffer cache in a similar manner as in step 8. An UPDATE statement to undo the user's UPDATE statement is generated and placed in the rollback segment. Undo for the update to the row's index is also generated and placed in the rollback segment.

11. The row of data is actually modified in the database buffer cache memory. Index and rollback segment buffers are also inside the buffer cache.

12. The server process finds space and writes the change to the redo log buffer. This includes both the modified data and the contents of the rollback segment.

13. At this stage the user who issued the statement can see the change with a SELECT statement. Any other user issuing a SELECT statement will see the row as it was before step 4. The block containing the modified row is now considered dirty because it has been modified but not yet committed. If another user attempts to issue a statement to modify the same row, that session will seem to hang because it is waiting on the first user to release the row exclusive lock acquired in step 6.

14. The user types the COMMIT command at the SQL*Plus prompt and presses Enter. This is considered an explicit commit and is a signal to Oracle to make permanent any

changes made by the user. What if the user types the word EXIT at the SQL*Plus prompt and presses Enter? This is an implicit commit because the user is exiting normally. The changes to the data will be made permanent.

15. The Oracle server process receives the instruction to commit the row update. A unique System Change Number is assigned to the transaction in the rollback segment transaction table and in the redo log buffer. LGWR writes everything in the redo log buffer to the active online redo log file(s). Once the data is written to the redo log file(s) and Unix has confirmed the write to be successful, Oracle considers the transaction complete and the change permanent. If a database crash were to occur, the changes to the data would still be recovered.

16. DBWR will eventually write every dirty block in the buffer cache to disk, but that may not necessarily happen yet. In fact, the modified blocks may already have been written to disk. This will occur at the normal time when DBWR writes. A user commit does not force DBWR to write. The modified blocks may still reside in the database buffer cache, but the transaction is considered complete by Oracle because LGWR successfully wrote to the online redo log.

17. The row-level lock held by the user is released. The user receives a message stating the commit was successful.

18. The other statement (in step 13) waiting to update the row will now receive an exclusive row lock, and the steps starting at step 6 may occur.

19. The first user issues an EXIT statement in SQL*Plus. This causes any new DML statements to be committed. Next the Oracle server process and the corresponding user process terminate. Memory resources and any locks held in the user's PGA/UGA are released back to the system.

Note that this was discussed only at the Oracle level and that we did not yet mention how the memory and disk are accessed at the Unix level. Relatively simple transactions such as this occur very frequently and involve many steps. This should underscore the need for a highly tuned system because any inefficiency could result in noticeable performance problems.

## Miscellaneous Database Files

Files that make up the physical database are not the only files the DBA manages. There are specific support files common to any Oracle installation that require configuration or monitoring. These files fall under two categories: database parameter/log files and Oracle software installation files. Each file discussed is a text file and can be edited by the DBA.

## Oracle Database Parameter and Log Files

Each database has its own parameter and log files. The DBA will monitor these files and customize them to meet the needs of the specific database. These files are common to Oracle databases regardless of platform.

### init.ora

init.ora is the parameter file containing configurable database parameters. Actually, the file is called init*SID*.ora, where SID is the name of the database instance. This mandatory file is read during database startup, and the database is configured accordingly. It is by editing this file that the DBA assigns memory pool allocations, number and types of processes, and other parameter settings.

Any configurable parameter may be specified in this file. If a parameter is not listed, the default value is used. With the SQL*Plus SHOW PARAMETER command, values in this file can be confirmed and values not listed in the file can be found. The DBA should become very familiar contents of this file because it determines how the database will operate. It should be backed up regularly, documented, and versioned in case changes need to be backed out.

Changes made to init.ora do not take effect until the database is shut down and started ("bounced"). The DBA should be careful when making changes because, if some parameters are given too outrageous a value, the database will not start. In that case the DBA hopefully knows what has been modified and will choose a more realistic value. Bad database performance can often be attributed to poorly set parameter values in init.ora.

### config.ora

config.ora is an optional file used by many DBAs. The init.ora file can read in parameters from another file called config.ora. Often an IT organization will have a standardized init.ora containing basic settings for use in each database. As individual databases develop specific needs, a config.ora file containing customized parameter settings is often created.

For example, a database may be used for OLTP during the day, but intensive batch processing occurs during the night. By using a basic init.ora file that calls a more customized config.ora, the DBA can run the database with OLTP settings during the day and then bounce the database using another config.ora file to set-up for evening batch operations. This practice is also common when running development/testing databases versus live production.

### alert.log

The alert*SID*.log file contains diagnostic and error messages about the database. This file is written to every time the database is started, stopped, modified or has problems. Routine activities such as checkpoints and redo log switches are also written to this file.

The DBA must monitor this file frequently to check for errors. Ideally the DBA will monitor this file in the morning, at the end of the day, and several times throughout the day. It is in this file that problems and warnings will usually first appear. This is the first place the DBA checks whenever database problems are reported.

## Oracle Software Installation Files

Any Oracle software installation on a Unix or Linux box has certain files that are shared by every database. The DBA must configure these files to meet the needs of the database while making sure that any changes do not affect other databases.

Like all database files, these should be backed up. They should also be versioned, and changes should be tracked. The greatest threat to these files is multiple DBAs making ad hoc modifications and overwriting each other's changes. Situations like this would not necessarily cause an Oracle error, but loss of database service could still result.

> **NOTE**
>
> Connectivity Files
>
> Database connectivity details and configuration of the `tnsnames.ora`, `listener.ora`, and `sqlnet.ora` files are covered in Chapter 5.

## oratab

`oratab` is a simple file that contains the name of each database, the database version, and a Y or N flag to indicate if the database should be automatically restarted after a machine reboot. Oracle initially creates this file, but the DBA needs to make sure it is updated as databases are created and removed.

Viewing this file represents a handy way for a DBA to identify what databases are on a server and their versions. Some clever DBAs also write shell scripts that use this file to identify databases and set up Unix environments.

## tnsnames.ora

The `tnsnames.ora` file is the client-side file an Oracle application reads to get database connection information. The file contains the database name, the server address it resides on, and a port number to connect to. The user will enter a username and password and a database name. Oracle on the client will take the database name given and find the correct corresponding entry in `tnsnames.ora`. It will then attempt to connect to the specified server and database. In effect, `tnsnames.ora` is a database lookup file. It is typically a client-side file, but it is configured on servers to provide database-to-database connectivity.

### listener.ora

listener.ora is the configuration file for the Oracle listener process. The listener process waits and listens for incoming user requests to connect to a database. If a request is technically valid, the listener routes it to the appropriate database. listener.ora contains each database's name and various connection parameters for the server.

### sqlnet.ora

There are many Net8 configuration options available to the DBA. These include encryption, load balancing, tracing, dead connection detection, and the method of user authentication. Many of these options are configured in the sqlnet.ora file. This file can be found on both the client and server. While tnsnames.ora and listener.ora are the most important files regarding connectivity, sqlnet.ora is used to configure the more advanced features of Net8.

## Summary

Understanding how and why Oracle works is a requirement for the Unix DBA. A great deal of problem solving and tuning is made possible by understanding what is occurring in the server. Once this knowledge is obtained, error messages and diagnostics will seem logical, and problems can be solved. Almost anyone can memorize facts, but having actual practical knowledge about the Oracle architecture is how a DBA can become valuable to an organization.

# Planning a Database

## ESSENTIALS

- Planning is the most critical part of any project lifecycle.

- There are many factors, both technical and non-technical, that impact the configuration of the system.

- The role of the database within the overall system will dictate many of the parameters when planning the individual database.

- Plan and configure the database to support the specific type of application to be implemented: OLTP, DSS, or a hybrid of both.

- Use established design and tuning principles, such as OFA, and avoid resource contention when planning and configuring the database.

The planning and design phase of a database is the most influential factor in determining its performance and integrity. At this stage, the DBA should have identified the major business requirements. Now is the time to design a database to meet those business requirements. The DBA will look at the system architecture to determine where to put the database. This will depend largely on the type of application(s) the database will need to support. Next, the Unix/Linux server supporting the database will be selected based upon both technical and non-technical considerations. The DBA will then determine the physical structure and layout of the database files while focusing on performance and integrity. After these steps are completed and a solid database design has been created and reviewed, the actual process of building the system can begin.

## System Architecture

A computer system is typically composed of at least three components: the applications, the data, and the network. A new component, the Internet (Web), is now in most systems as well. The location, configuration, and role of these components are what systems architecture is all about.

If each of these components (application, data, network, and Web) is designed properly from the outset, the system can run very well. If any of these components is mishandled or misplaced, technical tuning will most likely not prevent a large system from being slow.

This relates to the fact that even though a poorly conceived process can be sped up, it is still inefficient. These types of inefficiencies might be barely noticed on small systems, but they become major problems as the system grows. Poorly designed systems do not lend themselves to scaling regardless of the hardware or tuning thrown at them. There is a popular industry estimate that a $1 fix in the design phase costs $1000 to fix in a production phase. I'm not quite sure how that number was derived, but I will say that once a bad process or design has been moved into production, it is *very* difficult to fix.

The DBA needs to know where the database sits in relation to the other components in the system. This will dictate the inputs into the database, the outputs, and the processing requirements. How much of the database will support Web users? How much will be for OLTP users? When will batch jobs be executed on the server? Is this database the primary data store and what are its uptime requirements? These are questions the DBA should ask when examining the architecture.

Each of these architectural components is implemented as a tier on a machine. For example, the application tier can reside on a client's PC as a program while the data is on a Unix box in an Oracle database. The network simply connects these tiers.

An additional Internet tier composing a Web interface is now being introduced in many businesses, especially the dot-coms. Because there are already three tiers and the number of servers is scaleable, this is often referred to as the *n*-tier architecture. This architecture will be discussed in detail in Chapter 19, "9i Server New Features."

Next, take a look at some basic architecture types.

## Two-Tier Basic Client Server Architecture (2 Tier)

The basic client/server (2 tier) architecture was briefly discussed in Chapter 2, "Architecture of the Oracle Server." This architecture has been in existence for several years and will likely continue for the foreseeable future. It is, however, being modified with the addition of dedicated application and Web servers. This architecture focuses on simply two entities: the client and the server.

### Client

The client is the machine where the end user sits. It can be as simple as a dumb terminal with an Oracle Forms order entry application, or it can be a powerful PC with a Visual Basic application. The basic idea is that a user sits at this machine, enters requests, and data "auto-magically" appears on the screen. The user doesn't care where the data or application comes from, just as long as it appears when needed. This goal of transparency is what you want; the user should feel like everything is stored on his/her own local machine.

The role of the client has been in a state of flux. In mainframe times the client was just a dumb terminal with no processing power; it simply displayed information received from the server. This is referred to as a *thin client*. As PCs became more powerful, a greater deal of the workload was transferred to the PC. The idea was to split the processing between the client and server. This was termed a *fat client* because the client held at least some of the application.

> **NOTE**
>
> **Dumb Terminals Still Exist?**
>
> When the reference is made to dumb terminals, it is not solely a historical reference. Dumb terminals are still used by some companies, particularly telephone call centers. I don't see these terminals lasting for too much longer, but they still do exist in some businesses.

As of this writing, the trend appears to have shifted back in favor of the thin client. Some factors influencing this shift were the advent of Web browsers and more powerful servers but no corresponding jump in network throughput. Now most architects are attempting to move as much of the data, application, and processing to the server, thus leaving the client to only request and display information.

Author's Perspective: 20 years ago, the thin client was a terminal attached to a mainframe. Today, it's a Web browser connected to the Internet. In between these periods was the fat client phase. I view this as a pendulum swinging between thin and fat clients. I would be surprised if it stays this way forever, but for now, thin clients are the way to go.

## Server

In a modern two-tier architecture the server holds both the application *and* the data. In this case, the application resides on the server rather than the client. The reason for this is that a Unix/Linux box will have a great deal more processing power and disk space than a PC, so why not use those resources? In addition, if a distributed processing situation occurs where huge amounts of data are being sent from the server to the client for processing, the network will get choked. Also, now that so much of the client requests are directed towards the Internet, it is not really practical to download the results to the client for processing. Figure 3.1 shows the resulting thin client architecture.

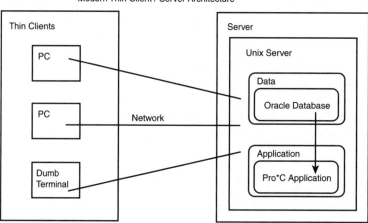

**FIGURE 3.1**
*Thin Client and Server Overview*

## Three-Tier Client Server Architecture

In a three-tier architecture, the data and applications are split onto separate servers. The client still is used as a front end, simply requesting and displaying data. The server-side processing, however, is distributed between a database server and an application server.

There are several reasons for splitting the application and data tiers. By having two servers, each can be dedicated to processing either data or application requests. If both tiers reside on the same server, contention for resources can occur. Also, this isolation of tiers makes for a more manageable system. It is easier to configure and manage a box specifically dedicated to database activities or to application needs.

Figure 3.2 shows how the three-tier architecture is implemented.

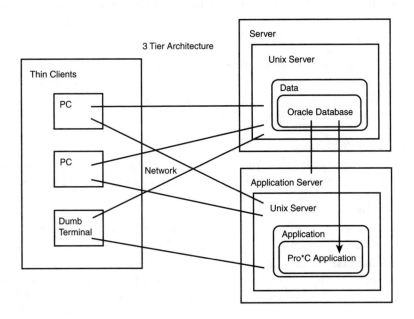

**Figure 3.2**

*Three-tier Architecture*

## Capacity Planning/Sizing

Capacity planning is the practice of sizing a system for the needs of the business. From the DBA's perspective, this means determining what kind and how big of a server and database are needed. The decision will normally be a joint one made by the DBA and SA, and then okayed by management. This is usually a tricky proposition because it involves estimating growth when there is often no baseline. This exercise often results in a potentially large purchase of expensive equipment, thus making the situation more difficult.

If the system is sized too small, more equipment will be needed just to keep the system going. This is expensive because of the lost performance, time to do an upgrade, and the equipment itself. Don't assume this will occur months or years later; an undersized system might become an issue very quickly, especially in a Web environment. If the system is sized too big, it looks like an expensive over-kill. Even if the system is sized perfectly for the first year or two, system resource requirements will change over time. If this looks like a difficult situation, it should, because it is.

The DBA and SA need to understand that their sizing will be questioned (as it should be) and will be second-guessed later (which is counter-productive). They have to make the best estimate possible based on the current (and usually incomplete) information. Make sure the estimate is reasonable, logical, and supported by numbers when possible. Finally, allow it to be analyzed by other technical people and management so they have their say.

Those are some of the issues I look at when I size systems. They fall into both technical and non-technical issues. In my opinion, it is better to error on the side of over-sizing rather than under-sizing. But remember, a well designed and tuned application will have a large impact on the size of machines needed for your system!

## Technical Sizing Issues

The DBA usually estimates the disk space needed over a period of time (at least one year) and the SA takes it from there. However, there are a few issues the DBA should have input on.

### Operating System

I won't get into a huge Unix versus NT debate here because it is safe to assume you've probably already decided on Unix because you are reading this book. Although Windows 2000 is now available and supposedly is improved, many IT people are still suspicious. Traditionally Unix has been viewed as being more stable, more configurable, and more scalable than NT. It will be interesting to see how Windows 2000 changes that perception.

Unix operating systems vendors such as Sun, HP, and IBM have enjoyed a strong position in the market. Most Oracle databases are on these operating systems. The DBA should consider this fact when selecting an operating system. Newer Oracle software releases will first appear on Sun and then on these other systems. It is almost inconceivable for Oracle Corporation to stop supporting any of these platforms. Bug fixes and new products will also come to these more common platforms before lesser-known platforms.

The DBA should also consider the skills and experience of the SA in these matters. It is preferable to run an operating system on a platform the SA feels comfortable with rather than experimenting. The DBA should also consider his or her own expertise on the operating system. Is it something new for the DBA? Are the differences between the OS's something the DBA is able to learn? When possible, the DBA should be willing to learn new platforms, as it will add to his or her own experience and marketability.

The growth and acceptance of the Linux operating system has provided another option to Oracle DBAs. Linux and the associated hardware is usually smaller scale and less expensive than the larger Unix machines. Therefore, Linux tends to compete more with NT than the large Unix systems do. In fact, based on what I have personally seen, Linux seems to be the system Unix people prefer when faced with going to Intel based systems. There are quite a few smaller systems such as individual Web servers and development/test boxes running on various flavors of Linux.

The guideline I've seen used for the most part is to use an established Unix vendor (Sun, HP, or IBM) for the large production machines and use a Linux distribution for smaller testing or development machines. Even this, however, is changing as more companies, particularly smaller dot-coms, are choosing to run everything on Linux. From a DBA perspective, I prefer an established Unix vendor to run anything production. If I'm doing work on my own (such as this book) or doing testing/development, I prefer Linux.

### Disks

This is typically a SA decision, but generally the more and faster the disks, the better. The DBA should request enough disk space for at least one year of database growth. From an Oracle perspective, having a larger number of disks to spread I/O across is far better than having a few large disks. I will show some examples of this later in this chapter. Also, having the disks spread out across multiple controllers is beneficial. The more controllers you can spread the I/O across, the better. The DBA should push for disks that are hot-swappable. The choice in disk brands and Logical Volume Managers (LVMs) is really an SA call, but the DBA should be familiar with the available products. If the database will be a production system, some degree of disk mirroring should be used.

Discussion of RAID, raw filesystems, and I/O caching is covered in detail in Chapter 13, "Unix Server Monitoring."

### Memory

In terms of memory, the more and faster, the better. Oracle likes disks, but it likes memory more. Production Oracle SGAs typically start around 200M and can easily reach 500M. And that is real memory, not swapped out to a disk. Also, one server will likely have several database instances. Don't forget to consider other applications running on the box besides Oracle. If there is only enough memory for Oracle, other applications might be continually swapped to disk because of memory shortages, which will affect the entire system. As a DBA, you should try to convince the SA to max out the memory on the box if at all possible.

### CPU

This really the SA's call, except that the box should have multiple processors (SMP). Oracle will take advantage of multiple processors and it is actually required for some features such as Parallel Query. Most systems are not CPU bound unless there is bad code running, in which case extra processors will not help. Regardless, go with multiple processors if possible to take advantage of Oracle's parallel processing. We will discuss more exotic architectures such as MPP and NUMA in Chapter 12, Unix Operating System Architecture.

## Non-Technical Sizing Issues

The non-technical aspects of system sizing are often overlooked. This includes more than just the price tag involved.

### Machine Cost

This is one item every manager considers. Often times when they see a server exceed $20,000 they go into a state of stock. After all, their PC only costs $1,000 so why should a slightly bigger computer cost so much more? At this stage, the technical person needs to explain in non-technical terms why a Unix server is in a different class than a PC. It helps if you justify the costs in terms of lost revenue because of downtime. I've been in this situation before and it's easy to get frustrated. Simply be professional and explain why this is a cost of doing business.

If purchasing a machine is impossible, look at other options. This means searching for leases, loaners, and special deals. Some vendors and hardware resellers will allow a shop to borrow a machine for a proof of concept. Once a server is actually installed and running a test system, it is easier to get managers to fund it. Server trade-ins and leases are also possible; check with the hardware reseller. Also look for special promotional deals. For example, there recently was a deal where Internet startups could get Unix servers cheap and database software at reduced cost.

When getting a new machine isn't possible, you are left to using what is already on hand. Often an IT shop has a server that *can* support the system, but it is usually less than optimal. In this situation, the server is usually older, not configured properly, and is already supporting system(s). See about getting such servers upgraded. Also, sometimes several machines can be cannibalized into a better server. Work such as this will have to involve the SA.

### System Maintenance

Supporting the system is often overlooked. Many times, companies purchase a state-of-the-art system (hardware and/or database), but don't have any one in the shop who can support it, so therefore it is even more unreliable than a basic system. This happens more often than you think. Being a "regular" DBA or SA is tough enough, but having to deal with new features such as Web servers or clusters will only add to the difficulty. Simply assuming that a technical person can "pick up" the specifics on the job is a costly assumption. Also, just because some-one goes to training doesn't mean they can manage a real system. Even if the DBAs and SAs can manage a complex system, remember that they are highly sought-after individuals and might leave for better opportunities.

---

> ## Keep Your Talented People or the System Will Suffer
>
> I was at one shop that had purchased an early high-availability Sun Cluster where we ran Oracle Parallel Server. The system itself was fairly stable when we had a highly skilled SA who knew about clusters. However, within days of that SA leaving, the system began crashing and the replacement SAs had a terrible time keeping it up. Although they were good SAs themselves, they lacked the skills with clusters. Ultimately, it was an expensive learning curve for the company.

I recommend using new technologies where they make sense; just don't assume that they run themselves. If you find yourself in a shop getting Oracle Parallel Server (OPS) or other advanced features, be prepared to do some extra work. Try to go to training if possible and do some reading and research on your own. If you can become proficient, you will find it a rewarding experience.

### Technology/Vendor

Become familiar with the technologies you are examining before you buy. That sounds obvious, but it is easy to skip. For example, if the hardware vendor is discussing SMP (Symmetric Multi-Processors) systems and MPP (Massively Parallel Processors) systems, do you know the difference? Are you willing to trust the vendor's explanation as to why you need one over the other? Time to do some research if you don't know.

Examine the vendor you are buying from. Sure, Sun, HP, and IBM are the big names in Unix today, but what about other options? This includes Linux. If you decide to go with a specific Linux distribution, will it still exist in the future? Don't go with an OS that is on the way out. Small, local vendors and resellers should also undergo this scrutiny.

From a DBA perspective, consider which versions of Oracle are supported on the OS. For example, Oracle develops and releases each new version on Sun Solaris. They then port to other popular OS's. When dealing with Linux, check on the Oracle online support pages (MetaLink and Technet) to see whether Oracle is certified for a specific distribution and kernel. This is where research on behalf of the DBA is necessary.

Ask DBAs and SAs at other shops about their experiences on a specific platform and database. These people can provide insights and technical advice that can be hard to find elsewhere. If you are making a case for or against a specific system, these kinds of testimonials can carry a lot of weight.

## Optimal Flexible Architecture

Now that you have planned and chosen your system, it is time to consider the Oracle-specific details.

**3**

**PLANNING A DATABASE**

Oracle Corporation has a recommended method of installing and configuring its databases on Unix. Originally written by Cary Millsap, this is called Optimal Flexible Architecture (OFA). This is a common method of installing Oracle and creating databases in a standardized manner. Another way to explain what OFA is would be to describe it as a recommended directory structure for Oracle software installations and database files.

OFA allows multiple versions of Oracle to be installed on one server. Many databases can be managed simultaneously with a minimum of contention. Benefits of OFA include:

- A standardized configuration across all servers
- Easily manageable installation and maintenance of different Oracle versions
- Separation of Oracle software files from database files
- Separation of database files from one another to improve manageability and performance
- Logical and distinguishable database file names
- Separation of files across multiple mount points to reduce I/O contention

The OFA is simply a set of recommendations, not a set of absolute rules. However, Oracle installs the software in an OFA-compliant manner *if* you create your filesystems correctly. Building the database in an OFA-compliant manner is discussed in this chapter and is demonstrated in Chapter 5, "Creating a Database." That chapter does not rehash all the points of OFA, but does cover what you need to know.

Create multiple filesystems to spread your files across as many disks as possible. At one shop I worked at, we had a Sun E450 with 16—18G disks available for the database. I specified disk mirroring (see Chapter 4, "Machine Setup and Installation"), which effectively reduced the number to eight disks. Based on that, a filesystem was created on each mirrored group. Mount points /u01 through /u08 were created to hold Oracle software, configuration, and database files.

---

**NOTE**

OFA Minimum Requirements

At a minimum, an OFA compliant database requires four mount points: /u01 for the software and /u02, /u03, and /u04 for database files.

---

A *mount point* is a Unix term for a filesystem. A filesystem is, from a DBA's perspective, a directory structure that holds files. It can span multiple disks and can be "mounted" from a different machine over a network (Network File System, NFS). Work with the SA to get multiple filesystems created. Each mount point is typically named with the convention /uN where N is the filesystem number (such as /u01).

The next section discusses the OFA structure by looking at what goes under /u01 and then examining the rest of the OFA.

## Files on /u01

Underneath the first mount point, create an app subdirectory. This is where the application runs. Next, on /u01/app, create an oracle subdirectory. Beneath the /u01/app/oracle directory, an important split takes place. The subdirectories /product, /local, and /admin are created, as shown:

```
/u01/app/oracle/product
   "    "    "      /admin
   "    "    "      /local
```

Under ../product, each version of the Oracle database is installed. For example, if you were running Oracle 7.3.4 and Oracle 8.1.6 on the same machine, you would have:

```
/u01/app/oracle/product/7.3.4
   "    "    "          " /8.1.6
```

This is an important distinction. You can have multiple versions of Oracle running simultaneously, but the software is stored in different locations. A common mistake is to try to load all the software in one directory and expect Oracle to figure it out. That won't work! Oracle knows which version you want to run by setting your Unix environment variable $ORACLE_HOME. This variable defines which Oracle software executables are used. For example:

```
echo $ORACLE_HOME
/u01/app/oracle/product/8.1.6
```

This shows that your Unix environment is set to run Oracle 8.1.6. All the Oracle software installation files for 8.1.6 are stored in this directory.

Under the ../admin directory are all the startup, configuration, and log files for each database instance, regardless of version. For example:

```
/u01/app/oracle/admin/prod_1
   "    "    "      "  /dev_2
```

This indicates there are two databases on this machine (prod_1 and dev_2). Prod_1 is an Oracle 7.3.4 production database while dev_2 is an Oracle 8.1.6 development database. If you examine dev_2, you might find the following subdirectories:

```
/u01/app/oracle/admin/dev_2/adump
   "    "    "      "     "  /bdump
   "    "    "      "     "  /cdump
   "    "    "      "     "  /pfile
   "    "    "      "     "  /udump
```

Each of these subdirectories hold files specific to the database instance dev_2. The directory structure and most of the files are created during database installation. You can now briefly examine the contents of each of these subdirectories.

```
../adump
```

**3**

adump contains trace files created by the database for auditing purposes. Every time a user connects internal to the database, this event is logged and a small, unique trace file is created.

`../bdump`

The bdump directory contains perhaps the most important file to the DBA: the `alert_sid.log` file. This file, commonly referred to as the alert log, contains diagnostic and error messages about the database. Every time the database is started or is shut down, messages and parameters are written to this file. The DBA needs to check this file several times daily.

Background dump (`bdump`) files are generated when an Oracle process experiences unexpected problems. A message stating a `bdump` file was generated is sometimes written in the `alert.log`. The DBA should examine the `bdump` trace files and try to determine what caused them. These files should not normally be deleted and, when serious problems occur, they can be sent to Oracle Support for detailed analysis.

`../cdump`

Core dump files are sometimes generated when an Oracle process has really big problems. These files are very large, sometimes filling up an entire filesystem. They are not much use to the DBA, but if needed, Oracle Support can analyze them. Unless there is a real need to keep and compress a core dump, it is usually best to delete the file.

`../pfile`

The `pfile` directory contains the `init.ora` file for the database. This is the configurable startup file that contains database parameters. The details of this file were discussed in the previous chapter.

`../udump`

User dump (`udump`) trace files can be intentionally generated by the DBA or developers. These files contain a wealth of diagnostic information, including the SQL being executed inside the database. The DBA and/or developers can turn on tracing to generate these files. The files are then analyzed to identify problems or tune SQL.

Under the `/u01/app/oracle/local` directory are general-purpose files for the Oracle user and DBAs. It is common to have a sql directory containing DBA SQL scripts here. Unix shell scripts for the DBA are sometimes stored here. The crontab file for the Oracle user (see Chapter 6, "Daily Activities") is usually stored here. Import and export dump directories can sometimes be stored under the `../local directory`, but that varies quite a bit from shop to shop. Export and import files are also often stored under the `../admin/database_sid/exp` directory.

Notice that nowhere under `/u01` have data files been discussed. That is because, ideally, database files will not be located under `/u01`. From an administration standpoint, it is easier to maintain the separation between actual data files and the Oracle installation/configuration files. This simplifies monitoring space usage, backups, and performing recoveries.

## Data Files and Other OFA Conventions

There should be at least three mount points dedicated to data files. An example is as follows:

```
/u02/oradata/prod_1/system_prd_01.dbf
  "     "      /dev_1/customer_dev_dat_01.dbf
```

Physical database files are stored under the ../oradata directory. Notice the subdirectory identifying the database each file belongs to. Also notice the descriptive file names identifying the database (dev or prd)—these aid in administration. In this case, there are no other files on /u02. It is okay to have additional database files on this filesystem, but do not include non-Oracle files or Oracle configuration/installation files.

File names can be in any form; Oracle doesn't care. However, it is a good idea to make them descriptive. Identify the tablespace, database, file number, and file type in the name. For example, customer_dev_dat_01.dbf tells you this is in the customer tablespace of the development database; it is a data (rather than an index) file; it is the first file in the tablespace (you don't know out of how many); and it is a .dbf (data) file.

Typically, a database will have a very similar core set of files for the SYSTEM, USERS, TEMP, and TOOLS tablespaces. When you're dealing with multiple data and index tablespaces, the names can get long.

Officially, the recognized file extensions are limited to .ctl for control files, .log for redo log files, and .dbf for all other data files. It's my opinion that this is a little restrictive. I have an even bigger concern about the redo log files being .log. This can give the impression that these files are viewable and somehow less important because they are *just* log files. In reality, if you lose one of these, you can be in big trouble. File extensions that I have seen used are listed here.

| File/Tablespace Type | Extension |
| --- | --- |
| Control | .ctl |
| SYSTEM | .dbf |
| USERS | .dbf |
| TOOLS | .dbf |
| TEMP | .dbf |
| DATA | .dbf, .dat |
| INDEX | .dbf, .idx |
| ROLLBACK | .dbf, .rbs |
| Redo log | .log, .rdo |

**3**

**PLANNING A
DATABASE**

Those are the basics of setting up an OFA database installation. As the database is actually configured, created, and managed, the benefits to this structure become apparent.

## Application and Database Considerations

To design and configure a physical database, you need to know what kind of transactions will be occurring and with what frequency. You can size and configure an Oracle database very effectively to handle long, intensive transactions, or you can set it up for many small quick transactions. Oracle can handle either situation very well. The trick is identifying what is actually being asked of your database and then making the appropriate settings. Keep in mind that these requirements are seldom clearly defined and they usually change.

There are two popular types of database setups: OLTP and DSS.

### Online Transaction Processing (OLTP)

OLTP is characterized by many, short transactions hitting the database with a high frequency. For example, the database can have hundreds of users in a call center taking orders from customers over the telephone. A sample transaction is as follows:

1. A customer calls the call center operator.
2. A selection on the customer's record occurs to get basic information.
3. The customer wants to order a product.
4. An insert is made into the ORDER and BILLING tables for the new order. An update to the CUSTOMER table might occur.
5. The operator commits the transaction and the customer hangs up. This is the end of the transaction.

This is not a long or intensive operation. All the data selected should be indexed and the INSERT statement is only one row in a few tables. This represents a typical OLTP transaction.

Designing for OLTP is not a problem when there are only a few users and a small CUSTOMER table. Problems start to occur when there are hundreds of users taking orders very rapidly. Problems increase when the users are spread out over a wide geographical area.

Another caveat of OLTP systems is the perceived need to be highly available. Many organizations are convinced their OLTP system needs to be fully operational 24 hours a day, 365 days a year. This brings on some very special needs and is quite expensive. Clustered servers, parallel server databases, and a very proficient staff are needed to provide this type of availability. Because of these reasons, most systems are not truly 24×7, but high availability requirements do exist.

Technical considerations for OLTP systems are as follows:

- Have many, small rollback segments. The standard is one rollback segment for every four active transactions. Each transaction will likely take one (maybe more) extents. This can be a problem, but the bigger problem is the rollback segment header. This header must be allocated initially to find an available block in the rollback segment. If several transactions are fighting each other over this header, the system will suffer.

- Size the redo log buffer appropriately. A redo log switch is a performance hit, so you don't want these occurring all the time. Size the redo log files to about 100M to start with.

- Have a large shared pool. Think about the previous sample transaction. Doesn't it sound reasonable for the same SQL to be executed many times, just with different customers? If you use bind variables for the customer name, the SQL will be cached in memory and the performance will improve.

- Have separate indexes from the data. Create your primary key and all other indexes in a separate tablespace and put that on a separate disk and controller.

- Use small temporary segments. Little sorting will be needed and most of it will occur in memory. If many large joins are part of the SQL, this can cause writes to the TEMP segment. In this case, see about tuning the SQL to use fewer joins or increase the memory with SORT_AREA_SIZE. OLTP transactions should *not* go to disk.

- Look at using MTS, especially when you have a large number of users. This can reduce the total amount of memory needed, but remember this comes at a performance hit.

OLTP is the most common application to manage. If it was the only type of transaction to plan for, the DBA's job could almost be easy. Unfortunately, the DSS transaction often finds its way into a system as well.

## Decision Support Systems (DSS)

Decision Support Systems (DSS) are, for the purposes here, business-oriented batch-processing systems. This chapter does not get into the caveats of running a data warehouse or number-crunching system for scientific research, even though the same principles apply. Batch processing involves a few, very large and intensive queries hitting many tables and requiring many sorts. Nightly processing tasks are considered DSS. A sample DSS job is as follows:

1. Create a report for management to identify sales over the past month. Update and cancel any orders that still have a "pending" status.

2. Select all the orders that were valid over the past month, group them by payment option, and sum the results. Also break this down by the customer's state of residence.

3. This requires a select on the ORDER table, as well as sorting and summing the data, which would likely require using the temporary tablespace. Queries against the CUSTOMER table also take place.

4. Update the orders with a "pending" status. These orders reside in the rollback segments for the length of the transaction.

5. Format the results and create the report.

This is a relatively simple report; most businesses have more complex needs and business rules. However, the idea behind this type of system is a few, very intensive queries hitting the database. These queries can take hours or even days to run. If the job fails, the rollback process can be quite lengthy before the job is restarted. In the meantime, management wants their reports and they frown on hearing "sorry, the job failed." This is even more critical during month-end or year-end processing.

Key components of supporting batch processing are as follows:

- Have fewer, larger rollback segments. DML in a DSS environment can take a large amount of rollback and can hold it for a long time. You do not want a job to die because the rollback segment ran out of space. Create an especially large rollback segment for the big jobs. Before the SQL statement, use SET TRANSACTION USER ROLLBACK SEGMENT *segment_name* to force a transaction to use a specific rollback segment. You learn about how to avoid SNAPSHOT TO OLD errors and rollback segment tuning in Chapters 10 and 11, respectively.

- Have a large temporary tablespace created for disk sorts and joins. DSS will often exceed the SORT_AREA_SIZE parameter and go from memory to disk. These sorts can be large and you don't want to run out of room.

- Use a smaller shared SQL area in favor of a larger database buffer cache. The SQL statements are not going to be executed so frequently that gains made by sharing the SQL are noticeable. Instead, increase the size of the database buffer cache so more data blocks and rollback segments can be cached in memory.

- Make sure you are running well-tuned and properly indexed SQL. This applies to both OLTP and DSS, but I have seen processing times reduced to a fraction of what they originally were simply by SQL tuning and indexing. This can save hours of processing per SQL statement and reduce stress on the rollback segments. Eliminating unnecessary sorts also helps reduce the use of the temporary tablespace.

- Use partitioning and the Parallel Query (PQ) option where applicable. If your CUSTOMER and ORDER tables are huge (millions of rows), partitioning and using PQ might provide some performance benefits. These options start getting into the realm of VLDBs (Very Large Databases) and data warehousing, but if they can help your batch-processing efficiency, use them.

Systems dedicated to DSS are not as common as OLTP systems, but they do exist. However, OLTP systems that have some DSS requirements are more common. These are called hybrid systems and are discussed in the next section.

# Hybrid Systems

Hybrid systems are those with a mix of OLTP and DSS needs. Although most applications are OLTP in nature, most systems are really hybrids. For example, virtually any business that takes orders from customers is OLTP. However, how long can those businesses exist without financial or sales reports? Although the OLTP application is where the company actually makes the money, there are back-end support functions that need DSS (batch) processing.

Review the needs of OLTP versus DSS. Do they look like they are in opposition? They should because the fundamental characteristics of OLTP are exactly the opposite of DSS. If you optimize a system to serve one, the other suffers. This can pose a dilemma for a DBA trying to please both the OLTP users (those who bring revenue to the company) and the DSS users (the managers who the DBA reports to).

There are three common solutions to this dilemma: throttle between OLTP and DSS on one system, run two separate systems, or run OLTP and DSS simultaneously on one system. Figure 3.3 shows how the different hybrid systems can be addressed.

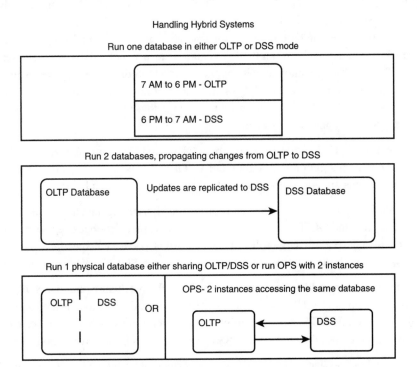

**FIGURE 3.3**

*Handling Hybrid Systems*

Run OLTP during the day and do batch processing at night. If the users are taking phone orders from 7-6, simply run the database configured for OLTP during that time. At 6PM, bounce the instance and bring it up using a DSS configuration. Whenever the nightly backups and batch processing are done, bounce the database again but restart it using an OLTP init.ora.

This works okay if a few assumptions can be made. The hours of OLTP need to be well-defined and not 24×7. Users *can* use the system after it has been bounced for DSS operations, but performance would be impacted. Depending on the call volume in the evenings, this might be acceptable from a business standpoint. Another issue involves Web users. The DBA needs to examine the impact that DSS and bouncing the server have on Web users. Remember, Web access and online ordering implies a 24×7 uptime requirement.

A second solution is to run two databases simultaneously, one for OLTP and one for DSS. Real-time updates are made to the OLTP database. At a regular time interval, these changes are propagated to the DSS database.

There are several methods available to do this. The DBA can perform nightly exports of some or all of the OLTP system and import into the DSS system. This method is conceptually simple, but is time consuming and might not meet the needs of the DSS system. A better solution is to use replication over database links to propagate the changes in a real-time manner. A third option available in Oracle 8i is to run the DSS database as a standby database. Archive logs from the OLTP database are automatically applied to the DSS database. This keeps the DSS system just a few steps behind the OLTP system, but as of now, only read-only queries are allowed against the DSS. The DBA will need to examine these options and perhaps use a mix of them to support a second DSS system.

The third option for hybrid systems is to run both OLTP and DSS simultaneously. This is probably the most common solution imposed by DBAs. Often times, a system starts off as OLTP, but DSS requirements are added gradually until the system becomes a hybrid.

In this case, the DBA must balance the needs of the OLTP users against the batch-processing tasks. I tend to favor the OLTP users in this case. Create as many rollback segments as you do for OLTP, but also have a few large rollback segments that you assign specifically to large transactions. Keep both the database buffer cache and shared SQL areas a reasonable size.

Make sure the temporary tablespace is large enough for the batch sorts, but use SORT_AREA_SIZE to keep the OLTP sorts in memory. I recommend using a dedicated server, not MTS in this situation. If MTS is used, configure it so batch job users have a dedicated server. It is possible to serve both the OLTP and DSS users, but it is a tricky proposition.

There is one final option that is really a derivative of running both OLTP and DSS simultaneously. Oracle Parallel Server (OPS) allows multiple instances to access one physical database. One instance is configured for OLTP and another instance is configured for batch processing.

Assuming the system is designed to handle this type of processing and assuming a qualified staff is available to manage the system, this is a good option because it provides both application partitioning and high availability.

---

**NOTE**

Multiple Applications in One SID

In large IT shops, it is not uncommon for a single database SID to support multiple, unrelated applications. This is necessary to keep from having to support hundreds of databases simultaneously. Even if the applications are different, try to separate OLTP apps from DSS apps and then design the databases accordingly.

---

### Avoiding Disk Contention

Designing the layout of the data files across the mount points is very important for performance. No matter how much memory your machine has, disk I/O will be necessary and it will hurt performance. However, if highly accessed files are on separate disks, this effect can be minimized. Take a look at each file type in terms of contention.

| File Type | I/O Activity |
|-----------|-------------|
| Control | Relatively little access. |
| SYSTEM | Relatively little access. |
| USERS | Little access if objects are created with a separate tablespace defined. |
| TOOLS | Little access. |
| DATA | Depends on the table. Can range from very high to very low. Identify and segregate high activity tables. |
| INDEX | Depends on the object indexed, but it often corresponds to the table activity. |
| TEMP | Depends on the amount of disk sorts. Low for OLTP but can be high for DSS or if the SQL is poorly tuned. |
| ROLLBACK | Very high. |
| Redo log | Very high. |

Based on this table, you want to separate the high activity data and index files, the rollback segments, and the online redo logs. After those have been assigned to separate disks, you spread out the rest of the less contentious files. Ideally, the DBA will know which tables/ indexes are used most frequently and will have many disks on which to allocate files.

**3**

**PLANNING A DATABASE**

Unfortunately, this is seldom the case and the DBA has to work with whatever information and resources are available.

Before you learn to review a sample layout, there are a few other items to remember:

- Mount points can be composed of multiple disks, and those disks might be part of several mount points. For example, disk A might have 9G allocated to /u02 and 9G allocated to /u03. If you put a rollback tablespace on /u02 and a redo log on /u03, you will have contention on the same physical disk even though you think you have distributed the files properly. Work with the SA and know which filesystems mount to which disks and which disks share which controllers. This will also affect your backup and recovery plans.

- Production databases are placed in archive log mode. This means that after every redo log switch, the online redo log files are copied by ARCH to another location (disk, tape, or optical media). This area will be highly active and needs to be large. If ARCH cannot write to this location (because the disk is full), the database will hang and no DML will be allowed. Therefore, make sure this disk has plenty of free space and monitor it regularly. Also, if there is so much I/O contention that ARCH cannot write the archive redo log before that online redo log file is needed, problems will occur. Therefore, make sure this disk (defined as ARCHIVE_DUMP_DEST) has plenty of space and is free from contention. Do not place online redo log files and archive log files on the same disk.

- Create at least three, perhaps even more, online redo log groups. Because the database will likely be in archive log mode, the extra groups will give ARCH time to write to the archive log before LGWR needs the group again. Also, multiplex the online redo logs.

- Consider multiplexing your data and index tablespaces. In this context, a tablespace will be composed of files on separate filesystems. For example, if you know a table will get big and you want to break it apart, place the data files for the tablespace on /u02 and /u03. The first data file created (*_1.dbf) will be used first, and then extents in the second data file /u03 will be used. Just be sure that you don't put the data and index files for the same object on the same disk.

- If a table will get really big, a better solution is to use partitioning. The table (and indexes) can be created across multiple tablespaces. This will spread out I/O and can be used to physically organize the data based on a logical value (using range partitioning).

- Consider backup and recovery when dealing with designing the database. Examine the impact on the database for the loss of each disk. For example, if disk A comprises filesystems /u01, /u03, and /u05, what is the impact of losing disk A? If your system is OFA compliant, you lose all the Oracle installation software on /u01. Hopefully you don't have all your control files or all the members of an online redo log group on /u03 and /u05. If you do, you're in trouble. This type of planning is well worth the time and will be very beneficial when developing your backup and recovery plans.

Take a look at a sample database layout, shown in Figure 3.4. Assume the system is a hybrid of OLTP and DSS. Also, it contains one data file per tablespace and the disks are mirrored with two controllers. It attempts to be OFA compliant, but some of the naming extensions vary.

This is typical of many Oracle installations, except there are more data and index tablespaces. A few *possible* I/O contention issues were intentionally introduced to make the design more realistic. Make note of the following:

- The mount points are separated by controller, using even and odd numbers to identify controller A and controller B. The DBA won't always have this luxury, but the DBA should dictate to the SA how many filesystems are created and the naming conventions when it pertains to Oracle.

- /u01 has been reserved for the Oracle installation files and the database parameter and configuration files. It is possible to add actual database files here, but it makes administration more difficult.

- Online redo log groups have been multiplexed. There are three groups with two members each. Each member is on a separate disk on a different controller. They are also named in a logical manner. For example, when group 1 is active, /u03 and /u04 will be written to frequently. When a log switch occurs, group 2 (/u07 and /u08) will be written to by LGWR and ARCH will read from the first group and write to the Archive Log Dump Destination on /u10.

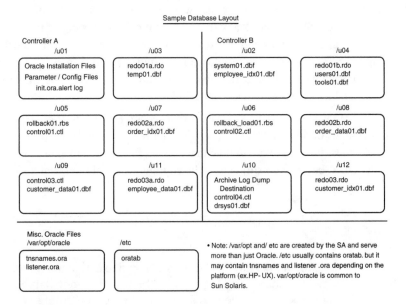

**FIGURE 3.4**

*Sample Database Layout*

- /u10 holds the Archive Log Dump Destination. This disk will continually be written to by ARCH, so only a small control file is placed on it. Monitor this location frequently to ensure that it does not run out of space.

- The control files are multiplexed across four disks and two controllers. Some DBAs would have even more than four copies, but if these disks are mirrored, that should be enough.

- Two rollback tablespaces are created on separate disks. /u05 holds the rollback segments for OLTP users. Depending on the number of users, there can be even more rollback tablespaces created if needed. /u06 holds the large rollback tablespace for large batch processes and data loads (for the DSS users). Remember, when dealing with batch jobs, that a transaction must be directed to a specific rollback segment. Otherwise, there is no guarantee that the transaction will choose the correct segment.

- The TEMP tablespace is located on /u03. This is a possible problem because that disk also contains a redo log member. In real life, there are usually not enough disks to dedicate one for each file. If the application is composed mostly of OLTP (few sorts and joins), this will be fine because TEMP will seldom be used. If the application is composed primarily of batch processes and uses the TEMP tablespace frequently, contention will occur.

- Data and index tablespaces are separated on different disks and controllers. The DBA will hopefully know which tables/indexes are active and which are not so I/O can be balanced. Notice that no data or index files were placed on disks with rollback segments. Avoid trying to compete with rollback segments as much as possible. If necessary, place seldom used or updated tables and indexes with rollback segments. Also, note that disks containing online redo logs are lightly loaded with index and data files. The DBA will often have to place data and index files with contentious online redo logs, but try to put the least used tables/indexes on these on these files.

- Miscellaneous Oracle files such as oratab, tnsnames.ora, and listener.ora are placed in default directories during the Oracle install. The DBA has limited control over the location of these files. It is important to note that they do fall outside the normal filesystems used by the DBA, but they do still need to be configured, monitored, and backed up.

---

### NOTE

Sharing Filesystems

The sample database shown in Figure 3.4 addresses only one actual database. Often times, the DBA will need to share the filesystems with more than one database. In this case, the DBA must coordinate the design and creation of any future databases with the needs of the existing database.

This database design is simply an example. In real life, more data and index tablespaces would be created and the diagram would be more cluttered. However, the OFA principles still need to be followed when applicable. Files would be separated based on contention and attention would be paid to the consequences of losing any given disk.

## Summary

This chapter covered basic physical database design. You need to spend some time analyzing the design before creating the database. The DBA needs to know the architecture of the system and understand how his/her database fits into the grand scheme. Knowledge of the inputs, outputs, and processing characteristics/requirements is absolutely essential. Otherwise, the DBA is really just shooting in the dark.

After you define the requirements, the database is designed to perform well, be easily managed, and withstand damage without data loss. By understanding the types of applications the database will support and following some basic tuning guidelines, the needs of the corporation can largely be addressed with a good design.

# Machine Setup and Installation

## ESSENTIALS

- There are multiple server and operating system requirements that must be met before installing Oracle.

- Work with the System Administrator to set up the server to make the database easily manageable, tunable, and simplify backup and recovery.

- Read and comply with the Installation and Configuration Guide for your particular platform and database version before performing the installation.

- Carefully install the software and note any problems or unexpected situations.

- Verify the installation was successful and apply patches as needed.

This chapter explains what it takes to get the Oracle software installed and running on a machine. You will start with a clean machine loaded only with the operating system and end with a box running Oracle 8.1.6 EE. For demonstration purposes, the box will be running RedHat 7.0 Deluxe Workstation. Differences between this and Sun Solaris and HP-UX platforms are highlighted as needed. The chapter assumes that the basic operating system has been successfully installed and network connectivity has been established.

# Pre-Installation Setup

In most shops, the SA will receive the new server, install the basic OS, configure the network, and add users. He or she will then ask the DBA what needs to be done for Oracle. At this stage, they are no longer talking about high-level system design or server sizing; they are discussing the exact technical needs of Oracle. The DBA will need to tell the SA which users and groups need to be created, how many filesystems to create and their sizes, and if there are any additional patches or server setup steps prior to installing Oracle. This information is found in the Oracle Installation and Configuration Guide (ICG) and Release Notes specific to your release of Oracle. These documents should be included with your software, but if they are not, you can find them on `http://technet.oracle.com` under the documentation section.

Depending on the size and culture of the shop and on the SA involved, the DBA might only be expected to provide this information. If the shop is small and the SA trusts the DBA, the DBA might be expected to actually set up the machine for Oracle. This is preferable because it gives the DBA the assurance of a proper setup. This chapter assumes that the DBA has been tasked with the actual setup, which is common in smaller and medium-sized shops.

## Gathering Information

When you need to install Oracle on a machine, the first step is to familiarize yourself with the machine. Hopefully you already know how the machine *should* be configured, but it is a good idea to verify the actual configuration of the machine. Some of this information will be needed to install Oracle and some of it will help later when creating and managing the databases. The next sections look at some of the machine characteristics of interest to the DBA.

### OS and Version

You need to determine which OS and version is installed on the machine. Do this by using the uname command:

```
$ uname -a
Linux mikehat.mike.com 2.2.16-22 #1 Tue Aug 22 16:49:06 EDT 2000 i686 unknown
```

As you can see here, it is a Linux machine running the 2.2.16-22 kernel and the machine is named `mikehat.mike.com`. Here is what the same command on a Sun and HP box yields:

```
Sun Solaris Machine Information
$ uname -a
SunOS vader 5.8 Generic sun4u sparc SUNW,Ultra-4
```

*HP-UX Machine Information*
```
>uname -a
HP-UX tiger B.11.00 U 9000/893 unlimited-user license
```

Make note of the machine name, its OS version, and the patch level. Ideally, start a spreadsheet for each machine showing the following information:

- OS and version
- Machine name
- IP address
- Database versions
- Database names
- Backup mode (Archive/No Archive)
- Major schemas/applications supported
- Points of contact (POC)

Keep this spreadsheet in your cube and keep a copy in your wallet/purse. Because this document contains potentially sensitive information, you might want to keep the IP address/machine name off the list. Certainly do *not* write down any passwords on this same sheet of paper! I have found a handy list like this especially helpful when I am "on call" and have to support many systems.

Verify that the OS, version, and patch level are compatible with the Oracle software you want to install. First, log in to Oracle's online support page MetaLink (http://metalink.oracle.com). Check under Product LifeCycle, and then Certifications to see which versions of the OS are certified with your Oracle release. As long as your combination is certified, you are pretty safe. However, if, for example, you are trying to load Oracle 8.1.6 on Solaris 8 before it is certified, don't expect a huge amount of help from Oracle Support. I had to do this once. It loaded and ran successfully, but because I was running in an "unsupported" configuration, Oracle was under no obligation to provide support.

Next check the README.TXT and Installation and Configuration Guide (ICG) for your Oracle release. See http://technet.oracle.com under documentation for this information. Read this *before* you try to install the software. Look for specific OS patch requirements and known bugs/issues. You need to verify that your OS is patched to or above the level specified in the Installation and Configuration Guide. Remember that just because the SA installed the operating system does not necessarily mean this same person also applied all the required OS patches to it (a common mistake).

**4**

**MACHINE SETUP AND INSTALLATION**

To check the patch level of your machine, type:

```
showrev -a (for Sun machines)
```

To see which packages are installed on your Linux machine, try this:

```
rpm -qa
```

If your machine meets or exceeds the level specified in the manual you should be okay. If it is deficient, find out what is missing and what it affects. Take this information to the SA and find out why the patch was not applied. Unless there is a compelling reason not to apply it, have the SA apply the patch.

## Memory

The DBA should already know from the server-sizing stage how much memory is on the machine, but it is good to verify the information. To do so, type:

```
$ dmesg | more
Linux version 2.2.16-22 (root@porky.devel.redhat.com) (gcc version egcs-2.91.66
...
Memory: 516136k/523264k available (1048k kernel code, 412k reserved, 5604k
data,
 64k init, 0k bigmem)
```

This gives you all the messages during boot time and this will contain the amount of memory on the machine. Remember, you want as much memory as possible to hold the SGA. In this case, there is 512M of real memory. Check your ICG for the minimum requirement for real memory and swap space.

### NOTE

**Verify Memory Is Recognized**

Sometimes on Linux, not all your memory is detected. On my machine, Linux thought I only had 64M to start with. If you are having these problems, edit (as root) /etc/lilo.conf to the total amount of RAM minus1M (511M in my case), and then issue the command /sbin/lilo, and reboot. After rebooting, the top of your /etc/lilo.conf should look like this:

```
append="mem=511M"
boot=/dev/hda
...
```

## Swap Space

Oracle documentation usually calls for a swap file that's two to three times the amount of real memory on a machine. To find the amount of swap space allocated, issue:

```
$ dmesg | grep swap
Starting kswapd v 1.5
Adding Swap: 1228932k swap-space (priority -1)
```

## Disks

Check the disk and filesystems available. Most likely they will need to be reconfigured to reflect the OFA requirements specified in Chapter 3, "Planning a Database." To check disk and filesystem sizes, enter the following commands:

```
Sun Solaris
$ df -k
Filesystem          kbytes     used    avail capacity  Mounted on
/dev/vx/dsk/var     3933982    46614 3848029     2%    /var
swap                3386832        0 3386832     0%    /var/run
/dev/vx/dsk/opt     3009327   397623 2551518    14%    /opt
/dev/vx/dsk/u01     5235898  3660752 1522788    71%    /u01
/dev/vx/dsk/u02     5235898  3169993 2013547    62%    /u02
/dev/vx/dsk/u04     5235898  4310880  872660    84%    /u04
swap                3387200      368 3386832     1%    /tmp
/dev/vx/dsk/u03     5235898  4132592 1050948    80%    /u03
```

```
HP-UX
>bdf
Filesystem          kbytes     used    avail %used Mounted on
/dev/vg00/lvol3      299157    91918  177323   34% /
/dev/vg00/lvol1       83733    34640   40719   46% /stand
/dev/vg00/lvol8     2003481   557889 1245243   31% /var
/dev/vg00/lvol7     1001729   638769  262787   71% /usr
/dev/vg00/lvol6      600571   254233  286280   47% /tmp
/dev/vg09/lvol1    17772544 11525424 6149564   65% /saveroot
/dev/vg05/lvol5     2048000  1381379  628015   69% /oracle
```

```
RedHat
$ df -m
Filesystem        1M-blocks   Used Available Use% Mounted on
/dev/hda5              3969    319      3448   9% /
/dev/hda1               220      5       203   3% /boot
/dev/hda15             1181      4      1117   1% /home
/dev/hda9              3150      1      2988   1% /tmp
/dev/hda6              3938      1      3737   1% /u01
/dev/hda10             1969      1      1868   1% /u02
/dev/hda11             1969      1      1868   1% /u03
/dev/hda12             1969      1      1868   1% /u04
/dev/hda13             1969      1      1868   1% /u05
/dev/hda8              3250   1888      1197  62% /usr
/dev/hda7              3351     34      3147   2% /var
```

This gives the filesystem layout and the space available in kilobytes for Unix and megabytes for RedHat. Later in the chapter, you learn how to configure these settings.

## CPU

The DBA really doesn't have control of the CPUs and they really are not tunable, but you should know how many you have and their speeds anyway. To get a quick count of the number on the box, issue this command:

```
$ dmesg | more
Linux version 2.2.16-22 (root@porky.devel.redhat.com) (gcc version egcs-2.91.66
19990314/Linux (egcs-1.1.2 release)) #1 Tue Aug 22 16:49:06 EDT 2000
Detected 801431 kHz processor.
...
Pentium-III serial number disabled.
CPU: Intel Pentium III (Coppermine) stepping 06
```

Once again, dmesg provides valuable information from system startup. Knowing the number of CPUs you have is beneficial if you attempt to use parallel processing features such as the Parallel Query (PQ) option.

## Network Information

This is not DBA territory per se, but you need the IP address to log in and the domain name to install Oracle. Check /etc/hosts to get network information. You can also use ifconfig -a to find information:

```
$ /sbin/ifconfig -a
eth0      Link encap:Ethernet  HWaddr 00:01:03:2D:4C:A2
inet addr:192.168.1.11  Bcast:192.168.1.255  Mask:255.255.255.0
...
```

Here, you can tell that the machine's IP address is 192.168.1.11.

There is one last command that will get a large amount of information about most of the previous topics, but it is a bit unwieldy. Try using /usr/sbin/prtconf. This will print a good deal of information if you are on a Sun Solaris box.

That covers it for obtaining basic system information. Just as there are many ways to write a program, there are many ways to get this information. System-monitoring tools exist which will give this information and more. These tools are discussed in Chapter 13, "Unix Server Monitoring," but they are not installed on every system nor are they always available to every user.

# Configuring the System

Now that the DBA has accessed the existing server, it is time to configure it for Oracle. This discussion works on the assumption that Oracle has never been installed on the server. Specific Oracle users and groups need to be created. Filesystems (/u01 ... /u0X) need to be built and sized. Shared memory parameters for the server need to be configured to handle the Oracle SGA. These are fairly standardized from one Unix server to the next except for adjusting the shared memory parameters. This is shown in this chapter, but you should find the actual numbers from your platform specific Installation and Configuration Guide.

## Root Password

To configure the system to install Oracle, you need a root password. This is the all powerful superuser account that allows you to do anything on the box. SAs normally don't just give this password out to anyone. Some shops will allow certain DBAs to have the password as long as they use it only for DBA purposes. You will need this password to create the users, groups, and filesystems for Oracle or you will need the SA to do it.

Giving the root password to non-SA staff can be a touchy subject. Many SAs and management will fight against it. There are many valid reasons why the root password should *not* be given to anyone except SAs because the risk to the system is so high.

My opinion is that, in a large shop where there are many SAs available, the root doesn't need to leave their control. If something needs to be done as the root user, an SA should be available. On the other hand, in a small shop I think the DBAs should have the root if they are competent and trustworthy. It should be understood that the DBA has the root only to act when time is an issue and the SA is not around, not to change settings on a whim. There are times when the SA won't be around, but something on the system will need to be done. Here, a Unix-savvy DBA can "save the day" and fix the problem. Ultimately, this is a decision for the individual shop to make.

## Groups

Users exist in Unix within groups. A user will have one primary group and can have multiple secondary groups. A group dba needs to be created. The root user can easily create groups via the command line, as follows:

```
[root@mikehat /root]# groupadd dba
```

Use more on the file /etc/group to see the groups in the system. The user oracle needs to have dba as its primary group. Other Unix users can be in the group dba as well. Being in the group dba gives the user the capability to connect internal in the database with full DBA privileges, so do this carefully. Do not put the root user in group dba. To see who is in the group dba, try this:

```
$ grep dba /etc/group
dba:x:504:oracle,mikew
```

The users oracle and mikew are in the group dba and will be able to connect internal into this system.

> **NOTE**
>
> Connect Internal Is Going Away
>
> The use of connect internal is being unsupported by Oracle Corporation because it is a perceived security risk. Many DBAs I've worked with don't agree with this change and like the ease of being able to simply connect internally. The change is scheduled to take effect in 9i.

Recent Oracle documentation talks about a new group: oinstall. This group is for sites with multiple Oracle installations that are trying to separate ownership of the database files and the software files. The documentation says to make this the primary group for oracle. Based on knowledgeable people I've worked with and on my own experience, you can go without creating this group. Simply create a user oracle and assign the dba group to it.

## Users

Oracle requires an oracle account, which owns all the software installation files, parameter files, and database files. This is the Oracle user.

This user can be created via the command line using the useradd command, but it is easier to use an admin tool to create the user. Use SAM on HP-UX and admintool on Solaris to create users and groups.

To create the oracle user on RedHat, use an admin tool such as KDE User Manager. See Figure 4.1.

Assign the user a home directory, name or comment, login shell, and assign the user to group dba. The choice of shell is up to the person using the account, but many DBAs prefer the Korn shell. Once the user is created, you can verify it by checking /etc/passwd. Use grep, more, or vi for the file (be careful!) to see the username and user information. If you are unfamiliar with these commands or with the vi editor, refer to Appendixes A and B.

## Disks

Filesystems need to be created for Oracle. They will follow the layout defined in Chapter 3. If you are on Unix and are going to use RAID and striping, you'll probably need the SA's help. This might involve the use of a Logical Volume Manager, which is the SA's territory. If the filesystems are simply going to be laid over the disks on Linux, it is probably simple enough for the DBA to do. During the Linux installation process, you can create your filesystems if you like using Disk Druid. Once the OS is installed, the Linux cfdisk utility can be used, as illustrated in Figure 4.2.

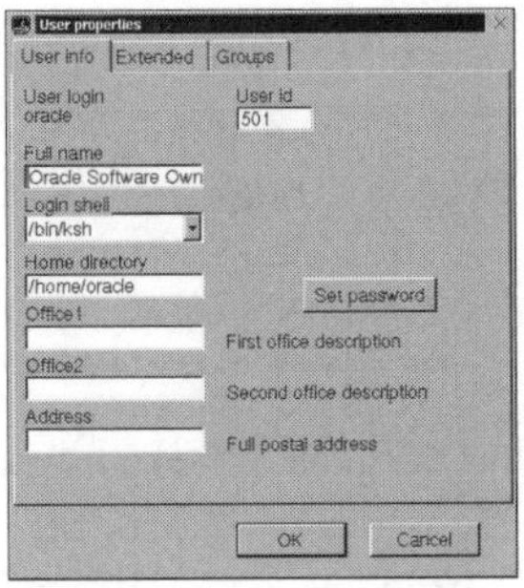

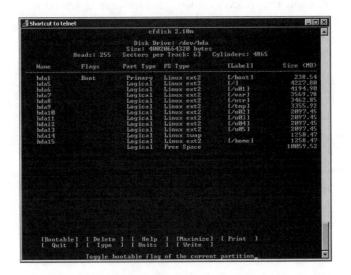

**FIGURE 4.1**

*Creating the User oracle.*

**FIGURE 4.2**

*Creating Filesystems.*

The user oracle in group dba needs read/write/execute access for /u01../u0X. The SA often forgets this step when configuring the system for the DBA. If this happens expect your install process to end very quickly, saying that Oracle cannot write to /u01. For example:

```
$ ls -l
...
drwxr-xr-x    3 oracle    dba              4096 Feb 16 17:06 u01
drwxr-xr-x    3 oracle    dba              4096 Feb 16 17:07 u02
drwxr-xr-x    3 oracle    dba              4096 Feb 11 16:21 u03
drwxr-xr-x    3 oracle    dba              4096 Feb 11 16:21 u04
drwxr-xr-x    3 oracle    dba              4096 Feb 11 16:21 u05
```

The Linux system in this example has only one physical disk. The use of a single disk limits the system to 12 actual filesystems including /, /boot, /tmp, /var, /usr, /home, and /swap. Therefore, you can only have /u01 ../u05 as actual filesystems. To simulate the 12 dedicated Oracle mount points covered in Chapter 3, you can create soft links to directories /u06../u12 on the /u02../u05 filesystems.

A true production machine (regardless of whether it uses Unix or Linux) should have more than one physical disk for size, performance, and fault-tolerance reasons, but this is a common setup for Linux testing and development boxes.

> **NOTE**
>
> Solaris Specific Directory
> Sun Solaris requires that a /var/opt/oracle directory be created and owned by Oracle.

## Kernel Parameters

You need to configure certain shared memory settings for Oracle. These affect the size and number of the shared memory segments and semaphores. They are stored in the /etc/system file on Solaris, which can be edited in vi. If you are on an HP, use the admin tool SAM to edit these parameters. In the Linux world, you will be editing /usr/src/linux/include/asm/shmparam.h and /usr/src/linux/include/linux/sem.h. Each Oracle Installation and Configuration Guide comes with a listing of minimum values for its platform. The following is a sample listing from a Sun /etc/system file:

```
set shmsys:shminfo_shmmax=805306368
set shmsys:shminfo_shmmin=200
set shmsys:shminfo_shmmni=200
set shmsys:shminfo_shmseg=200
set semsys:seminfo_semmni=4096
set semsys:seminfo_semmsl=500
set semsys:seminfo_semmns=4096
set semsys:seminfo_semopm=100
set semsys:seminfo_semvmx=32767
```

Make a backup of this file, edit (using vi) the real copy to have the values listed, and then bounce the box so the changes take effect. Each of these parameters is discussed in detail in Chapter 12, "Unix Operation System Architecture."

> **NOTE**
>
> Hexadecimal Parameters
>
> On Linux, some values can be in hexadecimal format. For example, file shmparam.h defines SHMMAX as:
>
> ```
> #define SHMMAX 0xF424000    /* max shared seg size (bytes) */
> ```
>
> The easiest method here is to just use your online calculator to determine that this is really 256M or .5 the value of physical memory on the machine, as required by the Installation and Configuration Guide.

## Oracle Environment Setup

After the machine is configured in accordance with the Oracle Installation and Configuration Guide and Release Notes, you are nearly ready to start the install process. The only remaining step is to set up your Unix environment for the user oracle.

This discussion assumes you are using the Korn shell, but a Bourne shell will also work. The environment for the Korn shell user is defined by .profile. This file is read every time you log in; it sets up your basic environment. From an Oracle perspective, it tells Unix which database software to use and which database to connect to.

> **NOTE**
>
> Shell Programming
>
> Comprehensive shell programming is outside the scope of this book, but it is necessary if you are a Unix DBA. You will write, modify, or use many shell scripts to automate database-management tasks. You don't have to be able to write complex programs from scratch, but you do need to be able to read, understand, and modify code.

**4**

MACHINE SETUP
AND INSTALLATION

If your account was created on a Unix system, you probably have a skeleton .profile file. Use `ls -al` in your home directory to see a long listing of all your files, including those starting with a dot. On Linux, you might need to copy your .bash_profile file to your .profile (for example, `cp .bash_profile .profile`). Your SA might have a standard .profile file to use as a template to get started. Figure 4.3 shows the basic settings you need to install Oracle for the first time. This is from a Linux system that created a .bash_profile, but I copied and modified it to be a .profile file.

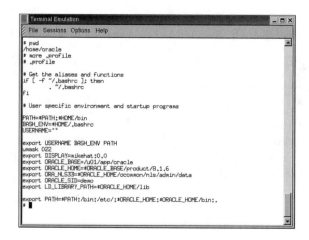

**FIGURE 4.3**

*Initial oracle .profile*

These are only the basic settings you need to install Oracle for the first time on a server. Once the software is installed and a few additional Oracle files are created, you can customize your .profile to reference these files. This is discussed in Chapter 5, "Creating a Database."

To determine your environment, type env. This will display all your current settings, even those not defined in your .profile file. Each value is identified by a variable such as $ORACLE_HOME. To identify the value of a specific variable, echo the variable name prefaced by the $ sign:

```
$ echo $ORACLE_HOME
/u01/app/oracle/product/8.1.6
```

This shows that you are set to use the Oracle 8.1.6 software. If you wanted to change the value of a variable, you must export the value to that variable:

```
$ echo $ORACLE_SID
demo
$ export ORACLE_SID=mh1tst1
$ echo $ORACLE_SID
mh1tst1
```

In this case, you just changed your environment to connect from the demo database to the mh1tst1 database.

Key Oracle environment settings include the following:

- **ORACLE_BASE** This is /u01/app/oracle. This is the starting point for your Oracle software. From this directory comes your admin, product, and local subdirectories. Assuming Oracle is not yet installed, there is no actual /u01/app/oracle directory structure. You need to create /u01 (with the correct permissions), but the app/oracle is created automatically during the installation process.

- **ORACLE_HOME** This is /u01/app/oracle/product/8.1.X. This is where each version of the Oracle software is installed. For example, you could have separate subdirectories for 8.0.5, 8.1.6, and 8.1.7. In fact, you are required to install each release in a different ORACLE_HOME, otherwise Oracle won't know which executable to run. Verify your ORACLE_HOME before you start any Oracle program. Although you can mess-up and use the wrong SQL*Plus to query information, you don't want to be connected to the wrong software when starting up a database.

- **ORACLE_SID** This is your Oracle System Identifier. It is an eight-character unique identifier that determines which database you are attempting to connect to. You'll learn about naming conventions and ways to circumvent this value in the next chapter.

**NOTE**

Always Verify Your SID

Verify your ORACLE_HOME and ORACLE_SID before you perform DBA tasks. It is *very* easy to accidentally connect to the wrong database (ORACLE_SID) or connect using the wrong software (ORACLE_HOME). This is particularly common when you have multiple screen sessions and versions of Oracle running. If you don't verify this often it is only a short matter of time before you do something to the wrong database. Using echo $ORACLE_SID every time before you log in is not being paranoid, it is being responsible.

- ORA_NLS33. ORA_NLS33 and NLS_LANG refer to the National Language Set used by Oracle. They are required only if you are creating a database in a character set other than US7ASCII. For the most part, they are not used.

- LD_LIBRARY_PATH. LD_LIBRARY_PATH provides a link to shared Oracle libraries in $ORACLE_HOME/lib.

> **NOTE**
>
> CLASSPATH Variable
>
> You need to set CLASSPATH to use Java, but Oracle documentation recommends not setting this variable during the install.

- PATH. This is your Unix path. It is the order of directories that Unix searches to find the executable for each command you enter. For example, if you issue ls, Unix will look through each directory listed in $PATH until it finds the *first* occurrence of ls. It will then use that particular executable. If it cannot find a copy of ls, it will issue a message "ksh: ls: not found."

  The same applies if you try to start SQL*Plus. Unix will look through every directory specified in $PATH for an executable called "sqlplus". If it finds one, it will start it, otherwise it issues the message saying it cannot be found.

  The last statement in the .profile file adds the $ORACLE_HOME/bin containing SQL*Plus to the path so Unix can find it. The statement export PATH=$PATH:/bin:/etc:$ORACLE_HOME:$ORACLE_HOME/bin:. sets PATH equal to the value already in $PATH plus the value in $ORACLE_HOME (the Oracle software directory for your version), $ORACLE_HOME/bin (binary executables directory), and your current directory (identified by the period). This will force Unix to search all these directories to attempt to find the program you want to execute before Unix gives up. To see which executable you are using, issue which *your_command:*

  ```
  $ which sqlplus
  /u01/app/oracle/product/8.1.6/bin/sqlplus
  ```

- DISPLAY. DISPLAY is used for XWindows when attempting to start a graphical program, such as the Oracle Universal Installer (OUI). It tells Unix which machine you are using to pop-up the program. It is the name or IP address of the machine you are physically sitting at, plus :0.0. Notice that it is the machine you are physically at, *not* the machine you are attempting to connect to. For example if I was trying to load Oracle on 192.168.1.11, but I was sitting at 192.168.1.10, I would do the following:

  ```
  $ export DISPLAY=192.168.1.10:0.0
  $ echo $DISPLAY
  192.168.1.10:0.0
  ```

## Don't Forget to Set Your DISPLAY

The most common errors when doing installations usually relate to either failing to comply with the ICG or not setting up your environment variables correctly. Of the environment variables, DISPLAY is most common.

I was once trying to install remotely over a network. However I made a classic mistake and didn't set the DIPLAY to the IP address of my client. When the graphical installer tried to start, it would fail every time.

Ultimately I figured out what was wrong and I fixed it. The install then went fine. However, since then I always double-check my environment and verify that my DISPLAY is set properly.

- umask. umask defines the default read/write/execute permissions on any file or directory you create. Every file and directory in Unix has a defined setting that can be viewed with ls -l. For example:

```
$ ls -l
-rwxr-xr-x    1 oracle   dba          65 Feb 16 21:45 tail-1
```

The file tail-1 is owned by the user oracle in the group dba. The rwxr-xr-x defines read (r), write (w), and execute (x) permissions for the file. This long string is better defined as:

```
        rwx               r-x               r-x
        owner oracle      group dba         all other groups
```

The file owner oracle has read, write, and execute (rwx) permissions on this file. Any other user in the group dba has read and execute (r,x) permissions on the file. All other users not in group dba have (r,x) permissions on tail-1. Each – means no permission is allowed for that value. The leading – indicates a file, whereas a "d" indicates a directory and an "l" indicates a link.

Each permission (r,w,x) has a numeric synonym, where read (r) = 4, write (w) = 3, and execute (x) = 1. These values are added within the owner, group, and others subgroup. Therefore, tail-1 is referred to as having 755 permissions where owner oracle has rwx (7), members of group dba have r-x (5), and all others have r-x (5).

umask comes into this by setting a default numeric value to any file or directory created. Every file or directory starts off with a default value such as 666 for this example. umask defines the value (permissions) to subtract from the 666. The standard umask for Oracle files is 022. Therefore, you start with 666, but umask subtracts 022, so the resulting permission value is 644. This way, only the oracle user can write (edit) Oracle files, but others can read them. The default value is normally 666 or 777. To find your default value reset your umask to 000. Then create a file and check its permissions. What you see there is the default value by the system and is what umask starts with, as shown:

```
[root@mikehat /root]# umask 000
[root@mikehat /root]# ls -l mike_test1
-rw-rw-rw- 1 root    root    0 Jun 29 06:49 mike_test1
```

As you can see, the resulting value is 666 with a umask of 000 being applied; don't always assume it is 777. You know the default value is also 666. Your umask is normally set in the .profile.

# Installing Oracle

Once the server, filesystems, and oracle user are set up, you are ready to install the Oracle software.

## Installation Process

Assuming you ordered your CDs from Oracle (rather than downloading them from Technet), you will likely have a box full of CDs. Some will be the extra utilities, whereas other CDs contain the actual Oracle database software.

Find the CD labeled *Oracle 8i Enterprise Edition Release X*. There will likely be several labeled like this, but some might be Standard Edition. If you are licensed for Enterprise Edition, make sure you load that version, and not Standard Edition (an easy mistake!). Also, some Unix CDs are labeled for either 32-bit or 64-bit. If you don't know what you are running, ask your SA.

Load the CD into the server and then mount the CD-ROM drive. Sun Solaris machines normally mount the CD-ROM automatically, but if you use a system that doesn't (such as Linux), simply type as root mount /mnt/cdrom. Then log out as root because you want to install as the oracle user, not as root.

Log in as Oracle and verify your environment variables. cd to /cdrom and read the Release Notes if you haven't already. To begin the actual installation, type:

```
. ./runInstaller
```

This begins the Oracle Universal Installer (OUI). This is a fairly standard Java-based program used to install Oracle software. If you get an error message stating the OUI could not start, check your DISPLAY settings. Remember, it is the IP address or name of the machine you are physically at, with a :0.0 at the end. You need to be on XWindows to run this OUI, normal telnet cannot run the GUI.

The OUI will start with a welcome screen. You will be given the option to deinstall products, check what is currently loaded via Installed Products, exit, or choose Next. Select Next and you will go to the File Locations screen. Leave the Source path as the default because you are loading from the CD. The Destination path should be set to your 8.1.6 ORACLE_HOME. If it is not correct, edit it now, as shown in Figure 4.4.

**FIGURE 4.4**
*Specify ORACLE_HOME.*

You are prompted for the Unix group that owns the software, as shown in Figure 4.5. This is the primary group you assigned to the user oracle. In this example, it is the dba group.

**FIGURE 4.5**
*Identify the Unix Group.*

Assuming this is the initial install, you will be prompted early to run (as root) the file orainstRoot.sh to create a directory (see Figure 4.6). If so, bounce out to a separate window, log in as root, and run the script. This script creates the file /etc/oraInst.loc, which specifies the location for oraInventory and identifies the Unix group dba.

**FIGURE 4.6**
*Run orainstRoot.sh to Create /etc/oraInst.loc.*

Assuming you have an Oracle CD with Enterprise Edition Server, you will have several installation options. You can install the Oracle Client, which simply contains database utilities such as SQL*Plus (no actual database), or you might load the Enterprise Edition, which is the actual database and utilities. Choose the Enterprise Edition, as shown in Figure 4.7.

**FIGURE 4.7**
*Product Selection.*

OUI will ask if you want a Typical, Minimal, or Custom installation, as shown in Figure 4.8. Unless you are having problems (some software isn't loading), are short on disk space, or just want specific products, install the Typical installation.

The Typical installation will attempt to create a demo database. This is not the actual database you want to create for normal use, but it is a good way to verify the installation. Set the SID to demo. The Global Database Name is your SID.domain_name. If you do not remember the domain name, go to another window and type uname -a. In this example, the Global Database Name is demo.mike.com, as shown in Figure 4.9.

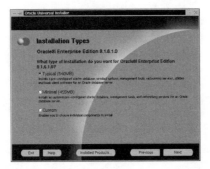

**FIGURE 4.8**

*Installation Options.*

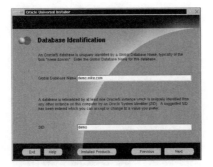

**FIGURE 4.9**

*Specifying the SID and Global Database Name.*

When the OUI asks for a location to install the database files, enter /u02, as shown in Figure 4.10. OUI is looking for a place to load the demo data, control, and online redo log files. Do not enter /u01, which is where the Oracle software will be installed. Also, do not specify /u02/ oradata; the OUI will create the oradata subdirectory automatically. Notice that because this is just a demo database, OUI does not prompt for mount points /u02../u04.

Next is a Summary page containing all the products you intend on installing, as shown in Figure 4.11. Verify that your Destination directory is your $ORACLE_HOME. When you are satisfied, click Install to begin the actual installation.

Once you specify all the installation parameters, OUI will install the Oracle software files. This might take a while to complete. If it seems as if the OUI is hanging for a few minutes, be patient. Figure 4.12 shows the installation progress screen.

**FIGURE 4.10**

*Enter the Location for demo Database Files.*

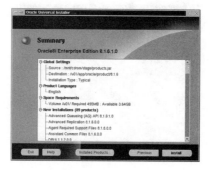

**FIGURE 4.11**

*Verify Install Options on Summary Screen.*

**FIGURE 4.12**

*OUI Installing the Oracle Software.*

At the end of the software installation, you will be prompted to run root.sh. Again, open another window and run this file as root. This time, the script is different and you will be prompted for some directories. Simply accept the defaults.

```
[root@mikehat /root]# cd /u01/app/oracle/product/8.1.6
[root@mikehat 8.1.6]# . ./root.sh
```

The OUI will quickly run the Net8 Configuration Assistant and will then move to the Oracle Database Configuration Assistant. At this stage it will copy the database files to disk for the demo database. Once this is done, exit the installer. Your XWindows screen will not have returned a prompt yet. This is not hanging; simply press the Enter key to get a prompt.

## Verification of a Good Install

After the install process, the GUI screen should report that the install was successful; it requests that you check the log file for errors. If you got to this point, good, you might have a valid install. In some cases if the database-creation process hangs, you might be forced to cancel out of this step. Even if the database creation and/or network configuration failed or was canceled, the installation of the software might be successful.

Check to see whether the demo database you created during the install is up. The existence of this database doesn't guarantee that everything is correct, but it will tell you if the install really went bad. Again, if you had to cancel the database creation because of hanging problems, do not expect the instance to exist. After a successful install and database creation, the instance is left running so you can check on the mandatory background process pmon:

```
$ ps -ef | grep -i pmon
oracle    1670     1  0 14:38 ?        00:00:00 ora_pmon_demo
danw          1826 1580  0 18:32 pts/0   00:00:00 grep -i pmon
```

If this process is up, you have a running database. If not, either something went wrong (check the install logs at $ORACLE_BASE/oraInventory/logs) or you decided to cancel the database creation.

If the install did go bad, check the install log for errors. Common mistakes include trying to write to filesystems you don't have permissions to or writing to a filesystem that is too small. More often than not, your system was not set up properly in accordance with ICG and Release Notes. Revisit these documents to make sure you complied with all the requirements.

Assuming that you have fulfilled these requirements and you still are having problems, it's time to look for outside help. Oracle on Unix is usually pretty stable, but installing it on Linux can be tricky. Although you should have already reviewed MetaLink and Technet *before* your install, now is definitely the time if problems persist. Technet and MetaLink both have separate forums for users to write in questions. These have proven to be extremely valuable, especially when working with Linux.

**4**

**MACHINE SETUP AND INSTALLATION**

## Always Have a Few Hacker Friends

If there is one thing I've learned it is that there is always someone who knows a little more about the kernel than you. There is nothing wrong with this; many people send their free time playing with operating systems. In fact, it is good to know these people when you have problems.

I was having some problems doing an operating system install. The help support line didn't know what was going on and basically told me I was on my own. The documents I had weren't much help either. Finally I simply asked for help from a colleague who plays with operating systems both on the job and in his free time. He explained the problem was in the operating system release rather than anything I had done. Next he explained a way he and a few other folks were getting past the problem. I tried his solution and it worked perfectly.

It's cases like this where networking with other technical people can save you time and headaches. Once you have exhausted your resources it's okay to ask for help as long as you don't abuse it.

Check out Technet first if you are trying to install Oracle on Linux and are having problems. The forums should tell you which library you are usually missing (which is not your fault) and how to find and install it. I personally have yet to see an install of Oracle on Linux work without some tweaking, so don't become frustrated if you experience problems as well. However, running Oracle on Linux is well worth any minor headaches you endure initially. If you fail to find information on Technet, try MetaLink. After that, try some of the many external Oracle-related Web sites. Just remember to take any advice with a grain of salt. If all else fails, call Oracle Support.

If you are installing on a major Unix release, the process usually goes fine. Most of the problems are because of mistakes by the user, not Oracle or Unix. Once again, check your Installation and Configuration Guide and the Release Notes. Make sure that your system meets the baseline requirements, your filesystems are not full, and that you can write to your directories.

MetaLink is the place to first start looking if you have problems when installing on Unix. Look under the bugs and patches sections for your platform and release. You will likely need to patch your release anyway, so you might as well see whether any of the related bugs affect the installation. Once you have exhausted the resources on MetaLink, call Oracle Support. I have received excellent support from the Unix group concerning installations. Often times they will have release-specific information and installation tricks that are not common knowledge, but will save you time and headaches.

---

### Persistence Is Good Up to a Point

I was once installing an earlier version of Oracle on Unix. However, every time I installed there were problems. I checked and double-checked my environment and settings, but each time the install didn't go right. I spent the better part of a day doing this.

Frustrated, I called Oracle Support. Within a couple of minutes, the support analyst told me there was a specific combination of products I had to install in a specific order. Otherwise I would run into a bug that wasn't documented for the general public. I followed the advice and the install worked perfectly.

On that day Oracle Support certainly paid for itself. They provided needed information I couldn't find anywhere else. Too bad I waited so long before using this resource.

---

## Applying Patches

It is often better to apply patches to the database after an install. For example, you might have just installed Oracle EE 8.1.6.1, but now you want to patch to Oracle 8.1.6.2. If you have to apply patches, now is the time to do so, before you have running production databases. Patches are covered in detail in Chapter 14.

## Summary

This chapter covered how to take a box only running Unix or Linux and install Oracle on it. Installing Oracle is not difficult, but it can be tricky. You have to read up on your platform to make sure it is compatible with your Oracle release. Next, you have to configure your machine in accordance with the Oracle Installation and Configuration Guide and Release Notes. Then comes the actual installation of the Oracle software, followed by verification.

Hopefully, the entire process will be uneventful and without errors. Otherwise, you get to dig into the details of what went wrong and search for solutions not listed in your install guides. Fortunately, there is a wealth of valuable online resources. If that fails, you can call Oracle Support.

**4**

MACHINE SETUP AND INSTALLATION

# Creating a Database

## ESSENTIALS

- Create a basic set of database scripts so each database creation is configurable and repeatable.

- Customize your database create scripts to meet the requirements of the database you need to create.

- Run the database create scripts and check for serious errors.

- Fix any problems with the database and configure your network files for the new database.

- Configure several Unix files to set up your Oracle environment when you log in.

Now that you have installed the database software, it is time to create your database. This involves creating the database data files, control files, and online redo log files. It also involves creating the necessary parameter (init.ora) and log (alert.log) files to support the database. Oracle will read the parameter file, open the database files, and allocate the SGA and background processes so you will have a fully functional database instance.

In terms of database design, this chapter creates a hybrid database (part OLTP, part DSS) and gives it the file layout described in Chapter 3, "Planning a Database." At the end of this process, you will have a running hybrid database suitable for OLTP and DSS use. Next, you will learn how to establish basic connectivity into this database from other machines. Finally, you will customize your .profile file to handle multiple database environments.

# Generating Creation Scripts

Scripts are a key part of any DBA's life. Their use cannot be overstated. There is simply no way any DBA, no matter how good, can type everything by hand. The most productive DBAs will attempt to script as much work as possible so it is reproducible and standardized. Given a choice between performing a task manually in five minutes or taking 10 minutes to write a short script, more often than not more time will ultimately be saved by writing the script. In fact, many sites operate largely on scripts. If you don't use your organization's scripts, you will get reprimanded. Individuality is normally a good thing, but when creating environments on many servers it does not work. Standard scripts are the way to go for any medium or large sized environments and creating databases are a good place to start.

## Use of Scripts

Databases are best created via a series of scripts. Although Oracle can create a database for you, or you can issue each command manually, both of these methods have drawbacks. If you let Oracle create the database for you, you lose the ability to finely customize the database. Creating a database manually takes too long, is prone to mistakes, and cannot be easily reproducible.

Many medium and large IT shops often have a set of standardized database-creation shell scripts. The DBA simply copies these scripts, modifies them to include the new database and filesystem names, and then runs them. This "plug-and-chug" approach ensures a level of standardization and allows a shop to use a set of "best practices" when creating every database. It permits virtually any DBA, regardless of skill, to create the necessary databases to support their applications.

Although this takes some of the "fun" out of being a DBA, it does make sense in larger environments. The only real drawbacks are if the original scripts are somehow flawed or if the DBAs are not allowed the degree of customization needed to serve their particular systems. If you are new to a shop, find out if there is a set of scripts you are supposed to use. Review these scripts to determine what they actually do and consider if there are any ways to improve them.

Just as many shops have a set of standardized scripts, many individual DBAs have a set of their own scripts. Particularly in consulting, where you frequently move from shop to shop, a DBA will develop a "tool box" of SQL scripts to monitor, tune, and create databases. These tools allow the DBA to always have a familiar, repeatable set of scripts available to perform tasks, such as creating databases. These scripts contain the tricks and best practices of that particular DBA, so every database he/she creates will have the same level of consistency and design. Regardless of whether you are in consulting or work for one shop, I strongly recommend you create your own "tool box" so you can enjoy these benefits.

## Database Configuration Assistant

The easiest way to get a basic set of database-creation scripts is to have the Database Creation Assistant (DBCA) generate them for you. The DBCA asks you a set of questions about the needs of your database and then offers to either create the database for you or to generate a set of scripts to create it. This chapter uses the DBCA to generate the set of scripts to create a basic hybrid database. You will then use these scripts as your template to create your real database.

The set of scripts DBCA generates are Unix shell scripts that execute SQL*Plus scripts to issue the database-creation commands. There is a master shell script that calls each of these scripts in order. Once the whole set is generated, you can use `vi` to edit certain scripts to reflect your desired database name, file structure, number of control files, number and size of online redo logs, and various other parameters. Once this customization is done, you can execute the scripts to create the database.

Create a temporary directory to store the scripts generated by the assistant. The default location for these scripts is $ORACLE_HOME/assitants/dbca/jlib. As the oracle user, create a directory for the database you plan to create:

```
$ mkdir $ORACLE_HOME/assistants/dbca/jlib/rh1dev1
```

DBCA is a graphical tool very similar to the Oracle Universal Installer used to install the software. Log in as Oracle and set up your environment just as you did in the previous chapter. To start the DBCA as the oracle user, simply enter the following:

```
$ dbassist
```

This takes you in to the Database Configuration Assistant. Here, you can create a new database, modify an existing database, or delete an old database. You want to create a new database, so select Create a Database, as shown in Figure 5.1.

**5**

CREATING A
DATABASE

**FIGURE 5.1**

*Database Creation Assistant Welcome Screen*

The next screen asks whether you want a typical or custom database. Either way, you will be editing the scripts manually, but selecting the custom option now will reduce the amount of work needed later. Select the Custom database design, as shown in Figure 5.2.

**FIGURE 5.2**

*Typical or Custom Database*

DBCA asks you which type of database to design. Remember from Chapter 3 that a hybrid of OLTP and DSS is the most common design. In this chapter, you will design for this type. You can later edit the scripts if you need to cater more towards OLTP or towards DSS. Select the Multipurpose option, as shown in Figure 5.3.

**FIGURE 5.3**

*Select a Multipurpose Database.*

The next screen asks you how many users will be connected simultaneously, as shown in Figure 5.4. This information is used to size your rollback segments. You can change this information later, but for now, enter 75 users. Be careful if you are ever in this tool again and select OLTP; DBCA will automatically set up MTS if you select 20 or more users.

**FIGURE 5.4**
*Enter Number of Concurrent Users.*

When prompted for dedicated server or shared server (which is really MTS), select the dedicated mode, as shown in Figure 5.5. This will give your larger jobs better performance and the set up and management processes are easier.

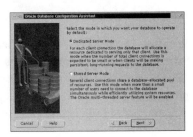

**FIGURE 5.5**
*Dedicated or Shared Server Mode.*

DBCA prompts you for the options to install. If you click Help, you get a description of each option. For your purposes, select everything, as shown in Figure 5.6. You will certainly use the JServer in the Java chapter and Oracle InterMedia will be used with iFS (internet File System).

The next screen prompts you for a Global Database Name and a SID. Before you enter the database name, which is unchangeable once the database is physically created, read the next section on SID/database names.

**FIGURE 5.6**

*Select Oracle Options.*

---

**NOTE**

Changing Database Names

There are a few "unchangeable" parameters such as the database names that can be changed after database creation. By generating a copy of the control file, modifying it, and then "recovering" the database you can change some parameters. Be warned that this is a more advanced technique and should not be attempted without proper research, backups, and practice.

---

A database name is really different than the SID (System Identifier), but most people use the terms synonymously. Each set of database files (the database) has a database name as identified in the CREATE DATABASE statement. The SID refers to that database instance (database plus memory and background processes). If you are like most people and only have one physical database that will be opened by one set of background processes and memory (SID), give each the same name.

In an Oracle Parallel Server (OPS) environment, this is different. Under OPS you will have one physical database name, but you will have two or more instances on different machines with different names (SIDs) accessing the same physical database simultaneously. Although OPS is gaining in popularity, it can be confusing initially. This chapter works on the assumption that you are using one physical database with one instance. Therefore, your database name and SID are one in the same.

Select the name of your database carefully. You are allowed up to eight characters, including letters and numbers. When the database supports only one application/major schema, you might be tempted to name the database after that application. For example, if your application is a production system that handles cable subscribers, you might call it subprod1. For small shops, this might be a good name.

If you are working in a larger environment with many databases hosting multiple applications, you need a more general naming convention. At one site I was at, we had dozens of HP and Sun machines hosting nearly one hundred SIDs supporting hundreds of applications. The method they used (which I think is a good idea) was to use the name to identify the server type, server name, instance name, and instance type. How can you get all this in only eight characters? Simple, use naming conventions to include server info and database info in the SID. Take the following example: HP4DEV2.

Use the first three letters to identify the server type and number. Use HP for HP-UX machines, SN for Sun, CP for Compaq, LN for Linux, and so on. Next, give each server a one-digit identifier. In our case, HP4DEV2 identifies the fourth HP server. A spreadsheet associates the server name to the number (4 in this case). Ideally, the server name will be something meaningful, such as hp4indy. If you are getting the idea that cute server names like Tigger (I've worked with several different Tiggers) are inefficient, you are correct. Name your servers something meaningful, and include the type (HP, SN, or LN), and a number (1-9, and then a..z) in the name.

Now that you have identified the server (HP4), you need to identify the database. You can tie the name to a specific application, but doing so restricts your database to only one application, which is inefficient in large environments. Identify the database by its function—production (PRD), repository (REP), development (DEV), or testing (TST)—followed by a number (1-9, a..z). In this case, HP4DEV2 refers to the second development database on the HP4. The database identification spreadsheet mentioned in the previous chapter will identify the HP4DEV2 and the applications it supports.

For the purposes here, you will name the database rh1dev1 for RedHat server #1, development database #1. Enter this name in the Global Database Name field, followed by a period, and then your domain (mike.com in my case), as shown in Figure 5.7. Your domain name can be obtained with the Unix command uname -a. Notice how the tool automatically fills in the SID value and the Initialization Filename fields with the your database name (up to the domain name). Leave the Initialization Filename (init.ora) as the default. The Compatible Parameter will be set to 8.1.0, but you will fix that manually after the database is created. Leave the Character Set as US7ASCII.

The next screen asks about control file location, as shown in Figure 5.8. Notice how the assistant puts all the three control files on /u01. Not only does that break with the OFA standard, but you would also be in a very tough situation if /u01's disk dies, because you would lose all your control files at once. You can fix this poor configuration manually, so leave it as is for now. Increase the Maximum Log Members from 2 to 4.

**5**

**FIGURE 5.7**
*Set the Global Database Name to RH1DEV1.*

**FIGURE 5.8**
*Define Control File Location.*

The next screen, shown in Figure 5.9, has a host of tabs: System, Tools, Rollback, Index, Temporary, and InterMedia. Each tab allows you to size the datafile(s) for the corresponding tablespace. Notice again that the default location is /u01, which is not optimal, but you will fix that once the scripts are generated.

**FIGURE 5.9**
*Size Each Tablespace.*

Click through each tab to view the options. For now, leave the default data file locations. Turn the auto extend feature off. This allows a data file to grow in size if it needs to allocate a new extent that wouldn't normally fit. However this is not a good policy to simply let files manage themselves. Leave the rest of the sizing parameters the same except for the following sizes.

| Tablespace | Size (M) |
|---|---|
| SYSTEM | 575 |
| TOOLS | 100 |
| USER | 104 |
| ROLLBACK | 675 |
| INDEX | 54 |
| TEMP | 100 |
| INTERMEDIA | 84 |

You will further adjust some of the parameters in the scripts (especially for rollback segments), but for now this is enough to get you started. Remember this is only a template, not your production system. Advanced topics regarding space management are covered in Chapter 6, "Daily Activities."

The defaults on the next screen regarding redo log files are a recipe for disaster. The redo logs are not multiplexed and they all reside on /u01. Not only is there contention between ARCH and LGWR, but a single loss of /u01 would cause the loss of all the log groups. They are also so small (at 500K) that they would be in near continual state of redo log switches during times of heavy transactions. You should certainly change these before you create the database. For now, make each redo log file a more reasonable 75M, as shown in Figure 5.10.

**FIGURE 5.10**
*Redo Log Files.*

The following screen asks you about Log Checkpoint Interval/Timeout. This refers to the init.ora parameters LOG_CHECKPOINT_INTERVAL and LOG_CHECKPOINT_INTERVAL. These parameters identify how often a system checkpoint (CKPT) will occur. For performance reasons, you want your checkpoints to occur only at redo log switches, so set the Checkpoint Interval to a value (in OS blocks) greater than your redo log size. Using 8K blocks and 75M redo log files, you can safely leave the value at 10000 because 8K×10000 is greater than 75M. Set the Checkpoint Timeout to 0 to disable this parameter.

**5**

You'll want to enable archiving eventually, but not for the database creation, so leave the Enable Archive Log option unchecked. See Figure 5.11.

**FIGURE 5.11**
*Log Checkpoint Interval and Archive Logging.*

The next screen addresses SGA parameters, processes, and block size, as shown in Figure 5.12. As a DBA, you will often analyze and sometimes change the SGA parameters, so these serve as preliminary values only. Leave the Shared Pool Size at its default value. For now, increase the Block Buffers to 6000. This will result in 6000 buffers times the database block size (8K), so the database buffer cache will be approximately 50M. Increase the log buffer to 540,672 bytes. The number of processes in dedicated server mode needs to be greater than the number of concurrent users (with one server process each), plus the number of background processes. Set this number higher; try 200.

The question about database block size has performance implications and it must be addressed now. Once you set this value (DB_BLOCK_SIZE) and create the database, it cannot be changed. The larger the block, the more data read into the database buffer cache for each read. Conventional wisdom is to use a larger block size for DSS applications because you are looking for larger amounts of data and this will improve your read efficiency. For OLTP, where you are looking for just a few rows to be returned, a smaller block size is more appropriate.

The single most important requirement is to make sure the database block size is a multiple of your OS block size, otherwise all your reads will be inefficient. For hybrid systems, I usually go with 8K blocks (8192 bytes).

The final configuration screen deals with Trace File Directories. The default settings are set correctly in an OFA compliant manner. Leave these settings alone and click Next.

After you have specified the basics of your system, DBCA will ask you whether it should run the creation now or save the configuration in scripts. Select the scripts option and put them in the $ORACLE_HOME/assistants/dbca/jlib/rh1dev1 directory you created before you started the assistant. A pop-up screen will appear stating the scripts will be saved as sql*sid*.sh, as shown in Figure 5.13. Click OK and exit the DBCA.

**FIGURE 5.12**
*SGA and Database Block Size.*

**FIGURE 5.13**
*Enter Path for Database Creation Scripts.*

## Customize the Scripts

As the oracle user, go to the $ORACLE_BASE/admin subdirectory. If you used the DBCA, it should have made your subdirectories for you. Otherwise, make a subdirectory named after the SID you plan to create. Then, type these commands:

```
$ cd $ORACLE_BASE/admin
$ pwd
/u01/app/oracle/admin
$ mkdir rh1dev1
$ cd rh1dev1
$ mkdir create
```

This create directory is where you edit your scripts. Copy the scripts created by DBCA to this location:

```
$ pwd
/u01/app/oracle/admin/rh1dev1/create
$ cp $ORACLE_HOME/assistants/dbca/jlib/rh1dev1/* .
$ ls
rh1dev1alterTablespace.sh    rh1dev1ordinst.sh
rh1dev1spatial1.sh           rh1dev1context.sh
```

```
rh1dev1replicate.sh        rh1dev1sqlplus.sh
rh1dev1drsys.sh            rh1dev1run.sh
rh1dev1timeseries.sh       rh1dev1iMedia.sh
rh1dev1run1.sh             sqlrh1dev1.sh
rh1dev1java.sh               rh1dev1run2.sh
```

There is a master script (`sqlrh1dev1.sh`) that calls all the other shell scripts in order. Use `more` on `sqlrh1dev1.sh` to see the order of the script execution. The main scripts you need to be concerned about are `rh1dev1run.sh`, `rh1dev1run1.sh`, and `rh1dev1drsys.sh`. Except for `rh1dev1run2.sh`, which runs some additional Oracle scripts, the rest of the scripts are used to install Oracle products and are not present if you did not select them during database configuration. Modification of `init.ora` is also required to configure control file locations. Modify the following scripts:

`rh1dev1run.sh`

This script performs the actual CREATE DATABASE statement. Open this file in an editor (such as `vi`) and make the following changes.

Give the system data file and online redo log files the location you created during the planning stage. Based on the sample configuration in Chapter 3, this should be changed to the following:

```
DATAFILE '/u02/oradata/rh1dev1/system01.dbf' SIZE 575M AUTOEXTEND OFF
logfile '/u03/oradata/rh1dev1/redo01a.rdo' SIZE 75000K,
    '/u07/oradata/rh1dev1/redo02a.rdo' SIZE 75000K,
    '/u11/oradata/rh1dev1/redo03a.rdo' SIZE 75000K;
```

Notice that the names of the redo log files now have an 'a' after them. The suffixes were also changed from `.log` to `.rdo`. In this configuration, these redo log files are not multiplexed. You will create the database with this configuration and then you'll learn how to add members to redo log groups in Chapter 6.

`rh1dev1run1.sh`

This script starts by running the catalog.sql, which creates data dictionary views (such as `V$SGA`). Next, it creates the basic tablespaces for the database. These include rollback, temporary, users, and any product-related tablespaces. If you know which application-specific tablespaces you need to create at this stage, you can add them here. For manageability reasons, I prefer to keep the creation of tablespaces separate from the database creation. For now, you can just create the basic tablespaces.

First, modify all the data file locations and give them an appropriate location (not `/u01`). Next, consider removing the INDEX tablespace. This tablespace isn't necessary unless you create a corresponding "DATA" tablespace. In this example, you will create application-specific tablespaces, so this INDEX tablespace is unnecessary.

> **NOTE**
>
> Be Careful with Initial Extents
>
> Resist the temptation to specify a higher initial extent size in an attempt to reduce contention within these tablespaces. Vendor-provided scripts often do not specify initial sizes for their tables and indexes so they default to the size specified in the tablespace. This results in many small tables allocating large initial extents until the tablespace runs out of space (it "blows out").

Next, examine the rollback segment allocations. Based on the number of concurrent users (75), DBCA decided to create 29 (0-28) rollback segments. Reduce this to 25 segments (0-24). Increase the extent size for each segment from 500K to 1M and adjust the optimal value to 20M. This will force the segment to shrink to 20M if it needs to extend during a transaction. Each segment starts with 20 extents at 1M each, so each rollback segment will take approximately 20M. If you size the tablespace at 675M, this configuration will take approximately 500M to allocate initially. This gives you extra room to add additional segments if needed and for existing segments to extend (allocate additional extents)

`.rh1dev1drsys.sh`

This script creates the tablespace DRSYS for the Context Option. Modify the script to place the data file in /u10.

`initrh1dev1.ora`

The init.ora in $ORACLE_BASE/admin/rh1dev1/pfile needs a minor modification before the database is created. Change the control file locations from /u01 to /u05, /u09, and /u10.

## Creating the Database

Once you create and edit the scripts, you are ready to run them to create the database.

> **NOTE**
>
> Filesystems Must Exist
>
> It is assumed that any filesystems not created during the initial machine setup have been created prior to this step. Each should have an ../oradata/rh1dev1 subdirectory owned by the oracle user.

**5**

**CREATING A DATABASE**

## Running the Scripts

Before you run the database, take a moment to verify a few parameters. Verify your $ORACLE_ SID and $ORACLE_HOME settings before you attempt to create the database. Also check that the CREATE DATABASE command refers to the new database you want to create, not a pre-existing SID you used earlier.

Go to each filesystem and create the ../oradata/rh1dev1 subdirectory for the data files and make sure it is writeable by oracle. Also check that your data files are not going to override any existing data files. Finally, verify that you have enough room (with some to spare) on each filesystem for the files you plan to create.

Once you have verified that the system is ready, cd to $ORACLE_BASE/admin/rh1dev1/create and execute the master shell script:

```
$ . ./sqlrh1dev1.sh
```

Expect this to seemingly hang for a few seconds to several minutes. Oracle is creating data files and allocating memory. This will impact the system. Oracle then has a whole list of scripts and subscripts to run. Your job is to sit back and watch for major errors. Huge amounts of text will scroll by far too quickly to read, but don't worry, as this data is being written to a series of log files.

This is the database creation. Oracle is starting with the first script and is running all the sub-scripts after that. This can easily go on for an hour. Once you kick it off and watch it for a few minutes (to ensure it is running), you can do something else because no further action is needed.

There will be many Oracle errors on the screen. There are "good" errors and "bad" errors. One good error you will see is ORA-01432: public synonym to be dropped does not exist. Before Oracle attempts to create an object (such as a synonym), it will attempt to drop it. Obviously if the synonym has never been created, it cannot be dropped. Hence, you get this "good" error.

An example of a "bad" error is a rapid succession of "not connected" messages. In this case, for whatever reason, Oracle failed to create the database or failed to connect to it. Oracle is still, however, attempting to run all the database-creation scripts even if the database cannot be created or doesn't exist. You can either press CTRL+C to get out of this or let it run. Either way, you need to look at your log files (start with the first one created) and determine why the script failed.

The database create will run for about an hour and will then finish. At this stage, you need to determine whether it was successful. This will involve several database-verification steps.

## Review the Create Logs

First, determine whether the database instance is still running.

```
$ ps -ef | grep -i pmon
oracle    1344    1  0 17:39 ?        00:00:00 ora_pmon_rh1dev1
```

Go to `$ORACLE_BASE/admin/rh1dev1` and look at the directories created. You should see the OFA-compliant subdirectories `adump`, `bdump`, `cdump`, `pfile`, and `udump`. The database-creation log files will be located in the create subdirectory. Skim through the `alert.log` in the `bdump` directory. Also determine whether any trace or core files were created in the `bdump`, `cdump`, or `udump` directories. Expect to see a few files in the `bdump` and `udump`; you may use `compress` on these files if they are large and delete them later if they are not needed. If you see any core files in `cdump` (you should not at this point), use `ls -l` to get an idea of just how big they are and then delete them with `rm`.

Next, go through the logs in the create subdirectory to determine whether there were any error messages. You can scroll through the smaller ones, but use a `grep` to search for Oracle errors in larger scripts.

```
$ grep -i ORA crdb2.log | more
ORA-01432: public synonym to be dropped does not exist
ORA-01432: public synonym to be dropped does not exist
ORA-00942: table or view does not exist
ORA-01432: public synonym to be dropped does not exist
...
```

Once again, you know that these errors are expected. What you want to look for are Oracle errors not like these. Investigate why any of these errors occurred. If they are related to a specific feature, such as Context Option, you might want to determine how important that feature is to you. If you can fix the problem and rerun the script, do so. That is one of the benefits of a modular design.

## Examine the Database Instance

The next step is to login to the database using SQL*Plus and look around. Use the default system/manager account for this.

```
$ sqlplus system

SQL*Plus: Release 8.1.6.0.0 - Production on Sun Feb 18 17:59:13 2001

(c) Copyright 1999 Oracle Corporation.  All rights reserved.

Enter password:
```

```
Connected to:
Oracle8i Enterprise Edition Release 8.1.6.1.0 - Production
With the Partitioning option
JServer Release 8.1.6.0.0 - Production

SQL> show user
USER is "SYSTEM"
SQL>
```

**NOTE**

Security Issues

There are two security issues here. First, Oracle always creates the SYSTEM account with manager as the password and the SYS account always has change_on_install as its password. This is public information and will be changed later in this chapter, but it is amazing how often these passwords are not changed. The second issue deals with not typing system/manager on the command line. Sure, you can log in with SQL*Plus system/manager, but don't do it! Not only can people look over your shoulder or scroll up on your screen when you are not there, but there is an even bigger problem. Anyone logged into the Unix system can use ps -ef to see your log in to SQL*Plus and some platforms will show the password. This information also goes into your history file.

Run SELECT statements from DBA_DATA_FILES, V$CONTROLFILE, and V$LOGFILE.

```
SQL> select tablespace_name, file_name, bytes
  2  from dba_data_files order by file_name;
```

| TABLESPACE | FILE_NAME | BYTES |
| --- | --- | --- |
| SYSTEM | /u02/oradata/rh1dev1/system01.dbf | 602,931,200 |
| TEMP | /u03/oradata/rh1dev1/temp01.dbf | 104,857,600 |
| TOOLS | /u04/oradata/rh1dev1/tools01.dbf | 104,857,600 |
| USERS | /u04/oradata/rh1dev1/users01.dbf | 109,051,904 |
| RBS | /u05/oradata/rh1dev1/rollback01.rbs | 707,788,800 |
| DRSYS | /u10/oradata/rh1dev1/drsys01.dbf | 88,080,384 |

```
SQL> select name from v$controlfile;

NAME
------------------------------------
/u05/oradata/rh1dev1/control01.ctl
/u06/oradata/rh1dev1/control02.ctl
/u09/oradata/rh1dev1/control03.ctl
```

```
SQL> select group#, member from v$logfile;

    GROUP# MEMBER
---------- ----------------------------------
         1 /u03/oradata/rh1dev1/redo01a.rdo
         2 /u07/oradata/rh1dev1/redo02a.rdo
         3 /u11/oradata/rh1dev1/redo03a.rdo
```

Compare the results of these queries against the files that you wanted to create. They should match, otherwise some file was not created. If this is the case, determine whether a filesystem is full (df  -k or bdf) and thus cannot create a data file. Next, ensure that the pathnames and filenames you specified in your create scripts are valid (a common mistake). Finally, exit SQL*Plus and cd to the directories where the files should be created. Verify that they are there and that the file structure is correct and OFA-compliant.

## Compile Invalid Objects

The next step of verification involves getting object counts and recompiling invalid objects. Login as SYSTEM into SQL*Plus and issue the following command:

```
SQL> select object_type, count(*) from dba_objects
  2  where status = 'INVALID' group by object_type;

OBJECT_TYPE          COUNT(*)
------------------ ----------
PACKAGE BODY             15
VIEW                     26
```

To get the names and types of each invalid object, type the following:

```
col object_name format a30
col owner format a10
SQL> select owner, object_name, object_type from dba_objects
  2  where status = 'INVALID' order by object_type, object_name
  3  /
```

In this case, you can see that there are some invalid objects, which is normal. My system had 41; if you see hundreds or thousands of invalid objects, you should be concerned. You simply need to recompile them. You can either recompile each manually, or you can use dynamic SQL to generate the SQL to compile the objects. Dynamic SQL is simply writing SQL to generate more SQL.

For example, you want to issue the following:

```
SQL> alter view SYS.USER_REPOBJECT compile;

View altered.
```

**5**

CREATING A
DATABASE

To use dynamic SQL to create a script to compile all the objects, do the following:

```
SQL> set heading off
SQL> set feedback off
SQL> set pagesize 200
SQL> spool compile_invalid_views.sql
SQL> select 'alter view ' || owner || '.' || object_name ||
  2  ' compile;' from dba_objects
  3  where status = 'INVALID' and object_type = 'VIEW'
  4  /
alter view SYS.ALL_REPCAT compile;
alter view SYS.ALL_REPCOLUMN compile;
...
SQL>  spool off
```

Then type *from within* SQL*Plus !vi compile_invalid_views.sql to invoke the vi editor. The ! allows you to enter Unix commands from the SQL*Plus prompt. Remove the SQL statement at the top of the file and the spool off command at the end of the file. Next, type ZZ to save, exit vi, and return to SQL*Plus. Then, run the script to compile the invalid views.

```
SQL> set feedback on
SQL> set heading on
SQL> @compile_invalid_views.sql
View altered.
View altered.
...
```

That's dynamic SQL. All your views should be compiled. Sometimes there is a dependency and not all the objects will compile the first time because they are depending on another object. If a few invalid objects remain, repeat this process a few times. If the object still won't compile, type show errors after the error message to identify the problem.

Write the dynamic SQL to recompile any other invalid objects. Use the following syntax for packages, package bodies, and procedures:

```
alter package package_name compile;
alter package package_body_name compile body;
alter procedure procedure_name compile;
```

**NOTE**

Dynamic SQL

Learn how to write dynamic SQL. Next to becoming proficient with vi and command-line editing, dynamic SQL is one of the biggest timesavers for the Unix DBA. It might seem a little awkward at first, but it is much faster and less prone to human errors than manual entry.

If you already executed the `initjvm.sql` file (within `rh1dev1java.sh`) to create the Java objects during the database create, there is no need to run it again. This is a system resource intensive script and sometimes it fails. If you already ran it, don't run it again. Simply get a count from the `DBA_OBJECTS where object_type like 'JAVA%'`. Your number should be around 9000 objects and none of them should be invalid.

## Clean Up a Failed Database

If, for some reason, the database create did fail, the problem can likely be found in the first few create database logs. Use `ps -efl` to see whether any of the background processes are still up (it's possible). If they are running and you cannot shut them down normally, you need to kill them and remove the shared memory segments (see Chapter 13, "Unix Server Monitoring") or reboot the server.

If some database files were created, you will have to either remove any files created or include the REUSE parameter in the database scripts (which should already be used). You might also have to delete or re-create the password file in `$ORACLE_HOME/dbs`. If you delete the `orapwrh1dev1` file, modify the init.ora parameter to `REMOTE_LOGIN_PASSWORDFILE = NONE`. Once those cleanup tasks are completed and you have fixed the original problem, try again to create the database.

# Post-Creation Activities

After you have created the database, there are a few things that you need to do. You need to change the passwords, verify the database is in oratab, and create a link for the `init.ora`. These steps will make your new database ready for normal use.

## Changing the Passwords

First, change the passwords for the users SYS and SYSTEM. You can use the SQL*Plus password-changing utility, which has a similar look to the Unix `passwd` command:

```
SQL> password
Changing password for SYSTEM
Old password:
New password:
Retype new password:
```

Alternatively, you can simply issue SQL to do this; just make sure no one sees it. Typing a `!clear` will enter the Unix shell, clear the screen, and return you to SQL*Plus. This, unlike using SQL*Plus `system/manager`, is not visible via `ps`.

```
SQL> alter user sys identified by superdba7;

User altered.

SQL> !clear
```

There are other user accounts that should be locked or have their passwords changed. Using DBA_USERS and selecting the username will yield approximately 15 standard accounts, depending on which features you loaded.

```
SQL> select username from dba_users order by created;

USERNAME
------------------------------
SYS
SYSTEM
OUTLN
DBSNMP
TRACESVR
AURORA$ORB$UNAUTHENTICATED
ORDSYS
ORDPLUGINS
MDSYS
CTXSYS

10 rows selected.
```

If you have any user test accounts such as SCOTT, ADAMS, BLAKE, CLARK, and JONES, they can be locked by this command:

```
SQL>  alter user scott account lock;

User altered.
```

Special accounts such as CTXSYS, TRACESVR, ORDSYS, and ORDPLUGINS can be locked if you are not using the Context Option. MDSYS is used for the Spatial Option so that can be locked if you don't need it.

## Change Default Passwords

Make it a point to change default passwords or people will circumvent your security procedures. There is a very popular story among DBAs of a manager traveling to a "secure" site to get some data from a system. Upon arrival he was hassled for hours about security clearance. Frustrated and desperate, when no one was looking, he tried logging in as SYS/change_on_install. To his astonishment he was able to get

> in. The manager then got the data he needed and left without ever telling the site about their huge security gap. I cannot tell for sure how much is exaggeration, but it's a safe bet this security hole exists in many systems.

You'll learn about changing passwords for the DBSNMP user in Chapter 7, "GUI Management Products." OUTLN should have its password changed, as it is used for database statistics and tuning. AURORA$ORB$UNAUTHENTICATED is a special case. Based on the information I have been given, you should not lock it nor should you change its password. This is supposed to be changed in a later release and currently it doesn't appear to have dangerous privileges, but some DBAs find this situation disturbing.

## Modifying oratab File

The file oratab contains a listing of each database, its ORACLE_HOME, and a Y|N flag to determine whether the database should be automatically restarted on machine reboot. It is used to determine which databases are on a server, their versions, and if they should be automatically started. Shell scripts often use this file when they set up a user's login environment. The oratab file is located in /etc on HP-UX and Linux machines, whereas it is in /var/opt/oracle on Sun Solaris platforms.

If you create a database completely with DBCA or use DBCA to generate scripts, the oratab file will be automatically updated. If you created and ran the scripts yourself, you need to add a line to this file containing your new database. Here are the key fields of an oratab file.

```
demo:/u01/app/oracle/product/8.1.6:N
rh1tst1:/u01/app/oracle/product/8.1.6:N
rh1dev1:/u01/app/oracle/product/8.1.6:N
```

Simply vi oratab, move to the last line, and then type yy to "yank" one line. Then type p to paste the line at the end. Edit the line to show your database name and the correct ORACLE_HOME. For now, leave the last column as N. You'll learn about setting a database to be restarted automatically on reboot in Chapter 9, "Backup and Recovery."

## Create a Soft Link for init.ora

Under $ORACLE_HOME/dbs, there needs to be a Unix soft link to the init.ora in $ORACLE_BASE/admin/*database_name*/pfile. To see what links already exist, do this:

```
$ pwd
/u01/app/oracle/product/8.1.6/dbs
$ ls -alt init*
lrwxrwxrwx    1 oracle    dba    51
Feb 17 11:55 initrh1tst1.ora ->
        /u01/app/oracle/admin/rh1tst1/pfile/initrh1tst1.ora
```

**5**

```
lrwxrwxrwx    1 oracle   dba  45 Feb 17 10:44 initdemo.ora ->
        /u01/app/oracle/admin/demo/pfile/initdemo.ora

-rw-r--r--    1 oracle   dba 835 Apr 11  2000 initsoxx.sql
-rw-r--r--    1 oracle   dba 9219 Aug 27  1999 initdw.ora
-rw-r--r--    1 oracle   dba 8385 Aug 27  1999 init.ora
```

Notice the "l" in first field for the permissions (such as lrwxrwxrwx). This indicates a soft link. In this example, the file initrh1tst1.ora is really just a pointer to the real file in /u01/app/oracle/admin/rh1tst1/pfile/initrh1tst1.ora. Oracle looks in this location ($ORACLE_HOME/dbs) to find the init.ora for the database you are trying to start. Oracle will find and use the soft-linked init.ora file in this location to start the database.

The links are created automatically if the DBCA is used to either create the database or generate the scripts. In this case, they were created automatically.

If you created the scripts without the DBCA, the only init.ora for the new database is in the pfile directory, so a link needs to be created to this file. The syntax is as follows:

```
ln -s where the file physically exists
        where you want the file to appear to exist.

$ ln -s /u01/app/oracle/admin/rh1dev1/pfile/initrh1dev1.ora  /u01/app/oracle/
product/8.1.6/dbs/initrh1dev1.ora
```

The file still physically resides in ...admin/rh1dev1/pfile, but it will also appear to be in $ORACLE_HOME/dbs.

> **NOTE**
>
> **Additional Scripts**
>
> Some additional scripts from $ORACLE_HOME/rdbms/admin might be executed to provide extra functionality or to prepare the database for special utilities. One example is locking scripts, discussed in Chapter 10, "When Things Go Wrong."

## Configuring Net8 for the New Database

Once the database is created, you need to include it in the Oracle networking files. Specifically, you need to make entries in the tnsnames.ora and listener.ora files. Then you need to start the listener process so the server can detect and route incoming requests to the appropriate database.

You can accomplish these tasks by either editing the files manually or by running the Oracle Net8 Assistant. Net8 is a GUI, like the Database Creation Assistant. To start the tool, type `netasst`. Once you have configured it for one database, manually editing the files to add additional databases is easy. Or, if you have working listener.ora and tnsnames.ora files from another server, you can copy them to your new server and edit them for the new databases.

> **NOTE**
>
> **Automatically Configured Files**
>
> If you used the DBCA to create your scripts or to create the database, you will find that the network files are automatically configured. You can use this method to quickly generate working tnsnames.ora and listener.ora files in your $ORACLE_ HOME/network/admin directories if you decide not to use the GUI network configuration tools.

## tnsnames.ora

The tnsnames.ora file initially resides in $ORACLE_HOME/network/admin. Copy this to /etc on HP-UX and Linux machines. If you are on Sun Solaris, copy the file to /var/opt/oracle. Oracle will work with the file in its original location, but as you install more versions of Oracle on the same machine, it is helpful to have the file outside a specific ORACLE_HOME. Because this file is outside the filesystems Oracle normally occupies, make sure it is not overlooked during backups. Figure 5.14 shows a sample tnsnames.ora file.

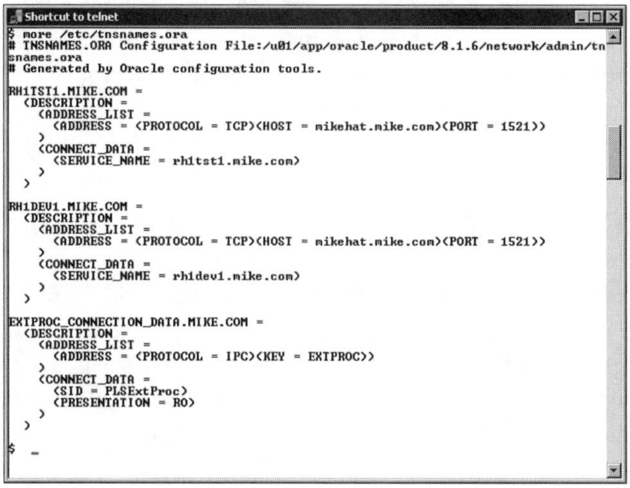

**FIGURE 5.14**

*The tnsnames.ora File*

The tnsnames.ora file is a client-side file. It is located on the server here to make connections to databases on other servers. When a user starts SQL*Plus and issues a connect string (for example, `sqlplus mikew@rh1dev1`), the tnsnames.ora file is examined to determine whether rh1dev1 exists. If rh1dev1 is found, a connection is attempted with the server specified on the specified port. Assuming that rh1dev1 is found and the username and password are valid, a database connection is established. If the value is not found, an Oracle message reports that the tnsnames could not resolve the service name (ORA-12154: TNS:could not resolve service name).

> **NOTE**
>
> **Connecting to Local Databases**
>
> If you are logged on the same server as the database and have your ORACLE_SID specified, you do not go through this process. Simply type `sqlplus username`; do not specify the database with the `@database_name`. You connect directly to the server via the bequeath protocol. You do not need the listener to be running to make this kind of connection. A `ps -ef` will show this connection as local.
>
> ```
> $ ps -efl | grep -i local
> oracle 2366  2365 18:45 ? oraclerh1tst1
> (DESCRIPTION=(LOCAL=YES)(ADDRESS=(PROTOCOL=beq)))
> ```

Once you have modified the server's tnsnames.ora, the copies on the client's PCs and other servers must be updated. If there are only a few such machines, the changes can be done manually. More likely, there are too many of these, so a new copy with the new database should be sent to each machine. This can become an administrative mess, particularly in a large environment. In such environments, a nightly or weekly job to refresh every client tnsnames.ora file with a copy of the master file might make sense.

## listener.ora

The listener.ora file, shown in Figure 5.15, is the parameter file for the listener process. The listener is a background process that listens for incoming connection requests and then passes those requests to the appropriate database. The listener.ora file specifies which port valid connections will come in on, which protocols to use, and which service name connects to which database. This file resides in $ORACLE_HOME/network/admin. Your connections will initially be through port 1521. The use of GIOP and port 2481 is for Java and will be covered in Chapter 16, "Java Inside the Database Server."

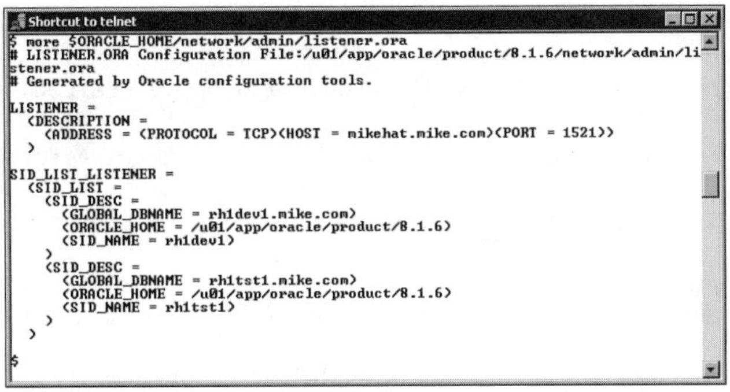

**FIGURE 5.15**
*The listener.ora File*

The key set of lines you need to copy and modify for the new database are as follows:

```
(SID_DESC =
     (GLOBAL_DBNAME = rh1tst1.mike.com)
     (ORACLE_HOME = /u01/app/oracle/product/8.1.6)
     (SID_NAME = rh1tst1)
   )
```

Make sure you have added the correct database name, and that it's spelled correctly. Next, you must consider the listener process itself.

# listener

The listener process must be running for connections from other machines to be successful. If the listener process is not running, you will be able to connect to the database locally, but outside connections into your database will fail. There is typically one listener process on each server that supports all the databases (regardless of version) for that server. To start the listener process simply type lsnrctl start, as shown in Figure 5.16.

You can use ps -ef to determine whether the listener process is running, or you can check the listener itself:

```
$ lsnrctl status
```

This will tell you whether the listener is running and for what databases (service handlers) it is listening.

After you modify the listener.ora file, you need to bounce the listener for the changes to take effect. You can either issue the lsnrctl reload command, or you can actually bounce it. To stop the listener, issue this command:

5

CREATING A
DATABASE

```
$  lsnrctl stop

LSNRCTL for Linux: Version 8.1.6.0.0 - Production on 19-FEB-2001 19:32:17

(c) Copyright 1998, 1999, Oracle Corporation.  All rights reserved.

Connecting to (DESCRIPTION=(ADDRESS=(PROTOCOL=IPC)(KEY=EXTPROC)))
The command completed successfully
```

Don't forget to restart the listener after you have stopped it if your intent is to bounce it.

Finally, to get a more comprehensive listing of the listener commands, try lsnrctl help.

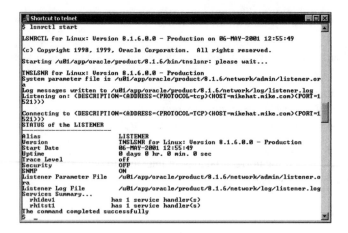

**FIGURE 5.16**

*Starting the listener Process.*

**NOTE**

**Don't Forget the listener!**

More than one DBA has started the production database in the morning, but has forgotten to start the listener. The result is confused users asking, "Is the database up?" Make sure that the listener process is running after you start your databases.

Remember that there are two ways to connect into the database, either locally or remotely. A local connection is when you are already logged into the database server, your ORACLE_SID is set, and you do not specify the database in your connect string:

```
$ sqlplus system
```

A local connection will use the bequeath protocol and does *not* require the listener to be running. Typically, this is how most DBAs connect to the database because they are already logged onto the Unix server via telnet or XWindows.

A remote connection involves the user connecting from a client machine to the database server. This requires the use of a connect string specifying the target database and a tnsnames.ora on their machine. The listener process must also be running on the database server. This is the type of connection used by most end users. An attempt to connect to a remote database looks like this:

```
$ sqlplus system@rh1dev1
```

That covers the basics of setting up Oracle networking. The more advanced features of Net8 always seem to be evolving, but these fundamentals will get you production-ready. Now that the database is set up and connectivity has been established you are ready from a technical standpoint. Some shops have procedures for documenting new databases, plus you need to update your own spreadsheet for the new database, so don't forget these final administrative tasks.

## Customizing Your .profile File

The .profile file you used to create the database will work, but it can be improved. Two popular modifications in the Unix environment are to provide a prompt for the database SID when you log on and to provide command-line editing.

To get a prompt for your SID and have your environment properly set up, you need to use the /usr/local/bin/oraenv file and have an updated /etc/oratab file. Simply add the following code to the end of your .profile file (located in your home directory):

```
echo "The SIDs on this machine are:"
cat /etc/oratab | awk -F: '{print $1}' | grep -v "#"
ORAENV_ASK="YES"
export ORAENV_ASK
. /usr/local/bin/oraenv
```

This code uses awk to extract and print the databases listed in /etc/oratab. You then select one of the SIDs and oraenv sets your environment using this value. Your next login will appear like so:

```
$ su - oracle
Password:
The SIDs on this machine are:

demo
rh1tst1
ORACLE_SID = [rh1tst1] ? demo
$ echo $ORACLE_SID
demo
```

**5**

The next common .profile modification uses the Korn shell feature of command-line editing and your history file. If you want to repeat a command you entered previously, simply type ESC+K. Then type K and each previous command you have entered will appear on the line. Each time you press K, the previous command will appear and you can then execute the command you want. Alternatively, you can edit the command as if you were in the vi editor. Simply use your normal vi commands—h and l—to move back and forth through the line. Use x to delete a character, and a or i to append or insert text. Although it might seem trivial at this stage, these features can be real timesavers.

To implement this, you must be set to use the Korn shell. Verify that you are set by default to use the Korn (ksh) shell.

```
$ grep oracle /etc/passwd
oracle:x:501:504:Oracle Software Owner:/home/oracle:/bin/ksh
```

In your .profile file, add the following line before you have the SID code:

```
export EDITOR=vi
```

By defining your editor, you can also edit your previous SQL statement in vi when you are in SQL*Plus. Log in to SQL*Plus and type SELECT * FROM V$DATABSE; and press Enter. Then type ed once the query returns. You should find yourself in vi with your SQL statement ready to be edited:

```
select * from v$database
/
~
~
```

You can type ZZ to save, exit vi, and return to the SQL*Plus prompt. Then enter a / to execute the command you edited. While in vi, if you want to, you can also save the SQL to a .sql file by typing :w file_name.sql. This is a quick and easy way to save your SQL as scripts. You will notice an afiedt.buf file in your directory; it contains the last SQL you edited.

## Summary

This chapter covered creating and customizing a database via scripts. It is easiest to have the DBCA create a basic template and then edit it to meet your needs. Expect the actual database creation to take a while and produce many errors, but still be successful. The chapter also covered troubleshooting and cleanup. You read about post-creation issues dealing with the oratab and invalid objects. Next, you took a brief tour of the Oracle networking environment, including tnsnames.ora, listener.ora, and the listener process. Finally, you learned a few pointers on setting up your login environment to support multiple SIDs and command-line editing.

# Daily Activities

## ESSENTIALS

- There are many different facets of database administration in which the DBA has to be proficient.

- There are several different ways to start up and shut down Oracle and the DBA needs to understand the differences between each method.

- Managing and tuning database structures and files is a core DBA responsibility.

- Creating and managing database users, their objects (tables and indexes), and security is another DBA responsibility.

- Monitoring the various logs and alert files for each database, their backups, and any nightly jobs is an important daily responsibility that cannot be skipped.

This chapter focuses on what a Unix DBA does on a "normal" day. It examines some the technical tasks performed by all DBAs (such as starting a database), but it also discusses some tasks not always covered in DBA school. It does not attempt to detail every conceivable option and syntax for basic Oracle commands. This information is best obtained from the Oracle manuals. Instead, this chapter attempts to impart unto the reader some the administrative knowledge and tasks of a DBA, not just the technical skills. It is this kind of "know-how" that separates people who can simply operate databases from people who are database *administrators*.

There are certain activities that DBAs are expected to perform on a daily basis. Most people might immediately suggest creating tables or adding indexes, but that is a bit short-sighted. The daily activities of a DBA usually center on either making the data safe or making it available. Tasks related to these tenants of database administration include checking backups, checking the status of previous night's processes, verifying the database is up and accessible to the users, monitoring the database for problems, and (hopefully) preventing the problems before they occur. Usually, only after these tasks are done, does the DBA have time to start creating tables and indexes.

## Database Views

One of the most effective tools the DBA has is access to the data dictionary. The use of V$, DBA_X, ALL_X, and USER_X views make a "real" DBA. A solid knowledge of database views from the command line is one common characteristic I've noticed with every good DBA I've worked with. By the same token, most of the DBAs I've worked with that have struggled usually had no real concept of these views. If their GUI management tool wasn't available, they were largely helpless.

Users with DBA privileges have access to all the views in the database. Normal users have access only to USER_X and ALL_X. The following table identifies the different types of information offered by each type of view.

| View Name | Information | Access |
|---|---|---|
| V$ | Dynamic performance information | DBAs |
| DBA_X | All objects in database | DBAs |
| ALL_X | All objects you have access to | All Users |
| USER_X | Objects you own | All Users |

The data dictionary provides a host of views with information regarding every object and statistic in the database. This information is provided in a read-only (not updateable!) format to the users. This represents a very good supply of information for anyone able to query it. In fact, most the GUI-management tools (covered in Chapter 7, "GUI Management Products") get *their* information from these views and then format it in colorful charts and graphs for the users.

One of the most beneficial activities I did as a new DBA was create an easy-to-read list of all the views available to me (as a DBA) and made a commitment to learning what some of the more common views were. By no means have I memorized all of them, but I know what many of them are and I know when to look for one even if I cannot remember its exact name.

To get a listing of all the standard views, issue the following command:

```
select synonym_name from dba_synonyms where
synonym_name like 'V$%' or
synonym_name like 'DBA%' or
synonym_name like 'ALL%' or
synonym_name like 'USER%'
order by synonym_name;
```

Spool this off to a file and edit it to remove unneeded or redundant information.

Some of the more popular views used by DBAs are:

```
v$database, v$datafile, v$controlfile, v$instance,

v$log, v$logfile, v$recover_file v$sga, v$session

dba_constraints, dba_data_files, dba_extents, dba_free_space,
dba_ind_columns, dba_indexes, dba_objects, dba_segments,
dba_sequences, dba_synonyms, dba_rollback_segs, dba_role_privs,
dba_roles, dba_tables, dba_tab_privs, dba_tablespaces, dba_users
```

To get a description of any of these views, use desc *view_name* from within SQL*Plus. Queries on many of these views will provide very large listings that can be difficult to read. It is almost essential to modify some of the default format masks and display options within SQL*Plus. To do this in an efficient manner, create a login.sql file that will exist in the directory from where you log in to SQL*Plus. This file will be read automatically when you start SQL*Plus and customize the display options for you. It will also issue a SELECT statement to identify the database and will identify the user. Figure 6.1 shows how this is done.

```
$ more login.sql
REM This file provides custom display settings with SQL*Plus.
REM Have it in the directory from where you start SQL*Plus.

set pagesize 25
col member format a60
col file_name format a60
col tablespace_name format a20
col owner format a15
col object_name format a30
col initial_extent format 999,999,999
col next_extent format 999,999,999
col bytes format 999,999,999
col sum(bytes) format 999,999,999,999
select name, created, log_mode from v$database;
show user;

$ sqlplus internal

SQL*Plus: Release 8.1.6.0.0 - Production on Mon Apr 23 19:07:04 2001

(c) Copyright 1999 Oracle Corporation.  All rights reserved.


Connected to:
Oracle8i Enterprise Edition Release 8.1.6.1.0 - Production
With the Partitioning option
JServer Release 8.1.6.0.0 - Production


NAME       CREATED      LOG_MODE
---------- -----------  -----------
RH1DEV1    24-FEB-01    NOARCHIVELOG

USER is "SYS"
SQL> desc v$sga;
 Name                                Null?    Type
 ----------------------------------- -------- ------------
 NAME                                         VARCHAR2(20)
 VALUE                                        NUMBER

SQL>
```

**FIGURE 6.1**
*Customizing the SQL*Plus Environment.*

# Oracle Startup/Shutdown

Database startup and shutdown requires more knowledge than just knowing the SQL syntax. There are several options and ramifications regarding database startup. Depending on what you need to do, you might start the database where only the memory and background processes are started or you might also include the data files. When it is time to shut down the database, there are also several options and ramifications you need to be aware of. This section examines how Oracle starts up and shuts down.

## Database Stages

Starting and stopping the database is as fundamental to the DBA's job as bouncing the server is to the SA's job. There are times when the DBA must shut down the database (such as during cold backups), and there are times when the database *should* bounce (such as when something goes wrong and hundreds of users need to be killed).

An Oracle database instance has four states of existence. Each state represents a stage, from taking a closed set of database files (no memory or processes), creating the instance (memory and processes), creating the instance and reading the control files(s), and opening the database files for normal access. During this evolution, each stage has its own set of characteristics. Certain database-maintenance and recovery tasks require the database to be in a specific state, so the DBA needs to understand each state and its implications.

The four states of an Oracle database instance are shutdown, nomount, mount, and open. Figure 6.2 shows the evolution from shutdown to open.

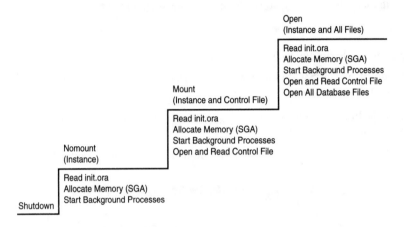

**FIGURE 6.2**

*Database Stages.*

As you can see, each stage has specific characteristics:

- **Shutdown** No database files are open nor are any processes or memory structures allocated. The database is not accessible. This is used for cold backups.

- **Nomount** During the nomount stage, only the instance (memory structures and background processes) is started. The init.ora file is read to get the parameters for the instance, but no data or control files are opened. During this stage, databases are created via the CREATE DATABASE statement. If you have sized your SGA too big or the expected memory resources are not available, an error will occur at this stage.

- **Mount** The init.ora is read, the instance is started, and the control file(s) is read. Application data and DBA_X tables/views are not available, but information from the V$ tables is accessible. At this stage, it is important to realize that the control file is read so Oracle knows about the database structure, but those files are not yet open. This allows maintenance on data files and redo log files to be performed. Database recoveries are also performed from this stage.

- **Open** The init.ora is read, the instance is started, and all the database files are opened and are accessible to users. This is the normal state of the database.

## Database Startup

When you start a database, you can specify which state it will open to. The default is open (STARTUP), but you can specify STARTUP NOMOUNT or STARTUP MOUNT depending on which tasks you need to perform. The database does not open directly to any one particular stage; it progresses from the nomount to mount to the open stage. If any problems are encountered along the way, the process stops and an error message is issued.

To start a closed database:

1. Log in as oracle (or any user in group dba).

2. Set your ORACLE_SID to the instance you want to start. Verify your ORACLE_HOME is set to the correct database version.

3. Start SQL*Plus and connect internal (desupport for this is covered in Chapter 15, "Migrations").

4. Start the database. Figure 6.3 shows an idle database instance being completely started.

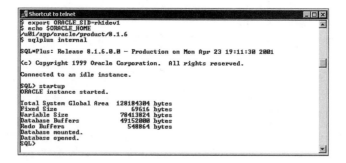

**FIGURE 6.3**

*Database Startup.*

Notice that Figure 6.3 says "Connected to an idle instance". This indicates the instance you are attempting to connect to is not started. Your database is not started if you start SQL*Plus and see the following:

```
SQL> select * from v$database;
select * from v$database
*
ERROR at line 1:
ORA-01034: ORACLE not available
```

This is a common mistake for beginners. It is also not what you want to hear over the phone from a user!

If you start the database in mount or nomount mode, you can continue to open the database from that stage:

```
SQL> alter database open;

Database altered.
```

Another handy startup option is STARTUP RESTRICT. When the database is started in restricted session mode, only users (such as those with roleDBA) with the system privilege RESTRICTED SESSION can connect to the database. Use this when you are performing maintenance or want only certain users to be able to log in.

If the database is already open, you can set it to restricted session even if normal users are logged in (no new users will be able to log in):

```
SQL> alter system enable restricted session;

System altered.
```

Once your task is completed, you can open the system to allow regular users to log in.

```
SQL> alter system disable restricted session;

System altered.
```

Oracle will, by default, use the `init.ora` specified in the `$ORACLE_HOME/dbs` directory. This is typically a database link to the `init.ora` in the `$ORACLE_BASE/admin/oracle_SID/pfile` directory. You can override this default by specifying a PFILE parameter on the startup line. Use this method when there is a special `init.ora` file you need to use. For example:

```
SQL> startup pfile='$ORACLE_BASE/admin/rh1dev1/pfile/initrh1dev1.ora'
ORACLE instance started.
```

# Database Shutdown

A database shutdown roughly goes in the opposite order of a startup. Oracle tries to shut down in the following manner:

1. Wait until all users log off or are killed so transactions are either committed or rolled back.
2. Issue a check point so all the redo log and database buffers are written to disk and the file headers are updated with the current SCN.
3. Close the database files.
4. Deallocate the memory structures and terminate Oracle processes.

Like the database STARTUP command, there are several options for database SHUTDOWN. Each option performs the shutdown steps listed previously in a slightly different manner. Use the least violent method you can while still shutting down the database within your time constraints and safety margins. Your shutdown options are (from least to most violent): SHUTDOWN, SHUTDOWN TRANSACTIONAL, SHUTDOWN IMMEDIATE, and SHUTDOWN ABORT.

## SHUTDOWN

The preferred method to shut down a database is simply the SHUTDOWN command. This kindly waits for each user to log off or be killed. Oracle then shuts down the database. If you can use this method, do so. However, there are seldom times when you (the SYS user) are the only one connected to the database. Remember, when using this method, Oracle waits until everyone except you logs off the database before the shutdown continues. The alternative to waiting for everyone to log off (often an unrealistic option) is to kill each user session, at which point Oracle will perform the shutdown.

You can kill users in the manner shown in Figure 6.4 until you are the only user left and shutdown can proceed.

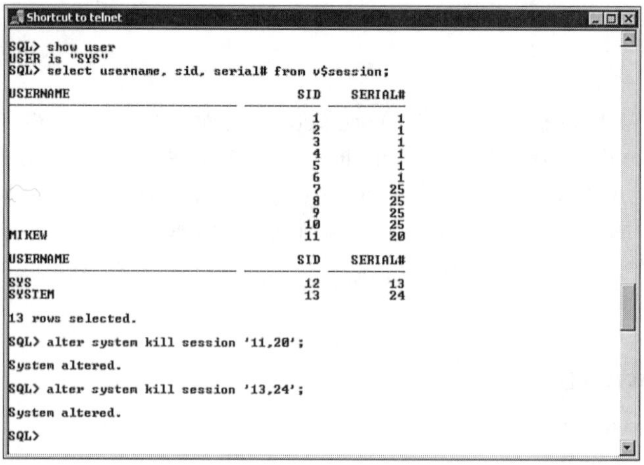

**FIGURE 6.4**
*Killing Users.*

The ALTER SYSTEM KILL SESSION '*SID,SERIAL#*' command kills the user session and forces a rollback of any current transaction. The problem is that it can take PMON a while (hours to days even) to remove the session. Even though the users status is 'KILLED', the user is still logged in and normal shutdown will not proceed.

---

**NOTE**

Know What Session You Are Killing

Be careful when specifying the SID (not the same as ORACLE_SID) and serial number to kill a user. Make sure you enter the correct SID and serial number for the user you want to kill. It is easy to accidentally enter the values for a background process. These are the first rows returned from V$SESSION where there is no value listed for the username (see Figure 6.4).

6

Use this method of shutdown to guarantee a "clean" shutdown where all the file headers are updated. If you are taking a cold backup, insist on this method. If many users are logged on and you must use a more drastic shutdown option, that is fine. After the shutdown, start the database normally and then do a regular shutdown, which should work because no one has logged on. This will guarantee a clean shutdown.

A normal shutdown should look like this:

```
SQL> shutdown;
Database closed.
Database dismounted.
ORACLE instance shut down.
```

## SHUTDOWN TRANSACTIONAL

This method is new to Oracle 8. Using this method, Oracle waits for each user to either commit or rollback their current transaction. Then Oracle kills their session and performs the shutdown once all the users are off the system.

This is an option, but it relies on waiting for the users to finish their transactions. Theoretically, this is a good idea, but if an OLTP user has gone to lunch or home for the weekend, you will be waiting for a while! For that reason, I typically skip this option and either kill sessions or use SHUTDOWN IMMEDIATE.

## SHUTDOWN IMMEDIATE

Using this method, Oracle kills all user sessions (forcing a rollback) and then performs the normal shutdown procedures. If you need a system down and more users are logged in than you care to kill manually, this is a good method.

SHUTDOWN IMMEDIATE is supposed to provide a clean shutdown (and it probably does), but many DBAs feel safer with a normal shutdown. If I need to shut down a database for cold backups with SHUTDOWN IMMEDIATE, I wait for the database to shut down, and then issue a startup and then a normal shutdown. This might not be necessary, but this extra step is worth it to me.

The problem with SHUTDOWN IMMEDIATE is that it can take a while (several minutes or more) for all the transactions to roll back and for the sessions to be killed. It will, however, finish sooner than if you entered the kill commands manually. If you find this process is taking too long and you really need the system down immediately, type CTRL+C to escape the shutdown, and read the next section on shutdown abort.

## SHUTDOWN ABORT

When I refer to a *violent* shutdown, this is it. This effectively slams the door on all the user sessions and kills the database. There is no automatic checkpoint or log switch before the database goes down. This results in a database that is in an inconsistent state and will require automatic instance recovery on the next startup. During this process, Oracle rolls back uncommitted transactions and makes sure committed transactions are applied. Control files and data files are resynchronized. Once this process is done, the database will be opened for normal use.

This normally occurs without problems, but it is not something experienced DBAs like to do. If you need to do a SHUTDOWN ABORT, at least try to force a checkpoint (ALTER SYSTEM CHECKPOINT) or redo log switch (ALTER SYSTEM SWITCH LOGFILE) before you issue the command.

Sometimes when the database is in a confused state or there are so many logins that killing them would take forever, SHUTDOWN ABORT is the only real option. I had one situation where a process went haywire and kept logging in. By the time it was stopped there were several hundred logins that had to be killed. I issued a shutdown immediate but after several hours I used CTRL+C to escape the command, issued ALTER SYSTEM CHECKPOINT, and then did a SHUTDOWN ABORT. Next I executed a normal startup and then shut down the database again. This worked; the checkpoint helped by flushing the buffers and updating the file headers. Instance recovery proceeded automatically and bouncing the database afterward, guaranteed any cleanup was finished.

Don't use a SHUTDOWN ABORT unless it's really necessary. If you issue this and then perform a cold backup, don't count on that backup being valid.

Shutting down the database is not always as simple as it seems. If you can get the users to log themselves off, that is best. If not, kill their sessions and hopefully their processes will be cleaned up quickly so a normal SHUTDOWN can occur. If this is not the case, use a SHUTDOWN IMMEDIATE. When writing scripts that involve database shutdowns, use the SHUTDOWN IMMEDIATE option. For times when a cold backup is needed, insist on a normal SHUTDOWN even if it was proceeded by a SHUTDOWN IMMEDIATE and STARTUP. Finally, if you have to use a SHUTDOWN ABORT, try to at least force a checkpoint before you abort the instance.

# User Management

Creating database users is a typical DBA task. Most users are simply that, database users; they do have any tables or other objects. These are the people logging on to the database to use the application. The key with these users is to make sure they have only the permissions they need, that password security is maintained, and that they are modified or deleted as necessary.

The database users requiring more attention are those relative few that actually own the tables, indexes, and other objects within the database. These are the schemas with the data that the DBA must monitor and keep available. Once these accounts are created, there is relatively little account maintenance. Most of the work involves creating or modifying tables and indexes at the request of the application developers.

# Creating Users

You must have the system privilege CREATE USER to create users. Typically, only DBAs have this power. The basic syntax to create a database user is as follows:

```
create user username identified by password
default tablespace tablespace_name
temporary tablespace tablespace_name;
```

If possible, make the username the same as the user's OS account. This helps tracking and auditing. It also permits the use of OS authentication, which is common in Unix environments. Set the password to something simple initially, but force the users to change the password by ALTER USER *username* PASSWORD EXPIRE. This allows the users to log in initially, but will force them to change their passwords. If you want to initially create the password with special characters, enclose it in double quotes (such as "newguy!2").

The default tablespace specifies where user objects, such as tables and indexes, are created when no tablespace is specified. Set this to the USERS tablespace. The specification for temporary tablespace indicates where disk sorts occur. Set this value to the TEMP tablespace. It is important to explicitly define both the default and temporary tablespace for all users because, if you don't, they default to the SYSTEM tablespace. You do not want users creating tables or sorting inside the SYSTEM tablespace because this will cause performance problems because of fragmentation, contention, and possibly running out of room.

Here is a sample user creation:

```
SQL> create user danw identified by "oracledan!"
  2  default tablespace users
  3  temporary tablespace temp;

User created.
```

The view DBA_USERS provides a great deal of useful information regarding users. The dynamic performance view V$SESSION also provides information on users currently logged in.

# Privileges

Even though this newly created user has an account, he cannot log in because he lacks the necessary privileges. Oracle maintains control over users by assigning privileges to every action and every user starts with no privileges. There are two types of privileges: system privileges and object privileges.

System privileges allow users to perform a database action. For example, being able to log in requires the CREATE SESSION privilege. This needs to be granted to a new user before they can log in.

```
SQL> grant create session to danw;

Grant succeeded.
```

This user can now log in, assuming he has the password. Other examples of system-type privileges include creating public synonyms, creating users, and modifying database structures such as tablespaces.

To see which system privileges exist, execute SELECT DISTINCT PRIVILEGE FROM DBA_SYS_PRIVS. As of Oracle 8.1.6, this command lists 115 different privileges.

Object privileges allow users to create, drop, modify, or execute an object such as a table, index, sequence, procedure, function, or package. If I have the privilege to create one of these types of objects, I can do anything I want with my object and no one else can touch it. By the same token, I cannot touch anyone else's objects without privileges to do so.

To be able to even view information in another user's table, you need permission on that object:

```
SQL> show user
USER is "MIKEW"
SQL> grant select on test_table to danw;

Grant succeeded.

SQL> connect danw/oracledan!
Connected.
SQL> select * from mikew.test_table;

F1 F2
---- -----------
   1 Hello World
```

In this case, the table TEST_TABLE was created and owned by MIKEW. For the user DANW to be able to select from it, MIKEW has to grant the object level select permission to DANW. Once that was done, DANW can select from MIKEW.TEST_TABLE, but DANW cannot insert, update, or delete data from it. To perform that kind of data-manipulation, DANW needs to be granted those privileges as well.

To view your object privileges, issue SELECT * FROM ALL_TAB_PRIVS. This command lists every insert, update, delete, and execute privilege you have on an object (not just tables) or that you have granted to other users.

## Roles

Obviously it would not be practical to grant explicit privileges for every action to every user. Oracle handles this by packaging groups of related system and object privileges together as a *role*. Oracle 8.1.6 comes with 22 predefined roles. Some roles are related to specific tools, but others, such as DBA and CONNECT, are more general and are intended to be granted to normal users. To identify these roles, issue SELECT * FROM DBA_ROLES. It is advisable to identify which privileges are being granted to the roles via SELECT * FROM DBA_TAB_PRIVS WHERE GRANTEE = '*ROLE_NAME*'.

On a generic system, it is standard procedure to grant the CONNECT role to users after you have created them. This role includes the CREATE SESSION system privilege.

```
SQL> grant connect to danw;

Grant succeeded.
```

In more security-conscious shops, these roles are recreated with different names and more restrictive privileges. It is common to create application-specific roles with only the privileges needed. This is an area where the DBA should work with the developers to identify a list of the privileges needed by the users. Assign only what the users need, this is not the time to be generous.

### NOTE

Roles as Flags

You can create a role but not necessarily assign any privileges to it. Developers will sometimes ask for a role to be created and assigned to a user so it can be used as a flag within their programs.

## Quotas

Quotas provide a way to limit a user's use of disk space on a specific tablespace. When users are initially created, they have no quotas on any tablespace, so they cannot create objects. If the user is not intended to create objects, it might be valid to just grant CONNECT to the user who does not require quotas. If the user needs to create objects, quotas must be provided to the user.

Granting the role RESOURCE will provide unlimited tablespace usage to a user. You can also assign users defined amounts of space on specific tablespaces. Typically, however, once it has been determined that a user *needs* to create objects, the necessary space is made available without the use of quotas to restrict size. It is more common to use quotas to completely restrict access to specific tablespaces rather than provide access only up to a specified amount of megabytes.

## Table, Index, Sequence Creation and Maintenance

It should seem odd that although a database exists to store data in tables, a DBA spends relatively little time working with individual tables. Unless the DBA is an Application DBA or doubles as an application developer, he or she spends a majority of the time managing schemas and databases rather than individual tables. Although many people initially cringe at this irony, most will agree it is true. More often than not, the developer or data modeler designs the table and the DBA just implements their request. The same holds true for indexes and sequences because it is the developers/programmers who are writing the code to use the index or sequence numbers.

Despite the fact the DBA most likely did not initially design the table, he or she is responsible for its efficient implementation. This means the DBA examines the developer's or designer's request, determines whether it makes sense, and only then decides how best to implement it. It is here where the DBA needs to exercise some discretion.

Not all table, index, or sequence requests are valid! Just because the DBA gets an email requesting a table or index, doesn't necessarily mean it should be created. Unfortunately, developers are often pressed by time and will design tables and indexes to expedite or optimize development of their particular piece of an application. This can come at the expense of data normalization and can conflict with the application's data model. I consider data models to be "living" objects that should be modified when needed, but not on a whim. I have managed systems that were solely at the mercy of the developer's whims for years and these systems became some of the most difficult environments to manage. In these environments, expect to see invalid, redundant, or ridiculous data tables that no one remembers why they were built. You should also expect to see a large number of poorly conceived and never used indexes. If you find yourself in this situation, expect a great deal of work ahead of you. Better yet, don't let yourself get into these types of situations in the first place.

### NOTE

Database Design Resource

One solid book on data modeling and design that recently came out is *Database Design* by Ryan Stevens and Ron Plew (SAMS Publishing, 2001 ISBN 0-672-31758-3). It provides the DBA with some valuable insights on design outside the scope of this text.

What do you do when a developer requests that a table be created or modified? First of all, don't just implement it. Look at the table and determine what is being created or changed. These requests are almost always emails with a CREATE TABLE statement or a CASE (Computer Aided System Engineering) tool generated with the CREATE TABLE script with the full syntax to create the table. Typically you will be given the syntax to create the table with X number of columns and Y data types. (The same goes for indexes and sequences). Attempt to determine what this object is for.

Next, examine the Entity Relationship Diagram (which should exist for your system) and determine whether this proposed table is redundant, breaks integrity rules, or is valid. If it is an index or sequence, review the data dictionary (using the DBA_X views) to determine whether the object already exists or whether another object exists that could be used instead.

Once you have done your homework on the object, approach the developer about it. Ask for an explanation for the new object. Ideally, you are part of the SQL code walkthroughs or design meetings where you can raise these issues, but if that is not possible you might need to confront the developer independently.

Unfortunately, some developers don't want to be "bothered" by the DBA nor do they want to justify their object. If you get this reaction, it should raise some red flags about the validity of the object. Do not waste the developer's time with questions that you can research yourself and don't demand explanations in the middle of crisis, but the developer should make the time to talk with you. If the developer isn't able to reasonably justify why a new table is needed, perhaps you should not create it. If the table will unreasonably danger the integrity of the data model or impose an unacceptable degree of data denormalization, do not create it. Instead, work out an alternative.

Assuming the table, index, or sequence is valid, you need additional DBA-specific information from the developer. Specifically, you should ask these questions:

- How big does this table need to be initially? How much will it grow over time (one to several years)?
- What type of activity will hit this table and how often? Are they primarily large inserts or will it be heavy query activity? What degree of updates and deletes will occur?
- Will this table be used heavily in conjunction with other objects?
- Are there any special objects in this table such as LOBs (Large Objects)?
- What kind of indexing is required? The size and activity on the table will influence this.
- If the object is a sequence (which is really just a unique number generator), identify the starting, ending, and interval values.
- Ask if there is any other information about the object you should know. Leave this open-ended and hopefully the developer will volunteer some information.

Do not expect complete answers to all your questions because often the developers and data modelers do not have all the information themselves.

Once you have all the information possible, it is time to create the object. Working off the assumption you have the basic SQL from the developers, it is best if you do *not* attempt to enter it manually. The chance for human error is simply too great plus this is simply not feasible in large, fast-moving environments. Logging into SQL*Plus, typing `spool scriptname.lst` to save the output, and executing the create script is the best policy. If there are errors, they are logged and can be more easily identified.

You'll learn about the performance-related technical details of table and index types and their advanced storage options in Chapter 11, "Oracle Server Tuning." If you need to create a table without the benefit of a script, a GUI tool is acceptable, especially when you can save the DDL to a script to execute from SQL*Plus. For times when you have to manually create a table, index, or sequence from the command line, the appendixes of this book contain the syntax and sample objects.

> **NOTE**
>
> **Check for Invalid Objects**
>
> When creating, modifying, or dropping objects, *always* check for invalid objects before and after you run the script. Query the view USER_OBJECTS WHERE STATUS = 'INVALID' to find any invalid object. This frequently occurs when working with PL/SQL packages and procedures. If necessary, generate dynamic SQL to recompile the objects.

You should store detailed information about the object in a repository for documentation purposes. In large shops where there are multiple releases of software, institute revision control over your DDL scripts and program code. This way, your database objects can match the application code. Just as the DBA must work with the SA on many issues, he or she should also work with the developers on this issue. Unix provides rcs (revision control system), which I have seen used successfully in small to medium sized shops. More comprehensive and complex third-party tools are also available and can be used in conjunction with CASE tools. If you are managing a large or complex environment, the use of these types of tools is almost mandatory. Just make sure that once these tools and their data become an integral part of your system, they are given the backup, recovery, and security attention they deserve.

# Identifying Objects and Synonyms

Earlier in the chapter, MIKEW created a table called TEST_TABLE and granted access to DANW to illustrate the use of privileges. I will now expand upon this example to show how users reference objects via schema names and synonyms.

The use of MIKEW.TEST_TABLE versus TEST_TABLE can be confusing for beginners. User MIKEW owns the table TEST_TABLE. Because it is his object, he can refer to it as either MIKEW.TEST_TABLE or simply as TEST_TABLE. He does not need to preface the object name (TEST_TABLE) with the schema/owner name (MIKEW). If MIKEW issues a SELECT statement on MIKEW.TEST_TABLE and on TEST_TABLE, the same data will be returned in both cases.

The user DANW does not own any tables. He has access to the table MIKEW.TEST_TABLE. Because DANW has SELECT access to that table owned by MIKEW (but no objects of his own), DANW must refer to the table as MIKEW.TEST_TABLE. If he simply looks for TEST_TABLE, Oracle will return an error message saying it cannot find TEST_TABLE.

For example:

```
SQL> show user
USER is "DANW"
SQL> select * from mikew.test_table;

  F1 F2
 ---- -------------
    1 Hello World

SQL> select * from test_table;
select * from test_table
              *
ERROR at line 1:
ORA-00942: table or view does not exist
```

The reason for this is because of how Oracle resolves object names. When a user issues a statement for an object without specifying an owner, Oracle looks for the object in the following order and returns the first one found:

1. If the user explicitly identifies the object with a schema name, it will use that object. In other words, MIKEW.TEST_TABLE always refers to the TEST_TABLE owned by MIKEW.

2. If the user owns an object by that name, Oracle uses that object if no schema name is specified.

3. When the user has created a synonym that basically says "TEST_TABLE really means MIKEW.TEST_TABLE", Oracle will use that synonym. Of course, that user must have permission to that table and the ability to create a synonym.

For example:

```
SQL> create synonym test_table for mikew.test_table;

Synonym created.

SQL> select * from test_table;

  F1 F2
  ---- -------------
     1 Hello World
```

4. When a public synonym points to an object, any user with permissions on that object will go through the public synonym to get to the object. Public synonyms are typically created by more powerful users such as DBAs to funnel users to objects owned by one particular schema. For example, assume the private synonym was dropped and a DBA creates the following public synonym:

```
SQL> create public synonym test_table for mikew.test_table;

Synonym created.

SQL> connect danw
Enter password:
Connected.
SQL> select * from test_table;

  F1 F2
  ---- -------------
     1 Hello World
```

As you can see from the previous examples, if you specify the schema/owner.object_name, you will always get that particular object, even when synonyms or public synonyms exist. Once you refer to the object name without the schema/owner, Oracle returns any object you own, and then objects that you have created private synonyms for, followed by any object with a public synonym. If Oracle cannot find the object after that, it issues an error.

If the object has a public synonym, but you do not have access privileges, Oracle returns an error. Assume MIKEW revokes access to TEST_TABLE for DANW.

```
SQL>  select * from test_table;
 select * from test_table
               *
ERROR at line 1:
ORA-00942: table or view does not exist
```

Notice how Oracle now acts like the object doesn't exist? That is because DANW no longer has permissions for that object. Once the use of permissions and synonyms is understood, manipulating access is easy.

---

**NOTE**

Running Multiple Schemas

In development and testing environments, it is common to run with multiple schemas with near identical sets of objects. If the testers want to test against User_A's objects, the DBA creates public synonyms to "point" everyone towards those objects. If the testers decide they want to switch and test against User_B's objects, the DBA drops the old public synonyms pointing to User_A and creates new public synonyms pointing to User_B. With the use of dynamic SQL to quickly make the drop and create synonym scripts, this sort of environment is relatively easy to manage.

---

Use the views DBA_SYNONYMS, DBA_VIEWS, and DBA_TAB_PRIVS to resolve problems involving object identification.

# Space Management

Space management is a major duty of the DBA. This typically involves creating tablespaces, adding data files to them, and then monitoring the free space in them as tables and indexes grow. The idea is to make sure that objects within the tablespaces have enough space allocated to contain their data without needing to grow dynamically, unexpectedly, or run out of room. Like so many tasks of the DBA, you know the DBA is doing his or her job if space management is never a problem.

## Storage Hierarchy

Managing objects is easier said than done. A single production schema can have 10,000 objects, including tables, indexes, sequences, synonyms, and PL/SQL packages, procedures, and functions. Obviously the DBA doesn't manage each of these individually, but the DBA is obligated to make sure each of these is in a reasonable tablespace and has enough space to grow if needed. Before you go any further, you should understand the storage hierarchy of Oracle objects, shown in Figure 6.5.

The storage hierarchy is from largest to smallest: tablespace, datafile, segment, extents, and blocks. Each unit is composed of one or more smaller subunits until you reach the Oracle block, which can be a multiple of OS blocks. Tablespaces, segments, and extents are logical constructs that organize and hold data. Data files and Oracle blocks are physical objects.

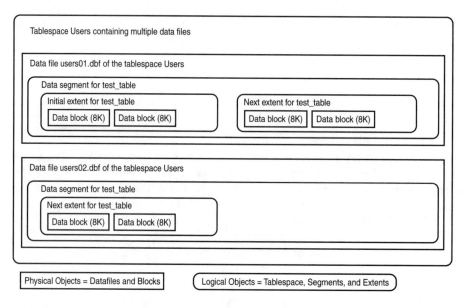

**FIGURE 6.5**

*Oracle Storage Hierarchy.*

Oracle reads and writes by the Oracle block, which is the smallest unit of I/O Oracle can manipulate. A block can hold several rows of data, or one long row of data can span several blocks. Having one row spanning multiple blocks is a possible performance hit and is covered in Chapter 11.

When a table (or index) is created, it is assigned to a tablespace. It is also assigned an initial extent size and a next extent size. A segment is simply the collection of all the extents for an object.

```
SQL> create table test_table (f1 number, f2 varchar2(20))
  2  tablespace Users
  3  storage (initial 16K next 16K);

Table created.
```

Generally, unless partitioning is used (covered in Chapter 11), a table will exist in only one tablespace. That tablespace can have one or more data files that are located on separate disks. When the table is initially created, the initial extent is created on a disk within the specified tablespace. In this case, the initial extent was set to 16K, which happens to be the size of two Oracle blocks.

As data is inserted (and committed) into the table test_table, each row is loaded into the 16K initial extent. If the rows are deleted, truncated, or updated smaller or larger, Oracle will automatically fit the rows within the initial extent. Ultimately, the first extent will likely run out of room and the next extent will need to be allocated.

When a new extent needs to be allocated to hold more data, this is called *dynamic space allocation*. If a user wants to insert more rows than can fit into the initial extent, Oracle will dynamically allocate however much space is specified for the next extent. In this case, Oracle would allocate another 16K next extent *somewhere* in either of the data files composing the tablespace USERS. This causes a performance hit because Oracle temporary has to pause the user's INSERT transaction, determine whether there is room left in either of the data files for the next extent, allocate that space, and then insert the data into the newly allocated extent of two blocks.

Notice that the new extent can be *anywhere* in the tablespace as long as the extent is *contiguous* (all the blocks are side by side). They do not even have to be in the same data file; the only rules are they must be in the tablespace USERS and the blocks of the extent must be next to each other. If the extents are located away from each other, this is called *fragmentation*.

---

**NOTE**

**Fragmentation an Issue?**

Few topics among DBAs draw as much heated discussion as fragmentation. For years, DBAs have worked under the assumption that fragmentation was a horrible performance problem. The recommended advice was to size your initial and next extents so large that all the data for the table (or index) would fit within just a few extents. The rationale was that if Oracle had to jump from extent to extent to retrieve rows (especially during Full Table Scans, FTS), performance would suffer. In recent years some people, notably those from Oracle, have been suggesting that fragmentation really is not as bad as once thought. Some have further indicated that trying to fit all the data into one or two extents is a waste of time considering the minimal performance gains. They suggest simply giving every extent one of just a few possible sizes (which optimizes storage) and not worrying about fragmentation. I haven't made my mind up on the issue yet. I don't lose sleep over a few extents, but I also don't let a table or index climb to hundreds or thousands of tiny extents either.

---

Tablespace and extent sizes are the two main storage parameters to be concerned about when creating tables or indexes. Other storage parameters can also be specified in the CREATE statement. These additional values, listed in the following table, become especially important when table access or free space becomes a problem.

| Parameter | Purpose |
|-----------|---------|
| pctfree | Percentage of the Oracle data block (8K) that's reserved for updates. This allows rows to grow within blocks so they do not need to spill into other blocks. Set high for tables with heavy update activity; set low for insert only tables. Default is 10%. |
| pctused | Once a block exceeds the pctfree percentage, no new inserts are allowed into that block. If deletes reduce the amount of space within that block to below the pctused percentage, that block will become eligible for new inserts. Set to a lower value to reduce fragmentation. Default is 40%. |
| minextents | The minimum number of extents for an object. Default is 1. |
| maxextents | The maximum number of extents for an object. Set this to unlimited. |
| pctincrease | A percentage increase in size of each next extent. Default is 50%, but change this to either 0 or 1%. If it is set to 1%, SMON will periodically coalesce (combine) contiguous free extents into larger free extents. |
| freelist | Identifies the number of blocks available for simultaneous inserts. Set this value higher to avoid contention on blocks during inserts. |

These values are tunable, but some of them require the object to be re-created with the new values. New advances in Oracle 8i and 9i allow an increasing number of parameters to be changed "on the fly" even if Oracle appears to be re-creating the object behind the scenes. One key factor that should be noted now, but is discussed in greater detail in Chapter 10, is locking.

Consider the effect you have on a table when you manipulate its parameters or add/drop/rebuild its indexes. It is possible to lock and prevent DML access to an object for normal users if the DBA is not conscious of how Oracle is modifying the table. Research what is actually going to happen to the table *before* you modify it so you won't unexpectedly lock a table that's being accessed by hundreds of users.

Good information about objects can be obtained from DBA_OBJECTS, DBA_TABLES, and DBA_INDEXES. Space-related information is available from DBA_SEGMENTS and DBA_EXTENTS.

## Tablespace Management

Tablespaces are a key logical unit within the database. They are composed of data files in which database objects are stored. You have already learned what they are and what they store in previous chapters. You have also learned why you should separate some types of objects so they will be in different tablespaces to avoid contention (such as data and indexes for the same table). Additionally, you have seen the basic create tablespace syntax in the create database scripts. Therefore, I will not rehash all this information, but will move onto the management activities rather than the theory.

In previous chapters, you planned a sample database layout and then created that database. You did, however, defer to this chapter to create the application-specific tablespaces. During database creation, the DBA should only be focused on getting a clean and solid database, not trying to build the application.

Creating tablespaces should not be taken lightly. Their creation is not difficult, but their characteristics and usage should be well planned. Once you have identified the need, the name, and the location for your tablespace, verify you have enough space to create it. If you lack the available disk space the creation will fail. To manually create a tablespace for employee indexes on /u02, do the following as a DBA:

```
SQL> create tablespace employee_idx
  2   datafile '/u02/oradata/rh1dev1/employee_idx01.dbf' size 100M
  3   minimum extent 128K
  4   default storage
  5   (initial 128K next 128K minextents 1 maxextents unlimited
  6   pctincrease 1);

Tablespace created.
```

## NOTE

### Raw Partitions

If your filesystems are on raw partitions (uncooked filesystems), you will need the SA to create a *volume* for your tablespace before you create it. This is common for Parallel Server DBAs.

The tablespace is now created and objects can be created in it. It took a few seconds to create because a 100M file had to be created. Be patient if you have to create tablespaces with files several gigabytes in sizes because it will take a few minutes. Notice that the example went to great lengths to specify the default parameters in the tablespace. If a table or index is created without a parameter (such as initial or next extent), that object is created with the default value for the tablespace. In this case, it is good to error on the side of being too small rather than accidentally creating a huge table that only holds a few rows.

Now that the tablespace is created, you can resize the data file. You can increase or reduce the size of the data file as long as there is still enough space for its objects.

```
SQL> alter database
  2   datafile '/u02/oradata/rh1dev1/employee_idx01.dbf'
  3   resize 125M;
```

Database altered.

If you decide you want to add a new data file to a tablespace, you can do that as well. Once again, verify you have enough space and that the new tablespace will not cause contention or recovery difficulties with other tablespaces on the same disk.

```
SQL> alter tablespace employee_idx
  2   add datafile '/u08/oradata/rh1dev1/employee_idx02.dbf'
  3   size 25M;
```

Tablespace altered.

At this stage, most literature on backup and recovery policies recommends a full database backup because you added a tablespace. Even if you only added or modified a data file, some DBAs would push for a backup. I find this somewhat excessive, but I would get a complete backup to use as a baseline before I start creating large numbers of objects. After that, I would recommend another backup before you open a database for production.

Moving data files from one disk to another (within the same tablespace) is also possible, but is a little trickier. This is usually done to eliminate I/O contention or in response to a disk problem. Data files can be named anything; Oracle does not care. A data file can be renamed, but this is also tricky and similar to a file move. Therefore, I will cover both in Chapter 10, "When Things Go Wrong."

If you have accidentally added a data file to the wrong tablespace or simply want to drop a data file, that's too bad. Unfortunately, there is *not* an "alter tablespace ... drop datafile" command. Many people would like one and I would assume the problem is being researched, but for now it is not possible. In this situation, the only options are to drop the tablespace (which *is* possible) or to resize the unwanted data file down to an insignificant size. Just be sure to remember to include this file in the backup scheme just like all the other database files.

**NOTE**

Locally Managed Tablespaces

Oracle 8i introduced a new type of tablespace. Locally managed tablespaces offer new ways to manage object sizes. By using these, combined with a different approach to categorizing tables, it is possible to manage large numbers of objects with a minimum of overhead. Because these types of tablespaces are still relatively new and are a departure from traditional tablespaces, they are covered in Chapter 11.

Tablespaces can be taken offline or made read-only. Taking tablespaces offline is typically done only when a disk has or is failing and a recovery is needed. Tablespaces are not often put into read-only mode unless there is a special situation where the data should not or cannot be changed.

Useful information about tablespaces can be obtained from DBA_TABLESPACES, DBA_DATA_FILES, and DBA_FREE_SPACE. The DBA should know what tablespaces are in the database, which data files they are composed of and their sizes, and how much free space is available in each tablespace.

# Monitoring

One of the most common, yet often overlooked, responsibilities of the DBA is monitoring. A production server supporting an application can be busy: there are normal users logged on, nightly batch processing, special processing such as month-end or year-end, backups of the server and of the database, plus all the little things specific to an application or shop. Most of these tasks can be automated and all of them should write to log files of some sort. It is often the DBA who is tasked with making sure everything runs correctly because all of it impacts the database. Remember, if it affects either the data or the data's availability to the users, it *is* the DBA's business.

When a DBA comes in the morning, he/she often has a list of processes to check. If any process failed, the DBA should ideally be the first to know about it and should know why. It is quiet embarrassing for a user or manager to call the IT department and inform the DBA that *their* database or application is down. Users are always going to call and complain when systems have problems, but it looks bad when the DBA needs to be told that the system has crashed. Therefore, the DBA should have a list of critical systems, subsystems, and jobs that he or she verifies every morning.

## Verify Database and Connectivity

This verification typically starts with the database. Log in to the Unix server and check for the PMON process for each SID.

```
$ ps -ef | grep -i pmon
oracle    1233    1  0 Feb26 ?        00:00:00 ora_pmon_rh1dev1
oracle    1961    1  0 06:57 ?        00:00:00 ora_pmon_rh1tst1
oracle    1987 1920  0 06:58 pts/0    00:00:00 grep -i pmon
```

If a database is not up that should be, find out why and get it started. If there is actually a database problem that will require time to fix, make sure the user community and managers are notified. No one wants to hear there are problems, but people get frustrated when they call to report a computer problem and find the IT department either didn't know about it or knew and decided not to tell anyone. This is a prime example of why IT departments and personnel sometimes have a poor reputation with other professionals.

Check the listener process. Either use `grep` to search for the process or use `lsnrctl status`. Remember, if this process is down, users will not be able to connect to the database. If there is any doubt about connectivity, the DBA should log in as a user to verify access into the system. This includes checking whether the application is available. Obviously, if the DBA cannot log in to the application, the users are probably having this same problem.

## Alert Log

Once the DBA has verified the database and listener are running and access into the application is possible, it is time to check the database log for errors. Each database's `alertSID.log` is located in `$ORACLE_BASE/admin/SIDname/bdump`. This file should be checked in the morning, before or after lunch, before the DBA leaves, and whenever there are problems.

The DBA will become very familiar with the contents of the `alert.log`. Many of the messages in the file are routine, such as database startup/shutdown, checkpoints, and redo log switches. The DBA should monitor the frequency of these messages to verify the database is operating as planned. Also, any non-default database parameters are listed in this file during database startup.

You are not interested in seeing the entire `alert.log`. Because this file is appended to, only the last 200 or so lines are important. Either use `tail -200 alertSID.log | more` or write a shell script such as:

```
$ more tail-1
tail -222 $ORACLE_BASE/admin/$ORACLE_SID/bdump/alert*.log | more
$ ls -alt tail-1
-rwxr-xr-x    1 oracle    dba              65 Feb 16 21:45 tail-1
```

This script makes it easy to routinely monitor the `alert.log`:

```
$ tail-1
Mon Feb 26 11:26:14 2001
Thread recovery: finish rolling forward thread 1
Thread recovery: 0 data blocks read, 0 data blocks written, 0 redo blocks read
Crash recovery completed successfully
...
Mon Feb 26 12:23:53 2001
Completed: ALTER DATABASE OPEN
Mon Feb 26 13:32:45 2001
alter tablespace users
add datafile
'/u02/oradata/rh1dev1/users02.dbf' size 100M
Mon Feb 26 13:32:45 2001
ORA-1031 signalled during: alter tablespace users
```

A database normally does not have a large number of ORA-XXXX errors in the alert.log. If you see error messages such as ORA-1031, you need to fully investigate. The DBA should check the error message number and find the cause of the problem. If the error is an ORA-600, a call into Oracle Support should be made. If anything is mentioned about media recovery or corruption, you should be ready to really earn your money because this is a serious problem.

To get more information about any Oracle error, use the error-checking utility oerr. This handy utility can look up most common errors related to Oracle and is much faster than using an error messages guide. See Figure 6.6.

```
Shortcut to telnet                                          _ □ ×
$ oerr ora 1031
01031, 00000, "insufficient privileges"
// *Cause: An attempt was made to change the current username or password
//         without the appropriate privilege. This error also occurs if
//         attempting to install a database without the necessary operating
//         system privileges.
//         When Trusted Oracle is configure in DBMS MAC, this error may occur
//         if the user was granted the necessary privilege at a higher label
//         than the current login.
// *Action: Ask the database administrator to perform the operation or grant
//         the required privileges.
//         For Trusted Oracle users getting this error although granted the
//         the appropriate privilege at a higher label, ask the database
//         administrator to regrant the privilege at the appropriate label.
$ _
```

**FIGURE 6.6**
*Checking Database Errors.*

The alert.log can get big over time. Sometimes it is advisable to archive and compress the file:

```
$ pwd
/u01/app/oracle/admin/rh1dev1/bdump
$ mv alert_rh1dev1.log alert_rh1dev1-20010227.log
$ compress alert_rh1dev1-20010227.log
```

There is no longer an alertSID.log, but Oracle will create a new one (with the same name as before) whenever it needs to write a new message. Therefore, the previous method is a safe way to archive your alert.log. If you don't want a copy of the file, simply cat /dev/null into the file and erase the file's contents:

```
$ cat /dev/null > alert_rh1dev1.log
```

## Monitor Database Objects

The DBA should monitor two particular types of database objects: tablespace allocations and invalid objects. These checks should also be done in the morning. A failure to do so will not destroy a database, but it can impact the availability of the data to the users.

Log into SQL*Plus and check the tablespaces you have created.

```
SQL> select tablespace_name, sum(bytes) from dba_free_space
  2  group by tablespace_name;
```

```
TABLESPACE_NAME              SUM(BYTES)
-------------------          ----------------
DRSYS                         84,074,496
EMPLOYEE_IDX                 157,270,016
RBS                          183,492,608
SYSTEM                       358,121,472
TEMP                         104,849,408
TOOLS                        104,849,408
USERS                        108,650,496

7 rows selected.
```

In a stable system, there is relatively little change in this from day to day. This is because most of the database objects already have their initial extents and will grow only when needed. Only when next extents are allocated or new objects are created should you see the amount of free space decline. Save and monitor these reports over a period of time. If you notice a trend where you expect to run out of space, either add more space to the tablespace, truncate or drop unneeded tables, or find out why a table or index is growing so much and stop it. If a table or index needs to allocate a next extent, but cannot find a contiguous free extent large enough, an error message will be issued.

Also get a count of invalid objects for whichever schema owns the application objects in the database. Inside SQL*Plus, a simple SELECT OBJECT_NAME, OBJECT_TYPE FROM DBA_OBJECTS WHERE OWNER = 'SCHEMA_OWNER' AND STATUS = 'INVALID' identifies invalid objects. Recompile these using dynamic SQL to improve performance and to verify that all the objects are valid. If you notice an increasing trend or an alarming number of invalid objects, raise this issue with the developers.

## Setting Up and Monitoring cron Jobs

cron is a very useful Unix/Linux job-scheduling and running facility. It allows you to specify that, at any given time on any given day, a specific script will be executed and a log file will be created. This provides a tremendous capability to set up jobs to execute without having to start them manually.

In the Unix world, most batch processing and automated tasks run via cron. From a DBA perspective, you can use it to schedule when your nightly backups begin, when exports/imports occur, when tables are analyzed, and what time nightly processing begins. You can also use cron to log in, check for the PMON process, and if it is not found send an email or page. There is virtually no limit to what you can use cron to do.

Setting up and running cron is very easy. Follow these steps:

1. First, create your shell scripts as normal. Be sure to fully define the environment variables within your scripts. If you don't set your environment variables, they will not be set automatically your script will fail. Scripts can call other scripts but make sure you declare the full path and filename in the scripts. SQL*Plus scripts can also be executed from within shell scripts.

2. Next, create a directory where your `crontab` (file with your jobs) will be stored. The user oracle will have a personal `cron` daemon, so create the directory `$ORACLE_BASE/local/cron_files`.

3. Create (using vi) a file called `crontab_oracle`. Any scripts (jobs) you want to run will be placed in this file along with when to run them and (optionally) the log file to be created.

4. Use `man cron` and `man crontab` for compete syntax on cron. The format for the `crontab` file is as follows:

```
0 22 * * 0-6 `/u01/app/oracle/backups/hots/hot.sh
1>/u01/app/oracle/backups/hots/hot.log 2>&1`
```

The script hot.sh will be executed at 2200 hours (0 for minutes, 22 for 22nd hour) on every day (the first *) of every month (second *) on days 0-6 (Sunday through Saturday). The log of the execution will be written as `hot.log`. Notice the use of back-tics (`` ` ``) rather than single quotes (`'`).

5. Currently this command only exists in the `crontab` file (`crontab_oracle`). It needs to be submitted to the `cron` process. To submit it, type `crontab` followed by the file you want submitted to `cron`. The file you submit will overwrite the current contents of `cron`, so make sure only one `crontab` file is used and it is up to date.

```
$ crontab crontab_oracle
```

6. To see what cron intends to run, execute `crontab -l`.

```
$ crontab -l
# DO NOT EDIT THIS FILE - edit the master and reinstall.
# (crontab_oracle installed on Tue Feb 27 09:25:42 2001)
# (Cron version -- $Id: crontab.c,v 2.13 1994/01/17 03:20:37 vixie Exp $)
0 22 * * 0-6 /u01/app/oracle/backups/rh1dev1_hots/hot.sh
```

That's it. `cron` will run the script `hot.sh` at the time specified until you tell `cron` to do otherwise.

The only negative aspect of scheduling so many jobs via cron is that someone (the DBA) should monitor their success or failure. Jobs in `cron` are not implicitly dependent on each other, so if one job begins failing, this could go on for a while before it is detected. The DBA should know which jobs are scheduled via `cron` (using `crontab -l`) and check the log files generated from the scripts to make sure they are running correctly.

> ## Always Check Your cron Job Logs
>
> As a DBA you should always check your database alert log, but after that the logs from your cron jobs should be checked. I have seen more than one occasion in which someone will change something on a system, causing my cron jobs to fail. The database will still be up and the alert log will be fine, but nightly processing will have failed.
>
> Each shop and system will have its own jobs; it is up to the administrators to set these up. However, just because they execute successfully once doesn't mean they will run forever without problems. Particularly if they deal with backups (such as exports) or some type of data loads, the DBA will be held accountable if they start failing but no one notices. Don't let that happen to you!

## Monitoring Backups

Backup and recovery is covered in Chapter 9, "Backup and Recovery," however monitoring the previous night's backups is clearly a daily task. Backups can be implemented in a variety of manners, but they all need validation by the DBA. On the Unix/Linux platform, the two most common methods are shutting all the databases down and then copying every file to tape or running a series of scripts to back up each tablespace while the database is running.

These jobs are typically executed by cron; therefore, log files from cron should exist and be reviewed. Because these cron jobs are implemented via Unix shell scripts, there should be a log which also should be reviewed by the DBA. In fact, if the scripts are well written, their logs might have more information than the logs generated by cron. Finally, the database alert.log can often be used to determine whether a backup occurred, especially if the hot backup mode was used. After all these logs are reviewed, you can always verify that the backup files are, in fact, residing in their backup dump location. Given all these indicators, you should have a reliable sense of whether the backups were successful.

You should also keep tabs on the success or failure of backups for the database server as a whole. If the SA reports that backups for a particular database server are often having problems, the DBA might justifiably be concerned. Repeated failures of tapes or other server backup components (including the SA!) should concern the DBA. The DBA needs to access how a recovery/restore of the server will affect the backup plans.

The DBA and SA should share a spreadsheet of each night's backups, the media they are on, and any special notes. If possible, the actual logs should be compressed (they are small) and saved so they can be reviewed as well. Once a recovery is needed there should be no question as to which day's backups should be used. If backup failures on both the database and server occur, but they are not logged, there is an unacceptably high risk of a bad backup being restored.

Although this doesn't seem likely in a small shop where there is only one DBA and one SA, what happens in a large or distributed shop? In large organizations, there are often teams of DBAs and SAs managing multiples systems that don't know each other or aren't even in the same city. Trying to remember which backup was good or bad is not realistic in these environments. Finally, for those organizations that really take offsite disaster recovery seriously, a log of valid backups might be the only information a recovery team has to work with after a disaster.

## Monitoring Exports

Exports and imports are covered in detail in Chapter 8, "DBA Utilities," but they do merit a mention here. Basically, an export dump (*.dmp) file contains the structure and data for the table(s), user(s), or database you have exported. These files are useful to DBAs when loading or unloading data. They are also used as a component of a shop's backup and recovery scheme. As a result, these files are important, their creation is often scheduled via cron, and they can be very large (in the gigabyte range).

Because of these factors, the DBA needs to monitor the creation and integrity of these .dmp files when they are created (typically overnight via cron).

Assuming a nightly cron job exists to export a user (and all his/her data) from a database, there are a few checks for the DBA.

- Make sure the cron job executed properly as defined in the previous section. This involves reviewing the execution log for that cron job.

- Exports generate log files that identify what was exported, by whom, and if there were any errors. The DBA needs to review this file (such as `more exp_customer_tbl.log`) to determine whether there were any errors or warnings. These will be clearly identified as they occur. The last line of the log file will have one of several messages: "export terminated successfully without warnings", "export terminated successfully with warnings", or "export terminated unsuccessfully". The DBA needs to determine whether there were problems and warnings, and if there were, to determine their severity.

- The last check is to see how much space is left on the filesystem after the export. Remember, export files can be very small for just a few tables, or they can be mammoth at several gigabytes or more. Use `df -k` or `bdf`, depending on your platform, to identify how much space is left on your filesystem. Feel free to use `compress` or `gzip` on your export .dmp files. Compression will not corrupt them and you will likely get much better than the normal 3:1 compression ratio. The use of compression on exports/imports is covered in more detail in Chapter 8.

Like backups, it is important to verify the validity of export files for the time when you actually need to use them. Although Oracle and cron will be happy to generate worthless files on an automated basis, it is up to the DBA to identify situations like this and take corrective action.

## Monitor Space on Filesystems

The DBA is better qualified than anyone to monitor the disk usage of his/her filesystems. Although the SA should have scripts that monitor and issue warnings if a filesystem begins running out of space, this is really the DBA's responsibility. If a routine backup or export fails because it ran out of disk space, it is the DBA who is accountable, not the SA.

On filesystems where you are dumping large export, log, or backup files, identify how much space you have and how much is used each night. Once again, use df -k or bdf. Next, project how long it will take for the filesystem to exceed 90-95% capacity or have only have a few hundred megabytes left. At this capacity, disk performance can begin to suffer, plus you run the real risk of running out of space. Do not let a filesystem reach this point before you attempt to take action.

Oracle files used for backup purposes and export .dmps can be compressed using compress or gzip without problems (testing is still a good idea!). Run a compression routine on any file you create in your backup or export dump directories. This should be the last part of any cron job, plus you might want a separate cron job that checks for and compresses any large file not compressed. By using compressing files in a sensible manner, you will save a large amount of disk space.

Work with the SA to identify when and how your filesystems are being backed up. The backup and recovery of databases is discussed in length in Chapter 9, but I am referring to Oracle filesystems/directories without databases. Most SAs will copy everything from a filesystem to a tape on a nightly basis. Those tapes then can be moved offsite in case a tornado, fire, or other disaster occurs. The tapes are then typically returned after a month or two to be recycled. This matters to the DBA because once a file has been copied to tape, it *theoretically* doesn't need to be kept on disk any more.

For example, the users want you to keep a backup of table data (typically in an export .dmp file) for 10 days. You can export that table nightly, compress it, and then let the nightly backup by the SA put the file on tape. You could deleted the data from the filesystem (saving disk space) because it is on tape and could be restored if needed. Even though your users might say they only need the data for 10 days, you have the benefit of knowing that if needed, you could have it for 30 days (or whatever the tape rotation dictates).

In reality, don't delete the file after the first night. Just as your backups will fail sometimes, so will the SA's jobs fail occasionally. If possible have a cron job automatically delete these types of files after three or four days. That should allow enough of a "fudge factor" for a bad tape, server crash, and so on. Also consider the impact of restoring files on the SA in terms of time, money, and hassle. If a tape is moved offsite, it usually costs both time and money to have it returned early. Plus the SA needs to do the restore unless he/she wants to empower the DBA to do this (which would remove dependency on the SA).

> **NOTE**
>
> Legal Requirements
>
> Many companies are legally required to maintain financial information for several years. From a DBA perspective this often means taking very large database exports on a month-end and year-end basis. Work with the SA to make sure these are backed up on clearly identified tapes and that they are stored properly. If you have not been approached about these types of legal requirements, ask your management if they exist. It might be possible that management *assumes* these backups are being taken even if they are not.

One final note about managing space on filesystems. Although these should be checked every workday, make absolutely sure there is enough space before a long weekend or a vacation. Especially just before these times, it is easy to overlook your disk space. Make sure you have enough space for normal activity plus a reserve.

## Electronic Monitoring and Notification

With many technical people carrying pagers and cell phones, it's a good idea to use automatic system tools that notify the DBA and/or SA when a database or system fails. The keys here are to make sure the monitoring tools are accurately diagnosing the system, to establish realistic thresholds for notification, to establish a plan of action for when problems do occur, and to ensure that the total process works.

The idea of setting a system to page the DBA if the database goes down seems so simple, yet many times there are problems. If the system is accidentally set to page all the time, this problem is noticed and fixed immediately. If, however, there is a problem where a page is not being sent or received correctly, this minor glitch might not surface until there is a major problem and the distress call is *not* received.

Testing and coordination between the SAs and DBAs is key. A good SA will have commercial monitoring software installed and running or will have customized monitoring scripts for key processes. Because there is such a dependency between the database and server, it makes sense to integrate monitoring and paging for both the database and server into one system. This often involves the DBA submitting to the SA's notification system. However, it is still up to the DBA to make sure the database monitoring and notification processes are accurate and tested. In other words, do *not* rely on the SA to monitor your database for you.

A clear understanding of what is and is not monitored needs to be established as well as who is notified when a specific problem occurs. For example, it seems obvious that if a server crashes, both the SA and DBA should be notified. But issues with email should not be sent to the DBA nor should a blown rollback segment trouble the SA. Be warned that this can become a touchy, political subject if one group or the other wants to get into the other's business and administration tactics. The situation becomes even more difficult when considering how and when management should be notified.

Have a plan and call list for when problems do occur. If all the DBAs, SAs, and managers get a page saying a script couldn't find PMON running, do they know what to do? If responsibilities are not clearly defined, chaos can occur. Half the staff is trying to fix the same problem and the other half is looking at the pagers saying "not my problem."

One final note of electronic notification: consider the impact it has on the staff. No one wants to be continually tied to a pager 24/7/365. If a system is truly that critical, it is critical enough to have more than one person available to be "on call." Do not make unrealistic expectations of people and then be surprised if they fail to meet those expectations. Also address what is considered "acceptable" response time and what happens if a page goes out but the DBA/SA cannot or does not respond. Remember, pages do legitimately get lost and people are sometimes out of range.

## Plan and Establish Paging Policies Reasonably

I have seen pager polices range from reasonable to ridiculous. If your system *really* needs to be up at 3AM a pager and perhaps a nighttime operator is necessary. Set this policy and enforce it. However, I have seen managers dictate to technical people that 7/24 support is "required" because it looks good from a business standpoint. Technical people are smart enough to know what is necessary and what isn't. As a result, technical people may well leave their pagers behind, even if they are expected to carry them. This is especially the case if the pager is assigned to an individual with no rotation or break from being on call. If the system pages the technical personnel at the slightest problem you can expect to develop a "Cry Wolf" syndrome as well. This can get to the point where administrators will leave their pagers behind because the notification policy is unrealistic.

Pagers and notification need to be taken seriously. However, this policy needs to consider people's personal lives as well. Administrators need to take carrying a pager seriously and respond in an acceptable time period. However, management cannot stick someone with a pager without compensation and expect personnel to base their lives (and that of their family and friends) around it.

# Summary

This chapter covered most common daily tasks of the DBA. Being a good DBA requires more than just adding users or building tablespaces. These are technical skills that should be mastered, but mastery of the skills makes one a good technician, not necessarily a good DBA. A good DBA has these technical skills, but more importantly has an understanding of the system, its processes, and how to manage and head off situations before they become major problems. Although it is an accomplishment to understand the finest details of creating tables, no one will really care if the database is down because the DBA never noticed the backups were invalid. Hopefully, you are leaving this chapter with a clearer understanding of technical issues regarding Oracle objects, but more importantly you know how to administer Unix and Oracle database *systems*.

# GUI Management Products

## ESSENTIALS

- GUI tools offer an excellent way to perform many tedious and routine tasks.

- GUI tools should not be expected to replace core skills and knowledge held by an experience DBA.

- There are several ways to configure Oracle Enterprise Manager to meet the needs of the DBA.

- OEM can be used to manage users, objects, and files as well as provide assistance when faced with tuning or locking issues.

- TOAD is another GUI tool that DBAs should be familiar with because they will likely encounter it at some point being used by developers.

Anything that needs to be done by the DBA can typically be done from the command line. This is especially true regarding complex tasks. A solid DBA will understand what he or she is doing, why he or she is doing it, and how Oracle and Unix implement it.

Having said this, Graphical User Interface (GUI) management products can fulfill a useful niche for the Oracle DBA. A GUI provides a layer of abstraction between the DBA and Oracle. This is only a presentation layer; because Oracle and Unix still perform the same tasks. The details are hidden beneath a GUI display.

Many simple, mundane tasks that cannot be scripted can be performed easily with the aid of a GUI tool. For example, you can add a new user or write a PL/SQL package from SQL*Plus, but it is often easier and quicker to use a GUI tool. A DBA might not remember the syntax or all the options for creating a table, but a GUI tool can generate the SQL for the DBA. It is in situations like these that GUI tools are advisable.

This chapter covers how to install and configure Oracle Enterprise Manager. It examines some of the more common tools and how they are useful to the Unix DBA, but a detailed coverage is outside the scope of this book. Finally, it looks at a popular OEM alternative: TOAD.

# Oracle Enterprise Manager

Oracle's main GUI management tool is Oracle Enterprise Manager. It comes standard with Oracle Client tools or Oracle Server. This makes OEM widely available to both DBAs and developers.

> **NOTE**
>
> Web-based Interfaces
>
> WebDB (aka Oracle Portal) does provide some OEM functionality via a Web browser interface. This is covered in Chapter 17, "Web DB/Oracle Portal."

## Architecture

OEM can take advantage of a multiple-tier architecture. In its barest form, you only need an Oracle database running on a server and the basic OEM tools installed either on a PC or on the server. This setup provides basic functionality; however, more advanced features of OEM require additional setup. For example, you can create a repository in an Oracle database to store data about the other Oracle databases. If you want to add even more functionality, you can connect to a middle tier running as an Oracle Management Server to store information about OEM jobs. To implement the more advanced features, you need to understand the architecture of OEM. The available architectures are outlined in Figure 7.1.

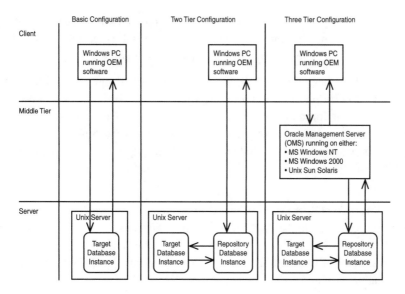

**FIGURE 7.1**

*Oracle Enterprise Manager Architecture*

As you can see in Figure 7.1, OEM can distributed across a client, a server, and a middle tier. The type of configuration you use depends on your needs. If you need basic setup where you connect to the database only to add users or modify objects, the basic configuration will be fine. If you need to perform more advanced tasks on multiple databases, it is necessary to create a repository database (such as rh1rep1) to store information about other databases. In a large environment where the database servers reside on Windows platforms, it makes sense to use the middle tier with Oracle Management Server (OMS). Let's take a look at each tier in detail.

---

**NOTE**

OMS

There seems to be a trend away from just using a client and a repository. Although it was common in previous versions of OEM and with some other tools, OMS is becoming more necessary.

---

## Client

There is typically a Windows workstation containing the OEM tools. From this machine, you start up and use the OEM utilities. You can log on directly to a single database, or you can connect to the middle tier to access all the databases in your enterprise. The installation process is simple and almost foolproof. It is customary to install at least the basic OEM tools on any DBA's machine on site, on any DBA laptops, and at home.

Just as you learned in Chapter 2 that SQL*Plus is a potentially dangerous tool to install freely to everyone, giving OEM out is even more dangerous. Because of OEM's easy-to-use interface, anyone with a minimum of knowledge can be dangerous. Make sure you control OEM's distribution and, more importantly, keep control of your passwords. Some sites have created users with read-only access and provide this with OEM to appropriate personnel. Developers often get OEM with the passwords to the schema they are developing in and read-only access to everything else.

You can install the basic OEM Database Administration Pack to cover your basic needs. If you have the proper licensing, add the Performance Tuning, Diagnostic, and Change Management Packs as well. These tools can act as great timesavers when examining user sessions or looking for locked users. Some of these utilities require a repository and an OMS server, so just because a product is installed does not mean it's available.

---

**NOTE**

OEM on Unix Platforms

Even though the basic OEM utilities are typically installed on Windows machines, they also come with the normal installation of Oracle Server on some Unix platforms (such as Sun Solaris). Verify this by looking in $ORACLE_HOME/bin for the utility oemapp.

---

## Middle Tier

The middle tier refers to the location of the Oracle Management Server (OMS). OMS runs as a service on Microsoft platforms and as a background process on Sun Solaris. You do not need OMS to run OEM, but if you want to connect to the OEM console, it is a requirement. From the OEM console, you can easily administrate multiple databases on different servers. OMS is also used to schedule jobs, monitor events, and to provide email and paging.

Oracle Management Server is as new as the OEM version 2.1. As of this writing, it currently requires access to Sun Solaris, MS NT, or MS Windows 2000. Many Unix DBAs don't even know about OMS yet, probably because they don't use OEM too much. Much of the OMS functionality is already available via Unix cron or via shell scripts to monitor events. Many Unix DBAs do not see any advantage to introducing an additional OMS tier to perform tasks already covered with Unix. For these reasons, not everyone is using it yet, but that will likely change as it becomes more powerful and supported on more platforms. I typically run OMS as a service on NT, but I have not seen any shops use it to replace established Unix monitoring and scheduling tools.

## Server

Under the OEM architecture, the server tier contains the target database, which is the database you are attempting to manage. The server can also contain a repository database, which contains information about one or more target databases. These databases might be one in the same or different physical servers and they might be different database server versions. Obviously, the repository database needs to be running to access it and to use any OEM features dependent on it, but even if that server/database is down, other databases can be accessed using the basic OEM tools.

Within each target database, there can be multiple user sessions for database intelligent agents. These agents provide a way to remotely administer databases even when you are not logged onto the OEM console. Oracle uses Intelligent Agents logged into each target database to detect OEM defined events and perform OEM scheduled jobs.

Oracle has one other optional service available on the server. Oracle Data Gatherer is a background process that collects information for Oracle Capacity Planner and Performance Manager.

Remember that OEM can be used with basic functionality when loaded on a PC accessing a target database. However, if you want to use the OEM's advanced features, you need to create a repository, add an OMS, start your Intelligent Agents, and finally start Oracle Data Gatherer. As you'll see in the next section of this chapter, once the initial setup is established and everything is working, OEM can be a useful tool.

## Installation

Installation of OEM is fairly simple. However, each tier has separate issues, each of which is examined in the following sections.

## Client

Installing the basic OEM client on a Windows machine is relatively simple and requires no server setup. For that reason, expect three consequences—there will many different versions of OEM floating around, it will be on every machine used by the DBA, and it will be on many machines used by people who are not DBAs. Your best bet is to institute a series of "authorized releases" and roll out OEM to the appropriate users when you are comfortable with it.

Unfortunately, the OEM genie is sometimes already "out of the bottle" and everyone in the shop has OEM and thinks they are a DBA. If you find yourself in this situation, you *must* step in and regain control, particularly if the DBA password(s) are no longer secure. Although a strong case can be made for SAs to have the Oracle password, developers and other users should not. Oddly enough, this is more common in smaller shops where there is often less stringent control of passwords and procedures.

The technical details of installing OEM on a client are as follows.

1. Obtain the CD "Oracle Enterprise Manager: Version 2.1 with Oracle Tuning, Diagnostics, and Change Management Packs."

2. Load the CD in any Windows machine 95 or higher. If you want to install and run the Oracle Management Server, the machine needs to be any version of either NT or Windows 2000.

3. The OEM load screen appears. Select the Install/Deinstall Products option, as shown in Figure 7.2.

4. The next screen (Figure 7.3) shows the familiar Oracle Universal Installer you used to install the Oracle Server in Chapter 4, "Machine Setup and Installation." Click the Next button.

**FIGURE 7.2**

*Oracle Enterprise Manager Installation.*

**FIGURE 7.3**

*Oracle Universal Installer.*

5. You will be prompted for file locations, as shown in Figure 7.4. It seems logical to create an Oracle directory, and then create a subdirectory for OEM and other Oracle product subdirectories at the same level. Unfortunately, I have experienced some problems with this method where the Registry on NT gets "confused." Instead, forgo the idea of creating an Oracle directory and simply install OEM as OraOEM21.

6. You will be prompted for what to install. If you are running NT or Windows 2000, your options will be OEM, Management Packs, and Management Infrastructure (which is OMS) or you can just Install OEM and the Management Packs. If you are running Windows 98 or Windows 95, you will receive the options shown in Figure 7.5. Assuming you are running Windows 95/98, select the Typical installation.

**FIGURE 7.4**
*OEM File Locations.*

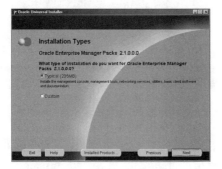

**FIGURE 7.5**
*OEM Installation Types.*

7

GUI
MANAGEMENT
PRODUCTS

Installing OMS and creating the repository are covered under Middle Tier and Server Installations.

7.  The next screen provides a summary of products to install, as shown in Figure 7.6. Once you have verified this is what you want, click OK.

8.  This installation of the products will occur, as shown in Figure 7.7.

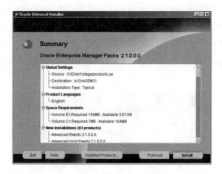

**FIGURE 7.6**
*OEM Summary Information.*

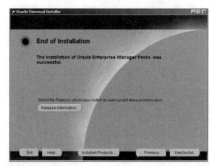

**FIGURE 7.7**
*OEM Installation Is Complete.*

9.  After the installation has occurred successfully, you will likely be placed in the Net8 Configuration Assistant to configure the client-side tnsnames.ora file. You did this for the server in Chapter 5, "Creating a Database," and you can proceed with this if you want. Another method is to exit from the assistant (it won't hurt your OEM installation). Then copy/ftp the tnsnames.ora file from your Unix/Linux server to your client in the $ORACLE_HOME/network/admin directory.

This is all there is to installing the OEM client. After the installation, your OEM software is available from Start, Programs, Oracle-OraOEM21.

## Middle Tier (OMS)

Installation of the Oracle Management Server is optional, but you can't schedule database jobs via OEM or monitor for events without OMS. As of this writing, to install and run OMS, you need either a Sun Solaris server or a Windows machine running any version of NT or Windows 2000. The Oracle Universal Installer determines whether you are running a Windows machine capable of running OMS and provides the additional OMS options. This section assumes that you are using Windows NT/2000. The installation process is very similar to the basic OEM except for the following OMS options.

OUI will provide you the option of installing the basic OEM and Management Packs or the OEM with the OMS infrastructure, as shown in Figure 7.8.

**FIGURE 7.8**
*OEM OMS Product Selection.*

OUI will then ask you whether OMS will connect to a new or an existing repository, as shown in Figure 7.8. In this section, you create the repository with the OEM Configuration Assistant covered in the OEM Server setup. Select New Repository when prompted.

**FIGURE 7.9**
*OMS Repository Selection.*

After the installation, Oracle Net8 Assistant will start and will be followed by the OMS setup, as shown in Figure 7.10.

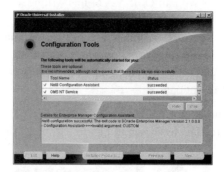

**FIGURE 7.10**
*OMS Setup.*

Once you reach this point, it is time to create the database repository and start the intelligent agents on the Unix/Linux server. Creating the repository on a database is a prerequisite for starting OMS. This is covered in the next section "Server Installation." Once that is completed, you can start the OMS service, as detailed next.

Assuming the database repository has been created and the intelligent agents are running, it is time to start the OMS service on your NT/Windows 2000 machine.

Go to Start, Settings, Control Panel, Services. As shown in Figure 7.11, you will find the service for Oracle Management Server.

**FIGURE 7.11**
*Control Panel Services.*

Next, highlight and double-click OMS get the service options. You can either start the service manually, or you can set it to start automatically on machine reboot. Select the manual startup for now, as shown in Figure 7.12.

**FIGURE 7.12**
*OMS Service Startup.*

After a few seconds, the service should start. You can verify this by looking in the status column for Services. At this stage you should be able to log in to OEM console. If the OMS server failed, check that the repository database and listener are started, the repository has been created, and that connectivity exists to that database. Basic OEM functionality is available if OMS or the repository is down, but advanced features will not be available.

---

**NOTE**

OMS Logins

The OMS will determine whether the repository database is accessible and whether the repository has been created before it starts. Expect to see multiple login sessions by the repository owner (OEM_OWN in this case) into the repository database once OMS is started. These sessions will terminate when OMS is stopped.

---

## Server Installation

Configuring the server tier for OEM is also optional; however advanced features provided by OMS are dependent on this. Also, some OEM tools require a repository, Intelligent Agents, and Data Gatherer even if you choose not to use OMS. Most Unix DBAs create OEM repositories and start Intelligent Agents even if they choose not to use OMS.

To create an OEM repository, you need to start the OEM Configuration Assistant, as shown in Figure 7.13. This is found on NT/Windows 2000 installations under Oracle-OEM21, Enterprise Manager. Select the option to create a new repository.

The next screen asks you which database you want to create the repository in. If you have created a database specifically for this, such as rh1rep1, enter that information now. Otherwise, the repository can go into a preexisting database, but that database will need to be continually running to support OEM's advanced features.

**FIGURE 7.13**
*OEM Configuration Assistant.*

Notice how OEM expects you to define the service name. It wants the service name in the format of *host:port#:sid*. If you cannot get the hostname to work, you can use the database server's IP address. The port will typically be 1521; you can verify this by checking the $ORACLE_HOME/network/admin/listener.ora file on the database server.

Figure 7.14 shows how to select a database to install your repository in.

**FIGURE 7.14**
*OEM Repository Configuration.*

The rest of the repository-creation process is fairly straightforward. The assistant creates a user (call it OEM_OWN), a tablespace called OEM_REPOSITORY, and the objects for the repository. The final screen before the repository is created is shown in Figure 7.15.

Once the repository is created, the OMS server can be successfully started. However, before OEM scheduled jobs and event monitoring can be implemented, Oracle intelligent agents need to be configured on each database server (referred to as a *node* in OEM documentation).

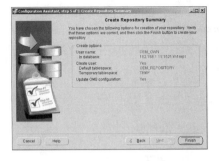

**FIGURE 7.15**
*OEM Repository Summary.*

## Intelligent Agents

Oracle Intelligent Agents exist on each node to provide the "lights out" administration by implementing OEM scheduled jobs and checking for events. Each target database instance will have two Intelligent Agents logged into it as the user DBSNMP.

```
SQL> select username from v$session
  2  where username is not null;

USERNAME
------------------------------
DBSNMP
SYS
DBSNMP

SQL>
```

This indicates that agents for this node have been successfully started. Every database instance on this node will have two DBSNMP sessions logged in.

Intelligent Agents are managed on each node through the `lsnrctl` utility. After you have started your databases and the listener process (`lsnrctl start`), it is time to start the agents:

```
$ lsnrctl dbsnmp_start

LSNRCTL for Linux: Version 8.1.6.0.0 - Production on 18-MAR-2001 17:55:05

$
```

This will start the agents for the *entire* node and all running database instances will now have two DBSNMP sessions. After this point any additional databases you start will have DBSNMP sessions login after about one minute.

To verify that the agents are running, you can check for their database logins in SQL*Plus by querying V$SESSION or you can use ps -ef to search for their background processes. You can also get the status of the Intelligent Agents using the command lsnrctl dbsnmp_status.

```
$ lsnrctl dbsnmp_status

LSNRCTL for Linux: Version 8.1.6.0.0 - Production on 18-MAR-2001 18:01:06

 Copyright 1998, 1999, Oracle Corporation.  All rights reserved.

The db subagent is already running.

$
```

Because these are actually login sessions, they must either be stopped or killed before you shut down a database instance. The best way to eliminate DBSNMP sessions is to shut them down via the lsnrctl dbsnmp_stop command.

```
$ lsnrctl dbsnmp_stop

LSNRCTL for Linux: Version 8.1.6.0.0 - Production on 18-MAR-2001 18:08:00

$
```

This forces the DBSNMP sessions to log out of *every* database instance on the node. You can then cleanly shut down the databases without having to kill any sessions. Problems arise, however, when you have multiple databases running on a node and want to shut one down, but you cannot stop all the agents on the node to do this. In these cases, it is usually best to use the SHUTDOWN IMMEDIATE option.

An Oracle Intelligent Agent is actually a default database user just like any other user created in a database. Therefore, it has a password that is a potential security risk. The default password for the DBSNMP user is dbsnmp. You can simply change the password as you do for any other user, but that can cause problems. A better method is as follows:

1. It is preferable to make these changes before you create any jobs or events. However, if any OEM jobs or events have already been created, remove the jobs and events for all the databases on the node.

2. Stop the Intelligent Agents if they are running. Use lsnrctl_stop.

3. Edit the file $ORACLE_HOME/network/admin/snmp_rw.ora to have the following two parameters:

```
snmp.connect.service_name.name = dbsnmp_name
snmp.connect.service_name.password = new_password
```

A modified snmp_rw.ora file looks like this:

```
snmp.contact.listener = ""
snmp.index.listener = 1
snmp.contact.rh1dev1.mike.com = ""
snmp.index.rh1dev1.mike.com = 2
snmp.connect.rh1dev1.mike.com.name = dbsnmp
snmp.connect.rh1dev1.mike.com.password = dbsnmppwd
snmp.contact.rh1rep1.mike.com = ""
snmp.index.rh1rep1.mike.com = 3
snmp.connect.rh1rep1.mike.com.name = dbsnmp
snmp.connect.rh1rep1.mike.com.password = dbsnmppwd
```

In this case, the service names are `rh1rep1.mike.com` and `rh1dev1.mike.com`. The Intelligent Agent login name is `dbsnmp` and the password is `dbsnmppwd`.

---

**NOTE**

**Include Future Databases**

You have to add two separate lines for each database. Be sure to add this file to the list of post-creation tasks for any database instance you later create.

---

4. Because this file has hard-coded passwords, it is necessary to change its permissions for security. Give it 700 permissions so only the `oracle` user can read it.

   ```
   $ chmod 700 snmp_rw.ora
   ```

5. Log in to each database and change the password to whatever you changed it to in the `snmp_rw.ora` file The syntax is as follows:

   ```
   alter user dbsnmp identified by "new_password";
   ```

   Putting the password in double quotations is necessary if you plan on using special characters such as !.

6. Restart the Intelligent Agents. Verify that they are logged on to each database you modified in `snmp_rw.ora`. If not, you most likely either mistyped a password or failed to change them inside the database.

   ```
   $ lsnrctl dbsnmp_start
   ```

   and

   ```
   SQL> select username from v$session;
   ```

7. Change the file `catsnmp.sql` to have the new password: `dbsnmppwd`:

   ```
   $ vi $ORACLE_HOME/rdbms/admin/catsnmp.sql
   ```

8. Modify the permissions on `catsnmp.sql` because it now has a hard-coded password.

   ```
   $ chmod 700 $ORACLE_HOME/rdbms/admin/catsnmp.sql
   ```

**7**

**GUI MANAGEMENT PRODUCTS**

That is all there is to working with Intelligent Agents. Once they are configured and started, they require little attention from the DBA. Just remember to add them to your normal startup routine and verify their status if you have reports of OEM jobs failing.

### Data Gatherer

The OEM utilities Performance Manager and Capacity Planner use Data Gatherer to collect and record information. It is possible to run Performance Manager without Data Gatherer, but it will run with reduced functionality.

Data Gatherer is installed with the Intelligent Agents. It can be found in $ORACLE_HOME/odg. Before you run it for the first time, clear any files out of the $ORACLE_HOME/odg/log and $ORACLE_HOME/odg/reco directories. A Data Gatherer alert log is created in $ORACLE_HOME/odg/log; you can view it if there are problems.

There are four basic commands to control Data Gatherer:

```
vppcntl -start        <--    Start Data Gatherer
   vppcntl -status    <--    Get status information
   vppcntl -ping       <--   Verify connectivity
   vppcntl -stop       <--   Stop Data Gatherer
```

To run and stop Data Gatherer:

```
$ vppcntl -start
The Oracle Data Gatherer is running.
$ vppcntl -status
The Oracle Data Gatherer is running.
$ vppcntl -ping
The Oracle Data Gatherer is running.
$ vppcntl -stop
The Oracle Data Gatherer has shutdown.
```

That is the basics of running Data Gatherer. It is not essential, but its setup is fairly simple.

# OEM Controls

Once Oracle Enterprise Manager has been installed and configured, you can begin working with its tools. There are two ways to run the basic suite of OEM products: via the OEM console or in standalone mode.

## OEM Console

Think of the OEM console as a master login where you can be logged onto all your databases simultaneously and can control them as an enterprise. It is from the console that you can perform advanced features, such as scheduling jobs and monitoring events. All the normal OEM utilities are also available from the console.

To start the console, the OEM repository database must be created, running, and accessible with the Intelligent Agents running. Also, the OMS service must also be running and accessible. To log on to the console, choose Start, Programs, Oracle-OEM21, Enterprise Manager, Console.

The first screen prompts you for the console administrator login and password, as shown in Figure 7.16 The username is sysman and the default password is oem_temp. You are also prompted for a running OMS server to connect to. If OMS is on your local machine, that version is normally listed as the default OMS. In cases where the OMS is on another machine, use the Add button to add the name of the remote OMS. Once this is done, click OK to log in.

7

GUI
MANAGEMENT
PRODUCTS

**FIGURE 7.16**
*OEM Console Login.*

Once successfully logged in, you will see a four-panel screen, as shown in Figure 7.17. The top-left panel labeled "Navigator" contains all the nodes and databases on each node. This is where you select the database to administer. The top-right panel is "Group" and allows you to logically group multiple databases. The lower-left panel is "Jobs" and it lists all the jobs you currently have scheduled. The lower-right panel is called "Events" and it displays all the events you are monitoring.

**FIGURE 7.17**
*OEM Console.*

All the tools installed are available via the buttons on the left side or by the drop-down Tools menu.

To gain access to the databases you want to manage, you must "discover" each node. Either use the Navigator drop-down menu or right-click the node's icon and select Discover Nodes. This will start a two-screen wizard that identifies every database on each node you want to discover. On the second screen, you enter the host name of the database server node you want to manage or its IP address, and then click Next. Once they are discovered, all the databases on that node will be identified every time you start the console. See Figure 7.18.

**FIGURE 7.18**

*Node Discovery.*

Once the node has been discovered every running database on that node is accessible if you have a password. By expanding the node and node name, and then clicking any of the databases, you will be prompted for a password. There will be a check box option to save the password as a Preferred Credential. If that option is selected it will not be necessary to enter the password again; this is the equivalent of "save password" for a database. This is possible because the passwords will be encrypted and stored on their PC. Once the DBA password has been entered, the database is accessible.

Figure 7.19 shows a view of databases accessible from the console.

**FIGURE 7.19**

*Accessible Databases via OEM Console.*

Detailed use of all the options provided by the OEM console is outside the scope of this book. Fortunately, however, OEM Help "Take a Quick Tour" provides a good overview of the features available. This feature off the Help menu provides a set of quick examples on how to use some features.

## Standalone

If the console seems overkill for your purposes, you can also use most of the OEM tools in standalone mode. Go to Start, Programs, Oracle-OEM21, Database Administration, DBA Studio. DBA Studio provides most of the tools commonly used with OEM. It provides the option to log in to the OMS server or log in in standalone mode. If not going to use the OEM console, it does not make sense to use OMS with DBA Studio. Simply select the standalone option.

DBA Studio displays all the databases as defined in the "tree," as shown in Figure 7.20. These are simply the databases found in your local tnsnames.ora that you have selected. If you add a new entry to your tnsnames.ora, DBA Studio will ask you if it should be added to the tree during the next login. Double-click any database listed and you will prompted for a password, which can be saved as a Preferred Credential in a manner similar to the OEM console.

**FIGURE 7.20**
*Accessible Databases via DBA Studio.*

A reduced tool set is provided with DBA Studio; however, you can also access these tools via the Windows Start, Programs menu. The Tools menu bar does have some useful features that manage database loads/imports/exports (under Data Management) and wizards that perform analyze and reorganizations. Once again, OEM provides some useful self-help information in the form of Quick Tours and Latest Features.

## OEM Tools

OEM tools are broken into different packs accessible from the Start menu. Some require the use of OMS, whereas others do not. The following sections cover the tools most commonly used by Unix DBAs.

## Application Development

The only tool available via Application Development is SQL*Plus. This is simply a Windows version of the normal SQL*Plus program started from the command line. There are several drawbacks to using the Windows version of SQL*Plus in the Unix environment. The largest disadvantage is that direct access to the Unix system is denied. The DBA cannot shell out to the Unix OS and all files accessed must be on the desktop. Any scripts must be on the Windows machine rather than the Unix server. This is not a problem if the DBA is dealing with small spool files, but if large files are generated or $ORACLE_HOME/rdbms/admin scripts are needed, problems will arise.

> **NOTE**
>
> **Shelling Out**
>
> "Shelling out" is the practice of using ! to escape SQL*Plus and to enter a Unix shell. Typing exit will return the user to the SQL*Plus prompt. Alternatively, a command sequence such as !ls from within SQL*Plus issues the ls command in the current directory without ever really leaving SQL*Plus.

## Change Management Pack

Oracle's Change Management Pack is a relatively new tool that allows schemas to be compared and changes outlined. For example, if a DBA wanted to compare the current production environment to the development environment, this tool provides that functionality. This tool is useful and deserves further examination, especially by Application DBAs.

## Database Administration

The Database Administration set contains SQL*Plus Worksheet and the DBA Studio. Developers might find SQL*Plus Worksheet useful, because it provides a more friendly input medium than SQL*Plus. Entire blocks of code, rather than single lines, can be written, edited, saved, and submitted.

DBA Studio is a suite of the most commonly used DBA tools. It can be used in either a stand-alone architecture or it can be combined with OMS. DBA Studio allows the DBA to identify multiple databases as a "tree" and connect to them simultaneously. Once connected, the DBA has four utilities to choose from: Instance Manager, Schema Manager, Storage Manager, and Security Manager. See Figure 7.21.

Instance Manager attempts to provide system-level DBA control over a database instance. If the correct password configuration is set, the DBA can start up and shut down a database from this tool. In the Unix world, however, every DBA I have worked with prefers to start up and shut down databases at the Unix SQL*Plus command line in case problems occur.

**FIGURE 7.21**
*DBA Studio Management Utilities.*

Instance Manager, shown in Figure 7.22, does provide the useful display screens for database state, parameters, and memory allocations. It provides an easy-to-use GUI representation of the SGA memory allocations and the init.ora parameters. Management of user sessions is also possible via the Instance Manager.

**FIGURE 7.22**
*DBA Studio Instance Manager.*

## Don't be a Point and Click DBA!

Most Unix DBAs understand the principles of Oracle and know when to use tools like OEM. However, I have been frightened to see too many "DBAs" who really know nothing about Oracle and survive only because of OEM tools such as Instance Manager and Schema Manager. My opinion is that if you cannot bounce a database or move files from the command prompt, you should not have OEM either.

*continues*

DBAs tend to be well paid, but that is largely because the position requires *knowledge*. Companies expect you to *know* what you are doing and why. Don't try to skate by just by relying on OEM to do everything for you. This policy does not work. Everyone I know who has operated like this pays the price sooner or later. You'll either end up with a corrupted database or just lose all respect from your peers. OEM truly is a great tool, but it is no substitute for knowledge!

Schema Manager, shown in Figure 7.23, is the most powerful and commonly used OEM utility. This tool allows the DBA to create, alter, or drop every object in the database. This includes tables, indexes, sequences, clusters, synonyms, objects, and so on. PL/SQL packages, procedures, and functions can also be managed from this tool.

In the example that follows, the table MIKEW.TEST_TABLE is displayed. Here, the DBA can add columns and any type of constraint, or can change the storage parameters. Schema Manager gives the DBA quick access to every type of object owned by any user. This allows the DBA to quickly create objects without having to remember the exact SQL syntax. The DBA uses the GUI to make the changes within the tool and then views the actual SQL via the Show SQL button. If you are satisfied with the SQL generated by the tool, you can use the Apply button to force the tool to submit the SQL to the database. Remember, Schema Manager is really just a slick SQL generation tool. Nothing is actually done to the database until you press the Apply button.

**FIGURE 7.23**
*DBA Studio Schema Manager.*

Oracle Security Manager, shown in Figure 7.24, is another tool widely used by DBAs. It is used to manage the users, roles, and profiles of the database. Most commonly it is used to add, modify, or delete user accounts.

As you can see, a database user has a password that can be changed or reset by the DBA (a common request). The account can also be locked or unlocked. Oftentimes, generic accounts are created and, later, no one remembers why they were created or if they are needed. In cases like this, it is common to lock the account for a few days or weeks and then delete it if no one complains about not being able to log in. The default and temporary tablespaces of the user can also be modified.

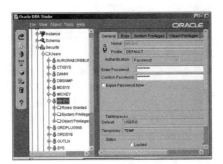

**FIGURE 7.24**
*DBA Studio Security Manager.*

Oracle Security Manager also provides an easy method to identify which roles, system, and object privileges a user has. Although this information can be found with the DBA_XXX tables, the GUI tool is a little faster and easier to use. If needed, new roles can also be created and privileges can be assigned.

Finally, one feature of Security Manager is a great time-saver: the create like option. Often, the DBA is asked to create a user, but no one knows what privileges are needed. Many times there are roles in the database that exist only as flags within an application, so even the DBA does not know what they really do. In cases like this the DBA needs to ask the person requesting the user "who do you want this account to mirror?" Basically the DBA gets the name of a current user who already has the necessary privileges. The DBA then highlights that user account, right-clicks it, and selects the create like... option. This will create a user with the same roles and privileges as the targeted user.

The final utility of OEM DBA Studio that is of use is Storage Manager, shown in Figure 7.25. This tool allows the DBA to add, modify, and delete access to the databases data files, control files, rollback segments, archive logs, and tablespaces. Obviously, there is a great deal of power associated with this tool. Unfortunately, many new DBAs have a tendency to rely on this particular utility too much.

OEM will let you modify these objects, but it won't tell you whether you *should* modify these objects. For example, you can drop a tablespace with this tool. It is up to the DBA to realize

7

GUI
MANAGEMENT
PRODUCTS

that all objects in that tablespace will also be dropped, so maybe dropping a tablespace is a bad idea. Given the magnitude of some of the changes this tool can be make, I prefer to make major database changes at the SQL*Plus command line, not within a GUI.

**FIGURE 7.25**
*DBA Studio Storage Manager.*

That covers it for the high points on DBA Studio. A DBA can use this tool with or without an OMS. It has many useful features, but you do need to understand the ramifications of any of your changes.

## Diagnostics Pack

OEM's Diagnostics Pack offers several tools, but TopSessions and Performance Manager are the most popular.

The DBA should always have a general idea of who is logged into the database and what they are doing. OEM TopSessions provides a graphical representation of which users are logged into the database. You can obtain more detailed information, such as the SQL being issued, by double-clicking a user. Simply start Top Sessions and connect to the database you want to monitor. Remember to edit the Sessions, Options, Count drop-down menu to show all sessions, not just the top 10 sessions. Also remember to refresh the view often to identify new logins.

TopSessions, shown in Figure 7.26, gives the DBA the capability to kill user sessions. This is a good idea to do before attempting a shutdown or if you notice that a user has been logged on for an excessive amount of time. To kill a user, you highlight that user, right-click it, and choose kill session.

The tool also provides the *very* useful feature of identifying locking sessions. Often, users call the DBA to complain about being locked. This usually indicates the user's session is hanging because someone else has already locked the same row or table. That locking user needs to either commit or roll back their changes.

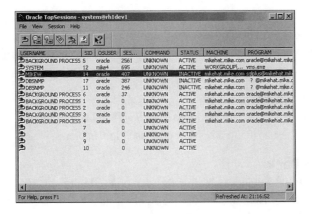

**FIGURE 7.26**

*TopSessions.*

To resolve this problem, get the user's ID/username. Highlight that user and double-click it to get more information. Then select Locks. This gives you the option of viewing All Locks or only the Blocking/Waiting Locks. Look under Blocking/Waiting Locks. Once you find the blocking session, either have the user commit their changes or kill their sessions. Figure 7.27 shows an example of normal locks because of a table update.

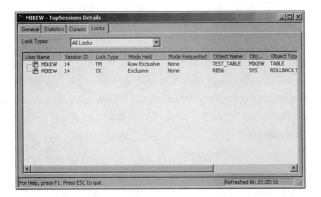

**FIGURE 7.27**

*Normal Locks because of a Table Update.*

Performance Manager is another popular tool provided by the Diagnostics Pack. Ideally it, along with Capacity Planner, should be used with an OMS. Performance Manager can, however, be used without attaching to an OMS. Data Gatherer should also be running on the database server when using Performance Manager.

OEM's Performance Manager is really just a tool to graphically represent what is going on in a database at a specific time. The tool uses tried-and-true SQL scripts to generate data and then merely charts that data. For these reasons, many Unix DBAs prefer just to run the scripts themselves. Many of these scripts are covered in Chapter 11, "Oracle Server Tuning."

## Network Administration

Both network configuration tools—Net8 Assistant and Net8 Configuration Assistant—are available via OEM. They have already been discussed in Chapter 5.

## Oracle Tuning Pack

The Oracle Tuning Pack provides two tools that can be used to tune your database: Oracle Expert and SQL Analyze. Both these tools are an okay place to get started, but this is an area where real knowledge of the database and its application is necessary. Before using these tools, you should have a solid foundation of tuning knowledge so that you know what is going on within the database, rather than relying on a GUI.

# TOAD

TOAD is a third-party alternative to OEM. It is owned by Quest (quest.com) and trial versions are available for download. Actually, there are many products in addition to TOAD that merit investigation, but they are beyond the scope of this book.

If you're a new DBA and have been trained using the traditional Oracle tools, it is possible that you've never been exposed to TOAD. This is unfortunate and is why it is being covered briefly here.

TOAD is basically an OEM alternative, but it is well regarded by Oracle PL/SQL programmers. Not many DBAs use it exclusively like they do OEM, but it is not uncommon to see developers use it to create or edit their PL/SQL. For these reasons, if nothing else, the Unix DBA should be familiar with it.

TOAD is easy to install. There is no OMS or repository, which is probably one reason it is popular. This comes at the expense of more advanced features, but most developers do not need those features anyway. You can create a few tables to support the use of explain plans, but this is not a complicated task, using the TOAD scripts provided by the install. TOAD uses the normal tnsnames.ora to connect, just like OEM does.

Once TOAD is started, there is only one screen to operate from, but all the utilities are available beneath drop-down menus. Many of these utilities are similar to the utilities provided by OEM, so it is up to you to decide which is best. Figure 7.28 shows a sample screen from a TOAD login. As you can see, many of the features available via the various OEM utilities are available here as well.

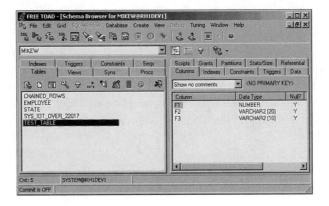

**FIGURE 7.28**

*TOAD Options.*

The best way to learn TOAD is to download it and play with it. In my experience, I have found the TOAD utilities to be quick and easy to use. I especially like the easy-to-use export utilities, which places my data in a script that I can edit, unlike Oracle Export utilities. The table editor is also good, just be careful with it. The fact that so many tools are quickly available on one screen makes accessing these tools and experimenting with them very easy. I have found that working with tables, data, and PL/SQL is particularly easy in TOAD.

The choice between TOAD and OEM is a personal one; they both provide similar functionality. It is my opinion that anything complex or critical should be done manually from the Unix box anyway, so the choice of GUI interface is trivial. I will say that it is safe to assume OEM will always be available and supported in any organization, so a DBA should be familiar with it. On the other hand, I find many DBAs are almost afraid to use any third-party tool or script not endorsed by Oracle because they are terrified something will break. I find this to be an irrational fear, especially because products like TOAD are so widely used. I encourage any DBA to at least be familiar with TOAD because it is very likely they will encounter it sometime in their career.

## Summary

The use of GUI tools such as OEM and TOAD do have their rightful place in database administration. They can and should be used to perform quick tasks that normally require a lot of typing. These tools can provide a quick overview of a database, its users, its objects, and how it compares to other databases.

The only caution I have against GUI tools is not to become too dependent on them. As you saw with OEM, there is a lot of functionality, but some of it is dependent on setting up and maintaining extra management servers and repositories. These extra layers require setup and can break or become unavailable. You need to be able to operate without them. OEM does offer some interesting monitoring and job-scheduling features, but these are duplicated in Unix with use of cron and shell scripts. The bottom line with any GUI tool is to use it to aid in doing your job, but don't expect it to do your job for you.

# DBA Utilities

## ESSENTIALS

- Using utilities to load, unload, and transfer data and objects are core DBA tasks.

- A solid working knowledge of Oracle's utilities will make life for a DBA much easier.

- Export and import are used to move data and objects from one Oracle database to another Oracle database.

- SQL*Loader is used to load data from non-Oracle flat files into Oracle databases.

- LogMiner is a relatively new utility that allows the DBA to view the contents of Oracle archive logs.

So much of what a database administrator does resembles the role of a system administrator or a programmer that it is easy to lose sight of the *data* itself. In reality, the DBA is expected to be an expert in loading, unloading, and manipulating data. Much of the unglamorous job of being a DBA is loading large amounts of data from one table to another. This isn't exciting work, but it is a core responsibility of being a DBA.

This chapter examines the two most common utilities for loading data: export/import and SQL*Loader. It includes a basic overview and some examples. The fundamentals are discussed, but more importantly, you'll get a good understanding of when and how to use these utilities. Best practices and a few tuning tricks are also covered.

The last part of the chapter covers a relatively new utility: LogMiner. This tool allows the DBA to examine the contents of archive log files. This capability to view the archive log files provides some much-needed options for undoing mistakes that logically corrupt data.

# Export and Import

Oracle data exists in tables, owned by users, residing in databases. Therefore, it makes sense that the data can be extracted (exported) from a table owned by one user and then loaded (imported) into a matching table owned by another user. This is the basic premise of export and import. All the data is exported from a table into a file and that file is later loaded into another table.

This section reviews the fundamentals of export/import. Next, it covers export and import processes in greater detail. After that, the chapter examines some of the common uses of export/import. Finally, it covers special situations that often arise when dealing with export and import in the Unix/Linux environment.

## Overview of Export and Import

Export provides the capability to extract all the table data from a single table, a group of tables, all the tables owned by a user, or an entire database. This information is placed in an export dump file called *filename*.dmp. This file, generically referred to as a .dmp file, is an individual file on the operating system that can be copied, moved, or FTP'ed as needed. It is not part of a database per se and can be treated as a normal file. The only restriction is that if you try to open it in a text editor it will likely be corrupted, but this issue is addressed later in the chapter.

Once the .dmp file has been created via export, the DBA copies it to the server that holds the database into which it will be imported. It is important to note that, while this must be an Oracle database, it does *not* have to be the same database version nor does it even have to be on the same platform. For example, if you wanted to create a small development environment on a Linux or NT system, you could easily export the tables from a production Oracle database on Solaris and use that .dmp file to build a new schema. The beauty of .dmp files is that they are highly portable and are largely version- and platform-independent.

Once the .dmp file is on the server that holds the target database, the DBA simply imports the data into the existing database. The DBA has the option to import all or just some of the tables in the .dmp into the receiving database. Plus this .dmp file is reusable so the same tables can be reimported time and again if needed.

Now that you understand the basic procedure of export and import, it's time to look at each phase in greater detail.

# Using Export

Exporting table data is relatively simple, but there are a few caveats you need to be aware of. Along with tables, other table-related objects such as indexes and grants can also be exported. Exactly which type of objects are exported varies depending on the level of export used. There are three levels of export: table, user, and database.

## Table Level Export

A table level export is simply an export of one or more tables owned by a user. This is the simplest form of export. The users conducting the export can export their own tables or can export any user's tables if the EXP_FULL_DATABASE role is granted (standard for DBAs). The biggest caution when dealing with table level exports is that, because tables are often linked in foreign key relationships, it is easy to miss a needed table.

The following objects are exported when a table level export occurs:

| | |
|---|---|
| Table data | Grants on the table |
| Table indexes | Triggers |
| Table constraints | |

## User Level Export

A user level export captures all the objects owned by a single user. This is the often the most practical form of export because it exports everything needed to re-create a user's schema. The only real caution when using a user level export is that the resulting .dmp file can be very large depending on the user's schema.

The terms user level and schema level are often used interchangeably, but Oracle expects the keyword to be user.

The following objects are captured with a user level export:

| | |
|---|---|
| Table data | Table indexes |
| Table constraints | Grants on the table |
| Triggers | Views |

8

DBA UTILITIES

| | |
|---|---|
| Database links | Private synonyms |
| Snapshots | Job queues |
| Sequences | Packages |
| Procedures | Functions |

## Full Database Export

A full database export will export an entire database, including every schema and object. Obviously, the resulting .dmp file can be huge.

I have not seen this level of export used much, although it is sometimes used to relocate entire databases. Typically, a database will have a few key schemas that need to be exported, but it is easier to re-create all the normal users and database structure without an export. The level of export is a matter of preference, but this chapter focuses on table and user level exports.

# Export Types

An export can be conducted in one of two ways: either interactively or using a parameter file (*parfile*).

## Interactive Export

An interactive export is best used for simple, one time exports of a user or a few tables. Once you start the utility you are asked a few questions to establish basic parameters, and then the objects are exported. It is important to note that only a few of the many parameters are tunable with an interactive export.

Figure 8.1 shows how you interactively export the DEPT and EMP tables from the default SCOTT schema. Make note of how simple this is when just dealing with a few tables.

The export occurred in the $ORACLE_BASE/admin/*SID*/exp directory. Exports can occur anywhere there is adequate disk space, but this is a logical location. Export is started with the command exp. The export was executed by the SYSTEM user, which has DBA privileges, including EXP_FULL_DATABASE. Therefore, SYSTEM was able to export SCOTT's objects. The export was fairly straightforward, as Oracle only prompted for a few parameters. Parameters for an interactive export are as follows:

- **Username/Password (USERID)** Oracle identifies the user executing the export in the form of Username and Password. Because the DBA SYSTEM has by default EXP_FULL_DATABASE, it was possible to export SCOTT.

- **Buffer Size (BUFFER)** Oracle will transfer bytes of data in the size specified. Obviously, the bigger the buffer, the better. Most Unix DBAs go with either 1024000 or 10024000.

- **Export File (FILE)** Develop a meaningful naming convention for the .dmp files generated. This example uses the schema name (SCOTT), identifies that tables are being exported (tbls), and includes the date (20010326). It is convention to always append a .dmp to the end of any Oracle export dump file.

- **Level of Export (FULL, OWNER, TABLES)** Interactive exports will permit database, user, or table level exports. In this case, table level export was used.

- **Export Table Data (ROWS)** Export provides the option just to export the DDL to create the exported objects, not including the actual data. This is useful when you want a bare schema or just want to copy a table's structure.

- **Compress Extents (COMPRESS)** This has nothing to do with the size of the resulting .dmp file. The Compress Extents option specifies that, upon import, all the table data will be placed in the initial extent. If a table was created with a smaller initial extent than can hold all the data, the imported table will have its initial extent expanded to contain all the data. This is useful to reduce table fragmentation. If you do compress into one extent, make sure the tablespace you will be importing into has enough contiguous space to handle the extent.

- **Table or Partition to be exported (TABLES)** Oracle 8i allows either entire tables or individual table partitions to be exported interactively. This example specified that SCOTT.DEPT and SCOTT.EMP tables be exported. After each export, a total identifying the number of rows exported is displayed.

The export terminates with a message stating the success or failure of the export.

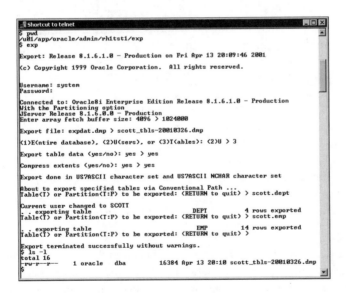

**FIGURE 8.1**

*Interactive Table Level Export.*

## Export Using Parameter Files

In cases where an export needs to be highly efficient, customized, or repeatable, a parameter file should be used. A parameter file is simply a text file containing a list of parameters to be used during the export. This allows you to customize certain options for a particular export. Because the parameters are specified in a file rather than entered manually, the export can be executed repeatedly as a cron job.

If a parameter is not listed in the parfile, its default value is used. The most commonly used parameters were already defined in the interactive export, however there are other options here. Figure 8.2 shows a listing of all the export parameters for Oracle 8.1.6.

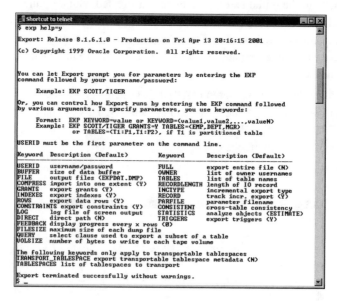

**FIGURE 8.2**

*Oracle 8.1.6 Export Parameters.*

As you can see, there are quite a few options available. In addition to the parameters explained earlier in this chapter, a few export parameters deserve attention. Remember, most of these options are available only when you explicitly define them in a parameter file or on the export command line.

- **PARFILE** Defining PARFILE=*filename*.par identifies that the export will not be interactive and will use the values defined in the parfile. Parameters can be defined in the parfile or on the command line; otherwise the default values are used.
- **FILE A** The name of the .dmp file to be created.

- **LOG** The name of the .log file created during the export. If this is specified, everything normally written to the screen is also written to this file. It is highly recommended to use this parameter.
- **FULL** Use of the FULL=Y parameter indicates a full database export will occur.
- **OWNER** Defining a value for OWNER identifies the schema to be exported. For example, OWNER=SCOTT signifies a user level export of the SCOTT schema.
- **TABLES** Use of the TABLES=(*table_name1, table_name2...*) indicates that a table level export will be executed and identifies the tables.

**NOTE**

Determine Level of Export

The use of the FULL, USER, or TABLES option is mutually exclusive. One and only one of the three options can be defined for the export. Attempting to specify more than one level will cause the export to fail.

**8**

DBA UTILITIES

- **FEEDBACK** When working with large table exports, an impatient DBA might wonder if the export is "hanging" because nothing is happening on the screen. If the FEEDBACK parameter is given a value, 50000 for example, one tic mark will appear on the screen for every 50,000 rows exported. This shows that the export is proceeding. The default value is 0, so this option is not used.
- **DIRECT** Setting DIRECT=Y changes the way Oracle reads and writes blocks to the .dmp file. Normally, Oracle will read each block from disk into the database buffer cache and will then write it to the .dmp file. If DIRECT=Y, Oracle will bypass writing the blocks to the buffer cache and will write them directly to the .dmp file. This parameter can speed up exports, but has no effect on import performance. The use of DIRECT=Y and the BUFFER parameter is mutually exclusive. The default value is no, so this option is not used.
- **CONSISTENT** Theoretically, an export should start and finish without any table data being changed. Unfortunately, on a busy database where many tables are being exported that is not likely to happen naturally. For example, if 50 tables are being exported it is likely for a user to update data in table 45 that conflicts with exported data in table 10. To resolve this problem, the CONSISTENT=Y parameter forces rollback segments to create a read consistent point in time view of the data at the start of the export. This way the export will have logically valid data, even if it changed during the export. Because this is not usually necessary and because of its stress on rollback segments, this option is off by default.

The best way to use exports and parameter files is to create a template parameter file and customize it for your needs. The following is a sample parameter file that creates a schema level export of the user SCOTT. It is a simple text file created in vi.

```
$ more scott_schema.par
userid=system
file=scott_user-20010326.dmp
log=scott_user-20010326.log
owner=scott
direct=y
$
```

Notice the password to the user SYSTEM is not included in this file. If executed from the command line, the export utility will prompt the user for the password. The .dmp file and the .log file have meaningful names. The OWNER=SCOTT parameter identifies this as a user level export. Using the DIRECT parameter prevents the use of the BUFFER parameter, but you are still getting a slight performance gain by bypassing the buffer cache.

Figure 8.3 shows a sample schema level export of the SCOTT schema using the parameter file. Pay particular attention to the non-table objects exported at the end of the export.

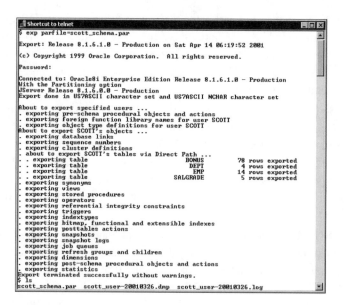

**FIGURE 8.3**

*User Level Export with a Parameter File.*

The export of the user SCOTT was successful. All four tables were exported. Many additional object types were listed as having been exported, but if SCOTT did not own objects of that type nothing was exported.

## Query Based Exports

There is one new feature in Oracle 8i that deserves separate attention: query based exports. Previously, when a table was exported, all the rows were exported. There was no way to selectively export only a few rows. This has changed in Oracle 8i with the use of the WHERE parameter.

It is now possible to include a WHERE clause in table level exports. If you can identify specific rows via a WHERE clause, export can be directed only to export those rows. The only drawback is that the clause must apply to *every* table being exported. You cannot export multiple tables and expect the WHERE clause to be applied to only one table. This effectively limits the export to one table at a time. The following is a sample parameter file to export only EMP rows where DEPTNO = 30.

```
$ more scott_emp_30.par
userid=system
file=scott_emp_30-20010326.dmp
log=scott_emp_30-20010326.log
tables=scott.emp
query="where deptno=30"
$
```

This export would be executed just like any other export using a parameter file, but it would export only those six rows in the SCOTT.EMP table WHERE DEPTNO = 30.

From a technical standpoint, you know everything you need to know to begin exporting data. However, more advanced techniques are often required in a real-world Unix environment. These are covered with advanced import techniques later in this chapter.

## Using Import

Importing data is the opposite of exporting it. As a result, many of the procedures and types of imports are similar to exports. Just like export there are three levels of import: table, user, and database. Also, you can execute an import interactively or with a parameter file.

The level of import is partially dependent on the level of export. Obviously if the export .dmp contains only a table you cannot import a schema. If, however, the export was of a schema you can choose to import only a few selected tables.

The user receiving the imported objects must be identified. If only a user ID is given for the import, objects will be imported into that user's schema. The only other alternative is to use the FROMUSER/TOUSER clause via a parameter file to identify who will receive the objects.

An import .dmp file is essentially a script with CREATE TABLE/INDEX/etc DDL and data. If you import a table into a schema where that table does not exist, the import will create the table with any indexes/constraints/triggers, load it with any data, and apply any grants necessary. If a table of the same name already exists, import will issue an error and will not attempt to create the table or load any data. This can be overridden by setting the parameter IGNORE=Y. By using this parameter, import will ignore the fact the table already exists and will load the data into it. All primary key, foreign key, and other constraints will be enforced unless they are disabled prior to the import.

## Interactive Import

An interactive import is similar to an interactive export. It is most appropriate when the import is ad hoc and does not require any special parameter changes. Just like the interactive export, this import will prompt you for a few parameters and will use the default values for the rest. Figure 8.4 shows an example of a table level import.

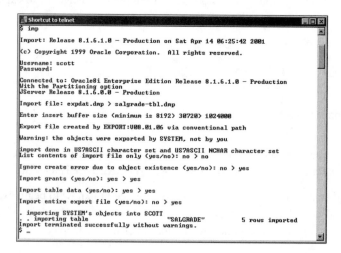

**FIGURE 8.4**

*Interactive Import of a Single Table.*

In this example, the user SCOTT imported the table SALGRADE into his schema. Take a look at the options in greater detail:

- **Username/Password (USERID)** This is the ID of the user conducting the import. If the user has IMP_FULL_DATABASE rights, he/she can import into any schema. That is normally a DBA privilege. Because SCOTT is just a normal user, he can only import into his own schema.

- **Expdat.dmp (FILE)** SCOTT identified the export .dmp file as salgrade-tbl.dmp.

- **Buffer Size (BUFFER)** Just like in export, this parameter determines how big each "chunk" of data is. Unlike export, there is no DIRECT option for import. Even if the export was taking with DIRECT=Y, a buffer value can be specified here.

- **List Contents of Import File Only** If this parameter is set to Y, the DML in the export DMP file will be displayed to the screen, but nothing will actually be imported into the database. Because SCOTT actually wanted to import the table, he accepted the default of N.

- **Ignore Create Error Due to Object Existence (IGNORE)** If import tries to import a table that already exists, it will generate an error message, skip that table, and move on to the next object in the .dmp file. The default action is not to import into a preexisting object. If the parameter is set to Y, the error will not be displayed and any rows of data will be inserted into the existing table. The only caveat of this situation is that any enabled constraints such as primary and foreign keys will be enforced. Also, any triggers on the table will also fire. No data will be overwritten, but an enabled primary key will prevent duplicate rows from being inserted.

> **NOTE**
>
> **Disable Constraints**
>
> For performance reasons, it is common to create the tables before importing the data. In cases like this, it is best to use Dynamic SQL to disable all the constraints, primary and foreign keys, and triggers on the user's tables before the import. After the import, the Dynamic SQL is modified to reset those constraints, keys, and triggers.

- **Import Grants (GRANTS)** Objects normally have grants to users or roles that should be included in any import. Typically it is best to go with the default of YES.

- **Import Table Data (ROWS)** Accepting the default value of YES will cause import to create any tables not existing and will import the associated data. A NO option will cause only the objects (tables, indexes, grants, and so on) to be created without any data. Use this option when you want to create a bare schema or set of tables with no data.

- **Import Entire Export File (FULL)** An import can import everything in a .dmp file or it can use individual objects. In cases such as this, it is best to know what is actually in the .dmp file, which can be a problem if it was created by another DBA. Based on the name (salgrade-tbl.dmp), you can assume it is a table so you can import the entire file. Had the NO option been selected, a prompt to identify the user that will receive the imported objects would have been issued and individual tables could have been selected.

Because this was an interactive import, there is no log file and the output is only to the screen. However, you can see the import was successful because it produced no warnings. This type of import is suitable for simple or ad hoc jobs, but most of the time, the parameter file method is preferable.

## Parfile Imports

Using a parameter file for imports provides maximum flexibility and makes the process repeatable. Indeed, to make use of the wide range of import options or to securely automate a job, a parameter file is necessary. To view the available import options, type imp help=y. See Figure 8.5.

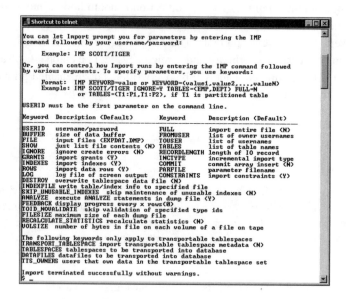

**FIGURE 8.5**
*Import Options.*

Key options used for import not discussed in the interactive import are as follows:

- **PARFILE** Defining PARFILE=*filename*.par identifies that the import will not be interactive and will use the values defined in the parfile. Parameters must be defined in the parfile or on the command line; otherwise the default values are used.

- **LOG** The name of the .log file created during the import. If this is specified, everything normally written to the screen will also be written to this file. It is highly recommended to use this parameter.

- **FEEDBACK** When working with very large imports, a DBA will want to check how many rows of an object have been imported. If the FEEDBACK parameter is given a value, 50,000 for example, one tic mark will appear on the screen for every 50,000 rows imported. This shows that the import is proceeding. The default value is 0, so this option is not used.

- **COMMIT** Oracle will, by default, wait until the entire import is finished before it commits any changes. During this time it keeps filling up the rollback segment until the import completes or the rollback segment runs out of room. Set this value to Y in your parameter file. It will force a commit after every table is imported, thus reducing the chance of blowing out a rollback segment. The only two drawbacks are a slight performance hit and the fact that you will be stuck with unwanted objects if the import later fails. If this happens, just drop everything imported (see your log file) and try the import again.

  It normally takes longer to roll back a failed import than to create it. For example, if you are six hours into an import and blow out your rollback segment, expect at least another six hours for Oracle to roll back the import. That represents 12 hours wasted on an import—time that most DBAs cannot afford. For this reason I almost always use COMMIT=Y.

- **FROMUSER/TOUSER** These parameters are used together. If you have the role EXP_FULL_DATABASE, you can log in as one user (SYSTEM for example), export another user's objects (such as SCOTT's SALGRADE table), and then import it into another user's schema on another database (ERIKH on rh1dev1). Simply set FROMUSER=SCOTT and TOUSER=ERIKH in the parameter file with USERID= SYSTEM. This is commonly done when moving schemas from one database to another.

- **INDEXFILE** Specifying a filename will force import to create a file containing only the DML from the export .dmp file. Nothing will actually be imported into the database when this option is selected. One use of this option is to create a file that can be edited by the DBA to change storage parameters. The edited file can then run via SQL*Plus to create tables and indexes with different storage values. Unfortunately, the resulting file is not easy to format by hand, but it can be useful if you are good with vi. Using this option to create indexes after an import is covered in the tuning export/imports section.

The following is an example of an import parfile of the user SCOTT from rh1tst1 into the user schema ERIKH on rh1dev1. The export is a user level one conducted by SYSTEM.

```
$ more scott-usr.par
userid=system
log=scott-usr.log
file=scott-usr.dmp
fromuser=scott
touser=erikh
commit=y
$
```

This parameter file will execute the import as SYSTEM. The DBA is prompted for the password at the start of the import. A log file scott-usr.log is generated containing the screen output. Because the export was taken by SYSTEM and the import will be conducted by SYSTEM, you use the FROMUSER/TOUSER clause. To execute the import, type `imp parfile=scott-usr.par` at the command line.

# Common Export/Import Uses

Now that you have an understanding of the syntax and options of export and import, you can learn how it is used in the Unix/Linux world.

## Logical Backups

The export utility can perform what is called a logical backup. The term logical is used because it differentiates between exporting table(s) or user(s) versus physically backing up all the files comprising a database. The pros and cons of logical backups are covered in Chapter 9, "Backup and Recovery," but two common types of logical backups are discussed here.

### Backing Up Individual Tables

There are times when a DBA is about to modify, drop, or load data into a table, but knows there is a chance that the change will need to be undone. For example, often times a data modeler or developer will identify a table that no longer needed and ask the DBA to drop it. Before the table is dropped, the DBA should export it just in case. The same applies when massive data inserts or deletes are scheduled. Although it is possible to recover an individual table from physical database backups, it is a major headache for the DBA. If there is any doubt, it is best to take a table level export because these are relatively easy to recover.

> **NOTE**
>
> **Always Export Before Dropping Tables**
>
> Don't ever drop a table without an export, no matter how much you are told "Oh, it's not needed. Just drop it." I have seen too many cases where data that is worthless today is needed tomorrow and the only thing that will save your skin is an export file. Also, it is often a good idea to request drop table and schema requests in an e-mail rather than acting on someone's verbal request.

### Backing Up Entire Schemas

A business does not actually depend on a specific database per se, but it does depend on the data in a user's schema. For this reason schema level exports are common in addition to normal physical database backups. If a database recovery is needed and, for whatever reason, the physical backups are invalid, the DBA can recover the necessary schemas into another database. This should be considered a last resort on production systems, but some development systems use this method exclusively.

A more practical use for schema level backups is to protect against accidental table drops, truncates, modifications, or deletes. A database doesn't need to lose data files to be rendered worthless—if the data is logically corrupted it is just as useless. One development system I was supporting was unexpectedly corrupted beyond repair when some software testers ran a series of scripts to modify data and messed up their WHERE clauses. They had no idea what they changed and deleted so the best option was to drop the user and re-import the schema from the previous night's export. Although this might not be acceptable in a production OLTP environment, it worked just fine for testing and development.

## Archiving Business Data

Many businesses face a legal requirement to store month-end or year-end data for several months or years. The DBA needs to work with management to determine whether this is a requirement. If so, a schema level export to tape can meet this need. In fact, an export .dmp might be even more useful than a database backup because the .dmp file can be imported into *any* later release of Oracle regardless of platform. Just make sure the tapes these exports are on are clearly labeled and stored properly.

## Migrations

Migrations are covered in detail in Chapter 15, "Migrations," but are also mentioned here in this context. A migration is the process of moving from a base release of Oracle to the next release. For example, moving from Oracle 8 to Oracle 8i is considered a migration. It might be on the same database server or it might be on a different physical server (aka *rehosting*). There are several ways to accomplish this, but using a schema level export is one accepted method.

## Building Schemas

Copying and moving schemas from one instance to another instance is a common task for the Unix DBA. Often there will be an existing production environment and the DBA will be expected to re-create that environment on another server to be used by developers and/or software testers. It is also common to create a training database for new employees to work with before they access live production data.

Make sure you understand your requirements before you start this process. Once word is out there is another database people will often want to use it for purposes it originally was not intended. You will be expected to provide a level of backup and recovery protection for this database, so do not forget to identify these needs. Training and development databases also need to be refreshed with data on a regular basis, so be ready to create a nightly cron job to drop the old schema and re-import a new copy of data. Finally, if you are dealing with sensitive data, institute controls on these smaller systems just as you would for the production system.

8

DBA UTILITIES

The process of re-creating a schema on another schema is conceptually easy, but there are a few details that can cause problems. First, execute a user level export for the schema you need to re-create. It is necessary to understand that this will get all the user's objects and grants but it will *not* get the user itself, public synonyms, database roles, or public database links. These objects need to be created on the target database before the import.

Next, create the user account on the target database. Grant the account the same roles and privileges as the original database. Use dynamic SQL to capture the roles and public synonyms on the original database and re-create them on the target database. It is important to note that you can create roles and public synonyms *before* you import the objects. Also make sure any users that have grants are created on the target database before the import. Otherwise, you will get import messages that state that grants to specific users and/or roles have failed because those users/roles do not exist. These are non-fatal errors, but your application may not work if the users/roles lack the correct grants.

> **NOTE**
>
> Grants
>
> During an import, any grants on objects are reapplied. If a table being imported has an insert grant to user CLERK, Oracle will look for a user named CLERK to apply that grant to. If that user does not exist, a warning message will be issued, but the import of the table will continue.

One common problem when moving schemas from database to database is dealing with table and index storage parameters. If you export a table with its indexes it will be imported with the same storage parameters. This is a problem when you have large initial and next extents from a production database, but you want to put them in a smaller development database. An even bigger problem exists when you have many, highly customized tablespaces. When importing an object, Oracle attempts to put it in the tablespace defined in the .dmp file. If that tablespace does not exist, Oracle places it in the user's default tablespace.

One of the best ways to deal with the storage parameter issue is to create the user's objects in the target database before you import the data. Get a copy of the user's DDL and edit it to include the necessary tablespaces and smaller extent sizes. Some work can be avoided if every database uses the same tablespace names, even if they are physically smaller. If you follow the belief that fragmentation is not a major issue and use small uniform extent sizes, you do not need to modify the initial and next extent sizes either. Otherwise, get a copy of the DDL for the user's objects from Oracle Designer, from various SQL scripts and tools, or from importing using an index file and then edit it as needed.

> **NOTE**
>
> Use the Same Tablespace Names Everywhere
>
> Because a schema can have hundreds of tables and thousands of indexes, it is often impractical to modify the storage parameters for each object. Many DBAs simply use the same tablespace names across all their databases. Tables and indexes are created only with a tablespace clause defined and therefore they default to the initial and next extent size of their tablespace. This greatly improves manageability.

Once the storage and tablespace issues are resolved, it is time to import the user's objects. There is a performance benefit if the objects are already created, but you have to use dynamic SQL to disable any constraints and triggers or they will fire during the import. As an alternative, if you import into a "clean" schema where there are no objects, you do not have to worry about existing PKs, firing triggers, or foreign key constraints. Import will create the tables, import the data, and then create/enable the constraints and triggers. Given a choice, I usually try to import into clean schema unless the tables/indexes are large or there are tablespace and storage issues.

When the import has finally completed and all the objects are successfully imported, there is one final step many DBAs often forget. It is necessary to recompile any PL/SQL packages, procedures, and functions because they will be invalid. Use dynamic SQL to recompile these and do not be surprised if you need to do this two or three times because of interrelated dependencies.

Once all the database objects are successfully imported, the PL/SQL is recompiled, and the public objects (synonyms, grants, database links) are resolved, look at the OS environment. Often, the DBA is responsible for setting up the OS file structure to support the application and move the executables. This can be difficult because it is not really "DBA work," but the DBA is responsible for it. Work with your developers and SAs if you have questions about what is needed here. I have found that using shell scripts to create directories and copy files to the correct locations is a good way to automate this tedious process.

## Maintenance Benefits of Export/Import

Exporting and reimporting tables inherently provides certain maintenance benefits. The savvy DBA will be aware of these benefits and use them when needed. The benefits fall into these categories: table rebuilds, corruption checks, and row count logs.

**8**

**DBA UTILITIES**

## Table Rebuilds

As a table changes over time, its rows might be stored in a sub-optimal layout on disk. Several inefficiencies can occur that impact performance. This is typically the result of frequent inserts, updates, and deletes. For example, if many rows have been inserted, there could be an excessive number of extents resulting in fragmentation. Other than fragmentation, there are other problems that occur.

The insertion of data results in a highwater mark, which indicates the furthest point in the segment that contained rows of data. Oracle uses this highwater mark to limit how far into a segment it reads during full table scans since it is useless to read where there are no rows. As rows in the segment are deleted by normal OLTP activity, gaps occur and data might no longer reach the highwater mark. Oracle, however, continues to read through the entire segment up to the highwater mark during the full table scans even though this in unnecessary. The segment begins to resemble a piece of Swiss cheese because of all the gaps, which result in a performance inefficiency.

Row chaining and row migration might develop over time because of long rows and/or high update activity. Chaining and migration are not the same thing. The differences are covered in Chapter 11, "Oracle Server Tuning," but basically these are when one row resides in two different data blocks. This creates a performance hit.

All these issues regarding table storage degradation can be addressed by rebuilding the table. This involves exporting the table, dropping it, and importing it back into the same database. It can be created in a different tablespace with different storage parameters. Exporting with the compress option will compress all the data into the initial extent during import. Gaps in the data are eliminated, chained/migrated rows are fixed, and the highwater mark is reset. Indexes are also rebuilt, which is beneficial because they too can suffer from storage degradation. I would not recommend doing this all the time, but a database suffering performance problems might benefit from rebuilding problem tables.

> **NOTE**
>
> 9i Improvement
> Oracle 9i promises to provide a new DDL to alter and rebuild objects "on the fly" without the normal export/import. These new features and their ramifications are examined in Chapter 19, "9i Server New Features."

# Corruption Checks

Database corruption is an advanced subject, but it does merit a mention here. Sometimes data or index information will not be written to disk in a way Oracle expects. There are many causes of corruption, but the end result is Oracle cannot read data or indexes that should be accessible and therefore this information is lost. As bad as losing data is, this problem is magnified by the fact that corruption can grow undetected for a long time.

Fortunately, an export will attempt to read all these blocks and if corruption exists an error is normally generated. For this reason, it is wise to examine your schema level export logs regularly and fully investigate when Oracle says it cannot read a block.

# Row Counts

The final way export and import is useful deals with monitoring table row counts. As unbelievable as it might seem, many DBAs do not have a real feel for how many rows are in their tables. They might know their tablespace sizes in megabytes, but they are clueless when it comes to how many rows are in each table.

Simple SQL*Plus scripts certainly can capture row counts every night, but this is unnecessary. Assuming schema level exports are taken every night and are written to a log file, you will always have an exact row count for every table. Because log files are relatively small, they can be kept on disk for an extended period of time.

Maintaining a log of row counts is beneficial not only because this is good DBA information, but also because it can be used to track table growth and deletions. It also provides protection for the DBA when someone claims "my table data is missing!" I have seen several cases where a developer or end user will suddenly "realize" they are missing table data, think there is a failure of some kind, and begin pointing fingers at the DBA. This is where a series of nightly export logs showing row counts can confirm or deny this accusation. If there is a problem, the date of the log file indicates which export .dmp file is needed to recover the data.

# Common Mistakes

Many DBAs write shell scripts to export or import data via cron. This is a reliable method, but there are a few common mistakes that pose a security risk. Too many DBAs do not protect their passwords when using scripts. Often there will be a line inside the shell script similar to this one:

```
imp userid=system/manager parfile=scott.par
```

This is a risk because when the script executes this command many Unix systems will display this line to anyone using ps -ef. The result is everyone will now know the SYSTEM password. For the same reasons you do not type `sqlplus system/manager` from the Unix command line, you should not do this within a script. This applies to SQL*Plus, SQL*Loader, and export/import regardless if the script is interactive or cron-driven.

A far better method is to hide the parameter USERID=system/manager in a parfile called by import/export or SQL*Loader. Make sure that file has appropriate permissions such as 740 or 700 to keep it secure. An even better method is not to embed a username/password at all and instead use an Oracle account with operating system identification. This way, the user connects with a "/" and no password is displayed or recorded anywhere.

One other common mistake people new to the Unix/Linux environment make is failing to place jobs in the background to execute. Unix/Linux allows a user to start a job (such as an import/export) in the background with the `nohup` (no hang up) option. This causes the job to execute in the background and text that normally goes to the screen will be redirected to a file in the local directory called nohup.out. The user is freed to issue additional commands in that login session and can even log out, but the job will continue normally in the background. If the user is still logged in to that session, a message will appear when the job is finished. The following example illustrates this:

```
$ nohup exp parfile=scott-usr.par &
[1] 9606
$ nohup: appending output to `nohup.out'

[1] + Done        nohup exp parfile=scott-usr.par
$
```

The user executed an export with a parameter file containing `userid=system/manger` so it would run automatically. By issuing the `nohup` option, you tell Unix/Linux to continue the job even if the login session terminates before the job is finished. The ampersand (&) pushes the job into the background and everything normally written to the screen is written to nohup.out, which can be viewed. Once the job is finished, the `Done` message is displayed.

## Test Your Exports and Imports

I know a couple of DBAs who had a schema that was corrupted and decided to restore it via export/import. Unfortunately, they never tested the parfile for the import. They set it up to run in cron that night and went home. Nor did they check its progress when it started (it was still early evening). Too bad the parfile had few errors in it that caused the restore to fail.

When they got in that morning to their shock their test schema supporting many people had zero tables and PL/SQL objects. After about five minutes of debugging the parfile was fixed and the import started, but it still took most of the day to restore the schema. No one got fired over this, but it was a silly mistake that did cost people time. The point of the story is to check and test *any* job you do, particularly then dealing with backup and recovery.

# Advanced Export and Import Techniques

In the Unix/Linux world, there are a few special cases where basic knowledge of export and import will not suffice. The situations covered here are exporting/importing large files, editing .dmp files, and a few tuning tricks.

## Export and Import with Compress and Pipe

Historically, Unix files were limited to a maximum file size of 2G (gigabytes). This limit posed problems when you attempted to export and the resulting .dmp would exceed 2G. On most modern Unix systems this limit no longer exists and most versions of Oracle no longer enforce this limit. However, the need to deal with large files still exists.

It is not uncommon to export a schema and have the .dmp file range from several hundred megabytes to several gigabytes. Even if the Unix operating system supports files this size they are still cumbersome to manage and can exceed the disk space on the filesystem. The obvious solution is to compress the .dmp file with the `compress` command for storage and moving/copying it, but Unix-savvy DBAs take this one step further. It is possible to export directly into a compressed file and import from a compressed file. This eliminates the step of compressing and uncompressing in the .dmp file, which is especially beneficial when the uncompressed file exceeds available disk space.

The idea is to create a Unix pipe redirected to a compressed file, which is the .dmp file. The export is then executed where the .dmp is defined as the Unix pipe. Data from the export goes through the pipe into the compressed file. The result is a .dmp.Z file, which is the export dump file in a compressed format. To do this, follow these steps:

1. Make a Unix pipe:

   ```
   $ mknod /u01/app/oracle/admin/rh1tst1/exp/p_rh1tst1 p
   $ ls -l
   prw-r--r--   1 oracle   dba        0 Apr  1 14:45 p_rh1tst1
   ```

2. Direct the pipe to the .dmp file and compress it in the background:

   ```
   $ compress < p_rh1tst1 > $ORACLE_BASE/admin/rh1tst1/exp/scott-usr.dmp.Z &
   ```

3. Create the export parameter file. Notice the file parameter points to the `pipe` p_rh1tst1.

```
$ more scott-usr.par
userid=system
compress=yes
direct=y
log=scott-usr.log
file=p_rh1tst1
owner=scott
$
```

4. Execute the export:

```
$ exp parfile=scott-usr.par
.....
$ ls
p_rh1tst1  scott-usr.dmp.Z  scott-usr.log  scott-usr.par
```

The export finished successfully and the resulting dump file is scott-usr.dmp.Z. This file is in a compressed format and can be handled just like any other compressed .dmp file. The pipe (p_rh1tst1) still exists and can be reused, but you have to repeat step 2 to point the pipe to the next dump file.

To import a compressed .dmp.Z file, follow the following steps:

1. Optionally move the .dmp.Z to a different location to conduct the import. If this is done, create a new pipe:

```
$ mknod /u01/app/oracle/admin/rh1dev1/exp/p_rh1dev1 p
$ ls -l

prw-r--r--    1 oracle    dba        0 Apr  1 15:12 p_rh1dev1
-rw-r--r--    1 oracle    dba     2564 Apr  1 15:01 scott-usr.dmp.Z
$
```

2. Uncompress the .dmp.Z file through the pipe in the background:

```
$ uncompress < scott-usr.dmp.Z > p_rh1dev1 &
```

3. Create a parameter file for the schema level import. Notice how the pipe is listed as the file in the parfile.

```
$ more scott-usr.par
userid=system
file=p_rh1dev1
log=scott-usr.log
ignore=y
commit=y
fromuser=scott
touser=danw
$
```

4. Conduct the import.

```
$ imp parfile=scott-usr.par
```

The compressed .dmp.Z file imported successfully through the pipe.

As you can see, working with pipes is fairly simple, yet necessary, if you are working with .dmp files in the gigabyte range. The only caveat is to be careful if you intend on manually uncompressing any .dmp.Z files. You can normally expect a 3:1 compression ratio on normal files, but this is not necessarily the case with .dmp files. Expect to get a much better ratio of compression (I have seen 500M .dmp files compressed to 50M). If you uncompress a relatively small file it could fill up your filesystem.

## Editing a Dump (.dmp) File

Oracle documentation and support personnel state that .dmp files are not editable and any attempt to open these files will corrupt them beyond repair. Furthermore, Oracle Support will not support you if you attempt to edit a .dmp file. Having said that, I will show you a way I have found to edit .dmp files to change storage parameters. Be warned, however, that this procedure is totally unsupported and that I am not responsible if you try it and it corrupts your files beyond repair.

If you export on Unix or Linux and attempt to edit the .dmp file in vi, the file *will* be corrupted beyond repair and import will reject it immediately. However, the following procedure has worked for me in the past. Try it at your own risk and remember to make backups of your .dmp file in case they become corrupted.

1. Export the file as normal. I have tested this with user level exports, no data (I just want the DDL), include grants, and no compress.
2. Make backup copies of the resulting .dmp file.
3. FTP one .dmp file in binary mode to a PC.
4. Open the file in WordPad.
5. Use Edit, Replace All to change your tablespaces and initial extent sizes.
6. Save the file as a .txt document.
7. FTP the file using binary mode back to the Unix/Linux machine.
8. Copy the file from .txt back to a .dmp file.
9. Import the file into the target database.

Once again, this works in some cases, but perhaps not in all cases. I do not rely on this method for production systems and I make backups before I attempt to modify any .dmp file. However, there are times when you need to create all the objects for a user with different storage options and this can work. A safer method is to use a script to extract DDL or export to an index file,

8

but those methods take longer and also require editing. This method is provided only as a possible alternative.

## Tuning Parameters

Large exports and especially imports can take hours or even days to complete. This is a frustrating reality for DBAs who are always trying to find ways to speed up the process. The following list includes a few methods I have used to improve performance of user level imports. These suggestions are tailored for large exports/imports, but will yield benefits even when you're working with small data amounts of data.

- When exporting data, use DIRECT=Y to bypass the evaluation buffer. Exports are relatively quick, but this will improve performance.

- Create all the user objects on the target database before data is imported. This way, there are no delays when attempting to allocate space and tablespaces can be sized more easily.

- Use dynamic SQL to disable all primary and foreign key constraints, as well as any other constraints on the tables. Also disable any triggers before the import to prevent them from firing.

- Import the data first, and then create the indexes. This is faster than importing data and indexes simultaneously. Run a test import first using the INDEXFILE option to create a .sql file to create the indexes. Next import the data with INDEXES=N. Once that is done, run the .sql file to create the indexes. This is highly recommended when working with large imports. Furthermore, the resulting index create file can be broken into multiple files to be run in parallel.

- Consider running multiple imports simultaneously. The same .dmp can be accessed by several import jobs at the same time. If you have multiple processors and disks, and can divide the tables into different imports, this might be an option. Just make sure you do not miss any objects.

- Use a large value for the BUFFER parameter. A value of 1024000 is not unreasonable.

- Analyze the tables after the import, not during the import.

- Set COMMIT=Y to commit after every table is imported to reduce the likelihood of blowing out a rollback segment. Remember it takes longer to roll back a failed import than to do the actual import.

- Set FEEDBACK to a value such as 100000 so you can track the progress of the import on large tables.

- Make sure you are familiar with using Unix pipes and compression to deal large files. Most large exports and imports will require these, so it is better to learn these concepts before you need them.

These suggestions should improve the performance of large exports and imports, but there is no one "magic bullet" to make the process go quickly. As with any important task, before you are faced with a large or critical export/import, you should test your procedures. You might find that some parameters yield larger results or are more difficult to implement than others under certain circumstances. Use whatever mix works best for *your* environment.

# Using SQL*Loader

SQL*Loader loads data from one or more flat files into Oracle database tables. It is the fastest and most efficient way to load large amounts of data, plus it allows for the data to be in any user-defined format. All that is needed is a flat file with the data and a DBA-created control file that tells Oracle the format of the data. In the Oracle world, export/import unloads data from one Oracle database and loads it into anther Oracle database. SQL*Loader takes the data from non-Oracle sources (flat files) and loads into an Oracle database for the first time.

For example, if a company had a list of several hundred perspective customers obtained at a trade show, these could easily be put a spreadsheet at the show. After the show, the spreadsheet can be dumped to a text file. That text file would be used as the data file for the SQL*Loader job. This is much better than having to manually enter the data twice (once into someone's laptop and then into the database).

On the other side of the spectrum, SQL*Loader is the preferred method of loading massive amounts of data. For example, imagine a legacy mainframe with volumes of data that someone wants to load into Oracle on a large Unix box. The mainframe people could dump the data (millions of rows) into CUSTOMERS, ORDERS, and so on, as flat files in any character-delimited or space-delimited format. The Oracle DBA would create corresponding SQL*Loader control files specifying the data's format and which Oracle tables to load the data into. He or she could then execute the SQL*Loader jobs in parallel to quickly load the data.

It is important to note that data is being loaded into preexisting Oracle tables. There is no user level or full database SQL*Loader job; you are simply loading data into table(s). There are, however, many ways to customize your SQL*Loader jobs. You might load the data into one or more tables, have null and check constraints, and include default values all within the SQL*Loader control file. This is *in addition* to the normal constraints and triggers in the Oracle tables. If you are going to be migrating many systems to Oracle, have complex data rules, or the data needs "scrubbing," I highly recommend delving deeply into all the options available. This chapter covers the fundamentals, but a highly detailed SQL*Loader study is outside the scope of this book.

SQL*Loader is a command-line utility executed in a manner similar to import. There many parameters that can be specified or the default settings can be used. A parameter file can be created containing standard options. Figure 8.6 shows the SQL*Loader options.

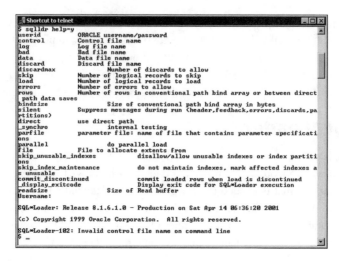

**FIGURE 8.6**

*SQL\*Loader Options.*

There are five types of files that can be used. Although they are called data and control files, they are not the same files composing a database.

- **Data** The data file is the flat file containing the actual data to be loaded. Each row in the file represents a record that's loaded as a row in a table. Within each record, individual columns are separated by either user-defined special characters, by fixed width, or by variable width. Because it is a text file, anyone can open it and edit it. Unlike export/import .dmp files, these files can be corrupted only if someone accidentally adds garbage data or control characters.

- **Control** The control file specifies the characteristics of the data. The data filename is specified and the corresponding database tables are identified. The format of the data record format is given. Any special default values, constraints, and WHERE conditions are provided. This file can be highly customized to scrub or validate data as it is being loaded.

- **Bad** Any rows that do not meet the size or format specifications for a record are written to this file and are not loaded into the database. After the data load, this file will contain rows that *cannot* be loaded into the table because they do not meet the format specification.

- **Discard** Rows that do not meet the logical requirements specified in the control file are written to this file and are not loaded into the database. Rows in this file could have physically been loaded, but business rules dictate they *should not* be loaded into the table. These rows can later be repaired and reloaded by the DBA.

- **LOG** Contains detailed results of the data load.

# SQL*Loader Load Types

Within SQL*Loader, there are two types of loads: conventional path and direct path. These differ in terms of how data is loaded and they impact the level of constraint checking and trigger firing. The default mode is conventional path, but specifying DIRECT=Y will force a direct path load.

## Conventional Path Loading

Conventional path loading essentially loads each row of data as an individual SQL INSERT statement. Ramifications of this include:

- It is slower than direct path.

- All the normal rules and processes for a normal INSERT occur. All constraints are checked, primary and foreign key relationships are maintained, sequences are used, and triggers fire as normal.

- Database buffer cache is used. The normal contents of this buffer could be flushed out as large numbers of data rows are read into the buffer. This will impact performance after the data load because the "normal" buffer contents need to be recached.

- Inserts are logged in the online redo log files and archive log files as normal. This is important to note because there is a danger that a large data load will cause a spike in redo log switches and creation of archive log files. Make sure there is plenty of free space in the archive log dump destination because if that filesystem fills up, the database will hang.

- Data is inserted into any free space available in the table's data blocks. New blocks are written to only if needed.

- The table is not locked so it remains available for DML.

- Indexes are built normally as data is loaded.

- Rows are inserted in groups (bind arrays) as defined by the ROWS parameter. Rather than loading one row at a time (which is inefficient), setting ROWS=100 would load data in 100-row units. For conventional path loading, this parameter acts as a commit.

Conventional path loading is best suited for small amounts of data in established databases. It essentially acts as a series of INSERT statements with all the associated ramifications of DML. This method is not the fastest way of loading data, but the DBA does not have to worry about constraints not being checked or locking a table.

## Direct Path Loading

When loading massive amounts of data, direct path loading is the best option. With this method, data is *not* loaded as a normal INSERT statement. This method has some implications you need to be aware of before you use it:

- Direct path loading is faster than conventional path.

- Normal table level insert processing does not occur, and only some constraints are enforced. Primary key, unique key, and not null constraints are enforced. Foreign keys and check constraints are disabled automatically so they are not applied during the load. Insert triggers are also disabled so they do not fire. After the load, you must re-enable any constraints or triggers not automatically re-enabled.

- Database buffer cache is bypassed. This improves performance and does not force Oracle to flush out blocks normally cached in the buffer.

- Redo information is not generated for the data loaded when the database is in NOARCHIVELOG mode.

- Current table data blocks are ignored during the load. As space is needed the next free table data block is acquired and data is loaded directly into that block. There is no attempt to load data into blocks that already contain data, even if they still have free space.

- The table and its indexes are locked during the load. No DML activity can occur; queries are the only access available. Obviously, this impacts the user availability. The DBA might be forced to run the load during non-production hours.

- Indexes are built after the load has completed, not during the load. Also, check the STATUS column of DBA_INDEXES after the load because, if there are problems during the load, an index might be left in direct load state. If so, drop and re-create the index.

- The ROWS parameter for direct path loading indicates how often to save the data. This is slightly different than a commit. If the database instance crashes, all the data protected by a data save will survive, but their indexes will be unusable. This is resolved by either finishing the load or dropping and re-creating the index. Data saves acts as performance hits, so do not set this value too low.

Direct path loading is most appropriate for new large tables whereby you can afford them being unavailable to the users. Just make sure after the load all the constraints and triggers are enabled without data problems.

The following is a basic example of a conventional load into the SCOTT.BONUS table. Before running the load, you have to define a control (.ctl) file, a data file (.dat), and a parameter file (.par).

The control file is as follows:

```
$ more bonus.ctl
LOAD DATA
INFILE bonus.dat
APPEND
INTO TABLE bonus
```

```
(ename position(01:10) char,
job position(11:19) char,
sal position(20:27) integer external,
comm position(28:30) integer external
nullif comm=blanks)
$
```

The parameters are fairly self-explanatory. The INFILE identifies the data file as bonus.dat. The next parameter, APPEND, tells SQL*Loader to insert data without disturbing any existing rows in the table BONUS. Other options here are REPLACE, which acts to delete any existing rows and TRUNCATE, which truncates any existing rows before the insert. The INTO TABLE BONUS code line indicates that the BONUS table will be loaded. Each field in the data file, its position, and the data type for the data file column are indicated. The last column in this example has a clause to set the table column to null if the last field is text blanks.

The sample data file is as follows:

```
$ more bonus.dat
Mike W      CEO      150000   10
Dan W       DBA      100000   25
Tige C      DBA      100000   25
Jeff J      SA       100000   25
John P      SA       100000   25
Mark P      SA       100000   25
Brian C     SA       100000   25
Bob G       PGR      100000   25
Becky G     PGR      100000   25
Kalynn H    PGR      100000   25
Zach H      PGR      100000   25
Josh H      PGR      100000   25
Erik H      G        100000
$
```

As you can see, each row corresponds to the format as defined in the control file.

The parameter file is optional because each value can be specified on the command line, but it makes running SQL*Loader jobs repeatable.

```
$ more bonus.par
userid=scott
control=bonus.ctl
bad=bonus.bad
log=bonus.log
discard=bonus.dis
rows=2
errors=5
skip=0
$
```

The user executing the data load is SCOTT and a password will need to be entered. Control, bad, log, and discard files are identified. SQL*Loader log files are lengthy and descriptive, but they should reviewed after a data load. ROWS=2 indicates a commit every two rows. ERRORS=5 specifies that if more than five rows are sent to the bad file, the SQL*Loader job will terminate. Any rows loaded and protected via row commits will remain in the table.

SKIP=0 indicates that the first 0 rows in the data file will be skipped during the load. If, for example, the first run of the load failed after successfully loading 35,000 rows, the DBA can fix the error and set SKIP=35000. When the data load restarts, SQL*Loader can resume where it left off.

Execution of the SQL*Loader job is similar to export/import, as shown in Figure 8.7.

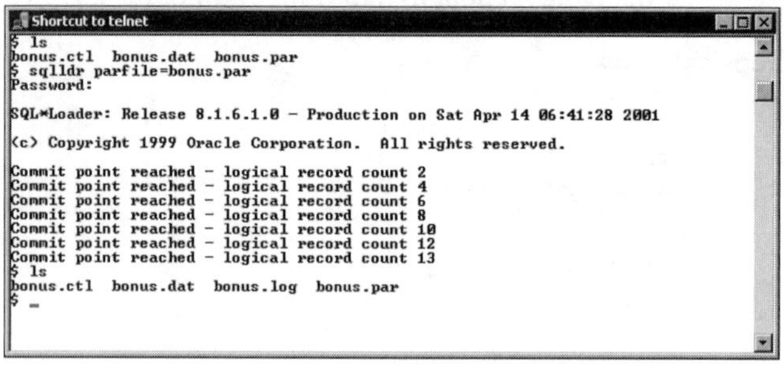

**FIGURE 8.7**
*SQL*Loader Execution.*

The most difficult technical issues in regards to SQL*Loader are writing a control file to correctly match the data format and resolving data integrity issues. What is really difficult is determining which data to load and verifying that it is valid. Especially when you're migrating legacy systems to Oracle, you should meet the data modelers and business analysts to verify that "garbage" data is not being loaded. Remember, just because data has been sitting in a legacy system for years does not mean it is valid in a new system.

# Using LogMiner

The online redo log files and any resulting archive log files provide a wealth of information because they are basically transaction logs. Any changes that occur within the database go to these files. Although this represents potentially useful information, the DBA historically had no way to view these files. All that changed with the advent of the LogMiner utility.

The contents of the online redo logs and archived redo log files can now be viewed by a DBA. If, for example, you know that critical data was changed sometime in the morning, you can examine all the SQL executed by any user during that time. Additionally, the utility can generate SQL to undo any DML in the database. This gives you the capability to undo any change within the database, even if it was committed. A classic example of how this is helpful is when someone updates data with a logically incorrect WHERE clause. You can track down exactly who made the change and when, and then fix it.

---

**TIP**

**Avoid Analyzing Online Redo Logs**

It is documented that LogMiner can analyze online redo log files without any problems. If you are like me and are uneasy about doing anything to your online redo logs, there is a simple solution. Use ALTER SYSTEM SWITCH LOGFILE to force the contents of your online redo log to a new archive log file that you can analyze.

---

LogMiner is conceptually simple, but the actual process is somewhat tedious. Everything past step 3 must be done from a single SQL*Plus session. If that session terminates for any reason, you must restart the entire LogMiner process from the beginning. Also, all files listed must be given full absolute paths. Hopefully, the process will be made more user friendly in the future, but for now these are the steps for using LogMiner:

1. Create a UTL_FILE_DIR directory. This is where Oracle will read the archive log files. For convenience, put this where your archive log files are stored. This example uses LogMiner with the database in archive log mode. Place the following line in the init.ora file and bounce the instance.

   ```
   # Location for Log Miner Dictionary files to be placed
   utl_file_dir = /ubackup/app/oracle/admin/rh1dev1/arch
   ```

   This cannot be set by ALTER SYSTEM or ALTER SESSION. The parameter must be in init.ora file and the database bounced. If you plan on using LogMiner, you should perform this step before a situation arises where data needs to be recovered.

2. Create the LogMiner Dictionary File, which will contain data dictionary info. This resolves object names in the archive log files. It might take several minutes to create the file, so be patient.

   ```
   $ cd /ubackup/app/oracle/admin/rh1dev1/arch
   $ sqlplus internal
   SQL> set linesize 400
   SQL> execute
   dbms_logmnr_d.build('rh1dev1dict1.ora','/ubackup/app/oracle/admin/rh1dev1/
   ➥arch');
   ```

3. Define a new list of log files to be analyzed. This might be online or archived log files. In this step you provide Oracle with a range of log files to analyze. Make sure the event you are searching for can be found in these log files.

```
$ cd /ubackup/app/oracle/admin/rh1dev1/arch
$ sqlplus internal
SQL> set linesize 550
SQL> col sql_redo format a350
SQL> col sql_undo format a350
SQL> execute dbms_logmnr.add_logfile
('/ubackup/app/oracle/admin/rh1dev1/arch/rh1dev1_arch_1_128.arc',dbms_logmnr.
➥new);

PL/SQL procedure successfully completed.

SQL> execute dbms_logmnr.add_logfile
('/ubackup/app/oracle/admin/rh1dev1/arch/rh1dev1_arch_1_139.arc',dbms_logm
➥nr.addfile);

PL/SQL procedure successfully completed.
```

Repeat this process for each archive log file to analyze. This example stops at arch_1_139.arc, which is the most current log file.

If you use the .new option, you create a new list of files to analyze (LogMiner disregards any previous list). After that, use the .addfile option to append log files to a list.

4. Begin the analysis of the specified logs.

```
execute
dbms_logmnr.start_logmnr(dictfilename=>'/ubackup/app/oracle/admin/rh1dev1/
➥arch/rh1dev1dict1.ora',
starttime=>to_date('07/03/2000:10PM','MM/DD/YYYY:HHPM'),
endtime=>to_date('07/07/2000:07:55:00AM','MM/DD/YYYY:HH:MI:SSAM'));

PL/SQL procedure successfully completed.
```

5. Use the following V$ views to interrogate the analyzed log files:

```
V$LOGMNR_CONTENTS    (especially the SQL_REDO and SQL_UNDO columns)
V$LOGMNR_DICTIONARY
V$LOGMNR_LOGS        (has SCN and time ranges)
V$LOGMNR_PARAMETERS
```

6. Query these views to identify SQL. Spooling the output to a .lst file for analysis is a good idea here.

```
SQL> select timestamp, username, sql_redo from v$logmnr_contents where
username in ('JOHNP', 'ERIKH', 'KALYNNH', 'JEFFJ');

SQL> select timestamp, username, sql_redo, sql_undo from v$logmnr_contents
where username = 'ZACHH' and seg_name = 'SUBSCRIBER';
```

> **NOTE**
>
> LogMiner Stresses the System
>
> These statements can take a long time to execute and are CPU-intensive. The Unix monitoring utility `top` shows the process as 48% CPU and 31 minutes. The load average identified by `uptime` also increased during this period.

7. Release the resources held by the analyzer. This is an important cleanup step done *after* you have made your LogMiner queries.

```
SQL> execute dbms_logmnr.end_logmnr;

PL/SQL procedure successfully completed.
```

LogMiner can be a useful tool for determining who changed what data and when, and then fixing it. I have used LogMiner several times to identify what exactly happened when a developer or user comes up and says "I was updating some data and I don't remember what I did, but now it's broke. Help!" In times like this, LogMiner can be a better solution than trying to guess what data to re-create or dropping and reimporting a logically corrupted table. Although LogMiner requires a little initial setup and is tedious to work with, it provides an important new level of functionality to the DBA.

# Summary

This chapter covered Oracle DBA utilities. It covered the basic syntax to use these utilities, but more importantly, addressed the situations when these utilities should be used. It is not enough to know that a utility exists, the savvy DBA knows *when* and *why* a specific utility should be employed to meet a technical need.

A majority of the chapter covered export and import because those are the most commonly used and versatile utilities. A solid working knowledge of export/import is a must for DBAs in the Unix/Linux environment.

SQL*Loader and LogMiner were also discussed. SQL*Loader is a great utility for loading data from a flat file into a database. This process can be done simply or can be made to enforce complex constraints and check conditions on the data as it is being loaded. LogMiner is a first-generation tool used to query the contents of online redo log files and archived redo log files.

# Backup and Recovery

## ESSENTIALS

- The first principal of database administration is data protection, which directly equates to backup and recovery. This is the most critical skill for a DBA.

- Oracle provides many features that can be used to implement a solid backup and recovery policy.

- The choice between ARCHIVELOG and NOARCHIVELOG mode will greatly impact your backup and recovery options.

- The type of damage your database suffers will also determine your method of recovery.

- No matter what policies you implement, they must actually be tested before you can rely on them.

Database backup and recovery directly relate to the first principal of database administration—data protection. This is the one area the DBA should never be deficient in and must aggressively promote. It is the most critical skill of a good DBA.

This chapter covers the fundamentals of backup and recovery in the Unix/Linux environment. It discusses the tasks required to create a reasonably secure database. Once you understand these procedures, you should practice them and be comfortable with them *before* a disaster requires you to use them. This point cannot be stressed enough. Backing up and recovering production databases is a little like working in an emergency room—during the emergency is no time to realize that the highly paid professional doesn't know what to do to save the day.

# Importance of Backups

It is important to realize that you are ultimately responsible for the organization's data. Unfortunately, that is said so often in marketing literature or job descriptions that many people overlook its significance. What it *really* means is that, if you (as the DBA) mess up and lose a database, you will likely get fired. In addition, those dependent on the data will suffer; customers lose a service they are paying for. Depending on the severity of the failure, the business could easily go under, meaning your coworkers are also facing unemployment. Finally, the owners of the business face a financial loss. Oracle DBAs are typically very well paid and one big reason is that they are expected to provide piece of mind that the database *will* be secure.

Ironically enough, data protection often comes at the expense of data availability. When systems are being backed up, they are either not available or they are available, but performance suffers. Not matter which backup scheme you implement, this is an unavoidable fact. Some backup methods have a smaller impact than others, but all have an impact even when it is not readily apparent. It is the DBA's job to understand the implications and develop a sensible backup schedule that meets the needs of the business. Be sure to document what will be backed up, who will be responsible for backups and recoveries, and the ramifications of potential problems. This is no place for assumptions.

Once a method and schedule have been established, the DBA must aggressively pursue its successful implementation. This is one area where you won't win any friends. You must check the status of your overnight database backups every morning. Once this is done, check with the SA to make sure the server backups are valid. If they aren't, you need to find out why and get the problem fixed. Ideally, this is not a problem, but some SAs get defensive when being questioned by the DBA. Also, business people and programmers sometimes prefer to forgo backups to complete a report or job more quickly. The DBA needs to step in before this happens and make sure backups are performed.

The final major impact is testing. It is not enough to simply implement backups. Everyone involved in the backup, restore, and database/server recovery processes should regularly practice their procedures. This ensures that the procedures are correct, sharpens the skills of the technical people, and builds the confidence of both the administrators and the technical staff. There is simply no substitute for backup and recovery drills.

# Backup Types

There are two types of backups: logical and physical. One is the process of backing up the raw data via Oracle's export utility (logical) whereas the other involves backing up the physical database files (physical). Most DBAs and SAs primarily think in terms of physical backups and that will be the main focus of this chapter. There are, however, some aspects of logical backups that merit discussion. Most DBAs use a mix of logical and physical backups to protect their systems because each method is used to recover from different types of failures.

## Logical Backups

Logical backups (exports) are used to recover from accidentally deleted or modified data. If, for example, someone accidentally deleted your production CUSTOMER table because they thought they were in a development database, you would use an export to restore the table. This is because there is nothing physically wrong with the customer01.dbf file on-disk, it's just that some human's logic was incorrect and data was destroyed.

Exports are easy to set up and schedule via cron so entire schemas can be backed up overnight. Because export and import are familiar utilities anyway, using them to back up and recover data is easier.

There are not any true problems with using exports for this purpose, but their usefulness is limited depending on the database and application. In large schemas if there is so much data that the export cannot finish in time (overnight), the export might be impractical as well as the import. Also, if the data itself is changing too fast or is highly entwined, the export might not be useful. Finally, because an export represents the database at a previous point in time, it might not be valid if transactions have occurred since that time.

In the previous example in which the CUSTOMER table was deleted, you would only need to reimport the table data back into the database. There would likely be triggers and foreign key constraints that needed to be disabled before the import, but these can be managed with dynamic SQL. The biggest issue here is what to do with the transactions that occurred after the export; these transactions are not recovered by the import. This is the largest problem with logical backups and brings the discussion to physical backups.

---

**TIP**

Use LogMiner to Undo Changes
The new utility LogMiner enables SQL to undo unwanted DML changes to the data. You should become familiar enough with LogMiner so you know when to use it instead of export/import.

## Physical Backups

The process of copying the Oracle database, configuration, and software files is a physical backup. A physical backup enables you to recover a database when a media failure, such as a bad disk, occurs. Physical backups are the primary form of database protection in the Unix/Linux world.

Fully understanding the architecture of the Oracle database is the first step to implementing successful physical backups. Going back to the emergency room example, a doctor who does not understand human anatomy cannot reliably diagnose a patient's illness. The same concept applies to DBAs because they are called to identify what is wrong with the computer system and determine the effect on the overall database instance.

Backup and recovery procedures make sense only when you understand *why* they are being done. Oracle architecture is complex and does change so you should review it on a regular basis. This chapter assumes that you have a solid understanding of the Oracle architecture and understand how each piece relates to the other. If you are not at this stage, a review of Chapter 2, "Architecture of the Oracle Server," is strongly recommended.

When dealing with physical backups, there are three distinct stages to be discussed: backup, restore, and recover.

- **Backup**   Backups are the act of copying the database files, database parameter files, and Oracle software installation files to disk, tape, or optical media (such as a writeable CD-ROM). Typically this is automated to run each night and is coordinated with the SA. The DBA (usually in conjunction with the SA) should verify the success or failure of these backups each morning and take action if they begin to fail. It is important that you understand when and how these backups occur, even if they involve backing up the Unix/Linux server files, which is traditionally not a DBA responsibility.

- **Restore**   Restore is the process of copying files from a previous backup to disk. Typically, a disk will fail, errors will occur, and the DBA will shut down the database if it hasn't crashed already. At this stage, the SA will replace the disk and ask the DBA what needs to be restored. The DBA should know what files were lost and when the last valid backup occurred. He or she should be able to respond with something like "Files for /u04 from May 23's backup". The SA will then retrieve the tape of May 23 and copy the files from /u04 to the replaced disk.

- **Recover**   Once the files are restored to disk, Oracle needs to be restarted and recovered so that it accepts the restored files. Depending on the backup method used, the database will either exist as it did at the time of the backup, or it will recover itself to the time of the failure. It is during this stage that you might need to provide instructions to Oracle on how far to recover and when to open for normal use.

These steps comprise the stages of a typical recovery of a lost disk. Most of the DBA's focus will be on planning the backups and performing the recoveries. The options available to the DBA during the recovery are determined by the type of backup(s) used, the validity of those backups, and the nature of the failure. The next section examines the technical details of this process.

# Incurring Damage on the Database

Before you look at ways to physically recover a database, you need to understand how it can be physically damaged. This section is no longer talking about a user accidentally deleting a table; it considers how files are destroyed or corrupted beyond repair.

The classic example is when a disk drive that holds a critical database file crashes. This is referred to as a *media failure*. There are many ways a file can become inaccessible, but this is the most common, so this section bases the discussion on this event. Remember that the impact is the same no matter how a file is lost, so these principles can be applied to most situations.

## Impact on the Database

Oracle's database control file(s) determine whether all is well within the database. Within the control file, there is a list of each file, its location, the current log file sequence number, and the timestamp and System Change Number (SCN) it *should* have. During a checkpoint, each file in the database is updated with timestamp and SCN information and the control file is included. If the information in the control file doesn't synch with what is actually on-disk, an error is issued to the alert log. For example, if a disk dies suddenly, taking with it customer01.dbf, Oracle should notice it is missing during the checkpoint.

**NOTE**

**Errors Might Not Show Up Immediately**

Most people would expect an error to immediately be logged if the customer01.dbf file is lost, but that is not the case. It might be a while before Oracle notices a file is missing. The problem is made even more confusing because the file might be deleted, but Oracle might still see it as open. In this case, it is not until a redo log switch that Oracle realizes the file is gone.

If any one file is missing or has an unexpected SCN or timestamp, Oracle will loudly issue warning messages in the alert log and the information in the missing file will be inaccessible. The impact on the database depends on what type of file is destroyed. Some files can be lost and the database will limp along, but the loss of other files can mean sudden death for a database instance. The following table contains guidelines for what to expect when you lose a database file. These guidelines are based on the assumption of a 1:1 ratio of data files to tablespaces. It is very important to note this chart contains *expected* results. Depending on the ARCHIVELOG mode of the database and how the file is lost, you might receive different error messages and the database might crash sooner than later.

| File Type | Expected Impact |
| --- | --- |
| System | Instance crash as soon as it is "noticed" by Oracle. |
| Control | Instance crash as soon as it is "noticed" by Oracle. Multiplexing control files does *not* prevent a crash, but they do allow for a much easier and faster recovery. |
| Online Redo Log | Depends on whether redo log files are multiplexed and whether the file is part of the active group. |
| | If multiplexed, an error message will be issued but the database instance will survive. |
| | If not multiplexed, the instance will crash and any data in that file will be lost if it has not be archived. |
| Rollback | If there is only one non-SYSTEM rollback tablespace, the database instance will crash. As long as at least one rollback tablespace is available, the instance should survive, but performance will suffer. If there were active transactions, data can be lost. |
| Temp | Database instance will continue to exist, but any operations requiring a disk sort will fail. |
| Data | Loss of access to objects in that tablespace. (USERS, TOOLS, DRSYS are treated as data files.) |
| Index | Loss of performance and capability to create/update primary or unique keys on corresponding table. Data will be accessible, but any DML requiring an index will fail. |

Oracle will react to a loss of a file as soon as it "notices" the loss. For example, when testing you can delete a system.dbf and still do some queries because that file is still considered "open" and Oracle does not know that it is missing. However, as soon as a log switch occurs and Oracle tries to access that file, the instance will crash because it no longer exists. All Oracle background processes (PMON, SMON, and so on) will terminate. Users will likely receive either "ORA-12571: TNS:packet writer failure" or "ERROR at line 1:ORA-03113: end-of-file on communication channel", indicating they have lost contact with the database. The alert log should have an entry such as:

```
Sat Apr 14 15:04:17 2001
CKPT: terminating instance due to error 1242
Instance terminated by CKPT, pid = 2676
```

At this stage you have a crashed database instance that cannot be opened. You also likely have one or more active transactions that need to be resolved.

The problem with losing disks is compounded by the fact that a crashed disk seldom takes just one file with it; normally it costs several files. For example, a failure of a disk holding /u02 would impact the files and databases shown in Figure 9.1.

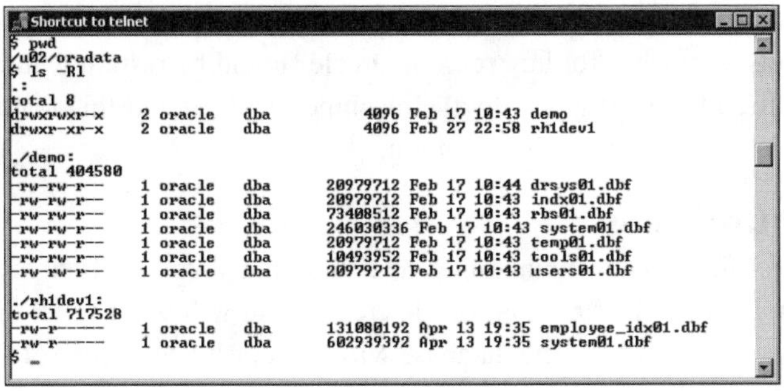

FIGURE 9.1

*Impact of Losing /u02.*

In this case, both databases would crash because the SYSTEM tablespace .dbf files would be lost. If, however, /u02/oradata/rh1dev1 only contained the EMPLOYEE index tablespace, the database would have survived the loss and the DBA would have only needed to drop the indexes on the EMPLOYEE table and rebuild them in another tablespace.

Obviously, you should know which files are located on which filesystems. Ideally, you will have identified what filesystems hold essential files and which filesystems are not as critical. If the SA comes to you and states "We're losing /u04 to a bad disk," you should have documented which files there are and know what the impact will be.

9

BACKUP AND
RECOVERY

> **NOTE**
>
> Impact of Losing One Disk
>
> On large Unix servers, one disk does not necessarily equate to one filesystem. This relates to RAID and will be covered in depth in Chapter 13, "Unix Server Monitoring."

## Adding Fault Tolerance

There is nothing you can do to prevent a disk from failing, but there are a few steps that you can take to make the database more fault-tolerant.

The two most advised practices are to multiplex the control files and to multiplex online redo logs. In the Oracle world, multiplexing means to have Oracle create and maintain two or more identical copies of a file. This is not the same as mirroring because mirroring is done at the operating system level, whereas multiplexed files are managed by Oracle. Only control files and online redo log files can be multiplexed.

Another common method of adding fault tolerance is to set the critical databases to restart automatically if the server crashes or reboots. This auto-start feature means that if a Unix/Linux server reboots or crashes for any reason, Oracle should be restarted automatically. The SA and DBA still need to investigate why the machine rebooted, but this feature allows Oracle to become available without human intervention.

## Multiplex Control Files

Multiplexing control files means maintaining several identical control files for the same database. Oracle will read from the first control file created, but will write to all the control files just as if there were only one file. The database will still crash if *any* control file is lost, but recovery is greatly simplified.

Typically, control files are multiplexed during database creation. The database-creation assistant and most scripts will automatically create the database with three control files. These are listed in your configSID.ora or initSID.ora files. If you want to add additional control files after the database has been created, follow these steps:

1. Shut down the database normally.
2. Edit the configSID.ora or initSID.ora files to have the new control filename and location.
3. Copy one good, preexisting control file to the location specified and give it the appropriate name.
4. Restart the database and verify that Oracle "sees" it by querying V$CONTROLFILE.

Control files are relatively small (about 4M each) and there is no real performance hit by having extras, so you should multiplex them. Just make sure they are placed on different filesystems with different controllers so one failure cannot destroy them all.

## Multiplex Online Redo Logs

Multiplexing online redo log files is conceptually very similar to multiplexing control files. Oracle automatically maintains one or more copies of a file. The key difference is that the loss of a multiplexed redo log file will generate an error message, but the database instance will still survive. Additionally, no data will be lost. Given these benefits, it is a very good idea to multiplex each redo log group on a different filesystem.

You normally multiplex redo log files after the database is created. Use the following steps to multiplex a redo log group:

1. Use V$LOG and V$LOGFILE to identify the members of each group and to identify which is the active group.

```
SQL> select * from v$logfile;

   GROUP# STATUS   MEMBER
---------- -------  ----------------------------------------
        1          /u03/oradata/rh1dev1/redo01a.rdo
        2          /u07/oradata/rh1dev1/redo02a.rdo
        3  /u11/oradata/rh1dev1/redo03a.rdo

SQL> select group#, members, bytes, status from v$log;

   GROUP#    MEMBERS            BYTES STATUS
---------- ---------- ---------------- ----------------
        1          1       76,800,000 CURRENT
        2          1       76,800,000 INACTIVE
        3          1       76,800,000 INACTIVE
```

2. Add a new member to the non-active redo groups.

```
SQL> alter database add logfile member
  2  '/u08/oradata/rh1dev1/redo02b.rdo'
  3  to group 2;
Database altered.
```

   Repeat this step for redo03b.rdo in group 3.

3. Use ALTER SYSTEM SWITCH LOGFILE to move to the next group. Then add the new member to the remaining non-active redo group.

4. Perform several log switches to remove the INVALID or STALE status for each new member, which can be seen via V$LOGFILE.

There is more maintenance and performance overhead associated with multiplexing redo logs than with control files. Specifically, if you have doubled the size of disk space needed for your redo log files and there will be more I/O because of the additional writes. However, this is a very small price to pay in return for not having the database crash and potentially losing data if a redo log file is lost.

## Automatic Database Startup

When a Unix or Linux server shuts down (planned or otherwise), any databases running on it are also shut down. Once the server is restarted, any databases will remain shutdown by default. This can pose a problem if the databases need to be restarted. Unless there is a DBA on call 7×24 just in case there are problems, the solution is to have the database automatically restart on machine startup.

Unix and Linux servers have a set of predefined stages they go through as they shut down or start up. Each run level can have a list of processes associated with it. The DBA can include shell scripts to start up or shut down one or more databases and listeners for a specific run level. This allows a database to be automatically shut down if the server is being shut down and allows the database to be restarted once the server has rebooted. Oracle instance recovery will automatically resolve most problems in the event the server crashed.

The controlling file to determine whether a database is restarted automatically is /etc/oratab (Linux or HP-UX) or /var/opt/oracle/oratab (Sun Solaris). Figure 9.2 shows a copy of the oratab file.

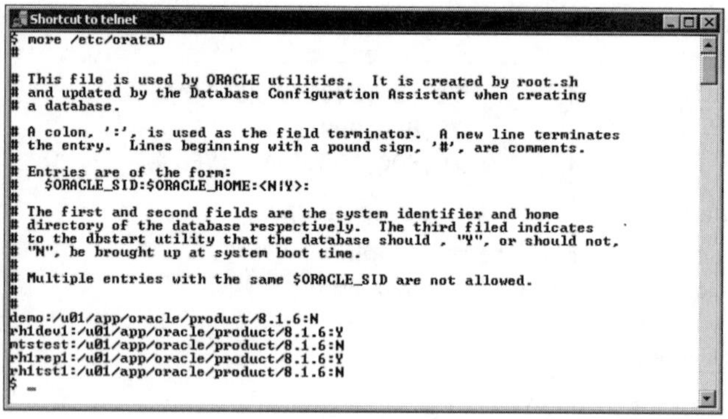

**FIGURE 9.2**
*The /etc/oratab File.*

The last field (Y or N) of each line indicates whether the database will be restarted at reboot. As you can see, only rh1rep1 and rh1dev1 are automatically restarted.

Oracle provides two scripts to automatically start and shut down the databases indicated in the /etc/oratab. The scripts are:

$ORACLE_HOME/bin/dbshut

and

$ORACLE_HOME/bin/dbstart

Work with your SA to implement these scripts because they do require root access. There can be platform-specific issues as well, so you should consult your Installation and Configuration Guide. However, the following steps provide one way to implement automatic startup and shutdown processes on Sun Solaris:

1. Edit (as Oracle) $ORACLE_HOME/bin/dbshut to use SHUTDOWN IMMEDIATE.

2. Create (as root) a file: /etc/init.d/dbshut.

   ```
   #!/bin/csh
   ```

```
su - oracle -c "/u01/app/oracle/product/8.1.6/bin/lsnrctl stop"
su - oracle -c "/u01/app/oracle/product/8.1.6/bin/dbshut"
```

3. Assign dbshut permissions 755.

   ```
   $ chmod 755 dbshut
   ```

4. Create (as root) a soft link for /etc/rc0.d/K01dbshut to /etc/init.d/dbshut.

   ```
   $ ln -s /etc/init.d/dbshut /etc/rc0.d/K01dbshut
   ```

   This link will force the script dbshut to stop the listener. The Oracle dbshut script will shut down immediate-running databases.

5. Create (as root) a file: /etc/init.d/dbstart.

   ```
   #!/bin/csh

   su - oracle -c "/u01/app/oracle/product/8.1.6/bin/dbstart"
   su - oracle -c "/u01/app/oracle/product/8.1.6/bin/lsnrctl start"
   ```

6. Assign dbstart permissions 755.

   ```
   $ chmod 755 dbstart
   ```

7. Create (as root) a soft link for /etc/rc2.d/S99dbstart to /etc/init.d/dbstart.

   ```
   $ ln -s /etc/init.d/dbstart /etc/rc2.d/S99dbstart
   ```

   This link will execute the dbstart script, which will start the databases indicated in /etc/oratab. This script will also start the Oracle listener.

These are only the basic steps for setting up automatic startup and shutdown in your databases. You can use the $ORACLE_HOME shell variable, but these scripts will explicitly call the 8.1.6/bin scripts, which sometimes need editing.

Once again, it's advisable to verify the filenames of your specific platform. Also, check Oracle's online support and installation guide for potential bugs or alerts with automatic startup/shutdown because they sometimes occur. If you still encounter problems, check the oracle .profile file, because this sometimes causes problems if it is interactive.

Ultimately you should test these scripts by actually rebooting the server.

# Performing Backups and Recoveries

There are two distinct modes of running a database: NOARCHIVELOG mode and ARCHIVELOG mode. In ARCHIVELOG mode, a copy of the active redo log file is made by ARCH and copied to a separate location after each redo log switch. This way, a copy of the redo log is always available in case it needs to be "replayed" to reconstruct the database to a specific point in time. This is in contrast to NOARCHIVELOG mode, whereby the online redo log files are never copied and are overwritten when they are needed again.

9

BACKUP AND
RECOVERY

The decision to place a database in ARCHIVELOG mode is important because it determines types of backups implemented and recovery options available. Ultimately, it determines the level of protection for the database. Let's now examine each type of backup in detail.

## Cold Backups and Recoveries

Cold backups (aka *offline* backups) are conceptually the simplest form of physical backup. Basically, you shut down the normal database and then copy *all* the control, online redo log, and data files to another location. It is key to note that the database is shut down while the files are being copied. The idea is that because the database was shut down normally, all transactions will neatly be closed, buffers will be flushed, and file headers will be properly synchronized. With a cold backup, you end up with a complete copy of your database at one specific point in time.

One common mistake people make is to back up the database while it is still running and think they have a valid cold backup. Unfortunately, that is not the case. If you back up a database file while the database is still running, your backup is worthless. You will not be able to recover your database if you try to restore a file that was copied while the database was running. Support personnel I have spoken with claim this is a very common problem, because people don't pay any attention to what they are backing up. Worse yet, they never test their recovery plans or their backups until a failure occurs.

Furthermore, databases should be shut down normally to guarantee the cold backup will be valid. Any other form of shut down (transactional, immediate, and especially abort) leaves doubt as to the validity of the backup. Some documentation states that shutdown immediate is fine, but I choose to be more conservative, when possible. If you must use shutdown immediate to kill user sessions, that's okay, but immediately restart it and then do a normal shutdown before cold backups.

---

### The Database Crashed!

I have seen more than one case where someone has panicked because the database went for cold backups, but they didn't know why it went down. They will claim the database crashed when in reality it was shut down as part of a normal backup script. What is even more common is for someone to schedule a nighttime job, but have it fail because the database went down. Particularly in large shops, it is very important to communicate changes in cold backup schedules to prevent jobs from failing.

---

How a cold backup is restored depends on whether a database is in NOARCHIVELOG mode or ARCHIVELOG mode.

## Cold Backups and NOARCHIVELOG Mode

Databases in NOARCHIVELOG mode can only be backed up and restored by full cold (offline) backups. If any data or online redo log file is lost or damaged and the database needs recovery, *every* file on the database must be restored.

The only file that doesn't require a complete restore is a control file. If you lose only a control file and still have a valid copy, you don't have to restore the entire database. Restoring control files is covered later in this chapter.

In this example, you shut down the database on Sunday night and perform a cold backup of all the control, redo log, and database files. On Monday morning, you restart the database and business runs as normal until Wednesday when /u07 fails. You know that /u07 only contains your customers_01.dbf file, but you still must restore the *entire* database from Sunday's cold backup. This means you lose all your transactions since Sunday night.

This is a severe loss of data, but that is a penalty of running a database in NOARCHIVELOG mode. You can only recover to the time of the last good backup.

Performing a recovery is conceptually simple. Delete all the control files, online redo log files, and data files of the damaged database. Then restore all the control files, online redo log files, and data files from the same backup to the exact same locations. Each file must be from the same backup and it must be in the same location. If any file is missing or was not "closed" during the backup, the database will not start up properly. Once the files are in place, simply start SQL*Plus, connect internal, and start the database. You will have the database exactly as it was before it was shut down for the cold backup.

## Cold Backups in ARCHIVELOG Mode

Cold backups of databases in ARCHIVELOG mode follow the same rule—the database must be shut down—but there is more flexibility in terms of what is restored. Specifically, you do not have to restore the entire database. Only restore those files that are damaged or lost. Oracle will recognize that the files restored from the backup have an earlier timestamp and will apply archived redo logs to bring those files up to date.

To start a cold backup, shut down the database normally. Next, copy all the data and control files to the backup location. Once all the files have been copied, the database can be restarted.

Do not copy the online redo log files of a database in ARCHIVELOG mode. You want to keep your online redo logs from the time of failure because they can contain transactions that need to be reapplied to the database. This is a key difference between cold backups of databases in ARCHIVELOG mode versus databases in NOARCHIVELOG mode. The following table summarizes what to backup.

| Backup Y/N | Control Files | Data Files | Redo Log Files |
|---|---|---|---|
| NOARCHIVELOG Mode | Yes | Yes | Yes |
| ARCHIVELOG Mode | Yes | Yes | No |

Backing up and restoring online redo logs is often a point of confusion, even with experienced DBAs. In fact, I have even seen Oracle documentation with conflicting information on this issue. The reason for this is that people often think that cold backups are the same for databases in NOARCHIVELOG mode and ARCHIVELOG mode. In reality, the requirements for each type of database are different.

Consider these three certainties in regards to cold backups:

- The database must be shut down cleanly before the backup
- The database is not available during the backup
- It is the only option for databases in NOARCHIVELOG mode

Cold backups are simple to understand, implement, and recover from. If used correctly, they provide full recovery to the point in time of the backup. However, because they require down time and because NOARCHIVELOG mode does not allow point-in-time recovery, many sites opt to use *hot backups* instead.

## Hot Backups and Recoveries

Hot backups (aka *online* backups) are copies of data files taken while the database is up and running. Only databases in ARCHIVELOG mode are eligible for hot backups. Furthermore, the backup is not simply an OS level copy of the entire database at once. Each tablespace is placed in "hot backup mode," which freezes the data file headers so the SCN does not increase. Then, each data file in the tablespace is copied to the backup destination. Once those files are successfully copied, that tablespace is taken out of backup mode and the file headers are unfrozen. The backup process then advances to the next tablespace and performs the same process. Once all the tablespaces are copied, the hot backup is complete. The result is a copy of each tablespace and its corresponding data files, whereby each set of data files has a slightly different timestamp.

Believe it or not, this method is the most flexible way to back up an Oracle database. Rather than backing up an entire database (as with cold backups), these hot backups save files at the tablespace level. If a disk fails and you lose a mount point, simply restore those lost files from the hot backup. During the recovery, Oracle will notice that they have an earlier timestamp than specified in the surviving control files. Oracle will go into recovery mode and prompt you for all the archive log files after the timestamp of the restored files. Oracle will then "replay" the transactions in the archived log files and eventually the online redo log files to bring all the data files to the current SCN. Oracle will then open the database for business as normal.

Conceptually, that is how Oracle recovers to the current point in time using archive log files. All that is needed is the archived log files, a current control file (to see how far to recover to), and valid copies of the data files. The restored data files can come from a cold backup, a series of hot backups, or a mixture of both. Oracle only cares whether the files were closed normally or were in hot backup mode when they were copied to the backup location.

Oracle does, however, require a continuous chain of valid archive log files. Conceivably, you can restore a backup of a data file taken the previous year as long as you have *every* archive log file since that backup. If you encounter a gap in your archive log files, your recovery will be halted at the last continuous file.

Hot backups only apply to data files that are part of tablespaces. Control files and online redo logs are not part of a hot backup per se. Rather, they are used to implement the recovery by providing guidance for what to recover (via the control files) and the most recent transactions (via the redo log files). The hot backup and recovery methodology is largely based on the assumption that at least one control file and one member of each redo log group will survive the initial failure. This is a big reason why you multiplex your control and online redo log files. If you lose all of either the control or redo log files, you must first recover them before you can attempt to recover the data files. A failure of this magnitude only adds to the complexity and time to recover the database.

## Putting a Database into ARCHIVELOG Mode

Databases are by default created in NOARCHIVELOG mode. After you build the database, create the application tablespaces, and load the initial data, you should put the database in ARCHIVELOG mode.

The first step is to identify where archive log files will be generated. This location is usually referred to as the archive dump destination or the LOG_ARCHIVE_DEST. The default location is $ORACLE_HOME/admin/*SID*/arch. This might not always be the best location, especially when it is not backed up regularly or is short in space. When choosing a location for the archive log files, consider two factors:

- Any loss of an archive log file will limit recovery to that point.
- If the archive dump destination fills up (no disk space left) or cannot be written to for any reason, the DML activity will "hang" on the database. In addition, new users might not be able to log in to the database.

Usually, you want your archive dump destination to be a very large filesystem reserved exclusively for Oracle. This filesystem should be mirrored and backed up on a regular basis. Preferably there should be a cron job to compress or gzip (either will work) these files automatically. Once they are on-disk, be sure to copy these files to tape or to a writeable CD-ROM, or to FTP them to another machine. If for any reason a file is lost, you need to take a new backup of the database and use that as your baseline because archive log files dated after that missing file are worthless.

Make sure the archive log files' destination is always available. If, for example, your filesystem fills up and Oracle cannot write the archive log file to that location, the database will hang on any DML activity. Normal queries will work, but DML will not be allowed because Oracle cannot archive it. Diagnosis of this problem will also be difficult because errors are not visible to the user, they will only appear in the alert log. Also keep in mind the speed at which files are being compressed or copied off the archive dump destination. I once started a big data load and archive log files were being written very quickly to the archive dump destination. Although we were writing to disk, the writeable CD-ROM could not keep up with moving the files from disk to CD fast enough. We almost hung the database.

To actually put a database into ARCHIVELOG mode, do the following:

1. Edit the init*SID*.ora file to contain the following values:

```
log_archive_start = true
log_archive_dest = "/u01/app/oracle/admin/rh1dev1/arch"
log_archive_format = arch_rh1dev1_%t_%s.arc
```

These parameters will start the ARCH process automatically, define the archive dump destination to $ORACLE_BASE/admin/rh1dev1/arch, and define the naming format of each dump file.

2. Start up the database in mount mode.

```
SQL> startup mount
ORACLE instance started.
```

3. Put the database in ARCHIVELOG mode.

```
SQL> alter database archivelog;

Database altered.
```

4. Verify the status of the database.

```
SQL> alter database archivelog;

Database altered.

SQL> archive log list;
Database log mode              Archive Mode
Automatic archival             Enabled
Archive destination            /u01/app/oracle/admin/rh1dev1/arch
Oldest online log sequence     37
Next log sequence to archive   39
Current log sequence           39
```

5. Open the database for normal use.

```
SQL> alter database open;

Database altered.
```

6. Force a log switch and verify the log has been created in the correct location.

```
SQL> alter system switch logfile;

System altered.

SQL> !ls /u01/app/oracle/admin/rh1dev1/arch
arch_rh1dev1_1_39.arc
```

The log file has the format arch_rh1dev1_*thread#_sequence#*.arc. The thread# only applies to Parallel Server installations in which there is more than one instance. Sequence# identifies the archive log file. For example, this file is given the value 39; the next log will be 40.

That covers the basics of putting a database in ARCHIVELOG mode. The only other parameters to consider are if you want to write archive logs to multiple destinations. The idea is that if one location cannot be written to, valid archive logs will also be written to a backup location. The old parameter was LOG_ARCHIVE_DEST, but now you can specify up to five locations with LOG_ARCHIVE_DEST_[1...5]. Also, successfully writing to each location might be optional or mandatory. These parameters are useful if you must have a high availability system and have plenty of disk space, but most databases do not need this level of protection.

One final note on archive dump destinations: they can be changed while the database is up. For example, if a dump location is filling up and you have another filesystem where they can be stored, this is a valuable option. Just make sure you don't lose any log files by writing to multiple locations. The syntax is as follows:

```
SQL> alter system archive log
  2   to '/ubackup/rh1dev1/arch';
```

## Putting Databases in Hot Backup Mode

Hot (online) backups require the database to be in ARCHIVELOG mode. Next, each tablespace is placed in hot backup mode, which effectively freezes the file header so it cannot change. The files corresponding to that tablespace space are then copied to the backup location. Once this process is completed, the tablespace is taken out of hot backup mode.

While the tablespace is in hot backup mode, normal database activity related to that tablespace can occur, but more redo logs will be generated. The reason is that changes will be logged at the block level, rather than the row level. Thus the increase in redo activity. This will impact performance, which is why hot backups should occur when the database is least active.

Also, there is no requirement to back up every tablespace nor is it required to back up each tablespace sequentially. However, if you can fit each tablespace in a nightly backup, do so. In addition, it is faster to back up each tablespace sequentially than to place all the tablespaces in hot backup mode at once. Remember, unlike cold backups in NOARCHIVELOG mode, you do not need to have data files with matching timestamps. This process restores valid backup copies of each data file (with differing timestamps), and lets the recovery process of applying archive log files bring the data files up to date.

The following steps are needed to back up a tablespace in hot backup mode.

1. Freeze the data file header by putting the tablespace into hot backup mode.

```
SQL> alter tablespace users begin backup;

Tablespace altered.
```

Remember that during this time, normal access to objects in the USERS tablespace is allowed, but at the cost of increased redo activity.

2. Next, use any OS command to copy the data files of the USERS tablespace to your backup location. This can be to disk, tape, or optical media. Also, once the file is copied it can be compressed.

```
SQL> !cp /u04/oradata/rh1dev1/users01.dbf
/ubackup/rh1dev1/hot_backups
```

3. Take the tablespace out of hot backup mode.

```
SQL> alter tablespace users end backup;

Tablespace altered.
```

At this stage, the next tablespace in the database can be backed up using the same procedure. Once all the tablespaces are backed up, perform the following tasks:

1. Back up the control file to a text copy. This will allow you to rebuild the control file if you lose all your control files or need to rebuild them with a different value such as max data files.

```
SQL> alter database backup controlfile to trace;

Database altered.
```

The trace file will be created in the udump location as defined by the parameter USER_DUMP_DEST.

2. Back up a control file to a binary copy. Provide it a location and unique name with a timestamp.

```
SQL> alter database backup controlfile to
  2  '/ubackup/rh1dev1/hot_backups/control.20010422';

Database altered.
```

3. Flush the online redo log files to make sure the changes during backups are archived.

```
SQL> alter system archive log current;

System altered.
```

Obviously, this is a task that is best scripted rather than performed manually. Scripts I've used in the past to dynamically generate the list of tablespaces are located in the appendixes of this book. I recommend testing them in your environment.

Notice that no attempt was made to back up online redo logs. Remember that you only back up online redo logs in cold backups on databases in NOARCHIVELOG mode. Backing up control files is not part of a hot backup per se, but it is logical to back them up at the end of the hot backup.

These steps comprise the fundamentals of taking hot backups. They provide a way to take reliable backups while the database is available. Once files are backed up, they can be used in conjunction with files from a cold backup or from another hot backup to recover the database.

## Recovering from a Crash During Hot Backups

Because it can take several hours to complete hot backups, it is logical to assume that at some point the database will crash during hot backups. If this happens, you cannot simply restart the database. Oracle will attempt to open its data files, will notice a tablespace is in hot backup mode, and will request media recovery for the file. Fortunately, although this is a common failure, it is relatively easy to fix.

In this example, assume the USERS tablespace was in hot backup mode and for whatever reason the machine rebooted. Upon startup, you will need to perform the following actions.

1. You start the database and encounter the following:

```
SQL> startup
ORACLE instance started.

Total System Global Area   128184304 bytes
Fixed Size                     69616 bytes
Variable Size               78413824 bytes
Database Buffers            49152000 bytes
Redo Buffers                  548864 bytes
Database mounted.
ORA-01113: file 5 needs media recovery
ORA-01110: data file 5: '/u04/oradata/rh1dev1/users01.dbf'

SQL>
```

2. Identify the filename needing recovery.

```
SQL> select * from v$recover_file;

    FILE# ONLINE  ERROR            CHANGE# TIME
---------- ------- --------------- ---------- ---------
        5 ONLINE                   247341 22-APR-01

SQL> select name from v$dbfile where file# = 5;
```

```
NAME
-----------------------------------------------
/u04/oradata/rh1dev1/users01.dbf
```

3. Because you know the database was in hot backup mode when it went down, this is not unusual. Simply take the data file out of hot backup mode and open the database.

```
SQL> alter database datafile
  2  '/u04/oradata/rh1dev1/users01.dbf'
  3  end backup;

Database altered.

SQL> alter database open;

Database altered.
```

That is about as simple of a "recovery" as they come. In reality, you didn't recover anything, you just changed the file status so Oracle could use it.

## Recovering from a Lost Data File

Losing a data file should not, by itself, crash the database. It will, however, make its corresponding tablespace inaccessible. Assuming that a valid backup copy is available, via a hot or a cold backup, and that all the archive log files since that backup are available, full recovery is possible. In this example, you will recover the USERS tablespace.

1. Identify that a problem exists. The data dictionary view V$RECOVER_FILE and the alert.log are the two best sources of this information.

```
SQL> select * from v$recover_file;

    FILE# ONLINE  ERROR            CHANGE# TIME
    ------- ------- ---------------- ------- -------
        5 OFFLINE FILE NOT FOUND          0
```

The alert.log shows the following:

```
Sun Apr 22 23:02:21 2001
Errors in file /u01/app/oracle/admin/rh1dev1/bdump/ckpt_9977.trc:
ORA-01171: datafile 5 going offline due to error advancing checkpoint
ORA-01116: error in opening database file 5
ORA-01110: data file 5: '/u04/oradata/rh1dev1/users01.dbf'
ORA-27041: unable to open file
Linux Error: 2: No such file or directory
```

2. At this stage contents of that tablespace are inaccessible. However, depending on the nature of the loss, the file might be listed as OFFLINE under DBA_DATA_FILES or DBA_TABLESPACES.

```
SQL> select * from danw.test_table;
select * from danw.test_table
       *
ERROR at line 1:
ORA-00376: file 5 cannot be read at this time
ORA-01110: data file 5: '/u04/oradata/rh1dev1/users01.dbf'
```

3. Take the corresponding tablespace offline.

```
SQL> alter tablespace users offline temporary;

Tablespace altered.
```

4. Restore the backup to the file that is missing or damaged. If it cannot be restored to that location, rename the file to a different location. In this case, you restore the file from the hot backup location.

```
$ cp /ubackup/rh1dev1/hot_backups/users01.dbf /u04/oradata/rh1dev1/
➥users01.dbf
```

5. Recover the USERS data file by applying archive logs. The simplest way to do this is using ALTER DATABASE RECOVER TABLESPACE AUTOMATIC. In this manner, Oracle will automatically apply the archive log files it needs without prompting the DBA. This assumes each archive log file is in the archive dump destination and is uncompressed.

```
SQL> alter database recover automatic tablespace users;

Database altered.
```

6. Verify the file no longer needs to be recovered and make the tablespace online.

```
SQL> select * from v$recover_file;

no rows selected

SQL> alter tablespace users online;

Tablespace altered.
```

7. Verify objects in that tablespace are available.

```
SQL> select count(*) from danw.test_table;

  COUNT(*)
----------
         1
```

The data file, and therefore the tablespace, is now available. Although only the data file was lost, this example recovered the entire tablespace. This method was selected because potentially you might have to restore several data files from one tablespace. However, the following statement could have been used for step #5.

```
SQL> alter database recover automatic datafile
  2  '/u04/oradata/rh1dev1/users01.dbf';
```

```
Database altered.
```

This recovery is a good example of how Oracle is robust. Although the tablespace was unavailable, the rest of the database remained open. Also note that no data was lost because, between the backup file and the series of archive log files, Oracle was able to reconstruct every change made to any object in the USERS tablespace.

## Recovering from a Lost Temporary or Index Tablespace

Theoretically, if you lose a temporary or index tablespace, you should just have to drop and re-create them. The procedure would be the following:

```
SQL> drop tablespace temp;
```

```
Tablespace dropped.
```

```
SQL> select * from v$recover_file;
```

```
no rows selected
```

```
SQL> create tablespace temp
  2  datafile '/u03/oradata/rh1dev1/temp01.dbf' size 200M
  3  minimum extent 64K
  4  default storage (initial 64K next 64K
  5  minextents 1 maxextents unlimited pctincrease 0)
  6  temporary;
```

```
Tablespace created.
```

The rationale is that because neither temp or index tablespaces contain truly critical data, they can be re-created easier than being recovered. I tend to agree with this when re-creating the temporary tablespace, but not when re-creating an index tablespace.

If you lose an index tablespace, data in the corresponding data tablespace will be accessible as long as indexes are not needed. For example, a full table scan will work, but inserting a new row with a primary key will fail.

```
SQL> insert into test_table values ('c', 3);
insert into test_table values ('c', 3)
            *
ERROR at line 1:
ORA-00376: file 8 cannot be read at this time
ORA-01110: data file 8: '/u08/oradata/rh1dev1/employee_idx02.dbf'
```

If you know which indexes exist in the lost tablespace and have a script to re-create them, this might be the fastest. Using an export .dmp file to create the index file script can be of use here. Otherwise, simply recover the index data file just like any other tablespace.

```
SQL> alter database recover automatic tablespace employee_idx;

Database altered.

SQL> alter tablespace employee_idx online;

Tablespace altered.
```

## Recovering from a Lost Redo Log Member

Losing an online redo log file is not a major problem if it is multiplexed. Theoretically, as long as the member is multiplexed, your database should not go down, although Oracle will issue error messages in the alert log. If, however, you lose an entire group, expect the database to crash. This section assumes that you did wisely multiplex your redo log groups and have at least two members each.

First, before a crisis occurs, let's look at the groups and members. As you can see in the following code, you have three groups of two members each.

```
SQL> select * from v$logfile order by group#;

   GROUP# STATUS   MEMBER
---------- ------- ------------------------------------
        1          /u03/oradata/rh1dev1/redo01a.rdo
        1          /u04/oradata/rh1dev1/redo01b.rdo
        2          /u07/oradata/rh1dev1/redo02a.rdo
        2          /u08/oradata/rh1dev1/redo02b.rdo
        3          /u11/oradata/rh1dev1/redo03a.rdo
        3          /u12/oradata/rh1dev1/redo03b.rdo

6 rows selected.
```

Next, you identify the current log group, which happens to be group 2.

```
SQL> select group#, members, bytes, status, archived
  2  from v$log;

   GROUP#    MEMBERS        BYTES STATUS             ARC
---------- ---------- ------------ ---------------- ---
        1          2   76,800,000 INACTIVE          YES
        2          2   76,800,000 CURRENT           NO
        3          2   76,800,000 INACTIVE          YES
```

If you lose the log file redo01a.rdo suddenly, you would see the following error in the alert log. This error would show up during the redo log switch, which attempts to make group 1 active.

```
Mon Apr 23 08:54:13 2001
Errors in file /u01/app/oracle/admin/rh1dev1/bdump/lgwr_10054.trc:
ORA-00313: open failed for members of log group 1 of thread 1
ORA-00312: online log 1 thread 1: '/u03/oradata/rh1dev1/redo01a.rdo'
ORA-27037: unable to obtain file status
Linux Error: 2: No such file or directory
Additional information: 3
Mon Apr 23 08:54:13 2001
Errors in file /u01/app/oracle/admin/rh1dev1/bdump/lgwr_10054.trc:
ORA-00321: log 1 of thread 1, cannot update log file header
ORA-00312: online log 1 thread 1: '/u03/oradata/rh1dev1/redo01a.rdo'
Mon Apr 23 08:54:13 2001
Errors in file /u01/app/oracle/admin/rh1dev1/bdump/lgwr_10054.trc:
ORA-00313: open failed for members of log group 1 of thread 1
```

At this stage, don't panic because the database is still up. Oracle is just letting you know it's missing a member. The important thing to remember here is to *not* restore a copy of a redo log file from any backup you have. If you do, you will lose whatever data was in the redo log you attempted to "fix." The proper way to address this problem is to drop the missing member and then re-create it in either the same or a different location.

1. Force a log switch so the group missing the file is no longer active. This is necessary because you cannot drop a "current" log member.

    ```
    SQL> alter system switch logfile;

    System altered.

    SQL> select group#, status, members from v$log;

        GROUP# STATUS              MEMBERS
    ---------- ---------------- ----------
             1 INACTIVE                  2
             2 CURRENT                   2
             3 INACTIVE                  2
    ```

2. Drop the missing member.

    ```
    SQL> alter database drop logfile member
      2  '/u03/oradata/rh1dev1/redo01a.rdo';

    Database altered.
    ```

As you can see, group 1 now has only one member.

```
SQL> select * from v$logfile order by group#;
```

```
    GROUP# STATUS  MEMBER
---------- ------- ----------------------------------------
         1         /u04/oradata/rh1dev1/redo01b.rdo
         2         /u07/oradata/rh1dev1/redo02a.rdo
         2         /u08/oradata/rh1dev1/redo02b.rdo
         3         /u11/oradata/rh1dev1/redo03a.rdo
/u12/oradata/rh1dev1/redo03b.rdo
```

3. Add the missing member back to group 1. This can be either to the same location or to a different location.

```
SQL> alter database add logfile member
  2  '/u03/oradata/rh1dev1/redo01a.rdo' to group 1;
Database altered.
```

4. Once the log file member has been added, it will show up as INVALID. Do not worry about this; cycle through several redo log switches to make the file valid.

```
SQL> select * from v$logfile where group# = 1;
    GROUP# STATUS  MEMBER
---------- ------- ----------------------------------------
         1 INVALID /u03/oradata/rh1dev1/redo01a.rdo
         1         /u04/oradata/rh1dev1/redo01b.rdo

SQL> alter system switch logfile;

System altered.
```

That covers the basic recovery process for online redo log files. As long as you do not lose an entire group or try to restore a redo log from a backup, recovery should be fairly simple.

## Recovering from Lost Control Files

If you lose a control file, your database will need to go down. Sometimes an instance will survive for a while before it crashes, but users will experience problems. The best solution is to issue a SHUTDOWN ABORT and then restore the control file. Although you might have lost a control file, as long as you still have a good copy of a control file, you have two very easy recovery options.

The easiest way to recover this is to edit the config*SID*.ora or init*SID*.ora files to only include the good control files. For example, if control file #2 was lost, simply remove it from the list of control files that are read during database startup.

```
control_files = ("/u01/app/oracle/oradata/rh1tst1/control01.ctl",
➥"/u03/oradata/rh1tst1/control03.ctl")
```

Then start the database as normal. V$CONTROLFILE will now show only the existing database files; you can continue with normal business.

A better long-term option is to replace the bad control file with a good control file. To do so, follow these steps:

1. Make sure the database is shut down, although in most cases it has already crashed.

2. Remove the damaged control file if it still exists. This delete is redundant, but it prevents you from accidentally copying the wrong file.

3. Copy (using `cp`) a good control file to the location of the bad or missing control file. Notice that you do not use `mv` because you do want to keep the good copy in its current location.

4. Rename (using `mv`) the restored control file to the name as listed in the `configSID.ora` or `initSID.ora` files.

5. Restart the database normally. Oracle will acknowledge the file's existence in V$CONTROLFILE and normal operations can continue.

If, however, you lose all your control files, recovery is much more difficult. Hopefully you had included `ALTER DATABASE BACKUP CONTROLFILE TO TRACE` in your hot backup scripts so you have a file to work with. You have to re-create a control file in order to recover the database; a task well outside the scope of this book. Help from Oracle Support is recommended in this case.

## Recovering from a Combination of Lost Files

The chapter has covered the basics of losing individual data, online redo logs, and control files. Individually, the recovery for each file is fairly simple as long as you have good backups and multiplex your control and online redo log files. Unfortunately, however, disk crashes seldom take just one file with them. Normally, you will lose several files at once and this complicates the recovery. This section looks at a sample recovery of a control file, an online redo log file, a SYSTEM tablespace, and an INDEX tablespace.

Assume a disk goes bad and you lose `/u02`.

```
$ ls /u02/oradata/rh1dev1
control02.ctl  employee_idx01.dbf  redo03b.rdo  system01.dbf
```

Because you lose both a control file and the SYSTEM tablespace, the database will crash.

This problem requires an offline database recovery. You need to restore and recover the files in the following order:

1. Restore the control file.

2. Restore the SYSTEM tablespace. Because you are restoring anyway, it's a good idea to include the INDEX tablespace in this step.

3. Drop the online redo log file. This will be re-created once the database is restored.

Recover the database by following these steps:

1. Make sure the database is shut down and all background processes are down. If the instance is still up despite the damage, use a SHUTDOWN ABORT.

2. Restore the control file. Copy the good control file from /u01 to /u02 and give it the name specified in the init.ora.

3. Restore the missing data files for the SYSTEM and INDEX tablespaces from the most recent valid backups. These can be from a cold or a hot backup, but the more recent the copy, the faster the database will recover. Also make sure that all the archive log files since those backups are restored to the archive dump destination and are uncompressed.

4. Log in to SQL*Plus, connect internal, and set autorecovery option on.

```
$ sqlplus internal

SQL*Plus: Release 8.1.6.0.0 - Production on Mon Apr 23 10:28:33 2001

(c) Copyright 1999 Oracle Corporation.  All rights reserved.

Connected to an idle instance.

SQL> set autorecovery on
```

5. Start the database in mount mode to allocate the SGA and open the control files. This step recovers the missing control file.

```
SQL> startup restrict mount;
ORACLE instance started.

Total System Global Area   128184304 bytes
Fixed Size                     69616 bytes
Variable Size               78413824 bytes
Database Buffers            49152000 bytes
Redo Buffers                  548864 bytes
Database mounted.
SQL>
```

6. Identify the missing/damaged data files.

```
SQL> select * from v$recover_file;

     FILE# ONLINE   ERROR            CHANGE# TIME
---------- -------  ------------- ---------- --------
         1 ONLINE                    288346 23-APR-01
         7 ONLINE                    288348 23-APR-01

SQL> select * from v$dbfile where file# in (1,7);
```

9

BACKUP AND
RECOVERY

```
      FILE# NAME
---------- ---------------------------------------
          1 /u02/oradata/rh1dev1/system01.dbf
          7 /u02/oradata/rh1dev1/employee_idx01.dbf
```

7. Identify the missing redo log file. Depending on the situation, the missing online redo log member might be identified as INVALID. You know, however, that because /u02 was completely lost, the member on that filesystem is also lost. The solution is to drop it and recover it after the database is opened. If Oracle complains that the file is a member of the active group and will not let you drop it, that is also okay, but you need to drop it after the next redo log switch.

```
SQL> select * from v$logfile;

    GROUP# STATUS  MEMBER
---------- ------- --------------------------------------------
         1         /u03/oradata/rh1dev1/redo01a.rdo
         2         /u07/oradata/rh1dev1/redo02a.rdo
         3         /u11/oradata/rh1dev1/redo03a.rdo
         3         /u02/oradata/rh1dev1/redo03b.rdo
         2         /u08/oradata/rh1dev1/redo02b.rdo
         1         /u04/oradata/rh1dev1/redo01b.rdo

6 rows selected.

SQL> alter database drop logfile member
  2  '/u02/oradata/rh1dev1/redo03b.rdo';

Database altered.
```

8. Recover the database automatically. This will cause Oracle to apply whatever archive log files are needed to bring the missing data files up to date. Because you set auto recovery on, the statement RECOVER DATABASE will apply the redo logs automatically. If you forgot to set autorecovery on, type AUTO at the archive log prompt.

```
SQL> recover database;
ORA-00279: change 288346 generated at 04/23/2001 09:55:39 needed for thread 1
ORA-00289: suggestion :
/u01/app/oracle/admin/rh1dev1/arch/arch_rh1dev1_1_101.arc
ORA-00280: change 288346 for thread 1 is in sequence #101

ORA-00279: change 288351 generated at 04/23/2001 10:16:58 needed for thread 1
ORA-00289: suggestion :
/u01/app/oracle/admin/rh1dev1/arch/arch_rh1dev1_1_102.arc
ORA-00280: change 288351 for thread 1 is in sequence #102
ORA-00278: log file '/u01/app/oracle/admin/rh1dev1/arch/
➥arch_rh1dev1_1_101.arc'
no longer needed for this recovery
```

```
ORA-00279: change 288352 generated at 04/23/2001 10:17:08 needed for thread 1
ORA-00289: suggestion :
/u01/app/oracle/admin/rh1dev1/arch/arch_rh1dev1_1_103.arc
ORA-00280: change 288352 for thread 1 is in sequence #103
ORA-00278: log file '/u01/app/oracle/admin/rh1dev1/arch/
➥arch_rh1dev1_1_102.arc'
no longer needed for this recovery

Log applied.
Media recovery complete.
SQL>
```

9. At this stage the database is "recovered," but you still need to open the database and re-create the missing redo log file. Disregard messages that state that the other redo logs are STALE; they will change status after a few redo log switches.

```
SQL> alter database open;

Database altered.

SQL> select * from v$recover_file;

no rows selected

SQL> select * from v$logfile order by group#;

    GROUP# STATUS  MEMBER
---------- ------- ----------------------------------------
         1 STALE   /u03/oradata/rh1dev1/redo01a.rdo
         1 STALE   /u04/oradata/rh1dev1/redo01b.rdo
         2         /u07/oradata/rh1dev1/redo02a.rdo
         2         /u08/oradata/rh1dev1/redo02b.rdo
         3         /u11/oradata/rh1dev1/redo03a.rdo

SQL> alter database add logfile member
  2  '/u02/oradata/rh1dev1/redo3b.rdo' to group 3;

Database altered.

SQL> alter system switch logfile;

System altered.
```

10. At this stage, the database is ready to be reopened for business. However, the smart thing to do is make a cold backup before proceeding. If, however, management demands the database be reopened, disable the restricted mode.

```
SQL> alter system disable restricted session;

System altered.
```

9

BACKUP AND
RECOVERY

The preceding example is one scenario of the events following a real disk crash. It was based on the assumption that the disk for /u02 filesystem was repaired by the SA and the files where properly restored. Also, notice how you knew what files where on /u02. It is important to have a cron job dynamically generate a list of every data, control, and redo log file in the database everyday. This way, you will know the impact when the SA informs you that /u02, is gone. Ideally, you will have documented and practiced your recovery procedures for a loss of /u02 before it occurs. This recovery plan should be stored next to plans for losses of /u01 through /u12. Because these types of recoveries can be complicated, it's important that you practice them *before* they occur.

Finally, if a situation occurs for which you have not prepared or which do not fully understand, call Oracle Support for assistance. Advanced backup and recovery techniques are well outside the scope of this book. If I need a tablespace point in time recovery or am encountering truly unusual errors, I will call support for help. Documentation on advanced recoveries is available, but like the emergency-room analogy, it is important to know when to ask for help. There are many tools and techniques Oracle Support has that the general public does not. Believe me, I know DBAs who have learned this lesson the hard way.

## Backup of Software and Parameter Files

The SA can back up Oracle software and database parameter files (such as tnsnames.ora) as part of a normal server backup. These files can be treated as any other normal file and there is no particular "state" or timestamp needed for them. If the OFA standard is followed and these files are placed on /u01 without any physical database files, the backup process is very simple. The SA might include /u01 with the backups of the rest of the non-Oracle filesystems.

Restoring the Oracle installation and database parameter files is just as simple as restoring any normal file. For example, assume that OFA is followed and /u01 is lost. The SA can replace the disk and copy /u01 restore from any valid backup. The DBA simply restarts the database and no special database recovery should be needed.

The only potential issue is when the database is in ARCHIVELOG mode. Be aware that if you are archiving your redo logs to /u01/app/oracle/admin/*SID*/arch (also standard OFA) and one or more is missing, they will not be restored because they were generated after the /u01 backup. The ramification is if they are later needed for a recovery, the recovery will stop at the last continuous log file. Remember, Oracle will not skip over a gap in archive log files during recovery. One solution is to take a full backup (preferably cold) after a recovery of /u01. An even better solution is to place your archive log files on a dedicated filesystem that is backed up very frequently.

> **TIP**
>
> Take a Backup After a Recovery
>
> Most prudent DBAs will take a full cold backup after *any* recovery just in case further problems develop. This can be a touchy situation if down time has already occurred and management wants the system up ASAP, but a backup is the responsible action to take.

## Comprehensive Planning and Testing

Now that you have identified how to implement different levels of backups, this section looks at ways they can be integrated to provide protection for a real system.

## Planning

First, look at the backup and recovery options available. You can use logical backups (exports), physical backups, or both. If your system has developers or users with access to SQL*Plus, logical backups are a good idea in case someone accidentally corrupts data. In fact, the only cases in which logical backups are a bad idea is in systems that are so large or changing so fast that any export would be hopelessly outdated by the time it is applied. For most systems, however, taking a nightly export is normally a good idea as long as there is sufficient disk space.

Because all databases are prone to hardware loss, physical backups seem necessary. The only exception is when it's easier to apply a logical backup to a new or different database than it is to restore and recover the old database. The only candidates I've seen that fall into this category are training and development databases.

Assuming physical backups are implemented, the next major decision is whether to choose ARCHIVELOG mode or NOARCHIVELOG mode. Pros and cons of each method are described, as well as recommendations, in the following table.

|  | *NOARCHIVELOG* Mode | *ARCHIVELOG* Mode |
|---|---|---|
| Online Redo Logs Archived | No | Yes |
| Overhead of Maintaining Archive Log Files | No | Yes |
| Point In Time Recovery Possible? | No | Yes |
| Cold (offline) Backups | Yes | Yes |
| Hot (online) Backups | No | Yes |
| Suitable for Production Systems? | No | Yes |
| Suitable for Non-Production Systems | Yes | Yes |

Next, examine the type of system you are supporting. The key questions are: Is it a production system? What is the acceptable down time? What is the acceptable data loss?

If a system is a training or development system, it probably does not need to be up 7×24 with point-in-time recovery. Therefore, NOARCHIVELOG mode is probably acceptable. Exports can be taken each night and every night the database can also be shut down for a cold backup. If a failure occurs, the database can be restored to the state of the previous evening. For development and training, this is usually sufficient.

Production databases normally require a higher level of protection. Any data loss usually translates to lost revenue and they normally also have higher availability requirements. This means ARCHIVELOG mode is a requirement. Depending on the business, the database might be able to be shut down for cold backups only once a week or even less often. This means hot backups will be required.

The following table shows a backup schedule of one shop I worked at that had relatively high uptime requirements:

| Day | Cold Backup | Hot Backup | Schema Export |
|---|---|---|---|
| Sunday | Yes: 9 PM | No | No |
| Monday | No | Yes: 9 PM | Yes: 12:30 AM |
| Tuesday | No | Yes: 9 PM | Yes: 12:30 AM |
| Wednesday | No | Yes: 9 PM | Yes: 12:30 AM |
| Thursday | No | Yes: 9 PM | Yes: 12:30 AM |
| Friday | No | Yes: 9 PM | Yes: 12:30 AM |
| Saturday | No | Yes: 9 PM | Yes: 12:30 AM |

This shop had people on the database from 7AM–12AM Monday thru Saturday. On Sunday, people went home at 9PM because there was little business on Sundays. When people were not working, batch jobs were being executed, but those did not change the data in the main schema.

In this situation, I could shut down the database Sunday night, take a cold backup, and still have enough time to restart the database and run the batch jobs that were relatively small. During the rest of the week people were on the system until midnight so I could not shut down the database, but I could start hot backups at 9PM because there was considerably less activity. At 12:30AM I knew for sure no one would be changing the transactional data so I kicked off a schema level export. Batch jobs proceeded, but were not severely impacted by the hot backups and they did not impact the export.

This scenario provided pretty good protection for most failures. If a disk went bad and files needed recovery, a maximum of one day of archive logs needed to be applied because either hot or cold backups were taken each night. If a logical error occurred, the schema level export provided a level of protection. In the event of a catastrophic failure, we always had a cold backup and schema level exports. Of course, all this was automated via cron and tapes were taken offsite on a daily basis.

## Testing

At another site I worked at, I was the first DBA to build the infrastructure. That meant everything was built from scratch and had to be tested before we went "live".

---

**NOTE**

**Try Working at a Startup**

From a career standpoint, if you ever have the opportunity to work at a new company, you should consider it. Few experiences are as enjoyable or as educational as working at a new IT company. You can expect to work some long hours initially, but the experience you gain is valuable.

---

I planned and built the database, put it in ARCHIVELOG mode, and implemented a mix of physical and logical backups. Because this site had to be available often, but was not yet in production, real testing was possible. The System Administrator and myself simulated each type of failure that was *likely* for our site. I documented my recovery procedures for each event and then tested them under real conditions. Not only did we find what worked and what didn't, we knew exactly how long it would take to restore the system for each type of failure. By the time we went live, the system was already backed up and the recovery procedures were documented so almost anyone could perform a recovery.

That is the way a system *should* be prepared. Unfortunately, that level of testing is normally not possible because it is rare to be on site before a system is live. Furthermore, the system, the requirements, and the technical staff change over time so your backup and recovery procedures need to be continually updated and tested.

If you do come to a site where backup and recovery standards have been established, it is your responsibility to test them. Testing verifies that the procedures are valid and familiarizes you with the procedures, the system, and the technical staff. Remember, testing is the only way to verify that a backup and recovery plan is valid.

**9**

**BACKUP AND RECOVERY**

# Conclusion

Database backup and recovery is a critical skill. If a database or data is lost, the ramifications are often significant. Every DBA will face a backup or recovery situation at some point in their career; therefore, it is best to learn what to do before a crisis occurs.

The chapter primarily focused on physical backups and recoveries. You learned that it's best to multiplex control and online redo log files in order to add a level of fault tolerance. Most production databases are in ARCHIVELOG mode because that promises the highest levels of uptime and recoverability. Next, the chapter covered the most common types of failures and how to recover from them. The steps described here should be used merely as templates on how to recover; there is no substitute for performing practice recoveries on your own system. Also, if you have *any* doubt about what you are doing, call Oracle Support because recoveries are too important to chance. Finally, the chapter discussed how to plan backups and the need to test recoveries. If no other point is taken from this chapter, let it be the need to continually practice and test your recovery plans.

# When Things Go Wrong

## ESSENTIALS

- When problems are reported, you should identify the who, what, when, why, how, and the impact of the problem.

- Check the server for obvious problems such as full filesystems, high system usage, and recent crashes and reboots.

- Managing data file locations, names, and sizes is a common DBA task.

- Locking problems within the database can be identified via scripts or GUI tools and then the blocking sessions can be terminated.

- ORA-01555 Snapshot too old **errors occur when Oracle cannot find a read-consistent image of the data.**

Problem-solving is one of the most important skills you need as a DBA. No matter how well your system is planned and implemented, problems will occur from time to time. These can be technical issues, or they can be business or human problems manifesting themselves into a technical problem. Often, the DBA is called to investigate a "database error" that is really a symptom of a more serious problem with an application, server, or network. Nevertheless, the DBA is often the person to diagnose a problem and begin developing a solution. Problem solving is often made more difficult because many sites have an associated dollar value for each hour of system downtime.

This chapter covers situations that normally start with "Help, the database is broken." It discusses what to do from a system perspective once problems are reported and identifies places to initially look. Then, it discusses the more common database problems involving file management, locking, rollback segments.

# Responding to Problems

It is quite common for users to call the DBA and claim that the database is down. First of all, don't panic. Normally there is some type of technical problem, but most times the database has *not* crashed. In fact, quite often, there is nothing wrong with the database per se; rather, the users cannot access their data. Regardless of the cause, the DBA must step in and determine the problem.

## Information Gathering

Before diving into a reported problem, the DBA needs to gather some basic information. This process relies as much on personal skills as it does technical skills. Unfortunately, when problems do occur, people often become frantic and act without thinking. As an administrator, you will receive these calls and must piece together an accurate picture of the situation. The standard series of questions—who, what, when, why, and how—are good places to start when diagnosing problems. Also, identify the impact of the problem.

- **Who** First, identify who the user is. Of equal importance, identify whom the user is trying to log in as. If the "who" is a process or job having problems, identify the owner of that job.

- **What** Next, clarify exactly which system is perceived as having problems. Exact server names (if known) and the error messages are very important. Often, a screen shot of the error message can be most helpful.

- **When** Find out when the problem occurred. Is it a current crisis? Or is it something intermittent, such as batch jobs failing? Also, how long has this problem been noticed? This is particularly important information because it allows you to search for anything that has changed that might be causing the problem. Finally, ask if this problem has happened before and, if so, how it was resolved.

- **Why** Ask why the user thinks there is a problem. Often, people think there is a problem even when the system is doing exactly what it is supposed to be doing. For example, if a user is getting the message "Invalid Password Login Denied," that is causing problems for the user but is not necessarily a system error. Also, end users are often the last people to know when a system will be modified or shut down.

- **How** Find out under what circumstances the problem is occurring. It is important to push for details here. Often, frustrated users will omit information they think is irrelevant, but is truly critical. If you can see the problem first-hand, this is best. Otherwise get as much step-by-step information as possible because often it is necessary to recreate a problem before solving it.

- **Impact** Ascertain whether this is a major problem worth working on all night or whether it is a minor inconvenience on a less important system. Do not ignore problems just because they are small, but do prioritize your problems according to impact.

In most real situations, you won't have the luxury of getting all this information, but it is a good goal. Sometimes by asking the user questions about the problem, a resolution appears. Other times, asking questions will resolve miscommunication issues, which can cause as much trouble as any technical error.

---

### Which "System" is Really Down?

I once had a user claim "the system," was down which sends shivers down the spine of any administrator. However, further questioning identified the user as the head of the training department and "the system" was really a tiny training database. It was during this time the main user schema was being imported so the database was in restricted mode. Had I just taken the report that "the system" was down at face value and started acting, I would have made the problem worse.

Remember; don't assume that you are on the same wavelength as the user. During crises, people often get excited and the chances of a costly miscommunication increase.

---

Hopefully, you'll have at least an idea of how the problem is appearing to the users and its frequency. From there, you can begin tracking it down from a technical perspective.

## Problem Identification at the System Level

Most technical problems originate from the database, the server, the network, or an application. However, a problem with any one of these elements normally impacts the performance of the entire system. If the DBA is called, it is normally because someone thinks it is a database issue, but in many cases it is not. It is up to you to look at the system as a whole and determine the real cause so you can fix it.

You need to understand the basic architecture of the system in order to be effective at diagnosing problems outside the database. A simple diagram outlining each server, its purpose, and what it connects to is very useful. This visually identifies all the pieces that can break; therefore each component can be individually checked. Figure 10.1 identifies the components of this system and what can break.

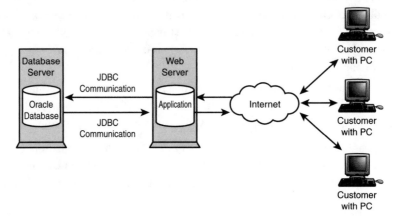

**FIGURE 10.1**

*Basic Architecture Diagram.*

For example, consider a database on a dedicated Unix server. The only connection into the database server is a Web server. The Web server contains the application code and connects to the Internet, which is how users access the system.

In a simple case like this, it's best to begin diagnosing the problem with the database and then work your way outward until you find the problem. First, make sure the Unix server is up. Next, make sure the database is running and users can connect to it. After you're sure your piece (the database server) is okay, start looking at the other components in the system. Verify that the Web server is up and that it is "talking" to the database server. Then check that the application on the Web server is running properly. Finally, look at the connections from the Internet into the Web server. If you reach this point without finding the cause of a problem, go back to examine each piece in more detail or look for something not represented on the diagram.

Although this is a conceptually simple example, it illustrates  an effective way to break big problems into small problems. Too many people only look at their piece of the pie and do not understand how it fits in the system as a whole. Each system is unique and has different points of possible failure that should be identified before they occur. Ideally, you have already done this during the initial system-design phase.

**TIP**

Benefits of an Architecture Diagram

Not only is this method good for diagnosing problems, it is a good way to look at performance tuning. By identifying bottlenecks at the system level, you can apply limited tuning resources to the areas where they will have the largest impact.

# Identifying Technical Problems

This section examines how to quickly identify obvious problems with the server, database, and applications. Use these methods only as a starting point. Each system has its own quirks and common problems that need to be identified differently. Remember, Unix and Linux systems tend to be highly customized and you, as an administrator, need to be aware of this. However, the following sections discuss common areas I have learned to check over the years. Don't necessarily go down each list sequentially either; use whatever combination of checks makes sense for *your* system given the nature of the reported problem.

## Server-Related Checks

When I receive a call that something is wrong with the system, I initially check the status of the server. For the most part, I include the network in this category as well. At this stage, look for anything that might be hindering the normal function or accessibility to the database, at a Unix server level. Verify that the Unix/Linux servers are available and running normally. Attempt to establish connectivity.

- Ping the box to establish basic connectivity. If this fails, contact the SA. Figure 10.2 shows there is connectivity to the machine. An IP address is used here, but if you have a DNS alias, be sure to test it also.

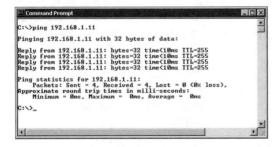

**FIGURE 10.2**

*Ping the Server.*

- Determine whether the Unix/Linux server is up. Try to log in to the machine with a simple Telnet window. If you cannot log in here, there is either a network or a server problem.

- See how long it has been since the server was rebooted.

```
$ uptime
  5:35pm  up 2 days,  5:22,  2 users,  load average: 0.00, 0.00, 0.00
```

In this case, you can see it has been two days since the box was down. If you notice it is only a matter of minutes, the problem probably stems from the server rebooting/crashing.

- If the machine has been rebooted or crashed, investigate this further. Use `dmesg | more` to see its boot messages. Other files worth seeing are /var/adm/messages and /var/log/syslog. This is SA territory, but by examining these files, you might be able to identify obvious problems.

- Determine who else is using the server. Depending on the system architecture, this might not be a valid indicator of problems. Look for any unusually high or low numbers.

```
$ who
oracle    tty1      Apr 22 17:22
oracle    pts/1     Apr 23 18:55
```

- Determine whether the system is being stressed more than usual. If a large, resource-intensive job is running, it might not be a problem per se, but it might be impacting user response time. This is particularly true when the server is being used to support more than just Oracle. Also look for runaway processes accumulating large amounts of CPU time.

  System-monitoring tools are covered in detail in Chapter 13, "Unix Server Monitoring," but one tool you can use to get a quick snapshot of the system is `top`. Figure 10.3 shows a small load on the server.

- Check for normal processes or locked files on the system. These are site-specific, but they include listeners, cron jobs, and any other process that is required for the system to perform its normal function. Ideally, you will know your system well enough to tell whether a process is missing. For example, one site I worked at had a home-grown replication routine and listener that had to be running. I learned to add that to my list of system checks. By the same token, also determine whether something is running that is out of place, such as a backup in the middle of the day.

- Pay particular attention to the response time from the command line. If it is noticeably slow, the server may be stressed or, more likely, the network is having performance problems. If you issue a command such as `ls` or `cd` and the command hangs, there is likely either a disk problem or a filesystem has become unmounted.

- The final check I normally do on a server is to determine whether any filesystems are filled up. Filesystems at 100% are immediately suspect, especially when they contain Oracle archive log files. Any other filesystem in the mid to high 90s is also investigated.

If you notice that available disk space suddenly decreases, determine whether it contains the cdump directory for any database. Often, a core dump resulting from a failed process is the culprit. Use either `bdf` (on HP-UX) or `df -k` to check on available space, as Figure 10.4 shows.

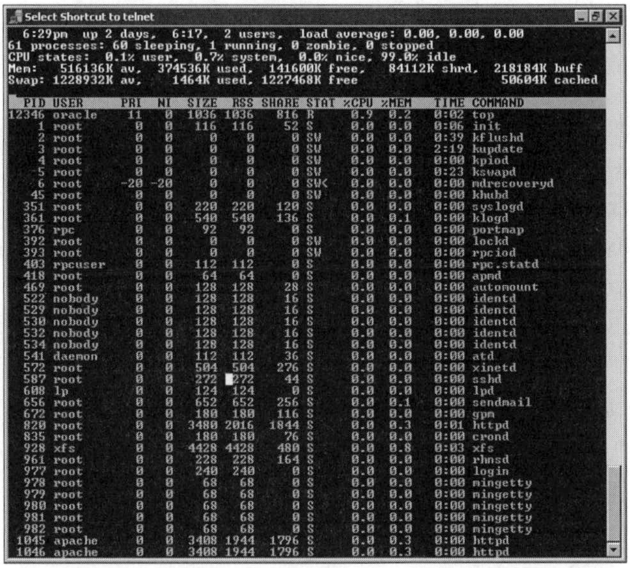

```
Select Shortcut to telnet
  6:29pm  up 2 days,  6:17,  2 users,  load average: 0.00, 0.00, 0.00
61 processes: 60 sleeping, 1 running, 0 zombie, 0 stopped
CPU states:  0.1% user,  0.7% system,  0.0% nice, 99.0% idle
Mem:   516136K av,  374536K used,  141600K free,   84112K shrd,  218184K buff
Swap: 1228932K av,    1464K used, 1227468K free                   50604K cached

  PID USER     PRI  NI  SIZE  RSS SHARE STAT %CPU %MEM   TIME COMMAND
12346 oracle    11   0  1036 1036   816 R     0.9  0.2   0:02 top
    1 root       0   0   116  116    52 S     0.0  0.0   0:06 init
    2 root       0   0     0    0     0 SW    0.0  0.0   0:39 kflushd
    3 root       0   0     0    0     0 SW    0.0  0.0   2:19 kupdate
    4 root       0   0     0    0     0 SW    0.0  0.0   0:00 kpiod
    5 root       0   0     0    0     0 SW    0.0  0.0   0:23 kswapd
    6 root     -20 -20     0    0     0 SW<   0.0  0.0   0:00 mdrecoveryd
   45 root       0   0     0    0     0 SW    0.0  0.0   0:00 khubd
  351 root       0   0   220  220   120 S     0.0  0.0   0:00 syslogd
  361 root       0   0   540  540   136 S     0.0  0.1   0:00 klogd
  376 rpc        0   0    92   92     0 S     0.0  0.0   0:00 portmap
  392 root       0   0     0    0     0 SW    0.0  0.0   0:00 lockd
  393 root       0   0     0    0     0 SW    0.0  0.0   0:00 rpciod
  403 rpcuser    0   0   112  112     0 S     0.0  0.0   0:00 rpc.statd
  418 root       0   0    64   64     0 S     0.0  0.0   0:00 apmd
  469 root       0   0   128  128    28 S     0.0  0.0   0:00 automount
  522 nobody     0   0   128  128    16 S     0.0  0.0   0:00 identd
  529 nobody     0   0   128  128    16 S     0.0  0.0   0:00 identd
  530 nobody     0   0   128  128    16 S     0.0  0.0   0:00 identd
  532 nobody     0   0   128  128    16 S     0.0  0.0   0:00 identd
  534 nobody     0   0   128  128    16 S     0.0  0.0   0:00 identd
  541 daemon     0   0   112  112    36 S     0.0  0.0   0:00 atd
  572 root       0   0   504  504   276 S     0.0  0.0   0:00 xinetd
  587 root       0   0   272  272    44 S     0.0  0.0   0:00 sshd
  608 lp         0   0   124  124     0 S     0.0  0.0   0:00 lpd
  656 root       0   0   652  652   256 S     0.0  0.1   0:00 sendmail
  672 root       0   0   180  180   116 S     0.0  0.0   0:00 gpm
  820 root       0   0  3480 2016  1844 S     0.0  0.3   0:01 httpd
  835 root       0   0   180  180    76 S     0.0  0.0   0:00 crond
  928 xfs        0   0  4428 4428   480 S     0.0  0.8   0:03 xfs
  961 root       0   0   228  228   164 S     0.0  0.0   0:00 rhnsd
  977 root       0   0   240  240     0 S     0.0  0.0   0:00 login
  978 root       0   0    68   68     0 S     0.0  0.0   0:00 mingetty
  979 root       0   0    68   68     0 S     0.0  0.0   0:00 mingetty
  980 root       0   0    68   68     0 S     0.0  0.0   0:00 mingetty
  981 root       0   0    68   68     0 S     0.0  0.0   0:00 mingetty
  982 root       0   0    68   68     0 S     0.0  0.0   0:00 mingetty
 1045 apache     0   0  3408 1944  1796 S     0.0  0.3   0:00 httpd
 1046 apache     0   0  3408 1944  1796 S     0.0  0.3   0:00 httpd
```

**FIGURE 10.3**

*Use `top` to Get an Overview of Performance.*

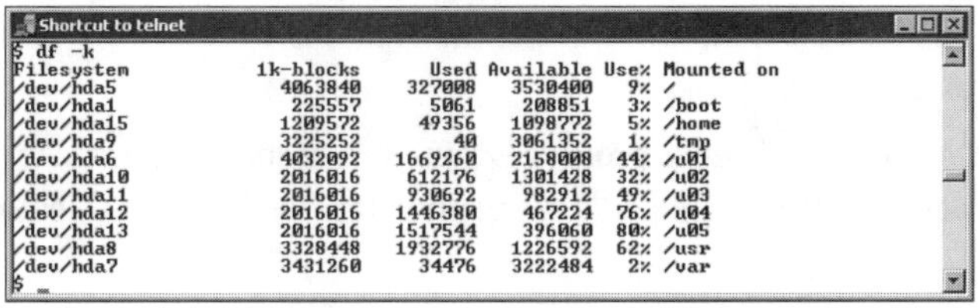

```
Shortcut to telnet
$ df -k
Filesystem           1k-blocks      Used Available Use% Mounted on
/dev/hda5              4063840    327008   3530400   9% /
/dev/hda1               225557      5061    208851   3% /boot
/dev/hda15             1209572     49356   1098772   5% /home
/dev/hda9              3225252        40   3061352   1% /tmp
/dev/hda6              4032092   1669260   2158008  44% /u01
/dev/hda10             2016016    612176   1301428  32% /u02
/dev/hda11             2016016    930692    982912  49% /u03
/dev/hda12             2016016   1446380    467224  76% /u04
/dev/hda13             2016016   1517544    396060  80% /u05
/dev/hda8              3328448   1932776   1226592  62% /usr
/dev/hda7              3431260     34476   3222484   2% /var
$ _
```

**FIGURE 10.4**

*Check for Full Filesystems.*

- If the Unix/Linux server is "average," the initial check for problems can stop here. However, if you are running a more advanced or complicated system, look further. For example, in a cluster, check the status of each node and the communications between them. If there are any site-specific quirks, consider these to be potential problems.

Unless the DBA has the root password, only the SA can fix most of the server problems. However, the more preliminary information the DBA can provide, the more likely the problem can be solved quickly.

## Database

Once you have verified that the Unix/Linux server is up and functional, turn your attention to the database. Many problems with the database fall into the following categories:

- Users cannot access the database as they expect. Usually, the database is down, a listener is not started, or there is a tnsnames/username/password issue.

- Users are not getting the results they expect in an acceptable timeframe. This is usually either a locking issue or a performance issue.

- An unanticipated change occurred at the schema level, which impacts the application. Often, objects are invalidated, or an object or grant is dropped.

- Routine database maintenance is needed. Perhaps tablespaces need more space, rollback segments need to be larger, or SGA or init.ora parameters need to be modified.

Most of what is checked is a repeat of the normal checks performed each morning. However, if the problem is with the database it will likely show up with the following checks:

- Determine whether the instance is running. Specifically, look for a required background process such as Process Monitor (PMON).

```
$ ps -ef | grep -i pmon
oracle   11385    1  0 Apr23 ?   00:00:00 ora_pmon_rh1dev1
```

  It is a near certainty that if PMON is up, the entire database instance is also up. If PMON is not running in the background, users will likely get an error ORA-01034 ORACLE not available. This is a clear sign that either the database is down or ORACLE_SID is set to a bogus value.

- Verify that the database listener process is running. A common mistake is to start a database, but forget to start the listener. The result is the database is up, but no one outside the box can connect to it.

- Either use ps -ef to search for the listener process or issue lsnrctl -status. Sometimes it is necessary to stop a listener, kill its dangling Unix process, and restart it if there were problems with the process.

- Check the user's tnsnames.ora file. These files are often managed by the users themselves, which make them prone to error. The problem is magnified by the fact that a PC or laptop often has a different tnsnames.ora file for each Oracle tool. Many end users do not know this. They might correctly configure tnsnames for one tool, but have problems connecting to another tool.

- Use `tail` to view the end of the alert*SID*.log file located in the database bdump directory. Do this multiple times daily whether or not problems are reported. The alert log contains the vital information a DBA needs to diagnose and solve database problems. Any serious errors encountered by Oracle will be reported in this file; you should investigate them all. The importance of checking the alert log cannot be overstressed, particularly when problems are reported.

- Force several redo log switches using `ALTER SYSTEM SWITCH LOGFILE`. Then check the alert log and the view `V$RECOVER_FILE` for any errors or files needing media recovery. If the database hangs during the log switches, determine whether the archive dump destination is accessible.

- Log into the database and determine how many user sessions exist. Note any particularly small or large numbers. If very few people are logged in, look at connectivity issues. A usually large number of logins can cause degraded performance because of stress on the system. A high number of logins can be caused by users being disconnected and logging back in.

- Check for database locks. Oracle is normally pretty good at handling locking. However, if the application is poorly written or if a user updated a row and never committed the change, locking problems can occur.

- Make sure each tablespace has an acceptable amount of free space available. If the view `DBA_FREE_SPACE` shows a low value for a tablespace, either add a new data file or resize the current files. Otherwise, users will get errors stating that Oracle cannot allocate another extent when a segment needs to grow. These errors also show up in the alert log.

  A problem related to this is the storage parameter MAXEXTENTS. If a table, index, or rollback segment was created without MAXEXTENTS being set to UNLIMITED, the value can be reached. If so, alter the object to increase the number of extents.

- Make sure that no tablespaces or data files are offline. Check the status column of `DBA_DATA_FILES` and `DBA_TABLESPACES`. Normally, nothing should be taken offline without a good reason and the DBA should be aware if this occurs.

- Look for `ORA-01555 Snapshot too old` rollback segment errors. These are discussed later in this chapter.

- Check for invalid objects (packages, procedures, triggers, and so on) within the database. Pay particular attention to the schemas owning application-related tables or PL/SQL. It is a common mistake to alter one object and accidentally invalidate others. If the DBA or developer is not in the habit of checking for this, the problem can snowball.

- Use dynamic SQL to create scripts to recompile invalid objects. Ideally, the DBA will have prepared scripts to generate the recompilation code before a problem occurs.

**10**

WHEN THINGS
GO WRONG

- Determine whether any application schema object or grant has been added, dropped, or modified. Tables, indexes, sequences, synonyms, and database links are frequently changed in development and testing environments. Also, necessary grants can sometimes be accidentally dropped and not reapplied in these environments.

- Determine whether anyone has changed the `init.ora`. If, for example, someone made a typo while changing a parameter, database activities can occur. Or, the intended change itself can cause problems. This is particularly common in larger shops in which multiple DBAs aren't communicating their changes to each other.

  Just as with any database file, be sure to back up the `init.ora` file. Ideally, it should also be locked in a version control system like RCS so changes are logged and can be undone if needed.

These are some of the more common database errors. Some are more serious than others, but any of these errors can cause user problems. Note that you can prevent the majority of these errors or at least minimize them by proactive maintenance, controlling access to the DBA password, and monitoring the `alertSID.log`.

## Application

Checking the application is normally the final step. The rationale for this is applications, particularly those developed in-house, tend to be modified frequently and have bugs, but identifying such bugs can be difficult. It can take a long time to track down, fix, and test a single program error. On the other hand, checking the server, network, or database for obvious problems can be done relatively quickly. Therefore, it makes sense to eliminate those areas that can be checked quickly before expending resources checking for bad code.

In most situations, the DBA will be familiar with the application. However, he or she won't know individual modules of program code well enough to instinctively associate a reported error with a specific module. At this stage, the DBA is largely at the mercy of the developers when it comes time to track down application code problems.

The developers, on the other hand, might not realize their code is causing problems. When problems occur, it is normally the help desk, SA, or DBA who gets the phone call, not the application developers. The first indication they have of a problem is when another IT person questions them about the code. At this stage, it is helpful to have supporting evidence of an application problem, rather than just a report that something is wrong with the system.

Consider the following application-related areas after you have ruled out a system, network, and database errors:

- Check the `alertSID.log` for errors indicating trace files have been created. Specifically, look in the `udump` directory for `.trc` files. These are typically generated when an individual user process fails when executing an application. The trace file is the best initial source of information when diagnosing application bugs. They contain a timestamp, userid, and the SQL executed at the time of error. This is normally enough information to start the debugging process.

- If the application has any log files, check those for errors. The administrator should be familiar enough with the application to check whether it is started and is writing any error messages to log files.

- Work with the user reporting the problem to create a documented test case that causes the error(s). This helps the developers to re-create the problem to aid in their debugging. If possible, place the user and developer in direct contact to discuss the problem.

- If the application has been purchased off the shelf, determine whether there are any known bugs. In cases where there exists a dedicated help staff for a particular product, use it.

One final tip on troubleshooting. Ask the question, "What has changed in the system?" In many small, unstructured shops, both administrators and developers will make changes to the production system without much testing or public announcement. Often, these changes cause problems, and you would not know any changes were made unless you specifically ask. To take this one step further, the parties who make these changes often quietly realize it was their change causing the problem. Do not, however, expect them to volunteer this information, especially when the work environment is hostile. Usually they will fix whatever they changed, but as far as you know the system mysteriously "fixed itself." Although this might be discomforting, don't be surprised to see it happen.

The next section discusses some of the database-specific troubleshooting activities performed by the DBA.

## File and Space Management

Managing Oracle data files is a common DBA task. Ideally, you should check the amount of free space available in each data file every morning. For performance tuning and backup and recovery purposes, be sure to run this job every night in order to record the name, location, and tablespace of each file.

**NOTE**

9i New Feature

9i has the capability to "manage" files by itself. You do nothing; you simply let Oracle handle everything, including the OS commands. This is optional in 9i; I doubt many DBAs will be willing to blindly give up control of the files to Oracle. Chapter 19, "9i Server New Features," covers this new feature in detail.

## Sizing Data Files

Most DBAs have SQL scripts to generate reports showing the amount of space. How much space should you keep free? That depends on the nature of your database. If you know an object is growing, keep enough space to allow for this, plus some overhead. Many DBAs run nightly cron jobs that report any data file over 90% allocated.

Use the view DBA_FREE_SPACE command to see the chunks of free space available in a data file. If the amount of contiguous free space is less than the size of the next extent for an object, an error will be generated the next time that object attempts to allocate an extent. This is a common, yet simple, problem that DBAs are often called to fix.

When it is time to add more space, you can either add a new data file or resize an existing file. Some sites have standards for this activity, so keep those in mind. Also, it is generally preferable to have several smaller files for a tablespace rather than one giant file (over 2G).

To add a data file to an existing tablespace:

```
SQL> alter tablespace users
  2   add datafile
  3   '/u03/oradata/rh1dev1/users02.dbf' size 100M;

Tablespace altered.
```

Alternatively, you can make the file larger or smaller as long as there is room for any objects in that file. Resizing a file to an insignificant size is sometimes necessary because there is no way to drop a data file from a tablespace once it has been added.

```
SQL> alter database datafile
  2   '/u03/oradata/rh1dev1/users02.dbf' resize 125M;

Database altered.

SQL> alter database datafile
  2   '/u03/oradata/rh1dev1/users02.dbf' resize 5M;

Database altered.
```

Pay attention to your disk usage. Look for patterns in database growth and determine the cause when the patterns change. Also, make sure there is enough disk space to support the growth. Work with the SA to make sure the server has the disk space available when the database needs it.

## Moving and Renaming Data Files

Moving and renaming Oracle data files is another task the DBA commonly performs. There are many reasons that a DBA moves or renames a data file. This might be in response to a SA request to clear off a filesystem. Or it might be necessary because a disk crashed and you need to restore the backup file from tape to a different location to perform the recovery. If there is a large amount of I/O contention on a particular disk, you can move one data file to another disk to reduce the contention. Finally, you might have just made a typo when adding a data file and you want to correct the mistake.

There are two approaches to moving and renaming data files: move them with the database open or move them with the database shutdown. The approach depends on the type of file you are moving.

| File Type | Online or Offline |
|---|---|
| System tablespace file | Offline |
| Rollback | Offline if it is only rollback tablespace |
| Online redo log file | Offline |
| Data or index file | Online or offline |

The rule of thumb is that if a tablespace can be taken offline, the file can be moved or renamed while the database is open. This means normal data and index files can be moved while the database is open. However, files in the SYSTEM tablespace and online redo logs cannot be taken offline; therefore, the database must be shut down. If there is more than one rollback tablespace and one can be taken offline, it can be moved; otherwise, it will have to wait until the database is shut down.

The following procedures explain how to move and rename a file. The procedure is the same even when the file is only being renamed.

The procedure for moving a file with the database open is outlined here:

1. Find the files associated with tablespace you need to move.

   ```
   SQL> select file_name, bytes from dba_data_files
     2  where tablespace_name = 'USERS';

   FILE_NAME                                BYTES
   ---------------------------------------- ------------
   /u04/oradata/rh1dev1/users01.dbf         109,051,904
   /u03/oradata/rh1dev1/users02.dbf           5,242,880
   ```

2. Assume, for example, that you want to place all the files on /u04. The next step is to verify that there is enough disk space to support the move and that the directory structure exists. You already know the directory structure exists, so just make sure there is sufficient disk space.

   ```
   SQL> !df -k /u04
   Filesystem   1k-block   Used    Available Use%  Mounted on
   /dev/hda12   2016016    851852  1061752   45%   /u04
   ```

3. Take the tablespace offline so it can be moved. At this stage it will be inaccessible to users:

```
SQL> alter tablespace users offline;

Tablespace altered.
```

4. Move the file to the new location using operating system commands. If it is to be renamed, do that as well. Be careful not to accidentally override any files during this process.

```
$ cd /u03/oradata/rh1dev1
$ mv users02.dbf /u04/oradata/rh1dev1/users02.dbf
```

5. The file needs to be renamed within Oracle.

```
SQL> alter database rename file
  2  '/u03/oradata/rh1dev1/users02.dbf'
  3  to
  4  '/u04/oradata/rh1dev1/users02.dbf';

Database altered.
```

6. Take the tablespace online so users can access it.

```
SQL> alter tablespace users online;
Tablespace altered.
```

7. Cycle through a redo log switch, and check V$RECOVER_FILE and DBA_DATA_FILES to verify the move was successful.

```
SQL> alter system switch logfile;

System altered.

SQL> select * from v$recover_file;

no rows selected

SQL> select file_name from dba_data_files
  2  where tablespace_name = 'USERS';

FILE_NAME
-----------------------------------
/u04/oradata/rh1dev1/users01.dbf
/u04/oradata/rh1dev1/users02.dbf
```

Backing up the database at this stage is a good idea. Also, if you used cp instead of mv, remember to delete the old Oracle file after you have verified the move. Oracle will not delete files at the OS level, so that file will remain there until you delete it.

Sometimes it is necessary to move a file when the database is shut down. This is common when you have to restore files because of a lost disk to a different location. In the following example, you move the SYSTEM tablespace, which requires the database to be closed. This procedure is also used to move online redo log files.

1. If needed, identify the location of the file to be moved. Then shut down the database normally.

```
SQL> shutdown;
Database closed.
Database dismounted.
ORACLE instance shut down.
```

2. Verify that the destination location exists and that sufficient disk space exists. Then move the file using OS commands.

```
$ cd /u02/oradata/rh1dev1
$ mv system01.dbf /u04/oradata/rh1dev1/system01.dbf
```

3. Start the database in mount mode so the file can be renamed inside of Oracle.

```
SQL> startup mount
```

4. Rename the file.

```
SQL> alter database rename file
  2  '/u02/oradata/rh1dev1/system01.dbf'
  3  to
  4  '/u04/oradata/rh1dev1/system01.dbf';

Database altered.
```

5. Open the database. Then verify that Oracle sees the file correctly in the new location.

```
SQL> alter database open;

Database altered.

SQL> select * from v$recover_file;

no rows selected

SQL> select file_name from dba_data_files
  2  where tablespace_name = 'SYSTEM';

FILE_NAME
-----------------------------------
/u04/oradata/rh1dev1/system01.dbf
```

The file has been moved successfully. Had this been part of a recovery process, you would have renamed the file and then proceeded with the recovery steps. Again, it's a good idea to perform a backup at this point, especially if this move was in response to a failure.

**10**

WHEN THINGS
GO WRONG

# Locking

When users report that they updated something and the database isn't responding, odds are it is a locking issue. The following section doesn't delve deeply into every type of locking situation inside Oracle, but it does show you what you need to know to solve the vast majority of locking problems.

*Locking* is the process of placing a hold on a table or row so that it can be changed while providing a read-consistent image to other users. Locking is a normal process that is handled automatically by Oracle. Based on the statement being issued, Oracle will automatically lock the rows being modified and then release the lock after the statement has been committed or rolled back. This automatic process requires no action by the user or the DBA.

Within the Oracle community there is a saying regarding locking: "Readers don't block writers. Writers don't block readers. And writers don't block writers unless they are trying to update the same row."

What this means is that, when a user attempts to read a table in the form of a query, no locks are acquired so no one is blocked. Oracle uses what is in the data file and in the rollback segments to provide a read-consistent view of the data for that user's query.

When a user attempts to update a row, an exclusive lock is taken only on that individual row. Another user can still query the entire table by seeing what is stored on-disk and in the rollback segment. Therefore, one user can update a row and another user can still query the entire table with a read-consistent image.

The only time one user's update impacts another user's update is when they are both trying to change the same row at the same time. In this case, whoever issued the statement first gets the lock. The second user will automatically wait *enqueue* for the first user to commit, roll back, or abnormally terminate. At that point, the second user is given an exclusive lock on that row and their statement is executed.

Locking is normally handled very well by Oracle with a minimum of problems. In a well-designed database, serious problems are rare. Locking can become a problem in the following situations:

- In Oracle Parallel Server (OPS) environments
- In shops in which application developers write code to explicitly lock objects or do not commit their transactions frequently enough
- When foreign key columns are not indexed

Locking problems in OPS environments are normally the result of poor application design and partitioning. If your developers are writing code to explicitly lock objects, find out why. This is often more of a bad habit than a programming necessity. Finally, *always* index the foreign key column in a parent-child relationship. Failure to do so will result in unnecessary locking of the child table whenever the parent table is updated or deleted.

## DML Locking

Because Oracle practices row-level locking, the most common problems occur when two users are trying to update the same row at the same time. As long as the first user commits or rolls back rapidly, this is usually not a problem. Problems occur when one user updates a row, but does not commit or roll back the change immediately. Any other user attempting to update the same row will issue their statement, but no response will come back from Oracle. It will look to them like the screen is "hanging." This is not an error per se, so Oracle will patiently wait for the first user to commit or roll back the change so the exclusive lock on that row will release. From a user standpoint, Oracle didn't come back immediately with a message saying "X rows updated" so they usually assume there is a problem and call for help.

For example, if User A opens a customer's account to make a change and then goes to lunch without committing or rolling back the change, that customer's record will be locked indefinitely. If User B issues a statement to update that same customer's account, nothing will happen. They will press Enter and no response will come back to the screen. There will be no message saying, "User A has locked Customer 123's account". User B will be stuck waiting on a response, which will not come back until User A commits or rolls back the original change.

At this point, user training can be very helpful. It is not impossible to train users about the basic idea of locking. They can be trained to know that two people cannot change the same piece of data at the same time. In cases like this, the users should know to call the DBA, identify who they are and what customer they are trying to update. This is all the information you, as the DBA, need to resolve the situation.

You can use a GUI tool such as OEM to determine who has the exclusive (blocking) lock and who is waiting to receive a lock on the row. You can then either ask the blocking user to commit or rollback, or you can kill their session. If you kill a session, it is considered a rollback. Also, if that user's session terminates abnormally for any reason, Oracle considers this a rollback and PMON will clear up the locks.

Oracle Enterprise Managers used to have a great tool called Lock Manager, which was designed specifically to monitor and resolve locks. Unfortunately, this tool is no longer included in new releases of OEM. If you happen to have an old copy of OEM, this tool makes it worth installing. New releases of OEM provide the same basic functionality via TopSessions, which comes with Oracle Diagnostics Pack. As you can see in Figure 10.5, TopSessions can identify users with locks.

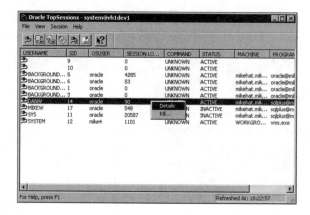

**FIGURE 10.5**

*Examining Users with TopSessions.*

In this case, the user DANW calls the DBA to report a locking problem. The DBA highlights DANW's session, right-clicks it, and selects the Details option. The DBA then selects the Locks tab, as shown in Figure 10.6.

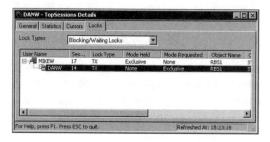

**FIGURE 10.6**

*Identifying Locks with TopSessions.*

The Lock Types drop-down menu has two options: All Locks or Blocking/Waiting Locks. Select Blocking/Waiting Locks to see any locks that DANW is waiting for. You can see that MIKEW already holds a row level lock (Lock Type TX) in Exclusive Mode. DANW has requested an exclusive lock on the same row, but is waiting for MIKEW.

At this point, you can take action. You can call MIKEW and ask him to either commit or roll back his update, or you can use TopSessions to kill MIKEW's session. Either way, DANW is next enqueue to receive the lock and his update will continue as soon as MIKEW's lock is released.

GUI tools are sometimes the easiest way to resolve locks when you know the identity of at least one locking user. However, sometimes you need to look at locking of an entire instance and, unless you have Lock Manager, you need SQL*Plus scripts to do this.

---

> **NOTE**
>
> Missing DBA_LOCKS?
>
> Sometimes, not all the locking-related data dictionary views are created when the database is. If you find that DBA_LOCKS does not exist, connect internal and run $ORACLE_HOME/rdbms/admin/catblock.sql to create the missing views. This is a prerequisite for running some lock-detecting scripts such as utllockt.sql.

There are many scripts in existence to identify locking issues. The views V$LOCKS, V$LOCKED_OBJECT, DBA_LOCKS, and V$SESSION are most useful when looking for locks, but prepackaged scripts makes this task much easier. One standard script is utllockt.sql, which resides in $ORACLE_HOME/rdbms/admin. Read over the script before running it. Basically, it creates a chart of the session IDs that have blocking locks and identifies the sessions waiting to acquire that lock. Once the blocking session IDs have been identified, you can use V$SESSION and the ALTER SYSTEM KILL SESSION command to kill the blocking session. Utllockt.sql determines the SID of the user process as defined by V$SESSION so you can use that value to identify the user session to terminate. Because the output can be lengthy, it is best to spool it to an output file and then review the results. Figure 10.7 shows the output of the utllockt.sql script.

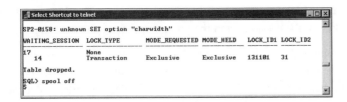

**FIGURE 10.7**
*Identifying Blocking Locks with utllockt.sql.*

As you can see, session 14 is waiting on session 17. These are the only sessions in the database currently having locking issues. By equating the number in the WAITING_SESSION to a SID, you can use the following query to identify the users. Then, you can kill the blocking session. As it turns out, DANW was waiting on MIKEW, so you need to terminate MIKEW's session.

```
SQL> select username, sid, serial#
  2  from v$session
  3  where sid in (14,17);
```

```
USERNAME              SID     SERIAL#
--------------     ----------  ----------
DANW                   14         33
MIKEW                  17         51

SQL> alter system kill session '17,51';

System altered.
```

## DDL Locking

You need to be aware that DDL actions can exclusively lock entire tables. Any type of ALTER, CREATE, or DROP command will lock a table and prevent DML for the duration of the command. ANALYZE statements will prevent all DML *and* queries, which is an exception to the rule that Oracle doesn't block readers.

This is an issue when the table is very large or accessed frequently. If the DML will take too long to perform during normal business hours, you might be forced to perform the action at night, assuming batch jobs can be delayed.

Another problem is that before a DDL lock can be acquired, *no* other lock can exist on the table. DML locks will patiently wait enqueue until they can acquire a lock, but DDL locks do not wait. If you issue a DDL command and another user has any type of lock on the object, you will receive an ORA-00054: resource busy and acquire with NOWAIT specified. You have to wait and try the DDL command later. The only other option is to put the database into restricted mode, kill all the sessions, and then reattempt the command.

Creating or rebuilding indexes also causes locking. Downtime because of this type of locking can be a big problem. I am aware of shops that have suffered because they could not withstand the downtime of rebuilding their indexes. The impact of creating indexes depends on the version of Oracle you are using. Oracle 7 and 8 always forced exclusive table locking during index creates and rebuilds. Oracle 8i is better because it allows some DML during indexing by using rollback segments. However, if too much DML occurs, it will revert to an exclusive lock on the table. Oracle 9i promises to alleviate some of these problems.

## "Snapshot Too Old" Rollback Errors

This section examines one of the most peculiar problems in Oracle: the ORA-01555 Snapshot too old error. This much-discussed problem relates to rollback segments. Rollback-segment fundamentals were explained in Chapter 2, "Architecture of the Oracle Server." Here, you are concerned with rollback segments in terms snapshot too old errors.

To understand the ORA-01555 error, you must first remember that Oracle demands a read-consistent image of the data for a query. This guarantees that once users start a query, they will not see changes that were committed during the execution of that query.

To do this, Oracle checks the current System Change Number (SCN) at the start of the query and does not display changes dated after that SCN. As Oracle is reading the data to be returned by the query, it will likely get most of this data from the table segments on disk. If, however, another user modifies that data during the course of the query, Oracle will need to reconstruct the "before image" of the data based on what is stored in the rollback segments. This is how Oracle provides read consistency: by using data from the table plus data reconstructed from the rollback segments.

For a long-running query, Oracle often needs to go to the rollback segments to reconstruct an old block of data. If Oracle cannot reconstruct a needed block of data from the rollback segments, it cannot provide a read-consistent view of the data. In this case, it rationalizes that its snapshot of the data is too old, therefore it issues the ORA-01555 error.

How can Oracle not find the older data in the rollback segments? Once the transaction that changes the data is committed, Oracle no longer protects the "before image" of the changed data in the rollback segment. This means that particular space is fair game and can be overwritten, at which point the earlier image is destroyed. If the data block on the disk has also been updated via delayed block cleanout, there is no way a long-running query can find the prior image. Thus, you get the error.

Long-running jobs are particularly prone to this error. Such an error occurs most often when there is a long-running query in an environment with many small OLTP transactions and equally small rollback segments. Under these conditions, before images do not last long after a commit, so a long-running query is a prime candidate for this problem.

Most DBAs resolve this error by reexamining their rollback segment allocations. The standard solution is to increase the size of the rollback segments. You might also find you are using too few rollback segments, which means the same segment is being reused frequently. In this case, add more rollback segments to spread out the transactions so each segment won't be reused so soon.

Another option is to run the query during reduced or nonexistent update activity. If the problem still exists, look at the application code to determine whether overly frequent commits are the cause before images to be overwritten too quickly.

## Summary

This chapter discussed what to do when problems are initially reported. Your life as a DBA can become stressful when problems occur. Especially in shops that lose large amounts of money for each hour of downtime, there can be excessive pressure to solve problems quickly. Unfortunately, situations like these are not conducive to clear thinking and silly mistakes can happen. Under these conditions, a problem-solving framework like the one provided in this chapter can be a great help. This chapter covered the major areas in which problems can occur (server, database, and applications) and looked at ways to examine each one. I recommend that you customize this list of common mistakes and problem-solving procedures to your environment. Once you do so, you will be more organized the next time a problem occurs.

The next portion of the chapter covered three common problems encountered by DBAs. Data file management was covered with a focus on sizing, moving, and renaming files. Next, you learned about locking both at the row level and table level, as well as ways to reduce its negative impact. Finally, you read about the cause of the infamous `Snapshot too old` error. You saw that by increasing the size and number of the rollback segments, you can reduce the frequency of this problem.

# Oracle Server Tuning

## ESSENTIALS

- Database tuning is an important skill that requires knowledge about both the database and the type of application it supports.

- Oracle's UTLBSTAT and UTLESTAT are solid, proven tools to obtain database statistics.

- The STATSPACK utility is a new Oracle product that provides B/ESTAT information in a more friendly format.

- There are many valuable SQL scripts available to monitor SGA, rollback segment, and data file usage.

- Performance can further be improved by monitoring Wait Events and by tuning tables and indexes.

Tuning an Oracle database is considered by some to be as much of an art form as it is a science. In reality, it is a little of both. This chapter tries to make it as scientific as possible. You will learn about tuning the parts of the Oracle database server that yield the greatest results. If you are not familiar with Oracle architecture, check out or review Chapter 2, "Architecture of the Oracle Server," first.

First, you'll look at how to approach tuning a database. Next, you'll find out how to get a snapshot of the database's performance so you can identify problems. You will then examine ways to monitor and tune the memory pools inside the SGA. You'll read about rollback segments from a performance standpoint, as well as ways to detect and avoid file contention. You will also learn how to monitor wait events inside the database. The chapter also provides an overview of a new Oracle feature: locally managed tablespaces. Finally, you will look at some different options when creating tables and indexes that can improve performance.

# Database Tuning Approach

Tuning should not start after a system is up and running, but it instead should begin during the system design phase. The sooner performance bottlenecks are detected, the easier they can be fixed. The DBA should be included in the system design meetings, but that doesn't always happen. You might just be called in to create a database for an application. If so, the guidelines in Chapter 3, "Planning a Database," will give the basis for creating a scalable database.

Having said that, more often than not the DBA inherits a preexisting database that might not have been designed and built correctly. In consulting circles, DBAs who specialize in tuning will be called in to tune databases of poorly performing systems. In reality, the root problem is often poorly written application code, an unscalable design, or poorly tuned SQL. However, before these issues can be addressed, problems with the database must be ruled out, which means the database performance must be examined. Therefore, this section focuses on the database itself.

Tuning a database starts by understanding what type of application(s) are running on it. Fundamentally, you need to know if it is an OLTP, DSS, or a hybrid. You need to know where the database exists within the entire system architecture so you can identify the inputs and outputs of the database. Understanding what a "typical" transaction entails is very helpful in understanding the stresses placed on the database. Once you understand what the database *should* be doing, you can find ways to get it there.

The next step is to get a feel for how the database is currently performing. This information will come from both technical and non-technical sources. Oracle supplied utilities and a host of scripts will tell you what is occurring inside the database. By speaking with end users and managers you will determine what the *perceived* problems with the database are. Both types of information are important because they will dictate where you apply your tuning resources.

The goal of tuning is to make the database meet the needs of the business, which means you address the problems identified by those relying on the system. This is an important point. Managers and end users really do not care how slick the internals of your database are. They just want their reports generated on time and the data returned to the screen quickly. Towards that end, you need to identify what *they* consider important and then tune to achieve that goal. For example, if your system is OLTP and it is performing badly, concentrate on getting data back to the screen quickly rather than trying to fix the occasional batch job.

Focus your attention on the areas that will generate the biggest gains and know when to stop tuning a particular part. There is usually not any one change that will make a slow database suddenly run quickly because most databases have several problems. However, initially focus your efforts on the biggest problems first. Once your goals have been met, assess whether it is worth your time trying to fine tune parts of the system that might not even be noticed by the end user. Once your tuning efforts reach the point of diminishing returns, you should probably move on to another area.

Finally, once a database is "tuned," the DBA needs to monitor it and make adjustments as needed. In reality, no database is ever "done" because systems are dynamic and the stresses on a database are usually changing. Therefore, keep running periodic reports on database performance to look for trends. Also keep in contact with the user population to verify the system is meeting their needs.

---

### Problems Are Often Tuning Opportunities

Often, fixing a database problem provides the opportunity to tune the system as well. One time a repository database I was managing suddenly started having problems allocating shared memory. Oracle ORA-4031 errors began occurring frequently, which is often an indicator of an under-sized shared pool. In our case, the shared pool was huge, but someone had added a small large pool, which Oracle started trying to use. However, since the large pool was too small to support the users, the ORA-4031 errors began occurring. This was verified by viewing V$SGASTAT, which showed almost no free memory left in the large pool.

After working with some highly skilled tuning experts, we determined our options were to either reset the large pool to zero so the shared pool would be used exclusively or to increase the large pool to handle the workload. At the same time, we could decrease the shared pool, which was far too large. In the end this turned out to be a "good" problem because it highlighted several suboptimal tuned init.ora parameters that were fixed in addition to the immediate problem.

---

Now that you know how to approach tuning, you can take a look at the technical details.

# Diagnostic Utilities: UTLBSTAT/UTLESTAT and STATSPACK

If you do not understand what is happening inside the database, you have no chance to make it better. There are several ways to look into a database such as with data dictionary views or using GUI tools like OEM Performance Manager. However, one of the most complete and time-tested methods for collecting information is running a series of scripts called UTLBSTAT and UTLESTAT. Starting in Oracle 8i, these scripts are being phased out with a similar utility called STATSPACK.

## UTLBSTAT/UTLESTAT

UTLBSTAT and UTLESTAT (hereafter called B/ESTAT) are scripts that capture and report statistics across an entire database for a defined period of time. Basically, you start the database and run UTLBSTAT to start capturing statistics. Let the database run for a while during the time you want to monitor. Then run UTLESTAT to stop the statistic-collecting process and generate a report.

The report generated by B/ESTAT contains a wide ranging and detailed listing of what happened inside the database. You can see detailed information regarding:

- Library cache activity
- Database statistics
- Events causing waits
- Latch statistics
- Rollback segment usage
- Dictionary cache statistics
- init*SID*.ora parameters
- I/O by tablespaces and data files
- Database version and when the scripts ran

This provides a wealth of information. Some of the information is not pertinent to the DBA and detailed coverage of each section is outside the scope of this book. However, this has historically been *the* method used when serious database tuning is required.

The best way to become familiar with B/ESTAT is to run it and then try to interpret the results. The report it generates is lengthy and can be overwhelming at first. However, much of the information captured in the report is the same as what is discussed throughout this chapter. Also, some sections of the report are commented with descriptions and explain what to look for. Therefore, run the report and then use this chapter to address each section.

When running B/ESTAT, consider these guidelines. First, run the report regularly and save the output so you have a baseline of information. Running the report only during poor-performing periods does not help you identify what has changed inside the database. You will get the most accurate results if you run the report only during the specific times you want to monitor. Also, let the database run a little while before running these scripts to allow for normal data to be initially loaded into the database cache.

Also, if the database is shut down or crashes between BSTAT and ESTAT, disregard the report because the statistics will be invalid.

Before you run the report you should alter the system to collect more detailed statistics regarding time. Either set the parameter TIMED_STATISTICS to TRUE in the init.ora or you can use ALTER SYSTEM to set the value. Theoretically, this change should incur a slight perfor-mance hit, but I have never noticed any problems. Also, running the scripts will not generate any additional performance overhead so there is no penalty for running them.

Start from the directory you want the report to be generated in when you run the scripts. The output report is simply called report.txt. Once it has been generated, you should rename it with a unique timestamp and save it for archive purposes.

Finally, you might want to change the default tablespace of the SYS user before and after you run the scripts. The reason is that UTLBSTAT creates temporary tables to store the statistics. These tables are dropped when UTLESTAT is executed. Some DBAs fear this can cause fragmentation of their SYSTEM tablespace. However, other DBAs feel that this small amount of fragmentation is negligible. I have run the scripts both in the SYSTEM tablespace and in the TOOLS or USERS tablespace and have never experienced problems either way.

Use the following steps to run UTLBSTAT and UTLESTAT:

1. Start SQL*Plus and connect internal.
2. Set TIMED_STATISTICS to TRUE to get detailed statistics.

   ```
   SQL> alter system set timed_statistics=true;

   System altered.
   ```

3. Run the script utlbstat.sql to create the temporary tables to store the statistics.

   ```
   SQL> @$ORACLE_HOME/rdbms/admin/utlbstat.sql
   ```

4. Let the database run normally so statistics can be generated.
5. After the period you want to monitor has ended, run utlestat.sql to drop the tempo-rary tables and generate the report.

   ```
   SQL> @$ORACLE_HOME/rdbms/admin/utlestat.sql
   ```

6. Set TIMED_STATISTICS back to FALSE.

```
SQL> alter system set timed_statistics=false;

System altered.
```

At this stage, the report.txt file is created and can be reviewed. Remember to change the default tablespace back to SYSTEM if you altered it to run the scripts.

# STATSPACK

Introduced in Oracle 8.1.6, STATSPACK is intended to provide similar functionality as UTLBSTAT and UTLESTAT, but with several improved features. Specifically, STATSPACK offers the following improvements:

- Reports are easier to read
- Resource-intensive SQL is identified
- Statistics are stored permanently in database tables
- Statistics can be captured with different levels of detail

Database statistics are captured by STATSPACK and are stored in database tables. Each time you capture statistics, you create a *snapshot*. You can capture multiple snapshots of data; they are saved indefinitely. For example, you can take a snapshot every three hours during a normal day of production—each snapshot is given a unique identifier. At some time later, you can then have STATSPACK create a report detailing the activity between snapshots X and Y. This allows you to collect statistics, but you do not necessarily have to generate a report at that time. The only restriction is that, like B/ESTAT, the report cannot span a database shutdown.

The reports generated by STATSPACK are also easier to read and understand. There is not as much extraneous information, the formatting is better, and many ratios are calculated for you. Overall, this is a much more user-friendly report.

STATSPACK does require a more involved setup and operation procedure, but it is not terribly complex. The basic steps require you to install STATSPACK, gather statistics, and generate a report. The details are outlined in the following sections.

## Installation

The first step is to install STATSPACK:

1. Start SQL*Plus and connect internal. Then add 50M to the TOOLS tablespace.

```
SQL> alter database datafile

  2  '/u04/oradata/rh1dev1/tools01.dbf'

  3  resize 150M;

Database altered.
```

2. Run the installation script statscre.sql. This will create a user PERFSTAT, who owns the tables used for storing the statistics. You will be prompted for both a default and temporary tablespace, so select TOOLS and TEMP. You will also be prompted for a tablespace for STATSPACK objects, so select TOOLS.

```
SQL> @$ORACLE_HOME/rdbms/admin/statscre.sql
... Installing Required Packages
...
Specify PERFSTAT user's default   tablespace: TOOLS
...
Specify PERFSTAT user's temporary tablespace: TEMP
...
Enter tablespace where STATSPACK objects will be created: TOOLS
```

In Oracle 9i the create script is renamed spcreate.sql. It is in the same location. Most of the scripts are the same, but instead of having a *stat* prefix they have a *sp* prefix. For example, statauto.sql is now spauto.sql.

3. The installation can take a couple of minutes to create the objects and about 30M from the TOOLS tablespace. The default password for PERSTAT is PERFSTAT.

4. Check the file statspack.lis for errors. This file is located in the directory where you ran the scripts. Assuming there are no errors, the installation is complete.

---

**CAUTION**

Be Careful Mixing B/ESTAT and STATSPACK

You cannot run UTLBSTAT/UTLESTAT and STATSPACK as the same user. They share a table called STATS$WAITSTAT, which will be overwritten by each utility. The solution is to continue to run UTLBSTAT/UTLESTAT as SYS, but run STATSPACK as the user PERFSTAT.

---

## Gather Statistics

The next step is to gather statistics in the form of snapshots:

1. Like UTLBSTAT/UTLESTAT, it is advisable to set TIMED_STATISTICS to TRUE.

```
SQL> alter system set timed_statistics=true;

System altered.
```

2. Connect as the PERFSTAT user.

```
SQL> connect perfstat/perfstat

Connected.
```

3. Execute STATSPACK.SNAP to capture a snapshot. It will take about 30 seconds to run.

```
SQL> execute statspack.snap;

PL/SQL procedure successfully completed.
```

That is all there is to creating a snapshot. This process can easily be automated via cron or as a DBMS_JOB using $ORACLE_HOME/rdbms/admin/statsauto.sql.

## Generate a Report

Once you have captured two snapshots, you can generate a report. The report is created in the directory where you start SQL*Plus.

1. Connect as the PERFSTAT user.

```
SQL> connect perfstat/perfstat

Connected.
```

2. Run the script statsrep.sql.

```
SQL> @$ORACLE_HOME/rdbms/admin/statsrep.sql
```

3. You will be prompted for a beginning snapshot ID. Select one of the snapshots available as a starting point.

```
    DB Id     DB Name    Inst Num Instance
---------- ---------- -------- ----------
3801419294 RH1DEV1           1 rh1dev1


Completed Snapshots

Instance   DB Name    SnapId    Snap Started         Snap Level
---------- ---------- ------ -------------------- ----------
Comment
------------------------------------------------------------
rh1dev1    RH1DEV1         1 27 Apr 2001 16:25:25          5


                             2 27 Apr 2001 16:31:27          5


                             3 27 Apr 2001 16:36:10          5


Enter beginning Snap Id: 1
```

4. Select an ending snapshot ID. Remember, the time between the snapshots cannot span a database shutdown.

```
Enter ending     Snap Id: 3
```

5. Name the output file. A default name is supplied or you can give it a more meaningful name.

```
Enter name of output file [st_1_3] : statspk_sp1_3.txt
```

STATSPACK will quickly generate the report in your local directory. The report will contain the following information:

- Database identification
- Snapshots used to create the report
- Buffer and block sizes
- Load information
- Calculated SGA ratios
- Wait events
- Most resource-intensive SQL statements
- Instance statistics
- I/O by tablespace
- Rollback segment usage
- Latch statistics
- Dictionary cache statistics
- Library cache activity
- Complete SGA composition
- init*SID*.ora parameters

The information in the reports generated by UTLBSTAT/UTLESTAT and STATSPACK is comparable. Certainly for the DBA just beginning to understand database tuning, STATSPACK reports will be easier to understand. For that reason I recommend using STATSPACK first, and then fall back on UTLBSTAT/UTLESTAT if you cannot find what you need.

## Tuning Memory Structures

Oracle's tuning utilities provide you the capability to capture information about the database. However, without accurate interpretation, that information is meaningless. This section looks at what the numbers mean within the SGA. First, it discusses how these values are measured. Then, it looks at the most common measurements of database performance.

## Ratios

A long-time measuring stick for DBAs has been the ratios of the memory pools inside the database. The idea is that every time a block of data is not found in memory and Oracle has to go to disk or a value has to be recalculated or parsed, the database is slowed. Therefore, DBAs rationalize, database performance can be measured by how many times a block is found in memory versus how many times it is not found. As a result, there are many formulas to measure the performance in terms of hits and misses. Furthermore, each category has an acceptable percentage that should be achieved.

Tuning a database solely on these types of ratios is dangerous. A database can meet or exceed all the recommended values and still have lackluster performance. High percentages can be deceptive depending on the type of application running. Just because you run a series of scripts and you have good numbers, does not necessarily mean your database is highly tuned.

On the other hand, poor ratios are good indicators of problems. If you notice a ratio with a low number, it can very well indicate a problem. The ratios are simply a quantitative means of measuring performance categories.

One final note on ratios: they work on the assumption that the database has been running for a while. Everything normally found in memory has to read into memory at least once. This takes time. For this reason expect your ratios to be lower immediately after database startup than after a few hours of normal use.

## Database Buffer Cache

The database buffer cache contains each block of data required by a user's operation. When an operation requires a block of data, it looks here first. If a good copy is found, that copy is used. Otherwise, Oracle has to go to a disk. Database buffer cache is sized by DB_BLOCK_BUFFERS.

The value for database buffers when queried from V$SGA is derived by:

```
Database Buffers = DB_BLOCK_BUFFERS * DB_BLOCK_SIZE
```

The efficiency is measured as the *cache hit ratio*. This is the number of physical reads versus how often a current or read-consistent image of a block is found in memory.

The value is derived by:

```
SQL> select 1 - (phy.value / (cur.value + con.value))
  2  from v$sysstat cur, v$sysstat con, v$sysstat phy
  3  where cur.name = 'db block gets'
  4  and con.name = 'consistent gets'
  5  and phy.name = 'physical reads';
```

```
1-(PHY.VALUE/(CUR.VALUE+CON.VALUE))
-----------------------------------
                         .973552222
```

The target value is 90% or higher for OLTP systems. In this case, it is 97%. If the value were less than 90%, you would add DB_BLOCK_BUFFERS as long as there was sufficient memory on the machine and the previous increase in DB_BLOCK_BUFFERS had an impact. In most databases the database buffer cache is the largest single pool. STATSPACK shows this as buffer hit ratio.

## Redo Log Buffer

The redo log buffer holds changed data until it can be written to the online redo log files. This buffer is cleared frequently so it does not need to be very large. However, it does need to be large enough so that server processes writing changes to it can find space quickly.

The redo log buffer is sized by LOG_BUFFER.

The performance is measured by the ratio of the number of redo log space requests to the number of redo entries. This represents how often a server process had to wait for space in the log buffer before it could write. This should not happen more than once every 5000 times.

```
SQL> select (req.value*5000)/entries.value
  2  from v$sysstat req, v$sysstat entries
  3  where req.name = 'redo log space requests'
  4  and entries.name = 'redo entries';

(REQ.VALUE*5000)/ENTRIES.VALUE
------------------------------
                             0
```

STATSPACK shows this as the redo noWait ratio.

## Library Cache

The library cache (sometimes called *shared SQL area*) stores each SQL statement issued and PL/SQL blocks. In the event the same statement is issued, the copy in the cache is reused and the costly process of reparsing is avoided.

This pool and the data dictionary cache are sized by the SHARED_POOL_SIZE parameter. There are two common measures of performance regarding the shared pool:

- How often an object has to be reloaded into the cache once it has been loaded. This should occur less than 1% of the time.

  ```
  SQL> select sum(pins) Executions, sum(reloads)
    2  Misses, sum(reloads)/sum(pins) Ratio
  ```

```
  3  from v$librarycache;

EXECUTIONS    MISSES      RATIO
----------  ----------  ----------
     53275          66  .001238855
```

- The hit ratio for the library cache. Conceptually, this is similar to the buffer cache. It should be in the high 90s.

```
SQL> select namespace, gethitratio
  2  from v$librarycache;

NAMESPACE         GETHITRATIO
----------------  ------------
SQL AREA          .974144487
TABLE/PROCEDURE   .831081081
BODY              .867924528
TRIGGER           .935483871
INDEX                      0
CLUSTER           .976284585
OBJECT                     1
PIPE                       1
```

These values are prone to distortion. For example, using Oracle forms can inflate this value. Increasing the value of the SHARED_POOL_SIZE parameter can help performance. However, an even better solution is to force the developers to write reusable code. Have your developers use bind variables in their SQL and enforce coding standards so the SQL can be reused more frequently.

STATSPACK measures library cache performance with library hit ratio.

## Data Dictionary Cache

The data dictionary cache stores definitions of data dictionary objects. This pool is tied to the library cache in that both are contained within the shared pool. As a general rule, if the library cache is performing well, the data dictionary cache will also be performing well. Most tuning focus is on the library cache rather than on the data dictionary cache.

The target ratio of GETMISSES to GETS for the data dictionary cache should be less than 15%. However, this ratio can be distorted if the database has not been running very long.

```
SQL> select sum(getmisses)/sum(gets)
  2  from v$rowcache;

SUM(GETMISSES)/SUM(GETS)
------------------------
              .080397678
```

## Disk Sorts

Whenever possible, sorts should take place in memory rather than on disk. This is fairly easy to obtain in OLTP environments, but it is more difficult when dealing with DSS or batch jobs.

The controlling parameter is SORT_AREA_SIZE, which is defined in bytes. Any sort requiring more space than specified by SORT_AREA_SIZE is done on disk in the TEMPORARY tablespace.

The target is to have not more than 5% of all sorts occur on disk.

```
SQL> select disk.value disk, mem.value memory,
  2  (disk.value/mem.value) * 100 ratio
  3  from v$sysstat mem, v$sysstat disk
  4  where mem.name = 'sorts (memory)'
  5  and disk.name = 'sorts (disk)';

    DISK     MEMORY      RATIO
---------- ---------- ----------
      11      3541   .31064671
```

Keep in mind that increases in the SORT_AREA_SIZE will increase the amount of memory in the PGA for dedicated server processes and in the shared pool when using MTS.

STATSPACK shows this ratio as its in-memory sort ratio.

This section covered the most commonly used indicators of performance. These values are not necessarily proof that the database is running well, but they can be used to highlight trouble areas.

# Tuning Rollback Segments

Tuning rollback segments is done differently depending on whether you are supporting OLTP or large batch jobs. The general guideline is to have more, smaller rollback segments for OLTP users and fewer, larger rollback segments for large batch jobs. The following sections discuss each.

## Rollback Segments for OLTP

The key for OLTP is to make sure each user can grab a rollback segment without waiting when they have a transaction. Because the typical transaction is not long, individual rollback segments do not have to be huge. However, they do need to be plentiful.

For years, the guideline has been one rollback segment for every four active transactions. For example, if you have 100 users at your peak time, create about 20 or 25 rollback segments. Ideally you should spread these out across several data files to distribute the I/O.

Once you identify the number of extents, you must come up with a number of minimum extents that each segment is created with as defined by the create parameter MINEXTENTS. You also need to determine how big each extent will be. Remember, rollback segments have the same size INITIAL and NEXT extents and the PCTINCREASE is 0. The main idea here is that each segment must be large enough so that a transaction will not likely need to wrap into the next extent. Also, create enough extents to reduce the likelihood of a single transaction having to extend the segment, a process called *dynamic space allocation*. This allocation is a performance hit, so once you create a rollback segment, you do not want to see it grow.

To start, I usually create my rollback segments with MINEXTENTS = 20 and with a size of 500K, or 1M each. Some might argue that 1M is large for OLTP, but I consider disk space cheap enough to justify not having to worry about wraps or extends.

## Rollback Segments for Batch Jobs

Create fewer, larger rollback segments if you anticipate long running jobs. The rationale is that you don't have to worry as much about a large number of transactions trying to grab rollback segments simultaneously. Your main concern is that once a transaction does grab a segment, it has enough room to grow without blowing out the tablespace. Preferably, each extent is large enough to avoid wrapping in the next segment.

I normally use between 1M-5M for my INITIAL and NEXT extent size. Create enough extents to reduce the likelihood of an extend, but avoiding these are sometimes not possible. I usually create all my rollback segments (OLTP and batch) with MAXEXTENTS set to UNLIMITED, but this is especially important with batch jobs. Remember to set the OPTIMAL parameter so the rollback segment will shrink after a long run, but don't set this so low as to incur a pattern of continuous growth and shrinkage.

Make sure there is a large amount of free space in your tablespace so a rollback segment can grow as needed without running out of room. The other option is to turn AUTOEXTEND on in your data files, but that can get dangerous if a runaway transaction occurs and starts consuming excessive disk space. Remember, running out of space in rollback segments while executing batch jobs is especially bad because not only does a large transaction fail, but there is also a large amount of rollback to be done.

Most shops run with a large number of OLTP sized rollback segments, but also create a few big segments reserved for batch jobs. Generally, you have no way of telling which rollback segment a transaction will use. Therefore if you want a specific transaction to use one of your large rollback segments, you must explicitly assign it to that segment.

You can assign a transaction to a specific rollback segment by using either of the following methods:

```
SET TRANSACTION USE ROLLBACK SEGMENT rollback_segment_name;
```

or

```
EXECUTE dbms_transaction.use_rollback_segment('rollback_segment_name');
```

Your transaction must start with either of these commands and the assignment only lasts until the end of the transaction. Be aware that if you are using loops to insert and commit data, you need to specify the rollback segment after each commit.

## Monitoring Rollback Segment Usage

There are two main areas you want to watch for regarding rollback segments: contention and size.

Contention is more common in OLTP environments. It occurs when several transactions are fighting for access to a rollback segment. Specifically, each rollback segment has a header containing a transaction table. This transaction table contains information about what is being written to the rollback segment. There are several extents in a rollback segment, but there is only one header. Therefore, this is a source of possible contention. If you see signs of contention here, you probably should create additional rollback segments.

Use the following query to check for contention. The popular guideline is if WAITS/GETS is over 5%, you need to increase the number of rollback segments. However, I usually look to increase the number if I find WAITS much larger than 0.

```
SQL> select a.name, b.extents, b.rssize,
  2  b.xacts "Active X-actions", b.waits, b.gets,
  3  optsize, status
  4  from v$rollname a, v$rollstat b
  5  where a.usn = b.usn
  6  /
```

| NAME | EXTENTS | RSSIZE | Active X-actions | WAITS | GETS | OPTSIZE | STATUS |
|------|---------|--------|------------------|-------|------|---------|--------|
| SYSTEM | 7 | 581632 | 0 | 0 | 389 | | ONLINE |
| RBS0 | 20 | 20963328 | 0 | 0 | 494 | 20971520 | ONLINE |
| RBS1 | 20 | 20963328 | 0 | 0 | 413 | 20971520 | ONLINE |
| RBS2 | 20 | 20963328 | 0 | 0 | 377 | 20971520 | ONLINE |
| ... | | | | | | | |
| RBS23 | 20 | 20963328 | 0 | 0 | 364 | 20971520 | ONLINE |
| RBS24 | 20 | 20963328 | 0 | 0 | 338 | 20971520 | ONLINE |

```
26 rows selected.
```

The next areas to monitor when dealing with rollback segments are wraps and extends. The existence of wraps can mean your extents are too small. Extends above the number of MINTEXTENTS can indicate too small and/or too few extents. Remember, every time Oracle has to allocate an extent, a new space is allocated on disk, and the database takes a performance hit. Also try to avoid excessive shrinks, which is a sign of too few extents and too low of an OPTIMAL value. The following query shows the number of wraps, extents, and other diagnostic information.

```
SQL> select name, extents, writes, optsize,
  2  hwmsize, shrinks, wraps, extends, curext
  3  from v$rollname name, v$rollstat stat
  4  where name.usn = stat.usn
  5  /
```

| NAME | EXTENTS | WRITES | OPTSIZE | HWMSIZE | SHRINKS | WRAPS | EXTENDS | CUREXT |
|------|---------|--------|---------|---------|---------|-------|---------|--------|
| SYSTEM | 7 | 10820 | | 581632 | 0 | 0 | 0 | 5 |
| RBS0 | 20 | 49278 | 20971520 | 20963328 | 0 | 0 | 0 | 16 |
| RBS1 | 20 | 55230 | 20971520 | 20963328 | 0 | 0 | 0 | 13 |
| RBS2 | 20 | 24218 | 20971520 | 20963328 | 0 | 0 | 0 | 15 |
| RBS23 | 20 | 28672 | 20971520 | 20963328 | 0 | 0 | 0 | 9 |
| RBS24 | 20 | 29810 | 20971520 | 20963328 | 0 | 0 | 0 | 10 |

```
26 rows selected.
```

This section explained rollback segment tuning. Make sure that there are enough rollback segments for every transaction that needs one. Also be sure that, once they are acquired, these segments do not extend excessively.

## Avoiding File Contention

Historically, spreading high-contention files across multiple filesystems has been a common way to tune a database. This process can improve performance if an I/O bottleneck exists. Ideally, competing files such as data and indexes will be identified and separated before the database is created. You learned about this principle and which files to separate in Chapter 3.

Once a database has been created, you should check to see which files are being frequently written to and read. Because you can determine which objects reside in a file, you can also identify which tables are being used heavily. If several high-contention data files reside on the same filesystem, it's a good idea to move one of the files to a less active location. Moving and renaming data files was discussed in the previous chapter.

There are several ways to identify areas of high I/O activity. You can either look from inside Oracle or you can use operating system utilities. I recommend a mix of both. Monitoring of disk I/O is covered in Chapter 13, "Unix Server Monitoring."

From inside Oracle, you cannot directly monitor contention at the disk level, but you can see which files (and their corresponding filesystems) are being heavily accessed. Oracle provides this information in both UTLBSTAT/UTLESTAT and STATSPACK. You can also run the following query to identify which files are being accessed:

```
SQL> select tablespace_name tablespace, file_name,
  2  PHYRDS, PHYWRTS, PHYBLKRD, PHYBLKWRT
  3  from v$filestat, dba_data_files
  4  where file_id = file#
  5  order by PHYRDS, PHYWRTS  desc
  6  /
```

| TABLESPACE | FILE_NAME | PHYRDS | PHYWRTS | PHYBLKRD | PHYBLKWRT |
|------------|-----------|--------|---------|----------|-----------|
| TOOLS | /u04/oradata/rh1dev1/tools01.dbf | 3 | 1 | 3 | 1 |
| USERS | /u04/oradata/rh1dev1/users01.dbf | 3 | 1 | 3 | 1 |
| EMPLOYEE_IDX | /u02/oradata/rh1dev1/employee_idx01.dbf | 3 | 1 | 3 | 1 |
| DRSYS | /u10/oradata/rh1dev1/drsys01.dbf | 3 | 1 | 3 | 1 |
| EMPLOYEE_IDX | /u08/oradata/rh1dev1/employee_idx02.dbf | 3 | 1 | 3 | 1 |
| USERS | /u04/oradata/rh1dev1/users02.dbf | 3 | 1 | 3 | 1 |
| RBS | /u05/oradata/rh1dev1/rollback01.rbs | 66 | 103 | 66 | 103 |
| TEMP | /u03/oradata/rh1dev1/temp01.dbf | 127 | 172 | 174 | 172 |
| SYSTEM | /u04/oradata/rh1dev1/system01.dbf | 1189 | 119 | 2023 | 120 |

```
9 rows selected.
```

As you can see, right now the SYSTEM tablespace—specifically the file /u04/oradata/ rh1dev1/system01.dbf—is most active. In a production system, this would not be the case, certainly after the database has been running for a while. As it stands now, no particular filesystem has a majority of the most active files. Therefore, there is no reason to suspect contention at this time.

## Wait Events

Oracle stores a good deal of information about its performance in views. V$SYSSTAT is a good example of general instance information. Other views, however, can provide information regarding potential bottlenecks within the instance. Specifically, you can look at the events occurring inside the database.

Oracle keeps information about how often and how long certain database events occur. These are not errors or problems; they are just normal events inside the database. Many of the types of events are cryptic to the average DBA, but some are useful. By finding the most frequent or longest running events, you can identify areas to be tuned.

To get a listing of the types of events, query V$EVENT_NAME:

```
SQL> select name from v$event_name
  2  order by name;

NAME
-----------------------------------------------
BFILE check if exists
BFILE check if open
BFILE closure
...
wakeup time manager
write complete waits
writes stopped by instance recovery or database suspension

212 rows selected.
```

Oracle stores the totals of each event in three useful views: V$SYSTEM_EVENT, V$SES-SION_EVENT, and V$SESSION_WAIT.

## V$SYSTEM_EVENT

This view stores the totals of each event in the entire database since the database started. Use this view to identify the longest running and most frequent events. The results can be sorted by the number of waits for an event or the total amount of time waited for an event.

```
SQL> select * from  v$system_event
  2  order by time_waited desc;
```

| EVENT | TOTAL_WAITS | TOTAL_TIMEOUTS | TIME_WAITED | AVERAGE_WAIT |
|---|---|---|---|---|
| rdbms ipc message | 46402 | 45522 | 2389696 | 51.4998491 |
| pmon timer | 14260 | 14258 | 317436 | 22.2605891 |
| virtual circuit status | 1421 | 1421 | 313344 | 220.5095 |
| dispatcher timer | 710 | 710 | 313344 | 441.329577 |

## V$SESSION_EVENT

Waits for individual sessions can also be identified in a similar manner. By identifying the session by its SID as defined by V$SESSION, you can see who is waiting on what.

```
SQL> desc v$session_event
 Name                                      Null?     Type
 ----------------------------------------- --------- ------------
 SID                                                 NUMBER
 EVENT                                               VARCHAR2(64)
 TOTAL_WAITS                                         NUMBER
```

```
TOTAL_TIMEOUTS                          NUMBER
TIME_WAITED                             NUMBER
AVERAGE_WAIT                            NUMBER
MAX_WAIT                                NUMBER

SQL> select event, total_waits, time_waited
  2  from v$session_event
  3  where sid = 11 order by time_waited desc;


EVENT                                   TOTAL_WAITS TIME_WAITED
--------------------------------------- ----------- -----------
control file sequential read                     1           0
file open                                        3           0
SQL*Net message to client                      347           0
SQL*Net more data to client                      1           0
SQL*Net message from client                    346           0
SQL*Net break/reset to client                    8           0
```

## V$SESSION_WAIT

The final view relating to wait events shows the cumulative statistics—it shows all the current sessions that are waiting. This is useful for determining which events currently are causing users to wait.

```
SQL> select event, wait_time, seconds_in_wait, state
  2  from v$session_wait;


EVENT                     WAIT_TIME SECONDS_IN_WAIT STATE
------------------------- --------- --------------- -----------
pmon timer                        0      1322890954 WAITING
rdbms ipc message                 0      3702286836 WAITING
rdbms ipc message                 0       502511022 WAITING
rdbms ipc message                 0      1301416113 WAITING
rdbms ipc message                 0         4294966 WAITING
rdbms ipc message                 0         4294966 WAITING
rdbms ipc message                 0               0 WAITING
smon timer                        0       223371349 WAITING
SQL*Net message to client        -2               0 WAITED UNKNOWN TIME
```

Wait events can provide valuable clues as to what is happening inside the database, and these views help you see and identify these wait events. Wait events are also identified when using UTLBSTAT/UTLESTAT and STATSPACK.

# Locally Managed Tablespaces

Introduced in Oracle 8i, locally managed tablespaces offer a new way to manage space within tablespaces. Traditionally, when using normal tablespaces, storage information regarding space allocation is stored in the data dictionary in the SYSTEM tablespace. When an object in a normal tablespace needs a new extent, Oracle looks inside the SYSTEM tablespace to determine where in the data file to create the next extent. Using this method, space allocation is managed from within the data dictionary. This can become a problem when dynamic space allocation occurs frequently. The result can be contention on the data dictionary inside the SYSTEM tablespace.

Locally managed tablespaces attempt to alleviate this data dictionary contention by managing space from within the tablespace's data file header. A bitmap containing the extent layout of the data file resides in the file header of the individual tablespace. When an object needs to extend, Oracle uses this bitmap inside the local tablespace to manage the space allocation rather than going to the data dictionary in the SYSTEM tablespace. Therefore, the space is locally managed inside the individual tablespace.

This new feature forces tablespaces to be defined based upon their space management technique: dictionary or local. Once a tablespace is created, there is no way to change its type. Unless a tablespace is explicitly created as being locally managed, it will default to the normal data dictionary management.

Within locally managed tablespaces, you have two options regarding how extents are allocated. Each extent can be either given a uniform size (UNIFORM) or you can allow Oracle to size the extent for you (AUTOALLOCATE). Once you have created the tablespace, Oracle will handle any object's INITIAL and NEXT sizes for you. If you have specified UNIFORM, *every* object extent will be that value regardless of the INITIAL or NEXT defined for it. Under the AUTOALLOCATE plan, the value defined as INITIAL will be used for the object, but all extent sizes after that will be determined by Oracle.

Where and why would you want to use locally managed tablespaces? The first place might be with tablespaces prone to frequent space allocation. This will reduce contention on the SYSTEM tablespace. Also, because data dictionary tables are not being updated, rollback generation is reduced.

Another place I have seen locally managed tablespaces used effectively is with data and index tablespaces where the DBAs don't want to spend time carefully managing extent sizes. You first create several tablespaces with small, medium, and large UNIFORM extent sizes. Then each table is created in the tablespace corresponding to its expected size (small to large).

Figure 11.1 shows the tablespace EMPLOYEES being created, which will be managed locally. Every object created in that tablespace will have an extent size of 500K. Even if you create an object with an INITIAL of 2M, it will be broken into four 500K extents, as you can see in Figure 11.1.

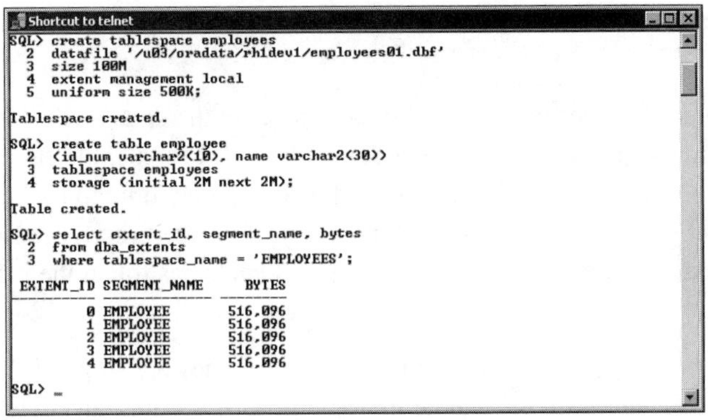

```
Shortcut to telnet                                           _ □ X
SQL> create tablespace employees
  2  datafile '/u03/oradata/rh1dev1/employees01.dbf'
  3  size 100M
  4  extent management local
  5  uniform size 500K;

Tablespace created.

SQL> create table employee
  2  (id_num varchar2(10), name varchar2(30))
  3  tablespace employees
  4  storage (initial 2M next 2M);

Table created.

SQL> select extent_id, segment_name, bytes
  2  from dba_extents
  3  where tablespace_name = 'EMPLOYEES';

EXTENT_ID SEGMENT_NAME      BYTES
--------- ------------      -----
        0 EMPLOYEE        516,096
        1 EMPLOYEE        516,096
        2 EMPLOYEE        516,096
        3 EMPLOYEE        516,096
        4 EMPLOYEE        516,096

SQL> _
```

FIGURE 11.1

*Creating a Locally Managed Tablespace.*

Locally managed tablespaces are an interesting feature. For those willing to sacrifice some control over the storage characteristics of their objects, they might be worth considering.

# Tuning Tables

You can include certain characteristics in your tables to improve performance. Not all the options for creating tables yield large performance gains nor are they all applicable in all situations. This section discusses some features that you might find useful for your environment. It also examines the issue of chained and migrated rows inside tables. Because fragmentation and basic storage parameters have been discussed in Chapter 6, "Daily Activities," they aren't discussed here.

There are two particularly interesting subsets of tables that are sometimes used to improve performance and manageability. They are Index Organized Tables (IOTs) and partitioned tables.

## Index Organized Tables (IOTs)

When creating normal tables, it is standard to have a column that uniquely identifies each row with an index created based on that column. As you probably guessed, this is the primary key. The table is stored in the data tablespace and the index on that column is stored in a corresponding index tablespace. Depending on the query issued, Oracle can use that index to quickly find any row in the table. Overall, this normally works well.

Index Organized Tables (IOTs) attempt to improve on this structure by combining the primary key index and the first column of the table. Rather than storing the data like a normal table, they store it as a B*Tree index. Basically, the index is stored as normal, but it has data stored with it. Each row starts with the index, but is followed by its row of data.

By combining the index and data, you save space. There is no separate data tablespace and index tablespace.

Access is faster because fewer reads are necessary to get to the data. Access via an index on a normal table requires an initial read on the index in the index segment to find the ROWID of the target row in the data segment. Then a second read is required to go to the ROWID in the data segment to get the actual data to satisfy the query. IOTs are faster because the second separate read on the data segment is not necessary. Once Oracle has found the index for the data, it has also found the data.

So you might wonder why IOTs aren't used all the time if they are so good. The reason is that their index-based structure does not handle multiple inserts, updates, and deletes too well. In addition, rows that grow too long are moved to a separate data segment called an *overflow area*. Also, prior to Oracle 8i, the only index you could have on the IOT was the one composing the first column. There is no ROWID for IOTs. Therefore, if your code references ROWIDs, IOTs cannot be used.

As a result of these restrictions, IOTs are not used very often. However, they do have a place in some situations. Specifically, if you have static lookup tables, they can be worthwhile. For example, a STATE table using postal abbreviations is a theoretical candidate for being IOT.

You create an IOT as follows:

```
SQL> create table state
  2  (code char(2), name varchar2(30),
  3  constraint state_pk primary key (code))
  4  organization index
  5  tablespace employees
  6  pctthreshold 20
  7  overflow tablespace users;

Table created.
```

The table creation is similar to a normal table, except for two IOT-specific parameters. ORGANIZATION INDEX specifies that the table will be an IOT. PCTTHRESHOLD 20 specifies that any rows taking over 20% of the block will have the non-index columns stored in the OVERFLOW tablespace. Specifically, columns exceeding that 20% will be stored separately. This is to keep rows from getting too long within the IOT segment.

## Partitioned Tables

When a row is inserted into a standard table, there is no relationship between the values in that row and where the row is physically stored. Oracle will place that row wherever it can find available space in a block. This is normally not a concern to the user because Oracle knows where the row is stored and makes access to the row transparent. However, when working with extremely large tables, it is often desirable to store the data in different tablespaces based on the characteristics of each row. This is the idea behind partitioning.

Partitioning allows you to replace one giant data segment with multiple smaller data segments in different tablespaces. This allows an I/O to be spread out more evenly. Also, by using parallel processing, Oracle can devote multiple processes to support a query or DML statement across the multiple partitions. This starts getting into data warehousing and supporting very large databases, which are outside the scope of this book. However, this section does discuss the basics of partitioning.

Data can be partitioned using one of two methods in Oracle 8i. *Hash partitioning* uses an Oracle algorithm to determine where to place each row to balance data evenly across all the partitions. *Range partitioning* allows you to specify a range of acceptable values for each partition. Each new row is evaluated to see which range it falls in and is then inserted into the appropriate partition.

Oracle 9i introduces *list partitioning*, which is similar to range partitioning. However, rather than specifying a range of values for each partition, you identify a list of specific values to be met. For example, instead of range partitioning based on orders placed on Monday to Wednesday and Thursday to Sunday, you could list partition for orders placed on Mon, Wed, and Fri and then Tue, Thur, Sat, and Sun. You can achieve similar results using either range or list partitioning, but this new feature makes the process easier to implement.

Indexes on the table data can also be partitioned. If you are going to partition your data, it makes sense to partition the indexes in the same way. One word of caution: it is easy to invalidate your indexes when using partitioning, so check their status regularly.

I have used range partitioning before to control the data in a new orders table. We knew it was going to get huge and did not want all the data stored in one big tablespace. I created twelve partitions corresponding to each month of the year. Each row was then inserted into the partition for the month it was created.

The idea was that once we got one year of data, we would create another set of twelve partitions for the next year. Oracle allows you to manage data at the partition level. Over time we would be able to export older, individual partitions and then drop those partitions. This would result in keeping the ORDER table at a manageable size because the data over one year old would be exported and dropped at the partition level. If any of the data was ever needed, it could still be retrieved via the export for that partition. However, we would not have incurred the overhead of storing old data that was likely never needed again. Plus, because the data was in smaller partitions, queries accessing it needed to go through a single small partition rather than a high multimillion-row segment.

If you are going to be dealing with very large tables, I recommend taking a serious look at partitioning. Partitioning is considered a separate option, so you need to purchase a license specifically to use it.

## Row Migration and Chaining

Oracle accesses table data fastest when it can go directly to a block and read the row needed for the query. For example, a data block defined by DB_BLOCK_SIZE as 8K will easily hold a row of data that is 3K long. The block will have not all 8192 bytes available to store data because a little is reserved for the block header. Also, whatever amount is defined by PCT-FREE will be reserved to store an increase in the row caused by an update statement.

If Oracle decides it needs to return the entire row for a query, it reads all 3K of the row located in this one block. This is normal and is what you want the database to do. However, what if that row was originally inserted as 10K or had been updated to be 12K? Where would it be stored? This opens up the issue of row migration and row chaining.

When a row of data exceeds the size of available space in a block, Oracle needs to either move it to a different block with more room or split the row into several pieces. Either of these represents a performance hit. When Oracle needs to read the row again, it will look in the location where the row was originally created. If that row has been moved (migrated), Oracle will see this, but will need to go to the new location of the row to get the data. This extra step hurts performance. If Oracle starts reading a row and finds that it has been split into two pieces, Oracle might need to jump to another block to get the needed data. Having to go to the block where the rest of the row resides also hurts performance.

Row migration occurs when an existing row within a block is updated and thus exceeds the amount of space remaining in that block. Basically, it can't fit. Oracle has a choice of either breaking that row into two pieces or moving the *entire* row to a new block. When Oracle chooses to move the row to a new block, it is called row migration. It will leave a pointer in the old block. This pointer gives the address of the row's new location. Future queries will still be able to find the row, although this requires an extra read.

Row chaining occurs when either a row is created that cannot fit in any block or when a preexisting row is updated to exceed the size any block. Oracle will be forced to break the row into two pieces. It will store what it can in the first block and then store the rest in another block. When a read occurs, the data in the first block will be read. If the column is found in the first block, the read stops. However, if the column is at the end of the row, Oracle will jump to the chained block to continue the read, of course with a performance hit.

Oracle will always try to migrate (move) a row before it will split (chain) a row. How can you prevent this? If the row is larger than the block size, there is nothing you can do to prevent chaining. However, row migration can be prevented or reduced by carefully setting the PCT-

FREE parameter. This reserves a percentage of each block to be used when a row grows because of updates. The default value is 10%. Increasing this reserves more space in case a row grows, but if the row never grows it is wasted space. You need to understand the DML characteristics of your table to set this value accurately. If you know there will be a high level of update activity, set this value higher. If you know data will never be updated, you can lower the value to pack the data in tighter.

Detecting row chaining and migration is fairly simple. In fact, it can be set up in a cron job and the results checked regularly. To check for this condition ANALYZE your table and then view CHAIN_CNT from DBA_TABLES. Use the most complete level of ANAYZE you can, but remember that it locks your table during this time. The column CHAIN_CNT will identify the number of chained and migrated rows. Another column that is useful is AVG_ROW_LEN; you can use it to see how long most rows are. If you notice they are smaller than your block size you probably have row migration. If they are larger than your block size, you are dealing with chained rows.

Fixing row chaining and migration is tougher than detecting it. The only way to fix chained rows is to increase your block size. Unfortunately, that can be be done only by rebuilding the database with a higher DB_BLOCK_SIZE value. If you detect row migration, increase your PCT-FREE value for the table. However, this adjustment will not fix rows that are already migrated. These migrated rows need to be identified, copied to another table, deleted, and then reinserted into original table. That process is outlined here:

1. Create the table CHAINED_ROWS to hold the ROWIDs for the chained rows. Use the script $ORACLE_HOME/rdbms/admin/utlchain.sql.

   ```
   SQL> @$ORACLE_HOME/rdbms/admin/utlchain.sql

   Table created.
   ```

2. Analyze the table with the migrated/chained rows. Use the LIST CHAINED ROWS option to load the ROWIDs into the CHAINED_ROWS table you just created.

   ```
   SQL> analyze table employee
   2  list chained rows into chained_rows;

   Table analyzed.
   ```

3. Create a temporary table holding the chained/migrated rows as identified in the CHAINED_ROWS table.

   ```
   SQL> create table employee_chained
      2  as select * from employee
      3  where rowid in
      4  (select head_rowid from chained_rows);

   Table created.
   ```

4. Delete the chained/migrated rows from the main table. Before you do this, you might want to disable foreign key constraints and triggers depending on your application and business rules.

```
SQL> delete from employee
  2  where rowid in
  3  (select head_rowid from chained_rows);

10 rows deleted.
```

5. Reinsert the rows back into the main table from the temporary table. If they are too big, they will be chained because they simply cannot fit in any one block. If they were only migrated rows, they will be inserted as normal rows and will be fine. After this, remember to re-enable any triggers or constraints you disabled in the previous step.

```
SQL> insert into employee
  2  select * from employee_chained;

10 rows created.
```

6. Drop the temporary table. Be sure not to drop the real one by mistake!

```
SQL> drop table employee_chained;

Table dropped.
```

7. Reanalyze your tables and confirm that the migrated rows have been fixed.

```
SQL> analyze table employee compute statistics;

Table analyzed.

SQL> select chain_cnt from user_tables
  2  where table_name = 'EMPLOYEE';

CHAIN_CNT
----------
        0
```

That is all there is to repairing migrated rows. Remember, you would have to recreate the database with a larger block size to fix rows that are truly chained. You should monitor for chained and migrated rows periodically. It is usually okay to wait until there several are migrated rows before fixing them, as shown previously, but do not let the numbers reach the hundreds or thousands before taking action.

# Indexes

A good indexing scheme is critical to application performance. If indexes are not created or aren't used by the application, performance will suffer.

Oracle automatically uses indexes to enforce uniqueness of primary keys and columns impacted by unique constraints. These also improve performance. When creating a primary key or unique constraint, Oracle will automatically create a unique index on that column. You can control the tablespace of the index by manually creating a unique index on the primary key or unique column and *then* creating the constraint. Oracle will use the index if it already exists.

Remember to always index foreign key columns. Failure to do so will cause unnecessary locking during DML. This was covered in detail in Chapter 10, "When Things Go Wrong."

The standard guideline is to create an index when fewer than 15% of the table will be returned by a query. If you think an index might improve a query, test it by using Oracle utilities such as TKPROF or AutoTrace.

However, before indexing all the columns on your tables, remember that indexes take up disk space and impact DML performance because Oracle must maintain them. There is also no guarantee that Oracle will use them once they are created. The point is to index columns that will be used by Oracle; do not create indexes blindly.

Verify that the SQL code being executed is actually using the indexes on the table. Getting an EXPLAIN plan for a statement will confirm or deny this. Indexes will not be used if a NOT clause or function is used on the indexed column. It is common for indexes to remain unused because the developer did not know his code was preventing their use.

Oracle 8i introduced a new type of index that can reduce the problem of unused indexes. You can now create an index on a column with a function applied to it. For example, if your SQL code always uses a WHERE clause with UPPER(LOC), any normal index on the LOC column would not used because of the UPPER function. Now, you can create a function-based index on UPPER(LOC), which will be used by Oracle. To create a function-based index, you need the system privilege QUERY REWRITE. Once you have that privilege, you create the index as follows:

```
SQL> create index dept_fk2
  2  on dept(upper(loc));

Index created.
```

Now, any query using UPPER(LOC) will make use of the function based on the index DEPT_FK2.

Indexes need to be maintained just like any other object. They require space and their data files need to have sufficient disk space. One key issue with B*Tree indexes is that they must be rebuilt on a periodic basis. Over time, as the index grows, the levels of index get deeper, which degrades performance for that index. You should analyze your tables regularly and then check the column BLEVEL (branch level) from USER_INDEXES to see how many levels exist. If this value is over three, you probably should rebuild the index as follows:

```
SQL>  alter index test_table_f1 rebuild;

Index altered.
```

Normally you have to be careful when creating or rebuilding indexes because they can lock your table and prevent DML from occurring. However, Oracle 8i allows you to create or rebuild indexes with the ONLINE feature. This option prevents the restrictive locking so you can use DML against the table. This feature comes at the expense of disk space during the rebuild. Also, because Oracle uses the existing index as the basis for the rebuild, it is sometimes better to drop and recreate the index if it is badly degraded.

Indexing is important and it needs to be done intelligently to compliment the application code. For this reason, you should work closely with the developers to have a solid indexing strategy.

## Summary

Performance tuning is considered by many DBAs to be "fun" work because it involves problem solving and is challenging. If you are successful, the users and managers are happy because the system runs better for them. Indeed, if you are good at it, a career in consulting might be a possibility. The demand for good tuning specialists is high.

The reason for the demand is that database tuning can be tricky. You've seen in this chapter that there is more to it than just changing parameters and hoping for the best. To be successful, you need an multifaceted approach to tuning. You need to know which areas are performing poorly, how to identify the technical causes within Oracle, and then how to implement a successful fix. Finally, you need to know when to stop tuning one area and move to the next.

This chapter covered some of the most common areas to tune within the database. It showed that you can use tools such as UTLBSTAT/UTLESTAT and STATSPACK to obtain valuable statistics regarding performance. The chapter also provided queries you can use to diagnose problems with your pools inside the SGA and rollback segments. Oracle stores information regarding events that have caused it to wait—the chapter looked at ways to view this information. Finally, you read about some ways to improve the performance of your tablespaces, tables, and indexes.

# Unix Operation System Architecture

## ESSENTIALS

- The Unix kernel manages processes, memory, files and I/O.

- Programs really execute as one or more parent and child processes managed by the kernel.

- Unix uses virtual memory which is a combination of real memory and swap space on disk.

- The kernel manages the various types of filesystems and any files they contain.

- There are several different architectures dealing with how multiple CPUs, memory, and disk are shared within and between machines and these can offer some benefits.

# Imperative Concepts

Understanding Unix architecture will help you better understand how and why Oracle runs as it does. The Unix kernel is key to the operating system as it manages processes, memory, files, and I/O.

For the same reasons you learned about Oracle's architecture, it is necessary to understand Unix architecture. When you understand why and how things happen at the OS level, the entire Oracle/Unix system becomes easier to understand and troubleshoot. Rather than looking at error messages as though they are in a foreign language, you can actually make sense of them because you understand the anatomy of the Unix operating system. Particularly when you're troubleshooting or tuning, a solid understanding of the operating system is very helpful.

This chapter looks at how Unix works. It examines the kernel, its main subsystems, and how they interact. The focus is theoretical in this chapter and more hands-on in the next chapter. An overview of startup/shutdown procedures and hardware architectures is also provided. Each flavor of Unix/Linux is different, so the chapter tries to be as general as possible when describing topics. However, preference is given to Solaris when describing architecture.

This chapter will not make you a Systems Administrator. However, it does give you an idea of what the OS is trying to do. Once the architecture and processes are explained in this chapter, you will be able to make the most of Chapter 13, "Unix Server Monitoring."

# Understanding the Kernel

The core of the Unix operating system is its kernel. This memory-resident program structure manipulates machine hardware and software resources to meet the user's requests. In a sense, it is the "brains" of the operating system. It does not, however, interface directly to service the user's request; the kernel operates through managing processes and hardware assets to do the user's work. The kernel is shielded from the users by several layers of abstraction. Figure 12.1 has long been used to show how Unix is layered.

As you can see, there are several layers operating above the kernel. At the outermost application layer, programs exist that are started by users. For instance, the Oracle database runs at the application level. This is the level users operate in. Beneath the application level is the shell, which is the user's interface into the operating system. At this level, commands from the user application enter the system to request a Unix service (such as to remove a file). The next layer is the process layer. At this layer, Unix processes fulfill the requests of the shell layer. Finally, beneath the process layer is the kernel. The kernel acts as an interface between the physical hardware and the processes requesting services.

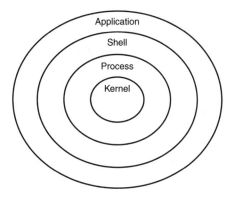

**FIGURE 12.1**
*Layered Unix Architecture.*

The kernel manages four subsystems consisting of processes, memory, files, and I/O. The combination of these subsystems composes a running Unix system, so this chapter examines each one in detail.s

## Unix Processes

Any "program" really executes as one or more processes. Within the context of a program, a process executes to perform a task. For example, the LGWR background process writes from the online redo log buffer to the online redo log files. That task is part of the Oracle "program." The same principle holds true whether the program is Oracle, a simple shell script, or a Unix command such as grep.

At any given time, there are usually hundreds of concurrent processes running on the system. Some are spawned by the users; others are supporting the system, such as those owned by root. Each process is trying to perform some unit of work, but "work" can only be accomplished when the process is actively running on a processor/CPU. Unless a process is actually running on a processor, it is accomplishing nothing. Additionally, only one process can be running per processor at any specific point in time.

How does anything ever get done under these constraints, especially when there are hundreds of processes demanding time on the CPU? Unix can support this by via multitasking, time-slicing, and using the scheduler. Basically, Unix forces each process to share time on the machine's CPU(s). One process will run on the CPU for a little bit, and then it will relinquish the CPU to the next process in line. A scheduling process allocates time on a CPU to each process based on its priority. This time-slicing technique is how Unix achieves multitasking.

Multitasking is the process whereby multiple processes can exist on a system at the same time. New programs don't have to wait until running programs end before they can start. A user can have multiple processes, corresponding to different programs, running simultaneously. Because Unix is a multi-user system, more than one user can have different processes running simultaneously. However, it appears to each user that he or she is the only person on the machine because the processes seem to run as soon as the user presses Enter. The fact that there are hundreds of processes by different users waiting in line to be executed is invisible to the user.

With all the processes demanding time on the processor, Unix must have a method for controlling access to this resource. Unix does this by classifying each process and then assigning it a priority. Then a scheduling process allocates slices of processor time to each process. In this way, every process gets CPU time, but more critical processes have priority over non-critical processes.

Unix processes have three general classifications. How much CPU time the process gets is based on these classifications. Within each classification is a number range further ordering the priority of each process. The higher the number, the higher the priority. The three types of processes are Time Share (TS), System (SYS), and Real Time (RT), described here:

- Time Share is the default classification. It is also the lowest level of priority. TS holds the priority range from 0 to 59. Processes in this range include your typical user processes, such as using Oracle. Within the TS range is a subset for Inter-Active (IA) processes. IA processes are used by GUI windows systems.

- System processes are those supporting the operating system, such as `init`. These processes command the range from 60 to 99. Any process of this priority class will receive CPU time before any time-share process.

- Real Time processes are allocated the highest priority on the system. They hold the range 100 to 159. These are common on systems that have critical applications requiring a hold on the CPU in order to complete processing, even at the expense of the system processes.

Information about each process is stored in a kernel array called the *process table*. Process information used by the kernel is stored in `/proc` and is always in memory. Given that each process has a classification and wants CPU time, there still must be some controlling authority that determines who gets the CPU and for how long. This controller is the scheduler process.

The scheduler process, `sched`, allocates a slice of CPU time to each process. `sched` is a daemon process. Daemons are operating system background processes that perform some sort of maintenance task. After the executing process has been run for its set amount of time, it goes to sleep and another process gets the CPU. This switching of processes is called a context switch. If a lower priority process is running and a higher priority process needs the CPU, `sched` will preempt the running of the less important process. This is how Unix implements preemptive multitasking.

As you can see, processes alternate between being run and waiting to be run. In reality, there are even more fine-grained classifications than these. A process can fall into the following states:

- **Idle**   A process needs to be scheduled in order to run.
- **Run**   The process is in the run queue.
- **Sleep**   The process is runable, but it is waiting on a system resource, such as I/O.
- **Stop**   A process has been stopped for some reason.
- **Zombie**   The process has been terminated; its resources have been released, and it is waiting to return its exit code to the parent process.

Now that you have looked at how processes are executed, you can examine their structure. A process exists to fulfill tasks determined by program code. In a sense, a user process is an individual entity whose sole purpose is to fulfill its program instructions. It does this by allocating memory, requesting services from the kernel such as I/O, and when necessary, spawning children processes to perform subtasks.

A process is a running representation of a program. This structure exists within the virtual memory of the machine. Although the program can be written in a high-level language, the process of compiling and linking the program ultimately breaks it down into machine-executable code. Just as the program is written to hold variables, these variables are contained in memory areas of the process. Also, a copy of the executable code is maintained within the process. Figure 12.2 shows a representation of a process's structure.

As you can see, the process has several areas. Each area has the following characteristics:

- **User Area**   Information about the process used by the kernel.
- **Text**   Sharable machine language code.
- **Initialized Data**   Variables with initialized values at program runtime.
- **BSS (Block Started by Symbol)**   Variables with undefined values at program runtime.
- **Stack**   Local variables within the process. It also contains parameters passed into it and the results of function calls.

Each of these areas is private to the individual process except for the text area. This is an important exception. Because the text area represents read-only executable code, multiple processes can and do share one copy of this area. Rather than having multiple redundant copies stored for each process (taking up valuable memory), all the processes running the same program can share the same copy.

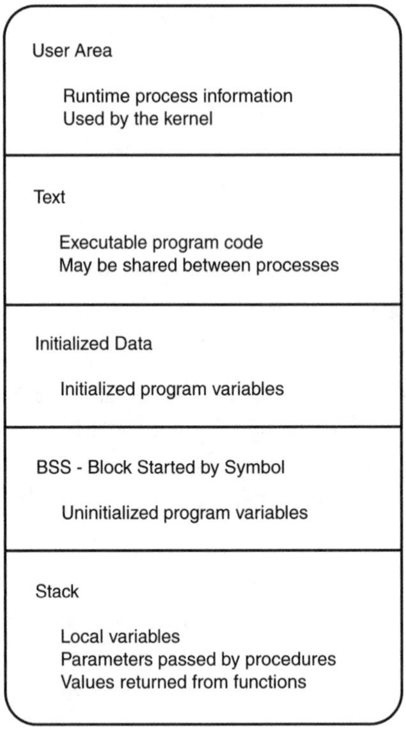

**FIGURE 12.2**

*Process Structure.*

For a process to be created, it must be spawned by another process (called a *parent*). This new process can, in turn, spawn children processes of itself to do work. This chain starts all the way with the `init` Process ID (PID) 1. Each successive child process has a unique PID, but the hierarchy can be traced by examining the child Parent Process ID (PPID). These are identified via the `ps` command.

The system called `fork()` is used to spawn a child process. The child is an exact copy of the parent. After `fork()` creates the child process, a new program instruction is laid on top of it with the `exec()` process. This is how a child process gets its instructions. Once a child process is spawned and has its instructions, the parent process has two options: pause until the child is done working or continue its work in parallel with the child. The course of action is determined by the specific program, but, by default, the parent process waits for the child process to execute and then resumes working.

All this information is interesting at a high level, but how does it apply to an individual system? How do you tell what your processes are doing? Use the Unix command `ps  -efc`.

Previously, you saw this command used to check on Oracle processes, but here, it's used to view non-Oracle processes:

```
[root@mikehat /root]# ps -efc
UID        PID  PPID   CLS PRI STIME TTY           TIME CMD
root         1     0    -  39 21:59 ?         00:00:05 init [3]
root         2     1    -  39 21:59 ?         00:00:00 [kflushd]
root         3     1    -  39 21:59 ?         00:00:00 [kupdate]
root         4     1    -  39 21:59 ?         00:00:00 [kpiod]
root         5     1    -  39 21:59 ?         00:00:00 [kswapd]
```

The expanded form of ps -efc provides the following columns:

- **UID**   User ID. This is the user ID owning the process. Keep in mind that a user does not have to be logged into have processes running.

- **PID**   Process ID. This is the process' unique identifying number. If you want to stop a process, you use the kill *PID#* command, where *PID#* is the process ID number.

- **PPID**   Parent Process ID. Every process except sched has a parent process. This number represents the process that spawned the child process.

- **CLS**   Classification of the process. If this is listed it is one of TS, IA, SYS, or RT.

- **PRI**   Priority number of the process within the classification. Remember, the higher the value, the higher the priority.

- **STIME**   The time the process was started. If the process is over a day old, the date rather than time appears here.

- **TTY**   The location of the process, if known.

- **TIME**   The total amount of CPU time in minutes accumulated for this process. This is not real time per se, but it is an indication of how much work a process has been doing.

- **CMD**   Command issued. This is the name of the process being executed. This can be a recognizable background process such as LGWR or it can be a command such as grep.

As you can see, there are many processes running. Some by root are always running—including sched, init, and pageout. Others can be owned by users, such as Oracle. As a DBA, you should become familiar with processes normally running and those that appear out of place. For example, if you notice that processes associated with nighttime backups are still running in the afternoon, you know there is a problem of some sort. Also, if you have reports of poor system performance and then see a process with an unusually large amount of accumulated CPU time, you have possibly found the culprit.

**NOTE**

*Windows NT and Threads*

Oracle on Unix works using processes as described previously. However, that is not the case with other operating systems. Windows NT uses multiple threads rather than processes to run Oracle. Threads are created to perform a process' subtasks. Rather than spawning a new child process, a thread will be created instead. One process can have multiple threads executing simultaneously. With NT, one process to support Oracle is started. From there multiple threads are created to support DBWR, LGWR, and so on.

## How Unix Manages Memory

Understanding how memory is managed within Unix is very important to being a DBA, particularly when you're performance tuning and troubleshooting. Knowing how the kernel will react when you create an SGA of several hundred megabytes is extremely relevant, especially when a novice SA insists it is Oracle making the machine swap. In situations like these, your knowledge of how Unix works is the best protection when people start complaining about performance.

Unix works on the principle of *virtual memory*, which is the concept that you can operate with a memory area composed of real memory and disk acting as one. The benefit is that active processes can run on the real memory and that inactive processes can be paged or swapped out to disk (to the *swap area*). This results in more "virtual" memory than what actually exists in terms of actual RAM.

Virtual Memory = Real Memory  +  Disk (Swap Area)

For example, assume you have 2G of real memory. Following the guideline of having two or three times the swap area as you have real memory, you need 4G of swap space. This would give you 6G of virtual memory.

Virtual memory also means more than just real memory plus disk space. Rather than assigning a process to a location of real memory, processes are assigned a virtual memory address. Address translation tables map the virtual addresses of each process to locations of real memory. This is transparent to each process.

This is relevant because for a process to be executed, it must exist in real memory. Therefore, before any work can be done, there must be enough room in real memory for the active pages of the process and they must be moved into that real memory area. By itself, this seems like a simple concept, but once again you need to realize that real memory is a finite resource and that the demand for memory usually exceeds the supply. For these reasons, real memory needs to be managed. In this case, the system daemon page manages the memory allocation.

Virtual memory is divided into units called *pages*. Each page is typically 4K or 8K. On Solaris, use the command pagesize to find the size on your system.

It is the job of the daemon page to determine which pages reside in real memory and make sure that there is enough room in memory for active processes to run. page does this by moving inactive pages and entire processes from real memory to the swap area on-disk. When individual pages of a process are moved from real memory to the swap area this is called *paging*. When entire processes are moved to the swap area this is called *swapping*.

Paging and swapping are Unix's way of responding to a deficiency in real memory. Either one represents a performance hit. However, some degree of paging can occur on most systems with relatively little negative impact. One the other hand, swapping is a negative sign that indicates a serious lack of real memory.

Paging and swapping do not occur randomly; there is a method to when Unix pages and when it swaps. Unix will always try to page first in order to free enough memory for the system to run. Depending on the kernel settings, page will attempt to maintain a certain amount of free space by moving non-active pages in memory to the swap area. It will identify pages that have not been used recently and will label them as such. Later, if they are still inactive, they will be freed to be used by other processes. This is actually done by the pageout daemon and thus, is called a page-out. Later when that page is needed back in real memory, it is read back in.

Hopefully, this level of paging will create enough room in real memory. However, if it doesn't work, swapping will occur. Unix will begin to swap out inactive processes in an attempt to free memory. This is often referred to as leisure swapping. If this fails to free enough memory, Unix begins "desperation" swapping where active processes are swapped out.

At this stage, things become serious because the machine will spend more time trying to manage swapping than it will letting processes execute. This is called *thrashing*. At this point, no productive work can be accomplished because the system is too busy swapping processes in and out of memory.

Figure 12.3 identifies the kernel parameters that determine at which level paging and swapping begin. These thresholds are based on the amount of real memory available and are typically determined by the SA. However, as the DBA, you should understand them.

These parameters determine at what level paging and swapping begin based on the amount for real memory available. Lotsfree indicates the level at which no paging occurs. If the amount of free memory drops to the desfree, leisure swapping begins. If this doesn't free enough memory and the minfree threshold is breached, desperation swapping will occur. In Solaris, these parameters are set in /etc/system.

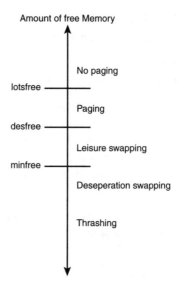

**FIGURE 12.3**

*Escalation from Paging to Swapping.*

There isn't much, as a DBA, you can do when the server reaches the point of desperation swapping because it simply needs more real memory. You can shut down or resize your SGA, but this example assumes the server was set up for Oracle in the first place, so stopping Oracle isn't an option. You can increase the amount of swap space, but this is really a Band-Aid solution if you are facing swapping.

Because paging and swapping represent disk I/O, you can try to have the SA spread the swap partitions across different disks and make sure they are not contending with your database files. You can also reevaluate which processes are running on the box and the size of the SGA to reduce memory usage. However, in the end, the best solution is to get more memory.

That covers the basics of memory management. There are, however, *very* important ramifications involving shared memory and the SGA, which are covered in the next chapter. For now, just understand that real memory is needed for processes to execute and how Unix tries to use paging and swapping to provide that memory.

## Filesystems and Files

Understanding how filesystems and files are managed and how they can be corrupted is useful information. It can help you troubleshoot your database when problems occur.

## Filesystems

Working on the assumption you know that Unix directories have a hierarchical structure, filesystems are a little easier to understand. For example, in Figure 12.4, you can see that there is a root directory (/) with subdirectories for var, usr, home, u01, u02, and u03.

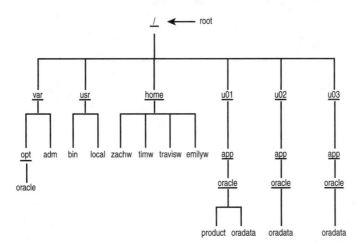

**FIGURE 12.4**

*Hierarchical Directory Structure.*

A filesystem corresponds to a directory with subdirectories and files located on a disk, called a device. In the DOS world this is conceptually similar to a partition. This device can be part of a one disk, an entire disk, or several disks combined to form one logical unit. The term device comes in because that is how Unix sees it. The Unix kernel will pass calls to it (I/O requests) and receive responses from it. For example, /u01 represents a device that happens to be a disk. Alternatively, devices can represent objects other than disks such as floppies or tape drives and CD-ROMs. For example, the devices /mnt/floppy or /mnt/cdrom correspond to floppy and CD-ROM drives.

Once a device has been created it is not necessarily available. To make it available it must be mounted so it is accessible by the kernel. Use the mount command to mount a filesystem. For example, the following command would mount /u01:

```
[root@mikehat /root]# mount /u01
```

The filesystem is mounted at its *mount point*. In this case the device name is /dev/hda6 and the mount point is /u01. When the operating system starts, it attempts to mount the root (/) filesystem and read from it. After some processing it will attempt to read the configuration file

/etc/fstab for most Unix and Linux systems and /etc/vfstab for Solaris. This is a text file containing the names and types of each of the remaining filesystems. Figure 12.5 is an example of a Linux /etc/fstab.

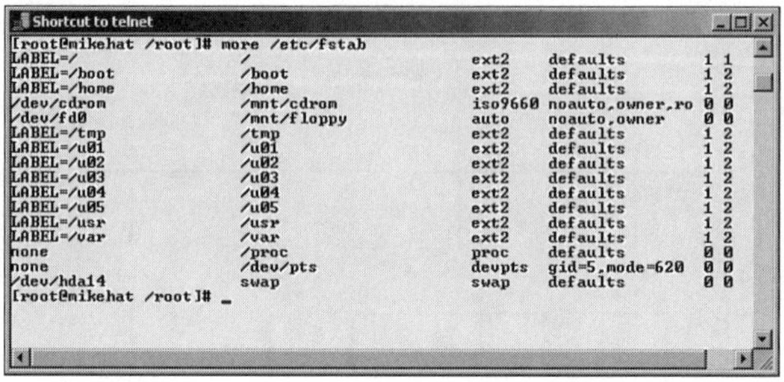

**FIGURE 12.5**
*The Linux /etc/fstab File*

Unix will automatically try to mount each filesystem. It will check each filesystem with the fsck utility for corruption. You can see the success or failure of this process on the console in the startup messages. After this, view /var/adm/messages or use dmesg | more to view these messages.

Once a filesystem is mounted it becomes accessible. A df -k or bdf will identify the device, its name, and the amount of space on it. Within the filesystem, directories can be created containing files. As files are added, the amount of free space for that particular filesystem decreases. Most people have multiple filesystems to provide a separation of duties, distribute I/O, and to contain growth. As you saw in Figures 12.4 and 12.5, the root / filesystem is mandatory, but you can also have /var, /usr, /home, and /u01 to /u03. For example, if you didn't separate / and /u02, all the disk access to the database files would conflict with root and there would be a greater chance that the root filesystem would become full (which is bad).

There are several types of filesystems, each with a different use, as follows:

- **ufs (the Unix ilesystem)**    This is the normal filesystem and is how most directories and files are stored. ufs is a disk(s) on your local machine. Root, /usr, and /var are examples of typical ufs filesystems.

- **ext2 (the second extended filesystem_**    The default Linux filesystem. Just as ufs is the Unix default, ext2 is the Linux default.

- **nfs (the network filesystem)**    In DOS terms, this is like mapping a network drive to your local PC. Conceptually nfs is similar to ufs, but it is physically located on a different machine. Once your server is started, Unix will mount this filesystem to your server. For example, the /home filesystem containing the home directories of all the users is a popular filesystem to nfs mount. This way, whenever users log into any machine, they are placed in the same directory with the same files. This eases the burden of maintaining multiple /home directories for each user and makes life easier for the user as well. Ramifications of this are possibly increased network traffic (because you are connecting to two servers) and increased impact when /home goes down because multiple servers are affected.

- vxfs (Veritas filesystem)—This is a vendor-specific type and it is very popular. What makes this different is it is a *journaled* filesystem. When writes are made to the disk, they are written to the Unix buffer cache *and* a redo log. The use of the redo log allows for faster filesystem recovery when the server crashes. Writes stored in the redo log are applied to the disk in a manner conceptually similar to that of an Oracle database.

- iso9660 (compact disk filesystem)—This is the filesystem type for CD-ROMs.

- swap—This is where processes are swapped out to. Ideally, there should be several swap partitions to distribute I/O and they should be separate from other high-contention disks.

- proc—This is a memory-resident filesystems containing information about each process running on the system. The kernel uses this filesystem to manage processes and the system.

**12**

UNIX OPERATION
SYSTEM
ARCHITECTURE

---

**NOTE**

*Oracle's New Filesystem*

Oracle has introduced its own filesystem, called iFS. The iFS (Internet filesystem) allows you to store your directories and files inside the database. You map a drive to the iFS location and access your files as though they are normally stored on disk. However, they are really stored within the database, which provides some benefits. All your data has the same level of protection as with any data in an Oracle database. When indexing documents, search access is also fast.

---

Just as you can mount a filesystem to make it available, you can also unmount it with the command umount. Maintenance on filesystems is possible only when the filesystem is unmounted. If a process is accessing that filesystem, you will get a "device busy" message. In cases like this, you have to find and kill the process using the filesystem. Then you can unmount the filesystem.

Filesystems that unexpectedly become unmounted or otherwise inaccessible often initially appear as "hanging" problems. If you use a command that attempts to access an inaccessible filesystem, the command hangs rather than returns an error. For example, if you issue the ls /u01 command to access a filesystem and the command hangs, you should first make sure the filesystem is mounted properly. If you notice that users log in and their login sessions hang, check whether the /home filesystem is an nfs mount. If the login process tries to place the users in a home directory that cannot be accessed, they will hang.

I remember one occurrence in which we had several filesystems stored on a SAN (Storage Array Network). (Basically a cabinet of disks attached to the server via a cable.) Somehow that cable became loose (someone probably tripped over it) and from that point on anyone trying to access those filesystems with an ls or cd or anything else became stuck. Unix was sending requests to access that filesystem and decided to wait (hang) patiently for a response that, it turns out, would never come. The fix was simple, but the problem did impact a large number of users.

## Files

Now that you know where files exist (in filesystems), you can examine the files themselves. Obviously Unix stores files in filesystems. Structural information about each filesystem is stored in the superblock. The superblock contains size information and information about the physical disk. This is critical information and is redundantly stored in several locations on disk.

Each individual file is broken into two components: the inode and the file itself. An individual inode exists for each file in the filesystem. The inode stores ownership and storage information about a specific file. Oddly enough, it stores everything about a file except for the filename and file contents. An inode for a file contains the following information:

- Owner (user ID)
- Group (group ID)
- Level of permissions
- Size
- Last access time
- Last modification time
- Block locations

The name of the file is stored at the directory level. The block locations point to where the file data is stored. Depending on the size of the file, single, double, or triple indexed block pointers indicate the location of the file data blocks.

Earlier, you read how the fsck utility is used to check filesystems for corruption. This utility checks superblocks and each inode. It makes sure each inode is valid and that it points to the correct file. Discrepancies create corruption and can be caused by bad/failed writes. fsck will attempt to fix these errors so the filesystem can be mounted.

## I/O Subsystem

The I/O subsystem simply describes how Unix reads and writes to disk. A user process will request a read or a write. The kernel will then take this request and forward it to the I/O subsystem. From here, things become more complicated. Unix doesn't immediately read or write directly to disk every time a read/write request occurs. Instead, it caches the writes and reads in a Unix buffer cache. This way the I/O can occur when it is optimal. Also during this time, the user process might be waiting for the result of the operation. If synchronous I/O is occurring, the user process will wait patiently until the kernel process returns a success or failure response. If asynchronous I/O is enabled, the user process will not wait for the result and will continue working. Ultimately, the kernel will receive an indication as to the result of the I/O and it will forward this to the user process.

I/O subsystems are difficult to describe past a generic level because so much depends on the specific vendor of your disk drives and disk storage arrays. Especially when dealing with large storage arrays and RAID, the differences between a Linux workstation containing one disk and a large HP or Sun box is great. Logical Volume Managers further make this a vendor-specific issue. The choice between "cooked" filesystems and raw disks also needs to be considered. All these factors impact performance and can be tuned and monitored.

For these reasons, detailed disk information and RAID are covered in the next chapter.

## Startup/Shutdown Processes in Unix

Normally, you don't start, shut down, or reboot Unix servers, but I have seen cases where it is necessary (normally because the SA is absent). Regardless, you should understand how the system boots, as is can aid you when troubleshooting. Understanding this process is a requirement if you plan on implementing startup/shutdown scripts, as outlined in Chapter 9, "Backup and Recovery."

The following steps occur when the Unix server starts up:

1. Firmware in the machine scans the server to determine what hardware exists.
2. The boot device, typically on-disk, is located.
3. The kernel is read into memory.
4. Server is scanned again and hardware is checked to see whether it is usable.
5. The init process is started and /etc/inittab is read. The init process is what spawns all the other processes.
6. More processes and daemons are started by init.
7. Filesystems are checked and mounted.

8. Run control scripts are executed. These start such services as SendMail, NFS, and Oracle, if it is configured.

9. Server will open to the default run level.

While this is happening, diagnostic messages are being written to the console and to /var/adm/messages. If you miss any of these, use dmesg | more. There is more to the startup process than this and it varies between platforms, but from a DBA perspective, these are the core steps. What is of particular importance to the DBA is the run level of the system and the run control scripts.

Just as a database has different levels of startup, so does a Unix/Linux server. These are listed in the /etc/inittab along with the scripts needed to reach each level.

| Run Level | Description |
| --- | --- |
| 0 | Shutdown or halted state. The server is physically shut down. |
| 1 or S | Single user mode. This is typically reserved for maintenance. |
| 2 | Multi-user for non-networked systems. |
| 3 | Multi-user with mode with file sharing and network connections. Typically the default level as identified in /etc/inittab. |
| 4 | User-defined run level. Typically it is unused. |
| 5 | Firmware state. The machine can be physically powered off. Used for maintenance. |
| 6 | Reboot state. The machine goes to run level 0 and then restarts to the default run level. |

How does Unix know when to start or stop specific services? Each run level has a series of shell scripts associated with it. The master script controlling each run level is called from /etc/inittab. The individual scripts for each run level are contained in subdirectories /etc/rc#.d where # represents the run level. These scripts determine which processes start or stop as the server moves through them. For example, run level 3 has certain scripts in the directory /etc/rc3.d that need to be executed, as you can see in Figure 12.6.

Each of these files is a shell script. Scripts starting with K are executed to kill the processes for this run level. Those beginning with S are executed to start processes. Within the K or S type, the scripts are executed in numeric order. For example, S10network is executed before S25netfs. When a run level is reached the K scripts are executed first to kill certain processes, and then the S scripts are executed to start the appropriate processes.

Unix/Linux does not jump directly to a run level on startup. For example, if the machine was going to run level 3, it would first start with the scripts in rc0.d and then proceed through rc1.d, rc2.d, and finally end with rc3.d.

**FIGURE 12.6**
*The /etc/rc3.d Directory.*

It is important to shut down the system in an orderly manner. Just like with Oracle, Unix has processes to kill, services to stop, and disk writes to complete. If you do not allow Unix to go through these process and, instead, simply turn off the power button, you are chancing problems when the server restarts. Always try to use the appropriate `shutdown` command to bring your Unix/Linux machine down.

# Understanding the Hardware Architecture

Hardware architecture is something best addressed *before* a system is built, but often you come into a preexisting environment and must work with whatever is there. However, you still need to understand the architecture of the machine, as well as its applicable characteristics. This section discusses at a high level the three most common architectures found today. It also defines two newer and less common architectures.

The most common machine architectures a DBA will encounter today are uniprocessors, Symmetric Multiprocessors (SMPs), and clusters. Each differs primarily in the number of CPUs and how memory and disk is shared. It is the distribution of these hardware assets that this section focuses on.

## Uniprocessor Machines

A uniprocessor machine is simply a box with one CPU. It can be anything from a SPARC workstation running a RISC (Reduced Instruction Set Computing) chip to an Intel-based box running Linux. The defining characteristic is that it has only one processor.

Uniprocessor machines, especially those running Linux, are very common. Most PCs meet this classification. They are so common because they are the least expensive and easiest to manage. This comes at a price in terms of performance and scalability. No matter how you analyze it, there is still only one CPU available to process work requests. This makes everything a serial process and eliminates the possibility of taking advantage of Oracle's advances in parallel processing. Although Unix is good at using time-slicing to provide the illusion that multiple users/programs are executing simultaneously, they are still only being executed one at a time.

Because they have only one processor, these machines are incapable of supporting resource-intensive systems. However, for small testing, training, or development systems, uniprocessor machines can be successfully deployed.

## Symmetrical Multiprocessor Machines

An SMP machine is a server with multiple symmetrical processors running simultaneously on the same physical machine. Although a uniprocessor workstation has only one CPU, an SMP server can have four, six, or eight processors (all at the same speed). Aside from the fact there are multiple processors, an SMP box is conceptually similar to a uniprocessor in that the same memory and disks are accessed on an equal basis. There is no memory or disk exclusively reserved for any particular processor. In this respect it is a *shared-everything* architecture.

Because there are multiple processors running simultaneously, these machines can take advantage of Oracle's parallel processing. For example, using Parallel DML, you can have four processes dedicated to executing one statement rather than just one in a serial manner. Or you can have several users/jobs running in a truly simultaneous manner. This becomes a requirement when you have a large user population trying to access data simultaneously. Don't forget that not only must Oracle and its users be supported, all the normal operating system processes must also be supported.

SMP machines are by far the most common type of production-class machine. These can range from fairly small machines, such as Sun E450s, to mammoth Sun E10000 or HP Superdome servers. Organizations willing to spend the money on SMP machines usually will also have a dedicated SA to manage them. Often there will also be a few uniprocessor machines around, typically for testing or development. Monitoring CPU usage is discussed in the next chapter, but for now you should know that if you are working an SMP machine you should try to take advantage of the multiple processors.

## Clusters

Clusters can be most easily described as two or more machines (typically SMPs) tied together and sharing a common set of disks. Figure 12.7 shows the basic architecture of a Sun cluster.

In this case, you have two SMP machines, each with their own processors, memory, and internal disk drives. What makes this a cluster is that the two machines are tied together and they also share a common disk array. Each SMP machine (aka *node*) has normal control over what's on its internal drives, but they share access to the shared disk array. Communication between the nodes occurs on the high-speed interconnect joining the two (or more) servers.

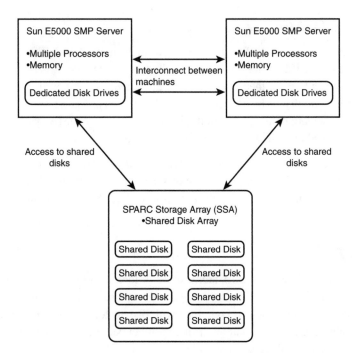

**FIGURE 12.7**

*Sun Cluster*

In terms of Oracle, you can put a physical database on the shared drive and have two instances (one on each machine) accessing it simultaneously. This configuration is called Oracle Parallel Server (OPS). Locking is handled by a Distributed Lock Manager (DLM), which manages locks between the two machines as each instance accesses the shared database. When running, both nodes access the database simultaneously. For example, you can have one node running batch jobs and the other supporting OLTP users. If one node fails, the database instance on the other is still accessible. This makes for a highly available system.

Clusters are common in environments where high availability is a must. However, they are expensive and complex. It takes a highly skilled SA to successfully manage a cluster. Also, Oracle Parallel Server requires an extra license charge, which drives the price up even further. Finally, managing the database and application is more difficult as well. However, if high uptime is truly needed, clusters and OPS are a viable solution.

## MPPs and NUMAs

Massively Parallel Processors (MPPs) and NonUniform Memory Access (NUMAs) are more complex architectures. MPP systems can be described as a collection of networked uniprocessor nodes with their individual memory and disks. Each node is composed of its private processor, memory, and disk. This is called a *shared-nothing* configuration. NUMA systems are similar in that they are composed of multiple processors, but NUMA systems share memory and disks, and operate with one operating system.

This section provided an introduction to the different hardware architectures you might encounter. Once you have identified what type of system you are on, by all means investigate it further. Particularly when working with clusters, you (and the SA) should understand how Oracle is implemented.

## Summary

This chapter covered the basics of Unix architecture. It looked at the kernel and the four basic subsystems it manages: processes, memory, files, and I/O. Programs are executed as processes. Memory is a valuable resource and is combined with disk to form virtual memory. If too little memory is available paging will occur and if the problem persists swapping might occur. Unix uses filesystems to manage directories and files. I/O is how Unix reads and writes to disk and is covered in greater detail in the next chapter.

The chapter also covered how Unix starts up and shuts down. Just like the Oracle database, there are different levels of startup and shutdown, which you should understand. Finally, the chapter introduced the three most common hardware architectures you will encounter: uniprocessors, SMPs, and clusters. Each has different characteristics in terms of how hardware resources (CPU, memory, and disk) are managed, which in turn influences how Oracle runs.

# Unix Server Monitoring

## ESSENTIALS

- The capability to monitor the Unix/Linux server is an important DBA skill.

- Oracle uses shared memory for the SGA and sometimes this, as well as semaphores, need to be cleared after a database crash.

- Key areas on the server to monitor are: memory, disk, CPU, and network.

- There are many tools that can be used to monitor performance and most differ slightly depending on your platform.

- Because each system is different and technology changes, there is not any one set of defined numbers that you can use to measure performance across all systems. This is where you need to understand your system and then apply tuning rules of thumb.

Server monitoring is an important skill for an Oracle DBA to have. The database and the server are inherently tied together. What happens on the server has a definite impact on the database. It is also true that what happens in the database impacts the server. Therefore the performance of the machine is the DBA's business.

As a DBA, you don't need all the skills of an SA, but you do need to understand the fundamentals, which were discussed in the previous chapter. This chapter looks at the four main areas to watch: memory, disk, CPU I/O, and network. By learning to monitor each of these subsystems, you will be able to identify what is impacting server performance. You will see how the server reacts to the demands placed on it by the database. By tying this information into what you learned in Chapter 11, "Oracle Server Tuning," you will be able to tune the system as a whole.

This chapter also explains in greater detail how Oracle and Unix handle shared memory and disk I/O. Also, throughout the chapter, there are multiple examples of situations I've seen so you can put the technical information into the context of the "real world."

# Need for Monitoring the Server

Monitoring the activity and performance of the server is traditionally an SA's job. This makes sense because the server is the SA's responsibility and theoretically this person understands Unix/Linux and hardware better than the DBA. For these valid reasons, the SA *should* be monitoring the server. However, there are reasons why the DBA also needs to monitor the server.

Most of the time when performance on a database server is poor, the first person people look for is the DBA. This is unfair in a sense that not all problems are caused by the database, but people will still come to the DBA first because it is a database server. The DBA needs to look at both the server and the database to identify where the problem is. For example, the DBA might be told "I entered a query and it's just sitting there." This might be a locking problem. Or, there might be a load on the server that it's taking a while for queries to be executed. The truth is, it often takes a look at both the database and the server to diagnose problems. If you can look at both areas, you can solve such problems faster.

The database and server are inherently tied to each other. Activity on the database impacts the server and vice versa. It takes a special skill set to examine both areas. If, for example, you notice the run queue on the server is high, you can hopefully trace it back to a specific database process. In cases where Unix memory is short, you might need to reexamine the size of the Oracle SGAs. In many cases it is easier to address these issues than it is to train the SA to have database skills needed to do so.

> **NOTE**
>
> Cross Training
>
> Keep in mind that many good DBAs were originally SAs and vice versa. As a DBA, you should train your SA in the basics of Oracle architecture: SGA, instance, file types, and so on. This way, the SA knows what issues you face and what the processes running on the box are. The SA should also train the DBA. The SA should show the DBA how backups are done, what other processes are running on the box, and how to monitor the server. This is especially true in smaller shops.

# Overview of Monitoring the Server

A Unix-savvy DBA is usually in the best position to tune the system (server, database, application) as a whole. This is because the DBA can interpret Unix statistics in terms of database or application activity. By being able to put all the pieces together, you will be able to solve problems quickly and tune the system.

Tuning strategy is covered in Chapter 11, so I won't rehash it here. However, it is important to note that you should monitor the server even when there aren't any problems. This is how you get a baseline for what is "normal." Throughout this chapter, I provide general guidelines and thresholds, but it is important to remember some of these baselines are system-specific. Numbers that I consider alarming might be okay on your particular system. This is where testing and understanding the characteristics of your particular system is important.

As you read your server statistics, try to tie them back to activity in the database. For example, if you notice a certain disk is getting a high level of I/O activity, cross check the V$FILESTAT file to identify which tablespace and data file is being used. As another example, if you notice one user process has accumulated a high amount of CPU time, investigate what it is doing. Use the combination of ps -ef and V$SESSION to identify the Oracle username, SID, and serial number of the Unix process. From there, you can put a name and "face" on the process that is hogging your CPU.

When monitoring the Unix server from a DBA's perspective there are four main areas to look at: memory, disk I/O, CPU, and network. The following sections discuss the tools needed in each of these areas. This chapter also provides expanded coverage of shared memory and disk I/O as it pertains to Oracle.

**13**

**UNIX SERVER
MONITORING**

# Monitoring Memory Issues

The previous chapter covered the basics of memory: virtual memory, processes, paging, and swapping. Here, you will learn how Oracle and Unix use shared memory, how to clean up allocated memory from an aborted instance, and how to lock it into real memory. It is important to understand how Oracle works with memory, which is why this section provides more detail. At the end of this section, you'll learn about a few commands you can use to check memory usage.

## Shared Memory and Semaphores

The SGA is a shared memory segment. What does this mean? First of all look at what the SGA really is—it contains the caches of data, such as the shared pool and data dictionary cache, as well as buffer areas such as the redo log buffer and database block buffers. In a sense, the SGA is the database loaded into memory. It contains all the background processes and server processes that access the data in the SGA.

The last sentence is key in that many database processes access the SGA. This means that the SGA is *shared* by all the Oracle processes; hence it is shared memory. When an Oracle server or background processes starts, it attaches to the shared memory of its instance, which is the SGA. This means that any background or server process can read or write to the SGA; therefore it *must* be shared.

Think about it in another way. Does it seem conceivable that you can have 100 users, each with his/her own private SGA of 300M? Obviously this exceeds the memory limits on a Unix or Linux machine. For this reason alone, shared memory is necessary, but there are other reasons for it as well. By attaching to a shared memory area such as the SGA, any process can read or write to it. This is how server processes work within the SGA and background processes such as LGWR and DBWR read and write from their respective caches. Oracle also has the dedicated process called PMON, which cleans up after terminated user processes.

Shared memory is not a concept limited only to Oracle; other applications can use their own shared memory segments. During Oracle's installation process, you read about configuring shared memory in files such as /etc/system for Solaris and Linux with /usr/src/linux/include/asm/shmparam.h and /usr/src/linux/include/linux/sem.h to match the Installation and Configuration Guide (ICG). The following key values are examples from a Sun box I worked on; however, you should get your values from the Oracle ICG and customize them for your environment.

### Shared Memory

```
set shmsys:shminfo_shmmax=805306368
```

SHMMAX is the maximum allowable size (in bytes) of an individual shared memory segment. Ideally, this should be larger than any single SGA on your box, so each SGA will have its own single contiguous memory segment. Otherwise, it will be broken into several smaller segments, which is not as good.

```
set shmsys:shminfo_shmmin=200
```

SHMMIN is the boundary for the smallest allowable size (in bytes) for an individual shared memory segment.

```
set shmsys:shminfo_shmmni=200
```

SHMMNI is the total maximum number of shared memory segments on the box at any given time.

```
set shmsys:shminfo_shmseg=200
```

SHMSEG is the total maximum number of shared memory segments of any one individual process.

## Semaphores

```
set semsys:seminfo_semmni=4096
```

SEMMNI is the maximum number of semaphore sets on the system.

```
set semsys:seminfo_semmsl=500
```

SEMMSL is the maximum number of semaphore identifiers for any one individual process/ semaphore set. This number needs to be greater than the PROCESSES parameter in the init.ora. Remember that PROCESSES is set to the number of Oracle background processes plus the maximum number of dedicated user processes on your database. Most DBAs set this value to at least 10 over their PROCESSES number.

```
set semsys:seminfo_semmns=4096
```

SEMMNS is the maximum number of system semaphore identifiers allowable at any one time.

This value should exceed the sum of init.ora PROCESSES parameters of all your simultaneously running databases. It should exceed this value because other processes on the box might need semaphores and Oracle needs additional semaphores during instance startup.

```
set semsys:seminfo_semopm=100
```

SEMOPM is the maximum number of operations per *semop* call.

```
set semsys:seminfo_semvmx=32767
```

SEMVMX is the maximum value of a semaphore.

Notice how some of these values seem a little high? I tend to use inflated values on purpose because once I set these for a box, I don't want to have to deal with them again. These values are only limits; they do not force memory to be allocated unless it is needed. This means there is no real penalty in using higher values for parameters such as SHMMAX or SHMMNI. Just as long as your machine can support the minimum values, you should be okay.

What you want to avoid is a case where your database hits an upper limit such as SHMMAX, SEMMSL, or SEMMNS. To fix these problems, you have to modify /etc/system and bounce the box, which imposes unnecessary down time. These values can be viewed either by examining the individual files or on Unix by using the sysdef | more command. Remember, however, that you have to reboot for any changes to take effect.

### Shared Memory Parameters Don't Cause Swapping

I once had an SA who was convinced that the server was swapping horribly and the shared memory parameters in the /etc/system were to blame. What really happened was that he misinterpreted the results of swap -s and thought the server was actively swapping. Then he blamed it on the shared memory parameters in /etc/system.

In reality, what he saw on swap -s was how much was *allocated* for swap, not what actually was being used. For the /etc/system parameters (supplied in the Oracle ICG), these allocations establish upper *limits* for shared memory. They do *not* necessarily impose these values or mandate that a certain amount of memory will be allocated whether it is needed or not.

This SA is a smart guy and just misinterpreted what he saw. Ultimately, it was a good learning experience for both of us. However, this is a good example of why the DBA *must* understand the Unix side of things. Had I not known he was wrong and had proof to support my case, we might have reset the parameters much lower and real problems would have occurred.

Processes lock and unlock shared resources via semaphores. A semaphore is simply a nonnegative integer value used as a counter. This is how processes synchronize the use of a shared resource with other processes. When a process wants to use a resource it will check the value of the semaphore for that resource. If it is greater than zero that resource is available. The process will then decrement the semaphore and use the resource. When it is done with the resource it will increment the semaphore. As long as the semaphore value is above zero, the resource is still accessible to other processes.

In terms of Oracle, each background and server process must be able to get a semaphore. It is through semaphores that processes can synchronize access to the SGA. This is why you set SEMMSL and SEMMNS in relation to the PROCESSES parameter in the init.ora.

## SGA Allocation

You need to set your shared memory parameters so Oracle can acquire the shared memory it needs to start up the instance. There are several SGA memory configurations Oracle uses to try to allocate the shared memory it needs, but if it cannot do this, an error message will be issued and the instance will not start. There are three configurations Oracle will use to allocate the

SGA after background processes have been started. In order of preference they are, one contiguous segment, multiple contiguous segments, and multiple non-contiguous segments, and are each discussed next.

## One Contiguous Segment

One contiguous segment of shared memory is found and the entire SGA is located within that segment. This is the optimal method, so Oracle tries it first. Intimate Shared Memory (ISM) is discussed in a later section, but for now you should know that this memory configuration is a requirement for ISM.

## Multiple Contiguous Segments

If the SGA cannot fit into one contiguous shared memory segment, Oracle will try to fit several segments together to hold the SGA. For example, if SHMMAX is smaller than the SGA, multiple shared memory segments have to be used. Oracle will attempt to put these segments next to each other.

## Multiple Non-Contiguous Segments

In cases in which Oracle cannot place the SGA into one segment or multiple contiguous segments, the final option is to break the SGA into parts wherever they will fit. Oracle breaks the SGA into fixed portion, variable portion, database buffer cache, and the redo log buffer. These can be seen via V$SGA. Oracle will attempt to combine the fixed and variable portions, but if the sum of the two exceeds SHMMAX, they will be split.

Next, Oracle will try to find a space for the redo log buffer and the database buffer cache.

If Oracle cannot allocate enough shared memory to satisfy any of the previous memory configurations, an error will be issued and the SGA will not be allocated. Assuming SGA is allocated, semaphores are allocated next. Then the appropriate files are opened and the database is opened as specified.

# Intimate Shared Memory

Intimate Shared Memory (ISM) is a Sun Solaris-specific option. It does two things for Oracle: it locks the SGA into real memory and allows processes to share the same page table entry. Both of these improve performance. Locking the SGA into real memory ensures that it will never be paged out to disk. Just keep in mind that this can cause other non-Oracle processes to be paged out instead. From Solaris 2.6 onwards, backing space is not allocated on the swap device for ISM pages so do not expect to see your SGA represented there. ISM also reduces the amount of kernel operations by allowing multiple processes to share the same address resolution table entry. This reduces the amount of work the kernel has to do when mapping virtual to physical memory addresses.

In more recent versions of Solaris (2.6 onwards) and Oracle (8i onwards), ISM is enabled by default. The init.ora parameter USE_ISM sets the parameter to TRUE by default in the database. It can be disabled at the operating system level in the /etc/system file. To use ISM, it must be enabled at both the database and operating system level. Also, the SGA must have been allocated in one contiguous shared memory segment, not the multiple segments previously discussed. There won't be any messages if this happens, but you might experience parts of the SGA being paged. Finally, beware that early on ISM required OS patches to prevent corruption caused by a bug, so check with your SA to make sure the OS is patched for this bug.

> **NOTE**
>
> LOCK_SGA Parameter
>
> You might wonder where you can use ISM if you're not on Sun Solaris. Is your SGA doomed to be paged out? Not necessarily. There is an init.ora parameter LOCK_SGA that you can set to TRUE in order to prevent the SGA from being moved out of real memory. Be warned that like ISM, locking an SGA into real memory can cause paging and swapping of other processes that can impact other applications.

## Cleaning Up Shared Memory and Semaphores

Although it happens infrequently, there are times when an instance crashes, but shared memory and semaphores for that instance still exist. In reality, the server and background processes have terminated and the files are no longer accessible, but memory is still allocated. This is a problem because before you can restart the instance, these shared memory areas and semaphores must be cleared out of the system. This is not just because they are a waste of resources; the new SGA will not allocate if the old memory segments still exist. The two ways to remove the old memory segments are to reboot the box or to remove them individually with ipcrm.

Most DBAs will attempt to remove the lingering remnants of the SGA via ipcrm. The trick is to make sure you remove the correct shared memory and semaphores. If you have two instances running and one crashes, there is a chance you could accidentally remove the wrong memory segment, thus creating two crashed instances. Fortunately, identifying and removing shared memory and semaphores is not as difficult as it might sound. Actually, just going through the process of identifying them will give you a better appreciation for the SGA as a memory structure and help you determine which configuration model it was allocated with.

There are several ways to identify which shared memory segments and semaphores belong to which database. If you have just one database running on a machine, simply remove all the segments and semaphores owned by the OS user oracle. In cases where you have multiple databases, it is often best and safest to list and identify the shared memory segments and semaphores for *each* database instance. Then you can identify segments of the crashed instance through the process of elimination.

For example, if you have three databases and one crashes, you can log into the two remaining databases and use Oracle utilities to identify their shared memory and semaphores. Then, you can go to the OS and identify all the Oracle shared memory segments and semaphores. Those owned by the `oracle` user that you cannot identify within the running databases are the ones you want to remove. Once you have identified everything, you can be sure you are removing the correct segments and semaphores.

The following example has two Oracle 8.1.6 databases running: `rh1dev1` and `rh1tst1`. You need to free the shared memory and segments for `rh1dev1` without impacting those for `rh1tst1`. You can use two Oracle utilities (`sysresv` and `oradebug ipc`) to get information about the instance's shared memory and semaphores. This example also uses the Unix command `ipcs` to get information about *all* the shared memory segments and semaphores on the system. Then, you can use `ipcrm` to remove the appropriate segments and semaphores.

1. Use the Oracle OS utility `sysresv` to determine what Oracle calls the shared memory for each instance. Remember to set your `ORACLE_SID` before running this utility for each instance. This utility exists for Oracle 8i and above.

```
$ export ORACLE_SID=rh1dev1
$ sysresv

IPC Resources for ORACLE_SID "rh1dev1" :
Shared Memory:
ID              KEY
5121            0x00000000
5122            0x00000000
5123            0x00000000
5124            0x00000000
5125            0x3cccf9f4
Semaphores:
ID              KEY
3584            0x03ec71b6
Oracle Instance alive for sid "rh1dev1"
$ export ORACLE_SID=rh1tst1
$ sysresv

IPC Resources for ORACLE_SID "rh1tst1" :
Shared Memory:
ID              KEY
5126            0x00000000
5127            0x00000000
5128            0xd5cdac04
```

**13**

UNIX SERVER
MONITORING

```
Semaphores:
ID              KEY
5121            0x0decb316
Oracle Instance alive for sid "rh1tst1"
```

As you can see from the shared memory report, each instance has the SGA allocated in multiple segments. Both instances have also acquired one set of semaphores. Make a note of the IDs of both the shared memory and semaphores associated with each instance.

2. Earlier versions of Oracle used the database utility oradebug ipc, which required logging into the surviving instances. This utility still exists in Oracle 8i. Depending on the version you are using, it either creates a trace file in the udump directory or displays output directly to the screen. The trace file is not huge, but it does contain information about both the database it was run against and the entire system (located at the end of the file). The values you want to find are those identifying rh1tst1's shared memory and semaphore IDs. The shared memory ID is identified by Shmid and the semaphore ID is identified by Semaphore List.

```
SQL> oradebug ipc
Information written to trace file.
SQL> exit
$ pwd
/u01/app/oracle/admin/rh1tst1/udump
$ more ora_12126.trc
/u01/app/oracle/admin/rh1tst1/udump/ora_12126.trc
Oracle8i Enterprise Edition Release 8.1.6.1.0 - Production
With the Partitioning option
JServer Release 8.1.6.0.0 - Production
ORACLE_HOME = /u01/app/oracle/product/8.1.6
System name:    Linux
Node name:      mikehat.mike.com
Release:        2.2.16-22
Version:        #1 Tue Aug 22 16:49:06 EDT 2000
Machine:        i686
Instance name: rh1tst1
Redo thread mounted by this instance: 1
Oracle process number: 0
12126

*** 2001-06-17 12:31:01.887
Dump of unix-generic skgm context
areaflags       00000027
realmflags      0000000f
mapsize         00001000
protectsize     00001000
lcmsize         00001000
seglen          00001000
largestsize  00000000f8000000
```

```
smallestsize 0000000000400000
stacklimit        0xbf87eed7
stackdir              -1
mode                  640
magic             acc01ade
Handle:           0x9400938 `/u01/app/oracle/product/8.1.6rh1tst1'
Dump of unix-generic realm handle `/u01/app/oracle/product/8.1.6rh1tst1',
flags
= 00000000
 Area #0 `Fixed Size' containing Subareas 0-0
  Total size 0000000000010ff0 Minimum Subarea size 00000000
   Area  Subarea    Shmid     Stable Addr      Actual Addr
     0       0       5126 0x00000050000000 0x00000050000000
                                Subarea size     Segment size
                                0000000000011000 0000000001411000
 Area #1 `Variable Size' containing Subareas 2-2
  Total size 000000000112e000 Minimum Subarea size 00100000
   Area  Subarea    Shmid     Stable Addr      Actual Addr
     1       2       5127 0x00000051800000 0x00000051800000
                                Subarea size     Segment size
                                0000000001200000 0000000001200000
 Area #2 `Database Buffers' containing Subareas 3-3
  Total size 0000000001000000 Minimum Subarea size 00002000
   Area  Subarea    Shmid     Stable Addr      Actual Addr
     2       3       5128 0x00000052c00000 0x00000052c00000
                                Subarea size     Segment size
                                0000000001000000 000000000102d000
 Area #3 `Redo Buffers' containing Subareas 4-4
  Total size 000000000002a000 Minimum Subarea size 00000000
   Area  Subarea    Shmid     Stable Addr      Actual Addr
     3       4       5128 0x00000053c00000 0x00000053c00000
                                Subarea size     Segment size
                                000000000002a000 000000000102d000
 Area #4 `Lock Manager' containing Subareas 5-5
  Total size 0000000000002000 Minimum Subarea size 00000000
   Area  Subarea    Shmid     Stable Addr      Actual Addr
     4       5       5128 0x00000053c2a000 0x00000053c2a000
                                Subarea size     Segment size
                                0000000000002000 000000000102d000
 Area #5 `Java' containing Subareas 1-1
  Total size 0000000001400000 Minimum Subarea size 00000000
   Area  Subarea    Shmid     Stable Addr      Actual Addr
     5       1       5126 0x00000050011000 0x00000050011000
                                Subarea size     Segment size
                                0000000001400000 0000000001411000
 Area #6 `skgm overhead' containing Subareas 6-6
  Total size 0000000000001000 Minimum Subarea size 00000000
   Area  Subarea    Shmid     Stable Addr      Actual Addr
```

```
                            Subarea size      Segment size
                    0000000000001000 000000000102d000
Dump of Solaris-specific skgm context
sharedmmu 00000000
shareddec        0
used region        0: start 0000000050000000 length 0000000004000000
Maximum processes:              = 50
Number of semaphores per set:   = 54
Semaphores key overhead per set: = 4
User Semaphores per set:        = 50
Number of semaphore sets:       = 1
Semaphore identifiers:          = 1
Semaphore List=
5121
------------- system semaphore information ------------
------ Shared Memory Segments --------
key         shmid      owner      perms      bytes       nattch      status
0x00000000 5121        oracle     640        69632       10
0x00000000 5122        oracle     640        29360128    10
0x00000000 5123        oracle     640        29360128    10
0x00000000 5124        oracle     640        24576000    10
0x3cccf9f4 5125        oracle     640        26755072    10
0x00000000 5126        oracle     640        21041152    13
0x00000000 5127        oracle     640        18874368    13
0xd5cdac04 5128        oracle     640        16961536    13
------ Semaphore Arrays --------
key         semid      owner      perms      nsems       status
0x03ec71b6 3584        oracle     640        204
0x0decb316 5121        oracle     640        54
------ Message Queues --------
key         msqid      owner      perms      used-bytes  messages
```

The easiest way to find the values you want is to vi the file and use /Shmid and
/Semaphore List to search for these strings. Make sure you keep searching (using the *n*
key), because in this case Shmid had several values—5126, 1527, and 1528—which
identify multiple shared memory segments. Semaphore List only had the value 5121,
which identifies one semaphore set.

3. Use the Unix command ipcs to find all the shared memory and semaphores on the system. Linux users can just use ipcs, but Unix users should use ipcs -b.

   ```
   $ ipcs

   ------ Shared Memory Segments --------
   key         shmid      owner      perms      bytes       nattch      status
   0x00000000 5121        oracle     640        69632       10
   0x00000000 5122        oracle     640        29360128    10
   0x00000000 5123        oracle     640        29360128    10
   0x00000000 5124        oracle     640        24576000    10
   ```

```
0x3cccf9f4 5125        oracle   640      26755072  10
0x00000000 5126        oracle   640      21041152  12
0x00000000 5127        oracle   640      18874368  12
0xd5cdac04 5128        oracle   640      16961536  12

------ Semaphore Arrays --------
key        semid    owner    perms    nsems     status
0x03ec71b6 3584        oracle   640      204
0x0decb316 5121        oracle   640      54

------ Message Queues --------
key        msqid    owner    perms    used-bytes  messages
```

This output shows all the shared memory segments and semaphores on the system. In this case, they are all owned by oracle. As you can see, there are eight shared memory segments belonging to two instances. If you were to add these for each instance, the result would be very close to what you'd get if you issued a sum from V$SGA. If you know the sizes of your SGAs and there is only one shared memory segment per SGA, you can usually guess which segment belongs to which SID. However, I recommend clearly identifying each SID's segments rather than making educated guesses. From this display, you can also see that two sets of semaphores have been allocated, one for each instance.

4. Once you have all the shared memory segments and semaphores identified, it is time to actually remove the crashed instance's shared memory segments and semaphores. Based on the output from sysresv for both instances, oradebug ipc for rh1tst1, and ipcs for the entire system, you can be sure rh1dev1 has the following shared memory IDs and semaphore IDs:

```
Shared Memory IDs:
1521, 1522, 1523, 1524, 1525

Semaphore IDs:
3584

Use ç to remove the shared memory segments:

ipcrm -m 5121 5122 5123 5124 5125        <- For Unix
ipcrm shm 5121 5122 5123 5124 5125       <- For Linux

Use ipcrm to remove the semaphores:

ipcrm -s 3584       <- For Unix
ipcrm sem 3584      <- For Linux
```

That is all there is to cleaning up shared memory and semaphores in Oracle 8i. Assuming that rh1dev1 had crashed in the first place and that shared memory segments and semaphores had survived, you could now restart the database because those segments and semaphores have been freed.

**13**

**NOTE**

Remove sgaSIDdef.dbf File

In earlier versions of Oracle, including Oracle 7 and Oracle 8, there was one additional step that was sometimes necessary. The file sgaSIDdef.dbf in $ORACLE_HOME/dbs needs to be deleted before removing the segments. Originally, this file stored memory and semaphore information and its existence indicated the instance was running. Early versions of Oracle needed to delete this file before the instance was restarted, after which the file would be recreated. However, in Oracle 8i, this file is not created so it becomes a non-issue.

## Monitoring Memory

The chapter covered how Oracle uses memory extensively because it's important to understand this when you're looking at memory usage. The SA will usually understand how memory is used (such as virtual memory); but more often than not, SAs are clueless about how Oracle uses memory. Understanding this is rightfully the DBA's responsibility. Now that you understand the fundamentals of memory and how Oracle uses memory, it's time to look at ways to monitor it.

**NOTE**

Available Monitoring Tools

There are many tools for monitoring system performance. This chapter focuses on those tools every DBA should have: sar, vmstat, swap, uptime, ps, iostat, and netstat. These are command-line utilities available on most Unix and Linux systems. Be warned, however, that each of these tools differs depending on your platform. Make sure you check your man pages for each utility because they will be different on Solaris, HP-UX, AIX, BSD, and Linux. This chapter focuses primarily on Solaris and Linux.

Other tools are more graphical in nature. Every system should have a version of top installed. This is a handy tool to be used with other tools. On HP-UX the tool glance provides a wealth of information and you should use it if you are on that platform. Other third-party tools such as Team Quest are available as well, but you need to work with the SA to get these tools.

There are several tools you should use when monitoring memory. In addition to memory usage, you also need to monitor swap usage because the two are inherently linked.

To see the size of your swap partitions and the amount used on Solaris, make use of the Unix command swap.

```
$ swap -l
swapfile               dev  swaplo blocks    free
/dev/vx/dsk/swapvol 162,8      16 6295216 6264976
```

The command swap -l shows the device that holds the swap partition and its size. You can obtain this information from df -k, where each filesystem and type is indicated.

The swap -s command shows the amount of swap space allocated, reserved, and used.

```
$ swap -s
total: 1328560k bytes allocated + 35856k reserved =
1364416k used, 3386064k available
```

This output can easily be misinterpreted. You have to understand how your particular operating system allocates swap space. Early operating systems mandated that if a process required a certain amount of real memory, that amount had to be allocated as a backing store on the swap device *in case* it was needed. Newer operating systems don't always require this. (Intimate Shared Memory on Solaris 2.6 onward is an example.) Also, keep in mind that when a process is created the necessary swap space is reserved/allocated, but not necessarily used. So just because you see a certain amount allocated doesn't necessarily mean you are actively swapping that amount.

Looking at the amount of memory used can be trickier. Many people like graphical tools, such as top or glance, and this chapter uses top later. For now, you can use the vmstat command to look at memory, although this tool provides useful CPU and disk I/O information as well. Remember to check your man pages to identify differences with this command between platforms. The following shows three snapshots taken five seconds apart.

```
$ vmstat -S 5 3
procs     memory            page            disk          faults      cpu
r b w   swap   free  si so pi po fr de sr f0 s0 s1 s2  in   sy   cs us sy id
0 0 0 3679944 647800 0  0 347 0  0  0  0  2  5  3 205  954 168  1  2 96
0 1 0 3385760 402368 0  0  0  0  0  0  0  0  1  1 146  212  82  0  0 100
0 1 0 3385760 402344 0  0  0  0  0  0  0  0  3  3 172  243  90  1  0 99
```

First check under the procs section for the w column. This column is covered in more detail in the CPU monitoring section, but for now, you should understand that values in the w column indicate processes that have been swapped out. If you see nonzero values in this column, you likely have a memory problem.

Next under memory, look at swap and free. The swap column indicates the amount of swap space allocated. Remember that operating systems like to allocate space on the swap partition in case it is needed, so this does not necessarily mean your machine is actively swapping. The free column indicates the amount of free real memory.

Paging is indicated under the page category. Remember that you can expect to see some paging on most systems, but if this becomes excessive or grows into swapping, you have problems. The most important columns here are pi, po, de, and sr. When a program starts, you can expect to see page-in activity under pi; such activity is normal. After program start-up, however, activity here indicates that processes have to page in from disk, which is not good.

po indicates that the system moved a process out in order to make room to run other processes. This is also not a good sign. If you have values under the de column, you have bigger problems. This value represents an anticipated shortage of memory; also a bad sign. Finally, sr represents the *scan rate,* which is the number of pages examined by the page daemon before it finds a free page.

> **NOTE**
>
> A Word About Thresholds
>
> Throughout all these monitoring examples, I can only suggest what to look for and what problems some numbers *might* indicate. The problem is that tuning is an art as well as a science. I cannot establish a set of concrete numbers and say with absolute certainty that if you see X number in the Y column you *always* have a Z problem. There are too many factors involved, including server size and architecture, and the OS.
>
> What I do give you are rules of thumb that I have used over the years. Based on what I have seen, read, and learned from some highly skilled Unix tuning experts I've worked with, I have never been able to find a concrete set of tuning numbers that fit *all* situations. But I do look for some key characteristics in order to determine whether a system is memory-, I/O-, or CPU-bound. Throughout this chapter, I share these rules of thumb, but make sure you apply them to your system in a reasonable manner. Remember, no one knows *your* particular system better than you and your SA, so remember to use your best judgment.

When looking at memory, keep in mind that Oracle performs best when it is in memory and not in disk. It is best if you can lock the SGA in real memory (via LOCK_SGA or ISM). However, this can come at the expense of paging for other processes. Obviously, you need to size your SGA relative to the amount of real memory available on the machine, but you also have to make sure it is big enough to keep your data blocks buffered. In many cases, this means buying more memory for the machine.

# Monitoring Disk I/O

You've read in previous chapters that disk I/O is orders of magnitude slower than memory access and that it should be avoided as much as possible. Both Oracle and Unix will go to great pains to cache data in memory in order to avoid disk I/O. Regardless, disk I/O does happen; it's your job to try to detect and eliminate needless I/O while reducing the impact of necessary I/O.

Work with the SA to plan and configure the disk layout on your machine. This involves both capacity planning and attempting to optimize performance. Typically, SAs get a box with a certain amount of disks to configure as they see fit. It's best if you can be part of the configuration planning too.

What you need to bring to the table are your plans for the database(s) you will build. Ideally, you will have a plan and sample layout of the data files, as covered in Chapter 3, "Planning a Database." Based on that example, you know you need 12 mount points and size requirements for each. From there, you and the SA start planning the disks.

Most likely the SA won't have the same number of disks as you have mount points planned. I can virtually guarantee that the SA's disk sizes will be different from your size specifications. That's okay because you don't want a ratio of one physical disk to one mount point anyway. Most likely, the SA will ask you what level of RAID you want for your disks. Therefore, you need an understanding of RAID.

## RAID

Redundant Array of Inexpensive/Independent Disks (RAID) is a method of creating filesystems across multiple physical disks. Basically, you have one logical filesystem, but it is composed of several underlying disks. The benefits of using RAID are two-fold: performance and fault tolerance.

Performance is improved with RAID because data is *striped* across multiple disks. Unix will issue a read or write to the device driver, but the actual read or write will take place over several disks, not just one. This way, no one individual disk gets hammered all the time. The amount of the data striped per disk is the *stripe size*. Speak with your SA when defining the stripe size because this value does have performance implications.

Fault tolerance is improved with RAID because, depending, on the level of RAID, if you lose one physical disk the data is still accessible on the other disks. This is possible either by disk mirroring (also called disk shadowing) or by using a parity bit. Disk mirroring is where you have data on one physical disk, but the OS keeps one or more exact copies on other disks. If you lose one disk, its data is still accessible via the mirrored disk(s).

Fault tolerance via parity bits work a little differently. The data is striped across all the disks, but each bit of data can also be recalculated from parity bits if a disk is lost. For example, you can determine that if $3 + X + 3 = 10$, X must be 4. Theoretically, the parity bits work the same way, because when a disk is lost, the remaining disks can calculate what is missing and recreate the missing data so nothing is permanently lost.

This all sounds fine, but there are some key issues that routinely come up when using RAID:

- You need multiple physical disks to implement RAID. If you are running Linux on your PC or if your Unix box only has a couple of disks, RAID isn't really an option.

- Disk mirroring provides the best fault tolerance because the data is copied exactly to multiple disks. However, this mandates that you buy twice the amount of disk you need. This gets expensive, especially as disk sizes grow.

- Fault tolerance via parity bits creates a performance hit. Every time you write, the parity has to be calculated. Supposedly if you do lose a disk, replace it, and the data is being recreated on the other disk it should still be available with degraded performance. However, one SA I know had this happened and he said his system was rendered virtually unusable because of the performance hit.

Those are just some of the issues associated with RAID. No doubt your SA will have opinions, which you will almost certainly hear. Furthermore, the use of intelligent disk array storage systems further complicates the matter. EMC is probably the biggest name among them, but there are others. When dealing with systems like these that have their own memory and configurations, you need to work with your SA and read the vendor-specific documentation. For now, this chapter focuses on the most common RAID levels in use.

## RAID 0

RAID 0 is stripping with no mirroring or parity of any kind. This adds to performance, but if you lose a disk, there is no protection and data will be lost. I have never seen this used by itself.

## RAID 1

RAID 1 is disk mirroring with no striping. If you want the safest, most fault-tolerant configuration, this is it. If one disk fails, the data is still completely intact on other disks. This does not provide any performance benefit because the data is not striped.

## RAID 0+1

RAID 0+1 is the combination of RAID 0 and RAID 1. It is mirroring with striping, which is the best of both worlds. Performance is improved because reads and writes occur across multiple disks. Fault tolerance is good because if one disk goes bad, it has a mirrored backup. This method is obviously expensive because you have twice the disk you physically need, but it is considered by many to be the best choice.

## RAID 5

RAID 5 is striping with parity. Just like in RAID 0, data is striped across multiple disks to improve performance. However, parity bits to recreate data are also striped across each disk. If one disk failure occurs, the data should still be safe because the parity bits can recreate it.

However, it should be noted that there is a performance penalty associated with recalculating the parity for each write. This level of RAID is often used when performance is not a big issue or when it is not possible to use RAID 0+1.

What about the other RAID levels, such as RAID 2, 3, and 4? Do these exist and is there anything above RAID 5? The answer is yes; they do exist. However, for the most part, they are just inefficient variations of the RAID levels previously discussed. They exist in a theoretical sense, but no one uses them because they have various flaws, which have been fixed in the levels discussed here.

In addition to RAID levels, there are two levels at which RAID is managed: hardware and software. Hardware RAID is managed at the disk subsystem level by an intelligent disk array. Software RAID is managed by the operating system; which incurs extra work for the OS. Hardware RAID is faster than software RAID and is preferable.

### NOTE

**Disks Are Getting Bigger**

Disk sizes are now exceeding the size of many databases. As of this writing, if I ask my SA for more disk space, he will ask me if I want a 18G or 36G disk. Too bad many of my testing and training databases are around 10G. This is an issue because for years DBAs wanted (and received) many small disks so they could spread out their I/O across multiple disks. Now most databases can fit one or two physical disks. And in most cases the SA or whoever is paying for the disks will laugh if the DBA asks for twelve 18G disks so he can spread out a tiny database across 12 mount points. The large size of these new disks and the economics involved are making the idea of "many small disks" a thing of the past.

So what are a DBA and SA to do? I/O still should be spread out even though the disks are relatively huge. My response is to work with the SA and stripe in an intelligent manner. Also expect to have to share the mount points with other databases. No SA is going to leave large amounts of disk unused because you are afraid of contending with other databases. This is where you, as the DBA, need to balance the different data files from multiple databases so no one disk or filesystem is getting hammered. Is this more difficult? Absolutely, but it is one consequence of having huge disks.

## Raw Partitions

There are other issues involved when deciding how to set up your disk subsystem. One issue that is not as common as it once was is the use of raw partitions. A misconception is that each disk needs to have a filesystem placed on it. That is not true. You can place data files on a raw "uncooked" partition rather than on a "cooked" partition. Most commonly this is done to improve performance. You can avoid much of the overhead of processing reads and writes by using raw filesystems. This comes at the cost managing those files as you normally would. You cannot use normal Unix commands such as `mv` or `ls` because they are not on a normal filesystem. This also requires you perform backups via the `dd` command.

The performance improvements gained by using raw partitions are not enough to justify the management headaches. For the most part, there is only one situation you will find raw partitions used: in Oracle Parallel Server (OPS) installations. OPS operates on clusters in which there is a *shared* disk array. The database files are located on this disk array so they can be accessed by each node in the cluster. However, for each node to access this shared disk array, it must be a raw partition, not a filesystem "owned" by one node. Except when OPS is used, I'd recommend against using raw partitions.

## Asynchronous I/O

The previous chapter stated that when a user process issues a request for a service by the kernel, such as an I/O, that user process will pause until the kernel returns a success or failure response to the user process. This is the default behavior for most platforms and is referred to as *synchronous I/O*.

Other platforms have an option that allows processes to proceed without waiting for the response from the kernel. This keeps the user process from needlessly waiting on an I/O and thus improves performance. Of course, it works on the assumption that the I/O subsystem is solid and that any writes will be successful. This practice is referred to as *asynchronous I/O*.

Platforms that support asynchronous I/O include Sun Solaris and HP-UX. This must also be enabled in the init.ora file. In Oracle 7.3 the parameters ASYNC_READ and ASYNC_WRITE must be set to TRUE. In Oracle 8 and above, the single parameter DISK_ASYNCH_IO must be set to TRUE. If you are on a platform that does not support asynchronous I/O, you can increase DBWR_IO_SLAVES to simulate asynchronous I/O.

## Monitoring Disk I/O

You can monitor disk I/O using several tools, but making sense of what you see and drawing accurate conclusions can be tricky. To be really effective you need to be able to tie what you see from these utilities to a particular database file and optimally to a table or index. This is the tricky part.

The tools you will see report on the activity of a particular disk. From there, you need to determine whether there is a problem with a particular disk and whether you want to pursue it further. If so, you must work with the SA to identify which mount point the problem disk corresponds to. If it is part of a striped set, it becomes more difficult to determine which mount point contains the files that are the subject of the I/O. Again, work with your SA on this.

Once you can identify the disk-to-mount-point mapping, you should be able to use a combination of your Oracle tuning tools and V$ views such as V$FILESTAT to identify which tablespace and data file is being impacted. Once you are at this point, you should be able to tell which table or index is the culprit. From there you can move the object to a "cooler" disk location or use any other method in your DBA bag of tricks to reduce the disk I/O on this object.

As complicated as this might seem, the first step is to look at your I/O using the following tools: sar, vmstat, and iostat. be sure to check the man pages for each of these tools because the options will differ between Unix and Linux. However, once you have a basic understanding of each command you should be able to use it successfully on your platform. Each of these commands has two numeric values to indicate the time in seconds between each snapshot and then the number of snapshots to take. For example, sar -b 3 5 displays statistics from five snapshots taken three seconds apart. Also, you should always ignore the numbers from the first snapshot because they are skewed.

You can use sar (System Activity Report) to check I/O. Use sar -b on Linux and sar -d on Unix. Here is a sample from a Linux box with little activity.

```
$ sar -b 3 5
Linux 2.2.16-22 (mikehat.mike.com)    06/23/2001

10:12:30 AM    tps    rtps    wtps    bread/s    bwrtn/s
10:12:33 AM    3.00    0.00    3.00       0.00      24.00
10:12:36 AM    5.66    0.00    5.66       0.00      45.33
10:12:39 AM    3.00    0.00    3.00       0.00      24.00
10:12:42 AM    5.66    0.00    5.66       0.00      45.33
10:12:45 AM    5.66    0.00    5.66       0.00      45.33
Average:       4.60    0.00    4.60       0.00      36.80
```

tps indicates the number of I/O transfers per second against a disk. rtps and wtps refer to read and write requests per second, respectively. The columns bread/s and bwrtn/s indicate the blocks read in or written out per second. As you can see from this example, there are some writes occurring, but no reads.

vmstat was used previously to check memory and it will later be used to check CPU, but here, it's used to check disk activity on a Sun box.

```
$ vmstat -S 5 3
procs     memory            page            disk          faults      cpu
r b w   swap    free  si so pi po fr de sr f0 s0 s1 s2  in   sy  cs us sy id
0 0 0 3679944 647800 0  0 347 0  0  0  0  2  5  3 205  954 168  1  2 96
0 1 0 3385760 402368 0  0  0  0  0  0  0  0  1  1 146  212  82  0  0 100
0 1 0 3385760 402344 0  0  0  0  0  0  0  0  3  3 172  243  90  1  0 99
```

Under the disk section, you want to look at s0, s1, and s2, which indicate the number of I/O operations per second on each disk.

13

UNIX SERVER
MONITORING

One tool I prefer to use is `iostat`. Again, you need to check your man pages for differences and additional options, but here is a sample from Sun Solaris.

```
$ iostat -D 5 5
     sd0            sd1            sd2            sd3
rps wps util  rps wps util  rps wps util  rps wps util
  1   1  0.5    2   3  3.7    1   2  2.1    0   0  0.0
  0   0  0.2    0   0  0.4    0   0  0.4    0   0  0.0
  0   0  0.0    0   3  2.2    0   3  2.1    0   0  0.0
  0   0  0.0    0   1  1.1    0   2  1.4    0   0  0.0
  0   0  0.0    0   1  0.8    0   1  1.0    0   0  0.0
```

Each disk is identified by sd0 to sd3. rps and wps correspond to reads per second and writes per second.

The following is how `iostat` is used on Linux.

```
$ iostat -d 4 2
Linux 2.2.16-22 (mikehat.mike.com)        06/23/2001

Disks:    tps   Blk_read/s  Blk_wrtn/s  Blk_read    Blk_wrtn
hdisk0   2.25         0.27       21.33    234014    18371058
hdisk1   0.00         0.00        0.00         0           0
hdisk2   0.00         0.00        0.00         0           0
hdisk3   0.00         0.00        0.00         0           0

Disks:    tps   Blk_read/s  Blk_wrtn/s  Blk_read    Blk_wrtn
hdisk0   0.00         0.00        0.00         0          72
hdisk1   0.00         0.00        0.00         0           0
hdisk2   0.00         0.00        0.00         0           0
hdisk3   0.00         0.00        0.00         0           0
```

tps is transfers per second. Then comes blocks read and blocks written per second and then totals for each.

So what do all these numbers mean? By themselves they are difficult to make sense of and draw conclusions. First of all, you are going to see activity on your root drive and swap partitions. Next, determine which disks correspond to the mount points with your Oracle data files. Those are the ones you want to monitor for increased activity. Finally, read about how your particular operating system buffers reads and writes and whether your disk arrays do the same. This will determine the degree to which each I/O request translates to a physical I/O (actual read/write) or a logical I/O (retrieved from memory).

# Monitoring the CPU

The previous chapter mentioned that only one process can actually be running on a CPU at any given time. However, by using time-slicing, Unix can service multiple processes nearly simultaneously to give the illusion of one CPU per user. By using SMP machines in which you have multiple processors executing simultaneously, the capability to service more processes without bottlenecks improves.

There are two ways to look at CPU usage: by using utilities to examine activity on the CPUs or by looking at the processes trying to access the CPUs. Most people immediately jump to using tools like vmstat and sar to monitor system-wide CPU usage. This chapter will certainly cover that method, but I often gain valuable information by looking at the currently running processes first to determine whether there are any "trouble makers."

If I find any runaway processes gobbling up CPU time with no end in sight, I will often kill them, thus freeing up the CPU. Just make sure you know what you are killing and are sure that they are runaway processes, not simply random jobs that you are not familiar with.

First, how do you recognize that a process has been running a long time on the CPU? Check the accumulated CPU time for the Unix process. From a DBA perspective, you obviously want to pay particular attention to user processes connected to the database. These tend to be far more problematic than any of the Oracle background processes such as LGWR or DBWR. Any process with over 10-20 minutes of accumulated CPU time will normally get my attention. Anything that exceeds several hundred minutes absolutely will be investigated and probably killed unless there is a good reason for it to exist.

**13**

Use any of the following commands to determine which processes are on the system and which ones have the highest amounts of CPU time: ps -ef, top, or glance. For example, the following code shows some Oracle processes, one of which warrants investigation.

```
$ ps -ef | grep -i ora
oracle 12574     1 0 Jun17 ? 00:04:00 oraclerh1rep1 (DESCRIPTION=(LOCA
oracle 12575     1 0 Jun17 ? 00:05:12 oraclerh1rep1 (DESCRIPTION=(LOCA
oracle 15624 15623 0 22:47 ? 00:55:04 oraclerh1rep1 (DESCRIPTION=(LOCA
```

Here, I used ps -ef to look for Oracle processes. Instead, you can use top or glance; which would have ordered the results based on the highest resource users. In this case, notice that process 15624 has 55 minutes of CPU time (shown in the seventh column), which is well worth investigating. Based on the oraclerh1rep1 and the partial description identifying the connection as LOCAL, you can determine that this is a user logged onto the database rh1rep1.

The next step is to log into SQL*Plus and identify which Oracle user session corresponds to this offending Unix process. Once that is established within Oracle, you can use your normal set of DBA tools to determine who the user is and what he or she is doing. If necessary, you can use the ALTER SYSTEM KILL SESSION command to terminate the session. From within SQL*Plus, issue the query shown in Figure 13.1 using V$SESSION and V$PROCESS.

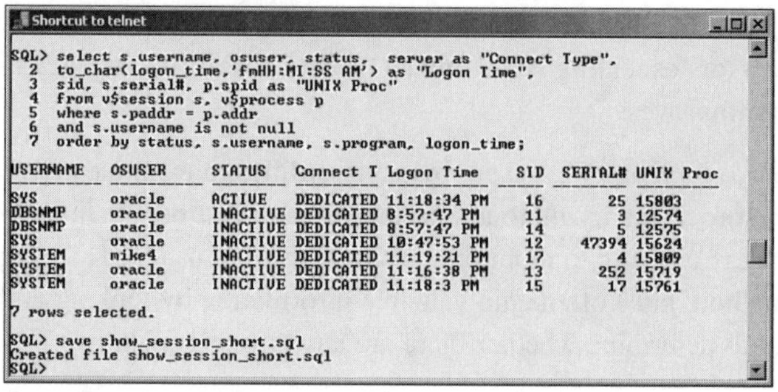

```
Shortcut to telnet
SQL> select s.username, osuser, status,  server as "Connect Type",
  2  to_char(logon_time,'fmHH:MI:SS AM') as "Logon Time",
  3  sid, s.serial#, p.spid as "UNIX Proc"
  4  from v$session s, v$process p
  5  where s.paddr = p.addr
  6  and s.username is not null
  7  order by status, s.username, s.program, logon_time;

USERNAME   OSUSER     STATUS   Connect T Logon Time     SID SERIAL# UNIX Proc
---------- ---------- -------- --------- ----------- ------ ------- ---------
SYS        oracle     ACTIVE   DEDICATED 11:18:34 PM     16      25 15803
DBSNMP     oracle     INACTIVE DEDICATED 8:57:47 PM      11       3 12574
DBSNMP     oracle     INACTIVE DEDICATED 8:57:47 PM      14       5 12575
SYS        oracle     INACTIVE DEDICATED 10:47:53 PM     12   47394 15624
SYSTEM     mike4      INACTIVE DEDICATED 11:19:21 PM     17       4 15809
SYSTEM     oracle     INACTIVE DEDICATED 11:16:38 PM     13     252 15719
SYSTEM     oracle     INACTIVE DEDICATED 11:18:3 PM      15      17 15761

7 rows selected.

SQL> save show_session_short.sql
Created file show_session_short.sql
SQL>
```

**FIGURE 13.1**

*Finding Unix PIDs for Oracle Sessions.*

As you can see in Figure 13.1, there is someone logged in as SYS with a SID of 12, SERIAL# of 47394, and the Unix PID of 15624. The PID identifies this user as the Unix process with 55 minutes of CPU time (identified with `ps -ef`) and the corresponding database information allows you to investigate what this user is doing. If necessary, you can contact the user or kill the session. Because this is a handy query to have, I saved it to a SQL script called `show_session_short.sql` for future use. It is also included in Appendix C.

The utility `top`, which you read about previously, also provides a plethora of good information regarding CPU usage and active processes. It breaks down CPU usage in an easy-to-read format as well as shows the most active processes. Figure 13.2 shows a sample `top` display.

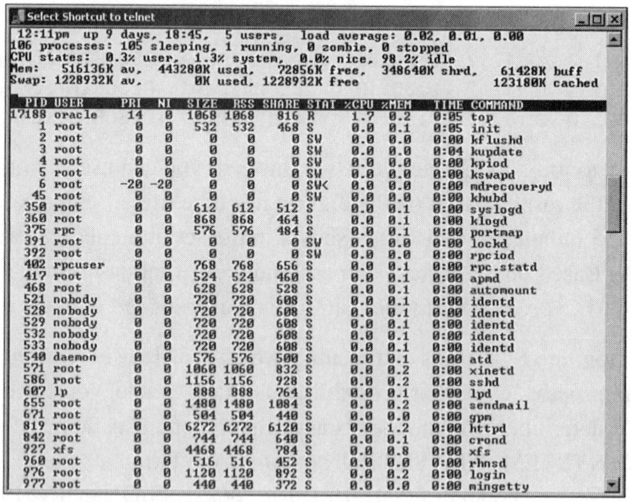

```
Select Shortcut to telnet
 12:11pm  up 9 days, 18:45,  5 users,  load average: 0.02, 0.01, 0.00
106 processes: 105 sleeping, 1 running, 0 zombie, 0 stopped
CPU states:  0.3% user,  1.3% system,  0.0% nice, 98.2% idle
Mem:   516136K av,  443280K used,   72856K free,  348640K shrd,   61428K buff
Swap: 1228932K av,       0K used, 1228932K free                  123180K cached

  PID USER     PRI  NI  SIZE  RSS SHARE STAT %CPU %MEM   TIME COMMAND
17188 oracle    14   0  1068 1068   816 R     1.7  0.2   0:05 top
    1 root       0   0   532  532   468 S     0.0  0.1   0:05 init
    2 root       0   0     0    0     0 SW    0.0  0.0   0:00 kflushd
    3 root       0   0     0    0     0 SW    0.0  0.0   0:04 kupdate
    4 root       0   0     0    0     0 SW    0.0  0.0   0:00 kpiod
    5 root       0   0     0    0     0 SW    0.0  0.0   0:00 kswapd
    6 root     -20 -20     0    0     0 SW<   0.0  0.0   0:00 mdrecoveryd
   45 root       0   0     0    0     0 SW    0.0  0.0   0:00 khubd
  350 root       0   0   612  612   512 S     0.0  0.1   0:00 syslogd
  360 root       0   0   868  868   464 S     0.0  0.1   0:00 klogd
  375 rpc        0   0   576  576   484 S     0.0  0.1   0:00 portmap
  391 root       0   0     0    0     0 SW    0.0  0.0   0:00 lockd
  392 root       0   0     0    0     0 SW    0.0  0.0   0:00 rpciod
  402 rpcuser    0   0   768  768   656 S     0.0  0.1   0:00 rpc.statd
  417 root       0   0   524  524   460 S     0.0  0.1   0:00 apmd
  468 root       0   0   628  628   528 S     0.0  0.1   0:00 automount
  521 nobody     0   0   720  720   608 S     0.0  0.1   0:00 identd
  528 nobody     0   0   720  720   608 S     0.0  0.1   0:00 identd
  529 nobody     0   0   720  720   608 S     0.0  0.1   0:00 identd
  532 nobody     0   0   720  720   608 S     0.0  0.1   0:00 identd
  533 nobody     0   0   720  720   608 S     0.0  0.1   0:00 identd
  540 daemon     0   0   576  576   500 S     0.0  0.1   0:00 atd
  571 root       0   0  1060 1060   832 S     0.0  0.2   0:00 xinetd
  586 root       0   0  1156 1156   928 S     0.0  0.2   0:00 sshd
  607 lp         0   0   888  888   764 S     0.0  0.1   0:00 lpd
  655 root       0   0  1480 1480  1084 S     0.0  0.2   0:00 sendmail
  671 root       0   0   504  504   440 S     0.0  0.0   0:00 gpm
  819 root       0   0  6272 6272  6120 S     0.0  1.2   0:00 httpd
  842 root       0   0   744  744   640 S     0.0  0.1   0:00 crond
  927 xfs        0   0  4468 4468   784 S     0.0  0.8   0:00 xfs
  960 root       0   0   516  516   452 S     0.0  0.0   0:00 rhnsd
  976 root       0   0  1120 1120   892 S     0.0  0.2   0:00 login
  977 root       0   0   440  440   372 S     0.0  0.0   0:00 mingetty
```

**FIGURE 13.2**

*Using `top` to View CPU Usage.*

Notice that `top` gives you information regarding memory and CPU, as well as detailed process information in a quick and easy to understand format. For those reasons alone, you will find `top` to be one of the most commonly used tools among DBAs and SAs.

---

### Determine Who Is Hogging Your CPUs

One morning I had a database that was taking a while to recover after a crash so I decided to check it out via `glance` (I was on an HP-UX 9000). I noticed that three of the six CPUs where pegged at nearly 100% utilization by three separate processes. Obviously each was climbing in terms of CPU time. This immediately raised some concerns about using half the processors on the machine to service three processes, which were likely runaway processes.

By using `glance`, `top`, and a combination of `ps -ef` with V$SESSION, I was able to determine one process was a backup that was running late, one was a runaway database process, and one was my database recovering. After consulting with the SA, we determined it was best to kill the backup and the runaway database job. We left the database recovery process alone. The end result freed two CPUs that were otherwise being wasted.

---

## Monitoring the CPU

When monitoring CPU usage, I first look at two similar metrics: system "load" and how many processes are waiting to run on a processor. Next I look at the percentage of user versus system verses idle processing so I can see where the processor is spending most of its time.

"Load" describes how busy or stressed a server is. Based on this number, you can tell relatively how busy a server is. Tools that provide this number also provide the average load from both five minutes and 15 minutes ago so you can tell whether the workload is increasing or decreasing. The easiest way to determine load is to use `uptime`:

```
$ uptime
2:09pm up 8 day(s), 21:55, 2 users, load average: 0.01, 0.02, 0.04
```

This gives you three very handy pieces of information. First, you can tell how long the box has been up. If you notice the machine has been up for an incredibly short amount of time, it's a reasonable bet that the machine bounced or crashed unexpectedly and that's why people are complaining. Believe it or not, this is sometimes how administrators find out their box has crashed at some point. The next piece of information is the number of users. Because people can connect to the server via Net8, this cannot be a reliable indicator of how many people are using the machine, but you should know your server well enough to notice if this is an especially large or small relative number.

Finally the load average is listed. As you can see, the average for that past minute was .01, the last five minutes it was .02, and over the last 15 minutes it was .04. Basically, this server is almost idle. On a "normal" system running Oracle during the day, I expect to see a load around 3.0. This might vary depending on your machine, but you should have an idea of what is "normal" for your system. That way if you see it spike to 10 you know something is happening.

How high can this value go? Again it depends on a variety of factors, but I start investigating if it gets above 5. On some systems I've seen it into the high teens, but at that point users are usually complaining.

Load information is also available via top and glance.

Most utilities report the usage of CPU on the machine as a percentage doing the following: being idle, servicing user processes, or servicing system processes. If the CPU has a high idle percentage, it is not doing anything. Generally, there is not a problem with a CPU having a high utilization percentage. However, you don't want to see an excessive amount of CPU time dedicated to system processing. This is because you want the CPU to service your user processes, which are the ones doing the application work for the system. As a rule of thumb, I like to see system processing around 20% or 30% and user processing around 70% or 80%.

The other characteristic similar to load that I look at when monitoring CPU usage is how many processes are runnable, but are waiting on a CPU. The tool I use for this is vmstat, which you used earlier to look at memory and disk I/O.

```
$ vmstat -S 5 3
procs      memory            page            disk          faults      cpu
r b w   swap   free si so pi po fr de sr f0 s0 s1 s2  in   sy  cs us sy id
0 0 0 3679944 647800 0  0 347 0  0  0  0  0  2  5  3 205  954 168  1  2 96
0 1 0 3385760 402368 0  0   0 0  0  0  0  0  0  1  1 146  212  82  0  0 100
0 1 0 3385760 402344 0  0   0 0  0  0  0  0  0  3  3 172  243  90  1  0 99
```

Once again, ignore the first line of statistics, as you have three snapshots five seconds apart. Next focus on the procs section. The values r, b, and w have the following meanings:

r       The count of runnable processes.

b       The number of processes that are blocked from executing because they are waiting on I/O or memory.

w       The number of processes that are waiting because they have been swapped out (memory shortage).

Under the faults section, you can see three statistics: interrupts in, system calls sy, and context switches cs. Each statistic is measured in number of times the event occurred per second.

The final section of vmstat is cpu. Here, you have a measure of time spent on user processes us, system processes sy, and the time idle id. As you can see, most of the time the CPU is idle and is not being used.

Another tool you can use to monitor CPU usage is sar.

```
$ sar -u 5 5

SunOS vader 5.8 Generic sun4u    03/15/01

14:14:39    %usr     %sys     %wio    %idle
14:14:44      0        0        50       49
14:14:49      0        0        51       48
14:14:54      0        7         8       85
14:14:59      0        1         0       99
14:15:04      2        4         1       93

Average       1        2        22       75
```

This report also shows the percentage of CPU use on user %usr, system %sys, and idle %idle. It also has another informative column indicating how much time was spent waiting on disk I/O %wio.

One Solaris utility I sometimes use displays a great deal of information—it's called mpstat.

```
$ mpstat 5 5
CPU minf mjf xcal intr ithr csw icsw migr smtx srw syscl usr sys wt idl
  1   33   1  184  283  181  83    3    4    5   0   459   1   2  8  89
  3   35   1  144   21   19  84    3    4    6   0   494   1   3  8  88
CPU minf mjf xcal intr ithr csw icsw migr smtx srw syscl usr sys wt idl
  1    1   0    4  309  209  90    0    3    0   0   164   1   0  1  99
  3    0   0    6    1    1  37    0    3    1   0    79   0  15  4  82
CPU minf mjf xcal intr ithr csw icsw migr smtx srw syscl usr sys wt idl
  1  291   0  195  270  167 155    5    7    7   0   935   4   3  0  93
  3  291   0   79    5    1 162    4    7    8   0   887   2   5  3  90
CPU minf mjf xcal intr ithr csw icsw migr smtx srw syscl usr sys wt idl
  1   12   0   16  262  162  47    0    2    0   0   172   0   1  2  98
  3   12   0   13    1    0  51    0    1    0   0   116   0   1  1  98
CPU minf mjf xcal intr ithr csw icsw migr smtx srw syscl usr sys wt idl
  1    0   0    5  250  150  35    0    1    0   0   110   0   0  1  99
  3    0   0    6    1    1  40    0    1    0   0    90   0   1  1  98
```

Just like with vmstat and sar, this utility provides percentages of CPU utilization. However, this utility also provides information pertaining to faults, interrupts, and context switches. Check the man page for a detailed description of each column.

**13**

## Consult Before Killing Sessions

I was wrapping up the day one Friday when the Sun E10000 I was working on was brought to its knees. Response time was slow and almost immediately several people came to my cube asking what the problem was. That server hosted several repository

*continues*

databases for Oracle Designer. Normally it ran like a champ, but for some reason it was crawling along at a snail's pace.

I quickly checked uptime and the load was around 15 and climbing. That is not good considering that it is normally around 3 or 4. Considering that this is a very large multiple CPU machine with abundant memory I knew something was wrong. Next I ran top and identified several Designer users, each with several hundred minutes of CPU time on the same database; these numbers were climbing. In the absence of any other unusual statistics, that was enough for me to determine that those people were indeed the culprits.

I traced the PIDs to individual database logins via SQL*Plus. Based on the IDs I knew who these people were and I also knew that they had been working on a project. Rather than just killing their sessions I decided to ask them what they were doing. It turns out that each one had some intensive processing to do within Designer and happened to start them at about the same time. This was just a case where people were not communicating or coordinating what they were doing with each other.

Did I kill their sessions and lecture them on scheduling resource intensive jobs? No. The timelines of this project dictated that these jobs had to finish. Management confirmed that, in this case, it was better to let their jobs finish at the expense of the rest of the users. This wasn't as bad as it sounds because on a Friday most people were going home anyway. So as a result, even though we knew who and what was causing the problem, there wasn't anything we could do to improve the immediate situation. It is cases like these where the DBA needs to use people skills and understand the needs of business in addition to technical skills to be successful.

Monitoring the CPU is not as difficult as monitoring other areas such as memory or the network. Perhaps this is because CPUs are easier to conceptualize rather than a swap area or network collisions. Regardless, this section has illustrated several tools that you can use to monitor CPU utilization.

# Monitoring the Network

Blaming the network for performance problems is a common tactic when the database, server, and application all appear okay. Like it or not, if everything else is "proven" to be fine, the network is usually the scapegoat when poor response time occurs. Part of this is because most DBAs, application people, and even some SAs have a tough time monitoring or tuning networks. Most have a good theoretical knowledge of networking principles, but not as many have the hands-on skills. This issue is exacerbated by not having as many tools on hand and used regularly by these people to monitor the network. DBAs and application people are busy enough trying to work their core areas. The goal is to get the DBA and application developers to think in terms of memory and CPU consumption while minimizing disk I/O. However, getting these people to think in terms of networking is a stretch because networking is largely out the hands of DBAs or developers.

For these reasons I recommend that if you suspect network issues, don't hesitate to enlist the help of people who deal with networks on a daily basis. As the DBA, you should be able to eliminate the database, application, and much of the server from the list of suspects when performance problems occur. With a little skill and investigative work you can perhaps suggest a network problem. However, to confirm the problem and get it fixed, you will need outside help. Just make sure you have your facts straight and have exhausted your resources before blaming the network for performance problems.

## Monitoring Network Usage

One tool commonly used by DBAs is tnsping. This is not a Unix network performance tool; it is actually an Oracle utility used to test database connectivity. However, it does provide timing statistics. You can use it as shown in Figure 13.3.

**FIGURE 13.3**

*Using* tnsping *to Test the Network.*

As you can see here, it is an Oracle utility that contacts the host and port used by the listener (1521). It returns a success or failure message and how long it took. Notice that this can be issued from a DOS prompt and that you don't need to be on a Linux or Unix box.

Another very similar and more common tool is the normal ping utility used by most people. Figure 13.4 shows a sample of its use.

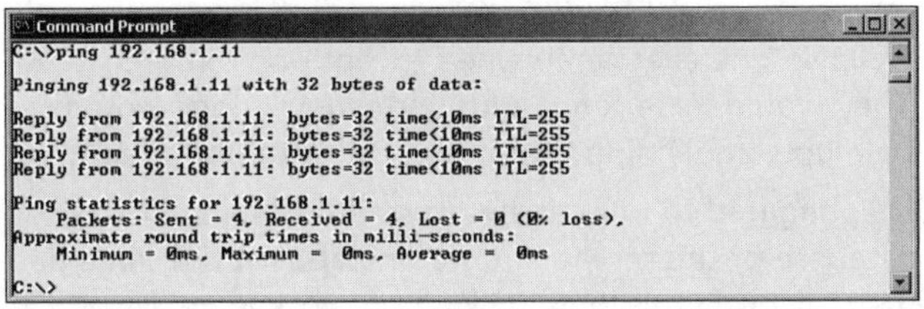

**FIGURE 13.4**

*Using* ping *to Test the Network.*

This provides a little more network-specific information than tnsping. You still get time statistics, but you also get the number of packets sent and received.

Obviously tnsping and ping provide some useful information, but not enough to allow serious network tuning. A more powerful tool is ifconfig -a. This command shows all network cards installed, the IP address, the number of packets sent (TX), the number of packets received (RX), and the number of collisions and errors.

```
$ ifconfig -a
eth0 Link encap:Ethernet  HWaddr 00:01:03:2D:4C:A2
     inet addr:192.168.1.11  Bcast:192.168.1.255  Mask:255.255.255.0
     UP BROADCAST RUNNING MULTICAST  MTU:1500  Metric:1
     RX packets:28589 errors:0 dropped:0 overruns:0 frame:0
     TX packets:17338 errors:0 dropped:0 overruns:0 carrier:0
     collisions:0 txqueuelen:100
     Interrupt:11 Base address:0xac00

lo   Link encap:Local Loopback
     inet addr:127.0.0.1  Mask:255.0.0.0
     UP LOOPBACK RUNNING  MTU:3924  Metric:1
     RX packets:686 errors:0 dropped:0 overruns:0 frame:0
     TX packets:686 errors:0 dropped:0 overruns:0 carrier:0
     collisions:0 txqueuelen:0
```

In this example, what you care about is the Ethernet card because that is where the network traffic is occurring. Look for high amounts of collisions and errors, which might indicate a problem to be further investigated by more skilled network specialists.

One final tool I will briefly mention is netstat. This tool is more useful, but it is also more complex and requires network knowledge outside the scope of this book. However, I want to acknowledge its existence and suggest you consult your man pages and network-specific resources for more information.

## Blame the Network or Blame the DBA?

I was managing some databases on a box and response time was good. All my database numbers (obtained using STATSPACK) were good and server statistics were generally good as well. No one ever complained except one remote site located hundreds of miles away. They would issue commands and when things would seem to run slow they would call me up complaining that it was the database's fault.

As a DBA you are obligated to investigate these claims and I did. I found nothing wrong on the database or the server. Plus no one else on the same database was having any problems. Obviously this looked like a network issue. Next I called the user back and by chance ended up speaking to someone else. This person volunteered

*continues*

that it was odd that one physical side the room was running fine, but the other physical side was horribly bogged down. This included everything, not just the database. I started laughing once I heard this because it was such an obvious network (not database) issue. Eventually they did have a dedicated network technician look at their network and made some changes. After that, everyone has been running fine. The moral of this story is that people will often blame whatever application they are using that seems to be running slow, regardless of the root cause. In this case, they were working on the database so they called me. Had these people be using another application, someone else would have probably been called even though it was really a network problem.

These are the tools I use to get a rough snapshot of the network. Use `tnsping` and `ping` to test connectivity and get sample times. Then use `ifconfig` to determine how many network cards your machine has, their IP addresses, the number of packets sent/received, and statistics relating to lost packets and collisions. Finally, if you really want more info, make use of `netstat`. However, my most common recommendation is to make use of your network technicians if you really think you have a problem.

## Summary

This chapter covered Unix server monitoring. At a high level, it looked at memory, disk I/O, CPU, and network consumption on the Unix server. Then, it took a deeper look at how Unix and Oracle interact in terms of shared memory, semaphores, and disk I/O. Understanding these topics and being able to apply them to real-world systems are truly key to being an effective Unix and Linux DBA. Many people argue that these skills separate Oracle DBAs on Unix/Linux from those on other operating systems. Indeed, these are critical skills to have if you want to be successful.

Within each category (memory, disk I/O, CPU, and network), you read about multiple utilities used to monitor performance.

Finally, I tried to include as many relevant examples and experiences from my past as I could in order to illustrate situations that might also happen to you. Remember, just like Oracle monitoring and tuning, Unix monitoring and tuning requires a mix of technical knowledge, problem-solving skills, logic, and people skills. This chapter attempted to provide the basis to succeed at monitoring and tuning your server.

# Patches and Upgrades

## ESSENTIALS

- Bugs and performance enhancements are common to any sophisticated software package and Oracle is no exception.

- Installing: patches to fix existing problems or to prevent future problems is part of the DBA's job.

- Upgrading the database release (such as from 8.1.6 to 8.1.7) is a common way to avoid bugs and improve the database's functionality.

- Installing: patches and performing upgrades normally are uneventful processes; however, you need to research, plan, and test these changes before incorporating them into production systems.

- Be aware of changes in the system as a result of a patch or upgrade.

It's commonly the DBA's job to apply patches and upgrade the database to newer releases. This is not normally done on a weekly basis, but it does need to be done periodically in order to fix or prevent bugs from causing problems and to keep the database up to date.

This chapter differentiates between applying a patch versus performing an upgrade. It explains how and why each is done. It also provides examples of how this is typically performed. It shows you how to apply a trivial patch to an 8.1.6 database, and upgrades another to 8.1.7. Issues regarding patch and upgrade policies are also discussed.

## What Are Patches and Upgrades?

Any sophisticated software package, including Oracle, is in a continued state of change. The competitive IT industry demands that companies always improve and update their products to improve sales. Software development is often at a breakneck pace—new product releases often occur every several months. Add to this the different operating systems that must be supported for any large product such as Oracle. As a result you can expect two consequences because of the fierce competition to release new products:

- Existing products will have problems (called "bugs").
- Vendors will push their customers to keep upgrading to the latest and greatest versions of their products.

These consequences happen with any software company you deal with, not just Oracle. This is simply the nature of the IT industry.

The first consequence deals with bugs. There is an old saying that if you fix one problem, you'll end up breaking something else. This is often true, especially in software development. Furthermore, as new features are added, you can expect there to be new bugs because these features haven't been tested yet in the real world. For situations like this, Oracle offers patches to fix the bugs.

The second consequence deals with upgrading. Each successive release of Oracle theoretically has new minor features and improvements, in addition to fixes for all the bugs in the previous release. If you want to take advantage of these new features and fix your existing bugs, you perform an upgrade.

When I say upgrade, I mean moving upward from one release in the same version to a higher release *within* the same base version. For example, going from Oracle 7.3.2.3 to 7.3.4 is considered an *upgrade*. However, if you wanted to go from Oracle 7.3.4 to 8.1.6, that is considered a *migration* because you are moving to a different version. Migrations are covered in the next chapter. Figure 14.1 shows the differences between version, release, and patchset numbers and how to differentiate between these.

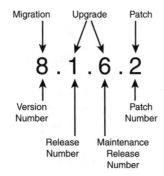

**FIGURE 14.1**

*Upgrades Versus Migrations.*

As you can see in Figure 14.1, a change in version is a migration and a change in release number is an upgrade. When you apply large patchsets, you can expect the patch number to increase as well.

When and why do you apply a patch or perform an upgrade? Usually this information is relayed to you by Oracle Support. For example, if you are encountering an unusual problem and call Support, they might well determine you are encountering a bug. They will normally tell you what patch you need to download and apply or what database version you need to upgrade to. You can also pay attention to new software announcements. For example, you might be running Oracle 8.1.6, but you have heard that Oracle 8.1.7 is out, so you decide to upgrade to 8.1.7.

Before you apply any type of patch or attempt an upgrade, you *must* do research and testing. It's not that installing:patches and doing upgrades is necessarily difficult, but they are detail-oriented processes and you need to follow the directions. Depending on the README file, you might just have to run a simple Unix shell script that will make the changes for you. In other cases, you have to start the Oracle Universal Install to make the changes, relink some or all of the executables, and then run scripts to rebuild the data dictionaries in each database. Again, none of this is difficult by itself, but you do need to know what you are doing.

In many cases, you will not need to apply the patch or perform an upgrade because they contain fixes to products you don't use. For example, assume there is a bug with replication. However, if you don't use replication and never plan on using it, applying a patch is not necessary and you should in fact probably avoid it.

**14**

---

> **NOTE**
>
> Patches and Upgrades Aren't Just for the Database
>
> *Any* product or tool you use might need to be patched or upgraded, not just the database server. As a general rule, it is a DBA responsibility if the product is owned by Oracle. For example, it is not uncommon for the DBA to install and patch Oracle Designer and/or Oracle Developer. The same guidelines that apply to the database should be applied when patching these tools.
>
> From time to time the operating system will also be patched or upgraded. This is typically an SA responsibility, but because it impacts the database you should be notified. Your job is to make sure there aren't any bugs or potential issues with the SA modifying the operating system. Check with Oracle Support and online forums to determine whether there are any known bugs. Also make sure the OS version the SA is upgrading to is compatible with Oracle. Specifically, you need to check the Oracle database and operating system matrix to ensure the database and OS are compatible and if there are any known issues. As a DBA you have to coordinate with the SA, developers, and designers to make sure that any planned patches or upgrades do not break other tools.

Installing: patches and performing upgrades *should* be uneventful and even boring. This is one area where you don't want unexpected results and excitement. Rather, you should be very familiar with the patch/upgrade instructions and have tested them on test databases. By the time you apply the patch to a production system, the process should be routine. I usually test what I'm doing on a development server, even if it only has the demo database installed. Even if the patch or upgrade runs correctly, I still need to know approximately how long the entire process will take and if there will be any invalid objects to recompile. Therefore, testing is a must.

# When and How to Apply Patches

This section examines when and how you should apply patches.

## Overview

Patches are small modifications made to the Oracle software to fix one or more bugs. If the bug is potentially serious, such as one that can cause database corruption, failure, or a security hole, you can expect a patch to fix that specific problem. When problems like this are discovered, Oracle will put a patch out immediately. Other times Oracle will wait and combine multiple bug fixes together into one larger patch. You might want the patch to fix a specific bug you are encountering, but in reality you might receive several bug fixes.

How do you know if you are encountering a bug and need a patch? Typically this happens in one of two ways. Either you or someone in your department notices something unusual and it turns out to be a bug or you see a bulletin from Oracle stating there is a bug.

In the first case, either you or someone notices some part of the database is behaving abnormally. An obvious example is if you try to start SQL*Plus and it performs a core dump. A lesser example is when you notice performance is unexpectedly bad or you receive a lot of warning messages. The trick is trying to identify whether the problem is your fault or whether it is because of a legitimate problem with the software. If you notice something that "isn't right," try to develop a test case for it. Determine whether it is a repeatable occurrence and document under what conditions it occurs. This is key; Oracle Support cannot do anything if you simply call and claim there is a bug. You need to provide them with documented proof of what you are seeing. Additionally, it needs to be documented so they can reproduce the same problem in their labs. Only after that is done can they determine whether the problem represents a real bug that needs to be fixed.

Once you have documented what you believe to be a bug, check with Oracle Support to see whether the bug has already been reported. Oracle has thousands of customers, so if you've found a bug, odds are it's happening to other people as well. If you are using Oracle online support such as MetaLink, try a search based on a short description of the problem. However, do not be surprised if it doesn't return any results. Oracle MetaLink has two versions: a public one with limited bug information and a internal version for Oracle employees with all the bug information. It may very well be that you are running into a bug, but Oracle doesn't have information about it posted for the general public on MetaLink.

The next step is to call Oracle Support and describe the situation. From there, the analyst will be able to access the internal MetaLink site to search for bugs. If there are any, the analyst will be able to tell you what the bug is, how severe it is, and how to fix it or a suitable workaround. Remember, you pay for Support as part of your license fees so don't be afraid to use it, particularly when dealing with bugs.

The other way you find out about bugs is because you read about them somewhere or someone tells you about them. For example, many times your developers will find bugs and will ask you to patch them. Other times you will read about Oracle bugs from third-party sources and you will pursue the problem from there. Other times by just browsing through MetaLink or talking to Oracle Support, you will find out about patches. Therefore, you should periodically check MetaLink's Patches section of your particular platform to find any new patches and bugs.

**14**

PATCHES AND
UPGRADES

**NOTE**

Check Your Installation CD for Patches

Sometimes your Oracle installation CD will contain patches included with it. After you mount the CD, do an `ls` to see whether there is a patches subdirectory. If so, investigate these patches because you might need to apply them after your installation.

Should you apply a patch for every bug you see? Absolutely not! Rather, you need to consider how the bug impacts your system. Remember, installing:patches requires system downtime and they do have the possibility of causing additional problems, so you don't want to apply patches if they are not necessary. As a guideline I wait for larger patchsets so I can squash multiple bugs at once. These larger patchsets have the benefit of being more completely tested for bugs than small "one-off" patches. However, if there is a serious bug or one that directly impacts my system, I'll apply it as soon as it is available. Finally, keep in mind that some IT shops attempt to have standardized versions of Oracle across all databases, so consider this before installing: patches.

## Applying a Patch to Your System

Once you have determined that a patch needs to be applied, the next steps are to read the README file, download the patch, FTP it to the server if necessary, create a backup, apply the patch, and perform any post patch validation.

The first step is to read the README file. This is available online via MetaLink and is included with the patch. I cannot stress enough how important it is to read and understand each step outlined in this document. Installing:patches often requires using the OUI, using shell scripts, manually relinking the executables, and running SQL scripts. If you don't thoroughly read the README file, you will not know what to do and you will likely mess up your database.

Next, download the patch to your server or to your PC where you can then FTP it to your server. Go to the Patches link at `http://metalink.oracle.com` unless directed otherwise. Remember to make sure the patch you are getting *exactly* matches your database version, operating system platform, and operating system version. In this case, close isn't good enough (unless directed otherwise by Oracle Support).

**TIP**

Don't Have Access to MetaLink?

Not everyone has a MetaLink account or can get to it all the time. If so, you can also download patches from:

```
ftp://oracle-ftp.oracle.com
```
I sometimes find more patches available on this site than on the normal MetaLink
site. If you are considering a move to a different version or platform, this site helps
you determine how many bug fixes there are. It's an easy-to-navigate site.

Patches are usually compressed, but they can be anywhere from 20K to several hundred
megabytes in size. Obviously, you need a reliable network connection to do the download.
Otherwise, call Oracle Support and see whether they can ship you the patch.

Create a subdirectory in your $ORACLE_HOME called patches or patchsets. In this location,
you should make a subdirectory for each patch you apply and reference it by the bug or patch
number. You need to place these files somewhere, and this system is a good way to keep track
of which patches have been applied. The following code shows how to do this.

```
$ cd $ORACLE_HOME
$ ls
JRE           install          ldap        odg       plsql
assistants    install.platform lib         oracore   precomp    slax
bin           javavm           md          ord       rdbms      sqlj
ctx           jdbc             network     otrace    relnotes   sqlplus
dbs           jlib             ocommon     owm       root.sh    svrmgr
$ mkdir patches
$ ls
JRE           install          ldap        odg       patches    root.sh
svrmgr        assistants       install.platform lib       oracore    plsql
bin           javavm           md          ord       precomp    slax
ctx           jdbc             network     otrace    rdbms      sqlj
dbs           jlib             ocommon     owm       relnotes   sqlplus
$ mkdir patches/bug_12345
```

Here, you have a patches subdirectory and a directory beneath that for a specific patch. After
you apply the patch, do not delete the directory or log files. If a tar file or a compressed copy
of the patch still exists and isn't needed anywhere else, you can delete them; but you should
keep your log files.

If you have to FTP your patches from server to server, make sure you use the correct form of
FTP. Corrupting files via FTP is a simple mistake, but it happens all the time.

**14**

## TIP

### FTP and Corruption

A common mistake I see all the time is FTPing files in the wrong mode. Specifically,
moving a file in ASCII when it should be binary and vice versa. If this happens with

SQL files or text files you might see control characters such as ^M at the end of each line if you vi the file. You can remove these manually, but a better solution is to FTP the file again. If you do this accidentally with an executable or a patch, you should consider that copy worthless and redo the FTP.

Remember to verify the type of FTP you are doing. For example, do not assume that a Unix-to-Unix FTP defaults to binary; I have seen cases where it does not. If you are unsure what you are set to use, issue the command status to see bin or binary (binary) or ascii (ASCII). In the following example, I switch from a default ASCII to a binary transfer.

```
ftp> status
Connected to 192.168.1.11.
Type: ascii; Verbose: On ; Bell: Off ; Prompting: On ; Globbing: On
Debugging: Off ; Hash mark printing: Off .
ftp> bin
200 Type set to I.
Connected to 192.168.1.11.
Type: binary; Verbose: On ; Bell: Off ; Prompting: On ; Globbing: On
Debugging: Off ; Hash mark printing: Off .
```

There are many GUI FTP tools available, many for free. However, you should still know how to use the command-line version of FTP on Unix, Linux, and Windows boxes because these GUI tools are not always available.

Before applying a patch and especially before doing an upgrade, it's a good idea to perform a backup. Preferably this is a cold backup of your database and all your OS software files. However, I must confess I don't always do this for "minor" patches, but I will also probably suffer for it sometime as well. Even though most patches I've seen come with or generate scripts to deinstall them, I have to recommend taking a backup if possible.

I approach installing:patches or doing upgrades just like I do performing installs. Read the documentation and set up your environment as you do normally. Make sure your ORACLE_HOME and your other environment variables are set properly or you will have big problems.

Applying the patch normally requires that you shut down the database(s). If your database needs to be shut down, be sure to coordinate this with your users. The actual process of applying a patch doesn't take too long, but there might be post-patch steps such as running data dictionary scripts and recompiling invalid objects that can be time-consuming. Therefore, make sure to allow yourself adequate time. Also, don't forget to shut down any database listener processes before applying a patch.

## The Databases Are Down!

Late one Friday afternoon, users at one of my IT shops reported that all the databases on a certain server were suddenly down. Users started calling and asking why their sessions had been killed and why Oracle wasn't available. DBAs and SAs began searching through their logs in an attempt to determine what happened. Finally, a new DBA seated far from the others heard the commotion, stood up out of his cube and said, "Oh, I shut them down to apply a patch."

It turns out this DBA was actually very experienced and quite good; he was just new to this shop. Someone had told him to apply the patch and that the databases on that server weren't really being used. Apparently he saw a few logins, but figured they were from people who'd left for the day so he killed them and then shut down the databases.

Because the databases were already down and the patch was basic, he quickly applied it and restarted the databases. This was nothing more than a miscommunication, but it should underscore the need to communicate effectively, especially with new people.

The way the patch is actually applied depends on the specific patch itself. I have used the following methods, as directed by the README files, to apply patches.

- Run a simple Unix shell script provided with the patch. In fact, sometimes the README *is* the script. Normally these scripts just make copies of old files, move new files to the correct locations, and then relink the appropriate executables. Installing:patches like this gives you the benefit of being able to read the shell script *before* you actually run it. This method is commonly used when the patch fixes one or a very small number of bugs.

- Manually move one or more individual files to the locations identified in the README file. Obviously, you need to make sure file ownership and permissions are correct.

- Use the OUI to apply the patch. After you unzip or untar the patch, a runInstaller.sh file is created in your patch directory. Set up your environment and use this script to start the OUI. Follow the instructions in the README to navigate through the OUI and apply the patch. This is a fairly simple method.

Once again, the README file will dictate which method you use to apply the patch. In the first two methods, log files might not be generated automatically. If they aren't, you should use the command `script` to create a log of what you have done. The OUI will generate logs of what it does automatically. Once the patch is applied, review these logs for errors.

After the patch has been applied, there may be post-patch steps to do for each database impacted. Typical examples of these include:

**14**

- Start the database, connect internal, and run the following scripts from `$ORACLE_HOME/rdbms/admin`:

  `catalog.sql`: Re-creates data dictionary views

  `catproc.sql`: Script for the procedural option

  `catrep.sql`: If you are running replication

  These scripts can run for a while and they need to be executed against every database impacted by the patch. Basically, they re-create data dictionary objects so the database can take advantage of the changes.

- Rebuild Java inside the database. Do this only if Java is installed. You can check this by either connecting internally and doing `DESCRIBE DBMS_JAVA` or counting the number of objects in `DBA_OBJECTS WHERE OBJECT_TYPE LIKE 'JAVA%'`. If you get a big package header called `DBMS_JAVA` or have roughly 8000 or 9000 Java objects, Java is installed and you need to perform the following step as internal:

  ```
  SQL> create or replace java system
  /
  ```

  The slash on the second line is important. Expect this command to run for a while. We cover this more in detail in Chapter 16, "Java Inside the Database Server."

- Check for invalid objects and recompile them. Preferably you should have a count of invalid objects before you apply the patch so you can see what has changed. After the patch has been applied and you have completed all the other post-patchsets, recompile any object from `DBA_OBJECTS WHERE STATUS = 'INVALID'`. I strongly recommend you use Dynamic SQL to accomplish this, as covered in Chapter 5, "Creating a Database."

Once the post-patch steps are done don't forget to start the listener so the users can log in.

These are the basic steps to follow when installing:patches. The next section goes through a simple Linux patch install step by step.

## Example Patch

The following is a simple patch that fixes one bug on Linux. The bug it fixes is not relevant to this discussion. What is relevant is the process used to apply the patch. At this point, you can assume the patch has been downloaded to your PC. You've verified that the patch is necessary and then made a back up of your database and software. From here, you perform the following steps:

1. Create the subdirectory in the `$ORACLE_HOME/patches` directory for patches if it does not exist. You did that earlier so now you can create the subdirectory for this specific patch.

   ```
   $ pwd
   /u01/app/oracle/product/8.1.6/patches
   $ mkdir bug_12345
   ```

```
$ ls -l
total 4
drwxr-xr-x   2 oracle  dba    4096 Jun 30 20:43 bug_12345
```

2. If necessary, FTP the compressed patch file from the PC to the `$ORACLE_HOME/`
   `patches/patch_12345` directory. Figure 14.2 shows how to FTP the patch from the
   PC to your `$ORACLE_HOME/patches` directory.

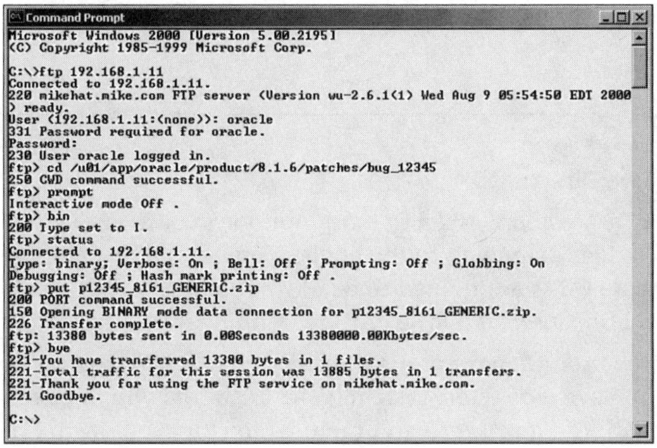

**FIGURE 14.2**

*FTPing the Patch File.*

3. The next step is to uncompress, unzip, and/or untar the file. When you download a patch,
   it is normally compressed and you must uncompress it. On Unix, you can expect files to
   normally be compressed with `compress`. In those cases use the command `uncompress` to
   uncompress the file. On Linux, they are sometimes zipped and you must unzip them as
   show here.

```
$ unzip p12345_8161_GENERIC.zip
Archive:  p12345_8161_GENERIC.zip
  inflating: prvtpidx.plb
  inflating: README.txt
$ ls -l
total 52
-rw-rw-rw-   1 oracle  dba    1583 May 16 08:49 README.txt
-rw-r--r--   1 oracle  dba   13380 Jun 10 21:19 p12345_8161_GENERIC.zip
-rw-rw-rw-   1 oracle  dba   31919 May 11 16:35 prvtpidx.plb
```

At this point, you can remove the ZIP file if you know the patch will not be needed
again. Sometimes larger patches will have multiple files and subdirectories. These are
compressed and transported in a tar file. Check the `man` page for `tar`, but basically it is

used as a way to compress a directory, its subdirectories, and all their files into one file. This one file can then be downloaded, copied, and moved to any location. Once it is in place, the file is untared and it expands to re-create the same directory, subdirectories, and files as before. The steps to uncompress and untar a patch are as follows:

```
$ uncompress 734_patchset.Z
$ tar xvf 734_patchset
```

In this case, I uncompressed the `tar` file `734_patchset.Z` and then untared it. You can then find the directory and subdirectories for the `734_patchset`.

> **NOTE**
>
> **Using tar to Move Directories**
>
> Oftentimes as a DBA you are asked to move not only a database, but also all the operating system files belonging to the application using that database. This can be a little tricky because DBAs are trained to deal with databases, but moving filesystems, Unix groups, and Unix users is a little outside traditional DBA training.
>
> One way I've seen used to move entire directory trees is with the `tar` command. For example, say you have a directory system under `/app` that you need to move to another server. You can go to `/app` and `tar` the directory you need, FTP it to the new server, and then untar it. This method will get all your files and subdirectories. You will still have to resolve differences in filesystem names, corresponding soft links, and hard coded directory names in scripts, but this gives you a good place to start.

4. Now that the patch is uncompressed (and potentially untared) in the correct location, reread the README. Make sure you know what needs to be done. Find out if it is simply a shell script to be executed, a SQL script to be ran, or if it requires the OUI to install the patch.

5. Next, shut down all the databases and listeners belonging to this ORACLE_HOME unless this is just a SQL script to be executed. In this case, it is just a SQL script so you can leave the databases up.

6. Execute the instructions for the patch. In this case, it is just a SQL script to be executed.

```
SQL> @prvtpidx.plb

Grant succeeded.

Package body created.

No errors.
```

```
Grant succeeded.

Commit complete.
```

7. Next, check for invalid objects and recompile them if necessary.

```
SQL> select owner, count(*) from dba_objects where status = 'INVALID'
  2   group by owner;

no rows selected

SQL>
```

In this case, nothing was invalidated so you are done with this database. The next step is to run the same script against every other database in this ORACLE_HOME. Once that's done, you are done.

As patches go, that was about as easy as it gets. Patches themselves are normally not problematic. Typically, you just run whatever shell or SQL scripts are indicated in the README. The tricky part is scheduling the downtime for all the databases in the ORACLE_HOME, running SQL scripts against *every* database in that ORACLE_HOME, and finally checking for invalid objects in each database.

This section covered the basics of installing:patches. It discussed what patches are, when to apply them, and how to do so. The next section looks at a more tricky issue: upgrades.

# When and How to Upgrade

This section examines when and how to perform upgrades.

## Overview

An upgrade involves increasing the database release number, but keeping within the same database version. Examples of upgrades include going from 7.3.2.3 to 7.3.4 or from 8.1.6 to 8.1.7. You do this to get all the bug fixes contained in the next release and to pick up new features within the same version.

There are multiple issues to be addressed before performing an upgrade. First, you should have a reason why you are upgrading such as acquiring new functionality or avoiding a set of bugs. One non-technical reason for upgrading is to move to the terminal release of a version so you will have Oracle Support longer for that release.

Next, you should verify that by upgrading your database, it won't break other systems or applications interfacing with it. This is a bigger issue with migrations, but it should be considered for upgrades as well. The upgrade process should be tested and applications should be re-certified to run on the new release. For example, there might be changes in application performance associ-ated with an upgrade so you need to investigate this issue before upgrading a production system.

I also recommend checking MetaLink, Technet, and any other forums you use to read about issues that other DBAs have encountered when performing similar upgrades. If bugs or other problems exist, these forums are a good place to learn about them *before* you encounter them. From these resources you can learn if the upgrade is going to cause problems with the listener, OEM, or other tools. Minor issues occur often enough with these tools that I strongly encour-age you to investigate them before doing the upgrade.

Finally, once you have tested your upgrade process and performance on a test system, you need to upgrade your production systems. Normally this involves scheduling downtime in the evening or on a weekend so you can shut the system down, perform the upgrade, and check that the system is handling the new database software without any problems. Hopefully, all will go well and your previous testing will have uncovered any problems, but make sure to fac-tor in some extra time to deal with any unexpected problems.

The next section looks at the basic steps of performing an upgrade.

## Performing an Upgrade

Upgrades are similar in many respects to patches, but they are more involved. First you install the new Oracle software (such as 8.1.7) using the same steps as outlined in Chapter 4, "Machine Setup and Installation." Key differences are that because Oracle is already installed on the server, you don't have to create the oracle user, group dba, or worry too much about your hardware requirements. You should still check the ICG for any changes such as with shared memory or semaphores, but once one version is installed, requirements for other releases within that version should be the same.

One key point, however, is that you must install Oracle in a different ORACLE_HOME than any other version or release. Starting with Oracle 7.3.4, this became a requirement. Fortunately, if you follow the OFA guidelines, this is simple. For example, under the $ORACLE_BASE/product direc-tory you would have an ORACLE_HOME for each version of Oracle installed:

```
$ ls $ORACLE_BASE/product
8.1.6  8.1.7
```

After the new database software is installed and you have verified that it is running properly, you need to upgrade the older databases. Remember you don't have to upgrade all your data-bases at once; you can do them one at a time. Don't forget that, before performing an upgrade, it is a good idea to perform a cold backup in case something goes wrong.

The next step is to log into each database you want to upgrade under the older ORACLE_HOME and shut them down normally.

> **NOTE**
>
> Multiple ORACLE_HOMEs
>
> You can run multiple databases of different versions on the same box with no problem. In fact, folks do this all the time. The trick is not to get your databases and software confused. For example, if you have 7.3.4 and 8.1.6 databases on the same server, you must have the software separated into different directories as shown:
>
> ```
> $ ls $ORACLE_BASE/product
> 7.3.4  8.1.6
> ```
>
> Remember that your ORACLE_HOME determines which database software you will use to access your database as identified by your ORACLE_SID environment variable. For example, here, the ORACLE_HOME is set for 8.1.6 databases.
>
> ```
> $ echo $ORACLE_HOME
> /u01/app/oracle/product/8.1.6
> ```
>
> Therefore, I can use this to access, start up, and shut down any 8.1.6 database, but not the 7.3.4 databases.
>
> It is *very* important that you verify and use the correct ORACLE_HOME for each corresponding database. Although you can normally use tools like SQL*Plus against different versions, you don't want to start up or shut down databases with the wrong software.

After you have shut down the older database you plan to upgrade, you need to set up your environment for the new database. This involves changing your ORACLE_HOME, creating a soft link in the $ORACLE_HOME/dbs to the $ORACLE_BASE/admin/*SID*/pfile/init*SID*.ora, and restarting the old database under the new ORACLE_HOME with new software.

Once the database is started you have a set of upgrade scripts to run as the user internal. These are typically located in $ORACLE_HOME/rdbms/admin. Once those are executed, you may need to rerun scripts such as catalog.sql and catproc.sql to rebuild the data dictionary. However, most upgrades to newer database versions include those scripts in the upgrade script so it is often not necessary to run them separately.

After all the database upgrade and data dictionary scripts have been executed, you need to check for invalid objects. If you find any, write Dynamic SQL as discussed in Chapter 5 to recompile them.

**14**

PATCHES AND
UPGRADES

Finally, modify your oratab, listener.ora, and any other Oracle parameter files to reflect the change in ORACLE_HOME. This includes application scripts, environment scripts, and the like. Change the COMPATIBLE parameter in the init.ora to reflect the upgrade. Also, you need to decide which listener you will use on the database. Typically, listeners have been backwards-compatible so you can just use the highest version available. However, sometimes listeners don't always work well that way so you may need to run multiple listeners on your server. They can share the same listener.ora file, but they will need to listen on different port numbers. Be sure to work this issue out and test it before upgrading a production system. The database won't be any good if users cannot log into it.

These are the basic steps in performing an upgrade. The next section shows an example upgrade.

## Example Upgrade

This example looks at moving from Oracle 8.1.6 to Oracle 8.1.7 on Linux. At the time of this writing, this is a very common upgrade. This section skims over some parts, such as installing Oracle, because that was covered in Chapter 4. Also, this section doesn't address application-testing or certification for the new version. What it does cover is the database-specific aspects of performing an upgrade. Finally, do not forget to take a cold backup of your database before performing the upgrade.

1. Install the new Oracle software. In this case, this is Oracle 8.1.7. Make sure you separate your software into different ORACLE_HOME directories. Also make sure that when you perform the install, your ORACLE_HOME is set for 8.1.7, not 8.1.6. Verify that all your other environment variables are also set to 8.1.7 where appropriate.

   Depending on your version, during installation the OUI will look at the oratab file and offer to upgrade/migrate older databases for you. Because you don't always want to do this, skip that step and install the software as normal.

2. Shut down the database you plan on upgrading and exit out of SQL*Plus. In this case, you have an 8.1.6 database called rh1tst1.

```
SQL> select name from v$database;

NAME
---------
RH1TST1

SQL> select * from v$version;

BANNER
----------------------------------------------------------------
Oracle8i Enterprise Edition Release 8.1.6.1.0 - Production
```

```
PL/SQL Release 8.1.6.0.0 - Production
CORE    8.1.6.0.0        Production
TNS for Linux: Version 8.1.6.0.0 - Production
NLSRTL Version 3.4.0.0.0 - Production

SQL> shutdown;
Database closed.
Database dismounted.
ORACLE instance shut down.
SQL> exit
Disconnected
```

At this stage, you should perform a cold backup of the database.

3. Set up your environment for the new database software. In this case, it is 8.1.7.

```
$ echo $ORACLE_SID
rh1tst1
$ echo $ORACLE_HOME
/u01/app/oracle/product/8.1.7
$ echo $LD_LIBRARY_PATH
/u01/app/oracle/product/8.1.7/lib
```

4. Create a soft link in the new $ORACLE_HOME/dbs to the init.ora in the $ORACLE_BASE/
   admin/*SID*/pfile directory. Also, remove the link in the old $ORACLE_HOME to reduce the
   chance of the database accidentally being started with the older software.

```
$ pwd
/u01/app/oracle/product/8.1.7/dbs
$ echo $ORACLE_BASE
/u01/app/oracle
$ echo $ORACLE_HOME
/u01/app/oracle/product/8.1.7
$ ln -s $ORACLE_BASE/admin/rh1tst1/pfile/initrh1tst1.ora .
$ rm /u01/app/oracle/product/8.1.6/dbs/initrh1tst1.ora
$ ls -l
total 24
-rw-r--r--  1 oracle  dba    8385 Oct 22  1999 init.ora
-rw-r--r--  1 oracle  dba    9219 Oct 22  1999 initdw.ora
lrwxrwxrwx  1 oracle  dba      51 Jul  1 15:15 initrh1tst1.ora ->
   /u01/app/oracle/admin/rh1tst1/pfile/initrh1tst1.ora
```

As you can see, there is now a link for the init.ora from the new $ORACLE_HOME/dbs to
the actual init.ora in the $ORACLE_BASE/admin/*SID*/pfile directory.

5. Connect internal with SQL*Plus and start up the database in restricted mode so no one
   else can log in. Make sure you do this using the new Oracle software. Also, you might
   have to change the init.ora parameter REMOTE_LOGIN_PASSWORDFILE to NONE to start
   and open the database without a password file for the first time.

**14**

```
$ sqlplus internal

SQL*Plus: Release 8.1.7.0.0 - Production on Sun Jul 1 15:32:11 2001

(c) Copyright 2000 Oracle Corporation.  All rights reserved.

Connected to an idle instance.

SQL> startup restrict;
ORACLE instance started.

Total System Global Area    55828640 bytes
Fixed Size                     73888 bytes
Variable Size               38805504 bytes
Database Buffers            16777216 bytes
Redo Buffers                  172032 bytes
Database mounted.
Database opened.
SQL>
```

6. Next, run the upgrade script in $ORACLE_HOME/rdbms/admin for your particular version.
   In this case, because you are upgrading from 8.1.6 to 8.1.7, you need to run the script
   $ORACLE_HOME/rdbms/admin/u0801060.sql. Notice that there are other scripts for
   upgrading from other versions as well in this directory. The directory also contains
   scripts to perform downgrades. Before actually running it, it's a good idea to actually
   read the script to understand what it's doing and what other scripts it calls. After reading
   it, run it while you are connected internal.

   ```
   SQL> @$ORACLE_HOME/rdbms/admin/u0801060.sql
   ```

   The script will run for a while, so be patient. Make note of any unusual errors and investigate them as needed.

7. In earlier versions of Oracle, such as in Oracle 7.3, you had to run scripts such as
   catalog.sql and catproc.sql to rebuild the data dictionary after the upgrade. In Oracle
   8i these scripts are executed automatically, as you can see in the upgrade script. However,
   after these scripts have been executed you might want to run utlrp.sql to automatically
   recompile any invalid objects.

   ```
   SQL> @$ORACLE_HOME/rdbms/admin/utlrp.sql
   ```

8. After the packages have been recompiled, double-check for any invalid objects and use
   Dynamic SQL to recompile them. Use the following statement to determine how many
   invalid objects each user has.

   ```
   SQL> select owner, count(*) from dba_objects
     2  where status = 'INVALID'
     3  group by owner;
   ```

9. At this point the database can be opened for normal use, but a better idea is to take a cold backup first. If necessary, you can open the database with `ALTER SYSTEM DISABLE RESTRICTED SESSION`.

```
SQL> alter system disable restricted session;
System altered.
```

10. The final step is to update certain files so that they include the new database information. These files include:

- **oratab**   Change the $ORACLE_HOME value
- **listener.ora**   Change the $ORACLE_HOME value and listener
- **init.ora**   Set COMPATIBLE = 8.1.7
- Any other miscellaneous scripts or files

This section assumes that you have configured the networking files during the installation of the new product. Simply remove references about the database from the old configuration files and put it in the new files.

That covers it for basic database upgrades. For the most part, upgrades are fairly simple and should be uneventful. This chapter didn't go into detail on upgrading other parts of the system such as the operating system, application, Web server, or other Oracle-specific products, but these elements should be addressed seriously because each has its own requirements. Make sure that you don't upgrade one part of the system so that it becomes incompatible with another part. I have seen this happen. It required multiple simultaneous upgrades and these are indeed tricky situations.

## Additional Considerations

Oracle normally recommends that you update with the latest patches and move to the newest releases. That way they can assume that any problems you have will be addressed by their bug fixes. It also keeps you moving forward with the latest and greatest of Oracle's products. From Oracle's perspective, this is a good thing. From your perspective, there are some additional considerations you need to consider before upgrading or installing: patches.

First, does your OS platform support this release of Oracle? Are there any special Oracle patches or operating system patches that need to be applied? This is normally a bigger issue when performing migrations, but it should be considered here as well.

Next, is every application and tool interfacing with your database certified to run on a higher version? Once again, this is often an issue to be addressed before performing a migration, but it needs to be discussed here as well. You do not want to upgrade your database only to find it is incompatible with some other application or system tool.

Why are you moving to a higher version or applying a patch? Make sure there is a valid reason to perform an upgrade or a patch. Sometimes people apply patches or do upgrades just to get new resume material. Other times it is someone trying to fix a problem and they are simply guessing that an upgrade or patch will help. Trouble-shooting by blindly installing:patches and upgrades is an ill-advised policy.

One legitimate reason Oracle will force you to upgrade or apply patches is if your database version is too old to be supported. It is unrealistic to expect any company to support every release of every product indefinitely. The line has to be drawn somewhere and Oracle enforces this by reducing the level of support for old database versions. For example, Oracle version 7.3.2.3 is no longer supported. You could call Oracle Support with questions and problems and they will answer them to the best of their ability. However, they will not write new bug fixes for that version or continue development on it. Instead they will suggest that you upgrade to a newer version.

With a seemingly endless chain of new versions, releases, and patches, is there ever a chance to stop upgrading? Yes and no. Oracle will always push you to upgrade to the latest and greatest, but you can usually settle on the terminal (last) database version release. For example, assume you are happy with Oracle 8i and you don't want to move to 9i. In this case, you should upgrade and patch to Oracle 8.1.7, which Oracle announced as the terminal release of 8i. Because it's the terminal release, it will be supported much longer than 8.1.6. Ultimately, you will have to move to 9i, but terminal releases such as 8.1.7 and 7.3.4 will be supported much longer than earlier releases within the same version.

## Summary

This chapter covered the basics of installing:patches and performing upgrades. Patches and upgrades occur in response to software bugs and as a way to take advantage of minor improvements. You should not rush to apply every patch and upgrade that becomes available; rather, you should selectively choose the ones that will help your system.

The actual process of installing:patches is usually easy. First, you carefully review the README file because the instructions for patches can vary greatly. Next, you download the patch and copy it to the correct `$ORACLE_HOME/patches` subdirectory and uncompress/unzip/untar it. When you are ready to apply the patch, you shut down the databases and the listener. Then, you perform the instructions in the README for patches. After that, you start each database and run any necessary post-patch scripts. Then check for invalid objects and recompile them as necessary.

If it is an upgrade, install the new software under a different `ORACLE_HOME` using OFA standards. Make sure the installation was successful by starting a demo database. Next, you shut down the old database and listener. You then set up your Oracle environment for the new software and restart the database and apply the necessary upgrade scripts out of `$ORACLE_HOME/rdbms/admin`. Next, you run any necessary post upgrade scripts to rebuild the data dictionary and rebuild the Java objects if needed. Then, you recompile any invalid objects. Finally, you have to modify any remaining configuration files such as oratab and the listener.ora to reflect the new environment.

# Migrations

## ESSENTIALS

- Migrating a database involves upgrading a preexisting database to a higher version.

- Careful planning and testing is necessary to ensure a successful migration.

- There are three methods used to migrate a database: export/import, mig utility, and ODMA (Oracle Data Migration Assistant).

- The easiest, most straightforward method is to use the Oracle Data Migration Assistant.

- This chapter shows you how to migrate from Oracle 8.1.6.1 to 9.0.1 using the Oracle Data Migration Assistant.

Migrations involve upgrading a database from one version to a higher one. Migrations require more planning, preparation, and are more difficult to perform than simple upgrades or patches. The three methods normally used to migrate a database are using export/import, using the mig utility, and using the Oracle Data Migration Assistant.

This chapter looks at what it takes to migrate a database. It discusses some of the planning and preparation issues needed to perform a migration. These issues need to be discussed because, all too often, DBAs migrate their databases without much planning and then suffer because they failed to examine other factors outside the database. The chapter also explores the three most common methods used to migrate a database. Finally, it provides an example migration from 8.1.6.1 to 9.0.1 using ODMA (Oracle Data Migration Assistant).

## What Is a Migration

A migration is simply an upgrade of a database to a higher version. This is different from a pure upgrade, which involves moving to a higher release within the same database version. Upgrades (and patches) were discussed in the previous chapter.

Don't confuse a migration with rehosting. Often, a DBA will be asked to "migrate" a database from server A to server B. Unless the database version is increasing during the move, the DBA is simply moving the database from one host to another. Incorrect use of the term "migration" is normally harmless, but it is good to understand the actual difference between the terms.

> **NOTE**
>
> A New Definition of Migration?
>
> Oracle's definition of migration now differs from the definition used in this book. New Oracle documentation now only uses the term migration when moving from Oracle 7 to a higher version. All other migrations, such as from Oracle 8 and Oracle 8i to higher versions, are referred to as "upgrades."
>
> For example, a move from Oracle 7 to Oracle 8i is a *migration*. However, a move from Oracle 8i to Oracle 9i is an *upgrade*.
>
> This definition differs with what I and other DBAs have been taught. Perhaps this is because the process of going from 8i to 9i is "simple" from an internal standpoint as compared to a move from 7 to 9i. Moving from 8i to 9i may be so simple internally that it is more like an upgrade than a full blown migration. In fact, the ODMA tool considers a move from 8i to 9i to be an upgrade. Additionally, the scripts to manually move from 8i to 9i resemble upgrade scripts.
>
> *continues*

I will still call this process a migration because you are moving from version to version but it's a good idea to note that Oracle documentation and the ODMA calls it an upgrade. Regardless of what you choose to call it, the main focus of this chapter is on using the ODMA tool to move your database from 8.1.6.1 to 9.0.1.

# Reasons to Migrate Your Database

Oracle is always coming out with new products with exciting features. Many DBAs enjoy learning about new products and technologies. From a technical standpoint, there are often valid reasons to use a new database—because of the completely new features and enhancements of older features. Sometimes businesses depend on these new features in order to fulfill a technical requirement within the system; other times they are considered interesting novelties. These new features typically come as a result of a new database version, not as part of a simple upgrade within the same version. Therefore, if you want to access new features, you have to use the newest version of the database. These new features are not back-ported to previous versions.

As discussed in the last chapter, Oracle will eventually force its customers to move to 9i by not supporting older versions. However, with releases of Oracle 7 and 8 still running in some shops, it might be years before this happens to you. Most DBAs don't want to wait until they have to migrate; they want to be using the newest software as soon as they are confident that it is stable and any major bugs have been resolved. For those reasons, you generally won't find a crazed rush of DBAs migrating all their production systems to the initial release of *any* software. Normally, they will get a copy of the new software and then take a few months to "play" with it and become familiar with the new features. In the meantime, Oracle will have a chance to come out with the next release and provide the first set of patches to fix any bugs. This conservative approach regarding new software is the more common and recommended one.

Ultimately, the time will come when you feel you're ready to start using the new version. By this point, you should know and understand its new features. Whether via structured training or simply on your own, you should be familiar with all the new features and be aware of which preexisting features have been modified or are no longer supported in the new version. Preferably, you should also have had the new version running on testing and development servers for some length of time. This way, you gain hands-on experience with the new database before using it on your production systems.

The next section examines some of the issues you need to consider when migrating databases to production systems.

# Preparation

You shouldn't migrate your production systems on a whim. Rather the migration process should be carefully planned and tested. This section discusses some of the issues involved with migrations.

## Planning

Treat migrating a production system like a project. You should consider the system-wide impact of migrating the database. Remember that the database interfaces with and depends on the Unix server, the application, and the Web. A change in the database can impact any of the other areas. You need to make certain you understand the impact on these other components. Consider, for example, these questions:

- Is the new database version compatible with the operating system version and do any patches need to be applied to either? Oracle's MetaLink has a Certification Matrix under the Project Lifecycle section that tells you whether your database/OS combination is certified and whether there are any known issues. I have run databases in uncertified configurations, but I knew there were potential consequences. You need to be aware that you'll receive limited support if you run into bugs because you are using an unsupported configuration. You also need to determine whether the new database will even work on your current operating system and whether the SA needs to perform any operating system upgrades or apply any patches.

- Is the new database version compatible with the application software? Many COTS (Commercial Off The Shelf) and GOTS (Government Off The Shelf) products are certified for a specific database version. In these cases, the DBA *cannot* upgrade or migrate the database until the application is certified for a higher version or release. If the application is in-house, the DBA might have some influence to get it certified. However, if someone else owns the application, the DBA might be at the mercy of the vendor. Many of the Oracle 7.3.4 databases in existence today fall into this category.

- Are there other version-dependent interfaces? Is there a Web interface that is version dependent? What about the backup software? These are examples of site-specific issues that the DBA must address before moving forward with a migration.

There are several distinct types of testing that should take place before any migration: database, application, and migration testing.

## Database Testing

Obviously, the DBA should be focused on the new database's characteristics. I'm a strong believer in DBAs going to "new features" training because it benefits the company. It does no good for Oracle to provide new features if the DBAs and developers don't know they exist. LogMiner is a great example of this. Many experienced DBAs do not know that they can use this tool to undo changes in the database or determine who made changes. They might be tempted to use tablespace point-in-time recoveries or restore from old exports to undo changes that can easily be done with LogMiner. However, unless the DBAs know about these features and are skilled enough to use them, they might as well stay with their old version of Oracle. In cases like this, the only reason to move to a new version is because of inherent improvements inside the database that don't require DBA expertise.

Ideally, you have installed the database on a testing or development box and worked with the new features so you know and understand the new features. Also be sure to review posts on Technet and MetaLink so you're familiar with any issues regarding the new database.

The next step is to set up the database as it will be used in production. This is where a test or development box is essential. By setting up the new database environment so that it mirrors the production environment, you can discover any problems. Additionally, you can test the new features of the database to see how they can be incorporated into your production environment. For example, be sure to consider any issues with locally managed tablespaces and the application. Here, you can test the new features to determine which ones you'll use in the production environment.

## Application Testing

The chapter has discussed situations in which the DBA cannot upgrade because the application won't be certified with a higher version. However, even when your database will be certified, you still need to perform rigorous testing, particularly when you're using homegrown applications. Structured testing should include:

- **Functionality**   Does the application still work? If you encounter problems, are they because of the database change or were they there originally? I worked on one database upgrade in which several application bugs were discovered only because we were performing the first real test cases executed in years.

- **Performance**   Is application performance better, worse, or the same? Common sense dictates that a newer database should make the application run faster, but that isn't always the case. Have you reanalyzed your database tables under the database version? Are there changes in the optimizer or execution plans under the new database? Any of these can impact application performance even without changing a line of code.

### Test for Performance
I once received an urgent flurry of emails from a DBA at a company I had once worked for. He had just migrated from Oracle 7.3.4 to Oracle 8i (I don't remember

the version) and performance was absolutely horrible. He had spent an entire weekend trying to find the problem. He was concerned that the migration had failed in
some respect so he emailed me.

I hadn't been at that company for a while and I wasn't there for the migration so I
didn't really know where to start. I asked him whether there were any obvious error
messages, which there weren't. I also asked him whether he had analyzed his tables
after the migration. It turns out that was the problem (although to his credit he
thought of that just as I was sending him the email). He never analyzed his data
tables after the migration. This must be done because after a migration all your statistics are worthless. After he reanalyzed the tables, his system's performance was
great and he was off the hook.

Because I wasn't there to witness how he preformed the migration, I really don't
want to make assumptions about his planning. However, the nature of the error sug-
gests he probably did not test his application much for performance before he
migrated. Although the technical problem had to do with failing to use ANALYZE
after the migration, the bigger problem probably had to do with not thoroughly
preparing for the migration.

- **New features**   Is the application taking advantage of any of the database's new features? If so, are they providing tangible improvements? Many of the enhancements inside
the database will improve overall performance and don't need to be specifically added to
the application. Other improvements, such as changes in PL/SQL, must be added directly
into the application. If you are lucky enough to have Oracle-savvy developers, you can
take advantage of new features more readily.

Those are the main areas to look for in terms of application testing. Typically, the DBA will
work with the developers and/or the vendor to make sure the application is ready for the new
database. Normally, the DBA doesn't have the background or familiarity with the application
to make this judgment alone. Therefore, use the expertise of your developers, testers, and vendors to make sure your application runs successfully.

## Migration Testing

Although testing the application and planning for the migration is essential for success, performing the actual database migration is the main focus of this chapter. It focuses mainly on
using the ODMA tool, but whatever method you use should be tested several times. This
should actually come as a natural part of your application testing. For example, if you have
testing, development, and production databases, it makes sense that you will have performed

the migration on the testing and development databases before you migrate the production system. Just make sure that you document your procedure and note any issues so when you do it for real there won't be any surprises.

After you have tested the database, application, and the actual migration processes, it is time to go live. Just like when performing upgrades, you need to schedule for the downtime. Depending on the migration method, downtime can be relatively minor if the database is migrated in place or it can take many hours if the database is created via export/import. However, do not forget to factor in the time for a backup because it is reckless to perform a migration without a backup first (unless you are using the export/import method). There is also the time required to verify that the migration was successful and the application is successfully restarted. Backups after the migration are also a good idea. Experienced DBAs will also factor in time to fix minor problems as they occur. This is normally performed late at night or over a weekend.

# Migration Methods

The DBA has several methods available to migrate a database. The most common three are using export/import, mig utility, and ODMA.

## Export/Import

You should already be familiar with the export and import tools. They were covered in Chapter 8, "DBA Utilities." You already know that you can use an export DMP file to move data and objects from one database to another, but additionally these databases do not have to be the same version. You can use your DMP file to import into a higher version database or even a lower version database in the event of a downgrade.

Key benefits of using export and import include:

- Conceptually simple for the DBA to understand.
- All objects are rebuilt thus improving performance. This includes indexes and Oracle 7 ROWIDs. Fragmentation is also reduced.
- This is an opportunity to reorganize tablespaces and disk layouts because the target is a different database.
- Selected portions of the database can be migrated and unneeded portions can be left behind.
- The source database still remains available.
- If the process fails, it can be reattempted with relatively little penalty.
- There is no need to take a full database backup before the migration.

**15**

Potential drawbacks using export and import include:

- The process takes a long time. There are ways to speed up the process, but there is no way to make it run as quickly as other migration methods.

- There is a chance of users, objects, roles, privileges, and database links being "missed" depending on the level of export/import used.

- The export must be consistent and transactions must be propagated to the new system so activity against the source database effectively stops after the export process begins.

For moving schemas from one testing or development database to another when time is not a factor, I like export/import. I'm already very familiar with it and as a result I know how to optimize its use. Plus I get the performance gains of rebuilding the objects. For those reasons, export/import is sometimes a good option.

There are not too many drawbacks to export/import, but those that exist are big. The single largest problem is the huge amount of time it takes to export one production database and import it into another. Many organizations simply cannot afford the time to do this.

---

### Upgrade and Rehosting with Export/Import

One of the first production systems I moved was using export/import. We wanted to move the system off the old server to a new server running a newer operating system. We also wanted to perform a database upgrade in the process. The method I selected was export/import.

Predictably, the export/import process took many hours to complete. However, everything was moved successfully. Because of a combination of new hardware and rebuilding the database, production batch jobs were much faster than before. In fact, originally we thought something was wrong because they finished in about one third the time. Obviously the new hardware helped, but rebuilding the database also contributed to the amazing increase in performance.

---

## mig

mig is a command-line Oracle migration utility that you can use to migrate Oracle 7.3 databases. This tool is actually called from the ODMA, but you have more control over the database-migration process by using this utility.

This utility has several steps. The benefit of this staged approach is that you can stop the migration process any time before the ALTER DATABASE CONVERT statement. Typically, after you start the ODMA, you are committed to going forward.

Ultimately, you get a binary file with the convert information stored in it. After you issue the `ALTER DATABASE CONVERT` statement, Oracle uses this file to create an Oracle 9i data dictionary and then update the data file headers and the control files. Notice that the data itself is not actually modified. After the database is migrated, you have to perform some cleanup steps, such as eliminating old `init.ora` parameters, creating a soft link in the correct `$ORACLE_HOME/dbs` directory, and recompiling all your invalid objects.

## ODMA

Oracle Data Migration Assistant walks you through upgrading or migrating a database. This GUI actually invokes the `mig` utility, but the GUI makes it much easier to use.

You can use ODMA to migrate Oracle 7.3 databases as well as Oracle 8 and 8i databases. After the database is migrated, the GUI will offer to run utlrp.sql to recompile your PL/SQL, update your listener.ora, and remove obsolete parameters from your `init.ora` file.

We have covered the basics of each tool available. Ultimately you must choose the best method for your situation. Factors influencing the type of method used are discussed next.

## Version of the Source Database

If database has the older ROWID type from Oracle 7, is badly fragmented, or has indexes in need of being rebuilt, using export and import is a valid option. The newer ROWID will provide benefits, but this doesn't happen if the database is migrated in place. Also, performance can significantly be improved by rebuilding all the database objects. Although export and import take longer, they will likely pay for themselves in performance gains.

## Time Available to Perform the Migration

Some shops have stringent uptime requirements that cannot be relaxed, even for migrations. If this is the case, export and import won't do. Furthermore, the `mig` tool might not be an option because it is not as fast as ODMA.

Remember, the time needed to perform the migration is determined by the number of data dictionary objects to be updated, not the size of the data files. Therefore, you can't use the size of the actual database as an accurate gauge to determine downtime. However, the size of the database is a factor when performing a backup before the migration. The best way to calculate a time estimate is by determining how long your migration tests take.

## Skill of the DBA

The skill of the DBA performing the migration is a factor. Every DBA is a beginner at some point; perhaps it's your first time migrating a database. As long as you test your processes and have prepared adequately, this shouldn't be a problem. The only recommendation I have specifically for less experienced DBAs is to use either export/import or the ODMA tool.

Typically, any DBA is already familiar with export/import so using this method to migrate a database shouldn't be difficult conceptually. The biggest points here are to optimize the speed of the export/import process and to make sure that all users, roles, privileges, and objects are indeed moved to the new database.

ODMA is probably the easiest migration method of the three. Assuming you know how to use the OUI to install Oracle, you can use the DBCA to generate database CREATE scripts, and have an understanding of the migration process, you can likely use the ODMA successfully.

# Using ODMA

This section shows an example of using the ODMA tool to move from an 8.1.6.1 database to a 9.0.1 database.

## Overview

This section assumes the Oracle 9i software has been successfully installed in a separate ORACLE_HOME. Furthermore, it assumes that you are not running Oracle Replication or OPS (renamed Real Application Clusters in 9i). If you are running replication, you need to make sure you don't still have any distributed transactions before the migration. As for OPS/RAC, the ODMA doesn't support migrating OPS/RAC. For this, you would need to use the mig tool.

---

**NOTE**

Migrating to a Base Release

Oracle documentation states that it only supports migrating to a base release without patches. For example, 8.1.6.0 is okay, but 8.1.6.2 isn't supported. Why? Oracle doesn't know how many patches it is going to release before a version comes out and it doesn't go back and retest direct migrations to every conceivable patch release.

This puts the normal DBA in a bind because theoretically you have to live with all bugs for a release until all your databases are migrated. Only after all the databases have been migrated can you patch your base release with approval from Oracle.

No doubt this will cause many DBAs to consider patching their databases to the level they need and then performing the migrations anyway. Theoretically I don't see why this would be a problem, except that Oracle says you're acting in an "unsupported" manner. However, I cannot recommend that you migrate your databases in an unsupported manner either. All I will say is that whatever you do, make sure you test it thoroughly before attempting a migration on your production systems. Make sure, as always, that you have valid backups.

# Migration Steps Using ODMA

The following example uses ODMA to migrate (or upgrade, using Oracle terminology) an Oracle 8.1.6.1 database to Oracle 9.0.1. In reality, the migration process for 8i to 9i is more like an upgrade (basically running scripts) than from Oracle 7.3 to 9i. You'll see where the two paths diverge once you're inside the tool.

The migration process can be broken into three steps: preparing the database, using ODMA to migrate the database, and performing post-migration checks.

## Preparing the Database

Before you migrate your database there are certain steps that you need to perform, as follows:

1. Modify the following `init.ora` parameters:

   ```
   DB_DOMAIN = mike.com
   ```

   (Your domain name will be different.)

   ```
   JOB_QUEUE_PROCESS = 0
   AQ_TM_PROCESSES = 0
   REMOTE_LOGIN_PASSWORDFILE = NONE
   ```

   These parameters are modified to stop advanced queuing, replication, and prevent the need for a password file. Make sure your `DB_DOMAIN` is properly set as well. After the migration is complete, you can reset the parameters and re-create the password file.

2. Increase the size of the SYSTEM tablespace so both data dictionaries can exist simultaneously during the upgrade. I usually like to have large SYSTEM tablespaces anyway, but make sure you have at least 100M free.

   ```
   SQL> select file_name, bytes from dba_data_files
     2  where tablespace_name = 'SYSTEM';

   FILE_NAME                              BYTES
   ------------------------------  ----------------
   /u02/oradata/demo/system01.dbf      246,022,144
   SQL> select sum(bytes) from dba_free_space
     2  where tablespace_name = 'SYSTEM';

        SUM(BYTES)
   ----------------
           720,896
   SQL> alter database datafile
     2  '/u02/oradata/demo/system01.dbf'
     3  resize 400M;

   Database altered.
   ```

3. Prepare the rollback segment inside the SYSTEM tablespace. You don't want this to blow out in the middle of your migration nor do you want it to shrink. Give it the maximum limit of 505 extents, turn off OPTIMAL, and set the PCTINCREASE to 50%.

```
SQL> alter rollback segment system
  2  storage (maxextents 505 optimal null next 1M);

Rollback segment altered.
SQL> alter tablespace system default storage (pctincrease 50);

Tablespace altered.
```

4. Make sure that the default and temporary tablespace for SYS and SYSTEM is SYSTEM. Most DBAs will change the temporary tablespace to avoid fragmenting the SYSTEM tablespace and others will move SYSTEM's default tablespace to TOOLS. During the migration, you need them both back inside SYSTEM. Also, if you moved SYS.AUD$ outside of SYSTEM tablespace, you must move it back.

```
SQL> alter user sys default tablespace system
  2  temporary tablespace system;

User altered.

SQL> alter user system default tablespace system
  2  temporary tablespace system;

User altered.
```

5. Make sure you do not have a database user called MIGRATE. This user is created and dropped during the migration process by ODMA. If you have this user, export and then drop the schema. You can bring the user back into the database after the migration.

```
SQL> select username, created from dba_users
  2  where username = 'MIGRATE';

no rows selected
```

6. Check whether you have a user named OUTLN. This user is created automatically in Oracle 8i onwards, so if you are already running 8i it is okay to have it. If you are running a previous version, such as Oracle 7, you need to export and drop this user, and then reimport it into another schema. Because this example is running 8i, it'll show this user.

```
SQL> select username, created from dba_users
  2  where username = 'OUTLN';

USERNAME                         CREATED
-------------------------------- ---------
OUTLN                            17-APR-00
```

7. Ensure that you do not have any data files that need recovery. Although it is doubtful that you would be performing a migration if your database needed recovery, some inexperienced people might think that by going to a newer version they can recover their database easier.

```
SQL> select * from v$recover_file;

no rows selected
```

8. Shut down the database normally and exit. Technically a SHUTDOWN IMMEDIATE will work, but I feel safer with a normal SHUTDOWN.

```
SQL> shutdown;
Database closed.
Database dismounted.
ORACLE instance shut down.
SQL> exit
Disconnected
```

9. Take a cold backup of your database. If something goes wrong during the migration, you will need this backup in order to recover. Do not skip this step.

Most of these preparatory steps are geared for migrating an Oracle 7 database, which is more involved than migrating an Oracle 8i database. However, nothing you've done here will harm your Oracle 8i database, so you are now ready to proceed with the migration.

## Use ODMA to Migrate

This series of steps comprises the actual migration:

1. Set up your environment to reflect the new software and ORACLE_HOME. Also set up your DISPLAY as if you were going to run the OUI. The ODMA is a Java GUI, so you will need the same settings as for running OUI.

2. Start the ODMA in the new $ORACLE_HOME/bin.

```
$ cd $ORACLE_HOME/bin
$ odma
```

3. After a few seconds a Welcome screen should appear, as shown in Figure 15.1. Click Next.

4. The next screen lists a few requirements to consider before attempting to migrate or upgrade, as shown in Figure 15.2. Click Next.

5. The next screen asks you to select an instance. This is generated by examining the oratab file, so make sure the database you want to migrate to is listed there with the *current* (premigration) version. Here, you want to select the demo database, as shown in Figure 15.3.

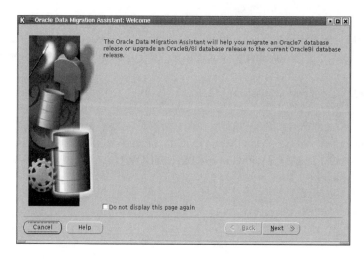

**FIGURE 15.1**

*ODMA Welcome Screen.*

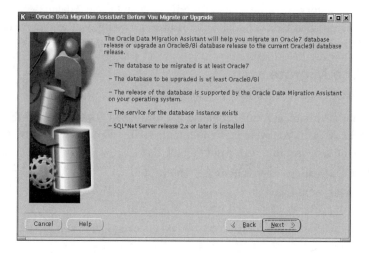

**FIGURE 15.2**

*Before You Migrate or Upgrade.*

6. ODMA will ask you to confirm both the old and new ORACLE_HOME. It will also ask for the location of the init.ora file, which should be in the old $ORACLE_HOME/dbs directory. This is shown in Figure 15.4.

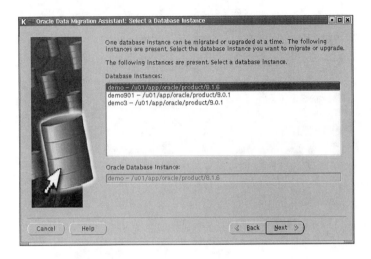

**FIGURE 15.3**

*Select an Instance to Migrate or Upgrade.*

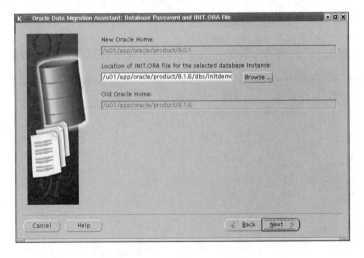

**FIGURE 15.4**

*Verify the ORACLE_HOME Directories and the init.ora Location.*

The ODMA will pause for a few seconds; you'll see a message stating that it is getting database information.

7. You can now choose a migration type: Default or Custom. The biggest benefits of the Custom option are that it allows you to change the database name and National Character Set. Select the Default option, shown in Figure 15.5.

**15**

**MIGRATIONS**

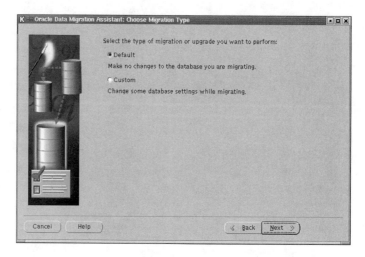

**FIGURE 15.5**

*Select a Default Migration.*

8. ODMA will ask you if you have backed up your database. If you have, click Next, as shown in Figure 15.6.

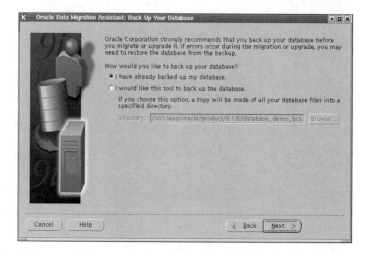

**FIGURE 15.6**

*Have You Backed Up Your Database?*

9. The next screen, shown in Figure 15.7, asks you if you are ready to start the migration or upgrade. Verify that the settings are correct and then click Next if you are ready to proceed.

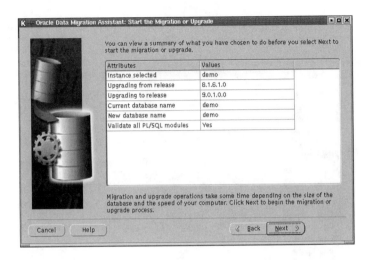

**FIGURE 15.7**
*Start the Migration.*

10. ODMA will ask you one last time if you are ready to continue. It specifies that, if necessary, it will use SHUTDOWN IMMEDIATE to shut down the database. Select Yes to continue.

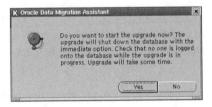

**FIGURE 15.8**
*Shut down the Database.*

11. The ODMA provides a status of the migration or upgrade as it occurs; see Figure 15.9.

    You can expect the migration or upgrade to take about 20 minutes to an hour. Remember, the ODMA is primarily working with the data dictionary inside the SYSTEM tablespace, not the actual data in your tables. Therefore, use the number of objects in your SYSTEM tablespace to estimate how long it will take, not the database's size in gigabytes.

12. The ODMA will offer to update the database entry in the listener.ora with the new version. You can do this manually later if you prefer.

13. The final screen will note that the process is complete. When you are done, click Finish to exit the tool.

**15**

The migration process should now be completed. Next, you need to perform the post-migration tasks.

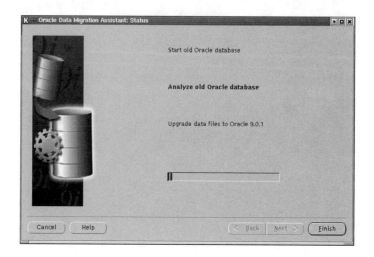

**Figure 15.9**
*ODMA Status*

## Post-Migration Tasks

In the best case, all went well with the migration. If there was a problem during the process, you might have to restore from your backups. However, even if everything appeared to go as planned, you have to perform the following steps. Notice how these steps are very similar to the ones you perform after an upgrade:

1. Check the logs in $ORACLE_HOME/assistants/dbma/log/demo directory. Use grep as a quick way to search for Oracle errors as follows:

```
$ pwd
/u01/app/oracle/product/9.0.1/assistants/dbma/log/demo
$ grep -i ora- *
```

2. During the migration, the ODMA examines the old init.ora, removes obsolete parameters, and places this revised copy in the new $ORACLE_HOME/dbs directory. This is the actual file; it is not a soft link. The old copy with obsolete parameters will still exist in the $ORACLE_BASE/admin/*SID*/pfile directory and the soft link in the old $ORACLE_HOME/dbs will also exist.

    Make a backup copy of the old init.ora and then delete the original. Then remove the soft link in the old $ORACLE_HOME/dbs. These steps are necessary because you want to reduce the possibility of the database being restarted with the old software.

```
$ cd $ORACLE_BASE/admin/demo/pfile
$ ls
initdemo.ora
$ cp initdemo.ora initdemo-816.ora
$ rm initdemo.ora
$ cd /u01/app/oracle/product/8.1.6/dbs
$ ls -l initdemo.ora
lrwxrwxrwx  1 oracle  dba  45 Feb 17 10:44 initdemo.ora ->
    /u01/app/oracle/admin/demo/pfile/initdemo.ora
$ rm initdemo.ora
```

Next, move the revised init.ora in the new $ORACLE_HOME/dbs to the $ORACLE_BASE/admin/*SID*/pfile directory. Then, create a soft link in the new $ORACLE_HOME/dbs to the init.ora in $ORACLE_BASE/admin/*SID*/pfile. This way the updated init.ora will always be used.

```
$ cd $ORACLE_BASE/admin/demo/pfile
$ mv /u01/app/oracle/product/9.0.1/dbs/initdemo.ora .
$ ls
initdemo-816.ora  initdemo.ora
$ cd /u01/app/oracle/product/9.0.1/dbs
$ ln -s $ORACLE_BASE/admin/demo/pfile/initdemo.ora .
$ ls -l initdemo.ora
lrwxrwxrwx  1 oracle  dba  45 Jul  3 21:27 initdemo.ora ->
    /u01/app/oracle/admin/demo/pfile/initdemo.ora
```

NOTE

**Server Parameter Files**

Oracle 9i allows you to replace the text-based init.ora file with a binary copy called an spfileSID.ora. You can create the SPFILE or you can continue to use the text-based init.ora file. The benefits of using this new type of file and how to create it are covered in Chapter 19, "9i Server New Features."

3. Review the init.ora; the ODMA should have removed obsolete parameters. You can use diff to compare the files.

```
$ diff initdemo-816.ora initdemo.ora
```

4. Set the COMPATIBLE parameter in the init.ora to represent the new version. Notice that this value is *not* automatically updated by the ODMA. In this case, you need to set it to COMPATIBLE = 9.0.0.

5. Start the database using the *new* Oracle software, as shown in Figure 15.10. Use STARTUP RESTRICT to prevent other users from logging in before you have verified that the migration was successful.

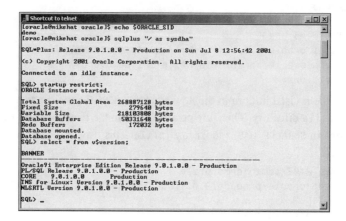

**FIGURE 15.10**

*Start the Database with the New Software.*

Notice how you have to use `sqlplus "/ as sysdba"`? That is because `connect internal` is no longer supported and will *not* work in 9i.

6. Check the alert log for errors.

```
$ pwd
/u01/app/oracle/admin/demo/bdump
$ ls *alert*
alert_demo.log
```

7. Run `$ORACLE_HOME/rdbms/admin/utlrp.sql` to recompile invalid objects.

```
SQL> @$ORACLE_HOME/rdbms/admin/utlrp.sql
```

8. Check for invalid objects manually and recompile them as needed. Use Dynamic SQL, as covered in Chapter 5, if needed.

```
SQL> select owner, count(*) from dba_objects
  2  where status = 'INVALID'
  3  group by owner;
```

| OWNER | COUNT(*) |
| --- | --- |
| CTXSYS | 3 |
| MDSYS | 15 |
| ORDSYS | 159 |
| SYS | 216 |

9. Check the status of your indexes. Look for any bitmapped indexes rendered unusable because of the migration. Rebuild them if necessary.

```
SQL> select owner, index_name, table_name from dba_indexes
  2  where index_type = 'BITMAP' and status = 'UNUSABLE';

no rows selected
```

Next look for any function-based indexes that might have been disabled or made unusable as well.

10. Use ANALYZE to reanalyze all your tables and indexes. You should have scripts and/or cron jobs to do this normally.

11. Shut down the database and perform another cold backup.

12. Verify that `oratab` and `listener.ora` reflect the migrated database. The ODMA should automatically modify your `oratab` file. Depending on what you selected in Step 11 of the migration, it might have also modified the `listener.ora`.

13. Restart the database and verify the application is running properly. If it is, open it for normal use.

Assuming all went well, you now have a solid Oracle 9i database!

## Summary

This chapter covered migrations. A migration involves moving to a higher version of Oracle. The first part of this chapter discussed the planning portion of the migration. It is important to have a tested migration plan before attempting a migration. Testing the database, application, and migration steps is essential to a successful migration. Each piece of the system should be tested against the new database to make sure it works reliably and with acceptable performance. If you skip this testing process, your system can be a mess even if your database migrates successfully.

The second half of the chapter discussed the three methods used to migrate a database: export/import, mig, and the ODMA. Factors influencing the choice of methods were discussed. The chapter then explained how to use ODMA to migrate from Oracle 8.1.6.1 to 9.0.1.

# Java Inside the Database Server

## ESSENTIALS

- Java is the language that provides scalable Internet development.

- Oracle has chosen to tightly integrate Java with the database.

- Java programs can exist outside or inside the database.

- The DBA must understand how to deploy Java outside the database and support the Java developers.

- The DBA needs to load Java programs and manage Java objects within the database.

Java is more than just another programming language; it is one of the building blocks of Internet computing. Just as TCP/IP is the standard for telecommunications and networking, Java is emerging as the language of the Internet. Because a large part of any vendor's future, including Oracle's, is tied to the Internet, it is not surprising that Oracle databases are built to be integrated with Java.

The goal of this chapter is to explain what the DBA needs to know about Java. It does not teach you how to write Java programs nor does it make you an Internet developer. These topics require an entire book to address it appropriately. Rather, this chapter is geared toward the DBA encountering Java for the first time. First, it discusses some of the Java technologies and how they can be deployed both inside and outside the database. This chapter serves to demystify Java so that you can focus on the tasks that you need to perform. The next part of the chapter provides hands-on examples of how to configure Oracle to support Java. It shows you how Java is built into the database, how to write Java programs to access the database, and how to deploy Java components inside the database.

## Understanding the Role and Future of Java Inside Oracle

Anyone involved with computers or the IT industry knows that the Internet is the key to staying competitive. Every computer vendor certainly knows this. As a result there has been a mad rush for several years to "Web-enable" virtually every aspect of computing. Oracle has embraced this idea and has gone to great lengths to make its database accessible and supportive of the Internet.

Oracle created several new products and restructured others to support this initiative. These products include:

- **WebDB**    This is Oracle's easy and lightweight method to Web-enable its database. This PL/SQL-based product is now called Oracle Portal. It is now being packaged with iAS. WebDB is covered in Chapter 17, "WebDB/Oracle Portal."

- **Oracle Application Server**    Oracle first created Oracle Application Server (OAS) to provide Web-based access into the database. This PL/SQL-driven product is being retired with a terminal release of OAS 4.0.8.

- **Internet Application Server**    Oracle's follow-up to OAS is iAS. This Java-oriented application Web server is covered in Chapter 18, "Internet Application Server."

- **Internet File System**    Oracle now allows you to store any type of file that normally resides on a typical hard drive inside your database. These files appear to the user as if they are on a network drive, but in reality they are stored within an Oracle database. Users access and edit their files as normal, for example using Windows Explorer.

However, because the files are inside the database, they can use all the indexing, locking, and backup features associated with Oracle databases.

- **JDeveloper**    Oracle built an integrated Java development tool called JDeveloper. This development tool allows programmers to quickly create Java programs.

- **Oracle Database**    Starting with Oracle 8i, a Java Virtual Machine exists inside the database. This allows Java programs to run inside the database. Furthermore, Java can now be used instead of PL/SQL. Finally, Java entry points into the database via JDBC and SQLJ are supported.

---

**NOTE**

### Changing Role of the DBA

These are quite a few changes involving Java, and more are likely coming. Although you don't have to know how to program Java, you do have to know how to *support* it. It's a very similar situation to what PL/SQL are currently. Some of the most effective DBAs aren't PL/SQL programming experts,but they know how to support their developers. The same holds true for Java. Just as you need to know what a PL/SQL trigger is, you need to know what an Enterprise Java Bean (EJB) is. Fortunately, if you already understand Oracle databases and PL/SQL, you should also be able to understand Java without too much trouble.

Unfortunately, Java, its related technologies, and the product names change much faster than Oracle and PL/SQL. Some of these changes reflect new technologies, whereas other changes are little more than marketing and sales ploys. For example, here are just a few name changes.

- Oracle Internet file system is now Oracle9i file system
- Oracle Portal is now Oracle9iAS Portal
- Oracle 8i JVM is now Oracle Enterprise Java Engine (EJE)

Keep in-mind these changes are just within Oracle! Other vendors change their names too. Regardless, you need to learn how Java plays a role within your environment and keep current with it. Although PL/SQL and "traditional" DBA work will still exist for years to come, those skills will become less valuable. COBOL and mainframe positions can still be found today, for example, but they don't usually pay as well as positions that deal with newer technologies.

---

Obviously, Oracle has invested a great deal of time and money into developing these Java-enabling products. These products keep changing with each release so trying to stay on top each product can be a full time job. Fortunately, you don't have to be a world class Java programmer or Webmaster. However, you should be familiar with the technologies involved and understand how they are deployed. Furthermore, at the points at which they interface with your database, you do need to be an expert.

## Java Overview

To learn about Java, the language, architecture, and its components, start by visiting www.java.sun.com. There you can find everything you need to get started, including software, tutorials, and white papers. Pay particular attention to the J2EE (Java 2 Enterprise Edition) specification and white paper. This paper outlines the Java architecture and specifications that inherently have a longer life span than many of the product names pushed by vendors. After you learn the fundamentals, learning the vendor-specific details is much easier. However, there are a few concepts and terms you should understand.

From a programming standpoint, Java is a highly portable, object-oriented (OO) language. Basically you can write it on any platform and run it on any other platform. Concepts of object-oriented programming are well beyond the scope of this book, but it is a powerful paradigm of programming and design that every IT professional should understand.

One of the confusing concepts about Java is that it can be deployed everywhere. If you take a simple three-tier architecture, as shown in Figure 16.1, you will see that Java can exist on every tier.

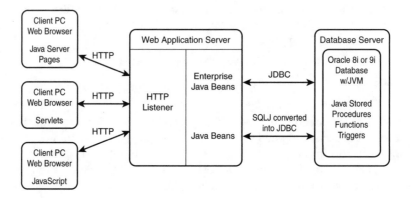

**FIGURE 16.1**

*Java Deployment*

This section explains each Java term. The middle tier is discussed in Chapter 18. The key point here is to understand that Java *can* exist on many different tiers. You don't have to set up your environment to use Java on the client, application/Web server, and database. In fact, you most likely will not use all the technologies identified in Figure 16.1. However, you need to know the differences between having Java in the client, the middle tier, or the database.

There are a plethora of Java terms flying around that you should be familiar with. Here is an explanation of the most common ones.

- **Applet**   A Java program that is downloaded and executes on a client's browser.

- **Java Virtual Machine**   The Java Virtual Machine (JVM) is the virtual machine and environment Java programs run in. This is described in greater detail later in this chapter.

- **Java Bean**   A Java bean is a piece of Java code on the middle tier. It can be graphical, lightweight, and accessed by Java Server Pages (JSP).

- **Enterprise Java Bean**   An Enterprise Java Bean (EJB) is a reusable, robust, scalable piece of Java code typically on the middle tier. It is *not* the same as a Java bean. There are two types of EJBs: session beans and entity beans. Session beans exist to serve one client and are not persistent across multiple sessions. Within that session they can be *stateful* (retaining information between calls) or they can be *stateless* (no information is retained between calls). Entity beans are persistent and do maintain information. For example, an entity bean can be mapped to an object, such as a customer, that exists longer than one session.

- **Servlet**   A servlet is a lightweight piece of Java code that resides in an HTML Web page, but runs on the server. Basically, it is an applet that runs on the server side. This code is executed based on actions by the Web user.

- **Java Server Page**   A Java Server Page (JSP) is a tag in an HTML page that compiles into a servlet when executed. Because it is only a tag in a Web page, it doesn't appear as Java code to the HTML developer.

- **JavaScript**   JavaScript isn't really Java. It is just a scripting language for use within HTML pages.

These are certainly a lot of terms that might seem foreign to you if you're new to Java or the Web. However, examining a diagram of your system's architecture to determine where Java is deployed will help demystify the whole Java/Web environment. Once you do this, you can manage it using similar principals used in any other environment.

Just as you do with any system, you need to identify the inputs and outputs related to the database and server. Although you might have a Web server between the users and database, you are still just dealing with connections into your database. In the case of Figure 16.1, these are JDBC connections into your database. Once a connection is established, SQL requests are hitting your database in a manner similar to any other connection.

# Supporting Java with Oracle

Rest assured that you don't need to be a Java programmer any more than you already are a PL/SQL developer. Although advanced skills in the respective languages are helpful, they aren't absolute requirements. However, there are some things you need to know about supporting the language and your developers. Among these are knowing where your program code resides and how it interfaces with the database.

## Java Outside the Database

Java code commonly resides outside the database. Sometimes the code resides in a Web application server, other times it is standalone. However the need to access data inside a database is still present. Since Oracle 7.3.4, Java can make SQL calls to a database. The two ways to do this are by using JDBC or SQLJ.

### JDBC

Java Database Connectivity (JDBC) is an open method that allows Java programs to issue SQL statements to *any* database, not just Oracle. Conceptually this is similar to ODBC (Open Database Connectivity) calls. Within the Java program, a JDBC code segment requests a connection to the specified database and issues a SQL statement. The statement is issued and results are returned to the program. This is a common method for interfacing with a database.

Oracle 8.1.6 and 8.1.7 databases comply with the JDBC 2.0 standard. There are three types of JDBC drivers used with Oracle databases. The nature of the application you are using determines which driver you use.

- **JDBC Thin Driver**   Connects a Web browser to the database. The key to this driver is that it does not require any Oracle network software (such as Net8) to be installed on the client. This allows the clients to be "thin" because they are just Web browsers. However, this lightweight method should not be used for SQL-intensive operations.

- **JDBC OCI Driver**   A more robust method of connecting to the database. Use this driver if you expect to be doing a lot of database calls. For example, if you have a Web application server that continually accesses the database, this would likely be the driver to use. The only drawback is that it requires Oracle Net8.

- **JDBC KPRB Server Driver**   Used with Java stored procedures located within the Oracle database.

Establishing a new JDBC connection, which is really a database connection, for each SQL call is expensive from a performance standpoint. Some Web servers allow connection pooling to avoid this expense. It's important to identify how your developers are using JDBC to access the database and to verify that they are using the right driver for the job.

## SQLJ

SQLJ is essentially Java with embedded static SQL. In many respects it is similar to Pro*C where a C program has embedded SQL statements. In fact, this product is sometimes referred to as Pro*Java. When the program gets to the SQL statement, the SQL statement is transformed into a JDBC call to the database. However, there are a few advantages to using SQLJ over straight JDBC calls, outlined here:

- The syntax is reduced and is more readable. This makes development faster and easier.
- You can use bind variables in SQL statements to improve performance.
- A precompiler checks the SQLJ syntax before it is executed, unlike in JDBC. This improves program debugging.

One drawback to SQLJ is that you cannot create dynamic SQL with it. This can only be done with JDBC.

---

**NOTE**

### MTS Is Not Always Necessary

One common misconception of DBAs new to Java is that they think MTS (Multi-Threaded Server) must be set up to run Java. That is only partially true. If you are running Java EJBs or CORBA servers *inside* the database, you must indeed configure and run MTS.

However, if the Java code resides exclusively *outside* the database, MTS is not required. For example, if you have a Web server containing EJBs that connect to your database via JDBC, you can (and perhaps should) run in dedicated server mode. The reason is that Java isn't really being executed inside the database; all the database sees are JDBC connections issuing SQL statements.

---

## Java Inside the Database

Oracle 8i is the first version to allow Java objects to exist inside the database, thanks to the Oracle Java Virtual Machine (JVM), which is inside the database. (Actually, there is also a JVM inside the iAS server, but this is discussed in Chapter 18.) To understand what this means, you need to know a little about Java and its JVM.

### JVM

Java programs are highly portable because they can be written on one platform and executed on a different one. This provides a big advantage over other languages. The main reason they are portable is that Java programs execute inside a Java Virtual Machine, which interfaces between the executing program and the platform.

Towards this end, Oracle has seen fit to include a special JVM inside both its database and iAS server. This JVM is tuned specifically to run within Oracle, which means it uses less memory than a standard JVM. Each Java program that runs inside the database gets its own JVM in which it executes. However, if your database had hundreds of Java programs running simultaneously, the required memory would likely exceed what was available. Oracle reduced the likelihood of this by reducing the memory needed for each session. Requiring MTS to be set up for Java running inside the database also reduces memory requirements.

Each new version of Oracle is compliant with different Java specifications and features. The readme.txt found in $ORACLE_HOME/javavm/doc is the best source for up-to-date information, but here are a few highpoints in terms of Java compatibility.

| Oracle Version | Compliant With |
| --- | --- |
| Oracle 8.1.5 | Java 1.1 |
| Oracle 8.1.6 | Java 2.0 |
| Oracle 8.1.7 | Java 2.0 |
| Oracle 9.0.1 | Java 2.0 |

The JVM is compliant with different versions of Sun's Java Developers Kit. The version of JDK is dependent on the version of the database:

| Oracle Version | Compliant With |
| --- | --- |
| Oracle 8.1.5 | JDK 1.1 |
| Oracle 8.1.6 | JDK 1.2.1 |
| Oracle 8.1.7 | JDK 1.2.1 |
| Oracle 9.0.1 | JDK 1.2.1 |

New in Oracle 8.1.7 is an improvement to the JVM called Oracle8*i* JVM Accelerator. This enhancement allows Java bytecode to be compiled and executed as native compiled C code. C code is faster than Java code, so this results in a performance improvement. Note that this does *not* impact the platform independence or portability of the Java code.

## Java Programs Used Instead of PL/SQL?

By running Java inside the database, you have a possible alternative to using PL/SQL. In fact, just about anything you write in PL/SQL can also be written in Java. Functions, procedures, and triggers can all be written in Java. This certainly provides you with some new options, but it is also begs the question: "Do you really want to write in Java?"

PL/SQL handles SQL operations very well. It is proven, robust, has a large code base, and a large skilled developer base. However, some tasks, such as interfacing with the OS, object orientation, and intensive processing, are better done with Java.

You don't have to choose to use either Java or PL/SQL; you can use both. Oracle has ensured that you can call SQL and PL/SQL from Java. Also, SQL and PL/SQL can call Java, as follows:

- Java calls SQL and PL/SQL via JDBC or SQLJ.
- SQL and PL/SQL have Java stored procedures placed in a PL/SQL wrapper so they can be called.

Therefore, I recommend using the following guidelines when choosing between PL/SQL and Java:

- If the task requires traditional database access, use PL/SQL.
- If the task does not require heavy database access and is more of a "number-crunching" program, use Java. Starting in Oracle 8.1.7, Java programs can be compiled and executed as very fast C code.

Oracle will likely continue to support PL/SQL. There is simply too much tied up in PL/SQL already and not enough people trained in Java. Plus PL/SQL does its job of database access and manipulation too well to justify converting to something else. I certainly wouldn't start migrating my PL/SQL programs to Java, but I would take a look at Java for new applications.

## EJBs and CORBA Inside the Database

Oracle allows Enterprise Java Beans and CORBA servers to be loaded into the database and executed. This comes in addition to having Java stored procedures, functions, and triggers. There are several advantages to having these objects inside the database, including faster execution and reduced network traffic.

To support the use of EJBs and CORBA servers inside the database, you needed to configure MTS. Each client session gets its own JVM and the connection to the database is managed by MTS. Although EJBs inside the Oracle database are not themselves multi-threaded, this is not a major issue because each client has its own JVM.

Starting with Oracle 8.1.7, Java Server Pages (JSPs) and servlets are also fully supported within the database. These are made possible by incorporating the Java Server Pages Engine and Servlet Engine inside the 8.1.7 database.

# Managing Java Inside the Database

Although you might never be called to *write* Java code, I can almost guarantee that you will have to *support* it at some point in your career as a DBA. This section covers some of the hands-on duties of the DBA who supports Java. Specifically, it covers Java-specific init.ora parameters, installing/uninstalling the Java option, writing and executing a simple Java program, configuring MTS and IIOP for Java, and loading EJBs and CORBA servers.

## Java Configuration Parameters

In Oracle 8i and 9i there are three init.ora parameters that specifically deal with Java.

```
SQL> show parameter java

NAME                            TYPE     VALUE
------------------------------- -------- ----------
java_max_sessionspace_size      integer  0
java_pool_size                  string   100M
java_soft_sessionspace_limit    integer  0
SQL>
```

They are discussed in detail here:

- **JAVA_POOL_SIZE**   Determines the size of the Java pool inside the SGA. This pool acts similarly to the shared pool except that it stores shared Java objects in memory. If you do not plan on using Java and want to conserve memory, you can set this value to 0 and Oracle will give it a minimum value of 32K. Otherwise, Oracle sets a default value of 20M, which is sufficient if you are using Java-stored procedures, functions, and triggers. However, if you are using stored EJBs and CORBA servers, this needs to be a larger value. When you install Java for the first time give this pool a large value such as 100M.
- **JAVA_SOFT_SESSIONSPACE_LIMIT**   This parameter is really just a threshold for warning messages regarding memory usage by a Java session. If the memory usage for a Java session exceeds this value, a message in the alert.log is written. The default is 1M.
- **JAVA_MAX_SESSIONSPACE_SIZE**   This is the hard limit for the amount of memory used for a Java program. It is a higher value than JAVA_SOFT_SESSIONSPACE_LIMIT. If a Java program exceeds this value, it is terminated. The default is 4G.

In addition to these three parameters, you must make sure that the SHARED_POOL_SIZE is sufficient. Oracle will use the UGA to store static Java variables so the shared pool must be sized accordingly. Fortunately, shared pools are usually large anyway so this shouldn't be a problem. For the initial install of Java I set the shared pool to 100M.

# Installing Java

Installing the Java option is not terribly difficult if you know what needs to be done. You must install this option if you want to run Java inside your database. Depending on your version of the database, there are between 8000 and 9000 Java objects. These are owned by SYS and are in the SYSTEM tablespace. These objects compose the Java option. They can be loaded when the database is created or afterward. Installing Java also results in the creation of the DBMS_JAVA package and a minimum of two roles: JAVAUSERPRIV and JAVASYSPRIV.

To load Java, follow these steps.

1. Set up your database environment. Loading Java is a resource-intensive process and takes about an hour. You do not want the process to fail halfway through because of a lack of resources. The default parameters are not normally sufficient to load Java. I usually increase the parameters as follows.

```
JAVA_POOL_SIZE        = 100M
SHARED_POOL_SIZE      = 100M
DB_BLOCK_BUFERS       = 35000 # Using 8K blocks
```

   After you have loaded Java and verified it was successful, you can reduce these parameters.

2. Make sure you have enough free space. I make sure I have about 500M of rollback space available and about 200M of free space in the SYSTEM tablespace. Use view DBA_FREE_SPACE to verify that you have enough free space.

```
SQL> select tablespace_name, sum(bytes) from dba_free_space
  2  where tablespacE_name in ('SYSTEM','RBS')
  3  group by tablespace_name;

TABLESPACE_NAME                       SUM(BYTES)
------------------------------ ----------------
RBS                                  568,311,808
SYSTEM                               230,023,168

SQL>
```

3. Get a count of invalid objects in the database before you run the script. This way, you can identify any objects invalidated due to the script.

```
SQL> select owner, count(*) from dba_objects
  2  where status = 'INVALID' group by owner;

no rows selected

SQL>
```

   The install generates many messages, which will scroll past the screen. Start a spool file to capture the output.

```
SQL> spool initjvm.lst
```

4. Connect internal (or as SYS) and run the script
   `$ORACLE_HOME/javavm/install/initjvm.sql`.

```
SQL> show user
USER is "SYS"
SQL> @$ORACLE_HOME/javavm/install/initjvm.sql
...
PL/SQL procedure successfully completed.

PL/SQL procedure successfully completed.

SQL>
```

Just like any install, you might see some harmless errors stating that objects don't exist before they are dropped. Expect the install to run 30 minutes to over an hour. Once the install is complete, stop spooling.

```
SQL> spool off
```

5. Once the install has completed, you need to take object counts and check for invalid objects. If you find any invalid objects, use dynamic SQL to recompile them as explained in Chapter 5, "Creating a Database."

```
SQL> select owner, count(*) from dba_objects
  2  where status = 'INVALID' group by owner;

no rows selected

SQL> select count(*) from dba_objects
  2  where object_type like 'JAVA%';

  COUNT(*)
----------
      8659

SQL>
```

You should see between 8000 and 9000 Java objects when you are done. You will have some variation depending on the version of Oracle you are running. Anything less than 8000 likely indicates a problem.

6. Verify that you can see the package DBMS_JAVA.

```
SQL> desc dbms_java
...
FUNCTION UNIQUE_TABLE_NAME RETURNS VARCHAR2
 Argument Name                   Type                    In/Out Default?
 ------------------------------  ----------------------  ------ --------
 PREFIX                          VARCHAR2                IN

SQL>
```

Assuming that you can see DBMS_JAVA, you have over 8000 Java objects, and none on them are invalid, you should be ready to start using Java inside the database. To get information specific to your database version, refer to the file $ORACLE_HOME/javavm/doc/readme.txt for details. Because each successive release of Oracle has increased support for Java, this readme.txt is critical.

## Uninstalling Java

There are rare times when you'll actually want to uninstall Java. I have run across this on several occasions. In one case, we didn't want to allocate any memory to JAVA_POOL_SIZE. I could have just set JAVA_POOL_SIZE to an insignificant value, but we wanted to make sure no one would try to use it, so we decided to completely remove Java. On another really odd occasion, full database exports were failing because so many Java objects were invalid (appearing as an ORA-04030 error). Because we weren't using Java at the time, we decided it was just easier to remove Java than to fix the problem.

1. The driving script to remove Java is $ORACLE_HOME/javavm/install/rmjvm.sql. Depending on your version of Oracle, you might have to make the following manual fix to the script. On line 38, change the following

   ```
   call rmjvm.run(true);
   ```

   to

   ```
   execute rmjvm.run(true);
   ```

   Although this is a simple change, it is probably a good idea to make a backup of your script before you edit any Oracle file.

2. Just as you did for the install, make sure there are several hundred megabytes of free space in your rollback segments. During the uninstall, a rollback segment MONSTER will be automatically created and then dropped once Java has been removed.

3. Connect internal (SYS) and run the script rmjvm.sql.

   ```
   SQL> @$ORACLE_HOME/javavm/install/rmjvm.sql
   ...
   set transaction use rollback segment MONSTER
   delete from obj$
   set transaction use rollback segment MONSTER
   All java objects removed
   alter rollback segment monster offline
   drop rollback segment monster
   flush shared_pool

   PL/SQL procedure successfully completed.

   SQL>
   ```

4. Verify that there are no longer any Java objects and nothing has been invalidated.

```
SQL> select count(*) from dba_objects
  2  where object_type like 'JAVA%';

  COUNT(*)
----------
         0

SQL> select owner, count(*) from dba_objects
  2  where status = 'INVALID' group by owner;

no rows selected

SQL>
```

Obviously, you can reinstall Java later if you decide you need it. Typically, I simply install Java whenever I create a database whether I know I'll use it or not. Although there is some overhead in doing this, I'd rather get the install out of the way during the database creation (unless the machine is really tight on resources).

## Creating, Loading, and Running Java Programs

Although the developers usually write the Java code, it is sometimes the DBA's job to load the Java code into the database. Therefore, this section shows you how to write a simple Java stored function, load it into the database, publish it so you can call from SQL or PL/SQL, and then execute it via SQL*Plus. Although this is a function, it could just as easily be a procedure or trigger. To load and use these types of Java objects, you do *not* have to be running MTS or IIOP. Note that the example does *not* load EJBs or CORBA servers at this point.

There are four basic steps to create a Java stored procedure, function, or trigger.

1. Write the Java program. This can be in any tool you want, but at this point the program still resides outside the database.

2. Load the program into the database as a Java program. There are two ways to do this. You can use the CREATE OR REPLACE JAVA SOURCE database statement or the loadjava command-line utility.

3. Publish the Java program into a PL/SQL wrapper so it can be executed by SQL or PL/SQL. This is done with the CREATE OR REPLACE [PROCEDURE | FUNCTION | TRIGGER] *PROGRAM_NAME* as LANGUAGE JAVA statement.

4. Call the Java program (contained in the PL/SQL wrapper) from SQL or PL/SQL.

The following is a simple example of creating the traditional "Hello World" program. This program has been written thousands of times in every language and this is the Java version. However, don't get too wrapped up in the code; the main emphasis here is on the processes used to load and publish a Java program inside the database.

Perform the following steps to load and publish "Hello World" in Java.

1. Write the program in Java. If you plan on loading the program into Oracle with the CRE-ATE OR REPLACE JAVA SOURCE database statement via SQL*Plus, you don't really need to write it beforehand. However, if you are using the loadjava utility, you need to save the file as a .java file as shown:

```
[oracle@mikehat oracle]$ more hello.java
public class Hello
{
    public static String world()
    {
        return "Hello World!!!";
    }
}
[oracle@mikehat oracle]$
```

2. Load the program into the database. There are two ways to do this.

Method 1: Load using the CREATE OR REPLACE JAVA SOURCE statement:

```
SQL> create or replace java source named "Hello" as
  2  public class Hello
  3  {
  4      public static String world()
  5      {
  6          return "Hello World!!!";
  7      }
  8  }
  9  /

Java created.

SQL>
```

Method 2: Load using the loadjava utility:

```
[oracle@mikehat oracle]$ loadjava -u system/manager -v -r hello.java
initialization complete
loading  : Hello
creating : Hello
resolver :
resolving: Hello
[oracle@mikehat oracle]$
```

3. Publish the Java program into a PL/SQL wrapper.

```
SQL> create or replace function hello
  2  return varchar2
  3  as language java
  4  name 'Hello.world() return java.lang.String';
  5  /

Function created.

SQL>
```

There is now a procedure called `hello` that SQL and PL/SQL can execute.

4. Execute the program from SQL*Plus. You might get a warning error ORA-29549 the first time you run the program. If so, re-execute the program to eliminate the message.

```
SQL> set serveroutput on
SQL> select hello from dual;
select hello from dual
                *
ERROR at line 1:
ORA-29549: class SYSTEM.Hello has changed, Java session state cleared


SQL> select hello from dual;

HELLO
------------------------------------------------------------
Hello World!!!

SQL>
```

At this point, you have successfully written, loaded, published, and executed a simple Java program inside the database. In this case it was a function, but it can also be a procedure or a trigger. The next logical step is to remove the Java objects from the database. As you can see, there are three Java objects related to the "Hello World" example.

```
SQL> select object_name, object_type from user_objects
  2  where upper(object_name) like 'HELLO%';

OBJECT_NAME                     OBJECT_TYPE
------------------------------  -----------------
HELLO                           FUNCTION
Hello                           JAVA CLASS
Hello                           JAVA SOURCE

SQL>
```

Dropping the function is just like dropping any other object.

```
SQL> drop function hello;

Function dropped.

SQL>
```

To remove the Java source and Java class, you can use the command-line utility drop-java. This is basically the opposite of loadjava.

```
[oracle@mikehat oracle]$ dropjava -u system/manager -v hello.java
dropping source  : Hello
[oracle@mikehat oracle]$
```

As you can see, all the "Hello World" objects have been dropped from the database:

```
SQL> select object_name, object_type from user_objects
  2  where upper(object_name) like 'HELLO%';

no rows selected

SQL>
```

Those are the fundamentals of creating, loading, publishing, executing, and dropping Java procedures, functions, and triggers inside the database. Obviously there is much more to the coding aspect, all of which is outside the scope of this book. However, these steps should be enough to get you started using Java inside the database.

## Configuring MTS and IIOP for Java

Oracle requires MTS (Multi-Threaded Server) to be running if you plan on using EJBs and CORBA servers *inside* the database. If you are simply running Java procedures, functions, and triggers inside the database, you don't need MTS because these components run in either dedicated or multi-threaded server mode. Furthermore, if you have EJBs external to the database (such as from a Web application server) that access it via JDBC, you do not need MTS.

You need to configure the MTS to use the IIOP protocol. Internet Inter-Orb Protocol is the TCP/IP implementation of the GIOP (General Inter-Orb Protocol) protocol. This protocol allows direct access to Java inside the database *without* using Net8. To set this up, perform the following tasks.

1. Modify the init.ora file to use MTS. Assuming you have used the DBCA to create a template database and init.ora, you have to uncomment only one line. Remember to bounce the instance.

```
mts_dispatchers = "(PROTOCOL=TCP)(PRE=oracle.aurora.server.SGiopServer)"
# Uncomment the following line when your listener is configured for SSL
# (listener.ora and sqlnet.ora)
# mts_dispatchers = "(PROTOCOL=TCPS)(PRE=oracle.aurora.server.SGiopServer)"
```

Here, you want to use `MTS_DISPATCHERS` with the TCP protocol because you are not using SSL (Secure Sockets Layer) at this point.

2. Next, configure the `listener.ora` file for GIOP presentation and RAW session. In this case, you use port 2481. Add the code under the default listener section. When you're done, it should look like this:

```
LISTENER =
  (DESCRIPTION_LIST =
    (DESCRIPTION =
      (ADDRESS_LIST =
        (ADDRESS = (PROTOCOL = TCP)(HOST = mikehat.mike.com)(PORT = 1521))
      )
      (ADDRESS_LIST =
        (ADDRESS = (PROTOCOL = IPC)(KEY = EXTPROC))
      )
    )

    (DESCRIPTION =
      (PROTOCOL_STACK =
        (PRESENTATION = GIOP)
        (SESSION = RAW)
      )
      (ADDRESS = (PROTOCOL = TCP)(HOST = mikehat.mike.com)(PORT = 2481))
    )
  )
```

3. Next reload the listener with `lsnrctl reload`.

```
[oracle@mikehat /etc]$ lsnrctl services | more

LSNRCTL for Linux: Version 8.1.6.0.0 - Production on 15-AUG-2001 19:10:40

(c) Copyright 1998, 1999, Oracle Corporation.  All rights reserved.

Connecting to
➡(DESCRIPTION=(ADDRESS=(PROTOCOL=TCP)(HOST=mikehat.mike.com)(PORT=1
521)))
Services Summary...
  PLSExtProc            has 1 service handler(s)
    DEDICATED SERVER established:0 refused:0
      LOCAL SERVER
  rh1dev1               has 1 service handler(s)
    DEDICATED SERVER established:0 refused:0
      LOCAL SERVER
  rh1dev1               has 2 service handler(s)
    DISPATCHER established:0 refused:0 current:0 max:254 state:ready
      D000 <machine: mikehat.mike.com, pid: 3633>
```

```
        (DESCRIPTION=(ADDRESS=(PROTOCOL=tcp)(HOST=mikehat.mike.com)
➥(PORT=41648))(P
RESENTATION=oracle.aurora.server.SGiopServer)(SESSION=RAW))
        Presentation: oracle.aurora.server.SGiopServer
    DEDICATED SERVER established:0 refused:0
        LOCAL SERVER
The command completed successfully
[oracle@mikehat /etc]$
```

MTS with IIOP is now configured so you can run EJBs and CORBA servers inside the database. You may connect either to port 2481 as identified in the listener.ora or directly to the dispatcher D000 through port 41648 as shown by lsnrctl services. You can also improve security by using SSL if needed.

## Loading EJBs and CORBA Servers

After the database is configured to run MTS with IIOP you can start loading and EJBs and CORBA servers. Because these objects are often placed on the middle tier rather than inside the database, this section doesn't go into a detailed discussion of the entire process. However, it does identify the steps needed to accomplish this task.

Both EJBs and CORBA servers need to be loaded and published inside the database. There are two command-line utilities that can be used to do this: deployejb and publish.

- deployejb is used for EJBS.
- publish is used for CORBA servers.

The syntax of the utilities is roughly similar to loadjava although there are differences and you need to investigate the details.

Once the EJB or CORBA server is loaded into the database it is published as a published object inside the session namespace. By using Java Naming and Directory Interfaces (JNDI), clients can find the published objects inside the session namespace.

You can navigate the session namespace as well. Once inside the shell, you can use Unix commands such as cd, ls, mkdir, and rm. You must first invoke the session shell as shown here:

```
$ sess_sh -u system -p manager -s sess_iiop://mikehat.mike.com:2481:rh1dev1
```

In this case, you invoke the session shell as SYSTEM/MANAGER. Then you connect to the hostname or IP address, the port, which is 2481, and finally the rh1dev1 database. This method uses the listener to connect to the database port.

Alternatively, you can specify just the hostname or IP address and the dispatcher's port number (41648), which you can determine using lsnrctl services. This method connects you directly to the dispatcher.

# Summary

This chapter covered the fundamentals of Java from the DBA's perspective. Java is a key to Internet computing and Oracle is incorporating it into as many products as possible. There are many ways to implement Java and an equal number of terms to understand. However, as long as you understand where Java is deployed in relation to your database, the environment is manageable.

Java code can exist inside or outside the database. If the code resides outside the database, Java will establish connections either by using straight JDBC calls or by using SQLJ, which is also JDBC. If the Java code resides inside the database, it will do so in the form of Java procedures, functions, and triggers, EJBs, and CORBA servers. As of Oracle 8.1.7, you can also use JSPs and servlets. All of these run inside a Java Virtual Machine (JVM), which has been optimized for Oracle databases.

Typically, the developers do the actual coding of Java programs. However, the DBA does have certain setup and configuration responsibilities, especially when Java programs are executed inside the database. First, the Java option must be installed. This involves using the initjvm.sql script to load over 8000 objects into the database. Depending on the type of Java programs running in the database, you might have to set up MTS with IIOP. Other DBA tasks can include loading Java programs and publishing them inside the database. Although there is a lot to learn if you're new to Java, it is not an impossible task as long as you are aware of your architecture and can see the big picture.

# WebDB/Oracle Portal

## ESSENTIALS

- WebDB has been renamed Oracle Portal starting in version 3.0.

- WebDB/Oracle Portal is the fastest way to Web-enable an Oracle database.

- WebDB/Oracle Portal allows users to connect to the database using any standard Web browser and execute PL/SQL packages inside the database.

- Many OEM-like DBA utilities become available to the DBA via the Web because of this tool.

- Application developers can use Wizards and PL/SQL to quickly create Web interfaces into the database.

WebDB (soon to be renamed Oracle Portal) can be used to quickly provide Web-based access into any Oracle database version 7.3 and higher. This software consists of an HTTP listener and PL/SQL packages that, once loaded into a database, allow users to access the database through any Web browser.

WebDB provides benefits to both developers and DBAs. Developers can quickly create Web-based forms and reports using easy-to-use Wizards and PL/SQL packages. DBAs benefit by gaining a set of OEM-like tools that they can access via any Web browser.

This chapter looks at WebDB/Oracle Portal primarily from a DBA's perspective. Complete coverage of what it can provide developers is outside the scope of this book. Instead, the chapter provides a quick overview of what it is, what it offers developers, and its architecture. The chapter then covers installation and basic maintenance procedures. Finally, you'll look at some of the database-management tools available.

# What Are WebDB and Oracle Portal?

WebDB and Oracle Portal are the same product. Right now, it is in the transition from WebDB 2.2 to Oracle Portal 3.0. The key functionality of WebDB still exists in Oracle Portal, plus the product is gaining some new features and improvements. Currently, Oracle Portal is being packaged with iAS, which is discussed in Chapter 18, "Internet Application Server."

## Purpose

WebDB purports to be the quickest and easiest way to Web-enable a database. After the tool is installed and running, the PL/SQL developer or DBA is presented with a multitude of templates and wizards from which he or she can create PL/SQL-driven Web forms to access the database. End users can access these forms using any Web browser as long as they have a valid URL, username, and password.

The main benefit of WebDB is that it is relatively quick and simple to implement without extensive training or setup. It uses a preexisting database. Installation of the product is normally straightforward and hassle-free. Because the forms are generated in PL/SQL and there is a wide array of wizards and templates to get started with, almost anyone with PL/SQL experience can use this product. For those who want to start using the Web quickly and with little overhead, this tool is a good choice.

### Developers Really Like this Tool

From my experience, any developer who uses this tool likes it. I made a mistake of mentioning I was going to install it at one site. One of the Java developers (who obviously had WebDB previously) was at my cube every few hours asking whether it was ready yet. He certainly was anxious to use it again.

Another developer I worked with said he wished he'd known more about the tool when we worked together. I had installed it, but because he didn't know much about it, he never messed with it. After he left our company he received WebDB training at his new company and wished that he had taken advantage of the tool sooner.

I also know of a PL/SQL-savvy DBA that thought he was going to have to hire a developer specifically to write an application using this tool. However, with a little work and trial-and-error he was able to write the application himself.

For the organization that has a limited need to Web-enable its database, this tool can be a viable solution. Especially if you have aggressive PL/SQL developers/DBAs like the ones I know.

## WebDB/Oracle Portal Architecture

There are three main components within the WebDB/Oracle Portal architecture: the client, the database server, and the WebDB/Oracle Portal server. Figure 17.1 shows how the WebDB architecture can be organized.

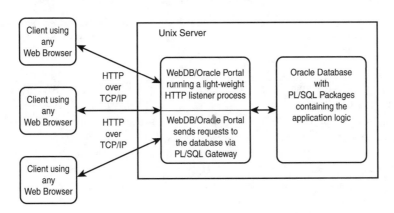

**FIGURE 17.1**
*WebDB/Oracle Portal Architecture.*

On the client side, all you need is a Web browser. No special Oracle tools or Net8 products need to be installed. This makes the database very accessible. All you need is the correct URL, username, and password.

On the database server side is an Oracle database with the WebDB PL/SQL packages installed. All the data, PL/SQL application logic, and user information is stored within the database. This inherently provides performance and backup and recovery protection because all the objects are in an Oracle database. Here, you can leverage your proven tuning and backup and recovery skills.

Between the client and the database server is the WebDB/Oracle Portal installation. It provides its own lightweight HTTP listener that takes requests from the client's browsers. Alternatively, it can also use the listener from an OAS server, iAS server, or another third-party Web server. This improves the scalability of the product. WebDB/Oracle Portal then relays the client's request via its PL/SQL gateway to the Oracle database, which in turn processes the requests via PL/SQL packages. The responses are then returned to the WebDB/Oracle Portal installation and then relayed back to the client's browser.

# Installation

This section discusses how to install WebDB/Oracle Portal. Installing this tool is normally straightforward. The install described here is WebDB 2.2 on RedHat Linux. The biggest issues normally deal with connectivity and getting the listener to run. You need to have the database you are going to connect to running because this tool loads objects into that database.

> **NOTE**
>
> ### Oracle Portal Is Now Installed with iAS
>
> Oracle has decided to start shipping Oracle Portal with iAS (Internet Application Server). WebDB, on the other hand, was shipped with the database. So why not cover it in Chapter 18?
>
> First of all, iAS is big enough that it deserves its own chapter, although this product is mentioned where necessary. Second, I have covered the use of the OUI throughout this book because I have been focusing on the latest releases of each product. However, this version of WebDB uses the older text-based installer, which every DBA should see at least once because older systems will continue to exist for some time. Finally, there are people who don't have iAS and just want to use WebDB. This chapter is intended to provide the fundamentals of WebDB/Oracle Portal from a DBA's perspective, not to cover all the technologies of the Internet.

Follow these steps to install WebDB 2.2 on RedHat Linux:

1. The database you will use with WebDB must meet the following minimum requirements:

    Have 25 or more MAX_ENABLED_ROLES

    Have 100 or more OPEN_CURSORS

    O7_DICTIONARY_ACCESSIBILITY must be set to TRUE

2. You must create a separate ORACLE_HOME for WebDB. Create the following directory and set your ORACLE_HOME variable.

```
$ cd $ORACLE_BASE/product
$ mkdir webdb22
$ export ORACLE_HOME=/u01/app/oracle/product/webdb22
```

3. Next, set up your other environment variables as follows:

```
$ export LD_LIBRARY_PATH=$ORACLE_HOME/lib
$ export SHLIB_PATH=$ORACLE_HOME/lib
$ export TNS_ADMIN=/etc
$ export WV_GATEWAY_CFG=$ORACLE_HOME/listener/cfg/wbsrv.app
```

Make sure your PATH has the correct $ORACLE_HOME. It is easy to accidentally include the wrong $ORACLE_HOME value at this stage.

```
$ echo $PATH
/usr/kerberos/bin:/usr/local/bin:/bin:/usr/bin:/usr/X11R6/bin:
/home/oracle/bin:/etc:/u01/app/oracle/product/webdb22:
/u01/app/oracle/product/webdb22/bin:.
```

4. Load and mount the CDROM. Then, cd to the CDROM. Some earlier software releases, including this version of WebDB, don't have OUI. Therefore, you will use the text-based install for this product. (You'll use the GUI installer when you install iAS in Chapter 18.) Here, you start the program orainst in the orainst directory.

```
$ mount /mnt/cdrom
$ ls
DST.LST      bin network oemagent otrace precomp sqlplus  upgrade
Extras       doc nlsrtl  oracore  owa40  rdbms   support  wwv21
RELDESC.TXT lib ocommon orainst  plsql  slax    unix.prd www21
$ cd orainst
$ orainst
```

5. The text-based installer should appear. This is what many installers looked like prior to the OUI. Use the Tab key and arrow keys to move through the installer's fields. You can use the Spacebar to highlight/select an item and the Enter key to issue your command.

The first screen, shown in Figure 17.2, lists the installation requirements. Tab over to OK and press Enter.

6. The next screen asks you to verify your ORACLE_BASE and ORACLE_HOME. Remember that you must use a different ORACLE_HOME for this install. Verify the values, as shown in Figure 17.3, and then Tab over to OK and press Enter.

7. The next screen asks you to select products for the installation. You want both WebDB and the WebDB Listener, but you'll install WebDB first. Highlight the WebDB product. This is shown in Figure 17.4. Then Tab over to OK and press Enter.

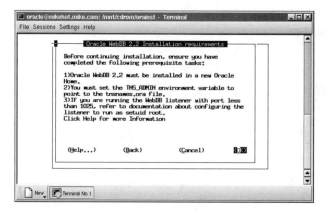

**FIGURE 17.2**
*Installation Requirements.*

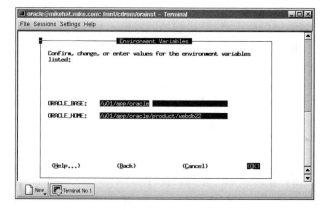

**FIGURE 17.3**
*Verify ORACLE_BASE and ORACLE_HOME.*

8. Figure 17.5 shows the installer in the process of installing all the products you selected. The installer will automatically advance after this screen.

9. The next screen asks you to select a database version. Here you should select Oracle 8i, as shown in Figure 17.6. Then Tab over to OK and press Enter.

10. Figure 17.7 shows the installer asking you for the SYS password and a TNS names alias. This is the database you want to store the WebDB objects in. Your password won't be visible when you enter it, but the database name will be. You might have to enter the full connect string, such as `rh1dev1.mike.com`, in order for the installer to connect. Enter the values and then press Enter.

**FIGURE 17.4**

*Select Oracle WebDB to Install it.*

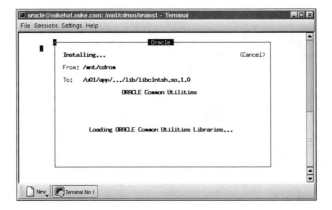

**FIGURE 17.5**

*Installation of Products.*

The installer will pause for a few seconds as it attempts to connect to the database specified using the SYS password.

11. The next screen will ask you for an owner of the PL/SQL Web Toolkit, and the default and temporary tablespaces. Accept the defaults, as shown in Figure 17.8.

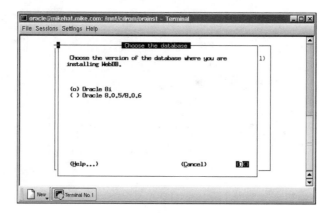

**FIGURE 17.6**

*Select a Database Version.*

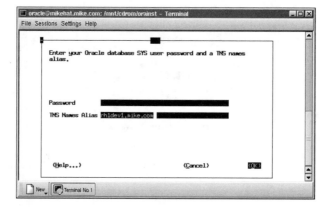

**FIGURE 17.7**

*Enter the SYS Password and the Database Name.*

12. Next the installer prompts you for a username, as well as the default and temporary tablespaces for the WebDB user. Select the defaults as shown in Figure 17.9.

13. The installer informs you that the default password for the WebDB user is WEBDB, as shown in Figure 17.10. Obviously, you should change this password as soon as possible.

14. The installer automatically loads English, but if you want to add additional languages, you can do so from the screen shown in Figure 17.11.

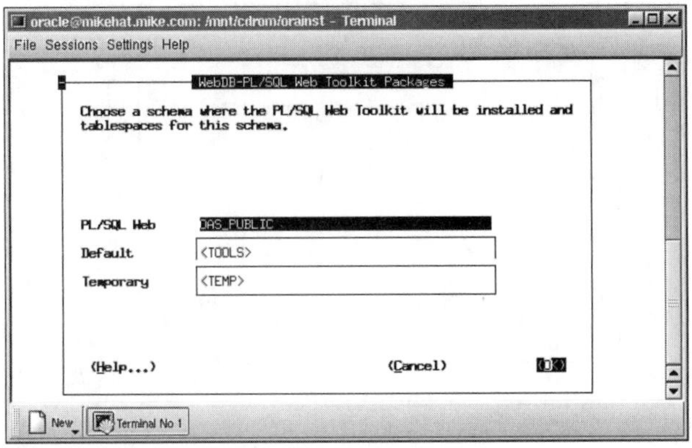

**FIGURE 17.8**
*Owner of PL/SQL Web Toolkit.*

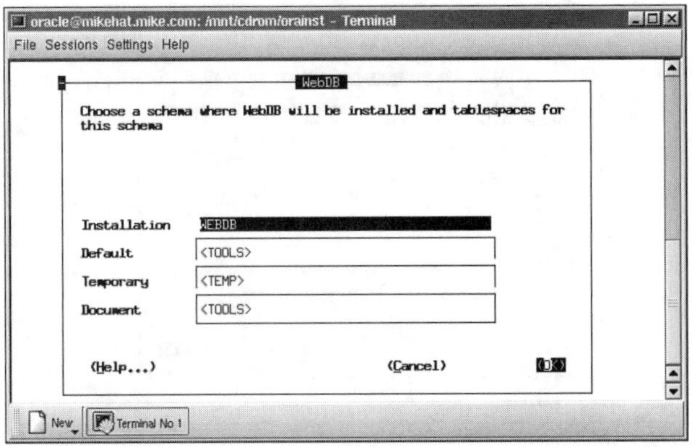

**FIGURE 17.9**
*WebDB User.*

15. The installer will then proceed to create the WebDB schema. This takes several minutes and involves multiple steps, as you can see in Figure 17.12.

16. The next screen notifies you that WebDB is successfully installed. It provides the default username/password of WEBDB/WEBDB, as shown in Figure 17.13.

17. The installer next asks you to log in as root and run root.sh after the install, as indicated in Figure 17.4. Unlike installing the database, you do not have to do this immediately. This represents the end of the WebDB PL/SQL product installation. Click on Cancel to continue.

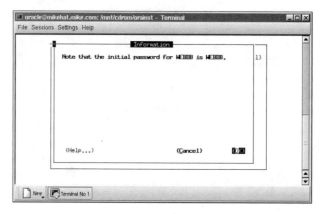

**FIGURE 17.10**

*The Initial WebDB Password.*

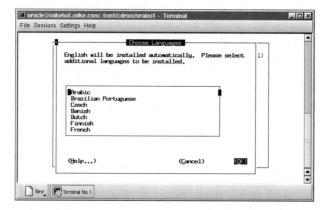

**FIGURE 17.11**

*Load Additional Languages.*

18. Next, you have to install the WebDB Listener. Highlight the listener and press Enter.

19. The installer will ask you for the Data Access Descriptor (DAD) information. Enter your hostname and accept the defaults for WebDB. Your hostname is your host plus the domain name. You can determine the hostname by using uname -a. You might, however, need to use a different port depending on how your server is configured. I used port 21093, as shown in Figure 17.16.

    The installer might pause for a while as it analyzes listener dependencies. If it returns an error at this point, try a different port number, such as 21093.

17

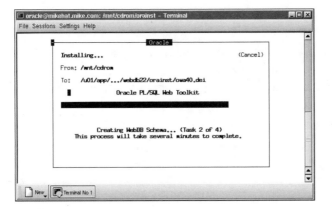

**FIGURE 17.12**
*Create WebDB Schema.*

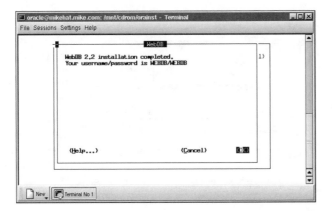

**FIGURE 17.13**
*WebDB Schema Has Been Created.*

20. The installer should return a screen indicating a successful install of the listener, as shown in Figure 17.17. It should include the URLs to get you started and instructions for starting the listener. If you are new to WebDB, be sure to print this page. Press ALT+PrtScreen to capture the screen and then paste it into a Word document to print. Just don't write any usernames and passwords on it since your URLs are listed there too.

21. Once again, the installer will ask you to run root.sh after you exit the installer. Highlight OK and press Enter to return to the main install screen. You can view the script from within the installer or exit.

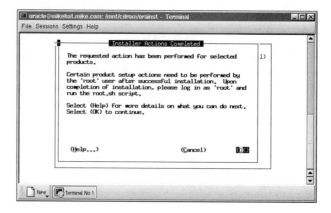

**FIGURE 17.14**
*You Are Told to Run root.sh.*

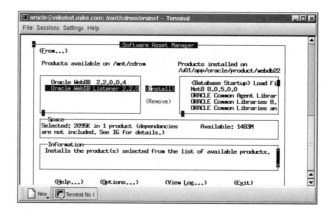

**FIGURE 17.15**
*Install the WebDB Listener Next.*

22. After you have exited, run root.sh as *root*. If the script immediately terminates without any messages, it was not executed as root.

```
[root@mikehat orainst]# pwd
/u01/app/oracle/product/webdb22/orainst
[root@mikehat orainst]# . ./root.sh
```

23. Continue to run the script even if you receive a message warning that the Oracle user's home directory is different from the $ORACLE_HOME value. Also verify that the local bin directory listed by the script actually exists; sometimes Oracle gives an incorrect location for it.

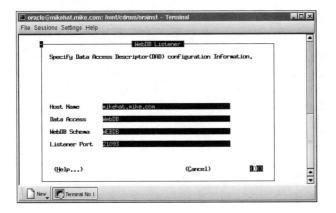

**FIGURE 17.16**
*Enter DAD Information.*

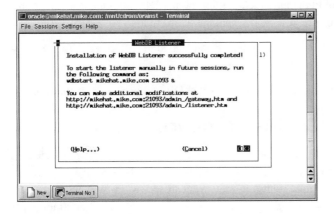

**FIGURE 17.17**
*Listener Install Successful.*

WebDB is now installed and the listener process is running. Note that the following users have been created during the install: OAS_PUBLIC, WEBDB, and SCOTT. Each user has the following roles:

```
SQL> select * from dba_role_privs
  2  where grantee = 'OAS_PUBLIC';

GRANTEE         GRANTED_ROLE                    ADM DEF
--------------  ------------------------------  --- ---
OAS_PUBLIC      CONNECT                         NO  YES
OAS_PUBLIC      RESOURCE                        NO  YES
```

```
SQL> select * from dba_role_privs
  2  where grantee = 'WEBDB';

GRANTEE          GRANTED_ROLE                    ADM DEF
-------------    ----------------------------    --- ---
WEBDB            CONNECT                         YES YES
WEBDB            DBA                             YES YES
WEBDB            RESOURCE                        NO  YES
WEBDB            WEBDB_DEVELOPER                 YES YES

SQL> select * from dba_role_privs
  2  where grantee = 'SCOTT';

GRANTEE          GRANTED_ROLE                    ADM DEF
-------------    ----------------------------    --- ---
SCOTT            RESOURCE                        NO  YES
SCOTT            WEBDB_DEVELOPER                 NO  YES
```

One of these should demand the attention of any DBA. Notice how the WebDB user has DBA privileges? Make sure you change that password to avoid a security hole.

The installation has also created a new role called WEBDB_DEVELOPER, which is just a flag. It has no system or object privileges granted to it.

The next section looks at how to access WebDB and use some of the DBA-related features.

# Basic WebDB Maintenance

There are a few basic maintenance tasks that you need to perform. Obviously, the database and its listener need to be running. Then WebDB needs to have its listener running. After you ensure that those requirements are met, you can access the Web page utilities inside WebDB in order to establish users and roles, create Web forms and pages, and monitor the database.

## Starting and Stopping the Listener

Before users can access the Web pages, you must start the HTTP listener and the database with its normal listener.

To start the WebDB/Oracle Portal listener, set the correct ORACLE_HOME. Next, you need to start the listener with the following syntax:

```
wbdblsnr hostname port# [start|stop]
```

In this example, you would issue the following command.

```
$  wdblsnr mikehat.mike.com 21093 start &
```

After this has started, you can verify the process is running by checking with ps -ef.

```
$ ps -ef | grep -i wdblsnr
oracle 5435 5434 0 12:51 pts/0 00:00:00 wdblsnr mikehat.mike.com 21093
oracle 5436 5435 0 12:51 pts/0 00:00:00 wdblsnr mikehat.mike.com 21093
oracle 5437 5436 0 12:51 pts/0 00:00:00 wdblsnr mikehat.mike.com 21093
oracle 5438 5436 0 12:51 pts/0 00:00:00 wdblsnr mikehat.mike.com 21093
oracle 5439 5436 0 12:51 pts/0 00:00:00 wdblsnr mikehat.mike.com 21093
oracle 5440 5436 0 12:51 pts/0 00:00:00 wdblsnr mikehat.mike.com 21093
oracle 5441 5436 0 12:51 pts/0 00:00:00 wdblsnr mikehat.mike.com 21093
oracle 5442 5436 0 12:51 pts/0 00:00:00 wdblsnr mikehat.mike.com 21093
oracle 5443 5436 0 12:51 pts/0 00:00:00 wdblsnr mikehat.mike.com 21093
oracle 5444 5436 0 12:51 pts/0 00:00:00 wdblsnr mikehat.mike.com 21093
oracle 5826 1478 0 14:06 pts/3 00:00:00 grep -i wdblsnr
```

To stop the listener, use this command:

```
$ wdblsnr mikehat.mike.com 21093 stop
```

## Log into the Site

To log into the site, you initially have two locations listed at the end of the installation. One is for gateway administration and the other is for listener administration. They are:

```
http://mikehat.mike.com:21093/admin_/gateway/htm
```

```
http://mikehat.mike.com:21093/admin_/listener.htm
```

The normal login location is:

```
http://mikehat.mike.com:21093/
```

At this point, you will be prompted for a username/password. Because you have only the WEBDB user, use that account, as shown in Figure 17.18.

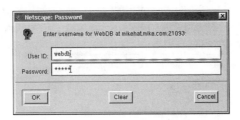

**FIGURE 17.18**
*Log into Site.*

You should now be logged into the main page of the WebDB user.

After you're logged into the Web site, you will see the corresponding login inside the database:

```
SQL> select username, program from v$session
  2  where username is not null;

USERNAME    PROGRAM
----------  ------------------------------------------------
SYS         sqlplus@mikehat.mike.com (TNS V1-V3)
WEBDB         ?  @mikehat.mike.com (TNS V1-V3)
```

The next section focuses on the utilities listed on the main page.

## WebDB Utility Links

WebDB has five utilities that you can access from the main page, as shown in Figure 17.19. Some utilities are geared toward the DBA and others prove to be more useful to the Web developers.

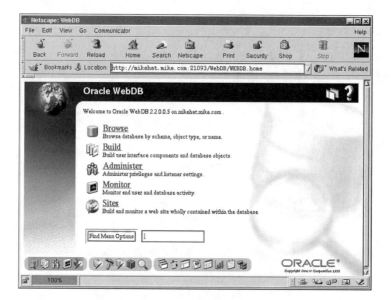

**FIGURE 17.19**

*WebDB's Five Main Utilities.*

## Browse

You use the Browse utility to search for and view any database object owned by any user. Figure 17.20 shows a list of objects owned by SCOTT that you could query.

17

WebDB/Oracle
Portal

**FIGURE 17.20**
*Browse Enables You to Look for Objects.*

If, for example, you selected Tables and clicked Browse, all the tables owned by SCOTT would be listed. Next, you can double-click any of those tables to view the details of that particular table, as shown in Figure 17.21.

With this GUI, you can see the columns and data types for the table. You can also issue queries and insert roles.

## Build

Under the Build menu, you can create objects. Figure 17.22 shows the available categories.

Most of these are of interest to the Web developers. For example, the easy-to-use tools to create forms are under User Interface Components in Figure 17.23.

This utility includes links to tools that enable you to build forms, reports, menus, and other objects. Technically, this isn't normally a DBA's responsibility, but you should be familiar with these tools.

From the Build page, you also access the Build Database Objects tool. As you can see in Figure 17.24, you can create tables, indexes, views, sequences, and PL/SQL objects using the Build Database Objects tool.

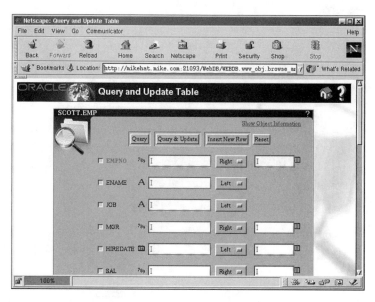

**FIGURE 17.21**
*You Can View SCOTT's EMP Table.*

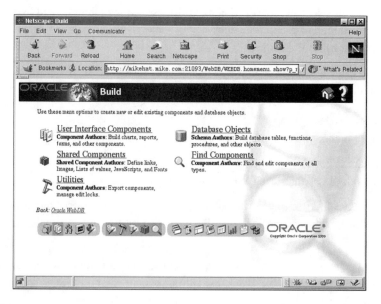

**FIGURE 17.22**
*Build Categories.*

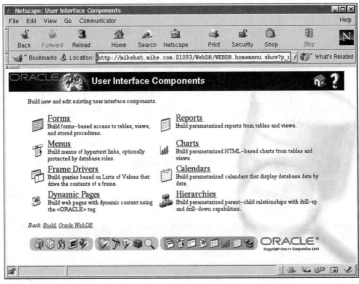

**FIGURE 17.23**

*User Interface Components.*

17

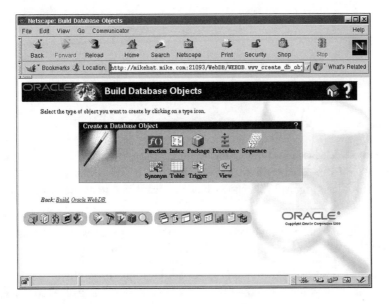

**FIGURE 17.24**

*Build Database Objects.*

By selecting any of these objects, you start a wizard that will help you create these objects. The look and feel isn't exactly like OEM, but the base functionality is there. Remember, this is available via a typical Web browser. Using just a simple Web browser, you can still do DBA work.

## Administer

From the Administer page, you have a more powerful set of tools. Figure 17.25 shows the several tools available.

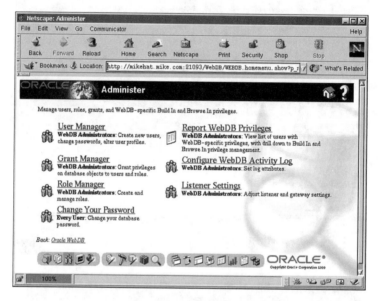

**FIGURE 17.25**
*Administrator Tools*

Most of these tools deal with user maintenance, roles, and privileges. Each tool is fairly straightforward, so I won't cover them all. User Manager is representative of what you can expect from these tools. Figure 17.26 shows how you can use it to create or modify existing users.

Because you want more than just the WebDB user to be able to access the Web site, you can create a user MIKEW. Later, you can add additional roles and privileges.

Another useful tool is accessed from the Listener Settings link. From there, you have the same functionality as if you went to the http://mikehat.mike.com:21093/admin_/gateway/htm link.

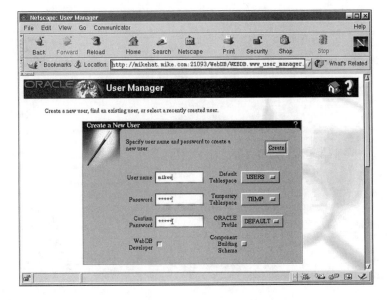

**FIGURE 17.26**
*User Manager*

## Monitor

The Monitor page provides a way to monitor the Web page components, usage, and the database. The DBA should be familiar with the Web components and be able to manage them. This involves using the User Interface Component, Activity Log, and Batch Results tools. These tools tell you who has logged into your page (database), from where, and what they accessed. It also calculates tuning and response time metrics. Although users are hitting a Web page, they really are also hitting your database; therefore, *you* should be monitoring this activity. Figure 17.27 shows a sample of the reports available to you via the User Interface Components tool.

As you can see, you can generate reports based on response time, frequency, user ID, IP address, and a host of other characteristics. This utility, combined with your other monitoring tools, can be used to gauge activity on the database and the server.

From a purely DBA perspective, you might be interested in the Database Objects tool, shown in Figure 17.28.

This tool provides much of the key reporting functionality provided by OEM, but it's accessible from any Web browser. You can generate information about user sessions, structure, parameters, and storage. You can also access blocking lock information, which can be a lifesaver when users are locked.

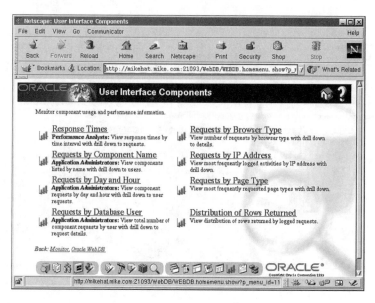

**FIGURE 17.27**
*Reports Available to the DBA.*

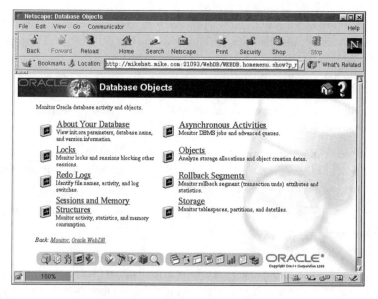

**FIGURE 17.28**
*Database Tools and Reports.*

You should familiarize yourself with these tools for times when OEM is down or otherwise unavailable. The layout of the reports generated by these tools is very readable. Although much of the information is in a report basis, you do have the ability to make some database changes. This chapter doesn't examine each category, but they all should look familiar to you. It's a shame that more DBAs don't realize the remote control and reporting power they gain over their database by installing and configuring WebDB.

### Remote DBA

This tool is great for the remote DBA. It provides most of the information normally available via OEM, only from a browser. But why would the DBA need this?

First of all, even as a typical DBA you are not at the shop all the time. Unless you carry a laptop, you are not always going to have a way to connect to your machine with all your Oracle tools. For example, you might be on vacation when you get an urgent call or page, and you don't have your PC with you. With this tool, you can simply use any computer with a browser.

Remote DBA support is a growing business that can make use of tools like this. Not all companies want to hire a full-time DBA to be on-site. However, they do have a legitimate need for *some* DBA support. So what can they do? Many consulting companies hire a DBA to remotely log in a few times a week and make sure everything is running correctly. This DBA might only work 20 hours a week for that client. Tools like this make remote support possible for smaller companies and DBA entrepreneurs.

## Sites

The Sites tool provides Wizards for creating new sites. It is primarily used by the developers. Figure 17.29 shows this tool.

From this page, you can query existing sites. To start the site-building wizard, click the Create button under Site Building.

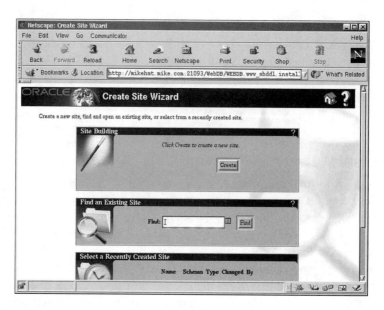

**FIGURE 17.29**
*Site Tools*

# Key Differences between Oracle Portal and WebDB

This chapter focuses primarily on WebDB because it is established and many people use it. Oracle Portal is being included with iAS, which means only those with iAS can use it.

The functionality and principles discussed here carry over into Oracle Portal. However, there are a few differences between the two products that you should be aware of.

- Oracle Portal uses a friendlier OUI rather than the text-based installer.
- Database users and Web users are separate. Oracle Portal users do not show up in the DBA_USERS table or when accessing SQL*Plus.
- Java is more prevalent in Oracle Portal.
- Oracle Portal makes heavy use of portals. These are more encompassing Web pages with many options. You will certainly feel more like a Webmaster than a DBA or PL/SQL developer when using this product.

People who have a limited need to Web-enable their database will likely be satisfied with WebDB. For what it is intended, it is a good product. However, for those wanting to get into true e-business, a more robust tool set and architecture is needed. For this, you will use iAS; its tools as described in Chapter 18.

# Summary

This chapter discussed WebDB/Oracle Portal as a standalone product. It offers a relatively quick and simple way to make an Oracle database Web-accessible. It does this by providing a lightweight HTTP listener that receives requests from any client's Web browser and then sending those requests to be executed by PL/SQL packages inside the Oracle database.

WebDB/Oracle Portal offers developers a host of wizards and templates that can be used to quickly create forms to access the database via PL/SQL packages. Developers can use these generated packages, modify them, or write their own as necessary.

Next, you learned how to install WebDB/Oracle Portal and how to get the listener running. Then, you navigated through a few screens, created some users, and assigned roles.

Although WebDB/Oracle Portal was designed to be used primarily by developers to quickly build Web applications, this chapter focused more on its uses as a DBA tool. Much of the basic functionality provided by OEM is also available via WebDB/Oracle Portal. This is a great benefit to off-site DBAs.

**17**

**WEBDB/ORACLE PORTAL**

# Internet Application Server (iAS)

## ESSENTIALS

- Web and application servers are key to Internet computing.

- The most common architectural design uses a client tier (Web browsers), a middle tier (Web and application servers), and a database.

- There are several pitfalls associated with some Web architectures including technical design, scalability, and availability.

- Oracle iAS is a highly functional Internet Application Server. It has many advanced features that integrate with Oracle 8i databases and development tools.

- Installation of iAS is fairly simple, but it does require substantial disk space.

This chapter looks at the Web architecture with a focus on Oracle 9i Application Server. First, it examines the Web environment. It covers the three-tier architecture and shows how each tier can be implemented to serve Internet users. You'll learn about the components of this architecture and learn how to avoid some common pitfalls.

Next, the chapter looks in detail at the Oracle 9i Application Server. It looks at what this product is, its architecture, and how it can be deployed. Finally, you'll learn how to install the product and some of the fundamental configuration steps.

This chapter discusses Java quite a bit. Unless you are already familiar with Java, check out Chapter 16, "Java Inside the Database Server," for an overview of Java and its components such as JVMs and EJBs.

# Web Environment

Anyone involved in computers knows that the Internet is a big part of most computer systems. It is difficult to imagine a new, large system that didn't interface with the Web in one way or another.

There are several ways to interface with the Web, but the most common method is using the generic Web application server. Although the details vary between vendors and implementations, Figure 18.1 outlines the basic architecture.

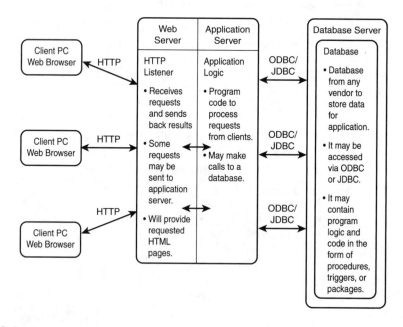

**FIGURE 18.1**

*A Simple Web Architecture.*

This is a three-tiered architecture with clients(s), a middle tier, and a database on the back end.

- **Clients**   Clients are Web browsers (such as Netscape Navigator/Communicator or Microsoft Internet Explorer) located on PCs. Because much of the customer base of Internet computing are desktop PCs, these are the main clients. However, with the advent of Web-enabled cell phones and PDAs, you can expect more attention to be paid to these devices.

  Their browsers send and receive requests via HTTP (Hypertext Transfer Protocol) to "paint" the screens of their Web browsers. Some processing can occur on the Web browser in the form of Java applets, but this tier is mostly used to display information.

- **Middle tier**   This tier receives requests from the client browsers, processes them, and then sends back the results. When you connect to a Web page, you connect to the middle tier.

  There are three main functions that occur here: browser requests are received, requests are processed, and responses are sent.

  The Web server component is responsible for receiving HTTP requests and sending responses. It examines the request and routes it to the appropriate application service to be addressed. It also returns any HTML files requested. The application server component is responsible for any type of program processing and logic needed to fulfill the request relayed to it by the Web server. Some of these requests can be fulfilled locally; others require access to a remote database.

  This tier can be on one physical machine or can be split. In some cases, high-availability systems such as clusters or fail-over systems are deployed. There can be several Web servers or application servers in order to improve performance, scalability, and fault tolerance.

- **Database tier**   The back end of this tier is a data store, which is typically a database. It receives SQL requests from the application server via ODBC or JDBC. The database processes and executes the SQL statement, and then it returns the results to the application server.

Optionally, there might be some program logic and computing inside the database. This is typically done via stored procedures, functions, triggers, and packages. Java can also exist inside Oracle databases to perform some processing.

The database component can be on the same machine as the middle tier. However, scalability and performance are improved by separating the database and middle tier so no one machine carries the burden of both tiers. It is also common to place the database component on multiple machines or clusters to improve performance and fault tolerance.

Web servers receive HTTP requests from a client, whereas application servers contain program code (such as EJBs) to service those requests. Many products combine both of these tasks into one product generically called either a Web server or an application server. I'll try not to blur the distinction and refer to this combination as a Web application server where appropriate. However, many new products combine these functions into one tool so the distinction between a Web server and an application server is sometimes difficult to make.

---

**NOTE**

### Alternatives to iAS

There are alternatives to Oracle's iAS and OAS. One such competing Web server I recently worked with is BEA's WebLogic Web server (go to www.bea.com or www.weblogic.com).

The Web application server sat on the middle tier between the database and the clients. Web browser requests from the client go to the middle tier. For our particular implementation, we chose to put the EJBs in the Web application server to handle the business logic. When data was needed, JDBC calls were made to the database. Because these were just JDBC using the JDBC-OCI driver, we needed to have Net8 configured, but MTS with IIOP was not needed.

We used JDBC connection pooling to keep a minimum number of database sessions open at all times to service requests. This prevented having to create a new database connection every time a JDBC request was issued. As the number of JDBC requests from the middle tier increased, more database sessions were automatically spawned. This architecture is shown in Figure 18.2.

From a DBA's standpoint managing the database was easy. No Java was actually used in the database. Rather the Java was outside the database and inside the Web server. Most of the connections into my database were in the form of JDBC connections accessing data. Connection pooling allowed a set number of connections to always exist, which improved performance because creating new connections require system resources. If the number of users increased, the number of connections would also increase. I found this architecture to be conceptually simple yet effective.

---

Those are the basic architectural fundamentals of a Web environment. Obviously, the technologies vary depending on the vendors involved and are always evolving. Common pitfalls in this environment include technological design, scalability, and availability.

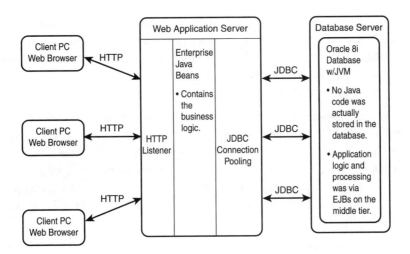

**FIGURE 18.2**

*A Sample WebLogic Implementation.*

## Technological Design

The chapter has so far covered the basic Web architecture, but there are many technical methods available to implement it. In fact, there are usually several ways that a system can be successfully built, but there are many more paths that lead to failure. The trick is knowing your requirements and then intelligently creating a design and architecture to meet those requirements.

People often use technologies for purposes they were never intended. Then they fail because the technologies cannot support their needs. This is the equivalent of using a hammer to nail a screw; it doesn't work very well! The key to avoiding this situation is to truly understand the technologies involved. Remember to focus on the product itself, not on the vendor's sales pitch.

Another related problem is selecting a design that is overly complicated, too reliant on a "bleeding-edge" technology, or is too obscure to be implemented and supported by an IT staff. Technical people often attempt to use the latest and greatest technologies, even when those are untested. They also sometimes settle on a technology like Java, but fail because they are not willing to find and pay enough for skilled and experienced Java developers.

## Scalability

Make sure your architecture, processes, and the underlining hardware are big enough to support your system. A very common problem involves building systems that are too small to support the users.

For example, suppose someone creates a flashy demo application on one or two small NT boxes and shows it to your manager. Your manager likes it and expects that same system to support everyone on the Internet. As ridiculous as that might sound, I've seen it happen several times. Some people just cannot understand what works well for 10 users in a testing lab will not work in a real implementation.

More often, an organization will spend relatively large sums of money to purchase several small- or medium-sized Unix or Linux servers. Then they will go live with the new system and within a very short amount of time (hours, days, or weeks), they find out the expensive system still cannot compete. Then they have to rebuild the system on a different platform and/or with more powerful machines. This is expensive in terms of money wasted on the initial purchase, money spent to purchase what should have been purchased initially, and the downtime experienced during the conversion.

The keys to avoiding this nightmare is accurately predicting your system load, performing intelligent capacity planning to meet that load, performing actual load testing to determine how your system performs, and remembering to scale big.

## Availability

Availability is closely tied to both scalability and technical design. Indeed, making sure your system can survive a crash should be part of the initial design and building process, not an afterthought. Business success in the Web environment is dependent on the system's availability. If you charge people for a service and then it is not available, you will lose customers. It's that simple.

Unfortunately, this isn't always realized or fully appreciated. At one Web-based Application Service Provider (ASP) I worked at, I was horrified to learn the production system was going live without any form of disk mirroring or RAID. Management and the system administration staff knew about this, but decided to gamble that the disks wouldn't fail anytime soon.

Silly mistakes and gambles like this are one factor in system availability, but there are others. Running all your key systems in one physical location, not using clusters or available fail-over technology, and designing systems with a single point of failure are other common mistakes. Although not every organization has the funding to take all these steps, it's surprising how often these precautions aren't implemented until *after* a problem occurs.

## Understanding and Using iAS

The Oracle product suite is constantly changing, both in terms of products offered and in terms of nomenclature. The product of focus here is commonly referred to as iAS (Internet Application Server). However, Oracle recently changed the name to Oracle9i Application Server and this is the product we are actually installing.

> **NOTE**
>
> ## What Existed Before iAS?
>
> Before iAS, Oracle had a product called OAS (Oracle Application Server). This tool also served as a Web application server. It was primarily used to run PL/SQL *cartridges*, but it also supported some Java. This product is being phased out with release 4.0.8.
>
> This move is not just a sales ploy or name change. iAS is a completely new product that's built into Java, uses a different Web server (Apache), and has many other features. Although OAS and iAS are similar in purpose, iAS is different internally and is more advanced. Oracle offers upgrade paths to iAS that reportedly do not require extensive modification of existing OAS applications.

iAS has many internal components, but I choose to conceptually separate them into two categories. Specifically, some parts fulfill the role of a Web server whereas others fulfill the role of an application server.

The key Web server element is the Apache HTTP listener component. Apache is itself a very popular open source product. It is very widely used and well liked. This component receives HTTP requests from clients and then routes them to be serviced. If only a HTML file needs to be supplied, it does just that. Otherwise it routes the request to the appropriate service on the application server. After the request has been fulfilled, Apache sends the request back to the client. From a high level, this is what a Web server does.

Application server-type components are those that perform the computing and processing to fulfill the client's request. Typically, this means program code in either Java or PL/SQL. It also includes products that use those languages such as Oracle Portal, Forms, and Reports, all of which are present in iAS. Supporting features such as the Oracle JVM, Database Cache, and Web Cache also fall into this category.

Unfortunately, however, that is about as far as this conceptual separation can go. In reality, all these components are linked to each other. As you can see in Figure 18.3, there are many components that make up iAS.

Figure 18.3 does not attempt to identify every component or relationship, but it does capture key points of this tool. As you can see, client requests come into the Apache HTTP Web server component. From there, they are directed based on request type to the appropriate application component. After the requests are fulfilled they are sent back to the Apache Web server where they are returned to the client.

Oracle has introduced and integrated some interesting components used to improve performance while providing the developers with as much flexibility as possible.

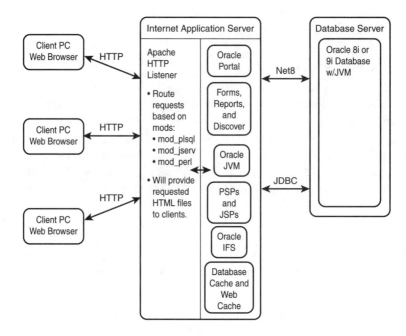

**FIGURE 18.3**
*Key iAS Components.*

# Modules

Modules (or mods) are the iAS equivalent of OAS cartridges. These are essentially plug-ins for the Web server that allow it to handle each type of client request. Each request is routed on the mod associated with it. The following list describes the more common mods available:

- **mod_plsql**    This mode is equivalent to the OAS PL/SQL cartridge. It routes requests for PL/SQL and stored Java procedures to the database.
- **mod_jserv**    This mod handles Java requests such as servlets and JSPs. It routes them to the Apache JServ.
- **mod_perl**    Perl requests are handled by this mod.

# Oracle Forms, Reports, and Discover

Each of these tools should be familiar to the DBA and PL/SQL developers. Oracle Forms have long been a key Oracle application tool and need little introduction. Reports create and display management reports and traditionally have been bundled with Forms. Discover is a query-creation tool that enables you to easily extract information from the database. Traditionally, these tools stood separate from the database. In iAS, these tools are bundled within the application server.

# Oracle Portal

Oracle Portal is the next generation of WebDB, which is covered in Chapter 17, "WebDB/Oracle Portal." This PL/SQL-based tool was originally used as a quick method for Web-enabling databases. Now, however, this tool has grown into a powerful way to design dynamic Internet Web applications. It is now bundled with iAS.

# PSPs and JSPs

iAS supports PL/SQL Server Pages (PSPs) and Java Server Pages (JSPs). These are basically HTML pages with embedded code tags used to generate dynamic content. When this code is started on the browser, it is compiled and then executed on the server side (not inside the browser).

# iFS

Internet File System (iFS) is Oracle's method for storing normal files inside the database instead of on normal file systems. Files stored in this manner appear as if they are on a mapped network drive, not in a database. The users can access such files normally, but iFS provides added features such as locking and version control. Also, because the file is inside the database, it can be indexed for faster access and protection, which is provided by Oracle's proven indexing and backup and recovery methods. Finally, by storing the files in the database, they are accessible to developers to manipulate using XML.

# Oracle 8i JVM

This is the same Java Virtual Machine you find in an Oracle 8i database and it serves the same purpose: to run Java programs. With this feature Java enables iAS to run EJBs, CORBA servers, Java Server Pages, servlets, and Java procedures on the middle tier. See Chapter 16 for more information.

# Database Cache and Web Cache

Oracle realizes that you can achieve large performance gains by caching database information and queries and Web information such as URLs. Many requests that come to the Web server normally require database access via SQL or PL/SQL. Normally these requests have to be relayed to the database, processed, and then returned. However, Database Cache can keep read-only database information on the middle tier, which reduces the accesses to the actual database. Web Cache is used to cache Web information, such as URLs. These caches reduce network traffic and processing on the database and Web application servers.

Those are the high-level features of iAS. There are many more exciting features such as its wireless option, which allows communication with cell phones and PDAs (outside the scope of

**18**

INTERNET
APPLICATION
SERVER (iAS)

this book). Also, each new release of iAS has many more features than the last. Therefore you need to keep up on the documentation and release notes to avoid missing out on new functionality.

As a DBA, you should work with the different parties of your IT staff to determine how best to use iAS. For example, coordinate with your HTML Web designers to determine how Oracle Portal can make Web portals. No doubt your PL/SQL and Java developers should be included in discussions about how and where the application code is developed and deployed. They will have valuable insight into using Forms, Reports, and PL/SQL in a Web environment as well as the various existing Java components. And don't forget to communicate with the SA staff so they know what to expect when they run iAS on their servers. Especially because iAS can (and should) exist on a separate server than the database and because it can be made fault tolerant, solid architectural planning is needed.

## Installation

This section outlines a simple installation of iAS 1.0.2.0 on RedHat Linux. An 8.1.6 database installation already exists on the server, but the iAS 1.0.2.0 database software is based on 8.1.7. For testing purposes the database and the iAS will be on the same physical machine, but normally this configuration should be avoided.

Read the installation and configuration guide (ICG) as you would before any software installation. The following steps install iAS:

1. Oracle iAS requires a substantial amount of disk space depending on which products you install. Enterprise Editions installations can take over 3G. Make sure that at least 2G is available for a standard installation.

```
[oracle@mikehat /u01]$ df -m .
Filesystem              1M-blocks        Used Available Use% Mounted on
/dev/hda13                   7875        4898      2578  66% /u01
[oracle@mikehat /u01]$
```

2. Unset the LD_LIBRARY_PATH environment variable.

```
[oracle@mikehat /u01]$ unset LD_LIBRARY_PATH
```

3. Create and set a new ORACLE_HOME specifically for iAS. Like all recent Oracle products, you must use a separate ORACLE_HOME for each product.

```
[oracle@mikehat /u01]$ export $ORACLE_HOME=/u01/app/oracle/product/
➥ias10210
```

4. If you plan on using iFS there are some database and network configuration steps you need to follow. Refer to the ICG for these steps if you need iFS.

5. iAS has three installation CDs. Therefore you have to change CDs during the installation process. Do not just cd to /mnt/cdrom and attempt to run the installer. Rather, execute the installer program from a different directory such as $ORACLE_BASE.

```
[oracle@mikehat oracle]$ cd $ORACLE_BASE
[oracle@mikehat oracle]$ /mnt/cdrom/runInstaller
```

This should bring up the OUI. Linux users might need to set LD_ASSUME_KER-NEL=2.2.5 and perform miscellaneous distribution-specific tasks to get this running. Check the ICG, release notes, MetaLink, and Technet discussion forums for details.

During the install you will be prompted for each CD when it is needed. Remember to unmount the CD-ROM, eject the CD, reload the CD, and then mount the CD-ROM drive before clicking OK.

```
[oracle@mikehat oracle]$ umount /mnt/cdrom
[oracle@mikehat oracle]$ eject
[oracle@mikehat oracle]$ mount /mnt/cdrom
```

6. A welcome screen appears as shown in Figure 18.4. Click Next to continue.

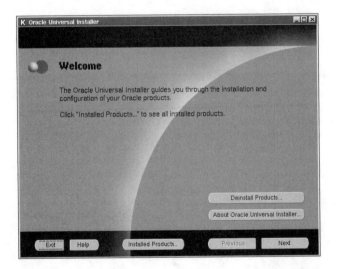

**FIGURE 18.4**
*OUI Welcome Screen.*

7. The next screen prompts you for a source and destination location. Do not modify the source. Verify that the destination is your $ORACLE_HOME as shown in Figure 18.5.

18

INTERNET
APPLICATION
SERVER (IAS)

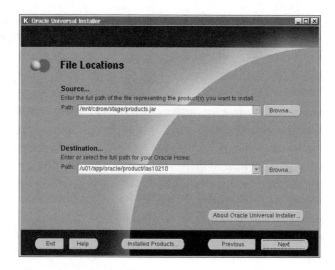

**FIGURE 18.5**

*Verify Source and Destination Locations.*

8. Next, you need to choose from Enterprise Edition, Standard Edition, or a Minimal installation. Because the Enterprise Edition requires over 3G of disk space, you should select Standard Edition unless you really need the extra features. Select Standard Edition as shown in Figure 18.6.

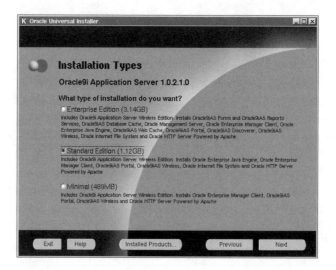

**FIGURE 18.6**

*Three Installation Options.*

9. The next screen is specific to iAS. It provides a list of installation tips that you can get help about. After you are satisfied that your system meets the installation requirements, click Next to see the screen shown in Figure 18.7.

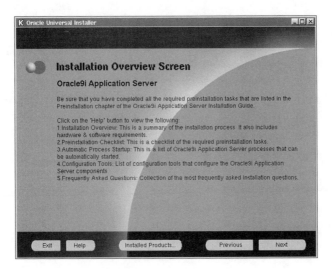

**FIGURE 18.7**
*Installation Checklist.*

10. OUI next asks you whether you want the installer to automatically configure the HTTP Server and Oracle Portal after the installation. Leave both products highlighted (indicating Yes), as shown in Figure 18.8. Then click Next.

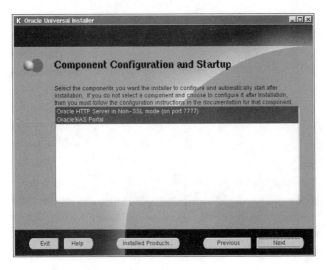

**FIGURE 18.8**
*Automatic Configuration Option.*

11. The next screen asks you for the DAD (Database Access Descriptor), schema name, and `tnsnames.ora` alias for the database that will be used for Oracle Portal. Accept the defaults, as shown in Figure 18.9. The database is `rh1dev1` so that will be the TNS connect string.

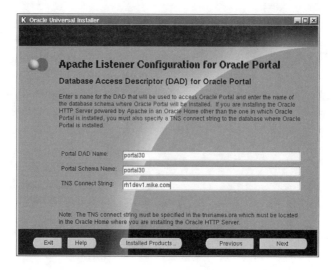

**FIGURE 18.9**

*Oracle Portal DAD, Schema, and Database.*

12. The installer will ask you for the same information as before, except this time for the single sign-on option. Accept the defaults of `portal30_sso` and enter your database name, as shown in Figure 18.10.

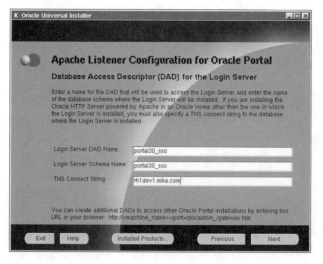

**FIGURE 18.10**

*Single Sign-On DAD, Schema, and Database.*

13. Oracle will ask you for a Global Database Name and SID of the database to be used for the Enterprise Java Engine (EJE). This is the renamed Oracle 8i JVM. Oracle states in the ICG that this database is created in the iAS ORACLE_HOME and that it should only be used for EJE. Use the default SID of ias1021 and Global Database Name of ias1021.mike.com, as shown in Figure 18.11.

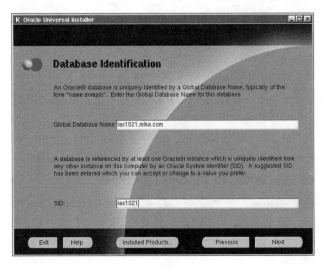

**FIGURE 18.11**
*Supply the EJE Global Database Name and SID.*

14. Next you are asked to enter the location of JDK 1.1.8. In my case it is in /u01/app/ oracle/jre/1.1.8. Enter your location as shown in Figure 18.12.

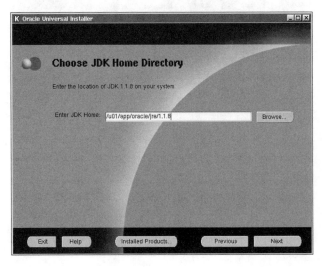

**FIGURE 18.12**
*Enter the JDK 1.1.8 Location.*

15. Portal-to-go repository information is requested next. Here you need to enter a hostname, listener port number, and SID. This is shown in Figure 18.13.

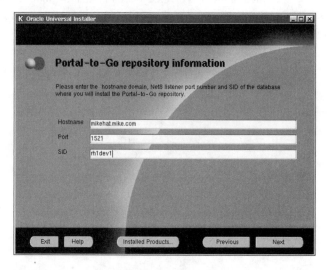

**FIGURE 18.13**

*Enter Portal-to-Go Repository Information.*

16. The next screen prompts you for an owner of the Portal-to-Go repository. Pick a memorable username such as PTG_MANAGER and a password as shown in Figure 18.14.

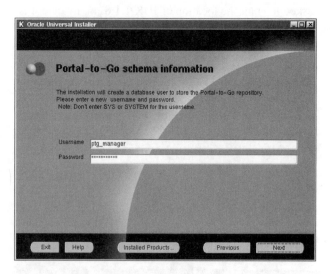

**FIGURE 18.14**

*Assign a Username/Password for the Portal-to-Go Owner.*

17. In Figure 18.15, Oracle asks you to supply the SYSTEM password for the Portal-to-go repository database. This password is used with the repository user.

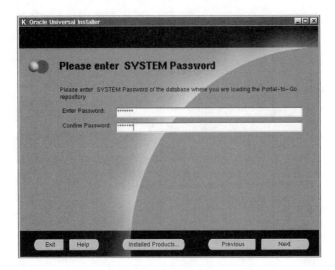

**FIGURE 18.15**

*Supply the SYSTEM Password.*

18. The next screen provides a summary of the products to be installed. This is shown in Figure 18.16. Click Install to continue the installation process.

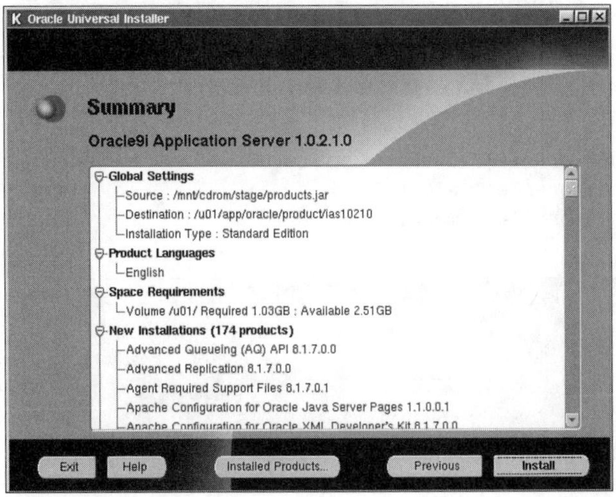

**FIGURE 18.16**

*Installation Summary.*

19. The installation process will take a while, usually over an hour. A status bar shows you the progress, as shown in Figure 18.17.

**FIGURE 18.17**

*Installation Status.*

20. Part of the way through the installation, the OUI will pause the installation and ask you for the next CD. Unmount the CD-ROM, eject the CD, place the next CD in the CD-ROM, mount the CD-ROM, and then press OK. This process is shown next and illustrated in Figure 18.18.

It might be necessary to find the session that started the installation, press Enter to get a command prompt, and log out as that user to free the /mnt/cdrom so it can be unmounted.

```
[oracle@mikehat oracle]$ umount /mnt/cdrom
[oracle@mikehat oracle]$ eject
[oracle@mikehat oracle]$ mount /mnt/cdrom
```

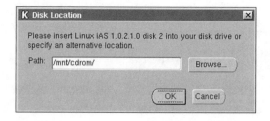

**FIGURE 18.18**

*Load the Next CD.*

21. The OUI will likely ask for Disk 1 again. If so, repeat Step 20. This process might occur several times.

22. After the installation and relinking process has completed, Oracle prompts you to run `root.sh`. After you have executed the script as `root`, click OK.

23. After a moment, iAS will start several configuration tools for Net8, DBCA, Oracle Portal, and finally it will attempt to start the Web server on port 7777. This is shown in Figure 18.19.

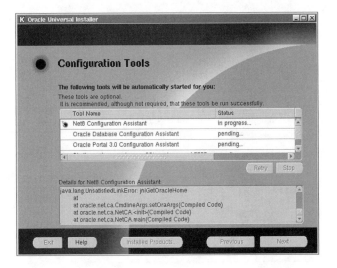

**FIGURE 18.19**
*Running Configuration Tools.*

At this point you can run the tools automatically or you can stop each tool and run it separately outside the installer.

24. It is interesting to note that although this is iAS, an Oracle database is actually installed. Therefore, you can use its JVM. The DBAC will automatically run as shown in Figure 18.20.

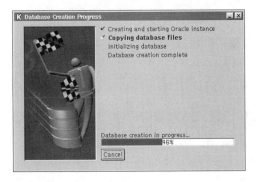

**FIGURE 18.20**
*Install the JVM Database.*

25. You identified the database earlier in the installation process as `ias1021.mike.com`. Oracle identifies the database and provides the default username and passwords in Figure 18.21.

**FIGURE 18.21**
*Confirm Database ias1021 and Username/Password.*

26. The Oracle Portal Configuration Assistant starts next. Choose to Install Oracle Portal and the Login Server and click Next to continue as shown in Figure 18.22. Because you have already installed WebDB in a previous chapter, I will not cover it again here.

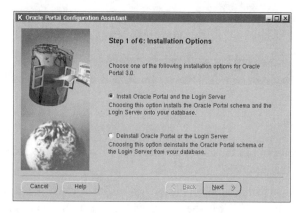

**FIGURE 18.22**
*Begin the Oracle Portal Configuration Assistant.*

Ultimately, you would configure Oracle Portal, start the Apache HTTP listener, and exit the OUI. Any of these tools and assistants can also be started from the command line, which means the OUI isn't mandatory. That concludes the fundamentals of an iAS installation.

# Configuration File Location and Apache Control

iAS has configuration and setup options you can access via Web browsers, which makes sense because it's a Web product. However, the Apache side of this product mandates configuration changes that cannot be made graphically. Rather, you have to edit configuration files using `vi`.

The main file you need to configure is `httpd.conf`. This is located in the `$ORACLE_HOME/Apache/Apache/conf` directory. This file controls parameters such as virtual paths, virtual directories, and virtual hosts. Other key configuration files can be found in subdirectories off of `$ORACLE_HOME/Apache`.

Finally, the Web locations for Apache and Oracle Portal are as follows:

`http://mikehat.mike.com:7777` for Apache

`http://mikehat.mike.com/pin/port130` for Oracle Portal

Don't forget to substitute your hostname for `mikehat` and your domain for `mike.com`.

This section covered iAS from a conceptual view, its components, and a sample installation. From here, you should have enough information to start experimenting with the different components and to begin developing Web applications.

# Summary

This chapter covered the three-tiered architecture of Internet computing. It explained the role of the client (Web browser), the middle tier (Web and application server), and the database on the back end. You also learned about key issues such as technical design, scalability, and availability.

Next, the chapter examined the Oracle9i Application Server, commonly referred to as iAS. The chapter looked at this product, its basic architecture (Apache Web server and an application server), and its key components. Finally, the chapter covered a standard installation and some of the configuration issues involved in such an installation.

**18**

**INTERNET APPLICATION SERVER (iAS)**

# 9i Server New Features

## ESSENTIALS

- Oracle 9i has many new features to improve performance and simplify database administration.

- The text-based init.ora parameter file can be replaced with a binary system parameter file.

- Many SGA parameters can now be adjusted "on the fly" without needing to bounce the database instance.

- 9i has the capability to create and manage database files without direct action by the DBA.

- Options regarding rollback segments have been expanded to include undo segments.

With every new version of Oracle, there are exciting new features and Oracle 9i is no exception. Some of these advances are inside the database and are largely transparent to the DBA. Other features impact the way the database is managed on a daily basis. It is those features that are the focus of this chapter.

This chapter covers new features roughly in the order you will encounter them. First, it looks at changes in the install processes. Next, it discusses what it takes to start the database and how to create a server parameter file. Then, the chapter covers ways to dynamically adjust SGA parameters. Use of Oracle managed files is then discussed. Ways that rollback segments have been modified and use of undo segments are next. Finally, the chapter addresses several miscellaneous changes.

## Installing the 9i Server

As with any installation you should check the Installation and Configuration Guide (ICG), but this is especially true when dealing with a new database version. Be sure to also review the release notes and any readme.txt files. Also, especially when working on Linux, review the discussion groups on Technet and the forums on MetaLink to identify the problems people are finding. I've used those discussion groups several times to get Oracle up and running.

Oracle 9i has a higher level of hardware and software requirements than previous versions. Especially on Linux, you need to verify that your server meets the 9i requirements. Check your own platform-specific notes for details, but expect to require considerably more RAM (512 M for Linux) and disk space (almost 2G). These represent roughly *double* the old requirements.

The OUI is still Java based and the basic screens and options are similar to 8i. However, it does have a new look, as illustrated in the Installation Type screen shown in Figure 19.1.

As you can see, you can still select between Enterprise, Standard, or a Custom install. Notice, however, that the software will take 1.79G. To do this 9i comes on three CDs and you will need to use each one during the installation. Because you will be using multiple CDs for the install, it is important that you do *not* start the installer process from within the CD. Do not just cd to /mnt/cdrom and attempt to run the installer. Rather, execute the installer program from a different directory, such as $ORACLE_BASE.

```
[oracle@mikehat oracle]$ cd $ORACLE_BASE
[oracle@mikehat oracle]$ ls /mnt/cdrom
doc  index.htm  install  oidupgrade  response  runInstaller  stage
[oracle@mikehat oracle]$ /mnt/cdrom/runInstaller
```

This should bring up the OUI. Linux users might need to set LD_ASSUME_KERNEL=2.2.5 and perform miscellaneous distribution specific tasks to get this running.

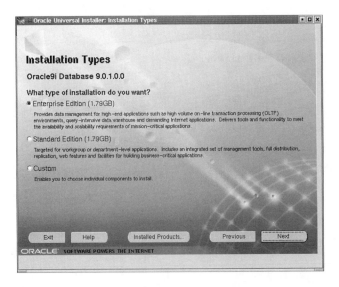

**FIGURE 19.1**

*9i Installation Type.*

During the install, you will be prompted for each CD when it is needed, as shown in Figure 19.2.

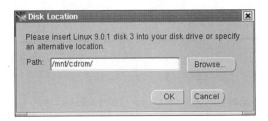

**FIGURE 19.2**

*Prompt for New CD.*

As you can see, OUI wants CD number 3. Remember to unmount the CD-ROM, eject the CD, reload the CD, and then mount the CD-ROM drive before pressing OK.

```
[oracle@mikehat oracle]$ umount /mnt/cdrom
[oracle@mikehat oracle]$ eject
[oracle@mikehat oracle]$ mount /mnt/cdrom
```

The OUI might ask you for the location of the Java Developer Kit (JDK). You might have to download a copy, install it, and then provide the location, as seen in Figure 19.3.

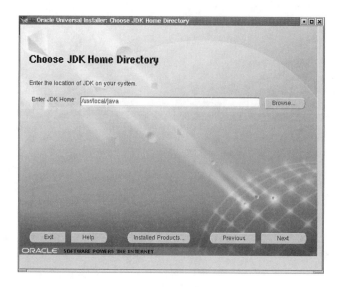

**FIGURE 19.3**
*Enter the JDK Location.*

Refer to your ICG guide for specifics regarding which JDK to download and install. However, this is a fairly straightforward easy task so you should not have many problems with it.

During the installation process you might be given a list of preexisting databases with the option to migrate them as part of the install. As mentioned in Chapter 15, "Migrations," I recommend avoiding this practice. A more conservative approach is to install and test the 9i software first, and then perform the migration as a separate process.

Those are the main differences between installing 8i and installing 9i. Expect 9i to require more memory and disk space, and be prepared to load from three CDs rather than just one.

## Setting Up Security and Logging In

There is an attempt at improving security for database installations. First of all, ServerManager (svrmgrl) and connect internal no longer exist. Oracle has been warning about this change for several years, and it is now a reality. If you try to connect internal, you will get the following error.

```
[oracle@mikehat oracle]$ sqlplus internal

SQL*Plus: Release 9.0.1.0.0 - Production on Sat Jul 14 15:10:52 2001

(c) Copyright 2001 Oracle Corporation.  All rights reserved.
```

```
Enter password:
ERROR:
ORA-09275: CONNECT INTERNAL is not a valid DBA connection
```

The description for this error is as follows:

```
[oracle@mikehat oracle]$ oerr ora 9275
09275, 00000, "CONNECT INTERNAL is not a valid DBA connection"
// *Cause:   CONNECT INTERNAL is no longer supported for DBA connections
// *Action:  Please try to connect AS SYSDBA or AS SYSOPER.
//
[oracle@mikehat oracle]$
```

To log in and start a database you must use SQL*Plus as shown here.

```
[oracle@mikehat oracle]$ sqlplus "/ as sysdba"

SQL*Plus: Release 9.0.1.0.0 - Production on Sat Jul 14 15:04:29 2001

(c) Copyright 2001 Oracle Corporation.  All rights reserved.

Connected to an idle instance.

SQL> startup
ORACLE instance started.

Total System Global Area   336356520 bytes
Fixed Size                    279720 bytes
Variable Size              268435456 bytes
Database Buffers            67108864 bytes
Redo Buffers                  532480 bytes
Database mounted.
Database opened.
SQL>
```

After you start the database you will find new users. Also, most of the default database accounts for the new database are expired. This is shown in Figure 19.4.

As you can see, most of the accounts are expired and locked.

Additional changes are planned in future releases. At some point the OUI will prompt you for passwords for SYS and SYSTEM so the defaults of change_on_install and manager will no longer exist. Also, the use of a SYSTEM user will no longer be supported some day and it will no longer be created automatically. No time frame exists for these changes, but they are *not* implemented as of Oracle 9.0.1.

**19**

9i SERVER NEW FEATURES

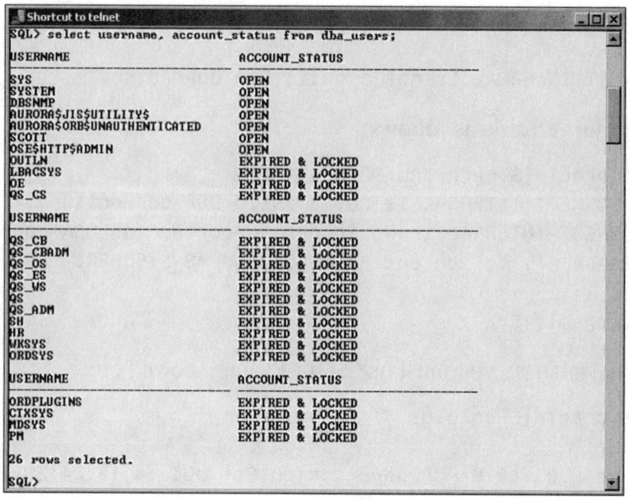

**FIGURE 19.4**
*Expired Accounts.*

# Creating a Server Parameter File (SPFILE)

In previous versions of Oracle the primary source of database parameters was the text-based init.ora. From that file it was common to read config.ora and initdef.ora files for additional parameters, but all of these files were text based. This changes in Oracle 9i.

A binary server parameter file (SPFILE) can now be created from the text-based init.ora file and used instead, if desired.

To create an SPFILE you must have a preexisting init.ora file to use as a starting point. Next, log in to SQL*Plus as the DBA and issue the CREATE SPFILE statement as shown here.

```
SQL> !pwd
/u01/app/oracle/admin/demo/pfile

SQL> !ls
initdemo.ora

SQL> create spfile='/u01/app/oracle/admin/demo/pfile/spfiledemo.ora'
  2    from pfile='/u01/app/oracle/admin/demo/pfile/initdemo.ora';

File created.

SQL> !ls
initdemo.ora   spfiledemo.ora

SQL>
```

This creates the SPFILE. Remember to make a soft link to it from your `$ORACLE_HOME/dbs` directory as you would with a normal `init.ora`. You can create this file when the database is running, but before it takes effect, you must bounce the instance. To determine whether you are using an SPFILE, examine the parameter SPFILE.

```
SQL> show parameter spfile

NAME             TYPE         VALUE
---------------  -----------  ----------------------
spfile           string       ?/dbs/spfile@.ora
SQL>
```

If no value is specified, but you have created a SPFILE in the `$ORACLE_HOME/dbs` directory, bounce the instance.

Because this is a binary file, you cannot change it manually. You can, however, view it using `more`.

```
[oracle@mikehat pfile]$ more spfiledemo.ora
__¥_

*.background_dump_dest='/u01/app/oracle/admin/demo/bdump'
*.compatible='9.0.0'
*.control_files='/u01/app/oracle/oradata/demo/control01.ctl'
,'/u01/app/oracle/oradata/demo/control02.ctl'
,'/u01/app/oracle/oradata/demo/control03.ctl'
*.core_dump_dest='/u01/app/oracle/admin/demo/cdump'
*.db_block_size=8192
*.db_cache_size=67108864
*.db_domain='mike.com'
*.db_name='demo'
*.dispatchers='(PROTOCOL=TCP)(SER=MODOSE)','(PROTOCOL=TCP)
(PRE=oracle.aurora.server.GiopServer)','(PROTOCOL=TCP)
(PRE=oracle.aurora.server.SGiopServer)'
*.fast_start_mttr_target=300
*.instance_name='demo'
*.java_pool_size='117440512'
*.large_pool_size='1048576'
*.open_cursors=300
*.processes=150
*.remote_login_passwordfile='EXCLUSIVE'
*.resource_manager_plan='SYSTEM_PLAN'
*.shared_pool_size=117440512
*.sort_area_size=524288
*.timed_statistics=TRUE
*.undo_management='AUTO'
*.undo_tablespace='UNDOTBS'
*.user_dump_dest='/u01/app/oracle/admin/demo/udump'

[oracle@mikehat pfile]$
```

Don't try to change this file with a text editor because you will corrupt the file. Changes to this file must be made through Oracle.

You must make parameter changes via ALTER SYSTEM commands within the database. These changes will be made to the instance and the SPFILE file will be updated. This eliminates the need to manually update an init.ora file to reflect a change. This is one of the biggest benefits of using a SPFILE.

Historically, the ALTER SYSTEM command impacted the current database instance, but the change did not persist across instance shutdown/startup. If you wanted to make the change permanent, you had to manually add it to the init.ora file. The ALTER SYSTEM command now has a new SCOPE clause that specifies whether the change is made to the current instance and SPFILE, just to the current instance, or just to the SPFILE. Using the COMMENT parameter, you can also include a text comment in the SPFILE. The structure of the SCOPE clause is as follows.

```
SCOPE = MEMORY
```

Here, the change affects only the current database instance. The SPFILE is not modified and the change will last only until the instance is bounced.

```
SCOPE = SPFILE
```

This change updates the SPFILE, but not the current instance. For the change to take effect, the instance must be bounced.

```
SCOPE = BOTH
```

The current instance is modified and the SPFILE is updated with the modification.

Rules regarding dynamic versus static parameters still apply. Static parameters are ones that require a database bounce to take effect. For example, you cannot specify a static parameter with a SCOPE of MEMORY or BOTH. Static parameters can only be specified with a SPFILE SCOPE.

The following is an example of a changing a dynamic parameter in both the SPFILE and in the current instance. Here, you change the value of TIMED_STATISTICS from TRUE to FALSE and add a comment.

```
SQL> show parameter timed_statistics

NAME                       TYPE          VALUE
-------------------------- ------------- --------------
timed_statistics           boolean       TRUE
SQL> alter system set timed_statistics = false
  2  comment = 'stop taking detailed stats'
  3  scope = both;
```

```
System altered.

SQL> show parameter timed_statistics

NAME                      TYPE         VALUE
------------------------- -----------  --------------
timed_statistics          boolean      FALSE
SQL> !more $ORACLE_HOME/dbs/spfiledemo.ora

___

...

*.timed_statistics=FALSE#stop taking detailed stats

...
SQL>
```

The change has now been made both to the current instance and the SPFILE, so it will be in effect after the instance is bounced.

After you are running the SPFILE it is wise to take text-based backups of it. This process is the opposite of creating the SPFILE.

```
SQL> create pfile='/u01/app/oracle/admin/demo/pfile/initdemo.ora'
  2  from spfile='/u01/app/oracle/admin/demo/pfile/spfiledemo.ora';

File created.

SQL>
```

It is possible to go back to using the text-based init.ora file after having used a SPFILE. Simply bounce the database, but on startup, specify the text-based parameter file.

```
SQL> shutdown;
Database closed.
Database dismounted.
ORACLE instance shut down.
SQL> startup pfile='/u01/app/oracle/admin/demo/pfile/initdemo.ora';
ORACLE instance started.

Total System Global Area   336356520 bytes
Fixed Size                    279720 bytes
Variable Size              268435456 bytes
Database Buffers            67108864 bytes
Redo Buffers                  532480 bytes
Database mounted.
Database opened.
SQL> show parameter spfile

NAME                      TYPE         VALUE
------------------------- -----------  ---------
spfile                    string
SQL>
```

**19**

You are now back to using the text-based init.ora file. However, it is necessary to create a link in `$ORACLE_HOME/dbs` to the correct initialization file.

Server parameter files offer a binary alternative to the older text-based files. The biggest advantage is the capability to change Oracle parameters and not to have to worry about updating a file manually. Drawbacks include the fact it is a binary file that cannot be manually edited. This file can become corrupted, so make sure you have a backup text-based file.

> ## Remember these Are *New* Features
>
> Whenever a new version of a software program is released, it is important to take them with a grain of salt. By that, I mean don't rush to use every new feature just because it is available. Especially when using production systems, I wouldn't trust a new feature from *any* vendor without testing it first.
>
> There are several reasons for this. First, new software obviously has a higher likelihood of containing bugs. I don't mind testing new software and finding bugs on test systems, but not on a production system. Next, if a technology is new, its optimal usage most likely hasn't been identified. It takes time and testing to identify how best to deploy a technology. This can be a painful process fraught with many false starts. This is okay, as long as it is not on your production system.
>
> Finally, some new features turn out being little more than gimmicks or are so narrow in their scope that very few people will use them in the "real world." Not every product or feature released by a vendor is going to be helpful. The trick is to make sure you don't buy into products that have no real value. Marketing buzzwords are everywhere. As a person evaluating these features, you must identify what it will actually *do* for you, not what is promised. If a feature isn't going to benefit your system in some tangible way, you probably shouldn't implement it. Some of the best technical advice I ever got was if a product doesn't seem to fill a business or a technical need it probably isn't a good idea. If you apply that rule to new features and products, your system will be better off.

# Using Oracle-Managed Files

Oracle 9i offers a new feature that attempts to free you from the details of managing database files. Oracle-managed files allow you to create data files and tablespaces normally, but Oracle manages these aspects:

- **Location**    Each file is placed in a default directory location. This parameter can be modified with ALTER SYSTEM.

- **Name**    Each file has a unique name within the database. It still follows OFA conventions and data files include the tablespace name, but each file is given a system-generated unique name.
- **Size**    Each file is 100M by default.
- **Growth**    Each file is set with AUTOEXTEND = TRUE to an unlimited size.
- **Deleting**    Once a tablespace is dropped, the file is automatically removed from the OS by Oracle.

The idea is to make managing files almost transparent. This way, you don't spend time worrying about name, file size, location, or growth. Oracle takes care of all this transparently.

This feature can be used for control, online redo log, and data files. You can have a mix of normal files and Oracle-managed files. Assuming you let the defaults of each file take effect, the single largest variable is determining the default location, which is controlled by two database parameters.

- **DB_CREATE_ONLINE_LOG_DEST_[1...5]**    If this parameter is specified, this is where control files and online redo log files are placed by default. You can specify up to five locations. If more than one location exists, the files are multiplexed automatically. Data files are not placed in this location. If this value is not set, control and online redo log files are placed in the default data file location.
- **DB_CREATE_FILE_DEST**    Data files are placed in this location when created by Oracle. Also, if DB_CREATE_ONLINE_LOG_DEST_[1...5] is not specified, a single copy of a control file and one member of the two online redo log groups are placed in this location.

If neither of these parameters is specified and you attempt to create a tablespace without properly specifying the data file, the statement will fail. The following steps show some examples of using Oracle-managed files.

To create a simple tablespace using Oracle-managed files, follow these steps:

1. First, set the location of your DB_CREATE_FILE_DEST file, which is where data files are created.

```
SQL> alter system
  2  set db_create_file_dest
  3  = '/u03/app/oracle/oradata/demo3';

System altered.

SQL> show parameter db_create_file_dest
```

```
NAME                        TYPE      VALUE
--------------------        --------  --------------------
db_create_file_dest         string    /u03/app/oracle/oradata/demo3
SQL>
```

2. Create the tablespace and accept all the defaults.

```
SQL> create tablespace data01;

Tablespace created.

SQL>
```

3. Examine the tablespace's defaults. Here, you can see it is in the DB_CREATE_FILE_DEST location, has a unique name, is 100M, will auto-extend, and it is locally managed.

```
SQL> select file_name, bytes, autoextensible
  2  from dba_data_files
  3  where tablespace_name = 'DATA01';

FILE_NAME                                                        BYTES AUT
------------------------------------------------------  ------------- ---
/u03/app/oracle/oradata/demo3/ora_data01_xotkdrnj.dbf   104,857,600 YES


SQL> select extent_management, initial_extent, next_extent,
  2  allocation_type, segment_space_management
  3  from dba_tablespaces
  4  where tablespace_name = 'DATA01';

EXTENT_MAN   INITIAL_EXTENT        NEXT_EXTENT ALLOCATIO SEGMEN
----------   ---------------   ---------------- --------- ------
LOCAL                 65,536                    SYSTEM    MANUAL

SQL>
```

4. Determine whether Oracle will automatically delete the file at the operating system level once you drop the tablespace.

```
SQL> !ls /u03/app/oracle/oradata/demo3
ora_data01_xotkdrnj.dbf

SQL> drop tablespace data01;

Tablespace dropped.

SQL> !ls /u03/app/oracle/oradata/demo3

SQL>
```

Oracle was able to create the data file in a default location, give it default values, and then remove it as needed. Alternatively, you could have provided some explicit values such as size.

```
SQL> create tablespace data02
  2   datafile
  3   size 250M;

Tablespace created.

SQL> select file_name, bytes
  2   from dba_data_files
  3   where tablespace_name = 'DATA02';

FILE_NAME                                                    BYTES
------------------------------------------------------ ------------
/u03/app/oracle/oradata/demo3/ora_data02_xotlhtwk.dbf  262,144,000

SQL>
```

You can also add to existing tablespaces and can add multiple files simultaneously as seen here.

```
SQL> select file_name from dba_data_files
  2   where tablespace_name = 'DATA02';

FILE_NAME
------------------------------------------------------
/u03/app/oracle/oradata/demo3/ora_data02_xotlhtwk.dbf

SQL> alter tablespace data02
  2   add datafile size 150M, size 150M;

Tablespace altered.

SQL> select file_name, bytes from dba_data_files
  2   where tablespace_name = 'DATA02';

FILE_NAME                                                    BYTES
------------------------------------------------------ ------------
/u03/app/oracle/oradata/demo3/ora_data02_xotlhtwk.dbf  262,144,000
/u03/app/oracle/oradata/demo3/ora_data02_xowlz7d0.dbf  157,286,400
/u03/app/oracle/oradata/demo3/ora_data02_xowlzc00.dbf  157,286,400

SQL>
```

As you can see, you added two data files with non-default sizes to an existing tablespace. This adds to the flexibility of Oracle-managed files.

Creating control files or redo logs is very similar to creating data files. The biggest difference is that if DB_CREATE_ONLINE_LOG_DEST_*n* is not specified, a single copy will be placed in DB_CREATE_FILE_DEST. Next, you can create a multiplexed online redo log group with two members.

1. Specify the default locations for your redo log or control files.

```
SQL> alter system
  2  set db_create_online_log_dest_1
  3  = '/u03/app/oracle/oradata/demo3';

System altered.

SQL> alter system
  2  set db_create_online_log_dest_2
  3  = '/u04/app/oracle/oradata/demo3';

System altered.

SQL> show parameter db_create_online_log_dest

NAME                           TYPE      VALUE
------------------------------ --------- ----------------------------
db_create_online_log_dest_1    string    /u03/app/oracle/oradata/demo3
db_create_online_log_dest_2    string    /u04/app/oracle/oradata/demo3
db_create_online_log_dest_3    string
db_create_online_log_dest_4    string
db_create_online_log_dest_5    string

SQL>
```

2. Identify the current online redo log groups.

```
SQL> select * from v$logfile
  2  order by group#;

GROUP#  STATUS   TYPE    MEMBER
------  -------  ------- -----------------------------------------
1                ONLINE  /u01/app/oracle/oradata/demo3/redo01.log
2                ONLINE  /u01/app/oracle/oradata/demo3/redo02.log
3                ONLINE  /u01/app/oracle/oradata/demo3/redo03.log

SQL>
```

Clearly this is not a good layout. Every member is on one disk, which represents a single point of failure and would result in I/O contention. Additionally, none of the members is multiplexed. This is probably the result of a hasty database creation and in a real system, you would likely fix these problems. For now, just add the new log group.

3. Create a new online redo log group.

```
SQL> alter database add logfile;

Database altered.

SQL>
```

4. Check to see what was created. In this case a new log group #4 was created. Because you assigned two locations for DB_CREATE_ONLINE_LOG_DEST_*n,* you will have two multiplexed members for the new group. Each file is uniquely named and is 100M in size.

```
SQL> select * from v$logfile
  2  order by group#;

GROUP# STATUS  TYPE    MEMBER
---------- ------- ------- --------------------------------------------------
1                   ONLINE  /u01/app/oracle/oradata/demo3/redo01.log
2                   ONLINE  /u01/app/oracle/oradata/demo3/redo02.log
3                   ONLINE  /u01/app/oracle/oradata/demo3/redo03.log
4                   ONLINE
/u03/app/oracle/oradata/demo3/ora_4_xotmkyyz.log
4                   ONLINE
/u04/app/oracle/oradata/demo3/ora_4_xotml1f5.log

SQL>
SQL> select group#, members, bytes
  2  from v$log
  3  order by group#;

    GROUP#    MEMBERS         BYTES
---------- ---------- -------------
         1          1   104,857,600
         2          1   104,857,600
         3          1   104,857,600
         4          2   104,857,600

SQL>
```

As you can see there is now a new online redo log group with two members at 100M each.

Oracle-managed files do seem to simplify administration, but it comes at a cost. Spreading out your disk I/O is more difficult with Oracle-managed files unless your logical volume is striped and preferably mirrored. Even if that is the case, having all your files in one location is dangerous because one misplaced `rm` command can destroy everything.

19

9i SERVER NEW
FEATURES

Another concern I have is "dumbing down" the DBA's role and promoting sloppy administration practices. Although DBAs with a solid background in previous releases of Oracle aren't likely to fall into this category, newer DBAs might fall into this trap. If they never learn to separate their files and rely on Oracle to specify all default parameters, they will never practice solid database design principles. This might be sufficient on small test systems, but performance will suffer greatly on larger systems. My advice is to use Oracle-managed files when they make sense, but never forget the fundamentals of file management.

## Using Dynamic Memory Parameters and Multiple Block Sizes

One of the most exciting new features of Oracle 9i is the capability to adjust the SGA without bouncing the database. Obviously this has large implications for systems with high uptime requirements. The process of defining the size of the database buffer cache has also changed. This section covers these changes.

Have you ever had a production database with lots of active users, only to find that you need to increase a parameter like the shared pool to meet an unexpected demand? It's a hassle to have everyone log off, increase the parameter to a higher number that you *think* is correct, bounce the database, and then have the users log back on. If your increase was sufficient, the users suffer a slight inconvenience and your image takes a small hit. If your increase was insufficient and performance problems continue, the whole problem snowballs. Fortunately, Oracle 9i allows you to change these parameters on the fly without having to bounce the instance.

The following parameters can now be changed using the ALTER SYSTEM command:

- **SHARED_POOL_SIZE**   Size of the shared pool.
- **LARGE_POOL_SIZE**   Size of the large pool.
- **DB_CACHE_SIZE**   New parameter in 9i. This is the size of the database buffer cache of the default database block size.
- **DB_*n*K_CACHE_SIZE**   New parameter in 9i. This is the size of the optional caches inside the database buffer cache dedicated to a specific database block size.
- **PROCESSES**   The number of processes on the system. This is an issue if the number of users logged in (plus the background processes) exceeds the processes number. Remember not to exceed the number of semaphores on your system when adjusting this value.

You can decrease or increase these memory pool values, but only up to the size identified by SGA_MAX_SIZE. You cannot increase a memory pool that will cause the SGA to exceed this value. Also, this value is not dynamic, so you must bounce the database to increase it.

Here, you modify the shared pool size.

```
SQL> alter system
  2  set shared_pool_size = 75M;

System altered.
```

If you attempt to increase the shared pool above the value set for SGA_MAX_SIZE, you'll get an error.

```
SQL> show parameter sga_max_size

NAME                      TYPE         VALUE
- - - - - - - - - - - - - - - - - - - -  - - - - - - - - - - -  - - - - - - - - - - - -
sga_max_size              big integer 336356520

SQL> alter system
  2  set shared_pool_size = 400M;
alter system
*
ERROR at line 1:
ORA-02097: parameter cannot be modified because specified value is invalid
ORA-04033: Insufficient memory to grow pool

SQL>
```

Related to dynamic memory pool allocation is the practice of using multiple block sizes in the database. Oracle 9i allows you to use up to four database block sizes for data files and segregate these as separate caches within the database buffer cache. Within the buffer cache, you can dynamically increase or decrease individual pools based on block size. The range of block sizes available are 2K, 4K, 8K, 16K, and 32K.

When you create a 9i database, you still define a DB_BLOCK_SIZE, which will be your default block size and will be the size used for the SYSTEM tablespace. For example, here you are set to use 8K blocks.

```
SQL> show parameter db_block_size

NAME                 TYPE         VALUE
- - - - - - - - - - - - - - - - -  - - - - - - - - - - -  - - - - - - - - - -
db_block_size        integer      8192
```

Now, for tuning purposes, you want a tablespace with a larger block size, you can specify that within the CREATE TABLESPACE statement. However, before you do this, you must allocate a pool within the database buffer cache to hold this different block size. Failure to create space in buffer cache for the different block size will result in an ORA-29339 error when you try to create the tablespace, so be sure to allocate the pool first.

**19**

**9i SERVER NEW FEATURES**

```
SQL> show parameter db_16k

NAME                    TYPE         VALUE
------------------      ----------   ---------------
db_16k_cache_size       big integer  0

SQL> alter system
  2   set db_16k_cache_size = 16M;

System altered.

SQL> create tablespace data
  2   datafile '/u01/app/oracle/oradata/demo/data01.dbf'
  3   size 100M
  4   blocksize 16K
  5   default storage (initial 1M next 1M);

Tablespace created.

SQL>
```

You now have DATA tablespace using 16K blocks and a pool in the buffer cache reserved for it. The database buffer cache now contains a pool for 16K blocks and a separate pool for the default 8K blocks. Keep in mind that when you add new pools, they come in addition to the buffer cache. By adding the new pool for 16K blocks, you do not implicitly increase or decrease the size of the default (8K) pool.

There is a catch when creating separate pools for different block sizes. You cannot define a pool with DB_$n$K_CACHE_SIZE for the default block size. In this example the default block size was 8K, but you never defined a DB_8K_CACHE_SIZE value. This pool is sized by setting the DB_CACHE_SIZE parameter, which is for the default block size. Oracle might initially let you assign a separate pool size for the default block size, but you will receive the following error when you bounce the instance:

```
SQL> startup
ORA-00380: cannot specify db_8k_cache_size since 8K is the standard block size
SQL> !oerr ora 380
00380, 00000, "cannot specify db_%sk_cache_size since %sK is the standard block
size"
// *Cause:  User specified the parameter db_nk_cache_size (where n is one of
//          2,4,8,16,32), while the standard block size for this database is
//          equal to n Kbytes. This is illegal.
// *Action: Specify the standard block size cache using db_cache_size (DEFAULT
//          pool) (and db_recycle_cache_size, db_keep_cache_size if additional
//          buffer pools are required). Do NOT use the corresponding
//          db_nk_cache_size parameter for the standard block size.
//

SQL>
```

Using multiple block sizes alters the way the buffer cache is sized. Prior to 9i, the formula for the buffer cache was as follows:

```
buffer cache size = DB_BLOCK_SIZE  *  DB_BLOCK_BUFFERS
```

Under 9i, this formula changes. You no longer measure the buffer cache in terms of DB_BLOCK_BUFFERS. Rather, you specify the size of the buffer cache for the default block size using the parameter DB_CACHE_SIZE. In addition to that value, you also add each pool for any non-default block sizes as well. The new equation is as follows:

```
buffer cache size = DB_CACHE_SIZE  +  DB_[2K...32k]_CACHE_SIZE
```

In this manner, you measure the buffer cache by the sum of each pool reserved for a specific block size.

## Using Undo Tablespaces

Oracle 9i also attempts to reduce maintenance duties involving rollback segments. If you want, you can still use traditional tablespaces, whereby you create rollback segments and manage the extents. However, 9i introduces a new type of undo tablespace that replaces traditional rollback segments. In fact, Oracle documentation states that the traditional method of creating rollback segments is being depreciated and strongly recommends using undo tablespaces.

Undo tablespaces perform the same core functions of traditional rollback segments. They provide the three Rs of rollback segments:

- Rollback of SQL statements
- Read consistency
- Recovery in case of a crash

Unfortunately, at the time of this writing, Oracle has not explained exactly *how* undo tablespaces work internally and in what way they differ internally from traditional rollback segments. Basically, we know how to create them and that Oracle automatically manages them, but the exact details haven't been released. Based on the queries from DBA_ROLLBACK_SEGS, it looks like they do use some type of segments, but how these differ from traditional rollback segments is still unknown. Therefore, this section focuses on what they do rather than how they do it.

A 9i instance can run using either traditional rollback segments or the new undo tablespaces. Changing between methods requires modifying the parameter UNDO_MANAGEMENT and bouncing the instance. UNDO_MANAGMENT has the following settings:

| Setting | Description |
| --- | --- |
| UNDO_MANAGEMENT = '' | Unset, defaults to rollback segments |
| UNDO_MANAGEMENT = MANUAL | Use traditional rollback segments |
| UNDO_MANAGEMENT = AUTO | Use new undo tablespaces |

**19**

9i SERVER NEW FEATURES

If you do not set UNDO_MANAGEMENT or set it to MANUAL, you can use and manage rollback segments as normal. However, if you decide to use undo tablespaces you must do the following:

1. Decide whether you will create the tablespace at database creation or after the database is created. Here, you create an undo tablespace after the database has been created. The key difference between creating this undo tablespace versus any other type of tablespace is the UNDO clause.

```
SQL> create undo tablespace auto_undo_tbs
  2   datafile '/u02/app/oracle/oradata/demo/auto_undo_tbs01.dbf'
  3   size 100M;

Tablespace created.

SQL>
```

Here, you now have an undo tablespace called AUTO_UNDO_TBS. If you let Oracle create it for you at database creation, the default name is UNDOTBS.

2. Currently, you are set to use manual (traditional) rollback tablespaces. Because you can have multiple tablespaces, you must identify which one you will use. Set the database to use the undo tablespace AUTO_UNDO_TBS once you start using undo tablespaces.

```
SQL> alter system
  2   set undo_tablespace = auto_undo_tbs
  3   scope = spfile;

System altered.

SQL>
```

Once you have set the database to use undo tablespaces, you can change UNDO_TABLEPSACE dynamically to switch between different tablespaces. New transactions will take place in the tablespace specified, whereas existing transactions will continue in the previous tablespace. However, here you can't set UNDO_TABLESPACE dynamically because the database is still in manual rollback mode. Therefore, you set it in the SPFILE using the SCOPE clause to take effect next time you bounce the instance.

3. Next, you must set the database to use the auto undo tablespace method rather than the manual method. This parameter is not dynamic so you must set it in the SPFILE so it will take effect when you bounce the instance. Set the database to use AUTO undo.

```
SQL> alter system
  2   set undo_management = auto
  3   scope = spfile;

System altered.

SQL>
```

4. Bounce the database so the changes take effect.

```
SQL> shutdown;
...
SQL> startup
ORACLE instance started.

Total System Global Area  420242700 bytes
Fixed Size                   279820 bytes
Variable Size             335544320 bytes
Database Buffers           83886080 bytes
Redo Buffers                 532480 bytes
Database mounted.
Database opened.

SQL>
```

5. Verify the database is using the undo tablespace.

```
SQL> show parameter undo

NAME                        TYPE         VALUE
-------------------------   ----------   --------------
undo_management             string       AUTO
undo_retention              integer      900
undo_suppress_errors        boolean      FALSE
undo_tablespace             string       AUTO_UNDO_TBS

SQL> select segment_name, tablespace_name, status
  2  from dba_rollback_segs
  3  order by tablespace_name;

SEGMENT_NAME     TABLESPACE_NAME  STATUS
--------------   --------------   ----------------
_SYSSMU11$       AUTO_UNDO_TBS    ONLINE
_SYSSMU12$       AUTO_UNDO_TBS    ONLINE
_SYSSMU13$       AUTO_UNDO_TBS    ONLINE
_SYSSMU15$       AUTO_UNDO_TBS    ONLINE
_SYSSMU17$       AUTO_UNDO_TBS    ONLINE
_SYSSMU19$       AUTO_UNDO_TBS    ONLINE
_SYSSMU20$       AUTO_UNDO_TBS    ONLINE
_SYSSMU18$       AUTO_UNDO_TBS    ONLINE
_SYSSMU16$       AUTO_UNDO_TBS    ONLINE
_SYSSMU14$       AUTO_UNDO_TBS    ONLINE
SYSTEM           SYSTEM           ONLINE

11 rows selected.

SQL>
```

**19**

9i SERVER NEW
FEATURES

As you can see, the database is using the undo tablespace. There are 10 segments automatically created in this tablespace. You cannot manually add additional rollback segments to this tablespace. The parameter UNDO_SUPPRESS_ERRORS is currently set to FALSE, which means Oracle will issue an error message if you attempt manually add rollback segments. If you set UNDO_SUPPRESS_ERRORS to TRUE and attempt that operation, Oracle will not display an error and it will appear that your command was successful, however the segments will not be used.

One final parameter of interest relating to undo tablespaces is UNDO_RETENTION. This parameter dictates how long, in seconds, the undo from a completed transaction is preserved in the undo tablespace before the space is reused. By keeping this undo information available, Oracle provides a read consistent "before image" of the data for other transactions to use. This is necessary to prevent the ORA-01555  Snapshot Too Old error. The default value is 900 seconds (15 minutes). To modify this value, issue the following:

```
SQL> alter system
  2  set undo_retention = 1800;

System altered.

SQL>
```

In this case, you double the retention period to 1800 seconds (30 minutes). Oracle will now attempt to retain committed undo data for 30 minutes in case a long running query needs it for read-consistency. However, if Oracle needs space in the undo tablespace, this retained undo is used. Therefore, you cannot entirely depend on the undo being available if you have an active database or a small undo tablespace.

Undo retention also supports the new package DBMS_FLASHBACK. This package allows you to view data as it existed previously, but only to the point that undo exists. If you plan on using this package, you need to set UNDO_RETENTION accordingly.

Oracle has provided a new view to monitor undo tablespace usage. The new view is V$UNDO-STAT. Previous views regarding rollback segments still exist in 9i.

## Comprehensive Sample Schemas

Oracle 9i has a new and more complete set of optional sample schemas for testing. Many DBA and developers originally learned Oracle on the SCOTT/TIGER account; this account still exists. However, the SCOTT schema is limited in terms of objects, complex referential integrity, and volume of data. Often trainers and instructors have to create their own schemas so students can train on realistic accounts.

Oracle 9i now allows you to create several new testing/training schemas. These include references to Human Resources (HR), Order Entry (OE), Product Media (PM), Sales History (SH), and Shipping (QS), as shown next. Notice how each account (except for SCOTT) is expired and locked by default.

```
SQL> select username, account_status from dba_users
  2  where username in ('SCOTT', 'HR', 'SH', 'PM', 'OE')
  3  or username like 'QS%';

USERNAME    ACCOUNT_STATUS
----------  --------------------
QS          EXPIRED & LOCKED
QS_ADM      EXPIRED & LOCKED
QS_CB       EXPIRED & LOCKED
QS_CBADM    EXPIRED & LOCKED
QS_CS       EXPIRED & LOCKED
QS_ES       EXPIRED & LOCKED
QS_OS       EXPIRED & LOCKED
QS_WS       EXPIRED & LOCKED
OE          EXPIRED & LOCKED
PM          EXPIRED & LOCKED
SH          EXPIRED & LOCKED
HR          EXPIRED & LOCKED
SCOTT       OPEN

13 rows selected.

SQL>
```

These schemas are created when you create the demo database. You can also find scripts to create each schema in $ORACLE_HOME/demo/schema.

Why make a big deal about training accounts? Aren't there other 9i features that will impact the DBA more on a daily basis? First of all, these training accounts represent most of the new default users, so you need to know what they are. Second, because many DBAs will attempt to learn 9i by experimenting, it is good to identify the "Guinea pig" accounts quickly. Finally, these schemas contain objects that the average DBA might not have experience with, including LOBs and queues. Fortunately, some schemas do have these types of more exotic objects.

```
SQL> select owner, object_type, count(*) from dba_objects
  2  where owner = 'QS'
  3  group by owner, object_type;

OWNER                 OBJECT_TYPE          COUNT(*)
--------------------  -------------------  ----------
QS                    INDEX                        15
```

**19**

9i SERVER NEW
FEATURES

```
QS                   LOB                    1
QS                   QUEUE                  6
QS                   SEQUENCE               2
QS                   TABLE                 15
QS                   VIEW                   5

6 rows selected.

SQL>
```

Use these schemas as you experiment with the 9i features. They will likely be used in Oracle training classes and probably future books.

## Miscellaneous Features and Changes

There are many more new features and changes that deserve mentioning. Use this list to identify features you should explore as you find the time.

- Oracle Parallel Server (OPS) is now called Real Application Clusters (RAC). RAC is the system of having a physical database on a shared disk array that's accessed simultaneously by multiple instances on separate nodes. This provides improved fault tolerance and can be used to partition the application. This feature has been available since Oracle 7, but Oracle is pushing it more aggressively in 9i. Because of recent improvements, this feature is now available on Linux systems.

- Net8 is now referred to as Oracle Net.

- The processes of locking and reorganizing database objects have been improved.

- You can now create tablespaces with automatic segment management. This eliminates the need to configure parameters such as FREELISTS and PCTUSED.

- LogMiner via OEM now has a graphical interface.

- DBMS_FLASHBACK allows you to view data as it existed previously in the database.

- Standby databases are improved and are now called Data Guard.

There are many more features you should be familiar with; you should explore the ones listed previously in greater detail. However, this should provide a good place to start. From here, you can start experimenting with the new database. Next, you should consider taking a 9i New Features class to better understand the new release and prepare for the OCP upgrade exam.

## Summary

This chapter covered some of the most interesting new features of Oracle 9i. Although there are many improvements that you should become familiar with, the focus of this chapter was on the changes that you will notice immediately.

The chapter covered changes to the installation procedure and what to expect during installation. Next, it looked at changes to security and how to log in using the "/ as sysdba" clause. Server parameter files (SPFILE) were discussed, as this new feature attempts to replace text-based init.ora files. Oracle-managed files were also discussed. Oracle is attempting to replace DBA managed rollback segments with automatic undo tablespaces. The chapter therefore showed how to create and implement this new type of rollback management. Next, it provided an overview of the new training schemas that you can create. Finally, the chapter touched on several miscellaneous changes and new features that you should be aware of. This information should help you get started using 9i.

# Growth of the DBA

## ESSENTIALS

- The key to advancing your career as a DBA is continuing education.

- Classes via Oracle University or third-party schools are a great way to learn new skills.

- Certification is very popular in IT and the best way to prepare for Oracle certification is to take Oracle University Classes.

- Learning on your own is a critical skill for any technical person because paid training is not always available.

- There are many lucrative opportunities for experienced technical people if they are willing to pursue them.

# Growth of the DBA

People in the technology industry often ask "How can I get ahead?" This is often tied to "How can I make more money?" These are fair questions because IT certainly is a business. However, although many technology people are driven by money, most also do gain a level of personal satisfaction by being good at what they do. Combined with the dynamic nature of IT, growing and learning is more of a requirement than an option.

This chapter discusses some common characteristics I've noticed among DBAs that I consider successful. It surveys some of the ways DBAs can become better at what they do. If becoming more skilled increases the salary base, even better. However, the main focus of this chapter is growing from a technical standpoint.

# Motivation

What drives a DBA or any technical person for that matter? The answers are as varied as the people. However, I have noticed some traits common among successful DBAs and SAs that I've known.

- They really like to understand how and why things work.
- The desire to keep learning extends far beyond the classroom.
- They want to make good money, but they know they won't get ultra-rich.

Obviously, motivating factors vary from person to person. However they reflect the nature of the industry so people possessing these characteristics tend to do well as administrators. Notice how learning and understanding the technology are central themes. That's why this chapter focuses on continuing education.

# Continuing Your Education

It is one industry in which a specialized degree is not a requirement. Unlike most other professional occupations, there is no rule (official or implied) that says you must have a college degree to practice. Some of the most successful people in IT don't even have college degrees. In fact, the CEOs of several of the largest software companies are college dropouts. Could anyone imagine this to be the case in the legal or medical professions?

What this means is that you should not feel inferior if you lack a traditional education in IT. However, it does not mean that learning isn't important. In fact continuing education is often the key to advancing yourself. It almost seems cliché to say that change is constant, but in IT, this really is true. Most DBAs realize this and want to stay on top. The following sections outline some of the more common ways to stay abreast of the changes in this field.

## Traditional Education

Many people leave school early to get into IT or have non-IT degrees. The point is they lack a computer degree and feel that one would help them. Once someone is established as a DBA with years of experience, the effort of earning a degree approaches the point of diminishing returns. Regardless, some people do leave the industry for a full-time education or (more often) take classes while working a full-time job.

You can get quality Oracle training at universities. In addition to the normal classes in programming, design, and networking, many programs require some level of database training. Initially, this is often taught in SQL using Microsoft Access. However, upper-level classes often teach PL/SQL, data modeling, and database design. Some of the better institutions also teach database administration.

## Oracle University Classes

Oracle Corporation offers a very good series of instructor led classes. The scope of these classes covers virtually everything related to databases. Very good training for SQL, PL/SQL, Oracle Designer, Oracle Developer, Oracle Discoverer, Web and Internet products, data modeling, and database administration is available. These classes are continually being updated; you'll find complete course descriptions on the Oracle University (formerly Oracle Education) Web page at `http://oracle.com/education/`.

The classes contain a mix of instructor-led lectures, discussions, and lab work. Most of the classes take place in special training centers, located in almost every city. As a student you have access to a workstation loaded with whatever software you are learning. You also are issued a student kit containing the lecture and lab manuals. Pay particular attention to the training manuals. These are *very* good manuals and will be useful once you return to your job.

| **TIP** |
| --- |
| Keep Your Manuals |
| If your company officially pays for training, the lab manuals are yours. If you later leave your company I recommend taking them with you. |

Each class takes between one and five days. However, most classes are four or five days. Most of the standard classes, such as those related to SQL and database administration, are offered regularly at any training center. However, if you want a class covering specialized products, such as Parallel Server or iAS, you will probably have to travel to a major city. The only other alternative is to have Oracle come to your organization and teach a class. If a large group of students attend, Oracle will send an instructor to a site to teach a specific class.

**20**

**GROWTH OF THE DBA**

Computer Based Training (CBT) CDs are also available. CBTs are interactive multimedia presentations designed to teach a topic. Over the years these have improved dramatically from plain text lectures and questions to fully graphical, audio training presentations. These CBTs are a good way to get introductory information on a subject. However, the full-blown instructor-led courses provide a more complete and in-depth education.

## Third-Party Oracle Classes

Quality training is also available from third-party organizations. Particularly for those who just want more training so they perform their jobs better, smaller schools are often better. Depending on the company, you'll pay about $600 for the lecture, a hands-on lab, and training materials. Many private individuals opt for these types of classes to advance their IT careers because they can be held at night. These types of classes are also popular with non-IT individuals looking to see whether they want a change in careers.

One such company that conducts this type of training is Perpetual Technologies (`http://www.perptech.com/`). They provide a full range of Oracle DBA, SQL, PL/SQL, and design classes. Unlike many training organizations, they also place an emphasis on the Unix/Linux operating system, which is very important. Classes in system administration and Korn shell programming are also available (these are also valuable skills for an Oracle DBA to have). Finally, training internships are also available so students can practice their skills in a work environment.

## Learning on Your Own

By far, most DBAs train themselves on the job when needing a new skill. Working DBAs seldom have time to take a class for every new skill they need just to survive. Most DBAs might get basic training on a new topic, such as performance tuning, and then use this basis to teach themselves the on-the-job skill.

DBAs typically read Oracle manuals, published books, and Technet (`http://technet.oracle.com`) and Metalink (`http://metalink.oracle.com`) Web pages to gain new information. In fact, it's not a bad idea to try to devote at least one hour a day reading or practicing new skills. Too many systems suffer because administrators fail to understand or implement their systems properly. Indeed, viable technical options to difficult problems won't be considered if you don't know they exist. This means that management *must* understand that computer administration is a technical position and their administrative staff needs the time to maintain and expand their technical skills.

> ### "Goofing Off?"
>
> I once had a non-technical manager who frowned on his technical people reading manuals or Oracle Web pages. He was convinced that if you were not typing rapidly at the keyboard, you obviously were not working. After about one month of getting dirty looks, the SA, a developer, and I let him know what we were doing and why. We cited examples of how training and what we learned on our own had directly benefited the company. After a while he started to understand the nature of an IT shop, but the culture still wasn't conducive to professional development. Ultimately we all left that company; the negative atmosphere we faced was a big reason for our leaving.

Many DBAs build a test instance on a Unix or Linux box to practice what they have learned. This is how most real learning occurs. If you cannot get a test box at work, get a Linux box at home. Many people become DBAs because they are willing to work and learn on their own. Obviously, you should not use production databases to test new skills. This is why a test box is great—if you crash it or lose a database, nothing of value is lost.

Make notes to yourself and develop a collection of scripts you know and understand. There is no reason to reinvent the wheel; when you do perform an interesting or complicated task, outline it. These notes are for yourself so the next time you are faced with a similar task you will be better prepared. By creating these personal white papers you become more familiar with what you did and increase your retention level. This makes you more valuable as an administrator because your experience stays with you. Also start creating a toolbox of scripts. These can be shell or SQL scripts that perform virtually any task. DBAs who travel and consult often rely on a common set of scripts they take with them. This improves efficiency and guarantees a level of repeatability because the same scripts are used each time.

## Emerging Technologies

After you have been trained and are working as a DBA, it is up to you to learn new technologies. In recent years, the roles of the Internet, LDAP, Java, and Web servers have become more important to the DBA. There is a big push to Web-enable many preexisting systems, which of course has an impact on the database. As Java supplements and replaces PL/SQL, you must understand how, why, and where it is used. Oracle is continually phasing these technologies into each new database release. The traditional tasks of the DBA are changing as the database becomes more self-managed. However, the responsibilities of data protection and data availability will remain, it's just they will be more Web-oriented. Progressive DBAs realized this and are acting accordingly.

This section covered continuing education. A formal education in computers is helpful, but not necessary. It is far more important what you do on the job than what you learned in school. Knowing this, you can use structured training classes to learn new topics. Then, you can work on your own to maintain and expand your skills. Once you have been "trained," it is up to you to stay on top of new technologies, because they will ultimately change the way you work.

# Getting Certified

Certifications have been part of the IT industry for some time. Novell certifications have been around for years; Microsoft has several certifications available; and now Cisco is expanding. Oracle is no exception with its Oracle Certified Professional (OCP) program.

## Available Certification Tracks

Until just recently, there were three categories of OCP: Database Operator, Database Administrator, and Application Developer.

Database Operator is the simplest certification. It has one test focused on basic database principles and OEM. Some people consider it the equivalent of a Junior DBA test.

Database Administrator is the main certification most people attempt. It has five tests covering the following areas:

- Introduction to SQL and PL/SQL
- Database administration
- Network administration
- Backup and recovery
- Performance tuning

By no mere accident, these correspond *exactly* to the classes offered by Oracle University.

Application Developer certifies that you can be a developer. This track is being modified for the new Developer 6i toolset. The exact number of tests depends on the track you are taking. Generally, it is composed of the following tests:

- Introduction to SQL and PL/SQL
- PL/SQL
- Forms 1
- Forms 2

As of this writing Oracle has expanded the program to include certifications for Java Developer and Financial Applications. The Java certification is one or two exams depending on the level of certification you want to obtain. The Financial Applications certification requires three tests, but it looks like this certification is being retired.

> **NOTE**
>
> **The OCP Program Is Evolving**
>
> New OCP tracks are added regularly and the requirements can change. Be sure to check the Oracle Certification (`http://www.oracle.com/education/certification/`) page to view the latest requirements.

The "Introduction to SQL and PL/SQL" test is the same for both the DBA and Developer categories. Each test is slated towards a version of the appropriate Oracle product—whether it be Oracle 7, Oracle 8, or Oracle 8i DBA. Rather than having to take all the tests of a specific release, as it used to be, you now can mix the versions of the tests to a certain extent. You can also take upgrade tests in order to go from one version to the next. For example, if you are an Oracle 8-certified DBA, you do not have to take the same five tests for 8i certification. Simply pass the Oracle 8i upgrade test and you will be certified for Oracle 8 and Oracle 8i.

## Preparation

These tests do require preparation; most people cannot pass the exams without preparing. These tests ask very specific, detailed questions about Oracle. Because these are multiple-choice questions, there is no way to give a bogus essay answer and get partial credit. You can normally eliminate one response, but you are still left with three or four other possible solutions. You really need to know the material.

Another reason these tests are challenging is that they deal with areas you might not have any hands-on experience with. You might be very successful using shell scripts to do many of the tasks that Oracle has separate products to do also. However, the test focuses on the Oracle products, not your scripts. You have to be familiar with each Oracle product whether you use it or not.

So how do you prepare for these exams? By far the best way to prepare is to take the Oracle University courses. I have found that if you take these classes, you'll have everything you need to pass the test. Just read the manuals from the class from cover to cover. Make sure you really know this material; if so, you'll do fine on the exam.

What about many of the third-party courses available? Personally speaking, I would skip them and go straight to Oracle University. Why go to a third-party group focusing solely on a test when you can get a good technical education plus the testing material from Oracle? One characteristic I especially like about Oracle University classes is that they focus on teaching the topic, not only on passing the test. In fact, most of the instructors I've had barely even mention the OCP and none structure the class around taking the test. However, by taking the class and knowing the manual, you'll be more than ready to take the test. This is a better way to prepare yourself for employment as a DBA. It is also much more respected in the industry.

There are also many books on the market that claim to prepare you for the tests. Many times, these books don't reflect the tests very well. There might be some exceptions out there, but none that I have seen. You can get some good information in terms of learning more about Oracle, but I think they pale in comparison to the real Oracle courses.

The only other source to consider is the official Oracle documentation set. As a DBA, you should be familiar with these manuals already. If you cannot make it to Oracle University courses, the documentation—free online from Oracle Technology Network—should suffice. The course material is tied closely to the documentation set. The only problem with the documentation set is that you risk getting information overload, but that will probably benefit you in the long term.

In terms of evaluating your readiness, there are practice tests available. Oracle offers short sample tests that are accessed online. These are worthwhile and are a good predictor of success. From my experience if you have studied and can pass the practice test with a 90% or more, it's time to consider taking the real test. Oracle also offers tests with more questions. I have not used these, but people I know who have are satisfied with them.

## Taking the Test

Each test costs $125 whether you pass or fail. If you fail and want to retake the test it costs another $125. Many companies will reimburse their employees who pass the test, so you might want to check with your employer. If you have Oracle training credits and don't have enough for a class or CBT CD, sometimes you can use them to obtain testing vouchers.

You have to find a location that hosts the tests and then register for a day and time. I recommend registering at least one week in advance to make sure space is available. Registration links and phone numbers are available online from the Oracle certification Web site.

Most of the tests are between 40 and 60 questions and you have 90 minutes to complete them. Expect between one and six questions per subject area. Although these tests are computer-driven, they are not adaptive. That means the test will not adjust the difficulty of the questions based on your strengths and weaknesses. At the end of the test, you will immediately receive your score, whether you passed or failed, and the subtotals of each subject area.

## Benefits of Certification

Certification adds a nice touch to any resume. Many companies give bonuses or raises for certification. Consultants sometimes have a higher billing rate when they are certified. However, most IT people consider it no substitute for real experience and I have to agree with that. Also, be aware of the fact that preparing for certification exams is a moneymaking opportunity for many people. Whether they are selling books or teaching the "Boot Camp" training classes, they are doing it for a profit. So keep that in mind before spending thousands of dollars to prepare for one test.

# Networking with Other DBAs

Administration of any type is often as much a human issue as it is a technical one. Many of the ways administrators grow professionally is by working with and learning from other administrators. Doing so can meet two objectives—it can help you become more technically skilled and find a better position.

## Technical Benefits

One of the best ways to become more knowledgeable about Oracle is to talk with other DBAs. No one person can stay abreast of every development regarding the database industry. It is by talking with other DBAs (or SAs for that matter) that you can learn how technology is implemented, what works well, and what doesn't work. This type of information usually isn't in a manual. By learning from other DBAs, you can avoid "reinventing the wheel" to a certain extent.

I usually try to work with as many DBAs as I can. By seeing what they are doing, getting their insights, and sometimes swapping scripts, both people become a little wiser. Most administrators I've worked with are more than willing to impart some of their knowledge, but you should be willing to return the favor at some point. I've also never had a problem teaching more junior DBAs either. It really is true that one of the best ways to learn a topic is to teach it. In these cases, both parties benefit.

Try to meet as many IT people as possible outside your organization or company. This is how you learn what other shops are doing. Learn how and why they have implemented a certain database, operation system, and programming language and consider the challenges they have faced. By doing this, you learn which technologies are doing well and which are not. This is helpful later, when you are called to evaluate a new platform, database, or language.

Classes, Oracle conventions, and user group meetings are good places to meet other DBAs and exchange ideas. I have yet to be at a class that didn't start off with a round of introductions. Because you will likely be in training for a few days, you have plenty of time to meet other

DBAs who are often working locally and are usually facing similar issues. Conventions such as Oracle's Open World are also good to attend so you can meet other technical people, as well as learn about newer technologies. Finally, user group conventions are good places to meet local DBAs and learn what they are doing.

## Professional Benefits

Another reason to network with other IT people, particularly DBAs and SAs, is to build your potential job contacts. A high percentage of technology people owe their positions to someone they know. Networking is how people find better jobs, especially among established IT people. The biggest reasons for this phenomenon are as follows:

- Word gets out about job openings before it ever reaches the want ads.
- More accurate and honest depictions of the job are available.
- You already have a reference from someone in that shop.
- The "middleman" is cut out, which might result in higher salaries.

Usually, when a shop has a need for an administrator, the other (often overworked) administrators are the first to know about it. Frequently, you will hear something like "We're not actively looking for someone yet, but my boss is thinking about hiring someone." At this early stage, you have a leg up if you can get an interview; they often are prone to hire you because they don't want to deal with a formal hiring process.

By knowing people at a shop, you'll get an idea how it is to work there. Even before a job opening is available, you can usually identify the technology used and how people are treated at that shop. Whether or not it's fair, some shops get a good reputation, whereas others are labeled sweatshops. These reputations carry a great deal of weight; be sure to find out how the company is labeled.

If someone you know is setting you up with an interview, it's pretty safe to assume *they* think you can do the job. Acting as a personal reference for someone can be risky if they don't turn out as promised, but it is a very persuasive way to get someone hired.

Do not lose sight in a market in which IT people are in demand; there is money to be made by meeting that demand. Finding and hiring any qualified IT person is expensive, time-consuming, and often frustrating for employers. Currently, Oracle DBAs, Unix SAs, and Java programmers are at the top of the list in terms of being hard to find and retain.

As a result, many companies turn to employment agencies, or "headhunters," as they are usually called, to fill IT positions. This costs the company money and time because they have to pay the headhunter for you plus they still have to perform interviews. On the other hand, you also pay indirectly because a percentage of your salary goes to pay the headhunter. This is reflected in a lower starting salary. Obviously, if you can directly contact the hiring company before a headhunter becomes involved, both you and the employer come out on top.

> **NOTE**
>
> Referral Incentives
>
> Be aware that many companies have incentive programs for employees who help hire other employees. IT people are highly sought after and they can bring a bonus of several thousand dollars. This does not necessarily mean the job is bad, but just keep in mind that your "friend" might also benefit from your employment there.

## Consulting/Contracting versus Salaried Employee

Many DBAs start off initially as employees at established companies. Many companies prefer to train DBAs internally because it's sometimes cheaper than hiring someone off the street. Plus, the DBA they get in the end already knows their systems. This makes sense and can work if both parties are truly committed to the program. However, once they are trained and have a few months or years of experience, many DBAs look for higher-paying jobs.

Many DBAs are then faced with a decision of working for another company on salary or consulting. This is a big issue that many people do not consider until they are faced with the situation. Some of the pros and cons of consulting follow.

Pros:

- Potentially much higher pay.
- Exposure to many different shops and environments.
- Great resume-building material.
- Travel to different states and even countries.
- Ability to sometimes avoid involvement in company politics.

Cons:

- Potentially unstable employment.
- Travel for extended periods of time.
- Long hours and aggressive project deadlines.
- Potential to work in hostile client environments.
- Pay and benefits might be less than expected.

Obviously, these are generalities and might not apply to everyone. However, with the majority of consultants I've worked with and from what I've experienced, these are common pros and cons.

Most of the consultants I know are glad they are or have consulted. They usually cite the variety of interesting work and higher pay as top reasons why they consult. The biggest complaint I've heard, particularly by those with families, is the travel. I know of consultants who go on projects out of state lasting over a year. Keep this in mind before signing up as a consultant.

## Learning Systems Administration and Architecture

After a few years as a DBA, some people branch out into other related IT fields. One of these is system administration. The duties are similar in terms of being responsible for complex systems. Plus the knowledge of Unix allows an easier transfer of skills. In smaller shops it is not uncommon for one person to be both the DBA and SA.

This transition goes both ways. Some of the best DBAs I've worked with have their roots in system administration. Needless to say, anyone who can claim a position as both the DBA and SA will command a very high salary.

Approach becoming an SA the same way you did to becoming a DBA. Take classes if possible, study and practice both on the job and at home, and work with the SAs on the job. Ideally, the DBA should be able to serve as a backup SA anyway, which can be good justification for learning the job.

Tied closely with administration is designing system architectures. After a few years of experience implementing, managing, and tuning systems, many administrators have a feel for what works and what doesn't. These skills tend to come more with experience than with classroom training. The key is understanding the different pieces of a system and how they work together. Once this and the project-management skills are obtained, the administrator can demand a high salary in many different organizations.

## Learning Java

Historically people usually grow from being developers (especially PL/SQL developers) into the DBA position. So why might you go back to development? Actually, there are a couple of reasons many people find this path appealing.

Some people do not like the stresses of an administrator position. It usually requires long hours and can be stressful. This can burn some people out so they go back to being a developer.

Another reason, perhaps even more common, is the money. A good Java programmer in the right job can make more than a DBA. Plus Java is new and exciting. Therefore it can draw many people away from DBA positions. Also, as Oracle and Java become more entwined the transition process becomes easier.

Regardless of whether you want to learn Java as a language, you need to know how it is used in your system. You don't have to be a serious Java coder to understand where and why it is deployed. Understanding the role of Java inside the database and how a Web server operates are important in today's market. In the future, Java will likely be a mandatory skill for the Oracle DBA.

## Summary

This chapter looked at how a DBA can grow professionally and technically. Learning the technology involved is tough enough. Once you have learned those skills, you have to keep them sharp and keep adding new skills. This is done via classes, manuals, books, Web sites, working on your own, and learning with others. It is truly a never-ending task.

Fortunately those who work hard to learn the technology, get certified, and network with others tend to do well financially. Oracle DBAs are at the top of list for the most sought-after IT staff. Whether you are a consultant or a salaried employee, you should expect to do well, if not, there are plenty of other jobs available. Most DBAs can also branch into other areas, including system administration, system design, or Java development.

# Basic Unix Commands

This appendix identifies and describes Unix commands commonly used by the DBA. It does not attempt to provide every possible option, but it does display commands in a useful context.

bdf — bdf displays all the filesystems and the amount of disk space on an HP-UX server. Use this command to determine what filesystems you have and how much disk space is available on each.

cat — cat `filename` displays to the screen the contents of an entire file. The output of the file will scroll past the screen if the file is large. Pipe this file with more to display the contents one screen at a time (for example, cat long_file.txt | more). Also use with /dev/null to erase the contents of log files (for example, cat /dev/null > alertdemo.log).

cd — cd `directory_name` moves you to the specified directory. Issuing cd without a directory specified takes you to the $HOME directory. The directory can be specified with an absolute path (for example, cd /home/mikew/scripts) or with a relative path (for example, cd scripts). To move up one directory, use cd ... and to move to a user's home directory, use cd ~username (for example, cd ~mikew).

chgrp — chgrp `newgroup filename` changes the group for the file specified. For example, chgrp dba test.sql changes the group of test.sql to dba.

chmod — chmod `644 filename` changes the permissions of the specified file. The first digit represents permissions for the owner, the second digit represents permissions for members of that group, and the final digit represents permissions for everyone else. Read permission = 4; write permission = 2; and execute permission = 1. Therefore, in this case, the owner has read and write permissions (4+2=6), members of the group have read permission (4), and everyone else has read permission (4).

chown — chown `newowner filename` changes the owner of the specified file. For example, chown oracle test.sql changes the owner of test.sql to oracle.

clear — clear clears the screen of all previous output and moves the prompt to the top of the screen.

compress — compress `filename` compresses the file to approximately one third its original size and adds a .Z extension to indicate it is compressed. You can expect DMP files to have a higher compression ratio of approximately one fifth the original size.

cp — cp `filename destination` copies the file to the specified destination. A copy of the file will exist at both the source and the destination. You can use a -p option to preserve the permissions and modification date of the file when you copy it to the new location.

crontab — crontab `filename` loads the file into a user's crontab to be executed by cron. crontab -e allows you to edit the crontab directly and crontab -l lists the user's crontab. The safest method is to use crontab -l > oracle.crontab, edit this file to include your changes, and then load it back into cron with crontab oracle.crontab.

`man`—`man` *command* displays the manual page of any Unix command.

`mkdir`—`mkdir` *directory_name* creates the specified directory.

`more`—`more` *filename* displays the contents of a file, one screen at a time. To keep scrolling one screen at a time, press the spacebar. To advance one line at a time, press Enter. To stop viewing a file, press CTRL-C.

`mv`—`mv` *filename_destination* moves a file from one location to another. The file can also be renamed in the process.

`nohup`—`nohup` *command* specifies the no-hangup option for a command. Basically, if you issue a long-running command or start a program and your session terminates before the command or program ends, your command/program will still continue processing until completion. This is commonly used with the ampersand (&) to put the command/program in the background so you can continue to issue more commands from the same prompt. For example, `nohup exp parfile=exp_customer.par` & starts an Oracle export using a parfile and places the job in the background. You can then log out of the machine, yet the export will continue to run.

`page`—`page` *filename* displays the contents of a file one screen at a time. To keep scrolling one screen at a time, press the spacebar. To advance one line at a time, press Enter. To stop viewing a file, press CTRL-C.

`passwd`—`passwd` enables you to change your password.

`pine`—`pine` invokes a Unix-based email system.

`ps`—`ps -ef` shows all the Unix processes running. The option `-elf` shows additional information. This is commonly used with `grep` to find Oracle background processes (for example, `ps -ef | grep ora`).

`rm`—`rm` *filename* removes a specified file. Use extreme caution when using `rm` with the * wildcard because it is very easy to accidentally delete files you did not intend to delete.

`rmdir`—`rmdir` *directoryname* removes a specified directory if it is empty. If the directory contains files, use `rm -r` *directoryname* to remove it and any subdirectories and files.

`rpm`—`rpm -Uvh` *packagename.rpm* uses RedHat Package Manager to install *packagename.rpm* on a Linux machine. To see which packages you have installed, issue `rpm -qa`.

`sar`—`sar` is System Activity Report and can show a variety of operating system statistics. This is frequently used for monitoring the server and it has several options.

`script`—`script` *filename.txt* creates a log of everything that is displayed to the screen until you press CTRL-D. This is similar to spooling output in SQL*Plus. This is good to run when applying patches.

su—su - *username* prompts you for a password to log in as the specified user. The hyphen indicates that the user's .profile will be executed and new environment variables will be established when you log in. If the hyphen is not specified, the user will inherit the environment of the previous user. There is normally not a good reason to log in as a user without setting up the proper environment, so generally you should use the hyphen.

tail—tail -*n* *filename* displays the last *n* lines of a file. To continually see the end of a log file that's being added to, use tail -f *filename*; this will keep displaying the end of the file until you press CTRL-C. The -f option is commonly used to monitor export or import logs, whereas the -*n* option is often used for alert logs.

talk—talk *username* *tty* requests an online chat session with the user with a specific tty. You can obtain this information using the who command. This is a handy means of communicating with another user logged in to the same server. The communication will continue until you quit with a CTRL-C. To refresh the screen display, use CTRL-L.

tar—tar cvf -`find . -print ` > *filename.tar* compresses a directory, its subdirectories, and all the files into one file called *filename.tar*. This TAR file can be compressed and transported via cp or ftp to a different location. Once it has been moved to its location, the directory, its subdirectories, and all the files can be recreated by issuing tar xvf *filename.tar* in its new location. This is a common way to move directory trees from one server to another. Oracle patches also are often in TAR files.

top—top invokes a Unix server monitoring utility. This is a handy utility to have as it gives a good snapshot of system performance and load.

touch—touch *filename* attempts to create an empty file in your current directory. Use this to determine whether you have write permissions on a directory. For example, after the oradata directory has been created, touch a file there as the oracle user to confirm it has the necessary permissions.

truss—truss -p *PID* traces all the system calls for a given process ID. This command is handy when you have to see exactly what a process is doing at the Unix level.

umask—umask 022 sets the default file permission mask to 644 if the default was 666.

uname—uname -a displays the operating system type and version, the name of the server, and the current time. This provides basic information about the server you are using.

uncompress—uncompress *filename.Z* uncompresses the file. Make sure you have enough space on your filesystem for the file once it is uncompressed.

uptime—uptime displays the current time, how long the server has been running since the last reboot, the number of users on the server, and the load average for the present time, five minutes ago, and 15 minutes ago.

vmstat—vmstat displays a variety of Unix server monitoring statistics. There are several options with this command and it is very useful.

wall—wall < *enter your message*> <*CTRL-D*> echoes your message to every user on the server. Use this for announcements such as "The database will be shutdown in five minutes. Log off now!" Once you type wall, your cursor will jump down a line. There, you type your message. To end your message and send it to everyone, type CTRL-D.

wc—wc -l *filename* gives a word count of the number of lines in a file. Use it in conjunction with grep to count the number of lines found. For example, to see the number of Oracle errors in your alert log, issue this command grep -i ORA- | wc -l. This will show you the number of lines with ORA- in them.

which—which *command* determines which executable you are going to use when you issue *command*. For example, which sqlplus might show you /u01/app/oracle/product/8.1.6/bin/sqlplus.

who—who shows you the users logged on the system, their tty, and the time they logged in.

# vi Editor

The vi editor is the most commonly used editor on Unix and Linux machines. Although it is a little tricky to learn initially, you need to know how to use vi because it is the standard editor on most machines. This appendix lists the common vi commands. However, the best way to learn vi is to practice editing files. Learning vi is a lot like learning how to type; it is difficult and awkward at first, but after a while, it becomes instinctive.

Follow these general rules when using vi:

- Do not edit with the CAPS LOCK key on.
- You can precede most commands by a number to indicate the number of times to execute a command. For example, 5dd erases five lines.
- vi has two modes: Insert Command mode.

  When you're typing text, you are in Insert mode. Before you can issue any commands or move the cursor, you must enter Command mode by pressing the ESC key.

  To leave the Command mode and begin inserting text, you must either press i for Insert or a for Append. Insert allows you to enter text before your cursor location, whereas Append allows you to enter text after your cursor location.

To invoke vi to create or edit a particular file, type the following:

`vi filename`

## Cursor-Movement Commands

| To move... | Press... |
| --- | --- |
| Left | h |
| Right | l |
| Up | k |
| Down | j |
| To the end of file | G |
| To line *n* | *n*G |

## Entering Text

| To perform this... | Press... |
| --- | --- |
| Insert | i |
| Append | a |

# Editing Text

| To perform this... | Press... |
| --- | --- |
| Delete one character | x |
| Delete one line | dd |
| Copy *n* lines | *n* yy |
| Paste | p |

# Saving and Exiting

| To perform this... | Type... |
| --- | --- |
| Save a current file | :w <ENTER> |
| Save with a different filename | :w *filename* <ENTER> |
| Save and exit | :wq <ENTER> or ZZ |
| Exit without save | :q! <ENTER> |

# Miscellaneous Commands

| To do this... | Type... |
| --- | --- |
| Display current line number | CTRL-G |
| Refresh the screen | CTRL-L |
| Read an outside file into the document | :r */path_to_file/filename* <ENTER> |
| Search | /*search_string* <ENTER> |
| Global search and replace | :1,$s/*search_string*/*replacement_string*/g (The above reads, start at line 1 (:1), search for *search_string*, replace it with *replacement_string*, and do so globally (g).) |
| Execute a Unix command from within the editor | :! command <ENTER> |
| Repeat a command | . |
| Undo a command | u |

# Scripts

# Scripts

The following scripts are some of the ones that I've used over the years. None of them is terribly complex so you should be able to understand them without much problem. Most are really just canned queries that save typing, therefore you will *not* find them nicely commented or documented. I've found that many of the ad hoc queries I make I end up needing again, so why not put them in a script? I usually put them on a floppy, take them with me on-site, and add to them as I go.

Feel free to modify these as you need, but make sure you understand them before using them. Remember, never blindly run *anyone* else's script before you have had a chance to read them yourself. Truly complex scripts are available via other sources and I recommend using those when possible instead of "reinventing the wheel" and writing your own. However, I wouldn't trust the integrity of *my* system to some mysterious script I picked up on the Internet or anywhere else.

Above all, I hope these scripts prove to be useful and help spawn ideas for your own scripts.

## login.sql

```
REM This file provides custom display settings with SQL*Plus.
REM Have it in the directory from where you start SQL*Plus.

set pagesize 25
col member format a60
col file_name format a60
col tablespace_name format a20
col owner format a15
col object_name format a30
col initial_extent format 999,999,999
col next_extent format 999,999,999
col bytes format 999,999,999,999
col sum(bytes) format 999,999,999,999
select name, created, log_mode from v$database;
show user;
```

## show_session_short.sql

```
select s.username, osuser, status,  server as "Connect Type",
to_char(logon_time,'fmHH:MI:SS AM') as "Logon Time",
sid, s.serial#, p.spid as "UNIX Proc"
from v$session s, v$process p
where s.paddr = p.addr
and s.username is not null
order by status, s.username, s.program, logon_time
/
```

## show_dba_rollback_segs.sql

```
select segment_name, owner, tablespace_name, initial_extent,
next_extent, min_extents, max_extents,
status, instance_num from dba_rollback_segs
/
```

## show_filestat.sql

```
set linesize 180
col tablespace_name format a20
col file_name format a52
col PHYRDS format 999,999,999
col PHYWRTS format 999,999
col PHYBLKRD format 999,999,999
col PHYBLKWRT format 999,999
spool show_filestat.lst
select tablespace_name, file_name, PHYRDS, PHYWRTS, PHYBLKRD, PHYBLKWRT
from v$filestat, dba_data_files
where file_id = file#
order by PHYRDS, PHYWRTS  desc
/
spool off
```

# show_index_depth.sql

```
REM B*Tree indexes should not go past 4 levels, performance suffers.
REM Rebuild anything greater than 3, but remember it will lock the table from
dml
REM unless you are using 8i online rebuilds (which take space instead).
REM Also remember to run analyze before running this
REM
col owner format a15
accept user_name1 prompt 'Enter index owner to examine: '
select owner, table_name, index_name, blevel, last_analyzed from dba_indexes
where upper(owner) = upper('&user_name1')
order by blevel
/
set heading off
select 'Note: blevel should not be greater than 3' from dual
/
set heading on
```

## show_redo_logs.sql

```
set linesize 180
col member format a50
col bytes format 999,999,999,999
```

C

SCRIPTS

```
select v$log.group#, members, member, v$log.status, bytes, archived
from v$log, v$logfile
where v$log.group# = v$logfile.group#;
```

## show_rollback_contention.sql
```
set linesize 180
col name format a15
select a.name, b.extents, b.rssize, b.xacts "Active X-actions", b.waits,
b.gets,
optsize, status
from v$rollname a, v$rollstat b
where a.usn = b.usn
/
```

## show_segments.sql
```
REM Note the hard coded owner, you will have to fix this for your system
set linesize 180
col tablespace_name format a16
col segment_name format a30
col segment_type format a6
col initial_extent format 9,999,999,999
col next_extent format 9,999,999,999
col bytes format 99,999,999,999
spool verify_import-2000.lst
select tablespace_name, segment_name, segment_type, initial_extent,
next_extent, bytes, extents
from dba_segments
where owner = 'CUSTOMER'
order by tablespace_name, segment_type, segment_name
/
spool off
```

## show_tablespaces.sql
```
set linesize 132
set pagesize 65
set heading off
set feedback off
set verify off
col tablespace_name format a30
col file_name format a60
col bytes format 999,999,999,999,999
col status format a15
spool tablespaces.lst
select to_char(sysdate,'MM-DD-YYYY HH:MM')from dual;
set heading on
select tablespace_name, file_name, bytes, status from dba_data_files
```

```
order by tablespace_name, file_name
/
spool off
```

## compare_users.sql
```
REM Get two database users and show their roles.
REM
accept user_1 prompt 'Enter the first user: '
accept user_2 prompt 'Enter the second: '
select grantee, granted_role from dba_role_privs where
grantee in (upper('&user_1'),upper('&user_2'))
order by granted_role, grantee
/
```

## create_analyze_script.sql
```
REM Note the hard coded owner. You need to modify this or use Dynamic SQL.
set heading off
set feedback off
set linesize 180
set pagesize 32767
spool analyze_customer_tables.sql
select 'analyze table CUSTOMER.' || table_name || ' estimate statistics;'
from dba_tables
where owner = 'CUSTOMER'
/
spool off
set heading on
set feedback on
```

## tail-alert
```
# The following is a handy shell script to check the end
# of the alert.log for a database identified by $ORACLE_SID
# I normally run this script several times a day and immediately
# whenever problems are reported.
# I usually give this script 755 permissions.

tail -150 $ORACLE_BASE/admin/$ORACLE_SID/bdump/alert*.log | more
```

# Hot Backup Script

The following is a small piece of code that enables you to initiate hot backups. Use this as a *sample* for your script. I used scripts to generate this dynamically, but it can be hard coded as well. I also could have made use of Unix environment variables for the copy and compress steps, but I wanted to keep it simple.

This script first spools to create a log. Next it puts a tablespace in hot backup mode. It uses cp to copy the file to a backup location. The -p option is probably not necessary. Next it uses gzip to compress the file. The tablespace is then taken out of hot backup mode. At the end of the script, I make a text copy and a binary copy of the control file. The timestamp for the binary copy is dynamically generated. Finally, I force a log switch and end the spool.

Especially when writing backup scripts, you *must* test the scripts to make sure they work and nothing becomes corrupt.

### run_hots.sql

```
spool hot_backup_run.lst
alter tablespace TOOLS begin backup;
!cp -p /u02/app/oracle/oradata/rh1dev1/tools01.dbf
/ubackup/hot_backup_dump/rh1dev1
!gzip -f /ubackup/hot_backup_dump/rh1dev1/tools*.dbf
alter tablespace TOOLS end backup;
alter tablespace USERS begin backup;
!cp -p /u02/app/oracle/oradata/rh1dev1/users01.dbf
/ubackup/hot_backup_dump/rh1dev1
!gzip -f /ubackup/hot_backup_dump/rh1dev1/users*.dbf
alter tablespace USERS end backup;
alter database backup controlfile to trace;
alter database backup controlfile to
'/ubackup/hot_backup_dump/rh1dev1/control.15062000135844';
alter system switch logfile;
spool off
exit
```

# Glossary

The following is a list of terms commonly used by Oracle DBAs in Unix and Linux shops.

**alert.log**—A log file containing informational messages about the database's status, health, and errors.

**archivelog mode**—Database mode in which online redo logs are copied to a separate location before they are reused. Later these logs can be reapplied to recover a damaged database.

**archiver process**—The background process that copies the online redo logs to the archive dump file location.

**background process**—Any process running in the Unix/Linux background. In Oracle terms, this is one of the background processes supporting the database.

**block**—The smallest unit of data managed by Oracle.

**bounce**—To stop and restart a database, server, or process.

**checkpoint**—An occurrence whereby Oracle flushes the redo log buffer and updates every file header with checkpoint and System Change Number information.

**Checkpoint process (CKPT)**—The background process that updates file headers during a checkpoint.

**cold backup**—A complete copy of every data, control, and redo log file on an Oracle database. The database must be shut down for the backup to be valid.

**commit**—The action of making DML changes permanent inside the database.

**config.ora**—An optional file called by the init.ora file that contains initialization parameters for the database.

**control file**—A binary file containing metadata about the database. It is also a text file used to manage SQL*Loader jobs.

**core dump**—The result of a failed process. The contents of the memory and variables are dumped to a text file. These files can be extremely large and can fill up a filesystem. Typically, core dumps should be removed and the failed process investigated.

**cron**—A Unix job-scheduling utility. This is commonly used to schedule batch jobs and backups for both Oracle and other applications.

**daemon**—A Unix background process.

**Data Definition Language** (DDL)—A SQL statement that creates, modifies, or drops an object inside the database. For example, ALTER TABLE or CREATE INDEX are DDL statements. A DDL statement issues an implicit commit and it cannot be rolled back.

**data dictionary**—The set of tables and views that contain metadata about the database.

**data dictionary cache**—A memory area in the shared pool containing data dictionary information.

**data file**—A file belonging to a tablespace that contains data tables and/or indexes belonging to a database.

**Data Manipulation Language** (DML)—A SQL statement that inserts, updates, or deletes table data. These statements can be committed or rolled back. If they are followed by a DDL statement or the user session exits normally, they will be committed.

**database**—A set of data, control, and redo log files identified by a SID.

**Database Administrator**—The individual responsible for the creation, maintenance, tuning, and backup and recovery of a database. Principle responsibilities are data protection and data availability.

**database buffer cache**—A memory area within the SGA that holds copies of data blocks.

**Database Writer process** (DBWR)—The background process that writes blocks from the database buffer cache to the data files.

**export**—An Oracle utility used to extract data and objects from an Oracle database into a .dmp dump file.

**extent**—A set of contiguous blocks inside the database.

**hot backup**—A backup of the data files while the database is running.

**import**—An Oracle utility used to load data and objects from a .dmp dump file into an Oracle database.

**index**—A structure within a database holding a pointer to a specific row of a data table. Indexes increase data access and enforce uniqueness.

**init.ora**—A mandatory text file containing database parameters read during database startup.

**instance**—The combination of Oracle memory structures and background processes running on a server.

**Internet Application Server(iAS)**—The newest Oracle Web server product. It replaces Oracle Application Server OAS.

**java pool**—A memory pool inside the SGA used to hold Java objects.

**Java Developers Kit (JDK)**—The collection of libraries and classes used to develop Java programs.

**Java Runtime Environment (JRE)**—This is the environment that Java programs run under after they are developed with a JDK.

**Java Virtual Machine (JVM)**—The Java "engine" inside an Oracle database.

**kernel**—An internal memory resident structure in a Unix or Linux operating system that manages processes, memory, files, and disk I/O.

**large pool**—A memory pool inside the SGA.

**Linux**—A relatively new Unix variant typically running on PCs with Intel processors. Linux now often runs on server class systems with non-Intel chipsets.

**listener**—A process that's waiting for incoming requests from clients. These requests are then routed to another process to be managed.

**listener.ora**—The configuration file containing parameters for an Oracle listener.

**log switch**—The point in time at which LGWR stops writing to one online redo log file and begins writing to the next online redo log file. A checkpoint automatically occurs at this time.

**Log Writer** (LGWR)—The process that writes from the redo log buffer to the online redo log files.

**man pages**—Online help for Unix commands. See the listing for man in the Unix command appendix.

**mirroring**—A method of writing data on two or more identical disks in an attempt to improve fault tolerance.

**mount**—A database state in which the init.ora file has been read, the instance (memory pools and background processes) has been started, and the control file(s) have been opened and read.

**multiplex**—A practice of having Oracle maintain redundant copies of either control files or online redo log files. This provides fault tolerance, so if one file is damaged, its mirrored copies will still exist.

**Net**—Oracle networking software in Oracle 9i.

**Net8**—Oracle networking software in Oracle 8 and 8i.

**noarchive log mode**—Database mode whereby online redo logs are not copied to a separate location before they are reused.

**nomount**—A database state in which the init.ora file has been read and the instance (memory pools and background processes) has been started.

**online redo log file**—The file written to by the Log Writer process.

**Online Transaction Processing (OLTP)**—A classification of an application in which short, frequent transactions are common.

**Oracle Application Server (OAS)**—An older Oracle Web server product. It is being replaced by iAS (Internet Application Server).

**Oracle Certified Professional (OCP)**—An individual who has successfully passed the required test(s) covering Oracle subjects such as database administration, operation, or development.

**Oracle Enterprise Manager (OEM)**—A GUI tool used to aid administrators in managing the database.

**Oracle Parallel Server (OPS)**—An Oracle product in which multiple database instances simultaneously access one physical database. This product is called Real Application Clusters in Oracle 9i.

**Oracle Universal Installer (OUI)**—A Java-based Oracle utility used to install Oracle software.

**paging**—An effort by the kernel to free real memory by moving a portion of a non-active process from real memory to disk. This happens normally on most systems, but if it occurs excessively, performance will be impacted.

**PL/SQL**—An Oracle proprietary structured programming language based on SQL used to access and manipulate data within an Oracle database.

**Process monitor process (PMON)**—A background process responsible for cleaning up after and freeing resources of abnormally terminated processes.

**RAID**—Redundant Array of Inexpensive/Independent Disks. A classification of several methods of striping and mirroring disks.

**Real Application Clusters (RAC)**—The new name for Oracle Parallel Server starting in Oracle 9i. This is where two or more instances on a cluster simultaneously access the same physical database located on a shared disk array.

**redo log buffer**—A memory area containing a log of all the change activity within an Oracle database.

**redo log file**—See online redo log file.

**rollback**—Undo information generated for a statement. Also the action of undoing a DML statement. Only DML statements can be rolled back; DDL statements cannot be rolled back.

**rollback segment**—An Oracle structure used to hold rollback information.

**D**

GLOSSARY

**root**—The all powerful superuser account on Unix and Linux systems. Be very careful when working as this user.

**segment**—The collection of Oracle extents belonging to a specific object.

**semaphore**—A Unix/Linux integer structure that is incremented or decremented as a means of controlling access to a resource.

**Server Manager**—An Oracle utility that submits database commands and SQL to the database. This tool has been phased out in favor of SQL*Plus in Oracle 9i.

**Shared Global Area (SGA)**—See System Global Area.

**shared memory**—A memory area in Unix/Linux that can be attached, read, and written to by multiple processes. The SGA is a shared memory area.

**shared pool**—A memory area in the SGA containing the shared SQL area and data dictionary cache.

**shared SQL area**—A memory area in the shared pool containing parsed SQL statements so they can be reused.

**SID (System Identifier)**—An eight-character identifier used to identify an Oracle instance.

**spfile**—A server parameter file is a binary copy of the init.ora file. It is an optional 9i feature.

**SQL*Loader**—An Oracle utility that loads data from flat files into an Oracle database.

**SQL*Net**—Oracle networking software prior to Oracle 8.

**sqlnet.ora**—A file containing Oracle network configuration parameters. Contrary to the name, this file survives past SQL*Net.

**SQL*Plus**—An Oracle utility that submits database commands and SQL to the database.

**striping**—A method of writing data across two or more physical disks in an attempt to improve performance.

**Structured Query Language (SQL)**—A non-procedural language used to read, insert, update, or delete data in a database. This is not Oracle proprietary, although there are some proprietary extensions added to it.

**swapping**—An effort by the kernel to free real memory by moving an entire process from real memory to disk. This happens in response to a shortage of memory; performance is negatively impacted. This should be avoided.

**System Administrator**—The individual responsible for the administration and management of a Unix or Linux server.

**System Global Area (SGA)**—Also known as Shared Global Area. This is the collection of the different memory pools comprising a running database instance. These include the database buffer cache, redo log buffer, shared pool (data dictionary cache and shared SQL area), large pool, and the Java pool.

**System Monitor process (SMON)**—A background process responsible for instance recovery, cleaning up temporary segments, and coalescing free space in tablespaces for objects with PCTINCREASE > 1.

**table**—A database structure used to store data.

**tablespace**—A logical collection of database objects stored in one or more data files.

**tnsnames.ora**—A client-side Oracle networking text file containing a list of database names, their host machine names or IP addresses, and port numbers so the client can attempt to establish a connection.

**truncate**—A command to immediately delete all data in a table, free the used space, and reset the high water mark. There is no rollback for this statement.

**Unix**—A robust, multitasking, multi-user operating system commonly used on servers to host critical applications such as databases and Web servers.

# INDEX

## SYMBOLS

# Get your Oracle Fix from Sams

## Oracle and Java Application Development
By Bulusu Lakshman
ISBN: 0-672-32117-3 • 400 pages • $39.99 • August

This book describes the advanced Oracle Java technologies,
building reusable components and deploying Java in a Web environment
* Describes Oracle's Internet Computing Platform
  for developing applications
* Outlines key Oracle Java technologies like Enterprise Java Beans,
  Business Components, Java Server Pages and Servlets.
* Describes the creation of dynamic Web content with Java.
* Describes database interaction with Java using Java stored
  procedures, JDBC and SQLJ.

## Programming with Oracle Developer
By Matthew Bennett
ISBN: 0-672-32110-6 • 450 pages • $39.99 • August

*Programming with Oracle Developer* is packed with expert advice,
detailed explanations, and complete solutions that show you how
to produce robust, precise, Internet-ready applications for Developers.

After reading this book, the reader will:
* Master design and prototyping issues including the new wizards and
  GUI design features of Developer Forms, Reports, and Graphics
* Extend the reusability and optimize the security of your applications
* Deploy Internet applications and integrate them with other tools
* Create Robust, Web-Enabled Oracle Applications

## E-Business for the Oracle DBA
By Megh Thakkar
ISBN: 0-672-32147-5 • 400 pages • $39.99 • September

This book focuses on discussing the issues that a DBA would face
in extending existing systems for e-Business. The book also discusses
how DBAs can prepare themselves for the challenge. An example
business 'DOeBIZ Corporation' is used to help the reader understand
the various issues involved and how an Oracle DBA can deal with them.

This book will teach readers how to:
* Successfully transition their business to e-Business
* Understand the challenges faced by an iDBA
* Achieve high availability in e-Business
* Achieve secure e-Business environments
* Achieve high performance e-Business systems

## Oracle Performance Tuning
By Ed Whalen
ISBN: 0-672-32146-7 • 450 Pages • $39.99 • November

Learn how to diagnose performance problems, and how to improve
and optimize an Oracle Database.

This book will teach readers how to:
* Set measurable performance tuning goals for databases and
  accomplish those goals.
* Understand how to use trace files, the alert log file and event
  sets to assist with tuning.
* Understand and be able to use utilities and dynamic
  performance views to assist with tuning.
* Understand how to tune applications using index structures and
  how to perform SQL statement tuning.

## Watch for these other exciting titles this year!

* Building Dynamic Websites with Oracle Portal
* Oracle Development with VB.Net
* Oracle and XML Development

For more information on these titles
or becoming an author, contact:

**Rosemarie Graham**
Executive Editor
rosemarie.graham@samspublishing.com

**Angela Kozlowski**
Acquisitions Editor
angela.kozlowski@samspublishing.com

## SAMS
www.samspublishing.com

# Hey, you've got enough worries.

## Don't let IT training be one of them.

Get on the fast track to IT training at InformIT,
your total Information Technology training network.

 | **www.informit.com** | *SAMS*

- Hundreds of timely articles on dozens of topics ▪ Discounts on IT books from all our publishing partners, including Sams Publishing ▪ Free, unabridged books from the InformIT Free Library ▪ "Expert Q&A"—our live, online chat with IT experts ▪ Faster, easier certification and training from our Web- or classroom-based training programs ▪ Current IT news ▪ Software downloads ▪ Career-enhancing resources

InformIT is a registered trademark of Pearson. Copyright ©2001 by Pearson.
Copyright ©2001 by Sams Publishing.